D0743508

BLUE GUIDE

BUDAPEST

ANNABEL BARBER

SOMERSET · LONDON

CONTENTS

PRACTICAL INFORMATION

MAPS & PLANS

Third edition 2018

Published by Blue Guides Limited, a Somerset Books Company
Winchester House, Deane Gate Avenue, Taunton, Somerset TA1 2UH
www.blueguides.com
'Blue Guide' is a registered trademark.

ISBN 978-1-905131-79-2

A CIP catalogue record of this book is available from the British Library.

Distributed in the United States of America by
W.W. Norton & Company, Inc.
500 Fifth Avenue, New York, NY 10110.

The author and publisher have made reasonable efforts to ensure the accuracy
of all the information in *Blue Guide Budapest*; however, they can accept no responsibility
for any loss, injury or inconvenience sustained by any traveller as a result of
information or advice contained in the guide.

Statement of editorial independence: Blue Guides, their authors and editors,
are prohibited from accepting any payment from any restaurant, hotel, gallery
or other establishment for its inclusion in this guide, or for a more favourable
mention than would otherwise have been made.

Your views on this book would be much appreciated. We welcome not only specific
comments, suggestions or corrections, but any more general views you may have: how
this book enhanced your visit, how it could have been more helpful. Blue Guides authors
and editorial and production team work hard to bring you what we hope are the best-
researched and best-presented cultural guide books in the English language. Please
write to us by email (editorial@blueguides.com), via the comments page on our website
(*blueguides.com*) or at the address given above. We will be happy to acknowledge useful
contributions in the next edition, and to offer a free copy of one of our titles.

Maps: Dimap Bt.
Floor plans: Imre Bába
Architectural line drawings and Coronation Mantle diagram:
Michael Mansell RIBA & Gabriella Juhász
All maps, plans and drawings © Blue Guides.
Photographs by James Howells (pp. 81, 116, 209, 227, 255, 260);
Fortepan (p. 70); courtesy of the Nagy Imre Emlékház (p. 90);
Kőbányai Helytörténeti Gyűjtemény (p. 279). All other photographs by the author.

Cover: The Fishermen's Bastion, by Michael Mansell & Gabriella Juhász © Blue Guides.
Frontispiece: 'The Union of Buda and Pest'. Detail from
István Kiss's Centenary Monument on Margaret Island.

All material prepared for press by Anikó Kuzmich.

This is the 3rd edition of *Blue Guide Budapest*. The first two (1996 and 2001)
were written by Bob Dent. This new edition, after the elapse of many years,
has been fully rewritten, expanded and re-designed.

Every effort has been made to contact the copyright owners of material reproduced in this
guide. We would be pleased to hear from any copyright owners we have been unable to reach.

Grateful thanks go to the many people and institutions who provided
support, inspiration, companionship, assistance and advice during the preparation
of this guide and who made corrections to the manuscript, in particular:
György Antall, Zsolt Átányi, Veronika Bánki, Zoltán Bolla, Nóra Demeter, Bob Dent,
Fanni Fodor, László Földényi, Balázs Fürjes, James Howells, Zsombor Jékely,
Robert Kenedi, Zsófia Kenesei, Szilvia Kinback, Júlia Kisfaludi, Eleni Korani,
Slomó Köves, Anikó Kuzmich, Róbert Hermann, Bettina Hinnekens,
János Mátyásfalvi, Ágnes Merényi, Mark Odescalchi, Anna Perczel, Beatrix Reményi,
Noémi Saly, Enikő Sípos, Tamás Szakács, András Török, Benedek Varga,
Lajos Verbai, Gábor Verrasztó, Andrea Weichinger, Anne and Sándor Zwack.

Printed in Hungary by Dürer Nyomda Kft., Gyula.

Annabel Barber is the series editor of the Blue Guides. She is the author of *Blue Guide Literary Companion Rome, Pilgrim's Rome* and co-author of *Blue Guide Rome*. She lives and works in Budapest.

Introduction

Budapest, the 'Queen of the Danube', is one of the world's most beautiful capital cities. Hilly Buda to the west and flat Pest to the east are both divided—and joined—by the Danube and its stately bridges. The river panorama, viewed downstream from Margaret Bridge, is one of the loveliest cityscapes on earth.

The city is also an ideal size. With some two million inhabitants, it is large enough to feel like a true metropolis, with grand buildings, rich cultural amenities, leafy parks and good restaurants; and compact enough to absorb and explore from end to end. Its exemplary system of public transport makes travelling around easy and efficient. Budapest is famous for its architecture, its music (and its beautiful Liszt Academy concert hall), its coffee houses and its thermal baths. Hungary also has a long tradition of wine-growing and there are plenty of places where you can sample the dry red, white and rosé as well as the famous sweet Tokaj dessert wine. Budapest is also a fun city, with lively bars and cafés, especially in summer, and festivals of music, dance, literature, folklore, food and drink held throughout the year.

ORIENTATION

The city is divided into 23 districts (*kerület*), each with its own local government. They are designated by Roman numerals and most also have familiarly used names. The districts with the highest concentration of major sights are:

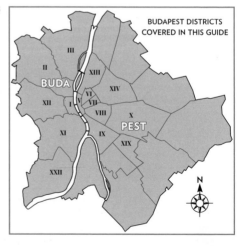

District I: Buda's Castle Hill, with the Matthias Church and Hungarian National Gallery

District V: Central Pest, with the Parliament and Danube waterfront

District VI: Liszt Academy and the Opera House

District VII: Great Synagogue

District VIII: National Museum

District XIV: Heroes' Square and City Park.

Historical Sketch

The site of modern Buda, fertile, accessible but easy to defend, lies on hill slopes above a narrow strip of land where streams of fresh water (now channelled underground) empty into the Danube. Unsurprisingly, it has been attractive to mankind since prehistory. A pair of fossilised footprints, left some 30,000 years ago by a Palaeolithic woman and child, have been found along the course of Buda's main street, Fő utca. We know that Castle Hill was inhabited in the Bronze Age and that before the Romans arrived, the Celtic Eraviscans occupied Gellért Hill.

The Romans brought considerable urbanisation. They built a military road along the Danube and stationed auxiliary legions there, first around the modern Víziváros and later in Aquincum, which swelled to become the capital of the province of Pannonia Inferior. Extensive remains of Roman occupation survive. As their empire dwindled and disintegrated, the Romans' place was taken by a succession of migrating newcomers: Huns in the 5th century; then Avars, then Magyars; who arrived in the late 9th/ early 10th century. Early 13th-century chronicles state that Árpád, the great Magyar chieftain, was buried at Óbuda—but no archaeological evidence for this has been found.

THE MIDDLE AGES

Under the early kings of the Árpád Dynasty (1000–1301), Óbuda remained the chief centre of this area, although the early Hungarian court was peripatetic and the kingdom as yet had no permanent capital. Óbuda was nevertheless favoured and important. A chapter of prebendary canons was set up there, an artisans' quarter grew up to serve them and a royal residence was also maintained. Pest grew up at this time too, once again around an old Roman kernel, the fort which had stood at the foot of today's Elisabeth Bridge. Graves suggesting early settlement close to the modern Szabadság Bridge have also been found. By the 13th century, both Óbuda and Pest were fully-fledged independent towns, with civilian and monastic populations and—in the case of Óbuda—royal status, since the itinerant court was regularly in residence there.

All this changed after the Mongol raids of 1241–2. The sudden death of the Great Khan Ögedei, son of Genghis, caused the Mongol hordes to retreat, but the ruins they left behind were not repaired; instead, King Béla IV (r. 1235–70) elected to configure things differently, bringing Pest under the jurisdiction of Buda and moving Buda to the safer, higher ground of Castle Hill. The court was still not permanently based there but it seems to have spent more time in the new site, resulting in quite rapid growth both in size and prosperity.

On the death of Andrew III in 1301, the House of Árpád became extinct in the male line. The throne of Hungary was bitterly contested by claimants from other powerful European dynasties. Caroberto of Naples, from the House of Anjou, eventually emerged victorious as King Charles I (Károly Róbert), in 1310. His wife, Elizabeth of Poland, founded and endowed a number of churches and convents in Buda. His son, Louis (Lajos) the Great, a formidable warrior king, ruled over Hungary, Croatia and Poland, eventually controlling territory that stretched from the Black Sea to the Adriatic. By the time of his death, in 1382, medieval Hungary had reached its territorial greatest.

By the early 15th century, the court had made Buda its permanent capital and Pest, independent once again, achieved the status of royal free town. This occurred during the reign of King Sigismund, son of the Holy Roman Emperor Charles IV, who assumed the throne on his marriage to Mary of Hungary, Louis the Great's daughter. He founded the Order of the Dragon, a league of knights committed to thwarting Ottoman expansion into Christendom, and succeeded to the title of Holy Roman Emperor in 1433. Portraits of him have been left to us by Pisanello (attributed) and (posthumously) Dürer.

King Sigismund left only a daughter, Elizabeth, whose husband, Albert of Habsburg, assumed the Hungarian throne. A period of uncertainty followed, with the Crown of St Stephen in pawn to the Holy Roman Emperor (*see p. 141*). Stability returned under Matthias Corvinus (r. 1458–90) and Buda entered its first golden age, becoming a centre of culture and learning, with a famous library and graceful buildings remodelled and extended in the Renaissance style, adorned with the works of Italian sculptors and artists. This flowering was due in great part to the influence of Matthias' queen, Beatrix of Aragon, daughter of the king of Naples, whom Matthias had married in 1476, after more than a decade of widowhood, pensioning off his mistress, Barbara, the mother of his illegitimate son János Corvinus. Beatrix made an enormous cultural impact on Hungary as well as on a husband who had previously been happiest in the saddle, in the jousting lists, on the battlefield or at the gaming table. Quite apart from the music and poetry, the textiles and woodwork, the stonemasonry and painting, she is said to have introduced the fork to the nation's dining tables (examples of cutlery from her era are on display in the Hungarian National Museum).

Throughout his reign Matthias, with the help of his Black Army of mercenaries, laboured to gain and consolidate the power that had gradually been lost since Louis the Great's time. By the time of Matthias' death, his realm had engulfed Vienna, stretching from Transylvania to Styria in one direction and from Bosnia to Bautzen (east Saxony) in the other. Many of these territories were tenuously gained and quickly gone and Matthias' critics have argued that he expended too much energy in expanding his borders west and north and not enough bolstering them against the Ottoman push from the south and east.

Crucially also, Matthias had no legitimate heir. In 1463 he had paid 80,000 gold pieces to get back the Crown of Hungary from the Holy Roman Emperor Frederick III of Habsburg, agreeing that the Hungarian throne would pass to Frederick's son Maximilian if Matthias should die without a successor. Matthias was young and lusty at the time and probably had no fears on that score. Alas, his bride, the Bohemian princess Katherine Podebrady, died in childbirth at the age of just 15. Beatrix, his second wife, likewise failed to produce a child.

Matthias died in 1490, leaving his vast realm to be squabbled over by rival claimants until the King of Bohemia, Vladislas of Jagiello, eventually triumphed, marrying Matthias' widow. The marriage was a humiliation for Beatrix: unconsummated, contracted purely to confer legitimacy on the husband, and ultimately declared null and void by the Borgia pope Alexander VI in 1500. Beatrix returned to Naples the following year. Vladislas was succeeded in 1516 by his son, the young Louis II, a ten-year-old boy, weak and inexperienced just at a time when Hungary badly needed determination and strength.

THE OTTOMAN ERA: 1541–1686

Louis II (r. 1516–26) was the last of Hungary's medieval kings. After his brief reign, the country changed forever. A portrait by Titian shows him gorgeous in damask robes, with a trim beard, a smile of quiet confidence playing about his lips. The reality is different. Louis was born prematurely in 1506. His mother, Anne de Foix, whom Vladislas II had married after his renunciation of Beatrix, did not survive the birth and was buried in the now-destroyed Church of the Virgin and St Sigismund on Castle Hill (*see p. 42*). To fulfil the role he was expected to play—a powerful monarch at the heart of Europe—Louis was brought up to speak Latin, German, Hungarian, Bohemian, Polish and French, to be a deft swordsman and an equally accomplished dancer. His hand in marriage was given to Mary of Habsburg, granddaughter of the Holy Roman Emperor Maximilian. At the age of eight he saw his father put down the peasant revolt of György Dózsa (*see p. 59*). Two years later, he was on the throne. Inevitably the boy-king's reign was dogged by faction. The Ottoman army seized its chance and the Hungarians were routed at the Battle of Mohács on the Danube in 1526. King Louis died trying to flee the field, drowned in a bog in his heavy armour. Suleiman the Magnificent entered Buda and sacked it (many treasures found their way to Constantinople), and though he did not hold on to it at this time, the city he left behind him was a smoking ruin. Its population fled.

In the ensuing turmoil the kingdom of Hungary was unable to coalesce under a single leader. Ferdinand of Habsburg, brother of Queen Mary, pressed his claim but it was unacceptable to many nobles, who at the Diet held on the Rákos Field in 1505, before King Louis' birth, had drawn up a covenant blaming the nation's ills on its foreign rulers and vowing in future only to accept a Hungarian-born king. The lords who had signed this covenant now came out in support of the Transylvanian claimant, John Zapolya (Szapolyai János) and both Buda and Pest were fought over by the two rival kings. Ferdinand took the towns in 1527 but Suleiman, allying himself with Zapolya, won them back in 1529 and placed them under Zapolya's control. There they remained until Zapolya's death in 1540, at which point Ferdinand at once attempted to resume lordship, entering Pest in the same year and in the spring of 1541 laying siege to Buda, where the widowed queen Isabella and her baby son John Sigismund were holding firm. Once again it was Suleiman who intervened. His troops seized Buda, from where the dowager queen and her son were sent in safety to Transylvania, with the promise that John Sigismund would be left free to rule it, in exchange for a sizeable annual tribute. (John Sigismund, incidentally, went on to become Prince of Transylvania, where he had proclaimed freedom of worship in his Edict of Torda of 1568. He himself was a Unitarian, the only monarch in history of this denomination.)

Buda and Pest, meanwhile, were in Turkish hands and this time Suleiman formally made them part of the Ottoman Empire. Buda once again became, as it had been under the Romans, the capital of an imperial province, ruled over by a proconsul, the Turkish pasha. The best known of the Buda pashas was Sokollu Mustafa, who held the position from 1566–78 and whose name is associated with the building of bath houses. Buda also became a city of minarets. Though both Christian and Jewish communities remained, large numbers of the Christians fled to Royal Hungary, the north and western part of the realm, which was under Habsburg control with its capital at Pressburg (modern Bratislava), and where Roman Catholicism held sway.

In the far east of Hungary, as well as in Transylvania, Protestantism flourished. Far away from Habsburg influence, Catholicism could not establish its hegemony and Ottoman indifference was tantamount to tolerance. In the Calvinist and Lutheran churches of the eastern regions, the Hungarian language was kept alive and the seeds of Hungarian sensibility were sown, seeds which would germinate in later centuries.

RECONQUEST AND REPOPULATION AFTER 1686

In 1683, the Ottomans were defeated at the gates of Vienna. To the victors, the time seemed ripe for an offensive against Buda. The cause was championed by the Habsburg emperor Leopold I, and by Pope Innocent XI, who convened the Holy League of Austria, Poland and Venice against the Turks. A first attempt to retake Buda, in 1684, was unsuccessful. Two years later, however, the city was conquered by a vast army, some ten times more numerous than the Ottoman defenders, commanded by Charles of Lorraine and others, with the troops of Eugene of Savoy securing the city against the arrival of a Turkish relief force. The three-month siege was destructive and bloody. The Christian soldiers raped and pillaged, taking as their victims not only Muslims but also Jews, who had fought alongside the Turks in Buda's defence. Not a mosque or synagogue—and scarcely any other building—was left standing. The elderly pasha of Buda, Abdurrahman, died in the fighting.

With the Muslims and Jews either killed or sold into slavery, the task of repopulating Buda and Pest was set in hand. The new settlers were mainly German-speaking Catholics; in fact, in the post-reconquest years it was only German Catholics who were permitted to live within the walls of Buda or to become citizens of Pest. Hungarians also returned and other settlers, notably Serbs and Greeks, arrived from the Balkans.

By 1703 Buda and Pest were once again royal free towns and Pest developed as a trading centre. The onion-spired churches and colour-washed houses with steeply pitched roofs all date from the Austrian-dominated 18th century, when Pest and Buda were small, moderately prospering Danube towns within the Habsburg empire.

ENLIGHTENED AND UNENLIGHTENED DESPOTISM: THE 18TH CENTURY

Although the Habsburgs had freed Pest and Buda from Ottoman control, Hungary has never viewed them as liberators and people chafed under the yoke of their rule. In

1741, harried by the ambition of Frederick of Prussia, who had captured Silesia, Maria Theresa made a personal appeal at the Diet of Pressburg, appearing before her subjects as a damsel in distress, holding up her infant son, the future Joseph II, and calling on the Hungarian nobility for support. Her efforts roused their natural gallantry and they vowed to serve her '*vitam et sanguinem*', pledging their lives and blood in defence of the integrity of her realm. The empress returned the favour by instituting the feast of the sainted King Stephen on August 20th, a specifically Hungarian national day. The holy relic of Stephen's right hand (*see p. 159*) was procured from Dubrovnik and placed in a purpose-built chapel in the royal palace of Buda, in the keeping of a company of nuns.

Despite all this, Hungary still lacked self-determination. The rule of Maria Theresa's son, Joseph II, who succeeded his mother in 1780, ushered in the era of enlightened despotism. Though an autocrat, Joseph sought to modernise his administration by weakening the power of the Church, reducing press censorship and limiting landowners' control over their serfs. Large numbers of religious orders were suppressed in the Habsburg dominions and the stranglehold of Roman Catholicism was loosened. In Buda, vacated monastic buildings were used instead to house the National Assembly, Hungary's early Parliament. The Edict of Tolerance of 1781–2 allowed Protestants, Jews and members of the Serbian Orthodox community to worship freely without having to answer charges of heresy and to build places of worship (modest and unassuming in appearance, without drawing attention to their function). Restrictions on non-Catholics' entry into certain professions was also lifted. Nevertheless, Pest and Buda never took Joseph to their hearts. He had refused to be crowned with St Stephen's Crown or to take his coronation oath to the Hungarian people, promising to rule them according to their ancient rights and usages. Against this, his inclination to a more liberal rule counted for little. The inclination was not in any case shared by his successors. Joseph (d. 1790) had recognised that the empire, politically overstretched and lacking a coherent internal structure, had become a tinderbox of ethnic tensions that could quickly erupt in flames. Watching the events in pre-revolutionary France, he had warned his sister, Marie-Antoinette, that if she and Louis XVI did not act prudently, the results would be 'atrocious'. He was proved right, but the French Revolution, far from inspiring a decision to rule with a lighter hand, terrified the Austrian monarchy back into full autocracy. A band of republicans, the Hungarian 'Jacobins', were tried and executed in 1795, the hall in which the trial was held the very vacated religious house to which the Hungarian assembly had been transferred under Joseph II (*see p. 33*). In 1796 the Hungarian Diet was convened in direct response to the events in France and subsequent sessions between then and 1811 took as their subject the military response to the threat posed by Napoleon.

The Napoleonic Wars were concluded by the Congress of Vienna in 1815. Peace and political stability were ushered in under Chancellor Metternich, but at the price of a strictly controlling and centralised state.

REFORM AND MAGYARISATION: 1815–48

The period between 1815 and 1848, under the irresolute emperor Franz I and his simple son Ferdinand, is known as the Biedermeier age. Government was authoritarian and the engagement in political affairs by the people, in Pest-Buda as in Vienna, was superficial. Painting, music, furniture design and literature flourished, but always at a safe, drawing-room level. Pest and Buda did not stagnate, however. Indeed, this was an age of considerable development and progress, the impetus for which was provided by Archduke Joseph, son of Joseph II's brother and successor Leopold II and younger brother of Franz I. In 1796 he had been appointed Palatine of Hungary. The Palatine acted as a sort of royal lieutenant and though the post had existed since the days of King Stephen, it was Archduke Joseph who really made use of it, becoming essentially a viceroy for the emperor and devoting his energies to modernising Hungary's chief cities. At last Hungary had again found a ruler with whom she was prepared to co-operate. Under the Palatine Joseph (*József nádor* in Hungarian), the Beautification Committee (*Szépítő Bizottmány*) was set up (*see p. 23*). The medieval walls of Pest were torn down and the city began to spread beyond them.

Hungary's Reform Era, stretching roughly from 1825 to 1848, was the age of István Széchenyi (*see p. 164*), the man who, in his financial treatise *Credit* (1830), had criticised those who harked back to Hungary's medieval past, claiming, 'There are many who believe that Hungary has been. For my part, I like to think that *she shall be*.' It was also Széchenyi who, in his maiden speech to the Upper House in 1825, had spoken Hungarian rather than Latin. His era became a time of burgeoning Magyarisation as the heterogeneous population of Buda and Pest became patriotically Hungarian in thought, word and deed. The Hungarian language flourished; Hungarian theatre, literature and journalism become fashionable. Even the topography of the cities was Magyarised as German place names gave way to Hungarian ones (*see p. 57*). Széchenyi also ushered in an age of technical progress, with steam boats, bridges, railways and the Hungarian Academy of Sciences. The growing sense of national identity of this era was not exclusive to Hungary. It was felt in Croatia, Italy, Austria, France and many other countries of Europe in the period leading up to the revolutionary year of 1848.

REVOLUTION: 1848

1848 was a testing year for Emperor Ferdinand, beset by rebellious subjects at a time when his mental powers were failing him. The Hungarian portion of his empire was in a ferment. National pride kindled by Széchenyi was now being fired into a revolutionary blaze by the radical rhetoric of Lajos Kossuth and the passionate poetry of Sándor Petőfi. The 'March Youth' of 1848, a loose group of intellectuals, were disseminating their ideas through the coffee houses. Earlier attempts by Emperor Ferdinand to snuff out the sparks of Magyar dissidence (Kossuth had been imprisoned in 1837–40 for publishing reports of parliamentary debates in defiance of press censorship) had only led to a swelling in numbers of reformists in the Hungarian Parliament as well as to the formation of the Liberal faction among the nobility, led by Count Lajos Batthyány and Baron József Eötvös. Latin was replaced by Hungarian as the official language of government. In 1841, Kossuth had founded a newspaper, the *Pesti Hírlap*, as a vehicle for his views. Political factions grew more bitterly opposed and Kossuth and Széchenyi clashed openly. Kossuth was a Lutheran, a son of the tradition that throughout the years of Habsburg absolutism clung fixedly to its ideals of literacy, education and the exchange of ideas. His egalitarian notions seemed modern and attractive beside the constitutional monarchism of the aristocratic Széchenyi. The nation was in the mood for revolt and news of revolution in Paris in February 1848 was quick to spread. On March 15th, rebellious crowds took to the streets of Pest, stormed the offices of Landerer and Heckenast, a printer's shop near the Danube, and ran off copies of the Twelve Points, which were loudly proclaimed at a mass rally in front of the National Museum. The points included demands for press freedom and an end to censorship, for independent government and an annual assembly, equality before the law irrespective of social status or religion, a standing army, the abolition of nobles' exemption from taxation, a national bank, the release of political prisoners and union with Transylvania. In haste, Vienna made concessions, appointing Batthyány Prime Minister of Hungary's first autonomous government. Széchenyi and Kossuth also held ministerial positions (*for a full list, see pp. 144–5*) but their visions for Hungary's future were too radically opposed. Széchenyi remained a champion of tradition, based on monarchy, aristocracy and an agrarian economic base. Kossuth was a separatist, protectionist democrat. Batthyány had no wish to break with the Crown and he tried to steer an even course but his government was inherently unstable. Its aim was to reconfigure Hungary as a nation state, linked to Vienna through the Palatine but otherwise autonomous. The Palatine Joseph had died in 1847 and his successor, Stephen, did his best to fill his father's shoes, in April 1848 obtaining Emperor Ferdinand's signed approval of the April Laws, legislation drawn up by the Hungarian government to secure provision of a national guard and control of national expenditure. The subtle mediation demanded by the role of Palatine required a shrewder and more experienced head than Stephen's, however, and the turbulent events of the autumn were to make his position untenable.

WAR AND COMPROMISE: 1848–67

Hungary's truculence—antagonistic to Austria and campaigning for a union with Transylvania that many in Transylvania did not want—soon found the country threatened with outright war. Matters were complicated by Josip Jelačić, Ban of Croatia and Slav patriot, who sought to serve his own country's separatist interests by driving a wedge between Hungary and Austria. His troops attacked Hungary in September. Batthyány had hoped that the Palatine Stephen would command the Hungarian defence but Vienna called him home. Kossuth quickly managed to muster an army and the Hungarians won a morale-boosting early victory. Seeing that war was now inevitable, Batthyány resigned and was replaced at the helm of government by Kossuth. He and the new emperor Franz Joseph, who came to the throne in December, remained implacable enemies for the remainder of their lives. Franz Joseph refused to recognise the April Laws. Hungary in return did not recognise him as her king.

In the early stages of the war the Hungarians won some important victories, prompting Kossuth to overreach himself and declare Hungarian independence together with the deposition of the Habsburgs. In May 1849, the Hungarians captured Buda by siege. While the siege was still raging, Count László Teleki, the Hungarian revolutionary government's ambassador in Paris, wrote to Kossuth urging him not to ignore the nationalities question in his zeal for Magyar freedom. 'Liberty, equality and fraternity are not enough,' he insisted, 'the ethnic groups want to live their own national lives. We must create a system that makes provision for this.'

In the end, Hungary's chances of victory were extinguished by the entry into the conflict of Russia. Kossuth fled the country, leaving General Artúr Görgei (*see p. 245*) in charge and with the unenviable role of surrendering—which he did, not to Austria but to the military representative of Tsar Nicholas I. Hungary admitted defeat, in other words, but it was Russia, not Austria, who had vanquished her. The Crown of St Stephen was buried to prevent it falling into Habsburg hands and Hungary braced herself for reprisals. The execution of 13 military commanders, the 'Arad Martyrs', on October 6th ushered in the so-called Bach Era (after the Austrian Interior Minister Alexander von Bach), which has a reputation in Hungary as a period of ruthless repression. Relations with Austria thawed only gradually. The 48-ers, supporters of Kossuth, remained intransigent but slowly (and greatly aided by Austria's struggles against Bismarck, Napoleon III and Vittorio Emanuele and the killing fields of Solferino and Königgrätz) the moderates, under Ferenc Deák (*see p. 250*), triumphed, leading to the Compromise of 1867, which established the Dual Monarchy of Austria-Hungary, two halves of a single realm (and customs union), each to be administered independently under a single head of state who was to go under the title of King in Hungary and Emperor in Austria. The first Prime Minister under this arrangement was Count Gyula Andrássy, an ally of the pragmatic Deák. To these two men, Hungary owes the great years of its late 19th-century prosperity and political consequence.

THE BOOM YEARS: 1867–1914

The period between 1867 and the outbreak of WWI was one of expansion and prosperity. It began with the long-overdue coronation of Franz Joseph in the Matthias Church. His beautiful wife, the Empress Elisabeth, crowned alongside him, has a special place in Hungarian hearts for the readiness with which she espoused Hungarian causes and took the Hungarian side against the instincts of her cautious and often reactionary husband. Many of those who had taken up arms against Austria in 1848–9 were pardoned and returned to their homeland to make careers for themselves under the new administration. Kossuth was an exception. Refusing to acknowledge Franz Joseph as his sovereign, he never returned to Hungary and died in Turin.

In 1873, Pest, Buda and Óbuda united to become a single capital city, Budapest. Supervised and controlled by the Metropolitan Council for Public Works, construction proceeded apace. More bridges were thrown across the Danube, wide streets and boulevards were laid out, suburbs were brought within the city's embrace, civic institutions were housed in grand Historicist buildings. The Opera House, Parliament, National Bank, Academy of Music, Customs House, St Stephen's Basilica, Technical University and the first underground railway line (to name just a handful of projects) all date from this period. In 1896 Hungary celebrated its Millennium—a thousand years since the Magyars had arrived in the Carpathian Basin—and Heroes' Square was laid out as a grand parade ground. Industry joined agriculture as the mainstay of the economy and the city's population ballooned as people flooded to the city to find work. All this was brought to a brutal and bloody end by the First World War.

THE FIRST WORLD WAR, RED TERROR AND TRIANON

The ethnic tensions within Austria-Hungary that had partly caused the First World War contributed greatly to the disintegration that followed it. Magyar-centric policies in Transylvania and the other Crown Lands led to bitter enmities. The collapsing economy by the end of the war had also given rise to radical socialist movements. Following the defeat of 1918 and the collapse of Austria-Hungary, the Aster Revolution in Budapest led to the dissolution of Hungary's union with Austria and the nomination of the 'Red Count' Mihály Károlyi (*see p. 246*) as President of the Republic, following the surrender of power by Charles IV (Franz Joseph's successor, who had been crowned in 1916). Károlyi, a pacifist and a fantasist, imagined that he could persuade Hungary's Serb, Romanian and Slovak neighbours to remain loyal. His hopes were dashed as the victorious Allied powers, in council in Paris, dictated new borders that stripped Hungary of large areas of her former territory in favour of those very neighbours. Károlyi resigned and power was seized by Béla Kun and his Soviet-style Republic of Councils, who unleashed a 'Red Terror' against those who opposed them, with gangs of 'Lenin Boys' recruited to eradicate unwished-for resistance. In an attempt to restore Hungary's pre-war borders, Kun and his Communist army of factory workers attacked first Czechoslovakia and then moved against Romania. Not only had Hungary lost the war, she was now a Communist belligerent. In retaliation the Romanian army occupied Budapest, in August 1919, and in the chaos Béla Kun fled, taking Hungary's gold reserves with him. Meanwhile, the Paris peace talks were continuing apace but Hungary had grievously damaged her chances of favourable treatment. Plebiscites in 1918 and 1919 resulted in non-Hungarian Transylvanians voting overwhelmingly to join the Kingdom of Romania. In June 1920 the Treaty of Trianon, aimed at promoting ethnic self-government in Central Europe, awarded large tracts of historic Hungary to Czechoslovakia, Romania and Yugoslavia. Hungary lost two thirds of her territory and over half her population, and with these went her coastline, forests, mines and mountains and a large part of the market for her manufactured goods, to say nothing of the means of manufacturing them. Budapest experienced a housing crisis as Magyar refugees, displaced from their homes, flooded to the rump that was left of the mother country. The wound inflicted by Trianon has never fully healed. The new borders, drawn up partly punitively but partly along ethnic lines, left many groups— Hungarians outside the new country borders, Jews almost everywhere—unprovided-for and vulnerable.

WHITE TERROR AND THE RISE OF FASCISM: 1920–41

When Admiral Miklós Horthy rode his white charger into Budapest in 1919, at the head of his National Army, he planned to 'call the city to account'. After Béla Kun fled, the Red terrorists gave place to a counter-revolutionary White Terror (some of whose leaders were National Army officers), which sought to liquidate Communists and their affiliates. Many fled into exile in Vienna or beyond. Horthy governed the country as regent, officially in lieu of the king (who had never formally abdicated but who was prevented from reassuming power despite two attempted coups). An air of ethnic hyper-awareness and Christian religiosity characterises the display devoted to this post-Trianon era in the Hungarian National Museum. Horthy's first Prime Minister, Count Pál Teleki, introduced a *numerus clausus* law in 1920, attaching ethnic quotas to university entry, a system which penalised the country's Jews. A later Prime Minister, Count István Bethlen, attempted to improve Hungary's relationship with the outside world, strengthening ties with Italy and entering the League of Nations, but as the decade wore on, particularly after the Depression of 1929, the climate became more inward-looking and more nationalistic. Communists were arrested and imprisoned, driving the movement underground. The Arrow Cross Party, which in many ways resembled the German Nazis, was formed in 1935. Under Prime Minister Gyula Gömbös, Hungary moved politically and economically closer to Hitler's Germany and Mussolini's Italy. There were economic reasons for this, but Mussolini also promised to lend military aid to a Hungarian effort to recapture territory signed away under Trianon. In March 1938, Hitler annexed Austria (the *Anchluss*). Two months later, Hungary passed its first Jewish Law, restricting Jewish participation in education, business and the professions. In November Germany announced the First Vienna Award, one of two inducements to Hungary to pledge its support for German military ambitions: part of Czechoslovakia was restored to Hungary. A second Jewish Law was passed in 1939. In 1940, the Second Vienna Award rewarded Hungary with a restituted portion of Transylvania. In 1941, after an ignominious failure to respect the Friendship Treaty with Yugoslavia by allowing German troops to cross Hungary to attack Belgrade (an event which led Pál Teleki, once again Prime Minister, to commit suicide), Hungary entered WWII on the German side.

THE SECOND WORLD WAR AND ITS AFTERMATH

Despite her position as a German ally, Hungary tried to avoid descending into full Nazism. Horthy's hesitance led Hitler to question his reliability; and in fact Hungary did begin secret negotiations with the US and Britain. On 19th March 1944, the Germans invaded Hungary and took control. Adolf Eichmann seized the chance to implement his Final Solution and within two months of the Nazi takeover, the transports of Jews to the concentration camps began. The fact that Horthy did not offer his resignation has exposed him to accusations of complicity. Both sides now saw him as incompetent, temporising and weak. By the end of June, most of Hungary's Jews, with the exception of those from Budapest, had been taken. In early July, Horthy ordered the suspension of the transports. On 23rd August, Romania changed sides, joining the Allies. Horthy, hoping to do the same, dismissed his Nazi Prime Minister, Döme Sztójay, and signed an armistice with the Soviets. Germany reacted by removing the vacillating Horthy altogether, occupying the country and assuming control. Ferenc Szálasi, an enthusiastic Nazi, head of the Arrow Cross Party, now came to power as Horthy's successor. Fascist mobs began rounding up Jews and anti-Nazis and shooting them into the Danube (*see p. 147*). In the absence of rail transports, Szálasi began force-marching Jews to the Austrian border. In November the Ghetto was set up in the Seventh District. It was left to brave individuals such as Raoul Wallenberg and Carl Lutz (*see pp. 300 and 215*) to do what they could to save lives in the International Ghetto in District XIII. The Siege of Budapest began in late December, lasting for two months during bitter winter weather. Aerial bombardment caused enormous destruction; and as the Soviets advanced, the retreating Germans blew up all the Danube bridges. Trapped in a cellar beneath the rubble of Castle Hill, Count Viktor Széchenyi wrote in his diary on 4th January 1945: 'Good news. The soldiers say that in 24 hours a large German army will arrive to liberate us. Pigs might fly!' In hiding across the river in Pest, the Jewish journalist Miksa Fenyő had hopes of an entirely different kind: 'I'm certain that the Russians will be here tomorrow. *Zdravstvuyte*: Greetings!'. Budapest was liberated by the Soviets in February 1945.

Once again a peace treaty was signed in Paris and once again Hungary was stripped of territory: all the gains made via the Vienna Awards were lost; Hungary's hopes of reversing the inequities of Trianon, for which she had entered the war, were dashed. Reprisals began. Szálasi and others were tried and executed and there were mass expulsions of ethnic Germans. The transition to Communism seemed muted at first, with an election held in 1945 which was won by the Independent Smallholders, a centre-right party with a strong rural constituency. The brief honeymoon of multi-party democracy and enthusiasm for post-war reconstruction was rapidly brought to and end when the Russian Marshal Voroshilov stepped in to ensure that affairs proceeded according to Soviet plans. A coalition government, with Soviets in prominent positions, was formed. Hungary was proclaimed a republic in early 1946 and a new unit of currency, the forint, was introduced in an effort to bring fiscal stability. The Prime Minister, Zoltán Tildy, was a Smallholder but his deputy was the hardline, Soviet-trained Communist Mátyás Rákosi. The Communist clampdown began as opponents of Rákosi's Stalinist policies were removed one by one (the famous 'salami tactics'). Following rigged elections in 1947, which still failed to return a Communist majority, Rákosi gave up all pretence at democracy, exiled or expelled recalcitrant Social Democrats, co-opted those who were prepared to be compliant and flung 'enemies-of-the-republic' slander at the Smallholders. He became head of the Hungarian Workers' Party in 1948. Opposition parties were outlawed in 1949 and Hungary officially became a People's Republic on the Soviet model.

THE COMMUNIST YEARS

The period immediately after the formation of the People's Republic was one of stringent Stalinism. Property was nationalised, religious organisations were outlawed and 'bad cadre' was ruthlessly hounded out. Two waves of internal deportations of the upper and middle classes took place in 1950 and 1951. Agricultural collectivisation and a move towards heavy industry, according to a series of Five Year Plans, did little for the economy and shortages became the norm. Behind Rákosi's genially smiling father-figure mask lay cruel megalomania. 'Class enemies' and 'agents of Western imperialism' were found to be everywhere, even within the Communist Party itself, as a bitter power struggle developed between the Soviet-educated guard and those who had been members of the Communist underground in Hungary. Show trials such as that of László Rajk sent many to their deaths or to interrogation, imprisonment and torture by the hated State Security police. After Stalin's death in 1953, the reformist Communist Imre Nagy came to power. Internal deportees were brought back from their labour camps and the activities of the secret police were curtailed. Rákosi, with Soviet support, fought back and Nagy was expelled from the Party. When Rákosi was finally undone by the collapse of his Soviet allies, his successor was the equally hardline Ernő Gerő. The events of the 1956 Uprising swept Nagy back to power. Student demonstrators demanded general elections by secret ballot, press freedom and the withdrawal of Soviet troops (who had been stationed in the country since 1945). Their attempt to get into the Hungarian Radio building to read their demands on air on 23rd October led to scuffles in the street that rapidly turned into a full-scale riot involving the tearing down of the giant statue of Stalin (*see p. 317*). Demonstrators were fired on outside Parliament. Imre Nagy promised free elections and a multi-party system. He also announced plans to withdraw Hungary from the Warsaw Pact. Appalled, the Soviets sent in the Red Army: tanks rolled into the streets of Budapest. Nagy was arrested and later executed and replaced by his erstwhile ally, former member of the illegal Hungarian Communist network János Kádár. Announcing that 'anyone who is not against us is for us', Kádár put down his opponents, made peace with Moscow and introduced a system that gradually evolved into 'Goulash Communism', the hotch-potch of Soviet ideology and Western ideas that came to characterise the long Kádár era. A relaxing of state control allowed a limited private sector to operate. Hungary became a country where you could buy things. Choice was restricted but there were no shortages. People had two-stroke-engine cars and little summer cottages among the vineyards: for many, life seemed safer and better and more predictable than in the free-for-all that descended after the fall of the Berlin Wall.

BUDAPEST TODAY

János Kádár's long career as Communist Party secretary came to an end in 1988. The following year was a momentous one in the history of Hungary, as the government introduced reforms aimed at further stimulating the economy. In June 1989, Imre Nagy was reburied and officially rehabilitated. Later in the same year, Hungary dismantled the fence along her border with Austria. This led to a flood of Easterners into the West and the resultant euphoria and chain of demonstrations ultimately led to the fall of the Berlin Wall. Hungary declared itself a republic—as opposed to a people's republic—in October. Free elections held in May 1990 resulted in a centre-right government led by the historian József Antall. Soviet troops finally left the country: the last detachment was gone by the summer of 1991.

Hungary joined NATO in 1999. Its currency, the forint, became fully convertible in 2001 and the country joined the European Union (though not the euro) in 2004. The sense of national unity that was joyfully felt after 1989 has failed to endure. Governments have swung back and forth between centre-right and centre-left and politics are bitterly contested. Budapest nevertheless continues to develop and thrive. Though in many respects and in many areas still a poor city where homelessness is a problem, its centre is beautiful, safe and well maintained, and, in this age of the low-cost airline, much visited. Where once it was rare to hear anything but Hungarian spoken in the streets, as you cross the Chain Bridge between Buda and Pest today, you will hear languages from almost all the continents of the globe.

Budapest Architecture

Budapest is an excellent city for looking at buildings. Despite extensive damage from shelling and bombardment in WWII—not to mention the assaults of Mongols, Ottomans, Counter-Reformers and urban planners—the fabric of the city has proved resilient. Medieval and Ottoman survivals are made all the more precious by their rarity. Reconstruction after 1945 was on the whole not brutal (nor was it Brutalist; Hungary's two great exponents of the art of building with raw concrete, Marcel Breuer and Ernő Goldfinger, both made their marks on other cities, New York and London). Very often the instinct has been to restore rather than to demolish and replace: from many vantage points the view of the cityscape today is recognisably the same one that appears in 19th-century lithographs.

Budapest is still essentially a low-rise city. Towers are springing up in a fairy ring around the perimeter but in the centre the Parliament and St Stephen's Basilica still dominate the skyline.

EARLIEST TRACES
Roman Budapest was a settlement called Aquincum, a civilian and a military town separated by a burial ground, on the west bank of the Danube in Óbuda (*map p. 97*). Much of the building would have been in wood and mud brick but plenty of stone foundations remain, showing the network of streets and with clear vestiges of numerous bath houses and two amphitheatres. Mosaics are scarce (there are a few) and wall-painting even more so, but there are some interesting lapidary remains, particularly funerary monuments. For detailed descriptions, see the relevant chapters in this guide (*pp. 94 and 230*). Traces of a Roman border fortress on the east bank of the Danube have also been found (*p. 176*).

THE MIDDLE AGES
It is bad luck that Hungary's period of political consequence under the Árpád kings (1000–1301) and Buda's splendour under Sigismund of Luxembourg (r. 1387–1437) and Matthias Corvinus (r. 1458–90) should have left so little material evidence. We know that there was some fine Romanesque and Gothic church architecture here, broadly following French models. Traces can be seen in the Matthias Church (*p. 38*) and under the former royal palace (*p. 51*). The fragments give no real idea what medieval Buda must have been like; it is like looking at it through a keyhole, where the wider picture is obscured. The same is true of the Buda—and Pest—of the Renaissance. Tantalising

vestiges in the Budapest History Museum and Hungarian National Gallery are all that remain, as well as two beautiful tabernacles in the Inner City Parish Church (*p. 177*).

THE OTTOMAN ERA

The Ottomans occupied Pest and Buda between 1541 and 1686. Their policy here—as it had been in Constantinople after 1453—was not to pull existing buildings down but to turn them over to new use. The royal palace seems to have become a gunpowder store and churches became mosques. Two reminders of this are the prayer niche in the southeast ambulatory wall of the Inner City Parish Church (*p. 179*) and a small doorway on Corvin tér (*p. 68*). Surviving examples of purely Ottoman architecture can be found in the bath houses along the Danube, built of alternating courses of brick and stone. There are four of these, three of which are currently in use (the Rudas, the Király and the Veli Bej) and all preserve a central domed hall with pools of varying temperatures around it. On the lower slopes of the Rózsadomb is the little octagonal mausoleum of the dervish Gül Baba (frequently subject to renovations and improvements funded by the Turkish government). Other funerary monuments are the little cluster of turban-topped gravestones above Szarvas tér (*p. 55*) and the stele of Abdurrahman, last pasha of Buda (*p. 35*). Not covered in this guide but of interest to those keen on tracking down Ottoman remains, is the minaret in the town of Érd, a short way to the southwest of Budapest (accessible by train and public bus).

THE BAROQUE ERA

After the Christian reconquest of 1686, Hungary was drawn into a lockstep march with Austria, architecturally no less than in other ways. Façades are rendered in coloured wash, roofs are steeply pitched, churches sprout onion-topped bell-towers and statuary shows emotionally charged saints, swathed in drapery and amply gesticulating, in a manner ultimately derived from Bernini though more primitive in execution. A sort of *horror vacui* begins to infect most surfaces, which crawl with stucco or squirm with frescoed martyrdoms. This is true certainly in ecclesiastical architecture but to a great degree in civic and domestic buildings too. Sumptuous Baroque church interiors can be seen at Szervita tér (*p. 172*) and Egyetem tér (*p. 187*). Votive statues erected to the Holy Trinity in thanks for the cessation of plague can be seen in three places: Fő tér (*p. 107*), Zsigmond tér (*p. 83*) and Szentháromság tér (*p. 40*). Statues of St John of Nepomuk (*see p. 69*) are also frequently found.

The so-called Zopf style of exterior decoration gets its name from the ornamental stucco swags resembling braids or pigtails (*Zopf* in German, *copf* in Hungarian), usually painted white against a coloured ground. There are several examples on and around Castle Hill, the Semmelweis Museum building (*p. 59*) being one of them.

For most of the 18th century, this architecture was the norm, a style that expressed the sentiments of the Counter-Reformation. After Joseph II issued his Edict of Tolerance in 1782, we begin to see a soberer model in church architecture, as Lutherans and Calvinists built places of worship. Both the first Lutheran and the first Calvinist churches were in Pest, on Deák tér and Kálvin tér respectively. Both have been much remodelled since the dates of their consecration: the original churches would have been even plainer, since Joseph II's Edict stipulated that non-Catholic places of worship must not proclaim their function in any obvious outward form.

NEOCLASSICISM AND HISTORICISM

We owe much of layout of Pest to the Palatine Joseph (*see p. 14*), who set up the Beautification Committee in 1808. The first architect on the board was János Hild, who planned the design of the expanding city. The old medieval walls were pulled down, the moat was filled in and replaced by a broad boulevard, and public and private buildings went up in the Neoclassical style, resulting in a network of graceful streets lined with houses that shared a common roofline. After Hild, the architect Mihály Pollack joined the committee, without whose agreement nothing could be built: it is to the committee's stipulations that we owe the lovely core of Pest. After the great flood of 1838, stringent building regulations were introduced, both regarding aesthetics and technical specifications. Pollack's masterpiece is the Hungarian National Museum, completed in 1847. The great architect of the mid-19th century is József Hild, son of János, who continued to build in a restrained, elegant Neoclassical style.

After 1867, Budapest began to fashion itself as the co-capital of an enormous empire. Buildings became larger, statelier and more grandiloquent. Just as the Renaissance in Italy was the age of the allegorical fresco and symbolic statue group, so was the neo-Renaissance in Hungary. The cycles of wall paintings in the Opera House and National Museum are examples, as are the statues surrounding the exterior of the Customs House (*p. 264*). The great architect of these later decades is Miklós Ybl, who built numerous town houses for the imperial Hungarian aristocracy in the 'Palace District' behind the National Museum. Neo-Renaissance was not the only Historicist style to take to the streets of Pest. As public buildings began to go up to house the institutions of the new co-capital, new styles were adopted to suit them. There is the Opera House (neo-Baroque), the Academy of Sciences (neo-Renaissance), the Museum of Fine Arts (Neoclassical) and the Parliament (neo-Gothic). In many cases the styles did not remain pure; eclectic mixes of Renaissance and Baroque elements became popular. Andrássy út (*p. 190*) is Budapest's supreme Historicist avenue.

THE SECESSION AND FOLK REVIVAL

Though the confident new Budapest of the Hungarian Millennium of 1896 (*see p. 368*) had filled up with grand and beautiful buildings, there was a sense that none of them was specifically Hungarian, and it is partly this that led to the Secession, the breakaway movement that turned its back on the derivative patterns of Historicism and instead began to plumb folk memory in search of a new, quintessentially native aesthetic. The name most associated with this is Ödön Lechner (*see p. 318*). His orientalising, folk-inspired architecture, a Hungarian version of Art Nouveau, had numerous followers, both those who adhered to it very closely (Sándor Baumgarten) and others who used it as a basis from which to develop a direction of their own (Albert Kálmán Kőrössy, who was inspired by French and Belgian models). Lechner's pupil Béla Lajta moved towards Art Deco and early Modernism, though still with ancient folk motifs a prominent feature.

Other architects of this period, responsible for their own elaboration of Art Nouveau and Secession principles, are the Löffler brothers (Kazinczy utca synagogue), József Vágó (Schiffer Villa) and Emil Vidor (Bedő-ház).

As Budapest boomed in the late 19th century, large numbers of people came to the city to work. Their housing needs were met by swiftly-erected tenement blocks, harmonious and well-proportioned externally but cramped and insanitary within. In the years immediately preceding WWI, however, a number of well-planned workers' housing estates were put in hand, in Óbuda and outer Pest, with leafy streets and low-rise semi-detached cottages. The Wekerle Estate (*p. 284*) is an example. Many new schools were built at this time too, and the Folk Revival style of Károly Kós and his follower Dezső Zrumeczky was popular in both social housing and school building projects.

MODERN ARCHITECTURE: THE '20s AND '30s

The years immediately following WWI were an impoverished time. The Treaty of Trianon, which stripped Hungary of most of her territory, led to immigration, as Hungarians from the former Crown Lands retreated within the new borders. Housing shortages were acute but paradoxically, many architects' careers were brought to an end. Partly this was due to a lack of money and patrons (the Art Nouveau master Albert Kálmán Kőrössy left architecture to become a civil servant), but partly also to the fact that many architects had allied themselves with the revolutions of 1918–19 and in consequence either left Hungary or did not receive public commissions. Building projects of the 1920s were generally conservative, adhering to tried and tested styles. This was the age of the 'Third Baroque', a restrained neo-neo-Baroque idiom that evoked past power and glory, comforting at a time of distress in a Hungary that had been shorn of land and status, vanquished and then humiliated.

Subdued Art Deco and Modern streamlined designs began to become a feature of the Budapest streetscape in the 1930s. József Fischer and Farkas Molnár built many Bauhaus-inspired villas in Buda. Other architects working in this vein were Lajos Kozma (a pupil of Béla Lajta) and Gyula Rimanóczy. Many companies invested in property. The Manfréd Weiss Steelworks, for example, built luxury flats for its pension fund in Újlipótváros (District XIII), the part of town that probably has the best concentration of architecture of this era. Not all the blocks were luxurious but they all shared the same system of apartments opening off a central stairwell, with windows on the street. The model of apartment buildings arranged around a central inner courtyard, with separate servants' and tradesmen's staircases, became a thing of the past.

THE COMMUNIST YEARS

World war once again interrupted things. Not only were many architects lost in the conflict (Farkas Molnár died in hospital after his house suffered a direct hit; Marcell Komor, Ervin Quittner and Béla Hofstätter were murdered by the Nazis; the Löffler brothers emigrated; Imre Francsek never returned from the Soviet gulag), but post-war political ideology intervened. Modern styles which had become established in the 1940s were repudiated under Communism as imperialist and Western. The construction industry was nationalised and responsibility for planning was assumed by the state, which controlled designs and commissions through bodies such as LAKÓTERV (responsible for residential building projects) and IPARTERV (public buildings). Just as Mátyás Rákosi demanded that the royal palace on Castle Hill be rebuilt as it had been 'but with less decoration', so everything else had to be divested of decadent, bourgeois ornament. Stripped Classicism became popular, as evidenced by the Second District Municipality on Mechwart tér, a typical example of the Socialist Realist ethos which between 1951 and 1954 sought to root out undesirable cosmopolitan influence. As in architecture, so in painting and sculpture. All privately-run art galleries were nationalised and it is interesting to follow the career development of many 20th-century artists as they tried to survive in the turbid waters of Communism. In 1954, the 'Two Thousandths' policy was introduced, whereby a small proportion of all state infrastructure funding had to be spent on art. The result was a glut of suitably-themed public sculpture and murals, showing a utopian world of hard work, happy families and peaceful, productive community living.

In 1958, state control was slightly relaxed and art became less inward-looking (Hungary once again participated in the Venice Biennale, for example) but, under the Culture Minister György Aczél, the system of the 'Three Ts' was introduced, dividing art into categories: *Támogatott* ('subsidised'), *Tűrt* ('tolerated') and *Tiltott* ('banned'). Themes that were banned included all reference to 1956 and defection to the West, criticism of the Party or praise for Western consumerism.

In the 1960s came *szanálás*, a neologism derived from the Latin word *sano*, in other words a cleansing. Whole areas of the city—Óbuda, Kőbánya—had their ancient hearts torn out and in place of the humble cottage dwellings went tall, prefabricated concrete blocks of flats, the 'panel apartments', all with central heating and mains water. The first of these were built in 1966 and suburban streets filled up with 'Kádár boxes', uniform square-plan houses with hipped roofs, which people received state funding to build.

ARCHITECTURE TODAY

In 1968, with the launch of the New Economic Mechanism, art and architecture were freed from central control. Post-Modern constructions, in a sober and sometimes slightly dowdy form, appeared in the 1980s, along with Organic Architecture, based on the forms of nature allied to native folklore. Modern office blocks arrived in the 1990s. New housing pressures today have led to wholesale demolition of 19th-century tenements in the Seventh, Eighth and Ninth districts and the erection of new and undistinguished apartment blocks. Contemporary trends have embraced the glass sheath, as seen by the development on the north corner of Kálvin tér and the shimmering multi-purpose block on Vörösmarty tér. Tall towers are beginning to sprout at the city rim. A Zaha Hadid project fell through in around 2008 but if Foster and Partners build their projected tower for MOL, the Hungarian oil company, on the Danube bank in District XI, then Budapest will have its first real taste of international starchitecture. A modern Historicism, meanwhile, is making itself felt in the reconstruction *ex novo* of buildings destroyed in WWII (the royal stables on Castle Hill and Casino on Margaret Island are examples). The time way well be ripe for a new Secession.

District I: Castle Hill

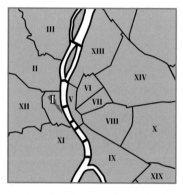

Castle Hill (Budai Vár) is a limestone outcrop about 1.5km long rising steeply on the west bank of the Danube and standing some 100m above the plain from which it springs. It is a scenic district, its cobbled streets lined with brightly-painted late Baroque houses with steeply pitched roofs. Every so often you will see a poignant vestige of medieval splendour and the many plaques and statues, stelae and spolia are constant reminders of battles lost and won: in its time Castle Hill has been fought over by Ottomans and Christians, Habsburgs and Hungarians, Soviets and Nazis. The main sights are the Matthias Church, the former royal palace (now the Hungarian National Gallery and Budapest History Museum) and the Fishermen's Bastion, famous for its panoramic views of Pest.

HISTORY OF CASTLE HILL

Buda was first fortified in the 13th century, as a precaution against Mongol raids—to which the royal centre of Óbuda, closer to the river, had proved vulnerable. A city grew up here, provided with religious houses belonging to the Dominicans and Franciscans, and with a Jewish community also. The royal court at this time was still peripatetic and it is not certain whether King Béla IV, who had fortified Castle Hill, ever used it as a residence. His successors, however, certainly did. Initially the royal enclave was on the hill's northern tip and it was here that the court moved from Visegrád in the 14th century. Queen Elizabeth, pious widow of Charles I and mother of Louis the Great, rebuilt and richly endowed the chapel of St Michael here. It was under King Louis (r. 1342–82) that the royal palace moved to the south end of the hill and from his reign on, Buda remained an important royal seat. It was used as such by King Sigismund (r. 1387–1437), who extended the palace and built a chapel. Under Matthias Corvinus (r. 1458–90) the court at Buda was famed throughout Europe for its splendour, culture and learning, almost a second Palermo, where the opulent East met the intellect and taste of the Italian Renaissance. After the disaster of Mohács in 1526 (*see p. 11*),

CASTLE HILL
View of the Matthias Church.

confidence tottered. Buda was sacked and Queen Mary, widow of the young king Louis II, who had died in the battle, fled from the palace with as much of the royal treasury as she could take. With her went a great part of Buda's populace.

In 1541 the troops of Suleiman the Magnificent took the city. It remained in Ottoman hands until 1686, when it was recaptured for Christendom by the Habsburg armies. The siege was bloody and destructive, claiming many lives and reducing houses, churches, convents, synagogues and palaces to rubble (the victorious soldiers were given the customary three days to loot and pillage the stricken town). It was rebuilt, in the Austrian Baroque style, but it never regained its medieval pre-eminence. Hungary was ruled from Vienna, and Buda, without a royal court, was forsaken by the aristocracy. Instead it became home to a mainly German-speaking community of shopkeepers, merchants and artisans. When the patricians returned after Franz Joseph's coronation in 1867, it was the old burghers' houses that accommodated them, and it is mostly those houses that line the Castle District streets today, rebuilt once again following huge destruction during the Siege of Budapest at the close of WWII.

In the interwar period, during the regentship of Miklós Horthy, Castle Hill was home to a number of government ministries (and Horthy himself took up residence in the royal palace). At the time of writing the Hungarian government planned to move two ministries and the Prime Minister's office to the hill. There were also proposals to move the National Gallery from the old royal palace. Though work had begun on some of the planned removals, no final outcome was certain. The descriptions below reflect the situation at the time of writing.

Getting to Castle Hill

From Clark Ádám tér (map p. 423, C3) you can make the ascent by funicular (see pp. 69–70), by bus no. 16 or on foot. From Széll Kálmán tér (map p. 423, A1), take bus 16 or 16A, or walk up Ostrom or Várfok utca. From the bottom of the hill to east and west, stepped streets and paths lead to the top and there are lifts to ease the climb (marked on the map on p. 423). The description below begins at the north end of the hill, at Bécsi kapu, the Vienna Gate.

BEFORE THE VIENNA GATE

On the triangle of grass at the junction of Várfok utca and Ostrom utca (*map p. 423, A1*), low down and difficult to see if the grass has not been mown, is a globe-shaped sculpture entitled **Earth Mother** (Nándor Wagner, 1983). To the right of the barriers that control traffic entering Castle Hill is a larger-than-lifesize **statue of Mihály Táncsics** (*see p. 30*), clad in a voluminous cloak (Imre Varga, 1969) and in a niche in the rampart walls, a polychrome relief of the reconquest of Buda (Margit Kovács, 1977).

Opposite, at the entrance to the **Europa Liget** park (*map p. 423, B1*), is a seated statue of the founders of the Jagiellonian dynasty, Jadwiga (or Hedwig), daughter of Louis the Great of Hungary, and Vladislas of Lithuania. The Europa Liget, on a narrow terrace below the castle walls, was once the garden of the Grünwald Villa (destroyed in the war). Today it takes its name from the trees that shade it, planted by representatives of 29 European capitals in 1973, to mark the hundred years since Pest, Buda and Óbuda had united to form a single capital. The trees had to be typical of each donor city's native flora and also able to flourish in the Hungarian climate. Not all of them survived (the London plane and the Moscow ash have done notably well) and some felling and re-shuffling took place when the park was rejuvenated in 2017. On the wall overlooking Hunfalvy utca, arranged as if sitting on a park bench, is another successful work by Imre Varga, a **statue of Zoltán Kodály** (1982).

Close to the entrance to the Buda Castle, to the left of the gateway, is a tall **flagstaff** bearing a legend in *rovásírás*, the ancient pre-Roman runic script of the Magyars. The symbols (which are read from right to left) spell out the word *Budavár*, Buda Castle.

THE NORTH END OF CASTLE HILL

The area between Bécsi kapu tér (Vienna Gate Square; *map p. 423, A1*) and Szentháromság tér (Holy Trinity Square; *map p. 423, B2*) is mainly residential, with a handful of museums, some cafés and restaurants but few shops. At the time of writing the Interior Ministry and the Ministry of the Economy were preparing to move here. The buildings are ranged along four main parallel streets, which fuse into two after the Matthias Church. The houses, with their attractive colour-wash façades, stucco details and arched carriage entrances, are typically amalgamations of two or more smaller medieval properties, joined together in the 18th century. Many of the houses bear plaques giving the date of construction, and sometimes naming the well-to-do artisan for whom they were built. On some of the façades you can see traces of medieval stonework, much of it probably brought to light after damage in WWII. Post-war reconstruction overwhelmingly followed the 'where it was and as it was' principle; occasionally you will see a completely modern building (Fortuna u. 15, Országház u. 26, Úri u. 41, Táncsics Mihály u. 20), but its height and proportions are always adapted to the dimensions of its neighbours.

BÉCSI KAPU TÉR

Bécsi kapu tér, Vienna Gate Square, is fronted by a **tripartite gateway**, the northern entrance to Castle Hill, facing the direction of the Austrian capital. A city gate has always stood here; in medieval times it gave onto a marketplace. The present structure was erected in 1936. Vehicular traffic uses the wide central archway; the two, much narrower, lateral arches are for pedestrians and also give access to the ramparts. As soon as you are through the gate, you are confronted by a colossal plaque on the left, whose Latin inscription honours the 'Christian heroes' who laid down their lives for Buda in the struggle to win it back from Ottoman control in 1686. On the right is a **bronze angel** (Béla Ohmann, 1936), surging forward apostolic cross in hand, likewise commemorating Buda's restoration to 'liberty from servitude'. It dates from the

250th anniversary of the Christian victory. The square itself is a pleasant cobbled space, dominated on one side by the towering façade of the **Lutheran church** (Mór Kallina, 1895) and on the other by the brooding neo-Romanesque bulk of the **National Archives** (Nemzeti Levéltár), designed by Samu Pecz. Building began in 1913 but was not completed until after WWI. Severe damage in WWII has been repaired but some elements, such as the tower, were not reconstructed. The roof tiles, by the Zsolnay manufactory, are replacements of the originals. The carved main doors, with stone owls above them, are particularly fine. Guided tours of the building are available on certain days (*for details, see mnl.gov.hu/angol*). Next to the National Archives is a glass-fronted building with a concrete tower, formerly an electricity distribution substation (Csaba Virág, 1979). Recent plans to demolish it were halted by protests from admirers of its architecture and at the time of writing it was to be used by the Interior Ministry.

Behind a **fountain** (János Pásztor, 1936) commemorating the Neoclassical sculptor István Ferenczy, who lived on the hill, the yellow house with fine wrought-iron over the windows was for a time the **home of Baron Lajos Hatvany**, literary critic and Petőfi expert (*see p. 252*). In the early 1930s, before the rise of Fascism prompted Hatvany to leave Hungary, writers would congregate here (their signatures, worked in metal, have been inserted into the pavement outside). The house next door has a statue of St John of Nepomuk (*see p. 69*) in an exterior niche.

TÁNCSICS MIHÁLY UTCA

The curving Táncsics Mihály utca (*map p. 423, B1*) is the most attractive of the four main streets of the northern Castle District, partially blocked to cars. From the late 14th century until the ousting of the Ottomans, this was the Jewish quarter. Excavations in 1964–5 revealed remains of the **main synagogue**, built in 1461 in the Gothic style, in what is now the garden of no. 23 (plaque on Babits Mihály sétány). During the siege of 1686 it burned and collapsed. The excavations have been backfilled but there are plans to bring the remains to light again. At no. 26, opposite, you can visit a small **prayer house** (*open Wed–Sun May–Oct 10–5, Nov–March 10–4; ring the bell for admittance*). In the entranceway, behind a barred gate (*open as museum*), is a collection of mainly 17th-century tombstones, all labelled. The columns at the back of the courtyard came from the synagogue at no. 23. The entrance to the prayer house is inside the courtyard to the right. Seventeenth-century paintings on the vault show a Star of David with a verse from the book of Numbers and a drawn bow pointed heavenward with a text from 1 Samuel. The style of the writing, which shows affinities with Arabic script, leads scholars to believe that this was the prayer house of a Sephardic community.

At **no. 17** plaques commemorate the politician Albert Apponyi (representative of Hungary at Trianon), who lived here until his death in 1933, and his son György, who was taken from here to Mauthausen by the Nazis in 1944. There are more plaques, and portrait reliefs, on **no. 9**, site of a former gunpowder store and prison, where Lajos Kossuth (*see p. 144*) was held in 1837–40 and Mihály Tancsics in 1847–8 and 1860–7. A radical pamphleteer and advocate of Hungarian autonomy, Táncsics was born into a peasant family in 1799 and trained as a weaver. His utopian, egalitarian views brought him into conflict with authority and he was placed behind bars. On 15th March 1848,

TANCSICS MIHÁLY UTCA

Wall painting of a drawn bow in the Jewish prayer house. Scholars have interpreted the text
('The bows of the mighty men are broken') as expressing the Jewish community's
hope that the Christians would not prevail against the Ottomans in 1686.

the revolutionary mob freed him and he was paraded through the streets in a carriage drawn by his own supporters. For many years forced to go into hiding he, together with many others who had opposed the Habsburgs, was granted political amnesty after the 1867 Compromise. To the end of his life he continued to campaign for the betterment of the working man's lot. He died in 1884 and is buried in Kerepesi Cemetery.

THE JEWS OF BUDA

A Jewish community established itself very early in Buda, around the time of its foundation in the 13th century. They settled at the southern end of the outcrop, with their cemetery at the bottom near today's Krisztina tér. Remains of a synagogue and mikveh came to light during building work in 2005. King Béla IV, the founder of Buda, issued a bill outlining the Jews' rights, awarding them certain privileges. Although they were not permitted to hold high office, they enjoyed royal protection and paid taxes directly to the Treasury. Louis the Great briefly exiled them in 1349 but within a few years they were permitted to return. When the royal court moved from the north part of the hill to the south, the Jewish district moved likewise but in reverse, settling on either side of the street that became known as 'New Jewry', today's Táncsics Mihály utca. During the reign of Matthias Corvinus the community grew in size, owing to an influx of Sephardim expelled from Spain, and the king (whose Master of the Treasury was a converted Jew) appointed a prefect to be the community's head. During the Ottoman period, from 1541, the Jews lived largely unmolested and represented slightly over ten percent of Buda's population. For them the Christian recapture of Buda was a disaster not a victory: the conquerors' zeal snuffed out four centuries of Jewish life on the hill.

At **Táncsics Mihály u. 7** is the fine former Erdődy palace (Máté Nepauer 1750–69), with an attractive cobbled courtyard with wrought-iron lamps. It houses the **Music**

History Museum (Zenetörténeti Múzeum; *open Tues–Sun 10–4; zti.hu*), which has a permanent collection of musical instruments, including a fine early Broadwood fortepiano. Concerts are frequently held here. The palace has an interesting history. Beethoven stayed here at least once as a guest of Anna Maria Erdődy (he was also practically a permanent lodger in her Vienna *palais* and dedicated a number of works to her). The house was bought by József Hatvany-Deutsch in 1912. His widow was deported in 1944 and the house was taken over by the Nazis. The family's valuable porcelain collection survived the war but was looted by the Soviets in 1945.

The **Koller Gallery** at no. 5 (*open 10–6; free*) offers the chance to see inside a Castle District house and appreciate how warren-like they are, with narrow stairways darting between different levels, a flagged courtyard in front, with access to a cellar underneath, and a garden at the back. At the very top is the former atelier of the sculptor Amerigo Tot (1909–84), born in Hungary but active mainly in Italy. A handful of his works are on display. There is a superb Danube view from his studio window.

Another fine old house at **no. 1** has a long inner hallway stretching unbroken to the riverward side, where glass doors give onto wide views, a style faintly reminiscent of a Venetian *palazzo*, where the courtyard stretches between street gate and water gate. Formerly the home of the British Legation, it housed the Swiss vice-consul Carl Lutz (*see p. 215*) in 1942–5.

HESS ANDRÁS TÉR

This pleasant square (*map p. 423, B2*), where Fortuna utca and Táncsics Mihály utca meet, is named after the printer in whose Castle Hill workshop the first Hungarian book, the *Chronica Hungarorum*, was produced in 1473. Facing the square and its little garden is the **former Vörös Sün** (Red Hedgehog) inn, complete with plaster sign over the entrance. At the time of writing the **Litea bookshop and tearoom** was preparing to move into the right-hand retail space (appropriate to have a bookshop on this square dedicated to the memory of printing). In the centre of the garden stands a **statue of Pope Innocent XI** (József Damkó, 1936), who helped convene the Holy League against the Turks, contributing both moral and financial support to the fight to expel them from Vienna and Buda. To the right (as you face the pope) is the **Hilton Hotel**, with a curious tower at its north end. The lower part is a survival from the medieval church of St Nicholas, founded together with an adjoining friary by the Dominicans in the 13th century. In 1477 King Matthias Corvinus founded a university in the friary, a fact commemorated by the elaborate **high relief** on the front of the tower, a copy of the one set up in 1486 by the town of Bautzen in Saxony, when it acknowledged Matthias' rule. The features of the king are supposed to be a portrait from life. Neither church nor friary nor university survived the Ottoman occupation, much less the siege which brought it to an end. From the windows of the Hilton hotel lobby, you can look down into the **'Dominican Courtyard'**, an outdoor function space occupying the ruined shell of the old friary church. The renovated hotel building and the top section of the church tower are by Béla Pintér (1976). The old friary cloister is also now part of the hotel, remodelled in '70s taste but preserving an original wellhead and masonry fragments.

The orange building opposite the Hilton has examples of **sedilia** in its entranceway. Many Castle Hill houses have this feature, some of them with quite fine Gothic canopies. Scholars are undecided as to their original purpose.

ORSZÁGHÁZ UTCA

Facing Szenthármoság tér between Fortuna utca and Országház utca is a large neo-Gothic building (1904, restored after damage in WWII), the **former Finance Ministry**. At the time of writing, there were plans to move the Ministry of National Economy here. A plaque on the Országház utca flank notes that the Egyetemi Nyomda (University Press) occupied the building between 1777 and 1926. Books by Samuil Micu-Klein and other members of the Transylvanian School (Şcoala Ardealană) were printed here in the late 18th–19th century. Opposite, a plaque at **no. 14** commemorates the Neoclassical sculptor István Ferenczy, who lived here.

Historically much of Országház utca was in the hands of the Franciscans, who had convents of both friars and nuns (the Poor Clares) here. The nunnery was at **no. 28**. Displaced from Óbuda by the Ottomans, the sisters fled first to Pressburg (today's Bratislava) before settling here, until their Order was dissolved by Joseph II in the 1780s. Subsequently the Hungarian Diet also moved here from Pressburg and established their Országház (lit. 'Nation House' or Parliament) in the old nunnery. At the time of writing there were plans to move the Interior Ministry here. A plaque on the building's façade commemorates prisoners of the Gestapo, of various nationalities, who were held here in 1945. **No. 30**, once the Franciscan friary, was also incorporated into the parliamentary complex. Its former refectory was used for court hearings: in 1795 the Hungarian Jacobins (*see p. 56*) were examined here.

The house on the corner of Országház utca and Nándor utca has its exterior corner pierced by a **sculpture of a nun**, hands clasped in prayer, a memorial to the two religious houses which once stood here.

KAPISZTRÁN TÉR

Kapisztrán tér (*map p. 423, A1–A2*) is a wide cobbled space partly occupied by the ruins of the 15th-century **church of St Mary Magdalene** (Mária Magdolna templom; *tower open daily 10–sunset; weekends only in winter*), its outline traced by a set of low walls. The church, first founded on this site in the 13th century, came to be used by the Hungarian citizens of Buda, while the German-speaking population used the Matthias Church. After the Ottoman conquest it was the only building allotted to the Christians and different denominations used it alternately until in time it too was converted into a mosque. After the conquest of 1686 it was given to the Franciscans, who used it until their Order was dissolved in the Habsburg lands in 1782. After that it was used as the chapel of the Nándor Barracks (*see below*). It was badly damaged in 1945 and subsequently demolished. Plans continue to be put forward for its rebuilding. At the time of writing there were plans to create a Visitor Centre here. A peal of 24 small bells mounted on the tower plays a carillon every hour. On the Úri utca side you can see the entrance façade that was built in 1792 when the church was used for the coronation of Franz I as King of Hungary. Set up at the former east end is a **bronze replica of**

the Coronation Mantle (Tibor Rieger, 2017), providing an excellent opportunity to study its details and to identify the various saints, prophets and apostles (*for more on the mantle, and a schematic diagram, see pp. 231–3*).

Kapisztrán tér takes its name from St John of Capestrano, the Franciscan friar and inquisitor whose fiery rhetoric brought the Hungarians out behind János Hunyadi to beat the Turks at Belgrade in 1456. The battle was a turning point, and ever since then, the noonday bells have rung from church steeples in celebration. A **statue of the saint** (József Damkó, 1922) shows him surging forward, pectoral cross swaying. By his side a defiant Magyar sounds a horn and beneath his feet lies a slain Turk. It was close to here that the Franciscans had their friary, before the Order was dissolved by Joseph II (*see above*). The statue was set up as part of the programme of celebrations marking the 700th anniversary of the founding of the Order by St Francis of Assisi in 1222.

On the north side of Kapisztrán tér is the First District Town Hall. Next to it, the **former Nándor Barracks** houses the Military History Museum and Archives (*described below; entrance around the corner on Tóth Árpád sétány*). In the angle formed by the L-shaped buildings have been placed a number of **cannons**, of various ages and provenances. One of them, '*Le Louis*', dates from the latter years of Napoleon's republic. It is signed (on the breech) '*Par Bouquero, Chef de Bon d'Artrie Le 4 Fror An XI*', indicating that it was cast by François Gaspard Bouquero, Chef de Bataillon d'Artillerie, whose foundry was at Turin, on the 4th of Fructidor in the 11th year of the Republic: so in August 1803.

THE MILITARY HISTORY MUSEUM
Map p. 423, A1–A2. Hadtörténeti Múzeum. Entrance on Tóth Árpád sétány. Open Tues–Sun 10–6; 9–5 in winter. The museum is well organised and well labelled.

Outside the main entrance to the Military History Museum stands a collection of **cannons**. Among them are two Chinese guns captured during the Boxer Rising and a very rare, slender cannon whose breech ends in a stylised elephant head.

On the first floor the exhibits cover the period from 1815 to 1948. A considerable part of the display is devoted to the **Hungarian revolution of 1848–9** and the capture of Buda in May 1849. During the battle, the Austrian commander, Heinrich Hentzi, who had angered the Hungarian general Artúr Görgei (*see p. 245*) by his bombardment of Pest and resulting destruction of some of its fine Neoclassical buildings, was fatally wounded. The keys to the southern city gate of Buda are part of the display. There are also some superb photographs and posters from the period of the **First World War and its aftermath**, with material on the Romanian invasion of Budapest, the growth of Communist groups, the Red Terror and succeeding White Terror, Trianon and the Irredentist Movement (including an Irredentist board game called *Mindent Vissza!*, Win it all back!), the two royal coups, Horthy, **WWII and the Nazi takeover**. The **Siege of Budapest** follows (December 1944–February 1945), and after that a display on Hungarians in **Soviet POW and labour camps**. The last prisoners only returned to Hungary in 1955. Around half a million camp inmates are estimated to have died.

On the ground floor is a separate exhibition on the First World War, including a fascinating **film of the coronation of Charles IV** in December 1916. This was a magnificent final curtain call by old Austria-Hungary, full of pageantry. The film footage shows skittish horses as the procession leaves the royal palace; ladies in voluminous skirts being bundled into carriages; shots of Queen Zita and Prince Otto in the glass state coach; plenty of lords spiritual sporting a fine variety of headgear and members of the crowd posing for the cameras. The lords temporal in their national costumes are extremely splendid. The solemnities of the coronation itself in the Matthias Church were not filmed but the subsequent oath-taking and the *kardvágás*, the ceremonial brandishing of the state sword to the four cardinal points from a specially constructed mound on Dísz tér, are all captured on film. King Charles nods and smiles to the crowd from under a St Stephen's Crown that looks much too big for him.

The final rooms cover the period from 1948, when **Communism** began to take hold, through the catastrophe of 1956, to the final lowering of the Iron Curtain.

THE NORTHERN RAMPARTS

Walking around the ramparts to the right from the Military History Museum, you pass a tall flagstaff on top of the corner bastion. Round the corner, past more military paraphernalia, you come to the **stele of Abdurrahman**, the last Ottoman pasha of Buda, who fell in battle near this spot in September 1686. The inscription reads: 'A valiant foe; peace be with him.' On top of the walls by the **Anjou Bastion** (behind the building housing the lift), a plaque marks the spot from where the Hungarian pennant was first flown after the Christian victory.

THE MATTHIAS CHURCH
& FISHERMEN'S BASTION

Map p. 423, B2. Usually open 9–5 unless services are in progress. Tickets online or from the booths built into the wall opposite the church's south flank (tickets to climb the bell-tower can also be purchased here). In high season the church can get very crowded with coach tours and groups from cruise ships. It is best to visit at the end of the day or first thing, if you can. For updates and online tickets, see matyas-templom.hu.

Although ecclesiastical tradition maintains that the Church of Our Lady on Buda's Castle Hill was founded by St Stephen, there is no documentary evidence for this: the first attested building is a basilica in the French Gothic style, dating from the reign of Béla IV (13th century). Subsequent monarchs added to the edifice. In the 14th century, under Louis the Great and King Sigismund, the church played a significant part in the Hungarian coronation ritual: after the crowning at Székesfehérvár, the new monarch showed himself to the people of Buda here, in full regalia. During the reign of Matthias Corvinus the church enjoyed a flowering, in large part because of the prominence of the royal court here on the hill. The southwest bell-tower, which bears Matthias' insignia, dates from this time (c. 1470). Following damage in the Turkish sack of 1526, the church was rebuilt but immediately after the Ottoman conquest of 1541 was turned into a mosque, the first church to undergo such a change. It was here that Suleiman gave thanks to Allah for his victory. When other churches on the hill also became mosques, the Matthias Church adopted the name *Eski Djami* (Old Mosque). After the reconquest of 1686, the church passed to the Jesuits, who repaired it in the Baroque style. Between 1873 and 1894, a full-scale programme of repair and reconstitution took place, directed by Frigyes Schulek. He dismantled all the Baroque additions and set about resurrecting the church in its Gothic glory, re-carving damaged elements, supplementing missing ones on existing models and, where these were lacking, giving free rein to his own imagination (for example in the crocketed spire which surmounts the 15th-century bell-tower). The result is a sumptuous Magyarisation of the Gothic idiom, opulently polychrome in the interior, where the walls and vaults are covered with decoration in richly-coloured geometric and floral designs, partly inspired by Hungarian folk motifs and partly by heraldic emblems. Noted artists were brought in to execute the work, including Károly Lotz and Bertalan Székely. Two coronations took place here: Franz Joseph's in 1867 and Charles IV's in 1916. The church was badly damaged in WWII. Restoration was finally completed in 2015.

The church is officially dedicated to the Assumption of the Virgin but is always familiarly known as the Mátyás-templom (Matthias Church). The description below corresponds to the plan opposite.

(A) The Lotz frescoes: Above the chapel arcades on the north side is a series of 19th-century painted scenes by Károly Lotz celebrating the divine intervention of the Virgin, patron saint of Hungary, in the fortunes of the nation. From left to right, they are: **(Ai)** St Stephen appeals to the Virgin and the troops of Emperor Conrad retreat; **(Aii)** The Virgin in a dream promises victory to Louis the Great if he fixes her image to his standard; **(Aiii)** On the recapture of Buda in 1686, a statue of the Virgin, walled up by the Ottomans, miraculously shows itself once more.

(B) Zichy Chapel: The chapel is dedicated to St Imre, son of St Stephen. The panels on the altarpiece doors are painted by Mihály Zichy and show scenes from the sainted prince's life. The three statues are of Imre (centre) flanked by his father and his tutor, St Gellért. On the opposite wall are frescoes of St Francis by Bertalan Székely and allegories of the monastic vows of the Franciscans: Poverty, shown in rags; Chastity, holding her gown tight across her bosom; Obedience, with head bowed.

(C) Chapel of Béla III: King Béla III (d. 1196) and his first wife, Anne de Châtillon, were reburied here, in a fine tomb by Ferenc Mikula, in 1898. Opposite is an altarpiece of the Holy Trinity. King Béla's second wife Margaret of France (*see p. 339*) outlived her husband and died in the Holy Land.

(D) Entrance to the Gallery and Royal Oratory: As you mount the stairs, you have a good view of Károly Lotz's large fresco of the *Coronation of Franz Joseph*, showing the king and his wife Elisabeth kneeling before the Virgin. It decorates the chapel of the Hungarian Knights of Malta. The balcony of the

Royal Oratory overlooks the chancel and has good views of the stained-glass windows of saints and apostles. An exhibition here includes a copy of St Stephen's Crown and the coronation regalia (orb and sceptre): you can study these copies much more closely than the originals in the Parliament.

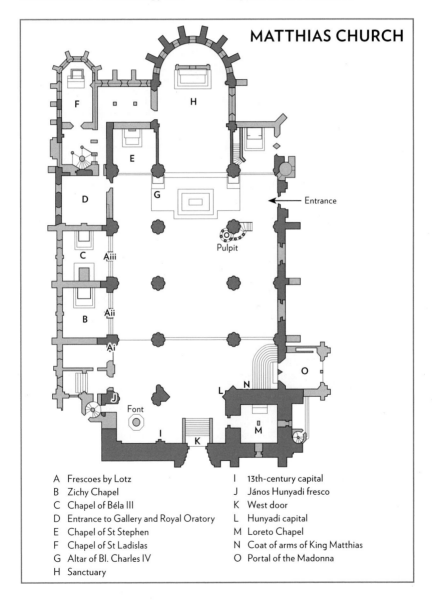

MATTHIAS CHURCH

Entrance

Pulpit

Font

A	Frescoes by Lotz	I	13th-century capital
B	Zichy Chapel	J	János Hunyadi fresco
C	Chapel of Béla III	K	West door
D	Entrance to Gallery and Royal Oratory	L	Hunyadi capital
E	Chapel of St Stephen	M	Loreto Chapel
F	Chapel of St Ladislas	N	Coat of arms of King Matthias
G	Altar of Bl. Charles IV	O	Portal of the Madonna
H	Sanctuary		

MATTHIAS CHURCH
Detail of the *Dormition of the Virgin* (14th century) from the Portal of the Madonna.

(E) Chapel of St Stephen: A reliquary here contains the foot of St John the Almoner, originally sent as a gift to King Matthias by Sultan Beyazit II in 1489 and placed in the chapel in the royal palace. The elaborate casket on the altar, designed by Schulek, was intended for the right hand of St Stephen, though it was never kept here and is now in St Stephen's Basilica (*see p. 159*). The walls have scenes from the life of St Stephen by Bertalan Székely.

(F) Chapel of St Ladislas: The walls are covered in Károly Lotz's fresco cycle of the life and miracles of Ladislas (László), who was canonised in 1192 on the initiative of Béla III.

(G) Altar of the Blessed Charles IV: Charles IV, the last Habsburg to sit on the throne of Austria-Hungary, was crowned King of Hungary in this church in 1916. After the collapse of the empire, Charles attempted to regain the Hungarian throne in two coups in 1921, encouraged by the Legitimists (the Hungarian royalist faction). Miklós Horthy quelled the attempts and Charles and Queen Zita were taken by British ships (HMS *Glowworm* and HMS *Cardiff*) to Madeira, where the king died of pneumonia in 1922. He was only 34. Historians differ in their assessments of Charles; what cannot be disputed is the unswerving ardour of his Catholic faith. He was beatified by Pope John Paul II in 2004.

(H) Sanctuary: The neo-Romanesque high altar is by Schulek. On it stands a statue of the Virgin crowned with a replica of St Stephen's Crown, added in 2000 and blessed by Pope John Paul II before it was installed.

(I) 13th-century capital: This capital, the oldest in the church (c. 1260), shows two male figures, one of them in monastic dress, pointing to pages in a book. It was discovered during the rebuilding of the church by Schulek and his team. As the information panel beside it notes, it is the only piece of medieval carving in Hungary still in its original position.

(J) János Hunyadi fresco:
Overlooking the font is a fresco by Károly Lotz telling the story of the Siege of Belgrade of 1456, with the figures of St John Capestrano and Pope Calixtus III, who commanded that noonday bells should ring in celebration (*see p. 34*).

(K) West door: The great doorway is flanked by painted angels. Note the wrought-iron lizard door handle.

(L) The Hunyadi capital: Beneath the organ loft is a capital decorated with four stylised faces: János Hunyadi, his sons László and Mátyás (Matthias Corvinus) and, facing the nave, Sigismund of Luxembourg. The Hunyadi family sought to legitimise their claim to the Hungarian throne by declaring King Sigismund to be János Hunyadi's father.

(M) Loreto Chapel: The chapel is named after the 17th-century copy of the Black Madonna of Loreto. Opposite the entrance is a stone statue of the Virgin which purports to be the very one that the Ottomans walled up and which by miracle revealed itself again after the Christian reconquest. Scholars doubt that it is one and the same; stylistically this statue seems to be a later work.

(N) Coat of arms of King Matthias:
The carved and painted coat of arms and profile of the king (restored and given a fine surround by Bertalan Székely) are the 1470 originals, formerly on the bell-tower (replaced *in situ* by a copy).

(O) Portal of the Madonna: This lovely Gothic porch and doorway, at the time of writing used as the exit, is a poignant survival from the 14th-century church. The carving in the tympanum above the door (reconstructed) shows the *Dormition of the Virgin*. At the bottom, the Apostles kneel in prayer. Above them is the Virgin's empty bed, and beyond it, her soul, represented as a swaddled infant, being received into heaven by her Son. Below, in the spandrels, are very ruined Evangelists. The original tympanum carving is excellently displayed behind perspex on the side wall, at eye level.

THE FISHERMEN'S BASTION

Map p. 423, B2. Between mid-March and Oct entry is by ticket only, between 9am and 7 or 8pm. Outside these times and hours there is usually free access.

The **Fishermen's Bastion** is a neo-Romanesque terrace overlooking the Danube, with seven conical turrets symbolising the seven Magyar tribes. It was designed by Frigyes Schulek and opened in 1902. The Guild of Fishermen was traditionally responsible for guarding this section of the battlements, hence the name. It has long been extremely popular with tourists (a restaurant has opened inside it) and to control the crowds a daylight-hours charge has been imposed (to the dismay of locals, though Castle Hill residents can get in free on presentation of the First District Card).

In front of the Bastion is an **equestrian statue of St Stephen** (Alajos Stróbl, 1906). The base is decorated with symbols of the Evangelists and reliefs showing scenes from King Stephen's life. The relief depicting the construction of the Matthias Church (which there is no documentary evidence to support) includes a self-portrait of Stróbl (behind the two monks on the far right).

CENTRAL CASTLE HILL:
SZENTHÁROMSÁG TÉR TO DÍSZ TÉR

SZENTHÁROMSÁG TÉR AND ÚRI UTCA (NORTH)

Szentháromság tér (Trinity Square; *map p. 423, B2*) takes its name from the tall **Holy Trinity monument** in its centre (restored), which was set up here in 1713 in thanks for the ending of a plague outbreak some 24 years previously. It took the place of a smaller statue, which was moved to Zsigmond tér (*see p. 83*). At the top are the figures of God the Father and God the Son, with the Holy Spirit appearing in a golden starburst between them. Around the base are saints and angels and below, on the plinth, reliefs show King David begging the Lord to end the plague in Israel (*2 Samuel 24*); the plague devastating Buda; and masons putting the finishing touches to this monument.

Szentháromság utca leads out of the square into Úri utca, past the tiny Ruszwurm café (*see p. 53*). At the junction with Úri utca is an **equestrian statue of András Hadik** (György Vastagh, 1936), commemorating soldiers of the 3rd (later Hadik) hussars. The horse has gleaming testicles because of the tradition whereby students stroke them for luck in exams.

Turn right into **Úri utca**. In 1951, the hunter and writer Zsigmond Széchenyi was internally deported from **no. 52** by the Communists. On Christmas Eve 1944 his parents had visited him here, only to find themselves unable to get away, because the Siege of Budapest began. Zsigmond's father Viktor wrote in his journal on New Year's Eve: 'Went to the Matthias Church in the morning [...]. Getting back to Úri utca saw a totally bombed-out house. Which one was it? Ours! It had suffered a direct hit in our absence. Wounded people lying groaning in the doorway. Horror—which members of my family? Thank God everyone was all right. German soldiers: nine dead, two seriously wounded. Everyone to the cellar. Rooms blown to shreds, upstairs and down. [...] A heap of ruins, not a single room to retreat to, only the cellar—and one candle!'

The building at no. 49, once part of the Poor Clares convent (*see p. 33*), houses the **Telephony Museum** (*closed for renovation at time of writing*). Its collection includes a letter from Edison acknowledging that Tivadar Puskás in fact invented the telephone exchange as well as two working examples of exchanges: a 19th-century one from Pest and an enormous rotary one from the old Post Office building on Széll Kálmán tér, in use from 1928 to 1985. Franz Joseph's phone and János Kádár's phone can also be admired.

From **no. 60**, on March 19th 1944, the day of their takeover of Hungary, the Nazis deported Count Antal Sigray to Mauthausen. Among those deported with him was the financier Ferenc Chorin, whose life Sigray is said to have saved, according to a family story, by giving him quinine. Both men escaped Hungary and died in New York. At no. 62 is the façade of the **former church** of the Poor Clares convent and opposite it, at nos. 64–66, the **German Embassy**.

ÚRI UTCA (SOUTH) AND TÓTH ÁRPÁD SÉTÁNY

Going south from the junction with Szentháromság utca, **Úri u. 24** (with a pretty courtyard) has a plaque commemorating Ferenc Erkel, composer of the Hungarian National Anthem, who lived here between 1851 and 1860. While he was here he wrote *Bánk bán*, a patriotic opera based on József Katona's play of the same name. **No. 13**, the 'Lion House', was originally a draper's shop and afterwards home to a religious confraternity. It now houses a cosy, friendly bar. At **no. 6** you can visit an exhibition of sculptures by Miklós Borsos, who made the Zero Kilometre stone in Clark Ádám tér (*open Sat 10–6; ring the bell, or T: +36 1 356 9981 to make an appointment*).

Móra Ferenc utca leads to **Tóth Árpád sétány**, a tree-shaded promenade along the top of the ramparts, with views over the city to the Buda Hills. At the bottom of the covered steps (or lift) at the end of Szentháromság utca is the entrance to the **Hospital in the Rock** (Sziklakórház), a museum of the hospital that operated in the tunnels under the hill during the Siege of Budapest in the closing stages of WWII. Admission, which also includes the Cold War-era nuclear bunker here, is by guided tour only (*tours last approx. 1hr; for information, see sziklakorhaz.eu*).

TÁRNOK UTCA AND DÍSZ TÉR

The wide Tárnok utca (*map p. 423, B2*) is lined with souvenir shops and has a modern school building on its east side. The **Arany Hordó** restaurant has a striking painted façade with a geometric design dating from the 16th century, which was rediscovered in the 1950s and restored. Outside no. 20 stands a **fountain** in the form of a woman bearing an overflowing platter (Pál Pátzay, 1975), an effective way to use the water. At no. 18 is the **Arany Sas Pharmacy Museum** (*open March–Oct 10–6, Nov–Feb 10–4; ticket allows discount at the affiliated Semmelweis Museum, see p. 59*), occupying the former premises of the Golden Eagle chemist's shop, which operated here until the First World War. The exhibits include Italian and Spanish pharmacy jars and a recreation of an alchemist's laboratory. Alchemy flourished in 18th-century Hungary until outlawed by Maria Theresa in 1768. 'Mummy powder', considered a cure for fever and other ailments, was an important component of the alchemist's and druggist's medicine chest. Here is displayed the mummy powder case from a pharmacy in Nagyszeben (Sibiu), Transylvania, with, on top of it, the mummified head of an ancient Egyptian woman, aged about 30. Traces of 18th-century *al secco* painting are preserved on the pharmacy ceiling and in one of the walls is an Ottoman-era lamp niche.

Facing Dísz tér (Parade Square; *map p. 423, B2–B3*) is György Zala's high-flown **monument to the 1849 recapture of Buda**. It was unveiled in 1893 on 21st May, the same day that the Austrian troops had surrendered the castle to the Hungarian rebels.

The unassuming building at no. 15, the **De La Motte-Beer Palace**, has an enfilade of elegant rooms on the first floor (*usually open 10–6*). They give a good idea of the gracious lives of the well-to-do in 18th-century Buda. The Baroque-style house was built after 1686, upon the rubble of two smaller dwellings. It came into the possession of the De La Motte family, who were ennobled by Franz I, and in 1773 was bought by the *K. und K.* army doctor Joseph Beer.

The south end of the square is closed by the stunted remains of the **former Ministry of Defence**, badly damaged in WWII and never rebuilt. At the time of writing, this area was a building site while the former Castle Theatre and associated buildings were being turned into offices for the Prime Minister. In 1686 the palace of Abdurrahman pasha, last Ottoman governor of Buda, stood here. It was destroyed during the reconquest and the site passed first to the Jesuits and from them to the Carmelites, who had a monastery here. When Joseph II dissolved the Carmelite Order, the monastery church was turned into a theatre. It continued to operate as such until 2016.

High on a tall plinth on the ramparts, across the bridge over the main access road to the castle from the west, is a **statue of Artúr Görgei** (László Marton, 1998), leader of the victorious assault on the hill in 1849 (*see p. 245*). Beyond an area of excavations and a statue of István Bethlen (Prime Minister in 1921–31; he died in Moscow in 1946), opposite a long row of tall flagpoles, is traced in the ground the **outline of the Church of the Virgin and St Sigismund**, built c. 1410. Two royal consorts were buried in it: Katherine Podebrady, first wife of Matthias Corvinus, and Anne de Foix-Candale, third wife of Vladislas II. Behind, across an expanse of lawn, is the Neoclassical **Sándor Palace**. Built in 1805 to the designs of Mihály Pollack, it has been a government residence since 1867, when Gyula Andrássy moved here as Prime Minister. Today it is the official home of the President of the Republic. Beside it is the upper station of the **funicular** or *sikló*, which runs from here to Clark Ádám tér (*see pp. 69–70*).

THE ROYAL PALACE & ITS MUSEUMS

Occupying the entire southern end of Castle Hill, the former Royal Palace (Budavári Palota), with its central dome and long wings on either side, dominates the Buda skyline as seen from the Pest side of the river. Home to several of Hungary's medieval rulers, most famously Matthias Corvinus, the palace fell out of use with the Ottoman conquest. After Buda was retaken, the court was in Vienna, and even following the 1867 Compromise, the Habsburgs never lived here permanently. Only the Regent, Miklós Horthy, used the palace as it was intended, but even then he only occupied nine rooms. The building was very badly damaged in WWII and what you see today is a post-war reconstruction of the complex designed by Miklós Ybl and Alajos Hauszmann in the 19th century (*for its history, see p. 51*). It houses the National Gallery, the country's most important collection of Hungarian art, and the Budapest History Museum. A curiosity is that the road which winds up to the former palace from the west side of the hill (Palota út) is still lit by gas lamps.

THE SAVOY TERRACE

An ornamental gateway with a sculpture of the Turul, mythical bird of the ancient Magyars (*see p. 372*), opens from Szent György tér (*map p. 423, C3*) onto a double stairway down to the Savoy Terrace, commanding superb **views of Pest** stretching far into the distance. Cafés operate here in fine weather and here too is the entrance to the Hungarian National Gallery. The **statue of Prince Eugene of Savoy**, on horseback with bound captives at his feet (József Róna, 1899), commemorates the great soldier who helped to liberate Buda from the Turks in 1686. Miraculously it remained undamaged during the siege of 1944–5. Contemporary photographs show it standing tall an obliviously proud, while the whole of the palace lies in rubble around it.

On either side of the entrance steps to the National Gallery are statues by Miklós Ligeti of Csongor (right) and Tünde (left), characters in a famous play by Mihály Vörösmarty.

HUNGARIAN NATIONAL GALLERY

Magyar Nemzeti Galéria. Map p. 423, C3. Open Tues–Sun 10–6, last tickets at 5pm. Closed Mon. Café and shop (visitable without a ticket). NB: There are long-term plans to move the National Gallery from Castle Hill to a new, purpose-built location. Work on this had not begun at the time of going to press and the description below reflects the status quo at the time of writing. For updates, see mng.hu.

Occupying the Danube-facing wing of the former royal palace, the Hungarian National Gallery is home to the country's major holding of Hungarian art from the Middle Ages to the 20th century. It provides a superb overview of the prevailing styles and genres and gives an excellent insight into the currents and trends that influenced Hungarian artists and sculptors. Works from all of historic Hungary are on display here, including important medieval sculpture from territory that is now Slovakia and *plein-air* painting from the Nagybánya artists' colony in present-day Romania. The display is thematic within a broad chronological framework. Highlights are given below.

MEDIEVAL, RENAISSANCE AND BAROQUE ART

This is shown on the ground and first floors. Access to the earliest works is to the left of the ticket desks, through the museum shop.

Renaissance sculpture

The exhibits are well displayed and captioned and beautifully lit. Highlights are a lovely limestone **relief from Nyitra** (modern Nitra, Slovakia) of 1520–30, showing Christ taking leave of his mother and Mary Magdalene. The buildings of the city in the background are incised rather than modelled, enhancing the plasticity of the figures.

Italianate Renaissance art arrived in Hungary during the reign of Matthias Corvinus. Here are displayed the splendid profile **reliefs of Matthias and his queen**,

Beatrice of Aragon, in white marble against a green jasper background. The king wears his hair long and flowing, bound with a garland of oak. The works, dated 1480–90 are attributed to Giovanni Dalmata and are remarkable survivals from the period. As if to demonstrate just how remarkable, a small fragment from a fountain is displayed close by, carved with King Matthias's raven emblem, by the workshop of Verrocchio. It gives a vivid idea of just how much was lost in the upheaval of the Ottoman conquest. The *Báthory Madonna* (1526) is the only such piece of its date (pre-Mohács) to have survived. It is derived from Florentine models, though the workmanship is much cruder.

Gothic sculpture and altarpieces

Works of the 14th and 15th centuries, spanning the Anjou to the Hunyadi dynasties, include many altarpieces and polyptychs, some of them painted on two sides: one side would have been turned to face the congregation on working days, the other on Sundays and feast days. Sculpture includes a stunning painted wooden *Madonna and Child* from Toporc (modern Toporec, Slovakia; c. 1420). Much of the original colour is now lost. The Virgin stands in graceful *contrapposto*, but there is nothing Classical in the atmosphere of this piece: it is entirely northern. Both Mother and Child hold an apple, symbol of Original Sin and of the redemption that Christ offers. There is a splendidly expressive *Dormition* group, pocked with woodworm holes, showing doleful Apostles clustering around the dying Virgin (1490–1500).

A winding stairway leads up to the continuation of the exhibition, with one room (the former throne room) entirely filled with enormous **late Gothic winged altarpieces**. Among them is the vast St John the Baptist altarpiece from Kisszeben (Sabinov, Slovakia), recently restored, with the Virgin and Child flanked by St John the Baptist and St Peter, all with magnificently gilded drapery (1490–1516). It must have been a truly awe-inspiring sight when *in situ* in its parish church. In a separate room is the exquisite *Visitation* (1506) by Master MS, tentatively identified as Marten Swarcz, who worked in Krakow with Veit Stoss. The sinuous curve of the Virgin's young body is remarkable. Note too the attention to the flowers and foliage: the purple iris by the Virgin's side and the strawberry at her feet. Both plants are replete with symbolism. Opposite, displaying a cheerful disregard for perspective, is an altarpiece of St Nicholas giving a dowry to the three poor sisters (1490).

Baroque art

Art of this period covers the 17th and much of the 18th century. Much of it is crude and many of the later works are firmly within the Viennese tradition. There are sculptures attributed to **Georg Raphael Donner** and his workshop, a portrait attributed to **Sustermans** of Ferdinand III as King of Hungary (1626) and another by **Pompeo Batoni** of Joseph II and his brother Leopold. There are still lifes with parrots and other birds by **Jakab Bogdány** (before 1660–1724) and **Tobias Stranover** and an amusing early 18th-century still life by **István Izbéghy-Vörös** showing a dish of shrimps and a loaf of bread, with a scavenging mouse just leaving the table. Expressive and lifelike portraits include a young woman by a painter from Spiš (1641) and a woman from the

Szalay family by **Stephan Dorfmaister the Elder** (1773). There is also a collection of works by the portraitist **Ádám Mányoki**, including his famous self-portrait in an open shirt and his well-known likeness of Ferenc Rákóczi. Religious works include striking Mannerist canvases by **Franz Anton Maulbertsch** (*St Paul*, *Death of St Joseph*) and Felix Ivo Leicher.

NINETEENTH-CENTURY ART

The gallery has a vast and excellent collection of 19th-century art, displayed on the first and second floors, in thematic and chronological sections.

History painting

On the first floor landing, arranged as a sort of pendant image to the equestrian statue of Eugene of Savoy which stands on the terrace outside, is Gyula Benczúr's triumphal *Recapture of Buda Castle* (1896). The date is that of Hungary's millennium year, when the country celebrated a thousand years since the Magyars arrived in the Carpathian Basin, and the painting reflects the optimism of the time. All eyes are drawn to the haughty face of Charles of Lorraine, who reins in his white horse over the sprawled, portly body of the dead Abdurrahman, his pistol undrawn, still in his belt, an ugly deep gash in his bald head. More **historical canvases** are displayed behind and around this one, and the collection continues in the exhibition hall to the right of the central atrium. The earlier works reflect Hungary's turbulent relationship with its history and its neighbours, whom it has tended to see as oppressors rather than as partners. The mood of the works is often defiant, sometimes lamentatory. Here are displayed works by the best-known names in Hungarian history painting: Mór Than (*Recruiting before 1848*); Bertalan Székely (*Discovering the Body of Louis II after Mohács*) and Viktor Madarász (*Mihály Dobozi*). Dobozi, according to folkloric and poetic tradition, was a Hungarian fighter who fled from Ottoman capture only to be pursued, overtaken and done to death. Before his pursuers caught up with him, he saved his wife from dishonour by stabbing her. The drama of the scene is vividly captured, with the terrified horse, the swooning woman, the pursuers against the streaked glare of the horizon, and the glint of the dagger in the husband's hand. A later work, from after the 1867 Compromise, is more cheerful, concentrating on Hungary's foundation story: Gyula Benczúr's *Baptism of Vajk* (1875), showing the pagan Magyar who was to become St Stephen, the founder of the Hungarian state in the year 1000, kneeling to be received into the Christian fold. To the right stands the Holy Roman Emperor Otto III, wearing the crown that can still be seen today in the Schatzkammer in Vienna.

The early 19th century and the Biedermeier age

Neoclassical sculptures include **István Ferenczy**'s famous *Little Shepherdess* (1820–2), a purely Italianate piece in candid white marble, carved when Ferenczy was in Rome in the atelier of Bertel Thorvaldsen. Other artists and sculptors influenced by Italy include **Lőrinc Dunaiszky** and the great painter of Romantic landscapes, **Károly Markó the Elder**. *Pigeon Post* by **Miklós Barabás** (1843) is a typical work of the Biedermeier age (*see p. 367*). A young girl in white satin, semi-décolletée, clasps a snow-white dove to her bosom. The bird has just flown in through the open casement with a letter, tied with blue ribbon and sealed with red wax. On the table beside the girl lies a Bible, unopened. The expression of frank satisfaction on the girl's face shows that her thoughts are far from pious.

Plein-air painting and portraiture

Italian and Oriental landscapes give way to *plein-air* scenes painted at home in Hungary. The great exponent of the genre is **Pál Szinyei Merse** (*Picnic in May*, 1873). He also introduced Impressionism to Hungary, as is clearly demonstrated in his work entitled *Swing* (1869), where the women's dresses are just smudges of colour.

Károly Lotz's *Spring* (1894) is a combination of *plein-air* painting and portraiture. An example of pure portraiture, with no backdrop at all, is **Philip de László**'s stunning likeness of the 90-year-old Pope Leo XIII (1900).

Portrait sculpture by György Zala, Miklós Ligeti, Alajos Stróbl and János Fadrusz is displayed alongside the paintings.

Genre painting and Symbolism

Genre scenes enjoyed great popularity in 19th-century Hungary and come in various guises, from frivolous through moralising to earnestly socially aware. Among the works on show here are Imre Révész's famous *Panem* (1899), showing poor would-be hired hands at a labour mart, and Ottó Baditz's *Angel-Maker* (1881), where a mother consigns her illegitimate child to the care of a crone in a squalid hovel. The unspoken understanding is that the child will soon be dead, hence the term 'angel-maker', which in Hungary was used to denote those who took in unwanted babies. László Tóth's Symbolist triptych *Beauty, Wealth, Intellect* (1894) mocks the hypocrisies of human values. The 'beauty' is a prostitute under a street lamp; 'wealth' is the worship of a golden calf and the hoarding of jewels in a box; 'intellect' an unshaven, greasy-haired anarchist experimenting with bomb-making in an unfurnished garret.

Late 19th-century Realism

Many Hungarian artists of the 19th century studied in Munich but, led by the example of **Simon Hollósy**, they began to break away from its academic traditions, experimenting with naturalistic depictions of town and country life. Examples here are by **Károly Ferenczy**, **István Csók** and Hollósy himself who, with Ferenczy, was a founder of the Nagybánya artists' colony (*see below*). Csók's *Bohemians' Christmas Eve* (1893), shows three young men in their bachelor flat huddling bleakly around a single lamp, the table bare, with no Christmas feast in sight.

Mihály Munkácsy is one of the best-known (and in his own lifetime the most famous and commercially successful) exponents of Hungarian realist painting. His subject matter can be frilly and feminine (*Paris Interior*, 1877) as well as brooding and dark (*Pawnshop*, 1874; *Last Days of the Condemned Man*, 1869–70). The darkness is exacerbated by the fact that he mixed his paint with bitumen, which over the years has turned tarry and pitch black.

Also uncompromisingly realist but in quite another style and productive of an entirely different atmosphere is **Adolf Fényes**, whose name, 'bright', perfectly suits his sun-drenched scenes. The sunshine should not be taken as a motif for untrammelled joy: his works mainly record the existences of very poor people. Examples include the moving *Mother* (1901), showing a ragged woman, head bowed, tightly clutching her small son (one gets the feeling that they have gone for some time without a meal); *Shelling Beans* (1904), a scene in a peasant courtyard; and *Small-Town Street* (1904), where a single old woman walks along a shabby, sunny lane, aided by her furled umbrella.

Also displayed here are genre scenes by **Sándor Bihari**: the vivid *Before the Judge* (1886) and *Sunday Afternoon* (1893), where the ladies sip tea and the men play cards.

Nude sculpture at the turn of the 20th century

The exhibits here, all small in scale, are of varying quality. They include József Róna's voluptuous *Standing Nude with Palm* (1892–4); Miklós Ligeti's *The Kiss* (1901), an embrace between man and mermaid partly inspired by Rodin and partly by Symbolist art; and Ö. Fülöp Beck's *Emese's Dream* (1922), inspired by Magyar myth. Emese, young wife of one of the Magyar chieftains, had a dream in which the Turul bird appeared, predicting that a river would flow from her womb and spread over many lands. Emese later gave birth to a son, Álmos, whose son Árpád led the Magyar tribes into the Carpathian Basin.

ART BETWEEN 1896 AND THE SECOND WORLD WAR

On the second-floor landing are three works by the eccentric, unclassifiable colorist **Tivadar Kosztka Csontváry**, notably his huge *Ruins of the Greek Theatre at Taormina* (1904–5). Csontváry, in his own words, set out to paint 'the path of the sun'. Here it is seen setting behind a ridge of hills, the sky below it the colour of Sicilian lemons, the ruins of the theatre rosy pink in the foreground, and Mount Etna a resplendent, dazzling white. It sets the tone for the rest of the display, which includes some of the finest works in the collection and shows how Hungarian artists, many of whom lived and worked outside Hungary after WWI—in Vienna, Paris, Munich, Berlin and Rome—responded to and adopted and adapted the artistic trends that they encountered. It is organised into chronological sections beginning with the art of the **Nagybánya artists' colony**, founded in 1896 in Nagybánya in Transylvania (now Baia Mare, Romania) as a development of the circle of artists that had gathered around Simon Hollósy in Munich. Essentially it was a naturalistic movement; many of the paintings are *plein-air* works, suffused with sunlight and Post Impressionist in style and atmosphere. Famous among the pieces displayed are several by **Károly Ferenczy**: *March Evening* (1902); *Bathing Boys* (1902), with the dappled light on their two naked bodies beautifully rendered; and *October* (1903), *Woman Painting* (1903) and *Sunny Morning* (1905), which all explore the interplay of sunshine and shadow.

Supreme among the works of the Hungarian Secession is **János Vaszary**'s *Golden Age* (1898), which caused a sensation when it was first exhibited. Two lovers stand naked and embracing in a dim, leafy grove, burning an offering on an altar before a statue of Venus (Capitoline type). The frame, with a design of leaves, a golden apple and smoking hearts, is also by Vaszary and is integral to the piece.

A section is devoted to the work of **József Rippl-Rónai**, the 'Hungarian Nabi', whose art was influenced by his time in Paris (he was a friend of Bonnard and Maillol), by the forms of Art Nouveau and by Pointillism. He worked both with a highly restricted palette (*Lady in a Black Veil*, 1896) and with bold daubs of bright colour (*My Father and Old Piacsek over a Glass of Wine*, 1907) that are allied to Fauvism, a movement which struck a chord in Hungary. Alongside Rippl-Rónai are works by **István Csók** and **Sándor Ziffer**.

A particularly interesting section of the display is devoted to the **Schiffer Villa**, a remarkable *Gesamtkunstwerk* designed by József Vágó for the railway magnate Miksa Schiffer in 1910–12. Three paintings that once hung in the villa, by Csók, Iványi Grünwald and Rippl-Rónai (*Mrs Schiffer and her Daughters*, 1911), are hung alongside archive photographs showing them *in situ*. There is also a study by Károly Kernstok for his huge stained-glass window in the villa's front hall, two surviving bronze statuettes from the ornamental fountain, also formerly in the hall, and a portrait of Vágó by Rippl-Rónai (1915). The villa itself can be visited (*see p. 202*).

The influence of Cézanne is clearly felt in the exploratory art of **The Eight**—Károly Kernstok, Béla Czóbel, Róbert Berény, Ödön Márffy, Bertalan Pór, Dezső Orbán, Lajos Tihanyi and Dezső Czigány—who produced landscapes, portraits, nudes and many bold and striking still lifes. **Dezső Czigány**'s *Funeral of a Child* (1907–8) is particularly memorable: a peasant scene, with neat white cottages in the background and the hay neatly stacked in the field, but far from pastorally idyllic in atmosphere, with its dark, threatening sky, the wayside Crucifix gleaming a ghastly white, the father, head bowed, with his child's coffin under his arm, and the weeping, inconsolable, bare-footed mother following behind him. Czigány himself suffered a nervous breakdown and ended his own life by suicide, having first killed his wife, daughter and grandchild.

Lajos Tihanyi was clearly also influenced by Cubism. Among his works is a portrait of the Constructivist artist Lajos Kassák. Kassák and his contemporaries produced art of a completely different aesthetic, born of the years of dissent and revolution and of currents felt in Vienna and Berlin. **Sándor Bortnyik**, who had studied at the Bauhaus, is represented here with works that are by turns Constructivist, geometric and Metaphysical. **Béla Uitz** (*Struggle*, 1922) moves clearly towards Abstraction. Other experimental interwar artists include **Jenő Barcsay**, with his *Workers* (*Red Boys*) of c. 1928. The boys are stocky, bare-chested manual labourers, bright red, with grey factory chimneys behind them.

The final section shows works from between the wars by artists of the **KUT** (New Association of Artists, founded in 1924) and **Gresham Circle**. Three key members of this were the sculptor Pál Pátzay and painters Róbert Berény and Aurél Bernáth, whose eerie *Riviera* (1926–7) is an excellent example of the group's style: work in which a *rappel à l'ordre* and return to classical forms is discernible, though often with sinister or grotesque undertones. There is a representative display of works by József Egry, Gyula Derkovits (working-class painter of the proletariat), Vilmos Aba-Novák and István Farkas (*The Madman of Syracuse*, 1930).

THIRD FLOOR: ART AFTER 1945

The display here aims to show how Hungarian art developed after being liberated from Socialist Realism. There are examples of the Post Surrealism of Margit Anna and the Surnaturalism of Tibor Csernus. From the 1980s there is one of László Fehér's famous outlines (*Looking into a Well*, 1988) and from the 1990s an example of the sparse *sfumato* of Attila Szűcs.

At the top of the stairs under the dome is Tibor Szervátiusz's huge and terrible *Dózsa* (1968–72), a bronze sculpture evoking the execution of the rebel leader (*see p. 59*), who was burned alive on a mock throne.

THE HABSBURG PALATINE CRYPT

The crypt under the National Gallery, where Archduke Joseph, Palatine of Hungary, and his descendants are buried, can be visited on request. (*To request a visit, write to muzeumpedagogia@mng.hu. Visits are accompanied by a guide. English-language tours are possible. A fee is payable.*) The crypt was originally the undercroft of the Sigismund Chapel, where the relic of St Stephen's hand was housed from 1791, when Maria Theresa had it brought from Dubrovnik. The sombre faux marble decoration of the walls, which dates from the early 20th century, is inspired by the Medici Chapels in Florence. Twenty-six members of the Palatine branch of the Habsburg family are buried here, in a total of 14 sarcophagi, all in the same style and dating likewise from the early 20th century (the original coffins are enclosed within them). The intention was to place a sculpted effigy on each sarcophagus but only five were completed. Among those buried here are:

Archduke Joseph, Palatine of Hungary (1776–1847), with a fine standing effigy by György Zala. He is shown wearing Hungarian military uniform (which he often wore in life) and with his right hand raised above St Stephen's Crown, symbolising his role as imperial representative in Hungary (*for more on the Palatine Joseph, known as József nádor in Hungarian, see p. 14*). In 1973 the crypt was ransacked by thieves, the sarcophagi opened and valuables removed. Archduke Joseph's Order of the Golden Fleece was a casualty.

Alexandra Pavlovna (1783–1801), Joseph's greatly loved first wife, daughter of the Tsar of Russia, who died in childbirth. Her entrails are enclosed within an urn but the sarcophagus is empty, her body being in the Russian Orthodox chapel built for her by her widow in Üröm, north of Budapest.

Princess Hermina of Anhalt (1797–1817), second wife of Archduke Joseph. Hermina, a Calvinist, also died in childbirth. Her twin babies survived (*see below*).

Maria Dorothea of Württemburg (1797–1855), the Lutheran third wife of the Palatine Joseph.

Abbess Hermina Amalia (1817–42) and **Archduke Stephen** (1817–1867),

Joseph's twin children by Hermina. After Archduke Joseph's death, Stephen (István) became Palatine of Hungary. He was not nearly as popular as his father; his attempts to mediate between Hungary and Austria were unsuccessful and caused him to be regarded with suspicion by both sides.

Archduke Joseph Karl (1833–1905), son of the Palatine Joseph by Maria Dorothea and author of the first Hungarian-Romany dictionary. He lies beside his wife, Clotilde of Saxe-Coburg Gotha. Their reclining effigies and the angel that looms above them are by Alajos Stróbl.

Archduke László (1875–95), Joseph Karl's son, who died after a hunting accident: he shot himself in the leg while trying to fend off a wild cat and died of septicaemia.

THE HUNYADI COURTYARD AND LION COURTYARD

A pair of curious gates fashioned to look like a cobweb, surmounted by the raven emblem of the family of King Matthias, leads to the **Hunyadi Courtyard**, surrounded on three sides by wings of the royal palace. On the fourth, west side, overlooking Krisztinaváros, stood the **royal stables** and palace guard house. Destroyed in WWII, at the time of writing they were being reconstructed *ex novo*. At the back of the courtyard is the impressive **Matthias Fountain** (Alajos Stróbl, 1904). In the grandeur of its composition, with bronze figures arranged against an architectural backdrop and the water forming an important part of the narrative, it has the air of a Hungarian Trevi. The central figure is King Matthias, shown out hunting, having just taken a stag. Below him, his hounds are slaking their thirst at a spring, beside which sits the shy figure of Szép Ilonka, the Fair Helen, a simple country girl who caught sight of the king at a woodland spring and instantly fell in love with him without realising who he was. Her love, of course, was doomed.

A gateway guarded by lions (János Fadrusz, 1902) leads into a third courtyard, the **Lion Courtyard**. The lions on the exterior of the gate, facing those who enter, are calm and placid, while on the interior, facing those who leave, they are roaring fiercely (one might have expected it to be the other way round). To the right as you enter is the entrance to the **Széchenyi Library** (Országos Széchenyi Könyvtár), the national repository for books published in Hungary and an important study resource. It was founded in 1802 by Count Ferenc Széchényi, father of István Széchenyi. A public corridor leads down its entire length, offering good views of the new stables and guard house. A bank of display cases shows relics from the old palace: stove tiles, pottery, weapons, photographs of the palace before and immediately after WWII, and examples of invitations to grand official balls and other functions. At the end of the corridor is a lift (*coins required*) down to Dózsa György tér (*see p. 59*).

At the far end of the Lion Courtyard is the Budapest History Museum, its entrance flanked by allegorical sculpture groups of *War* and *Peace* by Károly Senyei.

BUDAPEST HISTORY MUSEUM

Budapest Történeti Múzeum. Map p. 423, C3. Open March–Oct Tues–Sun 10–6, Nov–Feb Tues–Fri 10–4, Sat–Sun 10–6. Combined ticket with the Kiscell and Aquincum museums. btm.hu.

The collection is arranged in three sections: the history of the royal palace on the lower floors; the history of Budapest; and material from prehistoric and ancient Budapest.

THE ROYAL PALACE BUILDING

A royal residence was first constructed here during the reign of Louis the Great (r. 1342–82). It was extended by King Sigismund, the Holy Roman Emperor, who died in 1437. Traces of both palaces have been unearthed deep below the present building. When Matthias Corvinus came to the throne in 1458, he ushered in an age of great splendour for Buda. He had most of the Gothic palace rebuilt in the Renaissance style, with lovely marbles, decorative tiles on the floors, and carved woodwork. Only minuscule fragments of these things remain, but they are powerfully suggestive of what once was: spacious banqueting halls, bedchambers with gilded ceilings; lawns and fishponds, fountains and a columned summer loggia. Hungary was an important political centre and its court a magnet for scholars and artists.

During the Ottoman period, the palace suffered little structural damage (though many of its precious interior furnishings were carried off). The plundering had begun after Mohács in 1526, when Sultan Suleiman's brother-in-law, Ibrahim Pasha, took bronze statues of Hercules and Athena to adorn his Istanbul palace (they were later smashed for being un-Islamic). More destructive even than the Ottoman looting, however, was the bitter siege of 1686, when over the course of three months the Muslims and Christians slugged it out, before the Christian armies finally prevailed.

The first Habsburgs resided in a smaller palace, constructed on the foundations of what remained. Under Maria Theresa this was considerably enlarged and from 1790 it became the residence of the Palatine, the Austrian ruler's representative or viceroy in Hungary. The Holy Right Hand of St Stephen was brought here in 1791.

Following the establishment of the Dual Monarchy of Austria-Hungary in 1867, extensions to the building were carried out under the direction of Miklós Ybl. The Ybl wing now houses the Széchenyi Library. After Ybl's death the work continued under Alajos Hauszmann. He more than doubled the river frontage by adding a companion wing to the old palace of Maria Theresa and connecting the two by a central block surmounted by a dome. Completed in 1905, it was Hauszmann's greatest achievement (a bronze relief of it appears on his tombstone in Kerepesi Cemetery).

During the Siege of Budapest in 1944–5, the palace was completely gutted. Reconstruction began in 1950, as part of the first Five-Year Plan, to house the residence of Mátyás Rákosi. The work was supervised by Isvtán Janáky. After the 1956 revolution, however, it was felt inappropriate to use the palace for Party personnel and it was given a cultural function instead. The Budapest History Museum opened here in 1967, the National Gallery in 1975 and the Széchenyi Library in 1985.

History of the palace exhibit

The basement display makes use of the scant remains of the royal palaces of Louis the Great, King Sigismund and Matthias Corvinus. The **chapel**, only the lower section of which has survived, is thought to date from the reign of Louis (14th century). It was here that King Matthias placed his gift from the Ottoman sultan, the relic of St John the Almoner (now in the Matthias Church). The chapel was reconsecrated in 1990 and dedicated to St Stephen. The fine **Gothic hall** is from the restored and enlarged palace of King Sigismund (early 15th century).

There is also a display on **music at the court**, where you can listen to selected recordings, including a rendition of *Beatissima Beatrix* by Johannes Tinctoris, a Flemish composer at the court of King Ferdinand of Naples, where he dedicated a work to Ferdinand's daughter Beatrix, later to become the consort of King Matthias Corvinus. Another exhibit deals with King Matthias' celebrated humanist library, the **Bibliotheca Corviniana**. Of the many thousand volumes it is thought to have contained, including works by Classical authors and early Christian theologians, illuminated by Florentine masters, only some 200 now survive, dispersed in collections around the world.

Particularly interesting in this section of the museum are the medieval ceramic **stove tiles**, some of them extremely elaborate.

The story continues on the floor above, with the history of the palace under the Habsburgs and after WWII.

History of Budapest exhibit

The story of the city is told chronologically, from the times of earliest settlement to the 20th century, with detailed wall panels, maps, paintings, documents and other artefacts.

Material from the Palaeolithic to the advent of the Huns (top floor) includes stone tools, pottery, iron and bronze implements and weapons, domestic artefacts, jewellery, glassware and ivory. Maps show the location of the findspots.

The small museum café has tables outside on a raised terrace in fine weather. It is possible to leave the museum this way, from which the **ramparts** can be accessed. A walkway takes you all the way round the building to the Eugene of Savoy terrace overlooking the Danube.

EATING AND DRINKING ON CASTLE HILL

ON THE SLOPES OF THE HILL

fff **Arany Kaviár**. Excellent Russian restaurant in business here since 1990. Head chef Sasha offers exquisite caviar, sturgeon and lobster—and of course borscht and chicken Kiev. Good value bistro menu at lunchtime. Closed Mon. *Ostrom u. 19. T: +36 1 201 6737, aranykaviar.hu. Map p. 423, A1.*

ff **Riso**. The name means 'rice' in Italian and this family restaurant just outside the Vienna Gate serves good risotto and paella, as well as pasta dishes and pizza, Hungarian-inspired main courses and a set weekday lunch menu. Very popular, especially at weekends and in summer, when the outdoor terrace is full to bursting. Best to book. A good choice before or after sightseeing on the hill. *Lovas út 41. T: +36 1 224 7424, riso.hu. Map p. 423, A1.*

Just below the Vienna Gate, on Hattyú utca and Batthyány utca (*map p. 423, A1–B1*), there is a small cluster of places offering coffee and cakes: **Coco7**, **Takács**, **Pékműhely** and **MiniZso Bagel**.

ON THE HILL ITSELF

Finding good food at a reasonable price is not easy on Castle Hill. There are plenty of restaurants, many of them in lovely old buildings and some with stunning views across the city, but most have no real local clientèle.

Ruszwurm. Tiny *cukrászda* which has been in business since 1827, surviving war, siege and nationalisation. The Biedermeier furnishings are the originals, by a local carpenter and the sculptor Lőrinc Dunaiszky. It can get very crowded but turnover is usually quite quick. The *krémes* is famous. In summer they serve ice cream. It was bought by the Szamos family (*see p. 328*) in 1994. *Szentháromság u. 7. Map p. 423, B2.*

Walzer Café. Occupying an entrance hallway, with seating under ambient heaters in cold weather and a tiny closed space at the back. Good coffee, cakes, mulled wine in winter. A pleasant place to take the weight off your feet. Closes at 6pm. *Táncsics Mihály u. 12. Map p. 423, B1–B2.*

The **St George Residence hotel** has a vaulted café/restaurant with 18th-century wall paintings of birds and exotic plants. In the hotel courtyard are two ancient vines, of the indigenous Bakator variety, which survived the phylloxera outbreak of the 1870s. The hotel's house white is made of the Bakator grape. *Fortuna u. 4. Map p. 423, B2.*

From late spring, a number of **pop-up outdoor cafés** appear on the hill. The one with the best view is on Tóth Árpád sétány, at the end of Nőegylet utca (*map p. 423, B2*).

District I:
Krisztinaváros & Tabán

The part of the First District that lies west of Castle Hill, through the Alagút (Castle Hill tunnel), is Krisztinaváros: Christina Town. Until the mid-18th century it was an entirely agricultural area, acting also as a defensive glacis for Buda Castle; no permanent building, with the exception of one tiny votive chapel, was permitted to be erected here. In gratitude to Maria Christina, eldest daughter of Maria Theresa, for her part in getting the building prohibition lifted, the area was named after her. Development began in the late 18th century. Closer to

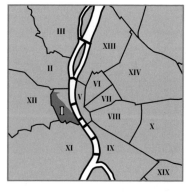

Elisabeth Bridge is the area known as Tabán, once densely packed with streets and cottages but now an open park. Beyond the bridge, at the far edge of the First District, are the Ottoman-era Rudas Baths.

KRISZTINAVÁROS

Logodi utca (*map p. 423, A1–A2*) runs along the lower west slope of Castle Hill. It takes its name from the medieval village of Logod, which occupied this slope and part of the plain at the bottom, until destroyed by the Ottomans. Stepped streets lead steeply up and steeply down: the zigzag Korlát utca, for example, with its iron lampstands; and **Bugát lépcső**, which takes you through a little paved area occupying the site of Logod's medieval parish church.

At the bottom of the steps is the busy **Attila út**, lined along this stretch by handsome blocks of flats from the 1930s. Cross it, and you are in the heart of the **Vérmező**, an attractively landscaped park. What greets you straight away is a bronze statue (László Marton, 2008) of the writer Mihály Babits. Favourite lines from his works, chosen by

TABÁN
Ottoman grave markers on the slopes of Castle Hill.

honorary citizens of the Castle District, are inscribed on a wall to the left of the statue. Olympic swimmer Krisztina Egerszegi's choice reads (loose translation): 'Hungarians must set an example to the nations: never cringe before shows of strength'. Babits was a translator of Dante and editor of the famous periodical *Nyugat*. At one time he lived in an apartment on Attila út. Other editors of and contributors to *Nyugat* who lived in this district include Aladár Schöpflin and Dezső Kosztolányi (whose novel *Anna Édes* is mainly set in the Krisztinaváros area). Another Olympic swimmer associated with the area is Alfréd Hajós (*see p. 292*), who in his later career as an architect designed the apartment building at no. 19. Behind the Babits statue, rather obscured by bushes, is Iván Szabó's 1967 memorial to the Buda volunteer regiment who fought alongside the Soviets in 1945 to liberate Budapest from Nazi control.

The Vérmező today is a pleasant place to stroll but its name, 'Field of Blood', recalls its history as the place of execution of a band of Hungarian republicans and their leader, Ignác Martinovics. Martinovics, born in 1755, began his career as a Franciscan friar and teacher of natural science. He was appointed court chemist to the emperor Leopold II and worked as an informant for the Habsburg authorities, reporting on the activities of secret societies, chiefly freemasons and illuminati. With time, however, he turned against his masters, becoming a freemason himself and espousing the cause of republicanism, organising a secret society of his own along the lines of the French Jacobin Club. He was beheaded here in 1795, together with his fellow conspirators, whom he had betrayed under interrogation. It is reported that he fainted on the scaffold after witnessing the beheading of Count Jakab Sigray, whom it had taken three strokes of the sword to dispatch. Martinovics and the other 'Hungarian Jacobins' are buried in Kerepesi Cemetery.

At the bottom (southwest) corner of the park is the **headquarters of Magyar Telekom**, a striking salmon-coloured building with five storeys of windows in equal bays. In pure Socialist Realist style (Pál Németh, 1951–4), it stands on the site of the Karátsony family mansion, which was pulled down in 1938.

KRISZTINA TÉR AND THE HORVÁTH KERT

Krisztina tér (*map p. 423, B3*) opens out at the west end of the tunnel through Castle Hill. Today it is noisy and filled with traffic, but in previous centuries its character was purely rural. Vines were grown on the slopes of Naphegy (Sun Hill) and after the tunnel was cut in 1857, rustic taverns sprang up to cater to families travelling to the hills to escape the heat of Pest. There are still popular eating places here: the Déryné bistro and Horváth Étterem (*see p. 63*).

KRISZTINAVÁROS PARISH CHURCH

The most important building on the square is the Krisztinaváros Parish Church (Kristinavárosi Havasboldogasszony-templom), dedicated to Our Lady of the Snow (*open 7.30–9 & 5.30–7*). It was constructed in 1795–7 by Kristóf Hikisch on the site of a small votive chapel, originally made of wood and built to house an icon of the Virgin and Child brought back from Italy in the late 17th century by a Buda chimney sweep, who had made a pilgrimage of thanks there after his family escaped the plague. When the wooden chapel burnt down, it is said that the icon refused to catch fire. It was transferred to Hikisch's new church and can still be seen above the high altar. In 1940 the east end of the church was placed on rollers and moved backward a few metres to incorporate the convex-walled transepts. In 1857 the doctor Ignác Semmelweis (*see p. 60*) was married here. In 1836 the church had witnessed the wedding of István Széchenyi and Crescence Seilern. The couple had waited over ten years for each other, being able to marry only after the death of Crescence's first husband. 'I am so very happy,' wrote Széchenyi in his diary the day after the ceremony, 'happier than I ever thought possible.'

THE HORVÁTH-KERT

The Horváth-kert (Horváth Garden; *map p. 423, B3*) is a narrow, grassy expanse between two busy roads, Krisztina körút and Attila út. It is named after the landowners from whom it was purchased when the tunnel was cut through Castle Hill. At its north end, facing Alagút utca, on the site of the old Buda Theatre, is a **statue of Déryné**, Mrs Déry, a contemporary copy of a famous 1935 original by Miklós Ligeti, showing the popular singer and entertainer with ringleted hair and bows in her dress, strumming a beribboned guitar. Herend porcelain figurines, modelled on the statue, are still commonly seen in antique shops.

> ## MRS DÉRY AND THE HABIT OF NAME-CHANGING
>
> The popular entertainer known as Mrs Déry was born Rozalia Schönbach in 1793. The name was later Hungarianised as Széppataki Róza, a literal translation. Hers was not an isolated case; the habit of name-changing has a long tradition in Hungary. There have been several waves of it over the centuries, for varying reasons but often rooted in questions of national identity. In 1848–9, at the time of the War of Independence against the Habsburgs, many people changed their German or Jewish surnames to Hungarian ones, to show solidarity with the anti-Habsburg cause and as a patriotic demonstration of Hungarianness. Later in the 19th century, many assimilated Jews elected to take a Hungarian name as a token of belonging. Changing one's name was also a way of facilitating career advancement. Between the wars, anyone working in the civil service or armed forces needed a Hungarian name in order to be promoted. With the rise of Fascism, Jews sought to Magyarise their names and, on the other side, there are cases of individuals with Magyarised names, confident of German victory, applying to get their German surnames back. At the end of the war, with the Germans defeated, Hungarian surnames became desirable again. Nor is this phenomenon a thing of the past: recently a Roma man was recorded as wishing to change his name, believing that it would give him better employment prospects.

In the park behind Mrs Déry is a fountain with a bronze **statue of a woman bather** by Béni Ferenczy (signed and dated 1956). Beneath the Horváth-kert, completely covered over, flows the Ördög-árok (Devil's Ditch) stream. At the park's southern tip is a **statue of St John of Nepomuk**, a 1999 copy of the original of 1838, which stood on

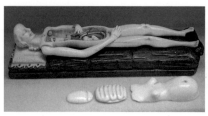 

TABÁN

Two variations on the Mother and Child theme: in ivory (Semmelweis Museum, 17th century; left) and terracotta (Attila út, by Alice Lux, 1936; right).

the parapet of a bridge across the stream. Because of the manner of his martyrdom (*see p. 69*), statues of St John of Nepomuk are frequently to be found on bridges. The most famous example is the one on the Charles Bridge in Prague.

TABÁN

The Tabán district today (*map p. 423, B3–C4*) is an area of parkland: pleasant grassy slopes and patches of verdant sward intersected by busy roads and tramlines (cross with care). The upper section of the park (no cars) is lovely in summer. The name Tabán probably derives from the tanneries which existed here during the Ottoman period. After the Great Migration of 1690 (*see p. 326*), many Serbs settled here and by c. 1700 over 90 percent of the population was Serbian. In September 1810, the whole district went up in flames when fire broke out in the house of a cooper, who was toasting staves. The conflagration reached Corvin tér (*map p. 423, C2*), engulfing hundreds of houses and claiming over 50 lives. Nevertheless, the houses were rebuilt and the Tabán was famous around the turn of the last century for its inns and taverns. The novella *Sipsirica* (1902) by Kálmán Mikszáth is largely set in one such tavern, the 'White Peacock'. Densely populated and poor, as well as unhealthy because the Ördög-árok had become little more than an open sewer, the Tabán nevertheless held a romantic appeal for some observers (including the young Le Corbusier, who on a visit to Budapest in 1911 was charmed to find in it the folkloric atmosphere he had so anxiously anticipated). Eventually deemed insanitary by the city authorities, the houses and narrow streets were swept away by the wrecking ball in the 1930s.

ALONG ATTILA ÚT

At **Attila út 37** is a plaque to the politician and journalist Endre Bajcsy-Zsilinszky (*see p. 256*), who was seized here by the Nazis in 1944. The quotation on the plaque, 'In future may the Hungarians have backbone', is said to have been his final message to the nation from prison. Further on on the left is **Dózsa György tér**, backed by the palace on Castle Hill. At the side of the road, defiantly confronting a coach park, is a huge statue group (István Kiss, 1961) of the peasant leader György Dózsa (*see below*).

GYÖRGY DÓZSA: REBEL LEADER

György Dózsa (b. 1470) was a Székely border guard from Transylvania appointed in 1514 by Tamás Bakócz, Archbishop of Esztergom and papal legate, to lead a Hungarian crusade against the Ottomans. The army assembled by Dózsa consisted largely of peasant volunteers, given some scanty training in how to fight but little in the way of equipment or rations. When their landlords recalled them to work in the fields at harvest time, the crusaders rapidly turned into a disaffected rabble who turned their ire on their overlords. As they marched across the country, burning manor houses and impaling the inhabitants, Bakócz distanced himself from the enterprise and King Vladislas II commanded the fighters to return to their homes. The rebellion by this time, however, was unstoppable and Dózsa and his men swept victoriously across the Great Plain and into Transylvania. An army was called out against them and they were defeated at Timişoara. Dózsa was put to death on a red-hot iron throne. His story became a potent symbol of class struggle and under Communism he was enthusiastically celebrated as a hero and a martyr.

Behind the Dózsa group, at the beginning of the access road to Castle Hill, a column stump against an acacia tree is a lone relic from Matthias Corvinus' **Aula Marmorea**, the marble hall of his garden loggia. Mounted on the end wall of **Attila út 25** is Alice Lux's terracotta *Mother and Child*.

SZARVAS TÉR AND THE SEMMELWEIS MUSEUM

The southern end of Tabán, before Gellért Hill, is filled with the access roads to Elisabeth Bridge. Vestiges of the old urban enclave nevertheless survive, the finest being the 18th–19th-century **Aranyszarvas building**, whose main doorway is surmounted by a painted relief of a golden stag (*arany szarvas*) attacked by two hounds. On the other side of the road are two other surviving houses (much restored). In front of them stands Pál Pátzay's 1971 monument to the poet Benedek Virág (1754–1820), who lived here: a statue of a girl bearing a disc with a cameo portrait.

At the foot of the grassy slope opposite, beside the entrance to an underground car park, is a **bust of József Antall**, who became Prime Minister after democratic elections in 1990. Before that he had been the director of the **Semmelweis Medical History Museum** (Semmelweis Orvostörténeti Múzeum or SOM; *map p. 423, C4*), which occupies the handsome early 19th-century Zopf-style house just next to the bust. The house was the birthplace in 1818 of the physician Ignác Semmelweis and is now home to the museum that bears his name (*Apród u. 1–3; open March–Oct Tues–Sun 10–6; Nov–March Tues–Fri 10–4, Sat–Sun 10–6; combined ticket gives discounted entry to the Arany Szarvas Pharmacy Museum; semmelweismuseum.hu*). As you go in, note the main door handles, which take the form of Aesculapian snakes. The museum is well displayed, with most captions also in English, and traces the history of medicine throughout the ages. Exhibits include instruments for cauterising and trepanning, a copy of the metal cilice supposedly worn by St Margaret (*see p. 293*); an exquisite mid-17th-century ivory obstetric model of a pregnant woman with a baby in her womb; and the interior furnishings, designed by Mihály Pollack, of the Holy Spirit Pharmacy, which opened on Király utca in Pest in 1813. Anatomical models include a splendid female waxwork of the 1780s, by Clemente Susini of the La Specola workshop in Florence. The woman is perfectly modelled in every detail: a voluptuous blonde beauty, sprawled full length with her abdomen open to display the workings of her insides—like a Renaissance Venus overtaken by a ripper murderer. There are also pharmacy jars; dentists' and oculists' equipment; an exhibit on mineral water spas (with a fine collection of souvenir drinking beakers) and mementoes of the great surgeon and early plastic surgeon János Balassa (1814–1868). The Semmelweis memorial room is decorated to recreate a typical interior of the mid-19th century, with period furniture, paintings and ornaments, some of them once belonging to Semmelweis and his family.

SEMMELWEIS, SAVIOUR OF MOTHERS

Ignác Semmelweis (1818–65) has gone down in history as the 'saviour of mothers' for his early grasp of the importance of disinfection to halt the spread of contagion, saving many women and infants from death by puerperal fever. Semmelweis' theories about the importance of hand-washing, borne out by significant decreases in the rate of mortality on obstetric wards under his supervision, were nevertheless rejected by the medical communities in Vienna, who were offended by the suggestion that it was a question of personal hygiene. Semmelweis's difficulty lay in the fact that he was a practitioner, not a scientist. His theory could be explained as a hunch that seemed to work but he had detected nothing through a microscope that could furnish scientific explanation and proof. He appears to have suffered some kind of mental and emotional breakdown, probably caused by syphilis, which he may have caught by medical contact from one of his patients. He began lashing out in print at the ignorance and obstinacy of the medical fraternity. It was Balassa who instigated his transfer to a Vienna asylum, supported by Semmelweis's wife, who was no longer able to cope with his tantrums. He died very shortly after his admission, perhaps as a result of ill-treatment.

Semmelweis's remains have had many resting places: he was buried first in Vienna, then in Kerepesi Cemetery in Budapest, and finally here, in the courtyard of his old house. Ironically, his theory is fully recognised today. He has even given his name to a phenomenon: the Semmelweis reflex, to describe the human tendency to reject or ridicule new ideas if they fly in the face of accepted conventions.

On the grassy slope above the Semmelweis Museum, behind an iron fence, are some turban-topped grave markers, remains of an old **Ottoman cemetery**. This is the only surviving old graveyard in this part of the city. The old Tabán cemetery was closed in 1885 and its land re-developed.

TABÁN
Floodwater plaque of 1838 in Hungarian and Serbian:
Tabán was historically a Serb enclave.

DÖBRENTEI TÉR

The **Tabán Church** (1728–36), dedicated to St Catherine (Alexandriai Szent Katalin-templom), stands on site of an Ottoman mosque. Enlarged over the course of the 18th century, the façade dates from 1880–1. Adjacent, in the square outside, is the **Asztalka café**, which has good cakes. Left of the café entrance, a narrow path beside the side flank of the church doglegs right into a tiny, stepped alleyway (Hegedűs köz), a vestige of old Tabán. It leads into **Döbrentei utca**, whose west side is lined by fine old early 19th-century houses (note the flood marker plaques on no. 15, one of them also in Serbian). Opposite, on the corner of Fogas utca, is a bust of Gábor Döbrentei (*see p. 85*), who gives his name to the square just south of here, the busy **Döbrentei tér**. Hemmed in by access flyovers to the bridge which bears her name is a seated **statue of Empress Elisabeth** (György Zala, 1932). Originally it stood on the Pest side of the river but was removed by the Communists. It was re-erected here in 1986. The **memorial tablet** on the ground at the west edge of the grassy area records that in 1944 Hungarian anti-Fascists blew up a statue of Gyula Gömbös, the national socialist politician who was Prime Minister from 1932–6. He was the first foreign statesman to visit Hitler after the latter came to power in Germany. The letters of his name have been hacked off the tablet in an act of *damnatio memoriae*.

IN THE PARK

The handsome building which houses the **Rác Baths** (now with a glass extension) is a survival of old Tabán. It takes its name from the Hungarian word for the ethnic Serbs: *rác*. The central wing is by Miklós Ybl but the domed Ottoman bathing pool survives in the interior. Plans to turn the complex into a hotel (there was even talk of

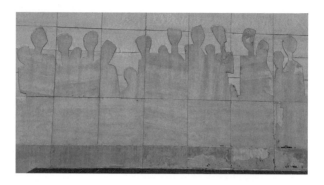

SZARVAS TÉR
Memorial to the victims of internal deportation. It is made of Litracon,
a light-transmitting concrete that is not only a Hungarian invention,
but was invented by the descendant of internal deportees.

a funicular to Gellért Hill) neared completion but the building has languished empty, the baths disused, for many years. The **low ruined walls** marooned on a green traffic island between the Rác Baths and the church are all that remain of the bridgehead of a medieval crossing place over the Ördög-árok, the brook which ran down from the Buda hills along the line of present-day Krisztina körút and emptied into the Danube about here.

Monuments in the green island opposite the Aranyszarvas house include a pale **shard-shaped slab** (Géza Szeri-Varga, 2010) commemorating the thousands of deportations of class enemies to internal exile on the Great Plain in 1950–3. It is made of light-transmitting concrete, invented by the architect Áron Losonczi.

A broad, curving sweep of evenly-spaced shallow steps cuts uphill through the centre of the park, past a cross erected by the Serb Greek Catholic community in 1865 on what was then a square in old Tabán, to the angular **1956 monument** marking the 40th anniversary of the Uprising. At the top of the hill is the L-shaped Czakó utca, with at no. 15 the charming **Czakó Kert** (*see opposite*).

THE RUDAS BATHS

Just beyond Elisabeth Bridge, at the foot of Gellért Hill, are the Rudas Baths (*map p. 428, C4*), a beautiful relic of Ottoman Budapest. Gellért Hill was in ancient times a cult centre of the Eravisci, who are thought to have chosen this spot because of its warm springs. They were later displaced by the Romans. In the Middle Ages the Knights of St John had a hospice here. The pasha Sokollu Mustafa built the Ottoman bath house c. 1572. Like the other Turkish baths of Budapest, the Rudas was an *ilidja*, a warm thermal pool, rather than a hamam or steam bath. In Europe's spa heyday the Rudas was known for its curative waters: with a significant fluoride and sulphur content, as well as radon, it is said to be good for the joints. The pump room or *ivókút* (tucked under Elisabeth Bridge), where you can drink the water, is open on weekdays.

The thermal baths are very well preserved and are the only ones where the sexes are still segregated (except at weekends). The central octagonal pool is surmounted by a dome borne on stout columns. Shafts of light penetrate the steam from hexagonal apertures filled with coloured glass. The temperature of the main pool is 36°C. At the four corners, which each have Islamic stalactite moulding, are plunge pools of varying temperatures from 28°C to 42°C (you are advised to stay no longer than five minutes in the hottest pool). At the side are a steam room and sauna. The cold plunge pool (16°C) is situated some way away from the sauna (at the rear of the main pool, off to the right—by the time you get there you may have lost your nerve).

The baths also have a swimming pool and wellness centre (*for details of tickets, entry times, men's days and women's days, see p. 358*).

EATING AND DRINKING IN KRISZTINAVÁROS AND TABÁN

KRISZTINAVÁROS

fff **Fáma**. Hungarian-Asian fusion cuisine. A fine dining experience. Closed Sun and Mon. *Attila út 10. T: 06 30 994 9000, famabudapest.com. Map p. 423, B3.*

ff **Déryné Bistro**. Lively and friendly restaurant and bakery on the site of the original Auguszt *pâtisserie* (*see p. 93*). Very popular, good food and good atmosphere. Outside seating in warm weather. *Krisztina tér 3. T: +36 1 225 1407, bistroderyne.com. Map p. 423, B3.*

f **Horváth Étterem**. The Horváth remains resolutely traditional in its bill of fare. As they say on their website: 'Trendy food doesn't make a square meal—and there's nothing trendy about us.' They are proud of their associations with the footballer Ferenc Puskás, who often ate here. Good value weekday lunch menu. *Krisztina tér 3. T: +36 1 375 7573, horvathetterem.hu. Map p. 423, B3.*

TABÁN

f **Asztalka**. Charming little café and cake shop tucked away beside the Tabán church. Closed Mon and Tues. *Just off Attila út. Map p. 423, C4.*

f **Czakó Kert**. Sister establishment of the popular Gerlóczy in downtown Pest, this is a re-imagining of the kind of vineyard tavern for which Tabán and the hill above it, Naphegy, were once famous. Here you can sit out with a *hosszúlépés* (spritzer) in the dappled pergola shade. One ancient vine survives and new ones have been planted. Hot and cold food is also available. A market is held here on Saturdays. There is indoor seating in the winter months. Closed Mon and Tues in winter. *Czakó u. 15. T: +36 1 501 4002, czakokert.hu. Map p. 423, B4.*

BATTHYÁNY TÉR
Detail of the dome frescoes in the church of St Anne, by Pál Molnár-C. and Béla Kontuly (1938).

District I: Vízváros

The Vízváros (literally 'Water Town') occupies the area on the Danube's right bank, on the east side of Castle Hill. It has always been a place of traffic, both by road, since Roman times, and by water. In the Middle Ages, after King Sigismund (r. 1387–1437) built his palace on Castle Hill, a fortified settlement grew up here. Scant vestiges of its walls remain today. Vízváros, being so close to the river, was one of the worst hit areas in the 1838 flood. The Palatine Joseph's court painter and illustrator Karl Klette produced drawings of the catastrophe showing people and cattle crowded into tiny boats, steering a precarious course between semi-submerged buildings. Today the Danube is embanked but the large number of floodwater plaques in the district survive to tell the tale.

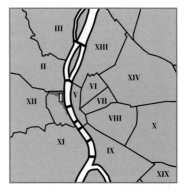

BATTHYÁNY TÉR

Opening out onto the river, with Fő utca, once the main Buda thoroughfare, at its back, Batthyány tér (*map p. 423, C1*) is the historic centre of old Water Town. It is a wide, busy space, filled with bus stops (it is the terminus of numerous lines) and a Metro station (M2, red), always busy with people scurrying from one appointment to the next and with numerous colonies of homeless, with no appointments to go to, sitting on the benches and around the drinking fountains. On the north it is bordered by the buildings of an ex-Franciscan convent, now occupied by charitable offices of the Knights of Malta. In front of these, facing the square, is a seated bronze statue (Ede Kallós, 1938) of the poet Ferenc Kölcsey, author of the Hungarian national anthem (the '*Himnusz*'). The statue bears lines from Kölcsey's poem *Huszt*, in which the writer, gazing gloomily at the ruins of a once-magnificent castle and mourning past glory, is assailed by a spirit who asks, what is the good of looking back? 'Look to the present and the future beyond. Be active, create, enrich, and your homeland will flourish.'

BATTHYÁNY TÉR
Relief of winemaking, representing Autumn, on the Hikisch house.

Attached to the old convent buildings, further north along Fő utca, is the mid-18th-century **Church of the Wounds of St Francis** (Szent Ferenc Sebei-templom), with a tall onion spire. Note the relief of stigmatised hands over the door, the emblem of the Franciscan Order. Today it is used by Budapest's German-speaking Catholic community (*only open for services*).

On the south side of Batthyány tér is the Angelika café (rather gloomy inside; the outdoor terrace, which functions in warm weather, is more congenial) and a **statue of Count Lajos Batthyány** (Géza Stremeny, 2007), namesake of the square and first Prime Minister of Hungary in the revolutionary government of 1848 (*see p. 15*). The statue recalls Batthyány's journey to Vienna by boat, to seek the emperor Franz Joseph's blessing on his government and its legal code. On the prow of the boat is a pelican it its piety, symbol of sacrifice (usually Christ's).

The double-spired **Church of St Anne** (Felsővízivárosi Szent Anna plébánia-templom) is the principal building on the square. Originally a Jesuit foundation, it was built in 1740–62 to plans by Kristóf Hamon and Máté Nepauer. The main portal is surmounted by statues of the Theological Virtues (Faith, Hope and Charity). Above them, in a niche, is a statue of St Anne with the young Virgin, and at the top, between the bell-towers, the symbolic Eye of God motif. After damage by earthquake, the church fell into disrepair. Restored by the stonemason József Hikisch (who built himself a house in the square; *see below*), it was reconsecrated in 1805. Damaged again by floods, its interior decoration today dates largely from the 1930s. Sadly it is only possible to get into the vestibule, from where the fine dome frescoes of the life of St Anne, by Pál Molnár-C. and Béla Kontuly, can be glimpsed through the glass doors.

The west side of the square, facing the river, is dominated by its **old market hall** (now occupied by a supermarket, a bank and a variety of other shops). Built in 1902, it was the first covered market hall in Buda. Its façade is adorned with the arms of Buda and, on either side, reliefs of fish and poultry and fruit and vegetables. Next to the market hall is a **sunken row of houses** indicating the original street level before the great 1838 flood. The larger building is the former White Cross Inn (c. 1770). Next to it is the house built by József Hikisch, stonemason and restorer of St Anne's church, as his own residence (1795). Reliefs of putti gardening, reaping, harvesting grapes and warming themselves by a fire represent the Four Seasons.

Just south of Batthyány tér, on the parapet wall overlooking the lower Danube embankment, is a **plaque commemorating the Kossuth Bridge**, built in 1946, 'in eight months, in a work of heroic self-sacrifice by our workers', to provide a river crossing after the Nazis had blown up all the Danube bridges. It remained in existence until 1960, when, 'its noble task completed', it was dismantled.

SZILÁGYI DEZSŐ TÉR TO CORVIN TÉR

Downriver south of Batthyány tér, Szilágyi Dezső tér (*map p. 423, C2*) is named after a late 19th-century politician who battled to reform ecclesiastical law. Szilágyi was a Calvinist: appropriately, the square is home to the first **Calvinist church** in Buda, consecrated in 1896. It was designed by Samu Pecz, an architect known for his Protestant churches. Neo-Gothic in style with a tall, slender spire, it is built of red brick with colourful Zsolnay roof tiles. In 1915, the poet Endre Ady married Csinszka here, much against the wishes of the bride's father. In 1940 István Horthy, son of the regent, was wed to Countess Ilona Edelsheim Gyulai. The church is not normally open, but in case you find it so, the furnishings were also designed by Samu Pecz. In the southwest corner of the square is a **drinking fountain** surmounted by a statue of the architect in the guise of a medieval master builder (Lajos Berán, 1929).

VÁM UTCA AND ISKOLA UTCA

Retrace your steps back towards Batthyány tér for a few paces and turn left into **Vám utca** (Customs Street; *map p. 423 B1–C1*). In the first short stretch it retains its old yellow cobbles, made of a durable clay-based material known as *keramit*. On the right are two interesting buildings from the 1930s: no. 1/b with elegant glass entrance doors (Loránd Sebestyén, 1937); and no. 1/c next to it (Ervin Quittner, 1936).

Cross Fő utca and continue up Vám utca to its junction with Iskola utca. On the northeast corner is a copy of the *Vastuskó*, a wooden post studded with iron nails, driven into it by travelling apprentices (original in the Kiscell Museum). The custom of hammering a nail into a tree stump, probably for luck or as an offering of thanks, was widespread in the former Austro-Hungarian Empire. The most famous (and oldest) such 'Nail Tree' is the *Stock im Eisen* in Vienna. The origins of the tradition are unknown but it seems to have been as popular among young apprentices then as attaching a padlock to a railing has become among young lovers today.

CORVIN TÉR

Iskola utca leads south to Corvin tér (*map p. 423, C2*). From the top of the stairway which drops down into the square, the cobbled Szalag utca winds up to Castle Hill. Corvin tér itself is a pleasant space opening off busy Fő utca, with the **Budai Vigadó** concert hall at its north end. Built in 1899 to plans by Mór Kallina and Aladár Árkay but much restored since, it now belongs to the Ministry of Human Capacities and its programmes are devoted to folk heritage. The centre of Corvin tér is laid out as a park, a mixture of grass and cobbles with benches and a little café. Here is the funerary stele of a Roman cavalry officer and (under glass) a copy of the **footprints of a woman and child** from c. 30,000 BC, fossilised in Danube mud. Upper Palaeolithic remains (including knapped stones as well as the footprints) were found here during building works in 1997. The original footprints are kept in the Budapest History Museum.

At the end of the grassy space, surrounded by horse chestnut trees, is the enormous **Lajos Fountain**, willed by a wealthy producer of soda water, Lajos Millacher, in his own memory. It is surmounted by a statue (Barnabás Holló, 1904) of the donor's namesake King Louis (Lajos)the Great, shown returning from the hunt having bagged a stag. During Millacher's life the output from his factory must have quenched many thirsts, but unfortunately the water in his memorial fountain is not drinkable.

It was the mother of King Louis the Great, Elizabeth of Poland, who founded the first **church on Corvin tér**, in the 14th century. Under the Ottomans it was converted into a mosque (a peaked doorway survives on the south side). After the reconquest of Buda, the site was given to the Capuchins and the church was restored for Christian worship. Following an earthquake in 1763 it was rebuilt, probably by Máté Nepauer, but burned to the ground during the struggle to recapture Buda from the Habsburgs in 1849: today's Romantic-Eclectic building is the work of Frigyes Feszl. Above the entrance is a statue of St Elizabeth of Hungary by Marschalkó (better known for the lions on the Chain Bridge). At the side, just outside the Ottoman doorway, is a statue of the papal nuncio Marco Aviano, who was sent to Buda by Pope Innocent XI to give spiritual succour during the battle for reconquest in 1686. An Italian Catholic community celebrates Mass here on Sundays. The former conventual buildings attached to the church were being restored as a hotel at the time of writing.

On the east side of Corvin tér, the **houses lining Fő utca**, now sunk below street level, are typical old Víziváros dwellings with steeply pitched roofs (rather garishly re-tiled). The green building has interesting reliefs from the 1920s. Over the doorway, satyrs flank a laboratory scene with an inscription that reads: 'Research means progress. Knowledge is power'. Above (difficult to see) are three reliefs showing King Matthias Corvinus as a farmer, scholar and warrior. The house next door (no. 3) has an 18th-century statue of St John of Nepomuk (*see opposite*), with an inscription in Latin invoking his protection.

FŐ UTCA

At **Fő u. 19** (east) is a plaque to the Nobel prizewinning biophysicist György Békésy, who lived here. Next door is the **Institut Français**, on the site of the mansion for which Tivadar Andrássy, elder son of the former prime minister Gyula Andrássy, commissioned his famous Secessionist dining room from József Rippl-Rónai in 1897 (designs for it can be seen in the Kiscell Museum; *see p. 102*). Opposite it, below street level, is the turreted **Kapisztory-ház** (dating in its current aspect from 1811), now housing a French restaurant. Pala utca is one of a number of stepped streets leading up to Castle Hill. Further up Fő utca on the left, the grey-green building at

no. 11–13 was built in 1880 for Count Gyula Andrássy. His daughter-in-law Eleonóra and granddaughter Klára allowed the Polish Red Cross to use part of the building during WWII. The doctors were murdered after the Nazi takeover in 1944 (plaque). Expropriated by the Communists in 1948, the building was home from 1949 to a dressmaker's co-operative (allegedly a front for a state munitions factory). It became a cultural centre in the mid-'60s (Frank Zappa rehearsed here before his last Budapest concert in 1991). At the time of writing there were plans to open part of the building as an Andrássy museum.

Opposite the Andrássy mansion, in the glassed-in atrium of a modern office building, are the **ruins** of an 18th-century house converted from medieval dwellings. At Fő u. 6, on the corner of Apor Péter utca, is the **Museum of Hungarian Applied Folk Art** (*open Mon–Sat 10–6; hagyomanyokhaza.hu*), with an open studio where you can try your hand at weaving.

ST JOHN OF NEPOMUK

Statues of St John of Nepomuk (c. 1345–93) are common in Central Europe. He was born in Bohemia and entered holy orders after studies at Prague and Padua. Following a disagreement with King Wenceslas IV over an ecclesiastical appointment, he was sentenced to death. In the popular imagination his death quickly took on the appearance of a martyrdom (he was flung into the Vltava and left to drown) and his cult spread. Apocryphal stories grew up around him, notably the one concerning Wenceslas' queen, whose confessor he is said to have been and whose secrets (if she had any) he refused to divulge, to the ire of her royal husband. He was canonised in 1729 and is the patron saint of Bohemia as well as of bridges. His aid is invoked against floodwaters, thus it is no surprise to find statues of him in Water Town, an area with such a history of inundation. One of the putti in the statue group on Corvin tér has a finger pressed to his lips, an allusion to the saint's posthumous reputation as a keeper of secrets.

CLARK ÁDÁM TÉR & THE VÁRKERT

Clark Ádám tér (*map p. 423, C3*), on the Buda side of the Chain Bridge, is largely taken up with a busy roundabout, brightly planted with flowers in its centre. It is named after Adam Clark, the Scottish engineer who supervised the construction of the Chain Bridge (*for the history of the bridge, see p. 164*). At the far (west) side is the Alagút, the **tunnel through Castle Hill**, which was another mighty engineering project masterminded by István Széchenyi and overseen by Clark. Work began in 1853 and the tunnel opened in 1857. Its parabolic archway is adorned by a Doric propylaion. Just inside the tunnel, the door on the right leads to the bridgemaster's office (still manned today). NB: Pedestrians are advised not to use the tunnel because of the heavy traffic fumes. To the right of the tunnel as you face it, on the corner of Fő utca, is the modern Hotel Clark (Anthony Gall, 2017–18), occupying a wedge of the circus like a slice of Trivial Pursuit pie. To the left of the tunnel is the **funicular railway** (Budavári

VÁRKERT BAZÁR
A picture from the Swinging Sixties, when the palace garden was a Youth Park. Photo: Fortepan.

sikló) up to Castle Hill (*open daily 7.30–10*). The second funicular in the world after the one in Lyon, it was built in 1870 on the initiative of Ödön Széchenyi, son of István. In its early years of operation it was powered by steam. The carriages in use today are replicas of the originals. Ticket queues can be quite long (gone are the days when a single public transport ticket was valid) but if you are on your way up to Castle Hill, the winding walk up through the ramparts is very pleasant. The elliptical limestone sculpture in front of the funicular (Miklós Borsos, 1975) represents a stylised zero: it is from this **Zero Kilometre Stone** that all road distances from Budapest are measured (the same concept as the *Miliarium Aureum* that stood in the forum in ancient Rome).

Across the park, a quiet lane leads between the backs of houses and the Castle Hill itself to the Várkert Bazár (Castle Garden).

VÁRKERT BAZÁR

Map p. 423, C3. Gardens open daily 6–midnight. Stairs, lifts and an escalator lead up to Castle Hill and down to Lánchíd utca (some of the stairways close at dusk). Café and WCs. varkertbazar.hu.

The gardens of the former royal palace, on the steep riverward slopes of Castle Hill, were laid out by Miklós Ybl between 1875 and 1883. Badly damaged in WWII, they were subsequently home to a Youth Park before finally collapsing into decay and finding themselves on the list of most endangered World Heritage sites. They were at last restored and opened to the public in 2014 and today are a pleasant place to stroll (particularly atmospheric at night). The so-called **Foundry Courtyard** is a walled sun-trap space with lounging chairs. The **Neo-Renaissance Garden** is an area of lawn and flowerbed with a central fountain and river views from the parapet walkway and its central twin-domed pavilion. At the top of the long escalator is a yard from which a spiral stairway takes you down (right) to the barrel-vaulted **Casemate Corridor**, which runs between two layers of the castle fortifications. Turning left at the bottom of the spiral stairs takes you down the 'Water Carriers' Stairs' to the gardens again.

From the south end of the gardens you can get down to **Lánchíd utca**, where at no. 6 Adam Clark spent the last years of his life (he died here in 1866). It and the next-door building (both fronted by colossal statues of soldiers of different eras) make up the **Southern Palaces** exhibition space, with temporary shows as well as a permanent display on the First World War (*open Tues–Sun 10–6*). A plaque on the back of one of the soldiers bears a quote by Cardinal Mindszenty: 'Time is the ally of Justice'.

Opposite is the **Várkert Kiosk**, built by Miklós Ybl in 1882 and now an events space. Its tower concealed a pumping mechanism to supply water to the royal palace (no more hauling it up the Water Carriers' Stairs). Water destined for the palace was formerly filtered through gravel in large underground cisterns here. In front of the kiosk is a square open onto the river with a **statue of Ybl**, erected just five years after his death (Ede Mayer, 1896) and a long line of benches beside the tram tracks. There is a good view of the Várkert's Oriental-turreted central stairway. Lánchíd utca leads past a parade of shops and cafés, occupying former artists' studios, back to Clark Ádám tér.

EATING AND DRINKING IN THE VÍZIVÁROS

RESTAURANTS

ff-fff **Csalogány 26**. Excellent modern Hungarian cuisine. Tasting menus and good-value lunch menu also offered. Closed Sun and Mon. *Csalogány u. 26. T: +36 1 201 7892, csalogany26.hu. Map p. 423, B1.*

ff-fff **Zóna**. Excellent food and wine, good value weekday lunch menu. Superb position overlooking the Chain Bridge. Sister restaurant of Liberté in Pest. *Lánchíd u. 7. T: 06 30 422 5981, zonabudapest.com. Map p. 423, C3.*

f **Corvin Kávézó**. Small, cosy place (outdoor seating in warm weather) offering good breakfasts, sandwiches, wraps, salads and very simple mains. *Corvin tér. T: 06 30 891 0019, corvincafe.hu. Map p. 423, C2.*

CAFÉS AND BARS

There are cafés serving drinks and snacks at the foot of the funicular on **Clark Ádám tér** and also in the **Várkert**. At Lánchid u. 5, **Zhao Zhou** offers speciality teas, meticulously prepared (closed Sun and Mon, other days open afternoons; *map p. 423, C3*). Beyond it are a handful of other cafés and places to get snacks, including a branch of the **Auguszt** confectioner (closed Mon and Tues; *see p. 93*). The **Lánchíd 19 hotel** has a restaurant overlooking the river and an outdoor plant-filled terrace.

District II: Margit körút, Rózsadomb & Pasarét

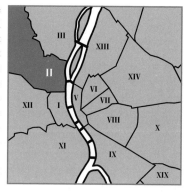

Budapest's Second District, on the Buda side of the Danube, has a small commercial section around Margit körút, with shops, offices and government ministries. The Ottoman-era Király Baths survive here. Much of the southeast part of the district was once covered with the buildings of the Ganz iron and electrical works, some of the which have found new uses as offices or cultural centres. As the district reaches northwest into the Buda Hills, it becomes leafy and residential, with some interesting examples of Bauhaus-style architecture.

NAGY IMRE TÉR

The busy Csalogány utca and Fő utca crossroads (*map p. 428, B2*) form the boundary between Districts I and II. Opening off Fő utca to the left is Nagy Imre tér, with a playground and dog run in the centre, its periphery thick with testimonials to Budapest's turbulent 20th century. The square is named after Imre Nagy, Prime Minister of Hungary during the 1956 Uprising, who was subsequently tried and executed by his own party (*see p. 91*). The brooding, massive building that occupies the north side of the square (Jenő Hübner, 1915) is the **former Military Law Courts**. It was here that Imre Nagy was subjected to a secret trial and condemned to death in June 1958. The building has a grim history. It was used by the Gestapo in 1944–5 and after that by Stalinist Hungary's secret police. During the 1956 Uprising, a number of armed groups were based here. Wall plaques commemorate all this.

The Post-Modern red-brick building facing the river (György Guczogi, 1987–90) houses the **Foreign Ministry**. At the river end of the park is a small patch of lawn with a bench in front of the so-called **Flame of Revolution** (Mária Lúgossy, 1996),

MARGIT KÖRÚT
Stairwell in the Manfréd Weiss building (1937–8).

NAGY IMRE TÉR
Relief of workers on the former Ministry of Light Industry building.

a black granite slab fashioned as if melted like a candle by the gas flame at the top. The monument was paid for by public subscription and originally stood in front of Parliament. When Kossuth Lajos tér was remodelled in 2014, the monument was removed. A campaign to have it re-sited, led by the politician Imre Mécs (whose 1956 death sentence was commuted to imprisonment), led to its re-erection here. Not everyone is pleased with the new location.

The south side of the square is closed by the (at the time of writing empty and derelict) geometric lines of the **former Ministry of Light Industry**, one of Budapest's earliest modern office buildings, built at breakneck speed (István Janáky and Jenő Szendrő, 1941–2) originally to house the Industrial Materials Office, a body responsible for sourcing raw materials during the war years. On the west façade overlooking Gyorskocsi utca is a large relief (Zoltán Borbereki Kovács, 1942) depicting workers weaving and harvesting fruit. A companion relief (construction workers) overlooks Fő utca.

Between Fő utca and the river rises the **Pontház**, a modernist block of flats partly raised on pillars. It was built soon after the war (1948, Pál Németh, with Jenő Szilágyi and János Scultéty) and for a time was held up as a symbol of resurgence (the building that formerly stood on the site was blown up in the war and those taking refuge in the air-raid shelter below were smothered by the rubble; a plaque commemorates this). As

Hungarian Communism became more hard-line, the building fell from favour and was branded decadent and Western in its inspiration. Marvellously, it still stands intact. A shop selling glazed earthenware made by the famous Herend manufactory operates on the ground floor.

Nearby **Kacsa utca** has a claim to immortality as the site of Hungary's first ever salami factory, which was set up here in 1880 by an Italian from Friuli, Pietro del Medico, in 1850. The factory and shop, which continued in operation until just before WWI, occupied buildings at nos. 15–17.

THE KIRÁLY BATHS & BEM TÉR

The **Király Baths** (*map p. 428, B1*) are one of Budapest's few surviving Ottoman-era buildings. Construction began under Arslan Pasha in 1565 and was completed after his deposition by his successor Sokollu Mustafa. Although it stands on the line of the seam of hot springs that rise beside the Danube, the baths have no thermal source of their own. Instead the water is supplied from the Lukács Baths further north. The surviving Turkish parts are in the wing which faces Ganz utca. The Neoclassical wing, with Ionic pilasters and a tympanum facing Fő utca, was built by the König family, who took over ownership of the baths in the late 18th century. The name Király derives from them (*király*, meaning king, is the Hungarian translation of the German *König*). The original 16th-century Turkish central pool is still in use. (*For times and entry requirements, see p. 357.*)

Next to the baths, across Ganz utca and a small park with a statue of the Ukrainian poet Taras Shevchenko, is the **Greek Catholic Church**, originally built (Máté Nepauer, 1760) as a chapel dedicated to St Florian.

Fő utca ends in **Bem József tér**, which has the Foreign Ministry building on one side and in the centre, a statue (János Istók, 1934) of the Polish general Jozef Bem, shown wounded with his arm in a sling. Bem (1794–1850) fought against the Habsburgs in the 1848 Vienna revolt and then joined the Hungarians during their War of Independence. Under his command the revolutionary army won significant victories in Transylvania, during which campaign Sándor Petőfi was his aide-de-camp (part of a poem written by Petőfi during the campaign is inscribed on the back of the pedestal: 'Fortune and God deserted us; Bem was our only friend'). In the summer of 1849, Bem's luck began to change and he was twice routed. He fled to Turkey, became an Ottoman subject and converted to Islam. He died in 1850, fighting for the Turks, and was buried in Aleppo. Low down on the corner of Bem József utca is a plaque marking the level of the floodwaters of 1838.

On the corner of **Fekete Sas utca** is the Bambi Presszó café and bar, a survival from the 1960s, still popular and with a large outdoor terrace. Further along Fekete Sas utca, on the corner of Tölgyfa utca (left), is a building housing a pulmonary clinic (Loránd Almási Balogh, 1931). On the roof is a row of Art Deco urns. The brick cladding hides a reinforced concrete core designed by Eszter Pécsi, Hungary's first woman engineer.

ALONG THE LINE OF THE BUDA CITY WALLS

The medieval town of Buda was bounded to the east by the Danube and to the west and south by Castle Hill. To the north it was defended by a wall along what are now Bem József utca, Margit körút and Vérmező utca.

Margit körút (*map p. 428, A1–B1*) is and always has been a major traffic artery. A Roman road existed here and in the early Middle Ages a busy highway led to a crossing place on the river near today's Margaret Bridge. Today it is dusty and noisy: but above the shopfronts there is some interesting architecture. The building at **no. 20**, just beyond the point where the road, coming from Margaret Bridge, makes a sharp bend south, still gives the street name as Mártírok útja, 'Martyrs' Road', the name it bore between 1945 and 1992, commemorating Communists who met their death in the military prison here (*see p. 78*). On the other side of the road, **no. 15–17** (corner of Rómer Flóris utca) is the **Manfréd Weiss Pension Fund Building** (Béla Hofstätter and Ferenc Domány, 1937–8), a magnificent example of Art Deco architecture. The door is kept locked, but if you are lucky, someone will be coming or going and you will be able to go in to see the delicate pale pink marble cladding in the entrance lobby, the twin cylindrical lifts, the wide stairway windows and fine elliptical stairwell, and the handsome entrance doors to the individual flats. From the Rómer Flóris side, there is a good view of the exterior with its staircase windows and sinuous balconies.

Across Rómer Flóris utca is a scruffy patch of ground unofficially known as **Csodaszarvas tér**, 'Miracle Stag Square'. A sculpture of a fallow deer (looking rather small and not at all miraculous; Róbert Csíkszentmihályi, 1982) sits in the centre. The legend of the miracle stag is part of Hungary's foundation myth.

THE LEGEND OF THE WONDER STAG

There are a number of versions of the story. The 14th-century Latin chronicle known as the *Képes Krónika* or *Chronicon Pictum* tells of two brothers, Hunor and Magor, forefathers of the Huns and the Magyars, who went out hunting in pursuit of a magnificent stag. The animal eluded them but as they gave chase, it led them into a beautiful land of marsh, lake and watermeadow. Realising the potential of the place as somewhere to pasture their flocks and herds, the brothers returned to their father and asked his permission to lead their sheep to water there. In such a land, they reasoned, with abundant running water full of fish, lush grassland and forests filled with game, protected on all sides and difficult of access, their people could prosper and multiply. The marshy lake is given as the Maeotis, in the land of the Scythians, a people famous for their animal art: two stylised golden stags are housed in the Hungarian National Museum and the stag motif is often reproduced in later Hungarian art. From out of the land of the Scythians came the ancestors of Attila and the lineage of Árpád.

Beyond the little stag rise the twin bell-towers of the **Franciscan church of St Stephen** (Budai ferences templom; Máté Nepauer, 1752–70), standing on the site of an earlier Augustinian chapel. Unless a service is in progress, it is only possible to get into the vestibule—which is a pity, because the side chapels have altarpieces by the Viennese artist Franz Anton Maulbertsch and 20th-century works by Béla Kontuly (*St Francis*) and his wife Hajnalka Fuchs (the stained-glass windows). It is sometimes possible to find someone from the next-door friary to let you in. Beyond the conventual buildings, across a narrow stepped street, at **Margit körút 27**, is a block of flats that was built as a Lottery House (*see p. 267*).

Diagonally opposite the Lottery House, the corner house with neo-Venetian balconies at the convergence of Bem József utca, Horvát utca and Margit körút (**Bem József u. 24**) is by Hugó Gregersen (1936–7), with a large statue of Hermes and other sculpture by his wife, Alice Lux. A short way down Bem József utca, behind railings, is the **Foundry Museum** (Öntödei múzeum; *map p. 428, B1; open winter Thur–Sat 10–4, summer Tues–Sat 10–4; mmkm.hu*), housed in an old factory built in 1858 to the design of the iron master Abraham Ganz.

ABRAHAM GANZ AND THE BUDAPEST IRON WORKS

Ganz was born in Switzerland in 1814. His family was humble and his father struggled to provide for nine children. After many years spent as a wandering apprentice, Ganz came to Hungary in 1841 where he found work in the Pest iron foundry, soon rising to become its manager. The girders for the Chain Bridge were made there. In 1845 Ganz set up his own foundry in Buda, which became known for its wagon wheels and steam locomotives. In 1848–9 the foundry made cannons for the anti-Habsburg war effort, for which Ganz was sentenced to prison (a sentence he never served; Franz Joseph pardoned him). In 1861 he was made an honorary citizen of Buda. Five years later Miklós Ybl, who at the time was designing a number of town palaces for the aristocracy, built him a stately mansion on the Danube bank in Pest. Ganz ran the business until his tragic death by suicide in 1867. Fearing that he was falling prey to the brain disease that ran in his family, he threw himself from the balcony of his own riverside palace (on the corner of Széchenyi rakpart and Széchenyi utca; the house was destroyed in WWI and its replacement is the only modern building in the row). Two years after his death, directorship of the foundry was taken over by András Mechwart, whom Ganz had hired some years before. It was under Mechwart's leadership that the Ganz works achieved worldwide renown. Both men are buried in Kerepesi Cemetery (*see p. 249*). In 1878 the firm gained an electric department, headed by Károly Zipernowsky. On the grass outside the Foundry Museum stands the sole remaining figure from a sculpture group made to commemorate Mechwart by Alajos Stróbl, which was destroyed in WWII. The elderly bearded man was modelled on one of the foundry workers.

The Foundry Museum building has a sawtooth roofline and fine old rafters inside. The display covers casting and die-casting processes, foundries for bells, cannons and baptismal fonts. Made in a characteristic chalice shape, few of these bronze fonts remain in modern Hungary, though there are a number in Transylvania and Slovakia (and one in the collection of the National Museum in Budapest). On show too are a great number of functional and decorative pieces, both large and small, from stoves, firebacks and lampstands to small inkwells and jewel boxes. There are even cast-iron grave markers.

The Ganz foundry functioned here on Bem József utca until 1964. Several of the houses in the neighbouring streets bear plaques commemorating engineers.

On the corner of Bimbó út is the **Mechwart Liget** park (*map p. 428, A1–B1*), with a fountain in its centre. It is named after András Mechwart, the German-born engineer who became head of the Ganz Works and was ennobled in 1907. He is commemorated with a bust, made in 1965 to replace a monument that was damaged beyond repair in WWII (*see above*). Behind the fountain, at the top of a high flight of steps, is the **Second District Municipality** (József Körner, 1952), a good example of stripped Classicism in the approved Socialist Realist style. The large corner building facing Bimbó út (Győző Czigler, 1898) is the **Central Statistical Office** (Központi Statisztikai Hivatal). From here, **Keleti Károly utca** leads west. It is named after the founder (in 1871) and first director of the Hungarian Statistical Office, Károly Keleti. Born Karl Klette, he was the son of a painter from Dresden, court illustrator to the Palatine Joseph. At the age of 15 he had joined the Hungarian revolutionary army but because of his youth escaped prosecution when the revolution was crushed. At Keleti Károly u. 26, Raoul Wallenberg (*see p. 300*) sat for his portrait to the artist László Dombrovszky in 1944.

Back on Margit körút, at no. 55 is the **Átrium Filmszínház** cinema (with a café), the first steel-framed building in Hungary, designed in 1935 by Lajos Kozma. Its upper floor is supported on slender pillars. The black and white tiles and the mirrors are true to the original design. The building next door (**no. 51–3**) is clad in *eau-de-nil*-coloured slats of *ongroplaszt*, a man-made material sometimes found on buildings from the latter part of the 1930s. On the corner of Fényes Elek utca, **no. 67** is also clad in *ongroplaszt*, in a bright shade of brick red. Opposite at **no. 69** is another house by Hugó Gregersen and Alice Lux (1939), with fish-tailed horses and the Zodiac symbol of Sagittarius, and lion-head corbels supporting the first-floor balcony.

The körút ends in **Széna tér** (*map p. 428, A1*), once a haymarket. In a clump of cypress bushes on the right, just before the Mammut shopping centre, is the **Martyrs' Memorial** (*Mártírok emlékműve*), three bronze blindfolds hanging from a lump of Tardos marble pockmarked to symbolise bullet holes (András Kiss Nagy, 1979). It commemorates the anti-Fascist Communist fighters who were executed in the military prison that once stood here. On the opposite side of the street you can see the sole surviving section of the old medieval **Buda city wall**. Further on, on the corner of Lövőház utca, is a little patch of lawn with a **monument to 1956**. It consists of some traditional wooden grave markers and a chrome steel figure of a broken body in front of a flag with a hole in its centre. Széna tér was one of the most important rallying points of civilian resistance during the Uprising. The fighters were led by the truck driver János Szabó, who lived in nearby Lövőház utca. Szabó was executed in 1957.

THE HOLE IN THE FLAG

The Hungarian tricolor with a central ragged hole became the symbol of the 1956 anti-Soviet uprising. Under Communism the Hungarian flag had sported the so-called Rákosi coat of arms: a garland of ripe corn surrounding a crossed hammer and ear of wheat, surmounted by the red star. In defiance of the regime, people cut it out of the centre of the flag.

FOUNDRY MUSEUM
Cast-iron paperweight in the form of a dachshund.
Made by Ganz & Co. (c. 1930).

MILLENÁRIS PARK AND LÖVŐHÁZ UTCA

On **Kisrókus utca** (*map p. 428, A1*) in 1934, the architects József Fischer and Farkas Molnár (*see p. 89*) opened a short-lived joint practice with Marcel Breuer in the plain Art Deco building at no. 5–7 (István Fenyves and Miksa Fried, 1930). A little further along, the Art Nouveau-influenced building at the corner of Kitaibel Pál utca is the headquarters of the **Hungarian Meteorological Society**, purpose-built for them by Kornél Neuschloss in 1910. The side wall bears a plaque (János Andrássy Kurta, 1944) to the street's namesake, the botanist and geologist Pál Kitaibel, with the motto *Gaude Hungaria quae talem tulisti*: 'Rejoice, Hungary, that you bore one such as he'.

In the **Millenáris Park**, a public area with lawns and fishponds, some of the buildings of the old Ganz electrical works (*see p. 77*) have been repurposed as events spaces. The **Invisible Exhibition**, where visitors experience a world without sight, occupies one of them (*lathatatlan.hu*). At the time of writing another was being adapted to house the **National Dance Theatre** (Nemzeti Táncszínház). The Ganz offices were in the handsome building that faces the park to the west. On its Lövőház façade (**Lövőház u. 39**) a plaque notes that the electrical engineer Károly Zipernowsky and his colleagues invented the electrical transformer here in 1885.

Lövőház utca is a lively, attractive street, pedestrianised in its entire central section (between Káplár utca and Fény utca). Notice the long building at **no. 19–31**, another work by Miksa Fried (1941), decorated at ground-floor level with numerous reliefs, including fruit harvesters, fishermen and a piper and dancer, by Géza Csorba, Tibor Vilt and Jenő Kerényi. At the top end of the street (corner of Alvinci utca) is the building that gives Lövőház utca its name, the **Lövőház**, former club house of the Buda gun club's shooting range. In its heyday the club was popular among the nobility (Count Gyula Andrássy was a member). Its motto was 'Learn here to defend your country and your king'. The club house was built by Antal Hofhauser in the 1880s and extended between the wars by Rezső Ray Jr. The site was being renovated and remodelled for mixed-purpose use at the time of writing.

SZÉLL KÁLMÁN TÉR

Széll Kálmán tér (*map p. 428, A1–A2*) is one of the busiest public transport hubs in Budapest. Formerly Moszkva (Moscow) tér, it reverted to its pre-Communist name in 2011. Kálmán Széll was Prime Minister of Hungary in 1899–1903. His wife was the daughter of the poet Mihály Vörösmarty. Despite these claims to patriotic approval, the name Széll Kálmán tér has been slow to catch back on and many people still refer to the square as 'Moszkva'. The mosaic name plaque on the wall of no. 3, showing Red Square and the Kremlin, had, at the time of writing, been reprieved. The square was completely re-landscaped in 2015–16 and most of the old booths and bus shelters were pulled down. The striking **corrugated roof** of the Metro station, known as the 'concrete fan' (István Czeglédi, 1972), was deemed iconic and allowed to remain.

At the top of the square (up the steps), near where the no. 16 buses leave for Castle Hill, some small **bronze sparrows** have appeared on the parapet. Other bronzes to discover here (unless they fall victim to metal thieves) are some snails, a wallet, an umbrella and a skateboard. The turreted **Buda Palota** office building was formerly a

SZÉLL KÁLMÁN TÉR
Bronze sparrows.

Post Office, built as such in 1922 on a site which ten years previously had been intended for a synagogue (plans were submitted to tender by Béla Lajta and the Löffler brothers but the First World War intervened). The building, which boasted the first paternoster lift in Hungary, was being renovated at the time of writing. There were plans to open the turret to the public, equipped with a lookout terrace.

RÓZSADOMB

The Rózsadomb, or Rose Hill (*map p. 424, C2*), historically Buda's most select residential district, rises above the Danube's west bank. The official Rózsadomb is bounded by Vérhalom utca and Bimbó út, though locally the entire area of hills and valleys both north and south of Bimbó út is referred to as Rózsadomb. Its development began around the turn of the last century, when well-to-do families commissioned summer villas here. Under Communism it was much favoured: János Kádár's house was here (commanding a superlative view across Pest) as was that of Imre Nagy.

FRANKEL LEÓ ÚT
Frankel Leó út (*map p. 424, D2*), which follows the course of the Danube and above which Rózsadomb rises, is named after a Budapest-born Communist revolutionary and activist who was a member of the First International, fought in the Siege of Paris during the Franco-Prussian war, joined the Paris Commune, worked for Karl Marx in London, was one of the founders of the Hungarian General Workers Party, died in 1896 and is buried in the Workers Movement Pantheon in Kerepesi Cemetery. He is one of

very few Communists still to have a street bearing his name. In the little square where Frankel Leó út meets Török utca, with benches in the form of huge flat boulders, is a statue on a very tall plinth: ***Motherhood*** by József Somogyi (1965). The house at **no. 21–23** bears a plaque to the sculptor Barnabás Holló, whose last home this was.

Next door are the **Lukács Baths** (Szent Lukács Gyógyfürdő; *for practical details, see p. 357*), on the site of a hospice founded in the 12th century by the Knights Hospitaller. The Ottomans used the waters to power a gunpowder mill. This was demolished in 1884 and the baths complex built over its remains to designs by Rezső Ray Sr, adapted in the 1920s by Rezső Hikisch (who worked in Ray's studio). It has been much altered since and the side facing the Danube was, at the time of writing, in need of restoration. A columned pump room (*ivócsarnok; open weekdays*) opens directly onto Frankel Leó út. The central drinking fountain no longer works but you can get a mug of the water from the dispensary on the right (or a coffee from the café on the left). The water is luke warm, faintly sulphurous and reputed to be efficacious in cases of acid reflux. At the time of writing, healing mud was also available.

Opposite the Lukács Baths, across the tramlines, is a derelict Ottoman building with an old mill pool at its foot (full of water lilies). Within the enclosure is the entrance to the **János Molnár Cave**, a deep underground hypogenic system (formed by the action of water rising up from below), with springs of thermal water that serve the Lukács Baths. It stretches for some 6km but has still not been fully explored. A diving centre was opened here in 2015 (*for details, see mjcave.hu*).

The **Veli Bej Baths** (*map p. 424, D2; entrance from the Danube side*) were built by Sokollu Mustafa Pasha in 1575. After the reconquest of Buda the baths took the name Kaiser Bad or Császár fürdő. In the early 19th century they passed to the Brothers Hospitallers of St John of God (known in Hungarian as the Irgalmas Rend), for use as a thermal hospital. The Neoclassical wing was built by József Hild. The complex was nationalised in 1951, becoming the state rheumatology hospital. In 2000 it was returned to the Brothers Hospitallers and is now restored and open to the public. The restoration has been particularly successful, with the old Ottoman baths and modern spa facilities excellently integrated. The domed Ottoman bath house is built of stone blocks interspersed with brick. A central octagonal hot pool is surrounded by four square ancillary pools in domed side chambers, all beautifully lit so that you experience the baths in a soft penumbra. Fountains of cold running water empty into small basins at the sides. The pools are marble-lined. Behind the Turkish bath is the *Régészeti folyosó* ('Archaeology Corridor'), with parts of the old foundations and interlocking clay pipes displayed behind perspex. (*For practicalities, see p. 359.*)

Back on Frankel Leó út, heading north, you pass the buildings of the Irgalmas Rend Hospital and its severe, Doric-fronted **Chapel of St Stephen** (József Hild, 1844). After that, beyond Kavics utca at no. 49, is a house with three narrow archways surmounted by a menorah and Tables of the Law. Within the courtyard, completely surrounded on three sides by flats rising through six storeys, is a tiny neo-Gothic **synagogue** (Sándor Fellner, 1888). The apartment blocks were built in the late 1920s, creating an extraordinary effect: the synagogue has something of the atmosphere of a cave chapel. Many of the apartments were occupied by members of the congregation. During the Holocaust, the Jewish tenants were corralled into apartments on the first two floors prior to deportation. A tablet on the courtyard wall commemorates them. The building opposite the synagogue, at Frankel Leó út 76 (corner of Kavics utca), was a **Lottery House** (*see p. 267*).

ÚJLAK

Two settlements lay outside the northern Buda wall in the Middle Ages. One of them, Felhévíz, occupied the area around where the Veli Bej Baths are now. The other, Szentjakabfalva, was further north. After the reconquest of Buda, the villages were re-founded as Neustift (in Hungarian Újlak). On **Zsigmond tér** (*map p. 424, D2*) stands a votive statue to the Holy Trinity, commissioned from Bernardo Ferretti following a plague outbreak in Buda and dating in its earliest parts to 1706. When Buda had a new Trinity statue made in 1713, this one was moved here, to the old market square of Újlak. It has been much modified and restored over the years.

From Zsigmond tér the old Vienna road, Bécsi út, begins, following the Danube upstream. On Kolosy tér (*map p. 424, D1*) is the main church of Újlak, the **Sarlós Boldogasszony Plébániatemplom** (Church of the Visitation), built in 1746–59 to designs by Kristóf Hamon and Máté Nepauer. Originally the bell-tower rose from the centre of the façade but it began to show signs of crumbling and was placed to the side in the 1760s. It is crowned by a steeple of 1877 by Miklós Ybl. The interior preserves a fine carved pulpit from the former church of the Poor Clares on Castle Hill.

District II ends here. On the other side of Kolosy tér you are in District III, Óbuda.

GÜL BABA'S TOMB

At the point where Margit körút makes a sharp, almost right-angled bend (*map p. 424, C2*), there are a number of streets with names commemorating Turkey and the Ottomans: Ankara utca, Turbán utca, Mecset (Mosque) utca and Török (Turk) utca. Nestling amongst all these, approached up a pretty cobbled lane (Gül Baba utca), is the türbe of Gül Baba, in a memorial garden (at the time of writing being restored and rebuilt with money from the Turkish government). Gül Baba was a dervish poet who accompanied Suleiman the Magnificent to Buda and died here in 1541, just after the city was first conquered by the Ottomans. His grave is a holy site for Muslims: the Turkish government has more than once provided funds to make sure it is properly looked after.

THE HEART OF RÓZSADOMB

On the corner of Áldás utca and Szemlőhegyi utca (*map p. 424, C2*) is a **school building** in the Hungarian Folk Revival style by Dezső Zrumeczky (1911–12). At Berkenye u. 19 (corner of Pajzs utca) is the fine Bauhaus **Magyar Villa**, built for the owner of a leather works by Lajos Kozma (1937). Two houses on **Cserje utca**, nos. 4/a and 12, are by Farkas Molnár (1931–2). At Cserje u. 21 is the Communist premier János Kádár's former house (much altered). The **Mansfeld Péter Park** (*marked 'M.P. park' on the map*) is named after the youngest victim of the reprisals that followed the 1956 Uprising. Péter Mansfeld, an apprentice iron turner, was condemned to death by hanging in 1959, only a few days after his 18th birthday.

THE CAVES OF BUDA

The János Molnár Cave (*see p. 82*) is only one of many riddling the hills in this part of Buda. The limestone bedrock is perforated with caverns running for tens of kilometres, and there may be more yet to discover. Two cave systems, Szemlő-hegy and Pál-völgy, can be visited on regular guided tours.

Getting to the caves

Szemlő-hegy: *Bus 29 from Szentlélek tér (map p. 421, B3) or Kolosy tér (map p. 424, D1) to Szemlo-hegyi barlang. Bus 65 or 65A from Kolosy tér (map p. 424, D1) to Szemlo-hegyi barlang (map p. 424, C1).*
Pál-völgy: *Bus 29 from Szentlélek tér (map p. 421, B3) or Kolosy tér (map p. 424, D1) to Csalit utca (map p. 424, B1), from where it is a short walk. Bus 111 from Batthyány tér also goes to Csalit utca.*

SZEMLŐ-HEGY CAVE

Map p. 424, C1. Open daily except Tues. Tours begin on the hour, first tour at 10am. Combined ticket with the Pál-völgy Cave. Tours last approx. 50mins. Dress warmly. To check for updates and times of the last tour of the day, see dunaipoly.hu.

The cave was formed about 1.5–2 million years ago, when an earthquake caused a crack in the limestone that allowed thermal water to seep up from below. The characteristic calcite plate crystal formations here were formed by calcium separating out in the water of the resulting cave lake. The other dominant formations are the so-called 'popcorn' crystals, possibly formed by the evaporation of bubbles of hot steam (though scientists are still not agreed on this point). The cave was discovered in 1930. It does not harbour life (no bats) and there is only one natural entrance. The tour takes visitors along a series of well-lit chambers and tunnels, artificially deepened through the clay rubble and scree. The so-called 'Eye of the Needle' is a tiny, diamond-shaped crevice through which only the young spelaeologist Mária Szekula could fit when the cave was first discovered. Because the cave was not formed by the dripping in of surface water, there are no stalactites—although intensive building on these hills since the 1980s has damaged the protective layer of clay and water is now entering. The tour guide will show you baby stalactites that are beginning to grow as a result. The Szent János Hospital uses the cave for respiratory therapy. The chamber known as the Chapel is also used for weddings.

PÁL-VÖLGY CAVE

Map p. 424, B1. Open daily except Mon. Tours begin hourly at quarter past the hour, first tour at 10.15. Combined ticket with the Szemlő-hegy Cave. Tours last approx. 50mins. Dress warmly. NB: The visit involves climbing precariously steep and narrow ladders. To check for updates and times of the last tour, see dunaipoly.hu. Adventure caving tours in the nearby Mátyás-hegy Cave can also be organised. See the website for details.

Set in an attractive dell (a former stone quarry), this belongs to the longest cave system in Hungary (almost 30km). It was discovered in 1904. Like the Szemlő-hegy

Cave, this was once a thermal lake. The crystals now caking it walls formed in different ways, partly depending on the water temperature. Unlike Szemlő-hegy, this cave is partly porous and the entrance of surface water has led to stalactite and stalagmite formations. A group known as 'Snow White and the Seven Dwarves' is shown, as well as the 'Zoo', with shapes resembling a crocodile, scorpion and elephant. There are shells and a sea urchin too, from 40 million years ago when the Pannon Sea covered Hungary. Large colonies of green 'lamp flora' are clustered around the electric lights, where they can photosynthesise. The cave has also become a popular hibernation site for horseshoe bats: some 400 overwinter here (the constant temperature of 10°C means that in winter it is warmer in the cave than it is outdoors). The tour covers some 500m of the huge extent of the cave system, new sections of which are still being uncovered. Rain that enters here will end up some 8–10,000 years later as thermal water in the Gellért or one of the other baths.

PASARÉT & BAUHAUS BUDAPEST

Pasarét, the 'Pasha's Meadow', derives its name from the 1847 'baptising' initiative of the antiquary, philologist and Crown Counsel Gábor Döbrentei. Before this, the hills and valleys of Buda had mainly German names; following the grand baptismal ceremony, they all emerged clothed with the Magyar spirit. The new names were either Hungarian translations of the German or allusions to episodes in Hungarian history. Thus *Ochsen Ried* (Ox Marsh) became Törökvész, an allusion to the crushing of an auxiliary force of janissaries that was making its way to Buda in 1686; and *Sauwiesen* (Sow Meadow) became Pasarét, in memory of the Buda pashas. Names that are simple mirror translations include the Hűvösvölgy valley (originally *Kühlental*, Cool Vale) and the name of the gully that runs down it, the Ördög-árok (*Teufelgraben*, Devil's Ditch). The Pasarét area is rich in examples of Bauhaus-style architecture.

Getting to Pasarét
Tram 61 from Széll Kálmán tér along Szilágyi Erzsébet fasor, or bus 5 from Astoria, Frenciek tere, Március 15. tér or Széll Kálmán tér to Pasaréti tér (map p. 424, A2).

SZILÁGYI ERZSÉBET FASOR
This tree-lined street (*map p. 424, A2–C3*), named after the mother of King Matthias Corvinus, has a **statue of Raoul Wallenberg** on the corner of Nagyajtai utca (*map p. 424, B2*). It is the work of Imre Varga (1986) and was created at the expense of the US Ambassador Nicolas Salgo, himself a Hungarian Jew, who had worked for the Manfréd Weiss company in Switzerland and later became a US citizen. Originally the sculpture stood in the US Embassy garden. On Salgo's departure, he offered the work to János Kádár, as a gift to Hungary. Since Wallenberg had disappeared in the Soviet Union, presumed to have been executed in Lubyanka prison, it was an awkward gift for Hungary to accept in the political circumstances of the time and it was set up here, in

this out-of-the-way site, without any public fanfare. The sculpture consists of a lifesize bronze statue of Wallenberg standing constricted between two Swedish granite slabs. The snake motif carved into the granite makes reference to the serpent-slayer memorial to Wallenberg that stood in the former International Ghetto (*see p. 300*). The Latin inscription is a quotation from Ovid and reads: 'So long as you are fortunate, you will have many friends; when times are troubled, you find yourself alone.'

PASARÉTI TÉR CHURCH

The Church of St Anthony of Padua on Pasaréti tér (*map p. 424, A2*) is a masterpiece of 1930s' design. Daringly modern for an ecclesiastical building of its time, it was built for the Franciscans in 1933–4 to designs by Gyula Rimanóczy. Though deemed by some to be more politically socialist than was appropriate for a sacred building, it was generally well received after its consecration in 1934. The main west façade has reliefs of St Francis and St Anthony by Tibor Vilt. To the right is the friary and to the left the slender bell-tower. The interior is basilica-shaped, with very narrow aisles separated from the wide nave by tall, exceptionally slender concrete arcades. The side walls are decorated with a painted frieze of Franciscan saints, while a procession of sheep on either side of a hill from which flow the four rivers of Eden adorns the organ loft. All of the iconography is clearly influenced by early Christian church mosaics in Rome and Ravenna. Symbols are everywhere: the strip lights on the ceiling have the Alpha and Omega worked into their wrought-iron casing; under the windows the Chi Rho is repeated. The lamps on the aisle columns are inscribed with the Beatitudes from the Sermon on the Mount. The side chapels in the south aisle have stained glass of the *Annunciation, Nativity and Flight into Egypt,* and *Crucifixion* by Lili Sztehlo.

BUDAPEST BAUHAUS

Bauhaus, Functionalist and International Modern architecture had some exceptional exponents in Hungary even though the styles were slow to receive official endorsement. In the anxious, nationalistic atmosphere of the 1920s, there were many who considered them too international: official culture was keen to reassert Hungarian confidence and pride, which had been undermined by WWI and the settlement of Trianon. Public, officially funded commissions from Modernist architects were in consequence rare. Churches were some of the earliest public buildings to embrace the style. In the 1930s, Bauhaus-inspired buildings begin to appear, many of them villas built for private individuals. Today almost all are still in private hands and many have been extended or modified, often in a style that is very different from what the architects would have desired. The crisp, geometric lines that look so good in architectural drawings and which are favoured by black and white photography create less of an impression with overgrown gardens and the paraphernalia of everyday living obscuring the deliberately contrived proportions (the organic forms of bushes and trees are in any case ill-suited to the Bauhaus aesthetic). The best time to look at the villas is in winter, when the trees are leafless (although many are hidden behind gloomy evergreens). Nevertheless, Bauhaus enthusiasts will enjoy seeking out these buildings.

SZILÁGYI ERZSÉBET FASOR
Detail of Imre Varga's monument to Raoul Wallenberg (1986).

The Pasaréti tér **bus station**, whose sweeping curve stands across the street from the church, is also by Rimanóczy (1937). It is occupied partly by a restaurant and partly by a pharmacy. Just outside the pharmacy, on the wall, is a relief of St Christopher (patron saint of drivers and travellers) with the infant Christ on his shoulder. Note the saint's shield, emblazoned with a winged bus wheel. The adjacent parade of shops includes a good place to get ice cream.

Behind the Aldi supermarket, at **Pasaréti út 96**, is another building by Rimanóczy. The house at **no. 97**, further down on the opposite side, is also his.

Above Pasaréti tér is the **Bartók Memorial House** (*Bartók Béla Emlékház; Csalán u. 29; map p. 424, A1; open Tues–Sun 10–5*), arranged in the house where the great composer and musicologist lived from 1932 until his departure for the US in 1944. Some of the rooms have Bartók's original furniture. It is here that he wrote his *Sonata for Two Pianos*, his *String Quartet no. 5* and part of *String Quartet no. 6*, in his small study (which originally had padded doors, to muffle exterior noise). The phonograph on display here is of the type that Bartók used on his travels, to record live folk singing and playing.

NAPRAFORGÓ UTCA

Built in 1931, Napraforgó utca (*map p. 424, A1*) was a model housing estate of small, mainly detached family units with gardens, inspired by the Weissenhofsiedlung in Stuttgart, built by the Deutscher Werkbund in 1927. The Budapest site was a challenging one: very narrow and on the banks of a steep ditch, the Ördög-árok. A total of 22 architects were involved in the project, including three of the best-known names of the Hungarian Bauhaus: Farkas Molnár, Lajos Kozma and József Fischer.

All the Napraforgó houses are different, though all essentially share the same principles: no inessentials, compact, well adapted to everyday living, comfortable. A number of the original street lamps survive, built into the railings. The houses have been altered over the years; garages have been built, windows and doors have been changed, balconies have been filled in to create more indoor space. To gain a full appreciation of the original design and concept of the whole, you need to look at archive photographs, although visiting the estate today still gives a strong impression of the architects' aims. In the small central park is a memorial stone listing all the architects, although it contains many errors. The correct attributions are as follows:

No. 1	László Vágó	No. 12	Ervin Quittner
No. 2	Gyula Wälder	No. 13	György Masirevich
No. 3	Péter Kaffka	No. 14	Ármin Hegedűs and
No. 4	Virgil Bierbauer		Henrik Böhm
No. 5	Lajos Kozma	No. 15	Farkas Molnár and Pál Ligeti
Nos 6–8	Lajos Kozma	No. 17	Alfréd Hajós
No. 7	Andor Wellisch	No. 18	Károly Weichinger
No. 9	K. Róbert Kertész	No. 20	József Fischer
No. 10	Aladár Münnich	No. 22	Béla Barát and Ede Novák
No. 11	László Vágó		

MOLNÁR, BREUER, FISCHER AND KOZMA

Farkas Molnár (1897–1945) began his career as a typographer and graphist. He studied at the Bauhaus in 1921 and worked in Gropius' office. On his return to Hungary he took a degree in architecture from the Technical University in Budapest. He became known for his designs for small apartment buildings and individual villas, pure examples of his watchwords of Functionalism and Rationalism. Molnár remained forever resistant to the temptation of moving abroad. In 1945 his house in the Pasarét area received a direct hit. He died a few days later in the hospital on Széher út.

József Fischer (1901–95) qualified as a master builder, never as an architect. His wife, Eszter Pécsi, was the first woman to receive an engineering degree, from the Budapest Technical University. Fischer designed villas and hotels, entering into partnership with Molnár in 1933. He was also an active politician, holding office a number of times, most notably in the 1956 government of Imre Nagy. He later emigrated to the US, returning to Hungary in 1978 after the death of his wife.

Marcel Breuer (1902–81) studied in Vienna, from where he went to the Bauhaus, then to Paris, then back to the Bauhaus to direct the furniture workshop. His tubular steel designs have since become iconic. In 1934 he returned briefly to Budapest, where he went into partnership with Molnár and Fischer. Together they formed the Hungarian wing of CIAM (Congrès Internationaux d'Architecture Moderne), renting an office on Kisrókus utca (*see p. 80*), but the collaboration was short-lived. Breuer had a carpentry qualification from the Bauhaus, but the Budapest authorities rejected it as insufficient for membership of the Hungarian chamber of architects. Thus it was that Breuer moved to London and then to US, where he set up in partnership with Gropius.

Lajos Kozma (1884–1948) belonged to an earlier generation than Fischer and Breuer. His early designs are more traditional and even his later work tends to be softer and less uncompromising. As a young architect, he worked in the design studio of Béla Lajta (*see p. 173*). He also designed furniture, setting up the Budapesti Műhely studio on the lines of the Wiener Werkstätte (*see p. 150*) He is buried in Kerepesi Cemetery.

THE IMRE NAGY MEMORIAL HOUSE

Map p. 424, A2. Orsó u. 43. Open Mon–Thur 10–4 (ring the bell). T: +36 1 392 5011, nagyimreemlekhaz.hu.

The Imre Nagy Memorial House (Nagy Imre Emlékház) is of great interest not only as the last home of one of the most interesting figures of the Hungarian Communist movement but also architecturally, being one of the few Bauhaus buildings in Buda which can be visited. Built in 1932–3 to designs by Lajos Kozma, it was the home of a Jewish lawyer and his family who escaped the Holocaust and emigrated to Australia. The house was still officially their property when Imre Nagy and his wife moved in in 1949. In 1952, following nationalisation, the house became the property of the state. The original owners petitioned for its return but their request was turned down. After Nagy's execution, the Hungarian state used it to house diplomats: for a long time it was the residence of the Austrian military attaché. Following a lengthy campaign and a programme of restoration led in part by Nagy's daughter, the house was opened to the public in 2002.

IMRE NAGY MEMORIAL HOUSE
Archive photograph of the villa, designed by Lajos Kozma, showing gardeners at work.

The house and exhibits

The visitor entrance takes you into the basement, formerly the garage and caretaker's quarters. A curved stairway leads up to the ground floor, where the living room, kitchen and maid's room were situated. The space would originally have been divided by screen walls but these have been removed to allow space for interactive boards and display cabinets. Stuccoes by the architect László Rajk, the son of another Communist executed by his own party on trumped-up charges, evoke the original use of the living space. The glassed-in veranda (internally much restored) survives. Detailed interactive boards (much of the text also in English) allow the visitor to explore the fateful course of events between the death of Stalin and Nagy's execution in 1958. Television screens show footage of Nagy's exhumation (members of the crowd are visibly moved as his bones, wrapped in tar paper, the hands and feet bound with barbed wire, are extracted) and reburial in 1989. Glass cases contain personal mementoes (including a pair of Nagy's trademark pince-nez) and copies of some of his publications (*What Does the Hungarian Communist Party Offer the Peasantry?* and others in a similar vein).

On the upper floor, at the top of the stairs, the original dumb waiter survives, just outside the room which Imre Nagy used as his study. It has been restored and furnished with some original pieces (the armchair and many of the books) and with other articles true to the period. A vase on the desk is shown as the one which Mrs Nagy filled each day with fresh flowers. Nagy's library consists of a few works of literature but is mainly political. The names on the spines are what one would expect: Marx, Engels, Lenin, Stalin, Webb.

IMRE NAGY

On 16th June 1989, several months before the fall of the Berlin Wall, an extraordinary event took place: the ceremonial reburial—and with it the political rehabilitation—of Imre Nagy, the Communist leader who had been executed by his own party on 16th June 1958. After a ceremony in Heroes' Square attended by over 100,000 people, Nagy's coffin and those of four of his colleagues, were taken to plot 301 in the Új Köztemető cemetery (see p. 283), where until then Nagy had lain in an ignominious, unmarked grave. It was the most public symbolic event of Hungary's political transition of 1989–90 and a cathartic moment for the nation.

Imre Nagy was born into a peasant family in 1896. During WWI he fought on the Italian and Russian fronts and was taken to a prison camp in Siberia. In 1919 he worked as a ship's carpenter on Lake Baikal. The following year, he joined the Bolshevik Party. After his return to Hungary in 1921, he joined the Socialist Workers' Party and was arrested on suspicion of Communist activity in 1927. He continued to be active, in journalism and broadcasting, from voluntary exile in Vienna and then the Soviet Union, joining the Red Army in 1941.

In 1944 he came back to Hungary, was appointed Minister for Agriculture in the provisional government set up in the eastern city of Debrecen. In this capacity he drew up a programme of sweeping land reform. He subsequently held posts as Interior Minister (during which time the deportations of the Swabians began; see p. 340) and President of the National Assembly but none of this was achieved without conflict: in the late '40s, clear signs of a rift began to appear as Nagy opposed the aggressively Soviet-style direction that Hungary was taking. He nevertheless continued to play a prominent public role, lecturing at universities, as Minister for Food and as a member of the Academy of Sciences. In 1953, after the death of Stalin, he became Prime Minister and announced a programme of reform, promising elections, a private sector, religious freedom and an end to internship camps: in other words, he vowed to rid Hungary of the Rákosi clique. Public support for Nagy, manifested by growing public restlessness and mass demonstrations, caused anxiety in Moscow. Nagy was removed from office in 1955.

On 6th October 1956, László Rajk was reburied in Kerepesi, in a ceremony at which Nagy was present. A silent revolution began to grow around Nagy, against a party leadership that was unable to break away from Stalinist methods. A week later, Nagy was re-admitted to the Party. On October 23rd, the anti-Soviet Uprising broke out and by the following day, Nagy was once again Prime Minister. He announced an exit from the Warsaw Pact and the introduction of a multi-party system. The brief and heady atmosphere of freedom was extinguished on 4th November with the arrival of Soviet tanks. Nagy and his loyal colleagues found refuge in the Yugoslav Embassy on Andrássy út. Tricked by false assurances given to the Yugoslav government, they emerged on 22nd November only to be arrested by the KGB and taken to Romania. From there, in April 1957, Nagy was transferred to the prison building on the square now named Nagy Imre tér (see p. 72). His secret trial, which began in early 1958, led to his execution in the prison courtyard at dawn on 16th June, the victim of a system which he had ultimately helped to create, but which he had tried to reform.

OTHER BAUHAUS VILLAS

Examples of more villas in the Pasarét area (and one in District XII) are given below as a list. Because so many have been altered and their original proportions and integrity damaged, and because tall trees partially conceal almost all of them, they will be of interest perhaps only to specialists.

Pasaréti út 7 (Bajai Villa and apartments) by Molnár, 1932 (*map p. 424, B3*)

Hankóczy Jenő u. 3/a (Balla Villa) by Molnár, 1932 (*map p. 424, B2*)

Herman Ottó u. 10 (Klinger Villa) by Kozma, 1933 (*map p. 424, B2*)

Lotz Károly u. 4/b (apartment block with the architect's own home at the top) by Molnár, 1933 (*map p. 424, A2*)

Harangvirág u. 11 (Tyroler Villa) by Molnár, 1934 (*map p. 424, A2*)

Csévi köz 7/a (Sommer Villa) by Molnár and Fischer, 1934 (*map p. 424, A1*)

Baba u. 14 (Járitz Villa) by Fischer, 1941–2 (*map p. 424, B1*). The statue by the former swimming pool is a copy of Ferenc Medgyessy's *Standing Woman* (1931) in the Hungarian National Gallery. The family had other Medgyessy statues but they were destroyed in the war. The villa is now a respiratory rehabilitation wing of the Szent János Hospital and it is possible to view the exterior. At street level a garage has been created by filling in the lower arcade.

Szépvölgyi ut 88/b (Hoffmann Villa) by Fischer, 1933–4 (*map p. 424, C1*).

In District XII

Lejtő út 2/a (Dálnoki-Kováts Villa) by Molnár, 1932. It won the prize for best villa at the Milan Triennale in 1933 (*map p. 424, B5*).

EATING AND DRINKING IN THE SECOND DISTRICT

RESTAURANTS AROUND MARGIT KÖRÚT

ff **Kacsa**. Traditional Hungarian restaurant: white tablecloths, upholstered dining chairs, parquet and carpeting and live gipsy music every night. The name means 'duck', and duck-based dishes are indeed a feature of the menu. *Fő u. 75. T: +36 1 201 9992, kacsavendeglo.hu. Map p. 428, B1.*

f **Márkus**. In business for decades and still traditional. Here you can eat an old-style Hungarian lunch of veal and tarragon soup, breaded carp and a dish of pickles on the side. Choose beer or a white wine spritzer to go with it. *Lövőház u. 17. T: +36 1 212 3153. Map p. 428, A1.*

The pedestrianised section of **Lövőház utca** (*map p. 428, A1*) is filled with small shops, cafés, snack bars and restaurants, all with outdoor seating in fine weather. This is a good place to look for a lunch spot. The **Szalonspicc café** at no. 17 is also a wine bar (*szalonspicc.hu*).

CAFÉS AROUND MARGIT KÖRÚT

For coffee and cake, go to the **Auguszt Cukrászda** (*Fény u. 8, closed Sun and Mon; map p. 428, A1*). With an over-the-counter cake shop downstairs and a café upstairs (and outside in summer), this historic family business was begun by Elek Auguszt in 1870, when he opened a shop in the Tabán area. The business flourished under his son, József Auguszt. It was nationalised after the war and the family was sent into internal exile. As things turned out, the Communists could not do without their cakes and the family was recalled in the 1950s. Later in the same decade they were able to open—and run—a tiny *pâtisserie* in Fény utca. Today the family is fully back in charge. The premises are much expanded and the cakes are as delicious as ever.

The **Bambi Presszó** (*Frankel Leó út 2–4; map p. 428, B1*) is a true survivor: the ceramic-chip floor and red plastic banquettes—even the waitstaff—have not changed for decades. Coffee, beer, toasted sandwiches, *pogácsa*.

RESTAURANTS IN AND AROUND PASARÉT

f-ff **Alessio**. Popular Italian restaurant serving good pizza. Also salads, *calamari fritti* and other specials. Friendly family atmosphere. *Pasaréti út 55. T: +36 1 275 0049, cafealessio.hu. Map p. 424, B2.*

f-ff **Pasarét Bisztró**. Occupying part of the 1937 bus stop building. Modern Hungarian cooking. Good wines. With a glassed-in front section. A good choice in an area where restaurants are hard to find. *Pasaréti tér. T: +36 1 200 0672, pasaretbisztro.hu. Map p. 424, A2.*

f-ff **Emile**. The Buda branch of Gerbeaud (*see p. 167*). Enjoy coffee and cake in the garden of a refurbished Buda villa, or eat lunch in the restaurant. The surroundings are somewhat over-designed but the menu (grilled chicken, breaded pork, stuffed cabbage) is well chosen and good value. *Orló u. 1 (corner of Gábor Áron utca). T: 06 30 585 0602, emile. hu. Map p. 424, B2.*

f-ff **Café 57**. Convenient for the Szemlő-hegy Cave. The outdoor terrace is pleasant in summer. Open for full meals or just for coffee. *Pusztaszeri út 57. T: +36 1 325 6078, cafe57.hu. Map p. 424, C1.*

CAFÉS IN AND AROUND PASARÉT

On Szépvölgyi út, visit the **Daubner cake shop**, still family-run after over a century. No seating; this is a place to come and buy a cake or a snack to take home for tea or eat on the run. Closed Mon (*Szépvölgyi út 50, corner of Pusztaszeri út; map p. 424, C1*).

District III: Óbuda

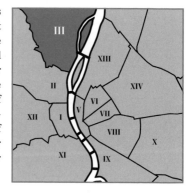

B udapest's Third District, Óbuda, is well off the beaten tourist trail but nevertheless has plenty to offer. The area has been inhabited since antiquity and there are extensive Roman remains. Other attractions include a clutch of handsome 18th–19th-century houses in an enclave of cobbled streets; a museum of Óbuda's once-important textile industry; an outpost of the Budapest History Museum in a former monastery; and atmospheric riverside beer gardens and fish stalls.

Getting to Óbuda

HÉV suburban railway H5 from Batthyány tér or Margit híd to Szentlélek tér (map p. 421, B3). Bus 9 from Deák tér or Nyugati station to Flórián tér (map p. 421, B3). Tram 17 from Széll Kálmán tér or Margit híd to Kolosy tér (map p. 421, B4) and subsequent stops.

HISTORY OF ÓBUDA

The name Óbuda means simply 'Old Buda', a reference to the fact that the settlement here is earlier (and formerly of greater importance) than the Buda that was later established on Castle Hill. The first traces of settlement are from the Palaeolithic. The Romans also chose to make their centre in this area and plenty of relics of their occupation survive. The conquering Magyars had a castle here (on the site of the Roman military amphitheatre) and tradition has it that their leader, Árpád, was buried in Óbuda on his death in 907. The kings of the ruling dynasty that bears his name frequently held court at Buda: between 1000 and 1241 (the year of the Mongol invasion) it was partly a royal estate and partly held by the Buda Chapter of prebendary canons. Their task was to issue authenticated documents and the deans or provosts of the chapter often held posts in the royal chancellery.

After the retreat of the Mongols in 1242, the court became inclined, for safety, to use the higher ground that is now Castle Hill. By the time of the first documentary

HERCULES VILLA
Mosaic of a defeated pugilist from
the bath house (3rd century).

mention of Óbuda, in 1261, it is already being referred to as *Buda Vetus*, 'Old Buda'. The area did not lose its royal connections, however, nor did Hungary's rulers cease to take an interest in it. In 1343 Louis I (the Great) made over the royal palace at Óbuda to his mother, Elizabeth, after which it remained the property of the Hungarian queen consorts. In 1395 King Sigismund founded a University here, the first in Hungary.

Almost all trace of medieval Óbuda was obliterated by the Ottoman conquest. After the reconquest of Buda, the town became a possession of the Zichy family and resettlement began, first by Hungarians and Swabians and later also by Serbs and Jews. In 1766 the widow of Miklós Zichy was constrained to hand over her estate to the Crown, which by this time had firmly been placed on a Habsburg head (Maria Theresa's). The terms of service for the inhabitants of Óbuda were harsher than under the Zichy overlords and in 1772 the so-called Óbuda Tumult broke out, a revolt against high taxes and back-breaking labour.

Up until the 19th century, Óbuda was predominantly a rural area, known for its wines (in 1766, 65 percent of families are recorded as being involved in viticulture). Although wine-growing revived after the phylloxera outbreak of the 1880s, it was never fully to recover and Óbuda instead became known for its industries, as a centre of textile manufacture, ship-building, brick-making, distilling and tobacco cutting. In the 1930s it was also known as an area of inns and taverns.

Following the repulsion of the Nazis in 1944–5, large numbers of the male population of Óbuda were taken to labour camps by the Soviets. In 1946 the ethnic Germans, for so long a defining section of the Óbuda population, were deported. In the 1960s many of the winding old streets began to be replaced by housing estates: the infamous 'panel apartment' tower blocks which now occupy so much of the skyline.

Today Óbuda is a moderately prosperous district, lively if not always lovely, home to a mix of commercial and residential life. It fills up with music lovers every August, who flock to Óbuda Island—an area of former shipyards (and also the site of the Roman governor's palace)—for the Sziget Festival (*see p. 361*).

THE ROMAN LEGIONARY CAMP & FLÓRIÁN TÉR

From Kolosy tér (*map p. 421, B4*), Bécsi út leads north along the tramlines, flanked on both sides by low-rise buildings with steeply-pitched tiled roofs. Most are modern reconstructions of earlier houses whose ground floors, once occupied by artisans' workshops, have now yielded space to restaurants, bars and beauty salons. Nevertheless, they give a good sense of Óbuda as it developed after the Ottoman defeat. Here too you will find 'Csopa', the Csodák palotája or **Palace of Wonders**, an interactive science museum popular with children (*Bécsi út 38–44; open daily 10–8, csopa.hu*).

Bécsi út meets Nagyszombat utca at a busy road junction. One part of it is now a small park named after the 'Martyrs of Katyń', Polish prisoners of war killed by the NKVD in 1940. On the other side of Szőlő utca are the remains (*accessible*) of the amphitheatre of the Roman garrison town.

AQUINCUM: THE GARRISON TOWN

The Romans arrived in the Danube area in the 1st century AD, overrunning and occupying the territory of the Eravisci, a Celtic tribe who had their *oppidum* on Gellért Hill. The land to the east, across the Danube, was occupied by the Sarmatians, with the river acting as a natural frontier. Though the Romans and Sarmatians are known to have traded with each other, their relationship was one of mutual suspicion and the Romans built a string of defensive border forts along the river. One such fort, occupied by a troop of cavalry, was at Aquincum. In AD 89 the emperor Domitian built a larger legionary camp or *castrum* here, at which were stationed soldiers of the Legio II Adiutrix, transferred from Syrmia (between the Danube and the Sava) and put in charge of defence against barbarian raids. To serve the camp, a garrison town grew up around it, populated by the soldiers' families, tradesmen, artisans, cooks and entertainers: an entire service industry to keep the troops clothed, fed, groomed and otherwise beguiled.

In AD 106, during the reign of Trajan, Aquincum became the capital of the province of Pannonia Inferior and a grand palace for the governor or proconsul was built on the Danube island (now Óbudai-sziget, Óbuda Island) opposite Aquincum. The first governor was Publius Aelius Hadrianus, later to become the emperor Hadrian.

The garrison town accordingly expanded to fit its new status: no longer a collection of haphazard shanties, it became a planned settlement with paved streets and cob or brick buildings on stone foundations. For the more important public structures, stone was used throughout. The southern districts were occupied by industrial and artisans' quarters, warehouses and docks. The cult buildings and residences of administrators and other officials lay to the north. The military amphitheatre—whose foundations are now landscaped as a public park—was situated at the town's southern tip. Inside the castrum was a huge baths complex, the Thermae Maiores, whose remains can also still be seen.

Pannonian troops were instrumental in bringing Septimius Severus to the throne in 193. The following year, Aquincum (both the military town around the camp and the separate civilian town to the north; *see p. 108*) was raised to the status of *colonia*. The towns attained the pinnacle of their prosperity at this time.

When Diocletian reorganised the Roman Empire in 296, Aquincum became an administrative centre of the new province of Valeria, whose capital was Sopianae (modern Pécs, south Hungary). From the mid-3rd century, the pressure of barbarian raids led to a dwindling population and steady decline. The castrum fell out of use and a new one was built further east. The civilian population retreated within the fortress walls, leaving the gardens of the former villas, as well as the now-deserted streets around them, to be used as places of burial. The Huns overran the province in 433.

THE MILITARY AMPHITHEATRE

The amphitheatre of the Roman garrison town (*map p. 421, B4*), thought to have been built in the mid-2nd century during the reign of Antoninus Pius, was an enormous structure. Its arena, measuring 89m by 66m, was larger than that of the Colosseum in Rome (84m by 48m), although its seating capacity of 12,000 makes it far smaller

FLÓRIÁN TÉR
Monument to the victims of road accidents.

(the Colosseum could accommodate six times as many). It had gates at four sides and animal pens to supply victims for *venationes*. Underground water pipes indicate that it could also be flooded for mock sea battles. When Roman power dwindled it was turned into a fortress and was used by various tribes during the time of the great migrations, including the Magyars. In the Middle Ages it was covered with earth and the resulting mound was known as Királydomb (King Hill). Workers' housing for the Óbuda textile mills was built here in the 19th century. Excavations began in 1935.

FLÓRIÁN TÉR AND THE THERMAE MAIORES

Flórián tér (*map p. 421, B3*), named after the patron saint of firefighters, a martyred Roman soldier born in present-day Lower Austria, is a wide space made up partly of busy roads and flyovers serving Árpád Bridge and partly, in its western part, of rough common planted with trees and overlooked on three sides by 'panel apartments', large prefabricated concrete blocks of a type common in the Budapest housing estates of the '60s, '70s and '80s. In the centre of the green space rises a tall **monument to the victims of road accidents** (Gábor Mihály, 1996): a winged angel holds a wreath above a copper car wreck. On the base are recorded the annual death tolls on Hungary's roads.

At the northeast edge of the green space are some reconstructed columns and sections of wall in *opus quadratum*, **remains of the Roman military camp**. In the underpass here are numerous copies of lapidary fragments, including Mithraic scenes and funerary monuments. Here too are the excavations of the military baths complex, the **Thermae Maiores** (*open April–Oct 10–6, Nov–March 10–4; closed Mon; aquincum.hu; access is along Exit B of the Flórián tér underpass*), which stood at the main crossroads of the castrum. Maps and information boards are posted throughout the site. The cold plunge pool (*piscina*), large frigidarium and the various rooms of the tepidarium and steam room can be clearly made out. Modern roads have prevented excavation of the caldarium. At the time of writing the latrines area and palaestra were not accessible. When in the 4th century the castrum fell out of use and was moved further east, the baths complex was reconstructed as a lavish palace, perhaps the seat of the military commander of the province.

ROMAN MILITARY TOWN MUSEUM

Táborvárosi Múzeum. Map p. 421, inset. Pacsirtamező u. 65. Open April–Oct Sun 1.30–2.30.

The sculpted bust of a Roman soldier (Gyula Gáldi, 1955) marks the entrance to the excavations of what are thought to have been a house and an inn. A series of very small rooms can be seen, with a hypocaust below (of a different system from those in the Thermae Maiores or Hercules Villa, the supports being constructed of piles of flat square bricks instead of monolithic stone struts). A vestige of downpipe shows that the building would have had an upper storey. Two tombstones are preserved here: those of the veteran Valerius Proclius and his wife (3rd century) and that of C. Aelius Alexander, keeper of the armoury (2nd century). A copy of the latter can be seen in the Flórián tér underpass.

HERCULES VILLA

Meggyfa u. 21. Map p. 421, B2. Open April–Oct Sun 11–1.

Squeezed between blocks of flats in an area that would once have been filled with the comfortable residences of Roman provincial administrators, the remains of the Hercules Villa were discovered in the 1950s, when land was being cleared for the building of the adjacent school.

The entrance path to the site leads between a section of tile-lined **water channel**, as well as later **sarcophagi** dating from the 4th century onwards, a time when the population had abandoned much of the town and huddled for safety within the walls of the military fortress. The main ruins, under cover, belong to a villa that was built in the 2nd century and extended and improved in the 3rd. The smaller of the protective buildings houses the remains of a **private bath house**, its floor mosaic showing two pugilists. The victor stands on the left while his vanquished opponent, bleeding from the head, sits crumpled on the ground. Behind him is the faint outline of a table or stand on which have been placed in readiness the victor's palm frond and other prizes. Both boxers appear to be wearing protective gloves or knuckledusters.

Under the billowing concrete roof of the second building is an enfilade of rooms ending in a large **apsidal hall**. The mosaic floors survive only in a fragmentary state but enough remains to show how fine they must once have been. The apsidal hall has traces of a Dionysiac scene: a panther and a putto still survive, along with bunches of grapes and the feet of the drunken Bacchus. In the room at the other end of the enfilade was found the mosaic that gives the villa its name: an *emblema* showing the centaur Nessus making off with Hercules' wife Deianeira. It is now on display at the Aquincum Museum (*see p. 109*).

THE CELLA TRICHORA

In the narrow angle where two streets, Hunor utca and Kunigunda útja, meet (*map p. 421, A3–B3*), in a patch of grass and clover, are the clover-leaf-shaped reconstructed remains (waist-high walls) of the so-called Cella Trichora, a three-lobed Palaeochristian chapel of the 4th century.

THE KISCELL MUSEUM

Map p. 421, A3. Open Tues–Sun April–Oct 10–6, Nov–March 10–4. Combined ticket with the Budapest History Museum (on Castle Hill) and the Aquincum Museum. kiscellimuzeum.hu.

The Kiscell Museum (Kiscelli Múzeum), part of the Budapest History Museum, occupies a former monastery in the hills above Óbuda. Its name, 'Little Zell', refers to its past identity as a pilgrimage site. Count Péter Zichy founded a chapel here to house a copy of the famous wooden image of the Madonna from Mariazell in Styria, held to be miraculous. The copy was ceremonially placed here in 1733.

Getting to the Kiscell Museum
On foot, in fine weather: *From Bécsi út, just west of the Military Amphitheatre ruins, Doberdő utca (map p. 421, A4) leads left, beyond a striking neo-Grecian housing development (Rezső Hikisch, 1926–8) with Ionic pilasters and a running meander frieze (one of its apartments was a former home of Árpád Göncz, first President of Hungary after the fall of Communism; the block was in fact built as part of a programme to create housing for the large numbers of refugees from Hungary's lost territory after WWI). The street leads uphill between buildings belonging to the Óbuda University and soon becomes a forest path, leading through maple woods past a small chapel dedicated to the Holy Blood. Follow the waymarks (blue crosses), which take you past painted Stations of the Cross (early 19th century, restored) and a couple of picnic sites, until the yellow buildings of the Kiscell Museum come into view.*

By public transport: *Tram 17 from Széll Kálmán tér or Margit híd to Szent Margit Kórház Hospital (map p. 421, A3) and walk up Kiscelli utca to the sharp right bend. From there a short stepped path leads to the museum. Bus 109 and tram 19 from Batthyány tér or Margit híd take you to the same place.*

HISTORY OF THE KISCELL MUSEUM

The museum occupies buildings that were originally a Trinitarian monastery, founded in 1738 by Zsuzsanna Zichy around the small pilgrimage chapel built by her husband. The conventual buildings and their church were completed in 1758, decorated with sculptures by Károly Bebo, the Zichys' court sculptor. When Joseph II dissolved the Trinitarian Order in the 1780s, the monastery and church furnishings were dispersed. The statue of the Kiscell Madonna is now in the Óbuda parish church (*see p. 103*) while Maulbertsch's *Death of St Joseph* hangs in the Hungarian National Gallery. The monastery found a new role as a storehouse for military uniforms. In 1910 it and its surrounding parkland were bought by the wealthy furniture designer and manufacturer Max Schmidt, who used it partly as his residence and partly as a workshop and showroom. Schmidt, son of the successful Viennese furniture maker Friedrich Otto Schmidt, was much sought-after by wealthy patrons in Hungary. He worked with a number of designers and in a wide variety of styles—neo-Baroque, English Georgian, Secessionist and Modernist (among those whose designs he used and who he in turn influenced were Joseph Hoffmann and Adolf Loos)—to create furniture, lamps, ceramic stoves and other fixtures for town apartments and country châteaux. His life was touched by scandal when in 1914 the body of his lover, a *demi-mondaine* known as Magnates' Elsa, was found bundled into a travelling trunk, washed up on the Danube bank near Bem tér. In his will, Schmidt desired that his house should be used as a museum and that its grounds should be given over to the public as a park. The Kiscell Museum is little-visited and under-curated and unfortunately the Schmidt material is only displayed as part of special exhibitions. Nevertheless, there are some interesting works of art on show here, with the additional attraction that you are likely to have the museum almost to yourself.

THE COLLECTIONS

At the time of writing there was a display of **old shop signs** on the ground floor, including a memorable one from the former Monkey Inn in the Tabán district. Here too is the original Iron 'Chump' (*Vastuskó; see p. 67*) from Iskola utca in Buda, and another, very similar one that once stood in Pest by the old gate in the city walls at the top of Váci utca (*map p. 428, C3*). In a room housing the Biedermeier (c. 1830) furnishings from the former Arany Oroszlán (Golden Lion) pharmacy in central Pest, a section of blue-and-white stencilled wall decoration from the time of Max Schmidt was uncovered in 2012.

On the first floor are pictures belonging to Budapest's **municipal art collection**. There are some fine works by some of Hungary's greatest late 19th and early 20th-century painters: József Rippl-Rónai, István Csók, István Réti, Károly Ferenczy and Dezső Czigány, an industrial Óbuda landscape by Uitz (*The Brickyard in Újlak*, 1916) and a portrait by Károly Kernstok. Small sculptures in bronze by Pál Pátzay and Ferenc Medgyessy include a version of the latter's delightful *Woman Scrubbing*. There are also drawings and poster designs by Róbert Berény, Farkas Molnár, Lajos Kassák and Aurél Bernáth.

The **Budapest history collection** includes furniture and artefacts from the 18th century onwards. Highlights are some superb architectural drawings and designs by Adam Clark (the tunnel under Castle Hill), Albert Schickedanz (Fine Arts Museum), Ignác Alpár (Hungarian National Bank), Imre Steindl (Pest New Town Hall), Rippl-Rónai (dining room for Tivadar Andrássy), Dénes Györgyi (apartment block at Nyáry Pál u. 10), Aladár Árkay (Városligeti fasor church), Lili Sztehlo (window for the Városmajor church) and Béla Lajta (the Vas utca school). Lajta made collecting expeditions to Transylvania, returning with examples of folk arts and crafts, whose forms and motifs found their way into his designs. A simple wooden chair for his Jewish Institute for the Blind on Mexikói út (*see p. 321*) is one such example.

ÓBUDA: THE ENCLAVE SOUTH OF ÁRPÁD BRIDGE

At the south end of Flórián tér, on a little hummock between Pacsirtamező utca and Árpád Bridge, stands the so-called **Votive Altar** (*map p. 421, inset*), a tripartite statue group invoking the protection of three saints: St Florian against fire, St Charles Borromeo against plague and St Philip Neri against earthquake. It was commissioned by the lord of the manor, Miklós Zichy, from his household sculptor Károly Bebo and the work was supervised to its completion by Zichy's widow, Erzsébet Berényi, between 1758 and 1763. It received its base in 1819. Damaged in 1919 during the Romanian occupation of Budapest, it was reduced to a single statue, St Florian, who was taken down in 1948 when construction of Árpád Bridge was underway. Completely restored and remade (the statue of Charles Borromeo is an entirely modern copy), it was re-inaugurated in 2012.

Behind the altar, on a blind wall facing Árpád Bridge, is a red-ochre village scene by Lajos Veszeli, based on drawings by Károly Kós. It acts as a sort of theatre curtain for the small, late 18th-century **Óbuda Calvinist Church** behind it, next to which is a priest house built in 1908 in the National Romantic or Folk Revival style to designs by Kós and Dezső Zrumeczky.

Further east towards the river is the so-called **Krúdy Quarter** (Krúdy-negyed), an area of town named after the great prose writer Gyula Krúdy, who lived here at the end of his life. His name is associated with the Kéhli Vendéglő restaurant on Mókus utca and with the building just around the corner on Korona tér, which now houses the delightful **Museum of Trade and Tourism** (Kereskedelmi és Vendéglátóipari Múzeum; *open Tues–Sun 10–6; mkvm.hu*). Two rooms on the ground floor have been arranged in Krúdy's memory. It is here that the great writer lived, ill, in poverty and hounded by creditors, until his death in May of 1933. Krúdy's writings had enjoyed great success before the First World War. He participated in the Aster Revolution of 1918 and after the fall of the Republic of Councils in 1919 found himself politically on the wrong side. His career faltered and he fell on hard times. Today he ranks as one of Hungary's most regarded writers and his name is often seen around Óbuda. The Sindbad stories are perhaps his best-known works, not least because of the 1971 classic film starring the great actor Zoltán Latinovits. Other rooms of the museum have recreations of a late 19th/early 20th-century patissier, confectioner, restaurant, inn, coffee house, hotel and nightclub, and from the domestic sphere a middle-class dining room, bathroom and kitchen with its tiny maid's box room. There is also a display on Communist-era retail and early department stores. Handbills in English are available in each room.

The **Óbuda Parish Church** (Szent Péter és Pál főplébánia-templom) was built for the Zichys in 1744–9 by János György Paur. The exterior has statues of St Sebastian (left) and St Roch, with St Peter and St Paul at either side of the tower. Above the door is St Rosalia, the Sicilian hermit saint, shown in her cave. All these are the works of Károly Bebo, as are the statues of St John of Nepomuk and St Florian at the east end of the churchyard and the richly carved pulpit in the interior. The *Kiscell Madonna* (*see p. 100*) and its altar, with angels by Károly Bebo, are on the north side. Just inside the main door, above the holy water stoup, is a plaque recording the Danube water level during the flood of 1838.

Outside the church are several **memorials**. Against the exterior church wall facing south has been placed a monument to Matthias Corvinus' chronicler Antonio Bonfini, who is thought to have been buried in the earlier chapel of St Margaret on this site. On the rear exterior wall is a WWI memorial (István Tóth, 1928). A little way to the south is a sculpture entitled *Peal of Bells* (Kornél Baliga, 1992), a memorial to those who lost their lives in the 1956 Uprising.

Diagonally across the cobbled car park behind the bell sculpture, you come into Lajos utca. The corner building, no. 158, on medieval foundations, houses the Budapest Galéria (*open for temporary exhibitions*). Opposite it stands the Neoclassical **Óbuda Synagogue**, built in 1820–1 to designs by András Landherr. It is the oldest synagogue in Budapest still functioning as a place of worship. The Jewish community in Óbuda is first recorded in the 14th century. Although after the reconquest the Jews of Buda generally found life harder than under the Ottomans, there was a sizeable community here and they seem to have enjoyed the protection of the Zichy family. The synagogue was taken over by the state in the 1950s but has since been restored to the community. It reopened for worship in 2010 (*obudaizsinagoga.hu; to book a tour, T: +36 30 396 9020*).

In the elbow formed by Perc utca and Kiskorona utca are the very scanty **remains of the Poor Clares convent and church**, founded in 1334 by Elizabeth, wife of King Károly Róbert (Charles I) and mother of Louis I. She was buried here on her death in 1380. In the convent's heyday the nuns undertook the education of daughters of the nobility. A particularly beautiful silver-gilt and enamel reliquary tabernacle, presented to the convent by Queen Elizabeth, is now in the Cloisters Museum in New York. The buildings were destroyed by the Ottomans and the nuns never returned, refounding their convent subsequently on Castle Hill.

THE GOLDBERGER TEXTILE MUSEUM

Lajos u. 138. Map p. 421, inset. Open Tues–Sun 10–6. Free 1st Sat of the month. Combined ticket with the Óbuda Museum. goldbergermuzeum.hu.

This excellent museum of the textile industry occupies the house where Ferenc Goldberger, an immigrant to Óbuda from Bohemia or Moravia, first set up his blue-dyeing business in 1784 (he and his family lived in the house and the dyeing vats were in the courtyard). Proximity to the Danube was essential, since a copious supply of water was needed for the dyeing process. The building later housed the offices of the Goldberger textile factory, whose premises expanded around and behind it, eventually occupying the entire block. The display traces the history of the Goldberger business, through six generations of the family and afterwards under Communism.

The first room illustrates the process of blue-dyeing (in a solution of indigo powder, slaked lime and iron sulphate), with wooden printing blocks and examples of finished cloth. By 1800 the Goldbergers had opened a shop in Pest (Sas u. 27). They were enthusiastic supporters of the 1848 revolution and the factory, by this time mechanised, undertook to supply cloth to equip 50 cavalrymen. They also produced patterns that made use of patriotic slogans and portraits of Széchenyi and Kossuth. The manufactory became a limited company in 1905. Under Leó Goldberger, who was head of the business from 1913, it went vertical, establishing weaving and spinning mills in south Buda to ensure a constant supply of its own cloth. The directors' offices and wholesale department moved to a handsome building in Pest (it still stands, as does Goldberger's town residence; *see pp. 154 and 168*).

Some way south of the Goldberger museum, at **Lajos u. 102**, is a house once occupied by another blue-dyeing manufactory, established by Gerson Spitzer in 1826. Following the establishment in 1844 of Lajos Kossuth's brainchild the *Védegylet* (Protection Association), aimed at promoting specifically Hungarian industry and products, Spitzer also became an enthusiastic producer of patriotic patterns. After nationalisation the Spitzer manufactory became a cotton mill. Diagonally opposite, the old brick façade of another former Óbuda factory building has been incorporated into the design of a building repurposed for modern urban use.

LEÓ GOLDBERGER AND HIS TEXTILE MILL

A small room in the Textile Museum, hung entirely in black, tells the story of Leó Goldberger. Scion of an ennobled Hungarian Jewish family, Goldberger presided over a cloth mill that was one of Budapest's largest employers. His pursuits were those of all men of his wealth and standing: he owned racehorses, became a Freemason, was president of the Lipótváros social club, had a seat in the Upper House, a town house in Pest (on Vörösmarty tér) and a summer villa on the Danube.

In 1919, with the establishment of the Republic of Councils, he and his family had temporarily fled to Switzerland. Not so in the 1930s. Goldberger always believed that his cordial relationship with Horthy would be sufficient to save him. Faced with restrictive laws limiting the commercial activities of Jews, he attempted to comply by making two of his directors redundant and forgoing his own salary. In 1944, immediately after the Nazi takeover, he was seized and deported to Mauthausen, where he died the following spring. On one of the walls of the little black room is a typewritten list, dated 1945, of those persons forbidden to set foot on the factory premises. At the top of the list are Leo Goldberger's widow and his son Antal.

Antal Goldberger, who had survived deportation and returned to Hungary in June 1945, attempted to keep the factory going but inevitably it fell to Communist collectivisation. A succession of three- and five-year plans were introduced to increase productivity (the plans of 1971–5 and 1976–80 focused on synthetic fibres). In a variety of guises, latterly as Budaprint, the factory continued in operation right through the Communist era but in 1992, with the disbanding of the Comecon market, it was heavily indebted and finally closed in 1997. Today, if you walk down Fényes Adolf utca, you can still see many of the old factory buildings. At the time of writing, the name Budaprint still appeared high up on one of them and a single outlet, Euro Textil, survived to bear witness to this once humming heart of the Óbuda cloth industry.

ÓBUDA: THE ENCLAVE NORTH OF ÁRPÁD BRIDGE

The wide, perpetually busy **Árpád Bridge**, is approached by a flyover supported on tall pillars, which divides ancient Óbuda in two. Construction began in 1939 but was interrupted by the war and the bridge was only opened in 1950. It bore the name Stalin Bridge until 1956, when it was rebranded with the name of the leading Magyar chieftain.

SZENTLÉLEK TÉR AND ITS MUSEUMS

Szentlélek tér, Holy Spirit Square (*map p. 421, B3*), lies immediately north of Árpád Bridge. In the white two-storey building behind the bus stops is the **Vasarely Museum** (*Szentlélek tér 6, entrance is through the courtyard and to the right; open Tues–Sun 10–6, last tickets 45mins before closing; vasarely.hu*), reorganised in 2017 and occupying two floors of a wing of the former Zichy Palace. It contains works largely donated to the city by Victor Vasarely (1906–97), who was born in Hungary. Vasarely belonged to the

FŐ TÉR

Tribal Magyar Atlas figure on the Óbuda Town Hall (1906).

same generation as Moholy-Nagy, Breuer and Farkas Molnár; in fact he studied at the Műhely, a school set up in 1928 by Molnár and Sándor Bortnyik, both of whom had been at the Bauhaus in Weimar. In 1930 Vasarely left for Paris, and was to spend the rest of his life in France. It was in Paris that he met Denise René: the first exhibition that she held at her new gallery in 1944 was dedicated to him. (René and Vasarely would later collaborate to put on a show of works by Lajos Kassák; *see p. 382.*) The ground floor has early graphic works and posters, experiments with Geometrical Abstraction and examples of his signature 'kinetic art'. The 1938 *Zebras* contains the seeds of what would later make him famous, the Op-Art that is displayed on the upper floor, with a number of very fine examples, many of them huge in scale. The final room presents his ideas on how art can be integrated into public spaces, which he outlined in his 1970 book *Plasti-Cité: L'oeuvre publique dans votre vie quotidienne.* An example of his public sculpture can be seen in Budapest, in the precinct outside Déli railway station (*map p. 428, A2*).

In another part of the Zichy Palace, entered from the cobbled western part of Szentlélek tér, is the **Óbuda History Museum** (*map p. 421, inset; open Tues–Sun 10–6,* *obudaimuzeum.hu*), with a display on the history of Óbuda from medieval times to the era of post-war reconstruction and the housing estates. Most of the wall captions are in Hungarian only.

Opposite the history museum is a school building with a plaque commemorating the founding of Buda University by King Sigismund and Pope Boniface IX in 1395. Also in the square is the Baroque **Trinity Statue**, set up by the Zichy family in 1740 in thanks for the ending of a plague outbreak, dismantled in 1950 and re-erected in 2000. At the three outer corners are statues of St Roch, St Sebastian and St Felix. The statues surrounding the central column are St Charles Borromeo, St Francis Xavier and St Florian. The column itself has the golden dove of the Holy Spirit at the top, God the Father and God the Son, and the Coronation of the Virgin below.

ON AND AROUND FŐ TER

Szentlélek tér opens out into the spacious Fő tér, the main square of old Óbuda, closed on its southern side by the steep-roofed Új Sípos fish restaurant and opposite by the **Town Hall** (Elek Barcza, 1906), its main doorway flanked by caryatids of tribal Magyars with walrus moustaches and long plaits, and bearing a plaque commemorating the citizens of Óbuda who were taken to Soviet labour camps in 1945. In the centre of the square, the Gázlámpa kiosk sells drinks (*closed in winter*). At the beginning of Harrer Pál utca, left of the Town Hall, is a statue of Pál Harrer, the first mayor of Óbuda. To the right of the Town Hall is a statue of Gyula Krúdy's famous fictional character Sindbad (bearing the features of Zoltán Latinovits, the actor who plays him in the 1971 classic film), shown seated at a table with a carafe of wine and a soda siphon. The statue is the work of Péter Szanyi (2013, signed on the tablecloth).

The right-hand (east) side of Fő tér is closed by the long, white **Zichy Palace**. An arched entranceway leads across wooden cobbles into an unkempt courtyard, at the back of which is the pink Baroque main palace façade (at the time of writing very shabby). It was built on the site of the family's earlier villa in 1746–8, when Miklós Zichy made Óbuda his principal residence. Today it houses the **Kassák Museum** on the first floor (*open Wed–Sun 10–5, kassakmuzeum.hu*), dedicated to the life and work of the Constructivist artist, poet and champion of the working man Lajos Kassák (*see p. 382*).

Another wing of the palace houses a little theatre, the Térszínház, and behind it is a secluded **beer garden**, the Kobuci kert.

THE IMRE VARGA COLLECTION

Laktanya utca (*map p. 421, inset*), one of the main streets of medieval Óbuda, leads off Fő tér past the sculpture group known as the ***Umbrella Women*** (Imre Varga, 1985): four female figures in thin coats, hunched against the cold and under deep umbrellas, are grouped around a lamp post. Inspired by similar women whom the artist saw on the streets of Paris, they are also known as the *Waiting Women*, prostitutes under the street light's sodium glare. At the end of Laktanya utca on the right (no. 7) is a branch of the Budapest Galéria (*open April–Oct Tues–Sun 10–6; budapestgaleria.hu*) housing the **Imre Varga Collection** of sculptures, paintings and models for large-scale public commissions by the prolific artist (b. 1923), including for his Hungarian Chapel under

St Peter's in Rome (1980), which features a Virgin and Child surrounded by gold panels embossed with the famous Scythian stags (*see p. 231*). Other works include the maquette for his willow tree memorial in the garden of the Great Synagogue (*see p. 217*) and for his Raoul Wallenberg memorial (*see p. 87*), as well as small-scale versions of the *Umbrella Women* and several workings and re-workings of his *Heroes Monument*, a one-armed, peg-legged soldier in a uniform coat, a row of medals nailed to his chest above his heart, ragged puttees on his remaining leg, but with no head and no face.

In the block between Vöröskereszt utca and Kórház utca is a small park with the partially reconstructed remains of one of the gates of the Roman castrum, the **Porta Praetoria**, which led down to the river to the crossing place over to the island where the governor's palace was located. Distances in the province were measured from this gate. Immediately behind, on the corner of Vöröskereszt utca and Miklós utca, are the very scanty traces (the outline of an apsidal building can be seen) of what was probably medieval Óbuda's **Franciscan church and friary**.

AQUINCUM

Map p. 421, C1. Museum open April–Oct 10–6, Nov–March 10–4. Ruins open 1hr earlier. In winter, check the website as the ruins are closed in wet or snowy weather. HÉV suburban train H5 from Batthyány tér or Margit híd to Aquincum (c. 15mins). Standard transport tickets are valid. There is a WC, tiny café and shop in the museum. The ticket office is at the south end of the site, close to the museum. Combined ticket with the Budapest History Museum and Kiscell Museum. aquincum.hu.

The ruins of the Roman civilian town lie beside the busy main road along the Danube. Much of the town still lies unexcavated under the asphalt. Immediately outside the ticket office are the children's play area and a reconstructed house used for activities during school visits. On a mound overlooking the site is the 'Chronoscope', where you look through an optical device to see a 3D reconstruction of the Roman town.

AQUINCUM'S CIVILIAN TOWN

North of the Roman garrison town and camp (*see p. 97*), a civilian town grew up, populated by veterans and wealthy Romanised Celts. In AD 194, together with the military town, it attained the rank of *colonia* and at its height, Aquincum had a population of around 40,000. The civilian and military towns prospered and expanded but never became contiguous, being separated by a necropolis. As Roman power and cohesion declined, so did Aquincum's fortunes. After a period of peaceful stagnation in the early 4th century, its population steadily dwindled until in the 5th century it was overrun by the Huns. The ruins called Aquincum today are those of the civilian town (*for remains of the military town, see p. 99*). Nothing remains to be seen of the governor's palace on Óbuda Island; the site was backfilled after excavation.

THE AQUINCUM MUSEUM

The building occupies a handsome former electricity substation by Dénes Györgyi and Ernő Román (1931) with an extension by László Rajk (2007). On the entrance wall is a replica of the *Tabula Peutingeriana*, the famous road map of the Roman world. On the ground floor are showcases of finds: pottery, metalwork, glassware and a **mosaic emblema from the Hercules Villa** (*see p. 100*) of the centaur carrying off Deianeira (Hercules' wife). The mosaic is by North African (probably Alexandrian) craftsmen and dates from the 3rd century. It is the only imported mosaic so far found in the territory of Roman Pannonia.

Upstairs is an **exhibit on the governor's palace** on Óbuda Island and more finds, including a 3rd-century silver-gilt brooch featuring gladiators in combat and a marble head of Juno with tiny traces of gilding on her headdress. Here too is a reconstruction of the 3rd-century **Aquincum water organ** (*hydra*), an instrument belonging to the firemen's *collegium*, whose remains were found in 1931 during the construction of this building. Displayed close by is the tomb-chest of Aelia Sabina, wife of the water-organist and a musician in her own right. The poignant inscription reads: '*Enclosed within this stone lies Sabina, dear and faithful wife. Excelling in the arts, she alone surpassed her husband. Her voice was sweet, her fingers plucked the strings. But she fell silent, suddenly snatched away. She lived three decades—five years fewer, alas, but three months more plus twice seven days. She herself lives on. She was a queen among the water organ players. May all you who read this be happy. May the gods keep you. And with a pious voice may you proclaim: Fare thee well, Aelia Sabina. Titus Aelius Justus, water-organist and stipendiary of the Second Auxiliary Legion, erected this monument to his wife.*'

THE RUINS

The ruins are confusing at first, but the maps and signboards are helpful. The description below covers the main things to see. Numbering corresponds to the plan overleaf.

(A) Large dwelling house: The remains of this once-luxurious and spacious dwelling are difficult to interpret but the sign-board helps greatly. Like most Roman town houses, its street-facing rooms were occupied by shops. In the same wing as the shops was the **private bath house (Ai)**, remains of which can be seen under cover (a plunge pool and mosaic floor showing two pugilists, one black and one white). The domestic area opened off a **peristyle courtyard (Aii)** and included a large pillared **reception hall (Aiii)**.

(B) Double bath: The twin apsidal caldaria of this bath house have led to the suggestion that it may have been used by men and women simultaneously.

(C) Merchant's House: The street entrance of this impressive house leads into a large central hall, presumably where the merchant conducted his business, with smaller rooms opening off it. Behind this, separated by a wide corridor, was the living area, some of it with under-floor heating.

(D) Butcher's House: Across a narrow lane from the so-called Merchant's

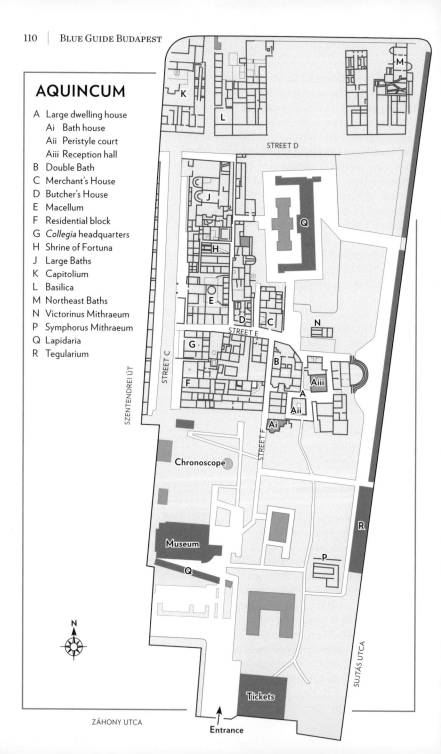

AQUINCUM

A Large dwelling house
   Ai   Bath house
   Aii Peristyle court
   Aiii Reception hall
B Double Bath
C Merchant's House
D Butcher's House
E Macellum
F Residential block
G *Collegia* headquarters
H Shrine of Fortuna
J Large Baths
K Capitolium
L Basilica
M Northeast Baths
N Victorinus Mithraeum
P Symphorus Mithraeum
Q Lapidaria
R Tegularium

STREET D

SZENTENDREI ÚT

STREET C

STREET E

STREET F

Chronoscope

Museum

Q

P

R

N

Tickets

Entrance

SUJTÁS UTCA

ZÁHONY UTCA

House is the Butcher's House, conveniently situated near the *macellum* or meat market. The living rooms were at the front. At the back was a stone flagged hall provided with running water and drainage, probably used for processing meat.

(E) Macellum: The meat market was a large complex occupying a plot at the corner of Street E and the wide Street C, which was lined on its far side with a row of *tabernae* or shops. The stalls in the meat market were of uniform size: in the thresholds you can still clearly see the slots for the shutters. At the centre was a circular tholos, perhaps a shrine and storehouse for the official weights and measures.

(F) Residential block: The development here belonged to the *collegia*, professional associations somewhat akin to guilds. It consists of a residential block with a central courtyard and communal lavatory. Some of the rooms were heated.

(G) *Collegia* headquarters: This corner block was a mixed-use development with ground-floor shops, a colonnaded porch opening onto the main street, an assembly hall, and a courtyard with a well. Adjoining it, with vehicular access from Street F, were two blocks of artisans' dwelling houses separated by a sewer.

(H) Shrine of Fortuna: In a pretty tree-shaded glade stand the ruins of a shrine built around an altar dedicated to Fortuna Augusta, the cult of imperial prosperity. The area backs onto the large public baths and a drainage channel leads diagonally across the site, taking water from the baths to the sewer under the street.

(J) Large Baths: This large public bath house is well enough preserved for the visitor to pick out the entranceway with its porter's lodge; the changing room (*apodyterium*), and progression of bathing halls from the apsidal frigidarium and tepidarium to the large, flat-ended caldarium. Remains of the blackened hypocaust and furnace are particularly well preserved and in the steam room (*laconicum*) you can see remains of hollow bricks cladding the walls, which would have carried hot air all around the space. Adjoining it, and also accessible from the street, is the public latrine with its rinsing channel.

(K) Capitolium: At the junction of Street D (the main decumanus maximus) and the north–south-running cardo, stood the forum, today at the very edge of the excavated area. At one end of the forum stood the Capitolium, the temple dedicated to the main gods of the state cult, together with municipal offices. Traces of wall heating can be seen in the main office (Curia).

(L) Basilica: Across the street from the Capitolium are the remains of the Basilica or court house.

(M) Northeast Baths: Next to the remains of the so-called 'Glue-boiler's House', in an area of town presumed to have been occupied by workshops and manufactories, are the Northeast Baths, with clearly traceable frigidarium, tepidarium and caldarium, and a small latrine.

(N–P) Mithraea: The cult of Mithras was popular among soldiers (*see below*) and there are likely to have been several Mithraea in Aquincum. One of them **(N)**, attached to the partly-excavated house of Marcus Antonius Victorinus, retains its once-subterranean dining chamber, lined with benches. At the far end would have stood the cult statue showing Mithras slaying the bull. The god was also worshipped in the **Symphorus Mithraeum (P)**.

THE CULT OF MITHRAS

Mithraism was one of the most popular of the foreign cults that spread across the Roman Empire in the 2nd and 3rd centuries AD. Its origins were in Persia, where worship of the god is said to have been founded by the sage Zoroaster. Mithras was associated with the sun and with cattle-herding or stealing, and the most common representation of him, found in relief or statue form in all Mithraic sanctuaries, shows him astride a large bull which he is stabbing in the neck.

There is a great deal of unresolved debate over how and why Mithraism spread from Persia, and the extent to which the Romans developed the cult for their own ends. In the Western Empire, Mithraism was especially popular among soldiers, slaves and ex-slaves. Women seem to have been excluded. Members met in small groups, up to 35, in sanctuaries which were designed to resemble caves, the traditional haunt of the god. At the eastern end there would be a relief or statue of Mithras, illuminated from above or by torches. This was the 'light' end of the sanctuary, which contrasted with the 'dark' western end and made the point that this was a saviour god who brought the initiate from darkness into light. During ceremonies the initiates would recline on platforms along the side walls and enjoy a ritual meal.

Some 400 Mithraea are known, a high proportion of them in Rome, but they are also found in army camps along the northern border of the Empire from Britain to the Danube, as evidenced here at Aquincum.

(Q) Lapidaria: Grave markers, altars, sarcophagi and sarcophagus fragments as well as elements of masonry are displayed at various parts of the site. Labelling is patchy. Of particular interest, in the lapidarium in the centre of the site, around the old museum building, are the tombstones of Eraviscan couples, shown adopting Roman customs and attributes, though the women still wear their native dress.

(R) Tegularium: An interesting display on Roman brick and terracotta, with fragments retaining hoof prints of a horse and a pig, cat and dog paw prints, a human footprint and the marks of a soldier's hob-nailed sandal (*caliga*).

THE AMPHITHEATRE

Right beside the train tracks at the Aquincum HÉV stop are the remains of the amphitheatre (*free entry*), built in the 2nd century during the reign of Antoninus Pius. It could hold around 6,000 spectators and was used for gladiatorial combats and animal fights, as well as for town assemblies. Today what you see is the basement level, with entrances east and west and remains of holding pens. The tiers of seating have

AQUINCUM

Tombstone of an Eraviscan couple. They adopt the Roman pose of the linked right hands (*dextrarum iunctio*), but the costume of the wife (headdress and torc) are native, not Roman.

disappeared. A single tree grows in the centre. In its heyday the beasts that were kept here are said to have been so fierce that a specially high fence had to be built to stop them from breaking out. Today the roaring of the lions and the yells of the crowd have been replaced by the roar of the main road and the sound of birdsong and crickets. It is an atmospheric spot.

THE ÓBUDA GASWORKS, RÓMAI PART AND CSILLAGHEGY

Behind the Aquincum museum is the former **Óbuda Gasworks** (its conical towers are a landmark) and adjoining gasworkers' housing estate, an important example of town planning on the English Garden City model. It was built in 1914, which is when the gasworks also officially opened, to plans by Loránd Almási Balogh and Kálmán Reichl, supervised by the Swiss expert Albert Weiss. The estate is in two parts, with housing for the workers and overseers. Immediately behind the Aquincum ruins, bordered by Sujtás utca and Gázgyár utca (*map p. 421, C1*), is the former **workers' housing estate**, designed by Almási Balogh. The houses are arranged symmetrically around a wide central avenue shaded by poplar trees and closed at one end by a kindergarten (still functioning). The buildings are of one, two or three storeys; there are no tenement blocks. All are painted yellow and have green wooden shutters in a variety of designs, evoking country cottages. Under the eaves of the largest houses is incised decoration of men and women in folk costume. The gasworks closed in 1984 and its former offices and administrative buildings (Kálmán Reichl and Albert Weiss, 1912–13) are now part of the Graphisoft business park. From inside the business park there is a good view of the gasworks' old water tower and coal tar silos. Development of this part of town is not easy owing to contamination of the ground.

Further south, reaching down to the river, is the **managers' and overseers' housing estate** of detached villas designed by Kálmán Reichl. The main north–south road, Ángel Sanz Briz út, is named after the Spanish diplomat (the 'Angel of Budapest') who saved thousands of Jewish lives in 1944.

RÓMAI PART

North of Aquincum and the railway line, the riverside stretch is known as Római part (the 'Roman shore'). Here, a shady promenade leads north as far as the city limits, past boathouses and rowing clubs as well as cafés and stalls selling beer, fried fish and *lángos*. You can sit here and relax with a drink and a snack after a tour of the Aquincum ruins. The Római fürdő public lido is popular with families in summer. The natural springs here have been exploited since Roman times and explain how it was possible to operate so many bath houses in the town of Aquincum. In fact the old Celtic name of the vicinity, Ak-ink, is thought to mean 'abundant water'.

At the time of writing the city had seen heated debates over the proposed construction of a mobile flood barrier, amid fears that Budapest risked losing one of its last wild spots (there is unimpeded access right to the water's margin).

CSILLAGHEGY AND ÜRÖM

The swimming lido at **Csillaghegy** (*beyond map p. 430, C1; csillaghegyistrand.hu*) is one of the oldest bathing establishments in Budapest, using natural thermal water. In the spring of 2017, close to the baths, a spectacular Roman chariot burial was found, including the skeletons of two horses. The chariot had been decorated with bronze figures representing a Dionysiac procession. Chariot burials were an Eraviscan custom that the local Romanised population seems to have retained for funerals of high-status individuals (others are known from the environs of Budapest and the finds are in the National Museum). The finds from this burial are expected to go on display in Aquincum.

From Csillaghegy, Ürömi út leads to the village of **Üröm**, where a chapel houses the coffin of Alexandra Pavlovna, daughter of Tsar Paul I of Russia and first wife of Archduke Joseph, son of Leopold II and Palatine of Hungary. Alexandra died, shortly after her baby daughter, of puerperal fever in 1801. She was not yet 18 years old. Her body was buried in Üröm according to the rites of the Russian Orthodox Church. Her entrails are in the Palatine Crypt in the former royal palace in Buda (*see p. 49*).

EATING AND DRINKING IN ÓBUDA

RESTAURANTS

f–ff **Kéhli**. Traditional Hungarian *vendéglő* (inn), in business since 1899 and famous for its associations with the writer Gyula Krúdy (who ate here when he could afford it). It is famous for its bone marrow. Dining outside in the courtyard in fine weather. *Mókus u. 22. T: +36 1 368 0613, kehli.hu. Map p. 421, inset.*

f **Csalánosi Csárda**. Traditional, old-style Hungarian restaurant just off Fő tér, serving hearty dishes such as smoked pork knuckle, oxtail soup and bone marrow. Outside seating in warm weather. *Hídfő u. 16. T: 06 20 955 5565. Map p. 421, inset.*

f **Gigler**. A traditional Óbuda tavern serving true Hungarian fare (grilled or breaded meat, for example, with a side order of grated cabbage and caraway seed). The dessert menu and the pasta menu are combined, in the old-fashioned way. The Gigler has a long history. A framed document on the wall records that Mrs József Gittinger (a member of a well-known family of Óbuda vintners) opened a wine shop here in 1909. In 1938 Mrs Ferenc Gigler (née Gittinger) ran a tavern here. It survived until nationalisation in 1951. The family reopened their business, on the same premises, in 1993. *Föld u. 50/c. T: + 36 1 368 6078, giglervendeglo.hu. Map p. 421, A3.*

f **Mókus sörkert**. Popular in summer with locals, this beer garden also serves salads, sandwiches, burgers, grilled meats and Hungarian favourites such as *marhapörkölt* (beef stew). *Mókus u. 1–3. T: 06 70 332 7108, mokussorkert.hu. Map p. 421, inset.*

CAFÉS AND BARS

Esernyős is a café (and simple restaurant) operating as part of a larger cultural centre. They have their own coffee blend, Esernyős 42, as well as a fine Florentine Marzocco espresso machine. Lunch menu on weekdays. In fine weather you can sample the coffee at the **Gázlámpa Kioszk** in the centre of the square. It occupies a tiny pavilion built in 1929 as a pressure-testing station linked to the Óbuda Gasworks (*see p. 113*) and it still has gas lamps attached to its exterior. *Fő tér 2. esernyos.hu. Map p. 421, inset.*

The **Kobuci Kert** beer garden in the courtyard of the Zichy Palace on Fő tér (*map p. 421, inset; open April–Oct weekdays from 4pm, weekends from 10am; kobuci.hu*) offers a programme of regular live music as well as drinks and street food (the name Kobuci is an abbreviation for *kolbászos buci*, a hotdog).

From spring to autumn, the river bank along **Római part** (parallel to Királyok útja; *map p. 430, C1*) is lined with stalls selling fried fish, sausages, grilled pork, *lángos* and cool beer.

Close to Aquincum and the gasworks estate, **This is Melbourne Too** is an espresso and brew bar belonging to the My Little Melbourne (*see p. 351*) family of modern cafés concentrating on the quality of the coffee (*Záhony u. 7; map p. 421, C1*).

Districts XI & XXII:
Újbuda & Budafok-Tétény

The Eleventh District, or Újbuda ('New Buda'), begins at Gellért tér, at the Buda end of Szabadság Bridge. It is made up of the districts of Lágymányos, along the Danube bank, Szentimreváros, centred on Móricz Zsigmond körtér, and the old industrial area of Kelenföld. The district is largely residential, with a couple of small museums. The chief attractions for the visitor are the Citadel and the Gellért Baths.

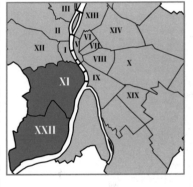

Budafok-Tétény, the Twenty-Second District, is known chiefly for its history as a wine-making area. The Törley sparkling wine cellars are still in operation, and here too is the Memento Park, with a collection of statuary from the Communist era. Nagytétény is home to the Applied Arts Museum's furniture collection, displayed in an 18th-century château.

DISTRICT XI: ÚJBUDA

The Budapest map of 1896 shows today's Eleventh District as an area of vineyards, watched over by the citadel on Gellért Hill, with a handful of scattered houses, a viticultural school, an isolated inn, a lake and two thermal baths. There is industry too, with a brick factory and a petroleum refinery on the Danube bank. Today the scene is somewhat different, although one of the baths, the Gellért, survives (and thrives), as do the citadel and the lake. The hillsides today are innocent of vines, being criss-crossed instead by urban streets lined with residential villas. Busy roads occupy the valleys. Yet on the site of the old viticulture school is Budapest's horticultural university and arboretum. Apart from the Citadel and Gellért Baths, the district is little visited by tourists.

GELLÉRT TÉR

In the centre of Gellért tér (*map p. 427, A5*), officially Szent Gellért tér (Saint Gellért Square), is a **drinking fountain**, sheltered by a somewhat ill-proportioned canopy. It caused a small stir when it was erected (2003), because it appeared that no permission had been sought or obtained (it has since been allowed to stay). From the central well, rivulets trickle out to drains marked with the names of the Budapest bathing establishments whose waters spring from here: Gellért, Rudas, Rác, Király, Lukács, Császár and Erzsébet. Of the seven, only one, the Erzsébet in Kelenföld, is no more. Around the inner architrave of the canopy is inscribed a poem by Sándor Weöres: 'Song of the Unbounded'. The fountain in fact serves tap water; but cross the road to look down at the river and you will see thermal water gushing from the embankment, forming a **natural hot tub** in the Danube in which people (often the homeless) like to come and soak, enjoying a free warm bath. Looking back, away from the river, you can admire the buildings of the **Budapest Technical University** (Budapest Műegyetem). Founded in 1782, the institution moved to this site in the early years of the last century. The first building (1902), on the corner of the embankment and Gellért tér, is by Győző Czigler, who was himself a teacher at the university. Facing the river is the main block (1909) by Alajos Hauszmann, also a teacher here. Its entrance façade is adorned with statues representing the university's faculties (Chemistry, Architecture, Engineering Science and Mechanical Engineering). They are modern copies of the originals by Károly Senyei, which were destroyed in WWII. Behind, on Budafoki út, is the library building (1909) by another member of the university's teaching staff, Samu Pecz. Students of the university played a major role in the Uprising of 1956; this is commemorated in the **1956 monument** facing the river, close to the junction of the embankment and Bertalan Lajos utca. The work of the sculptor Róbert Csíkszentmihályi, it was placed here in 2006 to mark the 50th anniversary of the Uprising. Further along the river towards Petőfi Bridge is **Building R** (1955), an exercise in Stripped Classicism by Gyula Rimanóczy, with a meander frieze along the string course and a Diocletian window in the central gable end. The lions on either side of the entrance are by Miklós Borsos.

THE GELLÉRT HOTEL AND BATHS

The Gellért Hotel and adjoining spa stand on the site of an earlier bath, greatly prized by the Ottomans and known for the healing property of its waters. The original Hungarian name was Sárosfürdő, because of the plentiful healing mud (*sár*). The buildings date from 1912–18, to late Art Nouveau designs by Ármin Hegedűs and assistants. The outdoor swimming pool with its wave machine was completed after WWI.

Allegorical groups representing Healing (by József Róna) flank the main entrance to the baths (on Kelenhegyi út). At the rear of the central ticket hall is a fountain in a mosaic niche, surmounted by a sculpture group of *Venus and Cupid* (Adolf Huszár) and above it to the right, stained-glass windows by József Baska (1974), replacing glass by Manó Róth, younger brother of Miksa Róth (*see p. 224*), lost in WWII. The modern glass shows bathing and sunbathing and something that looks like a pedicure scene.

GELLÉRT BATHS
Zsolnay glazed ceramic fountain
in the indoor thermal section.

The bathing halls themselves are lavishly decorated with mosaic, Zsolnay ceramics and statuary. The sculptural design of the former men's thermal baths (now unisex), with groups of snuggling children and a boy with a tortoise, is by Miklós Ligeti. Notable among the decorative elements around the swimming pool is the female nude entitled *Primavera* (János Pásztor, 1927), in a glazed ceramic niche. (*For practical details of the baths, see p. 357.*)

GELLÉRT HILL

The tall dolomite cliff known as Gellért Hill stands 140m above the Danube, a grand sight in itself and offering splendid views from its summit. Its commanding situation has been recognised since ancient times: before the Romans came, it was an *oppidum* of the Eravisci; after the 1848 revolution, the Habsburgs chose it as the site of a fortress.

The hill is named after the Venetian prelate Gherardo Sagredo, known in Hungarian as Gellért, who became a bishop in Hungary and was tutor to Prince Imre, son of King Stephen. According to legend, he was murdered here during a revolt, part of the unrest that followed Stephen's death (he is said to have been pushed down the hill in a handcart). Today a colossal bronze **statue of St Gellért** (Gyula Jankovits, 1904) presides over the landscape, brandishing a cross, the instrument with which he dragged the Magyars into mainstream European history. An ornamental waterfall cascades down the cliff face below. The statue can be reached by switchback paths and steps (populated by souvenir sellers in summer), which lead up past the waterfall. On reaching the statue, you will see that it is in fact a group composition: at the bishop's feet is a tribal Magyar, looking up at the prelate in awe. The ensemble is set off from the hillside by a columned hemicycle, the work of Imre Francsek Sr. The green shade of the hill is congenial to trees and plants (at the time of writing an invasive colony of Japanese knotweed had taken hold).

THE ROCK CHAPEL

On the Danube side of the hill, facing Gellért tér, is the entrance to the Rock Chapel (Sziklatemplom; *open Mon–Sat 9.30–7.30*), a church deep in the hill's cavernous interior. On the entrance grille is a badge showing lions on either side of a palm tree, onto which flies a bird with a round disc in its beak. These are the symbols of St Paul the Hermit, an anchorite saint to whom a monastery is dedicated on Mt Sinai. Paul lived in the Egyptian desert, his only companion a raven who would bring him bread. The Paulines, founded in the early 13th century by the Blessed Eusebius (Boldog Özséb) of Esztergom, are the only monastic order of Hungarian origin.

The idea to create a cave church here was born in the 1920s, during a pilgrimage of Hungarians to Lourdes, to pray for the restoration of territory lost after Trianon. The site selected already had a reputation for miracle-working: according to tradition, the cave had once been inhabited by a hermit named Ivan, who used the hill's thermal waters to heal the sick. The Rock Chapel passed to the Paulines in the 1930s and the remains of the poet Benedek Virág, himself a Pauline, were interred here. The Pauline fathers turned the cave into a place of sanctuary during the Siege of Budapest in 1944.

GELLÉRT HILL
Victorious torch-bearer, one of the sculptures at the base of the Liberty Monument
(Zsigmond Kisfaludi Strobl, 1947).

Under Communism it was walled up and Benedek Virág's remains were transferred to Kerepesi Cemetery (where they still lie). The chapel was restored to the Paulines and re-opened in 1991 (a lump of the concrete plug that once blocked its mouth has been preserved beside the entrance). The turreted, arcaded building beside the cave, overlooking the river, is the Pauline monastery (Károly Weichinger, 1934). The church is once again active and holds regular services.

THE LIBERTY MONUMENT AND CITADEL

A network of paths (with frequent benches) leads from Szent Gellért tér to the top of Gellért Hill. The main path, Verejték utca ('Perspiration Street'; the name might seem apt if you make the climb in high summer) ends in a broad lawn dotted with trees and three handsome sculpted amphorae (Ödön Metky, 1965; from time to time, one of them goes missing). From here, paths and steps lead to the summit. The hill is particularly lovely in autumn, when the leaves are on the turn.

At the top of the hill is a wide platform commanding magnificent views over Pest and Buda. On the Buda side, the tall windows of the Műteremház (*see p. 123*) are a landmark. Downstream on both sides of the river, the surviving tall smokestacks recall the districts' industrial past.

You will not be alone here. The Citadel hill is popular with coach parties, who come for the views and to see the famous **Liberty Monument**, one of the symbols of Budapest, a female Victory figure bearing aloft a palm branch. Zsigmond Kisfaludi Strobl's 29m-high sculpture, successful in silhouette from all angles, was erected in 1947. Known at the time as the Liberation Monument, it commemorated the liberation of Budapest by the Soviets in 1945. The Russian marshal Kliment Voroshilov, placed in charge of consolidating Communist control of Hungary, chose Kisfaludi Strobl because

CITADEL
Graffiti left by Soviet soldiers in 1956.

he was known for statue groups composed of grandiose, monumental figures. Twenty years previously he had produced a memorial to the fallen of World War One for the city of Nyíregyháza, its central figure a muscular youth beating down a many-headed dragon with his bare fists. Strobl used the motif again for this Budapest memorial, in the heroic nude dealing a death blow to the Hydra at the right-hand foot of the central Victory. On the left is a victorious figure bearing a flaming torch. Between them once stood an armed Soviet soldier (now in the Memento Park; see p. 125). A grateful inscription to the Soviet fallen has been picked off the statue base and the dedication now reads, 'In memory of all who gave their lives for the independence, freedom and prosperity of Hungary'.

The **Citadel** (Ferenc Kasselik, 1854) is a fortress built by the Austrians after the crushing of the 1848–9 revolution to keep watch over Buda and Pest and prevent further unrest. It occupies the site of an astronomical observatory which was destroyed during the conflict. The fortress ceased to be used after the 1867 Compromise, though the last Austrian soldiers only left it some 30 years later. It was used by German and Hungarian troops in 1944–5 and by Soviet troops in 1956. If you visit the public WC, note the Soviet graffiti on the stone jambs of the entrance.

SÁNC UTCA

Sánc utca, 'Rampart Street' (*map p. 425, D5*), leads downhill to the north. To one side of it is a **park** with good views over the Danube and Pest. Here too, at the edge of the park, is a covered reservoir topped by a sculpture (Márta Lesenyei, 1982) showing the Prince of Buda symbolically reaching across a cleft representing the Danube to take the hand of the Princess of Pest (the buildings of Pest seem strangely flattened, as if by a stiff gale). Close by is the so-called **Philosophers' Garden** (Filozófusok kertje), a sculpture group by Nándor Wagner (2001). Figures of Abraham (prostrated), Akhenaten, Lao-tsu, Buddha and Christ stand in a circle on a beautiful labradorite base contemplating a shiny metal ball. To one side stand Gandhi, Bodhidharma and St Francis. The ensemble is inscribed with the words, 'That we may better understand one another'. Three statues were stolen in 2006 but replacements have since been made.

MINERVA UTCA

The narrow, cobbled Pipacs utca and Rezeda utca (*map p. 425, D5*) still preserve the rural air of Gellért Hill, when once there was nothing here but mule tracks amid the vineyards. On the corner of Pipacs and Minerva streets is the large turreted **Bayer Villa**, the former Swedish Embassy. It is here that Raoul Wallenberg (*see p. 300*) began his work to save the city's Jews from deportation (plaque). Today the Danube Embankment below Gellért tér is named after him.

At Kelenhegyi út 12–14 (corner of Mányoki utca; *map p. 425, D6*) is the **Műteremház** (Gyula Kosztolányi-Kann, 1903), a large Art Nouveau building with well-lit artists' studios. Artists who have lived and worked here include Béla Czóbel and Béla Uitz.

BARTÓK BÉLA ÚT AND SZENTIMREVÁROS

The busy Bartók Béla út (*map p. 425, D6*), a major tram route, runs between Gellért tér and Móricz Zsigmond körtér. It is home to a number of cafés and art galleries. The early 20th-century building at no. 17–19 is the **Szent Imre kollégium**, with a chapel dedicated to St Imre, originally a Christian hostel and now a boarding house for the Technical University. Its cellars were used as a Swedish safe house during the war. A small **museum** at no. 31 (*open Sat 10–1*) is dedicated to János Csonka, an engineer at the Technical University, one of the inventors of the carburettor, who developed the first Hungarian gas engine as well as motor-assisted postal delivery tricycles, in use from 1900 (at the time of writing, one of these was on display in the Postal Museum; *see p. 205*). The idea for his gas engine is said to have occurred to him as he watched a flower girl spraying her blooms with an atomiser on a street corner near here. The museum occupies his former workshop. Opposite is a small park with a statue (János Horvay, 1932) of the novelist Géza Gárdonyi, author of *Stars of Eger*, a favourite school set text, which tells a heroic tale of Hungarian resistance to the Ottomans. The **Hadik café** is the successor to a literary coffee house of the same name, frequented in the early 20th century by the great humorist and writer Frigyes Karinthy (Hungarian translator of *Winnie the Pooh*). Next to it, at no. 40, is a **block of artists' studios** designed by Ödön Lechner (1899).

MÓRICZ ZSIGMOND KÖRTÉR

Bartók Béla út ends at Móricz Zsigmond körtér (*map p. 425, D6*), a busy transport hub at the heart of Szentimreváros, St Imre Town, a part of the Eleventh District named after the canonised son of King Stephen, who predeceased his father. A **statue of Prince Imre** (Zsigmond Kisfaludi Strobl, 1930) shows the young prince receiving the homage of contemporary Hungarians, while on the plinth is a relief of St Stephen offering his crown to the Virgin (*see pp. 158–9*). The circular structure in the centre of the square is known as the **Gomba** ('Mushroom'). Built in 1942 by József Schall, it was restored in 2014 and now houses cafés and a public transport ticket office. The arc of apartment blocks behind it is by Hugó Gregersen, Dénes Györgyi and others (1936). Móricz Zsigmond körtér was one of the centres of civilian resistance to the Soviets in the 1956 Uprising. A small plaque on the Bartók Béla út side commemorates this.

VILLÁNYI ÚT, FADRUSZ UTCA AND BOCSKAI ÚT

The view down Villányi út from Móricz Zsigmond körtér is closed by the rocky outcrop of the **Sas-hegy Nature Reserve** (*Visitor Centre on Tájék utca, map p. 425, B5, open March–Oct Tues–Sun 10–6*). It is home to many rare species of flora and fauna including the Pasque flower and Pannon lizard or Copper skink (*Ablepharus kitaibelii*; its botanical name honours the great Hungarian naturalist Pál Kitaibel).

Villányi út leads past a large school building, opposite which is a modern block of flats where the architect Imre Makovecz lived from 1935 until his death. **Fadrusz utca**, to the right, has some interesting buildings. No. 6 has attractive ceramic plaques. At no. 12 is a house (1928) designed by István Medgyaszay, who lived in this district, with sgraffito decoration by Ferenc Márton.

The reed-fringed pond known as the **Feneketlen tó**, the 'Bottomless Lake', occupies a flooded depression created by quarrying clay for the nearby brickworks. When the brickworks closed, the land passed to the Cistercians, in 1912. It is now an attractive public park. On the opposite side of Villányi út, the handsome neo-Baroque **Church of St Imre** (Gyula Wälder, 1938) is a good example of 20th-century Historicism, as is the school building next door (also by Wälder). It was restored to the church in 1997.

A detour south from Villányi út brings you to Bocskai út. On the corner of Bocskai út and Zsombolyai utca (Zsombolyai u. 6) is the **TIT Stúdió**, devoted to Natural History. It has operated here since 1969 but the building was built some 30 years earlier as a synagogue, to designs by István Hámor and Ede Novák (1936). It is cube-shaped and covered in tiny pale yellow tiles. Look closely at the garden railings: they are decorated with stylised menorahs. The original interior does not survive. Instead, the lobby has a mosaic (Lajos Kántor, 1970) showing a procession of people holding objects symbolising branches of Natural History: a microscope, for example, and a model of a molecule.

THE BUDA ARBORETUM AND MÉNESI ÚT

Szüret utca, 'Harvest Street', recalls the area's agricultural and viticultural past. It leads up to Ménesi út, where there is an entrance to the **Buda Arboretum** (*map p. 425, D6*), part of the Szent István University horticultural faculty. It now contains over 2,000 kinds of trees and shrubs, some of them over a century old, and several hundred flowers and perennials. The fallen leaves are not gathered until spring, so as not to disturb hibernating mammals and insects.

The simple cottage-style house at **Ménesi út 59/b**, former home of the architect István Medgyaszay, can be visited by appointment (*signed; access up a narrow path; T: + 36 1 365 2503*). Very close by, at no. 65, is the **Pál Molnár-C. Museum**, the former home and studio of the painter, which can also be visited (*map p. 425, C5; mcpmuzeum.*

hu). It has a representative collection of the artist's work and a small shop with prints and reproductions. Close to the two museums, opposite the junction of Bakator utca with Ménesi út, is a small grocery shop selling drinks, snacks, baked goods and fruit.

DISTRICT XXII: BUDAFOK-TÉTÉNY

This area of leafy, sprawling suburb includes the former wine-growing district of Budafok; the Memento Park, an outdoor museum of Communist-era statuary; and the former Danube-side village of Nagytétény, with its château museum.

BUDAFOK

Map p. 430, B4. Trams 47 from Deák tér or 56 from Széll Kálmán tér and Gellért tér to Leányka utcai lakótelep.

The suburb of Budafok is home to the Törley winery, known for its sparkling wines. Its history goes back a long way, to the foundation of a champagne works here by József Törley (1858–1907), who had learned the skill in Reims. The first automobile in Budafok was Törley's (used for transporting crates of champagne). Today the winery operates a **Törley Museum** on Anna utca (*open for visits, with a tasting, on alternate Saturdays; book in advance; shop open on Thur from noon; torleymuzeum.hu*). Above the museum, at Sarló u. 6, is the monumental but neglected **Törley Mausoleum** by Rezső Ray Jr, inspired by the Mausoleum of Theodoric in Ravenna.

BUDATÉTÉNY: MEMENTO PARK

Map p. 430, B4. Junction of Balatoni út and Szabadkai utca. Open 10am–sunset. Bus 150 from Kelenföld vasútállomás (map p. 430, B3) or Újbuda központ (metro line M4, green) to Memento Park. Also bus 101E from Kelenföld vasútállomás to Memento Park. From the bus stop you can see the park across the busy Balatoni út. Direct buses to and from Deák tér are also operated by the Memento Park. Tickets from the park ticket office, or consult the website, mementopark.hu.

This small open-air museum, created in 1992–3 by the architect Ákos Eleőd, gives a new public home to Communist-era statues, reliefs and plaques removed from their original locations across the city. Some of the works are by well-known sculptors. All are labelled. The main subjects are as follows: Communist leaders and Party members; key Communist tropes such as Power to the People, the Workers' Movement and martyrdom to the Counter-Revolution; the Republic of Councils of 1919; the Soviet liberation of Hungary from Fascism; honour to those who supported the Soviet regime in 1956. In the right-hand entrance archway stands a **double statue of Marx and Engels**, formerly on Jászai Mari tér (the Pest end of Margaret Bridge). In the left-hand arch is Pál Pátzay's **Lenin** (1965), of which the sculptor said, 'I have represented Lenin the way I see him, as a simple man, shining in the greatness of his ideas.'

Highlights inside the park include **statuary from the Liberty Monument on Gellért Hill** by Zsigmond Kisfaludi Strobl; Imre Varga's huge **monument to Béla Kun** (1986) from the Vérmező park on the west side of Castle Hill; and Jenő Kerényi's flag-waving **statue of Captain Ostapenko**, which used to be a familiar sight on the outskirts of Budapest at the beginning of the M7 motorway. Perhaps the most iconic is István Kiss's **Republic of Councils Monument**, celebrating its 50th anniversary (1969), which once stood on Dózsa György út (border of City Park). Taking the form of a muscular young worker, striding forward with his shirt open and chest bared, it is based on a famous poster of 1919 by Róbert Berény.

Outside the park, opposite the entrance gateway, is a lifesize reproduction in brick and concrete of the **tribune** which bore the colossal Stalin statue brought down by the 1956 revolutionaries (*see p. 317*). After the first phase of the destruction, only the boots remained fixed to the base, hence the symbolic representation here, where the empty boots (copies) stand for the death of tyranny. They were set up here in 2006, on the 50th anniversary of the Uprising. The original boots do not survive but two pieces from the statue, a hand and an ear, can be seen in the National Museum (*see p. 235*).

NAGYTÉTÉNY

Beyond map p. 430, B4. Bus 133E from Március 15. tér, Astoria and Ferenciek tere to the Petőfi Sándor utca/Kastélymúzeum stop. Alternatively, you can combine a visit to Nagytétény and the Memento Park. From Memento Park, take bus 101E or 150 to Budatétény vasútállomás (Campona), the final stop, from where you can change to bus 33 to Petőfi Sándor utca/Kastélymúzeum (or you can go on foot, but it is a not particularly pleasant 30min walk).

The former village of Nagytétény, on the boundary line between Budapest and Pest County, grew up on the site of the Roman border fortress of Campona. It is chiefly visited for the former **Száraz-Rudnyánszky manor house**, which stands on ancient foundations. A Roman *villa rustica* once occupied the spot. In the Middle Ages a castle stood here, destroyed by the Ottomans and successively rebuilt. The present Baroque building, in the style of a French château, dates from 1778. Its builder, József Rudnyánszky, was a nephew of Antal Grassalkovich (*see p. 330*), which may explain the similarity in design between this château and the one at Gödöllő. A later descendant of the Száraz-Rudnyánszky family, Vilma Hugonnay, was born in the château in 1847. She went on to become Hungary's first woman doctor.

The main part of the château is now an outpost of the **Applied Arts Museum** (*open Tues–Sun 10–6, imm.hu*), displaying furniture from the medieval Gothic to early 19th-century Biedermeier, well displayed and labelled. You are likely to have the entire museum to yourself (perhaps with a party of school children). A children's home used to operate in one wing; at the time of writing that section was very dilapidated and in urgent need of restoration.

Next to the château are the scant remains (*no access*) of **Roman Campona**. In the park in front of the château is a statue of St John of Nepomuk (*see p. 69*), inside a little shingle-roofed pavilion, and a **monument to the Battle of Tétény** (January 1849). It was not a decisive engagement but military historians agree that it acted as an important delaying tool, giving the Hungarian troops time to regroup, allowing them to pursue their struggle for independence and thus delaying their ultimate defeat.

On the north side of the main road, Nagytétényi út, is the main enclave of the former village, with its **church of the Annunciation**. The current building dates from the 18th century, though the base of the bell-tower is medieval. In the graveyard and built into the exterior church wall are tombstones and grave markers of Hugonnays and Rudnyánszkys. A little further north, on Petőfi Sándor utca (just beyond no. 40, after the junction with Pintyőke utca), is the **St Florian Well**, a spring of pure, chlorine-free water that is said to be particularly beneficial for babies and expectant mothers. Local people come here to fill their water bottles.

EATING AND DRINKING IN ÚJBUDA AND BUDAFOK-TÉTÉNY

ÚJBUDA

ff **A38**. Events and exhibition space on boat moored close to Petőfi Bridge, also with a bar and restaurant. International menu. Closed Sun. *T: +36 1 464 3946, a38.hu. Map p. 427, B6.*

f **Borpatika**. The 'Wine Dispensary' and cellar restaurant has been in business here since 1986, still with a very traditional menu. Loose and bottled wine. *Bertalan Lajos u. 26. T: +36 1 209 2644. Map p. 425, D6.*

f **Hadik**. Café and restaurant in a building which once housed a literary coffee house. The walls are bare brick with images of bygone writers and journalists. Lively atmosphere, a good place for a coffee, drink or light meal. Tables outside in fine weather. *Bartók Béla út 36. T: +36 1 279 02 90, hadik. eu. Map p. 425, D6.*

f **Kisvigadó**. Simple *vendéglő* that sticks faithfully to a traditional Hungarian bill of fare. Open daily.

Villányi út 34. T: +36 1 209 1660, kisvigado.hu. Map p. 425, D6.

f **Palack**. Lively, popular wine bar also serving sandwiches, sharing plates and good-value food. *Szent Gellért tér 3. T: +36 30 997 1902, palackborbar.hu. Map p. 425, D5.*

f **Tranzit**. In an old bus station, with a fun retro feel. Inside in winter, outside (with hammocks) in summer. Salads, snacks and sandwiches. *Kosztolányi Dezső tér. T: +36 1 209 3070, tranzitcafe.com. Map p. 425, D6.*

NAGYTÉTÉNY

f **Rozsdás Kakas**. In the centre of the old village, behind the church to the left, the 'Rusty Rooster' offers a daily lunch menu, ice cream in summer, and serves food in the inner garden in hot weather. Open midday–5pm Tues–Fri and Sun, midday–8pm Sat. Closed Mon. *Szabadság u. 1. T: +36 1 207 0186, rozsdaskakas.hu.*

JÓKAI-KERT
József Róna's portrait of the novelist Mór Jókai (disguised as Anacreon),
in the garden of his former summer villa.

District XII:
The Buda Hills

One of the great beauties of Budapest are its hills, easily accessible by public transport. They are popular all year round for hiking. Snowdrops, violets and corydalis grow here in profusion in spring. The trees are largely oak and beech, with scatterings of cornelian cherry, hazel and fine examples of manna ash, covered with clouds of white blossom in early summer. Fauna include nuthatches, black woodpecker, golden orioles, foxes, pine martens, red squirrel and wild boar (seldom seen, but their snufflings are often found at the path margins and they leave footprints in the snow).

The earliest houses in the Buda hills were agricultural or monastic. Then came the summer villas, to which wealthy families from Pest and the urban parts of Buda would decamp, bag and baggage, once the weather became warm. Some fine examples survive, built in the German hunting-lodge style or in imitation of Palladian villas. Pressure to build in the hills is great and enormous numbers of houses have gone up in recent decades. Fortunately conservation bodies are also at work and there are large tracts of forest still protected, criss-crossed with waymarked hiking trails.

VÁROSMAJOR & SVÁBHEGY

Just before the hills begin, occupying the former watermeadow of the Ördög-árok stream, is the Városmajor park (*map p. 424, B3–C3*). At its southeast edge, on Csaba utca, are two churches, a small one of the 1920s and the larger, main one beside it. Between them is a stele commemorating the architect, Aladár Árkay, who died in 1932, a year before the main church was completed.

THE VÁROSMAJOR CHURCH

Dedicated to the Sacred Heart of Christ (Jézus szíve plébániatemplom), the church, consecrated in 1933, is an interesting assemblage of geometric volumes, at the same time clearly inspired by early Christian architecture. The soffit of the **entrance arch** is decorated with a carved roundel with the Alpha and Omega and Chi-Rho. At either side is a procession of six sheep, reminiscent of mosaics in Ravenna and Rome. The ironwork of the sacristy window (exterior north side) contains a monogram of the name Maria, again inspired by similar monograms in Byzantine Christian churches.

The interior is not generally open, but you can get into the vestibule and look through the glass doors. The inscription above them is from Psalm 118: 'Open to me the gates of righteousness: I will go into them and I will praise the Lord.' A huge **mosaic window** fills the east end. The central figure of Christ points to his own bleeding heart. It and the other windows were the work of Lili Sztehlo, the architect's daughter-in-law (her husband, Bertalan Árkay, completed the building). Destroyed during WWII, the glass panes have been painstakingly recreated. On either side of the main window are **sculptures of the Apostles** by Pál Pátzay. The **ceiling**, made up of concrete coffers, has frescoes of the *Creation* with Evangelists, angels and prophets by Vilmos Aba-Novák (1938). Two painted **aluminium panels** in the sanctuary, showing St Stephen as founder of both Church and State in Hungary, are also by Aba-Novák.

The **bell-tower** is linked to the church by a covered arcade. Opposite the main entrance is a stele commemorating the first 'Pilgrimage of Expiation', which Cardinal Mindszenty (*see p. 151*) led from here just after the Second World War, in May 1946.

Behind the church stretches the **Városmajor park**, with benches where groups of men sit and play cards in sunny weather. On the south side, at **Városmajor u. 59**, is a primary school building in the Folk Revival style by Károly Kós and Dénes Györgyi (1910–11), which together with that on Áldás utca (*map p. 424, C2*) was constructed as part of the large-scale school-building programme that took place just before WWI. The reliefs in the triangular gables above the entrances (formerly one for boys and one for girls) are by Ferenc Sidló. Diagonally opposite the school, on the corner between Alma utca and Gál József út, is the house that Aladár Árkay built as his own residence (enlarged and altered).

THE COGWHEEL RAILWAY AND THE JÓKAI-KERT

The **Cogwheel Railway** (Fogaskerekű vasút; *map pp. 424–5, B3–A4*), officially tram no. 60, dates from 1874. Originally steam powered, it was built by a Swiss firm from Basel. It was electrified in 1929. There are ten stops in all and the total journey time is c. 25mins (at the time of writing, there were plans to extend it to Normafa). For the best views, sit on the right hand side facing away from the direction of travel. The grounds of the Szent János Kórház (St John's Hospital), one of the oldest in the city, stretch out by the side of the first stop. As the train climbs, you can see the modern buildings of the Kútvölgy Hospital, once an exclusive clinic for Communist Party members. The train slowly climbs **Svábhegy**, a hill whose name derives from the Swabian settlers who came to Hungary to repopulate it after the Ottomans had left. Construction of the railway opened up the hill and it soon became dotted with summer villas, many of them belonging to writers and artists. One such was the novelist Mór Jókai.

THE JÓKAI-KERT

Map p. 422, C4. Költő u. 21. Open mid-March–Oct Mon–Fri 8–6, Sat–Sun and holidays 10–6. Nov–mid-March closes at 4pm. dunaipoly.hu.

A few minutes' walk from the Városkút bus and cogwheel railway stop is a small public garden run by the Duna-Ipoly National Park. It occupies the grounds of a former villa owned by the popular writer Mór Jókai (the Hungarian Dickens). Jókai bought the property in the mid-19th century, when Svábhegy was an area of vineyards, dotted with rustic taverns. The villa no longer stands but its former wine cellar and press-house now has a small room with memorabilia of the novelist. A semicircular stone bench supported by lions survives from the old villa garden and next to it, hidden by trees, is a sculpture (József Róna, 1903) of the Greek poet Anacreon, famous for his bacchanalian lyrics. The face is clearly modelled on Jókai's. At the bottom of the plinth are carved the words of Goethe's *Anakreons Grab* and a line from the musical setting of the same by Hugo Wolf. In the rest of the park are nature trails and a small shop run by the Hungarian Ornithological Society. Behind the shop, vines have been replanted.

THE SZÉCHENYI-KILÁTÓ

At a crossroads by the Svábhegy railway stop is a **café and cake shop** run by Szamos (*see p. 328*). A short walk southwest of here is the **Széchenyi-kilátó** (Széchenyi Lookout), at the junction of Széchenyi-emlék út and Rege út (*map p. 422, C4*). The hemicycle or gloriette, designed by Miklós Ybl, used to stand in Heroes' Square but was moved here when the square was re-designed for the Hungarian Millennium celebrations of 1896. The bust of Széchenyi at the foot of the steps is by Alajos Stróbl (1891).

ZUGLIGET, JÁNOS-HEGY & NORMAFA

The area around János-hegy is a good place for walking. You do not have to go far before you leave the houses and streets behind and you could be forgiven for thinking yourself in the heart of the countryside. The main east–west roads, Tündérhegyi út and Jánoshegyi út are closed to private cars and are popular with runners and cyclists.

Getting to the hills

Cogwheel railway (map p. 424, B3) to Széchenyi-hegy (map p. 422, B4), the southern terminus of the Children's Railway. Bus 21 or 21A from Széll Kálmán tér (map p. 424, C3) to Normafa (map p. 422, B4). Bus 291 from Nyugati Station (map p. 426, A2) to Zugliget-Libegő (map p. 422, B3), for the chairlift to János-hegy. Bus 22, 222 or 22A from Széll Kálmán tér to Szépjuhászné (map p. 422, A2). Tram 61 from Széll Kálmán tér to Hűvösvölgy (map p. 422, B1).

ALONG THE LINE OF THE CHILDREN'S RAILWAY

The Children's Railway (Gyermekvasút) is a narrow-gauge line built between 1948 and 1950. It winds through the hills and woods for just over 10km between Széchenyi-hegy (*map p. 422, B4*) and Hűvösvölgy (*map p. 422, B1*). The complete journey time from end to end is c. 40mins. Both open-sided and closed carriages are in operation, and occasionally there is a steam locomotive. (*Services run year-round, daily in May–Sept and Tues–Sun in Oct–April. For timetables and details, see gyermekvasut.hu.*)

Originally known as the Pioneers' Railway, after the Communist equivalent of the Boy Scouts and Girl Guides, whose Youth Camp was at Csillebérc (*map p. 422, A4*), the railway was ceremonially opened by Ernő Gerő, hardline early Communist, former KGB agent and, at the time, Hungarian Minister of Transport. The trains, stations and ticket offices are entirely staffed by children between the ages of ten and 14 (the train drivers are adults). The children still wear traditional blue uniforms and red peaked caps and enthusiastically salute the trains in and out of the stations. They also make the loudspeaker announcements and pass up and down the carriages announcing stations and checking tickets. Participation is conditional on getting good marks at school and securing the permission of the head teacher. There is a training course and an exam to pass before the young guards and station masters are permitted to assume their duties. The Children's Railway is particularly pleasant in spring, when the trees are in new leaf, or in autumn, when the leaves are on the turn.

NORMAFA

Normafa (*map p. 422, B4*) takes its name from a celebrated occasion in 1840, when a singer from the National Theatre, Rozália Klein, sang the grand aria from Bellini's *Norma* to a gathering of the opera company here. The beech tree under which she sang it became known as the *Normafa* ('Norma Tree'). It was brought down by a gale in 1927 but the name has stuck. Close to the bus stop on the corner of Konkoly Thege Miklós út and Eötvös út is a wide sloping meadow (the Anna-rét; *map p. 422, A3*), where an opening in the trees gives fine views out across the hills. In snowy winters the spot is popular for skiing and sledging. There are buffets at the top of the meadow selling strudel, coffee and beer, and mulled wine in winter. The house at Eötvös út 48, on the other side of the road from the Normakert restaurant, was once used by the State Security Office (ÁVH) as a detention centre for sensitive political prisoners. László Rajk was among those held here. At the time of writing there were plans to turn it into an information centre.

THE 'MÁRIA ÚT' PILGRIMAGE ROUTE AND MAKKOSMÁRIA

The Mária Út or Marian Way is a pilgrimage route that crosses central Europe from north to south and west to east. The cardinal points are: Mariazell in Austria (west), Şumuleu Ciuc in Romania (east); Czestochowa in Poland (north) and Međugorje in Herzegovina (south). The route is flagged by painted waymarks in the shape of a crossed letter M. The **Makkosmária Chapel** (*just beyond map p. 422, A4*), on the border of Budapest and Pest County, is one of the way stations. It was built in the mid-18th century on the site of a tree where a young man, miraculously cured of an illness,

JÁNOS-HEGY
Young station master salutes the down train on the Children's Railway.

had hung a votive painting of the *Madonna and Child*. The site became a popular place of pilgrimage and gained a reputation for answering the supplications of those praying for the safe return of prisoners of war. Today the yellow church with its onion-domed spire stands on the edge of a wide picnic field dotted with oak trees (Makkos, the name of the site, alludes to an abundance of acorns, *makk*). There is a very pretty forest walk to Makkosmária from Normafa. The walk begins at the Eötvös utca/Konkoly Thege Miklós utca crossroads. Go through the wooden 'Székely gate' and follow the green cross waymarks. The walk takes about half an hour.

JÁNOS-HEGY, THE ERZSÉBET-KILÁTÓ AND THE LIBEGŐ CHAIRLIFT

János-hegy, or János Hill (527m), is the highest point in Budapest. You can reach it on foot from the Children's Railway stop of the same name, an invigorating climb of c. 10mins (red waymarks) on a path above the **Béka-tó** ('Frog Pond'), a natural clay-bedded pool that is home to frogs, newts and dragonflies. From Normafa you can also walk to János-hegy along the flat ridge that runs through the woods. There is a buffet selling drinks and snacks and here, at the upper station of the Libegő chairlift (*see below*). A stepped path leads to the top of János-hegy, where you can climb the **Erzsébet-kilátó**, a neo-Romanesque lookout tower (*open daily 8–8*). Built in 1908–10 to designs by Frigyes Schulek (who also built the Fishermen's Bastion), it is named after Empress Elisabeth, whom Hungary had always seen as a friend and whose assassination in Geneva had taken place ten years previously. Narrow spiral staircases lead to the top and down again, one-way in each direction. The one to the top is marked '*Salve*' in the terrazzo floor; the one down is marked '*Vale*'. From the top there are excellent views. At the bottom is a cosy café.

The **Chairlift (Libegő)** is an open ski lift that runs between János-hegy and Zugliget, a distance of just over 1km. Built in 1970, an open competition was held to find a name for it. Thousands of suggestions were received, including 'Space Bus', 'Hillycopter' and, less felicitously, 'Electric Chair'. The name Libegő, 'Hoverer', was eventually chosen. The journey (12mins) offers spectacular views (as well as glimpses into people's gardens), particularly on the way down. The chairlift operates all year round except in strong winds and heavy rain or when it is closed for maintenance (*for details and timetables, see bkv.hu/en/en/zugliget_chairlift*).

Close to the lower station of the Chairlift, on Zugligeti út (*map p. 422, B3–C3*), is the recently restored and reconstructed station building of the old **Lóvasút** or horse-drawn tramway, which once brought ramblers up to the foot of János-hegy. The building is now an events space and has a small local history display on the horse-drawn tram (*open Wed–Sun 10–6*).

HIKING TRAIL SYMBOLS

The hiking paths in the Buda Hills are well signed, with symbols painted on tree trunks, telegraph poles, walls and buildings. The symbols refer to the type of trail:

 Coloured stripe between white stripes. Denotes a main hiking trail.

 Coloured L. The trail leads to a ruin.

 Coloured cross on a white background. Secondary, intersecting trail.

 Solid circle. The trail leads to a spring or water source.

 Coloured triangle. A trail that leads to a hilltop or peak.

 Stylised archway or tunnel. The trail leads to a cave.

 Broken circle. A circular trail.

 Purple or blue letter M with a crossed central bar. The Marian Way pilgrim trail.

SZÉPJUHÁSZNÉ

At **Budakeszi út 71**, hidden behind trees, is a faithful rebuilding in the German hunting-lodge style of the Kochmeister Villa, where Crown Prince Rudolf and his sister, Archduchess Gisela, stayed in 1866 after the Austrian defeat at Königgrätz, when Vienna was deemed too dangerous. Their mother, Empress Elisabeth, stayed in the palace on Castle Hill, where she had also taken the Crown Jewels. The royal children also stayed here at the time of their father Franz Joseph's coronation in 1867. The villa fell into complete disrepair in the 20th century and was entirely rebuilt in 2001.

At **Szépjuhászné** (*map p. 422, A2*) there is a stop on the Children's Railway and a small roadside buffet. The main road runs through a pass between two hills, János-hegy and Nagy-Hárs-hegy. In the 18th century this spot was an important halting place on the coach road to Budapest and an inn stood here, named Szépjuhászné, 'Beautiful Shepherd's Wife', after a mythical incident in the life of King Matthias Corvinus. From the mid-19th century it became a fashionable country resort for Pest citizens. Franz Joseph brought Bismarck on a diplomatic luncheon here in 1852.

Just beyond the car park are the scant **ruins of the Budaszentlőrinc monastery**, founded c. 1290, which once held the relics of St Paul the Hermit (*see p. 120*). It was generously endowed by several Hungarian kings, including Matthias Corvinus, during whose reign around 500 monks lived here. One of them made Hungarian translations of the Bible in a nearby cave. The monastery was destroyed by the Ottomans. King Matthias had a hunting lodge near here (traces on Fekete István utca; *map p. 422, C2*).

BUDAKESZI WILDLIFE PARK

Beyond map p. 422, A2. Bus 22, 22A or 222 from Széll Kálmán tér (via Szépjuhászné) to Szanatórium utca (Vadaspark). From there it is a short walk up Szanatórium utca (follow the signs). Ticket office open 9–3.30, later in summer; vadaspark-budakeszi.hu.
The small Wildlife Park (Vadaspark), popular with children, has examples of animals that live—or once lived—in the Buda Hills, including pine marten, boar, brown bear, lynx, mouflon, edible dormouse and golden jackal (*Canis aureus*), a native species that is returning to its habitat in Hungary (and beginning to pose a threat to smaller species).

EATING AND DRINKING IN THE BUDA HILLS

RESTAURANTS

ff **Fióka**. Small friendly restaurant with a varied menu in a former post office. Garden in summer. Good wines. *Városmajor u. 75. T: +36 30 458 9406, fiokaetterem.hu. Map p. 424, B3.*

f–ff **Bajai Halászcsárda**. This is the place to come for fish soup (*halászlé*) and pike perch, carp and catfish. A country-style inn just by the Svábhegy stop on the Cogwheel Railway. *Hollós út 2. T: +36 1 275-5245, bajaihalaszcsarda.hu. Map p. 424, A4.*

f–ff **Normakert**. Popular restaurant occupying the old Normafa ski lodge. Hungarian cuisine. Outdoor seating in summer. Enclosed terrace and garden at the back. Best to book Sun lunchtime. *Eötvös út 59. T: +36 1 391 7151, normakert.hu. Map p. 422, B4.*

CAFÉS

Majorka is a cosy café-bar in an old electricity station at the edge of Városmajor park. They are proud of their hamburgers (*Szilágyi Erzsébet fasor 16. T: +36 1 224 0055, majorka. hu. Map p. 424, B3*). The **Kilátó Kávézó** inside the Erzsébet Lookout Tower (*map p. 422, A2*) is a nice place for a drink (mulled wine in winter). There is a branch of **Szamos** (*see p. 328*) on Svábhegy (*Szépkilátás u. 1; map p. 422, C4*)

District V: Lipótváros

Lipótváros (Leopold Town) is the area of central Pest's Fifth District that stretches between Margaret Bridge and Vörösmarty tér. Its name dates from 1790, when Archduke Leopold, second son of Maria Theresa, became emperor. Lipótváros is a stately part of town, an area of broad streets and imposing buildings, the administrative heart of the country. The Parliament building is here, government ministries are situated here, the chief law courts are here, as is the National Bank. The district is also home to the great basilica church dedicated to Hungary's first king, St Stephen, the nation's founder.

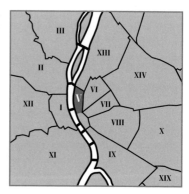

PARLIAMENT & KOSSUTH LAJOS TÉR

Map p. 428, C2. Visits to the Parliament building are by guided tour only. Tours last 45mins. Direct ticket sales from the Visitor Centre are for same-day visits only. To avoid disappointment, it is best to book in advance, especially for the English-language tours, which fill up quickly. The website for bookings is jegymester.hu. You will be sent an e-ticket to print out. Café, WC (free if you use the café) and shop in the Visitor Centre. Go to the Visitor Centre to begin the tour, a few minutes before the start time. You will be asked to pass through a security check. Photography is allowed except in the Dome Hall.

The Hungarian Parliament Building (Országház), self-confident and massive, is one of Budapest's best-known landmarks, deliberately constructed to become such. Predominantly neo-Gothic in style, the work of Imre Steindl, it is one of the largest administrative buildings in the world.

HISTORY OF THE HUNGARIAN PARLIAMENT

From its earliest beginnings until well into the 19th century, the Hungarian Parliament had no permanent seat but was convened in varying locations by royal summons. By the

HOLD UTCA
Detail of the glass doors of Ödön Lechner's ex-Post Office Savings Bank.

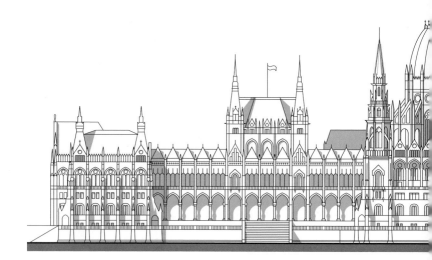

early 19th century, the favourite site had become Pressburg (Bratislava). As Hungarian national sentiment and the desire for independence grew, so calls began to be made for a permanent location to be chosen. Pressburg was rejected as being too close to Vienna. Pest became the allotted city. The first plan for a building was submitted by Mihály Pollack (architect of the National Museum) in 1840. His proposal was as massive as Steindl's eventual incarnation was to be, but heavily neo-Florentine, inspired by the massy grandeur of Palazzo Pitti. Nothing came of his plans, nor of the scores of others that were received, from architects all over Europe, because of the turmoil of the 1848–9 War of Independence. It was not until 1865 that another committee was set up to deliver a parliament building. They commissioned one from the foremost architect of the day, Miklós Ybl, and construction proceeded with haste. In just eleven months the building was completed, on Bródy Sándor utca opposite the National Museum (it is now the Italian Cultural Institute; *see p. 236*). The lower house met there while the lords met in the Museum (the Hungarian Parliament was bicameral until 1945). Hasty construction had delivered an imperfect building, however, with notoriously bad acoustics. In 1880 the project was put out to tender again. The requirement was a building to hold both houses, upper and lower, under a single roof and it was to be a symbolic edifice representing the entirety of the Hungarian people, 'to soar above all other buildings, to express the power of the Hungarian nation on the banks of the Danube.' When Imre Steindl's Gothic Revival design emerged the winner, critical voices grumbled that there was nothing quintessentially Hungarian about it. Nevertheless,

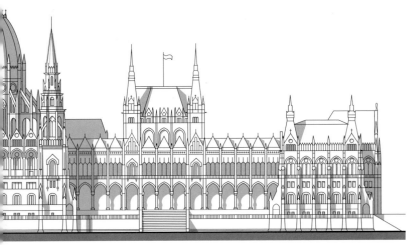

HUNGARIAN PARLIAMENT: RIVER FAÇADE

it was built, and now stands proud, 265 metres long, 96 metres high at the top of the dome and containing some 700 rooms. Work was completed in 1902 and the first parliamentary session was held in October of the same year. Sadly, Steindl had died a few weeks earlier and so did not live to see his great building finally fulfil its purpose.

A SYMBOLIC BUILDING FOR THE NATION

Despite the early critics' complaints that Steindl's building was not notably Hungarian in style, it does much to allude to Hungary throughout its fabric. The height of the dome, 96m, is unfailingly mentioned by the tour guides as being an allusion to the year 896, when the Magyar tribes occupied the Carpathian Basin. In the details of the decoration, motifs of Hungarian flora are constantly used. The seating in the two debating chambers is of Slavonian oak and everywhere else too, mainly Hungarian materials were used and Hungarian craftsmen and artists were employed to execute it all: Zsolnay, Róth, Lotz.

Despite its vastness and thus its capacity to accommodate representatives of all the Hungarian people, the fact remains that in its early years it did not. Before WWI, only a small percentage of the population had the vote and non-Magyars within the realm (Slovaks, Croats, Serbs and Romanians) were greatly under-represented. The franchise was extended after the First World War and though universal adult suffrage had arrived by 1945, it was swiftly extinguished by the single-party state. A multi-party democratic parliamentary system came into being in 1990.

PARLIAMENT

Bronze cigar holders, helpfully numbered, in the corridor outside the debating chamber. MPs would leave the chamber for a smoke and when recalled to vote, would place their cigar in a holder, mentally noting the number so as to be able to resume smoking when the vote was cast. On occasion an MP found himself remaining in the chamber for longer than planned, returning to the corridor to find his cigar burned to the nub. This gave rise to the expression 'worth a havana' to describe a particularly lively debate.

THE TOUR OF PARLIAMENT

Only a small part of the building is shown and what visitors see will depend on which parts of the house are being used. The tour leaves from the Visitor Centre, through the old brick-lined cellars and up a long flight of steps (lift available) to the main floor. Pause if you can while going up the steps to admire the great quantity of **gold leaf** used in the decoration. The details of the carving on the pillars and cornices are very fine and the stained-glass windows, here and throughout the building, by the workshop of Miksa Róth (*see p. 224*), are extremely beautiful.

At the top of the stairs you come into the long **City Corridor**, which runs the length of the building overlooking Kossuth Lajos tér. On the side ledges and window sills you will see brass **cigar holders**, all numbered (*see illustration*).

At the end of the City Corridor you emerge at the top of the wide **Main Stairway**, lavishly decorated and gilded, with a bust of Imre Steindl (Alajos Stróbl, 1904) set into the wall at one side. The ceiling has allegorical frescoes by Károly Lotz of the *Glorification of Hungary* (with István Széchenyi and Sándor Petőfi at her feet) and the *Apotheosis of Legislation*.

The Lower House formerly used the **debating chamber** in the south wing. This is the chamber now used by Parliament. The paintings on either side of the Speaker's podium show the coronation of Franz Joseph in 1867 and the Palatine Stephen (*see p. 15*) opening the Hungarian assembly in 1848.

From here you proceed into the sixteen-sided **Dome Hall**. Here, in the centre, in a stout glass case guarded by a pair of soldiers with drawn sabres, are the Hungarian crown jewels. The ceremonial changing of the guard takes place every hour.

THE HUNGARIAN CROWN JEWELS

As the sacred fire of the Vestals was to ancient Rome, so, in its way, is the Crown of St Stephen to Hungary. More than just a kingly appurtenance, it is the physical symbol of the continuity of the Hungarian state and of its independent governance. To those who object that the trappings of monarchy have no place in the house of legislature of a republic, this is the justification offered for keeping it in Parliament's Dome Hall: the Crown of St Stephen is no mere trapping of monarchy; it is a sacred talisman of Hungary's autonomous existence. Because of the meaning invested in it, it has been subject to more than ordinary trials and tribulations over the course of its long life.

Symbolically, the crown represents the diadem sent to King Stephen in the year 1000 by Pope Sylvester II. In reality it dates from somewhat later and is made up of two seemingly separate pieces. A Byzantine circlet, adorned with small pearls, cabochon gems and cloisonné enamel plaquettes, is attached to a cross-piece, with delicate gold filigree work and semi-precious stones. The enamel plaques on the circlet show Christ Pantocrator at the front and the Byzantine emperor Michael Ducas (reigned 1071–8) at the back (though his image may have been fixed on later, in place of an original plaquette of the Virgin). The gold cross-piece has an enamel image of God the Father, Creator of Sun, Moon and Stars at the top, and eight of the apostles down the sides. The cross at the top was at some time bent by accident but theories persist that it was fashioned like that deliberately, mimicking the angle of the earth's axis (23.5°).

The crown has been in danger more than once. In 1440, Elizabeth of Luxembourg (daughter of King Sigismund and widow of King Albert), had smuggled the crown to her infant son's clandestine and disputed coronation. Later, she pawned it to the Holy Roman Emperor Frederick III. In 1464 Matthias Corvinus succeeded in getting it back (for almost six times the price that Frederick had paid for it). As soon as his coronation had taken place, he began to rule by right of the crown, summoning parliament only twice more.

In 1848, some zealous revolutionaries advocated offering it to Russia or throwing it into the Danube—anything to prevent its falling into Habsburg hands. In the end it was buried, along with the Coronation Mantle, in a damp willow grove, and was retrieved in a terrible state in 1853. When the Communists first came to power in 1919, there were numerous calls for the crown to be melted down. Béla Kun planned to auction it off in Germany, but his regime was toppled before this could happen. When the Communists again came to power after the Second World War, the crown was smuggled out of the country and out of their reach. Its journey took it to Fort Knox, where it lay incarcerated until 1978, when President Carter formally returned it to Hungary. Today it is once again honoured as the symbol of the Hungarian state and a treasured piece of the nation's patrimony.

The Crown Jewels consist of an exceptionally rare and beautiful sceptre, 10th-century Fatimid work, consisting of a large lump of crystal housed in filigree gold casing with an elaborate Solomon's knot at the top. The orb dates from 1301. The sword, traditionally brandished by a new king after his coronation as he vows to defend Hungary from her enemies, is from the 15th century.

At the top of the dome hangs the largest chandelier in Hungary (when a bulb blows, electricians have to access it from outside). Around the hall are statues of the monarchs of Hungary, from Árpád, founder of the first royal dynasty, to Leopold II, son of Maria Theresa. Beginning with Árpád (immediately in front of you as you enter the hall), the figures are as follows: St Stephen; Louis the Great; King Kálmán; Andrew II; Béla IV; Ladislas the Great; János Hunyadi and King Matthias. Then follow four princes of Transylvania, István Báthory, István Bocskai, Gábor Bethlen and György Rákóczi. The last group are from the House of Habsburg: Charles II, Maria Theresa and Leopold II.

From the Dome Hall you can usually enter the **lobby of the former Upper House** (now used for conferences). Its great carpet has a blue background, said to symbolise the blue blood of those who once met here. The paintings on either side of the Speaker's podium in the chamber itself show Andrew II promulgating the charter known as the Golden Bull in 1222 and Maria Theresa's famous appeal at the Diet of Pressburg in 1741, when she threw herself upon the chivalry of her Hungarian subjects in a bid to save her crown (*see pp. 12–13*).

The route to the exit takes you along the **River Corridor** (more cigar holders), from where there are good views of the Danube and Castle Hill.

KOSSUTH LAJOS TÉR

Kossuth Lajos tér (*map p. 428, C2*) is a vast piazza bounded on its west side by the Parliament building with the river behind it. In front of the central section of the Parliament building is a wide paved forecourt with a tall **flagstaff** in its centre. From the top flutters the Hungarian tricolor, ceremonially posted and retired every day. Parliament's central flight of steps leading to the ceremonial entrance is flanked by two **seated bronze lions**. At first glance they appear to be a pair, but close inspection reveals that one is smooth while the other is rough. The left-hand lion is the original (Béla Markup, 1902). The right-hand lion was destroyed in WWII and replaced with a near-identical copy (József Somogyi, 1949).

Facing Parliament beyond the tramlines is the neo-Renaissance **Ministry of Agriculture**, the best-known work of Gyula Bukovics (1885–7). It has busts of eminent agriculturalists under its arcades and two bronze statues in front on the left, the *Boy Reaper* and the *Girl Agronomist* (Árpád Somogyi, 1956) and on the right a statue of István Nagyatádi Szabó (István Szentgyörgyi, 1932), peasant smallholders' representative and Agriculture Minister during the Horthy years. The statue was removed in 1945 but reappeared in 1990. The little bronze balls embedded in the walls commemorate the shooting and volley fire of 'Bloody Thursday', 25th October, 1956, when a mass protest outside the Parliament turned to violence as shots were fired into the crowd from the Ministry of Agriculture roof.

On the other side of Alkotmány utca, also facing Parliament, is the Curia or **Supreme Court building**, built as such in 1893–6, to designs by Alajos Hauszmann, although until the end of 2017 it housed the Museum of Ethnography (*see p. 317*). The façade is decorated with statuary by the great masters of the age, including József Róna, János Fadrusz and György Zala. Above the central columned porch is a triga (three-horse

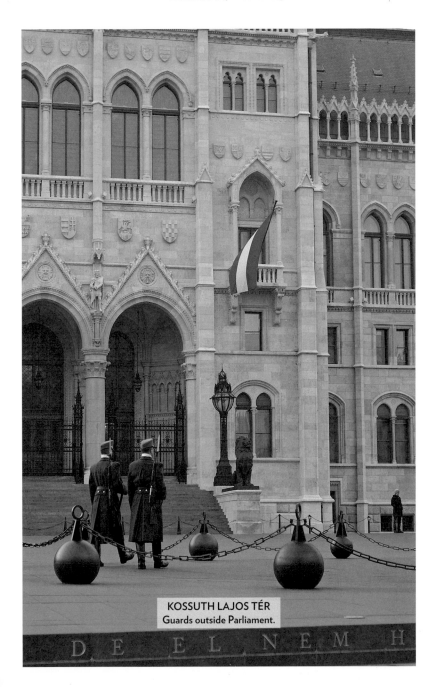

KOSSUTH LAJOS TÉR
Guards outside Parliament.

chariot) by Károly Senyei, in which Justice rides, bearing a flaming torch and a palm of Victory. In the interior, the central hall is extremely grand (for many years popular for film shoots), with a ceiling fresco of *The Triumph of Justice* by Károly Lotz. A statue of *Justice* by Alajos Stróbl used to stand here; if, as was planned at the time of writing, the Supreme Court moves back into the building, the statue will doubtless be returned.

COMMEMORATIVE STATUARY IN THE SQUARE

The commemorative statues in Kossuth Lajos tér have changed over the years, as the country's governing regimes have changed. One figure who remains constant is **Lajos Kossuth** himself, the politician and patriot who gives his name to the square which is the administrative heart of the nation. A statue group commemorating him stands on the right as you face Parliament, at the edge of the planted area.

LAJOS KOSSUTH

Most towns in Hungary have a street or a square named after György Dózsa, Sándor Petőfi, Endre Ady, Attila József or Ferenc Rákóczi. All of them—surely without exception—have a Kossuth Lajos utca. Kossuth (1802–94) is Hungary's most fêted hero, the Lutheran lawyer-turned revolutionary activist whose zeal and oratory made him into the greatest figure of the Hungarian independence movement of the mid-19th century. Appointed Minister of Finance in the first independent government of 1848, he was shortly afterwards elected Governor-President, in which role, among other things, he plotted the dethronement of the Habsburgs. In August 1849, when it became clear that the Hungarian cause was lost, Kossuth fled the country leaving the military commander Artúr Görgei in charge. Kossuth spent the rest of his life abroad, some of it in England and the United States, making speeches and writing articles explaining his country's cause. His English—which he had taught himself through reading Shakespeare—was by all accounts archaic but stirring. Although popular in Britain, he refused an invitation from the Chartists to speak at a working men's dinner, a decision which prompted Karl Marx to write that Kossuth was 'all things to all men. In Marseilles he shouts: Vive la République!, in London: God save the Queen!' It was an unfair assessment. To his own ideals, Kossuth was unyieldingly true. Until the end of his life he remained implacably opposed to any kind of Hungarian accommodation with Austria, forfeiting his Hungarian citizenship as a result. He was an opponent of Deák (*see p. 250*) and news of the Compromise was a bitter pill for him to swallow. He spent his last years in Turin, putting together a collection of Pliocene-epoch snails and seashells, meticulously labelled (the collection came to the National Museum but was lost following damage in 1956). Kossuth died in 1894. Shortly afterwards, his remains were repatriated to Hungary, where they lie in a magnificent mausoleum (*see p. 250*). A wax cylinder recording of his voice (1890) survives as a powerful relic for posterity.

The sculpture group is a modern reworking of a 1927 original by János Horvay. Kossuth stands flanked by the eight members of the short-lived autonomous Hungarian government of 1848: Count Lajos Batthyány (Prime Minister; *see p. 15*); Bertalan Szemere (Home Secretary); Ferenc Deák (Minister of Justice; *see p. 250*);

KOSSUTH LAJOS TÉR
Detail from the Lapidarium, of original stone carvings from the Parliament building.

Lázár Mészáros (Minister of Defence); Count István Széchenyi (Transport and Public Works; *see p. 164*); Baron József Eötvös (Education); Gábor Klauzál (Trade and Agriculture) and Prince Pál Esterházy (in charge of relations with the court in Vienna). All nine men look subdued, their eyes cast down as if chidden by history.

Beyond this monument, towards the river, is a gigantic **memorial to Count István Tisza**: a Doric-columned plinth is surmounted by a lion, raging in the toils of a serpent. Tisza was Hungary's Prime Minister twice, before and during WWI. Always a divisive figure, he was assassinated in the Aster Revolution of 1918, which brought Count Mihály Károlyi, the 'Red Count' (*see p. 246*), to power. The original monument to Tisza (György Zala and Antal Orbán, 1934), damaged during WWII, was dismantled and replaced by a statue of Mihály Károlyi. In 2014, Károlyi was displaced and a replica of the original Tisza monument went up instead. Both the new one and the 1934 original were criticised for the disproportionately massive scale of their composition.

Between the two memorials is the entrance, down steps, to an underground exhibition space, the **Lapidarium** (*open daily 10–6*), with a display on the exterior stone decoration of the Parliament building. It occupies part of the brick-vaulted former ventilation and heating tunnels for Parliament. At the other end of the square, a mirror-image underground exhibition space (*same opening times*) houses **In Memoriam 1956**, with photos and film footage of the events of 25th October during the suppression of the anti-Soviet uprising.

On the grass to the east is János Pásztor's 1937 equestrian **monument to Ferenc Rákóczi II**, Prince of Transylvania and leader of the failed anti-Habsburg rebellion of 1703–11. The Latin inscription on the left side of the plinth reads, 'With God for Fatherland and Liberty' (the words 'with God' were removed in the early 1950s but reappeared in 1989). On the opposite side are the opening words of the rebel manifesto in 1703: 'The wounds of the noble Hungarian nation burst open'. Equestrian experts have noted that the horse looks uncomfortable, with its mouth open in response to too much pressure exerted on the bit.

DANUBE EMBANKMENT
Shoes, by Can Togay and Gyula Pauer (2005, detail).

Towards the river is another equestrian monument, once again a replacement of a destroyed original, to **Count Gyula Andrássy**, the first Prime Minister of Hungary following the 1867 Compromise with Austria. The original statue was removed and melted down after WWII. Part of its metal was used to make the giant statue of Stalin, which stood at the edge of the City Park and was famously torn down during the 1956 revolution. Part of its metal, in turn, has now gone back into in the renewed Andrássy monument, which was unveiled in 2016. The plinth relief facing the river shows Andrássy placing the Crown of St Stephen on Franz Joseph's head.

MONUMENTS ON THE DANUBE BANK

Behind the Andrássy monument, steps lead down to the Danube embankment, where a plaque commemorates the **Kossuth Bridge**, a temporary crossing built in 1949 after all the other bridges has been blown up by the retreating Nazis. At the bottom of the steps, on the left, is a seated statue of the great poet **Attila József** (László Marton, 1980), with a line from his famous poem 'By the Danube' on the plinth: 'onward it flowed, as if from my heart: the restless, wise, great river.' Further down, right on the rim of the river wall, is a moving monument to those shot into the freezing river by the Arrow Cross in the winter of 1944–5. It consists of a **collection of sculpted shoes**, of all styles and sizes, men's, women's and a toddler's pair, placed haphazardly as if the victims had just taken them off. The monument was conceived by the Hungarian film director Can Togay and was set up in 2005. Visitors leave flowers and candles inside the shoes (particularly the toddler's pair), and fill them with stones.

THE RED DANUBE

During the chaotic summer of 1944, Hungary ordered the suspension of Jewish rail transports to the death camps. Miklós Horthy then ousted his Nazi quisling Prime Minister, Döme Sztojay, leading the Germans to launch Operation Panzerfaust, which removed Horthy from power. The Hungarian Arrow Cross then took matters into their own hands, raiding houses and rounding up Jews and other anti-Nazi victims. Many were marched to the Danube bank, where they were roped together, ordered to take off their shoes, and shot into the water. Those who received the gunshot died; the others were left to the mercy of the river. In that terrible winter, the Danube was stained with blood. Among those who suffered in this way were the pharmaceuticals pioneer Gedeon Richter, who did not survive, and the sculptor József Róna's daughter Erzsébet, who did.

THE STREETS AROUND KOSSUTH TÉR

Balassi Bálint utca (*map p. 428, C1*) runs between Kossuth Lajos tér and Margaret Bridge. The building closest to Kossuth tér, on the left, is the Biarritz House, an apartment block built in 1938 for the Bauxite Industrial Company, by Andor Wellisch and others. Opposite it is a building designed by Imre Steindl to house ancillary offices and apartments for Parliament staff (including the ceremonial guard) as well as a huge furnace to supply heating for the entire building. At the far end of the street, the last building on the left before Margaret Bridge is the former headquarters of the Hungarian Socialist Workers Party, humorously known as the 'White House' (1949, Lajos Gádoros, Gábor Preisich et al). It is now home to MPs' offices.

Parallel to Balassi Bálint utca is **Falk Miksa utca**, filled with antique shops. A number of notable auction houses have their showrooms here (Judit Virág and Kieselbach). At no. 13 is the shop of jewellery designer Vladimir Péter, known as Wladis. The son of the painter Margit Anna, he makes beautiful and original objects in silver.

Alkotmány utca, Constitution Street (*map p. 428, C2*), is just one of a procession of wide, stately streets that lead away from the Parliament building and into the heart of Pest. At the junction with Honvéd utca, on the right, is a house with a tower of corner rooms and diagonally opposite, a building with elegant balconies born on consoles (Győző Czigler, 1886). Its roof turrets, in the style of a rural hunting lodge, and the masks of wild animals above the windows, testify to its original function as the headquarters of the Forestry Commission.

HONVÉD UTCA

Honvéd utca (*map p. 428, C1–C2*) is one of the finest streets for architecture in this part of town, offering a wonderful scrabble-bag of styles, superb examples of late 19th- and early 20th-century Budapest eclecticism. Turn left to see an enclosed loggia decorated in colourful mosaics at **no. 16** (Emil Vidor, 1912). The building opposite, at **no. 13–15** (József Körner, 1947), is a good example of post-war Modernism, before the Proletarian movement and cheap building materials turned the style bleak and depressing. At the time of writing it housed the Ministry of the Economy (formerly the

Finance Ministry) but there were plans afoot to move it back to its inter-war premises on Castle Hill. At **no. 22** (corner of Markó utca) is an apartment block built for the Metropolitan Electricity Board by Dénes Györgyi and Ernő Román (1931), with a red-brick former electricity substation building behind. On the façade facing Honvéd utca is Béla Ohmann's allegorical *Electricity*, a statue of a man in a loincloth clutching two diminutive lightning bolts.

Turning right at the Alkotmány junction, walk two blocks to Báthory utca, where the pale yellow building on the right-hand corner (**Báthory u. 5**; Ignác Alpár, 1904) is worth a look. It bears a plaque commemorating Alfréd Hajós (*see p. 292*), who lived here. The façade is covered with moulded details. Above the doorway lours a hideous mascaron, with two grotesque peacocks above, apparently squabbling over a worm. The entrance gates are decorated with wrought-iron daisies and huge knapweeds. If you get a chance to go inside, note the marble spittoons in the corners of the stairway at floor level.

The remainder of Honvéd utca, the short block between Báthory utca and Szabadság tér, has some splendid buildings in a mixture of neo-Venetian, Romantic and Art Nouveau styles. The **Bedő-ház** at no. 3 is one of the finest examples of Hungarian Art Nouveau, with wrought-iron sunflowers on the balcony rail and mascarons with Assyrian beards framing one of the windows at the top. It was built by Emil Vidor in 1903 for the wealthy factory owner and art collector Béla Bedő (1862–1916). The entrance hall, stairway and all the flats are equally richly designed in the Secession style. It houses a café and a collection of Art Nouveau pieces. An amusing tradition asserts that when the house was under construction, the architect Alfréd Hajós, who lived around the corner and who was never a convert to Art Nouveau, would stand in the street and harangue the masons loudly, protesting at the building's preposterous ugliness.

SZABADSÁG TÉR

Szabadság tér, Freedom Square (*map p. 428, C2*), is a wide public space shaped a little like a Roman hippodrome, though it was never used as such. In 1786, the emperor Joseph II gave orders for a huge building to be erected here. Known as the *Neugebäude* or *Újépület*, it occupied the entire site and was used as a barracks. Count Lajos Batthyány (*see p. 151*) met his end in the courtyard of this building, which came to be seen as a symbol of Austrian oppression, much like the Citadel on Gellért Hill. To universal delight it was demolished in 1897 and the fine buildings that line the square went up after this. Today the square's role is somewhat in question. A number of its grand buildings stand empty and the proportion of local residents is quite small.

THE SOVIET MEMORIAL, VÉCSEY UTCA AND AULICH UTCA

In the top centre of the square stands the **Soviet Memorial**, erected in 1946 to the perpetual memory of the Soviet soldiers who laid down their lives on Budapest soil during WWII. The inscription reads: 'Glory to the liberating Soviet heroes', a sentiment that is distasteful for many; but despite numerous protests and attempts to

SZABADSÁG TÉR

Detail of Ferenc Medgyessy's wine harvest relief (1940). In the sculptor's original submission, the figures were naked. He won the commission but was asked to clothe them, hence their rustic garb (which he himself admitted was an improvement). The figure on the far right bears a pitcher inscribed 'In Vino Veritas' in *rovásírás*, the ancient Hungarian runic script.

tear the monument down, under the terms of a Hungarian-Russian agreement signed in 1995, the monument is to stay. It has become a popular visitor attraction and is by no means anathema to all. On important anniversaries, the Hungarian Workers' Party lays wreaths here.

LIBERATION AND COUNTER-LIBERATION

After 1897, when the hated barracks were torn down (*see above*), the name Freedom Square was selected in honour of the heroic victims of the struggle for independence from Austria in 1848–9. As you stand facing the Soviet memorial, the corner building on the left (**Szabadság tér 15**), now housing a bank on the ground floor and with stout rustication going all the way up to the top (a very curious sight) has, in its tympanum, a lifesize figure of Lajos Kossuth (Károly Fleischl, 1900), arm outstretched in acclamation. This was the first ever public statue of Kossuth erected in the city. The streets that lead diagonally away from here, Vécsey utca and Aulich utca, are named after two of the 13 Hungarian army generals who were executed in Arad (modern Romania) on 6th October 1849, the same day that Batthyány was shot in the barracks courtyard here. The little square at the end of Vécsey utca is named Vértanuk tere (Martyrs' Square) to commemorate them.

The statue in Vértanuk tere, though, honours a martyr of a different kind: **Imre Nagy**, the Communist leader who promised reforms in 1956 and was executed by his own party in 1958 (*see p. 91*). The statue (Tamás Varga, 1996), showing Nagy standing on a curved bridge as if in a Japanese garden, provides a popular opportunity for people to photograph each other standing next to him.

Turn and turn again: back on Szabadság tér, beside the Soviet monument to the liberation of Budapest from Nazism, is another monument recording another liberation: the fall of the Iron Curtain, evoked by a cheery, lifesize **statue of Ronald Reagan** (István Máté, 2011), shown walking out across the square, his hands shaped so that one can reach out and shake either one. People do, and take photographs of each other in the process. Malicious tongues hinted that the date of the statue's unveiling was chosen deliberately: Secretary of State Hillary Clinton was in town on an official visit.

The **Vécsey utca** flank of the rusticated building with the Kossuth statue has a beautiful doorway carved with the words '*Budapesti Műhely*', commemorating Kozma Lajos' interior design studio, which opened here in 1913, inspired by the Wiener Werkstätte. The studio went out of business in the 1920s and its decoration was lost. The doorway was recreated from photographs.

Aulich utca leads diagonally out of Szabadság tér to the northeast. High up on the façade of no. 3, the **Walkó-ház**, is a ceramic design of a woman picking an apple, by Albert Kálmán Kőrössy (1901). The first-floor balcony is borne on twin frogs and there are other sculpted details to discover (squirrels, birds in a nest, an owl's head), all by Géza Maróti. At the end of the street, both corner buildings house cafés. That on the left, the Liberté, is named in commemoration of its predecessor, the Szabadság (Liberty) coffee house, where the poet Endre Ady wrote *Harc a Nagy úrral* ('Battle with the Grand Seigneur') in 1906. In the centre of the square which opens out of the end of Aulich utca is a bronze casket on a tall plinth, in which burns an **eternal flame** (in fact an electric light) commemorating Lajos Batthyány, prime minister in Hungary's revolutionary government, who was executed in the former barracks here in October 1849. The eternal flame stands on the site of the hated building's northeastern corner, where the execution took place. Appalled by the idea of death by hanging, to which he had been condemned, Batthyány attempted to take his own life. The dagger he used was too small and brittle and he succeeded only in making a bad wound in his neck, from which he lost much blood. His sentence was commuted to death by firing squad.

THE US EMBASSY

Behind impressive railings on the east side of Szabadság tér is the **US Embassy building**, occupying an entire block. It was here, on 12th December 1941, that the Hungarian Prime Minister informed the US Ambassador that a state of war existed between their respective countries. It was also here, between 1956 and 1971, that Cardinal Mindszenty lived in internal exile (*see below*). In the grassy area outside the Embassy, facing the park, is a statue of the US Army general Harry Hill Bandholtz (Miklós Ligeti, 1936). Bandholtz was in Budapest in 1919, during the chaotic collapse of Béla Kun's Republic of Councils and it was thanks to his intervention that the Hungarian National Museum was spared looting by Romanian troops. After 1945 the statue was kept in the garden of the US Embassy residence.

CARDINAL MINDSZENTY

József Mindszenty was born in 1892, the son of a farmer. He entered the Catholic Church in 1915, became Bishop of Veszprém in 1944, Archbishop of Esztergom in 1945, and was made a cardinal by Pius XII in 1946. Despite the success of his career, he was to find himself throughout his life at the forefront of dissent and conflict. He was first imprisoned in 1919, for speaking out against the Communist Republic of Councils. During the Second World War, he was imprisoned again, for denouncing the deportation of the Jews. After refusing to support the Communist system in 1948, he was accused of actions that threatened to overthrow the republic and was taken to Andrássy út 60 (*see p. 200*) for questioning. He was detained there, tortured, subjected to a show trial in 1949, found guilty of treason and sentenced to life imprisonment. Released by rebel forces in 1956, he subsequently took refuge in the US Embassy. His presence here was publicised around the world and is thought partly to have inspired the film *The Prisoner* (1955), starring Alec Guinness, which turns on the interrogation and show trial of a Catholic primate. After 15 years of internal exile, the Hungarian government reached an agreement with the Vatican, under the terms of which Mindszenty left for Austria. He died in Vienna in 1975 and was buried at Mariazell. His remains were reinterred in the crypt of Esztergom cathedral in 1991.

THE BANK AND FORMER STOCK EXCHANGE

The building of the **Hungarian National Bank** (Magyar Nemzeti Bank; *map p. 428, C2*) was designed by Ignác Alpár. When it was built, in 1905, the institution it housed was the Austro-Hungarian Bank. Although the creation of a national financial

SZABADSÁG TÉR

Béla Markup's limestone likeness of Ignác Alpár (1905), architect of the National Bank
and former Stock Exchange buildings. He wears the costume of a medieval master builder.

institution had been one of the nation's Twelve Points in 1848 (*see p. 15*), it was only
in 1924 that the Hungarian National Bank came into being. Fine limestone reliefs by
Béla Markup, Ödön Moiret, József Róna, Károly Senyei and others, run all the way
round the exterior forming a frieze that traces the history of commerce and finance.
The architect himself appears costumed as a medieval master builder (as you stand
in the square, facing the building, he is on the right-hand corner bay, facing inwards).
Further along, a rather moving relief shows a bankruptcy scene.

On the other side of Szabadság tér is the vast bulk of the **former Stock Exchange**,
also built by Alpár in 1905. The stock and commodity exchanges were closed down
in 1948 and from the mid-1950s the building was the headquarters of Hungarian
Television. There have been numerous attempts to find a use for it since the TV left
in 2009. At the time of writing, it was to be turned into office and retail space. In the
centre of the square is the Hütte café, with seats outside in fine weather.

Behind the National Bank, on Hold utca, is the **State Treasury** (Magyar
Államkincstár; *map p. 428, C2*), Ödön Lechner's famous former Post Office Savings
Bank (1900–1), decorated in vivid yellow, green and white pyrogranite Zsolnay
encrustations, the façade one of his 'Turkish carpet' designs, the roof like a snakepit
of writhing sinuous forms. From the street, the wealth of decoration is almost

impossible to see and appreciate and seems almost gratuitous (but Lechner was famous for pointing out that birds have eyes too). Note the bees crawling up the piers to pyrogranite beehives at roof level, a symbol of productivity and provident saving. The building housed the Post Office Savings Bank until 1924 and has been the State Treasury since 2004. It is not open to the public but you can go into the entranceway and foyer and admire some of the details, including glass panels by Miksa Róth.

On the other side of the road at no. 13 is one of the series of covered market halls built in the 1890s (*see p. 264*). As the **Belvárosi Piac** it is still in use (*open daily except Sun from 6.30am*) and there are a number of lunch spots on the upper floor.

A detour along Nagysándor József utca (named after one of the Hungarian generals executed in 1849) takes you to Vadász utca, where at no. 29 (turn left and walk past the back of the market) is the so-called **Glass House** (Üveg-ház; Lajos Kozma, 1934). This former shop and showroom of a manufacturer of plate glass became a safe house under Swiss Embassy protection in the last months of 1944: over 3,000 Jews were crammed into the building, where members of the Zionist underground also worked producing false papers. A plaque commemorates Carl Lutz (*see p. 215*) and there is a memorial room which can be visited (*open daily 1–4; ring the bell*).

THE BOTTOM OF THE SQUARE

The south end of Szabadság tér remains unenclosed by buildings. Although a number of monumental designs were submitted in the 1930s, none ever came to fruition and instead, today, there is an interactive fountain here, where children like to play in hot weather. The public space is cluttered, though, by a **controversial monument** (2014) and by the exhibitions of dissent that it has engendered. The ensemble shows the Angel Gabriel being descended on by an eagle with fearsome talons, symbolising the Nazi takeover of Hungary on 19th March 1944. Even before the monument was completed, it became a focus of protest and it was erected stealthily, before first light. Officially it commemorates the victims of Nazi persecution but this has not reconciled its opponents to it: there are objections that it falsifies history by trying to suggest that all the blame should be laid at the feet of the German invaders and that Hungary bears no responsibility. The protest is still ongoing: memorial stones and pebbles, photographs and hand-written notices draw public attention to the debate, so that this has in fact become a sort of ever-changing installation rather than a static monument.

In front of the contested memorial, to the left in a patch of lawn, is the **'Virulj' fountain** (Ede Telcs, 1930). In the early days of Pest's development, Szabadság tér was little more than a sandy marsh. Count István Széchenyi drew up plans to fill it with trees and the relief on the fountain shows his wife, Crescence Seilern, planting a sapling. The exhortation *Virulj!* means 'Flourish!'

The building behind the fountain (1937, István Nyíri and László Lauber; *see illustration on p. 149*) is adorned with a large **relief of grape harvesters** (Ferenc Medgyessy, 1940). On the other side of Arany János utca is the **Homecoming Church** (Hazatérés temploma), built for a Calvinist congregation in 1939 in the contemporary Rationalist style (it looks more like a block of flats or offices than a place of worship). The congregation was originally formed of ethnic Hungarians from the ex-Crown Lands who came to Budapest after the Treaty of Trianon apportioned their homelands to other countries. The name 'Homecoming Church' was given to it after the First Vienna Award of 1938, when Hungary was given back some of its former territory in Slovakia and the Ukraine. The church was erected soon afterwards. Today it retains an unabashedly irredentist flavour and a bust of Horthy has been erected in the entranceway.

HERCEGPRÍMÁS UTCA

Hercegprímás utca, 'Prince Primate Street', takes its name from the princely title traditionally borne by the Archbishops of Esztergom during the days of the Dual Monarchy. It links Szabadság tér with Szent István tér and the great basilica of St Stephen, but it is worth strolling slowly along it, taking time to admire some of its buildings. The house on the corner of Arany János utca on the right (**Arany János u. 25**), now government offices, was built for the Salgótarján coal mining company (Alfréd Wellisch, 1905–7). Its façade has reliefs of crossed hammers and toiling miners. Turn left down Arany János utca to see, at no. 32, the **Goldberger house** (Dávid and Zsigmond Jónás, 1912), the former shop and offices of the Óbuda-based textile concern (*see pp. 104–5*), with the family name still emblazoned on the façade. Another old shopfront nearby is that of the former imported goods merchant Sándor Schmidl at **Hercegprímás u. 11** (Béla Lajta, 1905/6). At Hercegprímás u. 9, on the corner of Szent István tér (left), is the neo-Venetian **Pichler-ház** (Ferenc Wieser, 1855–7). Around the corner at **Szent István tér 15** is the Zsolnay-tile-clad storefront of the textile wholesaler Jónás Hecht (also Béla Lajta, 1907). The fish motifs are a play on the proprietor's name: Hecht means 'pike'. At the time of writing, the old shopfront was in poor condition.

SZENT ISTVÁN TÉR

Szent István tér, St Stephen's Square (*map p. 428, C2*), is a wide, pedestrianised space, always crowded with groups of tourists (often on segways or in cycle-rickshaws) and filled with cafés, whose seating spills outside in fine weather. It is the scene of frequent open-air fairs and markets, including a popular Christmas market in December, when a spectacular light show plays on the façade of the mighty basilica from which the square takes its name.

ST STEPHEN'S BASILICA

Open Mon–Sat 9–7, Sun 7.45–7. Free. From the porch there are stairs and a lift (expect long queues in high season) to the panoramic terrace, from which there are excellent views. The Chapel of the Holy Right Hand has shorter opening hours; see p. 159.

The basilica of St Stephen (Szent István Bazilika) is the largest and tallest church in Budapest, covering an area of over 4000m square and with a dome that soars to 96m, the same height as the dome of Parliament. It was planned originally as the

ST STEPHEN'S BASILICA

parish church of Lipótváros and was to be dedicated to St Leopold, an Austrian saint of the 10th–11th century who gave up a career as military governor to pursue a life of piety and charity within the cloistered walls of Klosterneuburg monastery, which he founded. Construction of the Lipótváros church began in 1851, to a Neoclassical design by József Hild. Hild died in 1867 and the following year, the dome, as yet unfinished, collapsed. The project passed to Miklós Ybl, who modified the plans and began work again in 1875. The present neo-Renaissance structure is his design. When Ybl died in 1891, a third architect, József Kauser, was brought in to complete the interior. The church was finally consecrated in 1905 and dedicated not to the Austrian Leopold but to the Magyar Stephen (István; *see below*), thus firmly establishing the Hungarian pantheon of saints within the universal Catholic tradition. The final stone was lowered into place in 1906, at a ceremony attended by Franz Joseph. Mindful of the disaster of 1868, the emperor is said to have spent much of the time looking nervously at the ceiling. In 1931 Pope Pius XI granted the church the title of Basilica Minor. It hosted a Eucharistic Congress in 1938, the 900th anniversary of St Stephen's death. Since 1993, the basilica has been co-cathedral of the archdiocese of Budapest-Esztergom, a status conferred on it by Pope John Paul II.

The dome has been subject to more vicissitudes since its first collapse in 1868. It caught fire during repair work following damage in WWII, and in 1982 part of it was blown down in a storm. A long programme of restoration of the entire fabric of the basilica was completed in 2003.

Exterior of the basilica

The basilica is approached up a wide flight of steps at the bottom of which, on either side, are fountains dedicated to St Imre, Stephen's son, and the Blessed Gisela, his wife. The design is eclectic, but clearly inspired by Italian prototypes. A tall Palladian-Serlian porch with giant Corinthian pilasters bears a tympanum in which is a high relief of the Virgin, patroness of Hungary, surrounded by Hungarian saints. At the base of the lateral bell-towers are niches with statues of the Doctors of the Church, SS Ambrose, Gregory, Jerome and Augustine. All these sculptures, as well as the Evangelists around the dome and the Apostles on the top of the balustrade around the exterior of the apse, are by Leó Fessler. Under the windows immediately left and right of the porch are low reliefs commemorating the 1938 Eucharistic Congress and showing the Coronation of King Stephen. Inside the porch, the lunette is filled with a mosaic of *Christ in Majesty* by Mór Than. Above the main doors is a tondo filled with a stern-faced relief of King Stephen (Károly Senyei) wearing his crown and holding both orb and sceptre.

STEPHEN I, KING AND SAINT

Stephen (István) was born c. 975, son of Prince Géza of the House of Árpád and Sarolt, his wife. The young Stephen, born a pagan and given the name Vajk, later received Christian baptism but we do not know when. In 995 or 996 he married Gisela, daughter of Henry of Bavaria. Stephen is credited with founding the Hungarian state, with dismantling the Magyar tribal system and with introducing the feudal model. To do this, he had first to prove his primacy among the Magyars and to defeat his rival, Koppány, also of the House of Árpád and some years Stephen's senior. According to Magyar rules of seniority and inheritance, Koppány was Géza's natural successor, entitled to claim Géza's widow as a wife. Stephen defeated Koppány in battle in 997, had his body quartered and the quarters sent to the four corners of the realm. From then on, Stephen was the Magyars' undisputed leader. He introduced the European system of descent within the ruling family, by right of primogeniture rather than seniority. He also set about reorganising his realm and Christianising his people. He contracted useful political alliances, marrying his sister to the Doge of Venice and his son Imre to a Byzantine princess. He himself was crowned King of Hungary, according to tradition with a crown sent by Pope Sylvester II in 1000.

The first three decades of Stephen's reign brought peace and prosperity. He founded numerous monasteries and churches and built a string of defensive fortresses. His realm became precarious after the death of his brother-in-law, the Holy Roman Emperor Henry II, in 1024. The new emperor, Conrad II, attacked Hungary in 1030 and Stephen was only able to prevail by applying scorched earth tactics. He died in 1038, predeceased by his son and leaving an uncertain succession. He was canonised in 1083.

ST STEPHEN'S BASILICA
St Theresa of Lisieux (1949) by Béni Ferenczy.

Interior of the basilica

The interior of St Stephen's basilica is opulent and shimmering, bathed in dappled coloured light from the stained-glass windows and suffused with a rosy glow from the copious use of Tardos marble. The ceilings are resplendent with mosaics and with coffers decorated with gilded rosettes. The side chapels hold paintings by noted artists of the day and against the columns are statues by well-known sculptors. All are labelled *in situ* as well as on the plan below. The structure of the church is not basilican: the nave and transepts form a Greek cross, pierced by narrow aisles, and with an apsidal sanctuary to the east. The name of the church refers rather to its ecclesiastical status as Basilica Minor.

The most famous painting is in the south aisle: Gyula Benczúr's ***King Stephen Places his Realm under the Virgin's Protection*** (4). King Stephen was left without a successor when his son Imre was killed in a hunting accident in 1031. According to

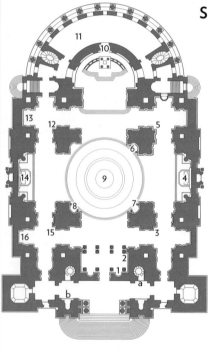

ST STEPHEN'S BASILICA

1. Bust of Cardinal Mindszenty by Tibor Rieger
2. *St Theresa of Lisieux* by Béni Ferenczy
3. *The Virgin* by Pál Pátzay
4. Gyula Benczur's *King Stephen Places his Realm under the Virgin's Protection*, flanked by statues of *St Imre* and *St Margaret* by Béla Ohmann
5. *St Anthony of Padua* by József Damkó
6. *St Ladislas* by János Fadrusz
7. *St Gellért* by Alajos Stróbl
8. *St Elizabeth of Hungary* by Károly Senyei
9. Dome (*described opposite*)
10. Apse (*described opposite*)
11. Chapel of the Holy Right Hand
12. *The Sacred Heart* by József Damkó
13. *St Joseph Teaching the Young Christ to Read* (flanked by SS Peter and Paul) by Árpád Feszty
14. Altarpiece of the *Crucifixion*, flanked by statues of *St Louis* and *St Francis* by Alajos Stróbl
15. *St Joseph* by Pál Pátzay
16. Altarpiece of *St Adalbert* by Ignác Roskovics. Beneath it is a reliquary bust of the Blessed Charles IV containing one of his ribs (2012)

a   Stairs to panoramic terrace
b   Lift to panoramic terrace

tradition, he elected to offer his kingdom to the Virgin Mary rather than to the Pope or Holy Roman Emperor. The painting shows him symbolically laying his crown before the Madonna, Hungary's protectress and patron saint.

The **dome (9)** is magnificent, clad in mosaic, with the Evangelists in the pendentives. Under them are statues of three Hungarian saints: Gellért, Elizabeth (shown giving bread and milk to a poor boy) and Ladislas. Under St Matthew is the pulpit. The mosaic of *God the Father* in the dome is to a design by Károly Lotz. In the crypt beneath the dome is the **tomb of Ferenc Puskás** (d. 2006), Hungary's most celebrated football player. He played for Real Madrid after defecting from Hungary in 1956.

In the **apse (10)**, above a splendidly illuminated statue of St Stephen by Alajos Stróbl, are mosaics by Salviati & Jesurum depicting the *Allegory of the Holy Mass*, based on designs by Gyula Benczúr.

A curiously secular note is struck by the figures bearing thick swags, high up in the aisles at either end of both transepts. In the south aisle they are seen from the front and are discreetly draped. In the north aisle they are seen from behind, entirely nude.

The Chapel of the Holy Right Hand

Behind the high altar is the chapel housing Hungary's most sacred relic, the mummified right hand of St Stephen (*entrance from the top of the north aisle, along a corridor past a lovely Della Robbian lavabo; chapel open Mon–Sat April–Sept 9–4.30/5, Oct–March 10–4; coin-operated light*). The hand has become desiccated in such a way that it is clenched into a fist. This is not the only surviving relic of St Stephen. The hand and part of his skull were placed for safekeeping in the care of the Dominicans in Dubrovnik, perhaps by Louis the Great. The hand came to Budapest during the reign of Maria Theresa, who instituted the celebration of St Stephen's Day on 20th August and built a chapel to house the relic in the royal palace on Castle Hill. During the Second World War it was hidden in a cave near Salzburg and was repatriated to Hungary by a US military mission in time for the St Stephen's Day celebration of 1945. For most of the Communist era it was locked away in a safe, until 1987, when this chapel was consecrated and it was placed here on public view. It is housed in a silver-gilt coffer borne on dragon-shaped feet. Every year on 20th August it is ceremonially paraded around the city. The reliquary of St Stephen's skull is still in Dubrovnik.

NEOCLASSICAL LIPÓTVÁROS

Hild tér (*map p. 428, C3*) is a good place to begin a tour of the part of Leopold Town that was once famous for its homogenous, graceful and unostentatious Neoclassical buildings. The small square has a fountain with benches beside it, where you can sit and contemplate two buildings in front of you (and one behind): excellent, restrained examples of the style (there are more around the corner in **Mérleg utca**). It was János Hild who first drew up plans for the development of this part of Pest but it was Hild's son József who really placed his stamp on the area, creating streets and squares that were lined with well-proportioned façades featuring regular bays, generous window apertures, handsome doorways and sometimes colonnaded porches with tympana above them.

The parallel streets here, Sas utca, **Október 6. utca** and Nádor utca, are always busy with locals and tourists, and are filled with cafés, restaurants and bars. At Október 6. u. 11 is **Bestsellers**, an excellent English-language bookshop, in business here since 1992. The name of the street commemorates the fateful date in 1849 when 13 Hungarian generals of the anti-Habsburg War of Independence were executed in Arad, present-day Romania, after the struggle finally came to its inglorious end. Further up the street, at **no. 19** (a Neoclassical building by József Hild), you can peep through a small window in the main door to see, in a niche at the back of the courtyard, a statue of a woman with a water jar (Lőrinc Dunaiszky, early 19th century). The statue, sometimes known as Abigail, is also referred to as the 'Suicide statue': legend has it that a gentleman once shot himself for love of the beauty who had served as the sculptor's model.

NÁDOR UTCA

Nádor utca is particularly rich in buildings of architectural interest. **No. 6**, with its corner tower of windows, is an important precursor of Modernism (Béla Málnai et al, 1911–12). The Neoclassical building across the street at **no. 5** (József Hild, 1839) is the former Tigris (Tiger) Hotel: note the sculpted tiger couchant, above the main doorway. The Tigris restaurant, around the corner in Mérleg utca, pays tribute to the old hotel. Other surviving Neoclassical buildings are Mihály Pollack's **no. 7** (1821) and József Hild's **no. 12** (1844).

At **no. 10**, the main façade of which overlooks Zrínyi utca, is the **Duna Palota** (Vilmos Freund, 1897), the former Lipótváros Casino, favourite club of Budapest's Jewish elite. In 1941 it had 1,800 members, almost two thirds of whom perished in the Holocaust. Leó Goldberger (*see p. 105*) was club chairman in the 1930s. Today it is a cultural centre and its interior is open to the public so you can go in and admire its (somewhat shabby) neo-Baroque lines.

The building diagonally opposite, at **Nádor u. 9**, is a former palace of the Festetics family (Mihály Pollack, 1827), now part of the campus of the **Central European University (CEU)**, a postgraduate institution founded by the financier George Soros in 1991. For the first two years the University was based in Prague. It moved to Budapest in 1993. In 2017 it sprang to prominence in the news when the Hungarian government passed amendments to its higher education laws that threatened the university's freedom to operate. The blue-and-white 'I stand with CEU' hashtag became a common sight. The CEU campus extends for some way up Nádor utca: the building at **no. 11** (Béla Jánszky and Tibor Szivessy, 1915) has three strange reliefs by Ödön Moiret on the theme of human conflict. In 2016 the CEU completely redeveloped the buildings at **no. 13–15**. The Irish architects, Sheila O'Donnell and John Tuomey, in partnership with M-Teampannon, retained some of the original elements but essentially created an entirely modern addition to the campus

Across the street at **no. 16** is a large, neo-Renaissance bank building with a striking and highly decorated façade (Albert Kálmán Kőrössy and Géza Kiss, 1912). It was built as a bank and still operates as such today, which means you can go inside to see the richly decorated banking hall with its fine metalwork, stained glass and opulent columns.

The red and yellow building at **no. 19** (József Hild, 1861) is home to the Terv bistro. Terv means 'Plan'; the bistro (formerly the Terv Presszó café) has been in business here for many years (*see p. 169*).

SZÉCHENYI TÉR

Busy Széchenyi tér (*map p. 428, C2–C3*), named after Hungary's great reformer István Széchenyi (*see p. 164*), is in practice a giant roundabout, always filled with cars and as a result somewhat difficult to enjoy and appreciate (there is a distinct lack of pedestrian crossings). There is a bus stop here, and the departure point for the River Ride amphibious bus. There is also a taxi rank (the drivers who wait here are not always honest; *for information on taxis, see p. 344*). Nevertheless, it is surrounded by fine and important buildings and filled with monuments. After his coronation in 1867, King Franz Joseph rode down from the Matthias Church on Castle Hill, proclaimed his coronation oath in front of the Inner City Parish Church and then galloped to the top of a small mound here on Széchenyi tér, which had been built of earth brought from each of the counties of Hungary. From the top of this knoll he performed the *kardvágás*, the solemn flourishing of Hungary's ceremonial sword to north, east, west and south while promising to protect Hungary from her enemies, whencesoever they may come.

The square was originally used as a place for docking and unloading goods and was surrounded by elegant Neoclassical buildings, each of them designed by József Hild. Today, largely as a result of war damage, the ensemble of buildings is much more jumbled.

BUILDINGS ON SZÉCHENYI TÉR

Facing the south end of Széchenyi tér (on the site of Hild's Lloyd Palace, built for the Hungarian Trade Association) is the **Sofitel building** (Lajos Zalavári, 1981). Moving anti-clockwise from there, the large building on the corner of József Attila utca is the **Interior Ministry** (Zsigmond Quittner and Ignác Alpár, 1907), occupying the former headquarters of the Pest Hungarian Commercial Bank, itself built on the site of Hild's popular public bath house, the Diana Bad. At the time of writing it appeared that the building would once again change hands as there were plans to move the ministry to Castle Hill. The next block, between Mérleg and Zrínyi streets, is filled by the Art Nouveau Gresham Palace, now the **Four Seasons Hotel**. It was completed in 1907 to the plans of Zsigmond Quittner and the Vágó brothers, to house the overseas headquarters of the London Gresham Life Assurance Company. At the top of the façade is a relief of Sir Thomas Gresham (d. 1579), merchant and financier and founder of the Royal Exchange in London, after whom the life assurance company was named. When built, the Gresham Palace was designed with the latest technology available. The luxury apartments above the offices were equipped with a modern dust extraction system and a form of central heating. Some of the original glory can still be sensed in the hotel lobby, though the original asphalt floor (a daring and modern material at the time) has now been replaced with mosaic. The beautiful wrought-iron gates at the two side entrances have been preserved.

The office building that occupies the next block, with restaurants on the ground floor, occupies the site of Hild's Europa Hotel, demolished in 1949. The only one of Hild's buildings to survive stands just off the square at **Akadémia u. 3**, a building of 1836 that is now occupied by the Ministry of Human Capacities. Its upper part consists of an octastyle pseudo-temple front, with engaged columns and pilasters. The first-floor balcony is supported on stucco consoles. The birthplace of Nobel prizewinning chemist György Hevesy, it overlooks the side of the Hungarian Academy of Sciences building, where a **relief by Barnabás Holló** (1891) depicts the scene at the Diet of Pressburg in 1825 when Count István Széchenyi pledged a year's income from his estates for the founding of a Hungarian association for the advancement of learning.

GYÖRGY HEVESY

György Hevesy, who was to win the Nobel Prize for chemistry in 1943, was born in the house at Akadémia u. 3 in 1885, the son of a well-to-do family of Jewish origin. Hevesy studied first in Budapest and then Freiburg. Much of his career was spent in Denmark, at the Institute of Theoretical Physics founded by Niels Bohr, whom Hevesy had met in Manchester, while working for Rutherford. When Denmark was occupied by Nazi Germany in 1940, Hevesy's chemical knowledge meant that he was able to devise a method for saving the gold Nobel medals of two colleagues from looting by the Nazis. Hevesy dissolved them in aqua regia, a corrosive mixture of two acids, nitric and hydrochloric. Raiders of the laboratory would be unlikely to see any value in two jars of liquid. They did not. When the war ended, Hevesy was able to precipitate the gold back out of the acid solution and have the medals remade. Hevesy died in 1966 and was buried first at Freiburg and then, in 2001, in Kerepesi Cemetery.

THE HUNGARIAN ACADEMY OF SCIENCES AND ITS BUILDING

On 3rd November 1825, Count István Széchenyi astounded his fellow deputies at the Diet of Pressburg (modern Bratislava) with the announcement that he would give an entire year's income to the founding of a learned society for the advancement of Hungarian art, science, language and literature. This was the era of Hungary's Great Reform and the Learned Society (today the Academy of Sciences, Magyar Tudományos Akadémia or MTA) was seen as a national project to revitalise the intellectual life of the country and give it a specifically Hungarian as opposed to a German character.

In the early decades of its existence the society had no permanent home. It was only in 1859 that a committee was established to organise the construction of a new building. A closed tender was offered to three architects: Imre Henszlmann, an Academy associate; Heinrich Ferstel, designer of the Votivkirche in Vienna; and Miklós Ybl, who had designed a number of mansions for the Hungarian nobility. Henszlmann insisted that all the designs should be neo-Gothic. Ybl found himself unable to comply and withdrew his submission. Another architect then entered the fray, Antal Szkalnitzky,

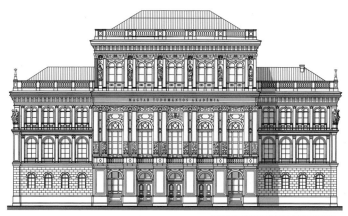

HUNGARIAN ACADEMY OF SCIENCES

who submitted a largely Neoclassical design on the grounds that it would harmonise better with the existing buildings around the square. However, the committee found itself dissatisfied with all the proposals and invited further contributions from Leo von Klenze of Munich and Friedrich August Stüler, the architect of the Neues Museum in Berlin and the Museum of Fine Arts in Stockholm.

In the end Stüler's neo-Renaissance design was accepted, a decision which caused great public controversy. Some were dismayed that a non-Hungarian architect had been chosen; others objected that the neo-Renaissance style reflected nothing of the Hungarian spirit. Construction went ahead nevertheless, and the new building was formally inaugurated in 1865. On the main façade are statues representing the original six departments of the Hungarian Learned Society: law, science, mathematics, philosophy, philology and history. Statues of noted scientists and philosophers (named) adorn the two lateral façades.

STATUES IN THE CENTRE OF SZÉCHENYI TÉR

In front of the Academy of Sciences building, close to the road, are bronze busts by Gyula Jankovits of the philologist **Gábor Szarvas** (a lissom nymph reaches up to offer him a laurel branch) and the historian and man of letters **Ferenc Salamon**. In the grassy island in the centre of the square is a colossal **statue of Széchenyi** (József Engel, 1880). Széchenyi stands at the top, with below him seated gods and goddesses symbolising the progress he bequeathed to his country in the fields of learning (Minerva); waterways and shipping (Neptune); agriculture (Ceres) and industry and railways (Vulcan). Unfortunately Széchenyi did not live to see the completion of his Academy of Sciences building, though he had earlier taken lodgings in one of the hotels on the square and would have been able to watch the progress of work on the Chain Bridge.

The companion colossal statue at the other end of the square (Adolf Huszár and Albert Schickedanz, 1887) is of **Ferenc Deák**, architect of the 1867 Compromise with Austria (*see pp. 16 and 250*). His companion figures represent Justice, Education,

Patriotism and Unity. Between the two statues, propped up on stilts, is an ancient acacia tree, over 200 years old.

THE GREATEST HUNGARIAN

Count István Széchenyi (1791–1860) was instrumental in conceiving and seeing through some of the most important projects of the Reform Period of 1825–48. As becomes clear from his famous diary, he made it his life's aim to bring the country he loved and devotedly served into the industrial, commercial, forward-looking 19th-century. Széchenyi visited Britain more than once and introduced many of the advances that he encountered there to Hungary. Gas lighting and water closets were two examples (the first gas lamp was tested in 1816; he installed a flushing commode in his manor house at Nagycenk in 1840). Horse racing was another: Széchenyi set up the country's first stud and encouraged English trainers and jockeys to move to Hungary. On a larger and more significant scale, in terms of the nation's infrastructure, he brought engineers and shipping experts to help extend the Danube's navigation potential. His major projects included the building of the Chain Bridge, the first permanent crossing over the river in Budapest; the founding of the Academy of Sciences; and the establishment of a modern financial and banking system. His instinct for how national prosperity should be gauged involved a courteous nod to the artisan classes: 'A country can only be said to be going well if the tailor, the soap-maker and the patissier etc. are firmly convinced that the national happiness depends on their skill and acumen.'

Széchenyi is fêted today as *a legnagyobb Magyar*, 'the greatest Hungarian' (an epithet bestowed on him by Lajos Kossuth). The admiration was not entirely mutual: although Széchenyi joined the revolutionary government of 1848, he remained a monarchist and opposed Kossuth's call for the overthrow of the Habsburgs. The events of the catastrophic War of Independence turned his wits. Blaming himself for his country's predicament, he ended up in an asylum at Döbling (now a northern suburb of Vienna). In April 1860 he took his own life. His funeral deeply moved the whole country. He is buried in the family vault at Nagycenk, western Hungary.

THE CHAIN BRIDGE

The Chain Bridge (Lánchíd; *map p. 428, B3–C3*), built in 1839–49, was the first permanent river crossing linking Buda and Pest across the Danube. Today its outline is one of the most commonly used symbols of Budapest.

The idea of a permanent bridge was strongly promoted by Hungary's great 19th-century reformer, Count István Széchenyi (*see above*). In the winter of 1820, in a hurry to reach Vienna for his father's funeral, he had waited for over a week to cross the river. As he notes in his diary, he arrived in Pest on 29th December after a tiring journey from Transylvania, his feet frozen inside too-tight boots, to find the Danube impassable because of ice. It was not until January 5th that he managed to have his carriage taken across on a grain wagon. The day before he had confided to his journal that, 'I would give a year's income to build a bridge between Buda and Pest, even if I

THE CHAIN BRIDGE
Viewed looking downstream from Margaret Bridge.

myself never derive a single groat of profit from it. To have served my country would be recompense enough.' In 1836 a bill was passed allowing for the building of the bridge and a national committee was set up to supervise the procedure, chaired by the Palatine Joseph. Széchenyi, who was also a member of the committee, approached a number of financiers with a view to collecting the necessary funds. The wealthy Greek-Austrian merchant and banker Georgios Sinas (György Sina) became head of the Chain Bridge joint-stock company in 1837 and he, together with Solomon Rothschild and Samuel Wodianer, purchased most of the shares. Their names are inscribed on one of the piers on the bridge's west side. The English engineer William Tierney Clark was commissioned to design the bridge and the Scotsman Adam Clark (no relation) came to Hungary to supervise its construction. The similarity to London's first Hammersmith Bridge and to the bridge over the Thames at Marlow is not coincidental: Tierney Clark designed those too.

The building of the bridge aroused much public interest and was seen as a symbol of Hungary's economic and social progress. However, the fact that many of the construction materials were brought from Britain generated some local resentment and there was even a public demonstration with demands for the dismissal of foreign workers employed on the project.

In May 1949, during the War of Independence and before the bridge was finally completed, the Austrians planned to blow it up. Adam Clark thwarted their plans by having the chain lockers flooded. When it finally opened, on 20th November 1849, it was one of the largest suspension bridges in the world. But the opening was a sober affair. By this time Hungary's rebellion against Austria had ended in defeat, the prime minister Lajos Batthyány had been executed and poor Széchenyi, suffering from a nervous breakdown, had been taken to an asylum in Vienna. The bridge was formally opened by the 'Austrian butcher', Julius Jacob von Haynau, the general who had upheld Batthyány's death sentence.

Up until the end of the First World War, a toll was payable to cross the bridge. Controversially, the charge was levied on all, regardless of rank, thus putting an end to noble privileges (nobles had previously been exempt from such taxes). The young Englishwoman Mary Elizabeth Stevens, governess in the household of Count Gyula Andrássy in Buda in the 1860s, remarked in a letter that, 'I am afraid I shall spend all my revenue crossing the bridge as it is two kreutzers each way!'

The bridge was reconstructed during WWI, since when it has officially been called the Széchenyi Chain Bridge. Destroyed by the Germans in January 1945, during the siege of Budapest, it was reconstructed and reopened in November 1949, the centenary of its original inauguration.

Urban legends have grown up around the lion statues at either end of the bridge (János Marschalkó, 1852). It was pointed out that they have no tongues, for the shame of which the sculptor is supposed to have drowned himself in the river. Another version of the story claims he made a bet that when real lions open their mouths, their tongues sit compactly below the teeth and cannot readily be seen. He even took a party of people to a travelling circus to prove it—and won.

ERZSÉBET TÉR & VÖRÖSMARTY TÉR

South of the busy József Attila utca is **Erzsébet tér** (*map p. 428, C3*), a wide public area shaded by trees. After WWII it saw service as a bus terminus and the **station building** (István Nyíri, 1949) is now a listed structure, with cafés on the ground floor and upper level. If you decide to have a drink here, an appropriate choice would be Unicum (*see p. 268*), since Joseph Zwack set up his first distillery in a building on this square in 1840. Plans to build a new National Theatre on the site of that building came to nothing after protests in the 1990s. The foundations had been dug and became known as the 'National Ditch'; an events space, bar and nightclub has now found a home in it. On the other side of the square, in 2013, a mobile ferris wheel was erected as a temporary attraction in conjunction with the Sziget Festival. It proved popular and at the time of writing the **'Budapest Eye'** was firmly in place, with a lease to remain until 2020. The fountain in the centre of Erzsébet tér is a reconstruction of the **Danube Fountain** that stood in Kálvin tér until its destruction in WWII (one original statue still survives; *see p. 262*). Erzsébet tér is also home to a playground, a dog run, skateboard park, and to another monument, ***Folk Song*** (*Népdal*), a sculpture group of a shepherd piping to his sheep (János Horvay, 1929), originally intended for the tomb of the singer Lujza Blaha. It takes as its inspiration a poem by Sándor Petőfi: 'My flute, my little weeping willow twig, cut from the branch of a graveyard tree; is it any wonder your note is so plaintive?'

Two large hotels close the south side of Erzsébet tér, the Kempinski (József Finta, 1992) and the **Ritz-Carlton**. The latter occupies the former Adria insurance company building of 1918, which in 1949–50 became the headquarters of the Budapest police. A tiny plaque facing Deák tér commemorates the founding of the revolutionary committee here in October 1956. The sculptures on the façades are modern copies of the originals, by Miklós Ligeti and Ede Telcs, representing the different branches of insurance. The figure of St Florian facing Erzsébet tér (corner of Miatyánk utca) symbolises insurance against fire, for example, while Atropos cutting the thread (just round the corner facing Miatyánk utca) symbolises life insurance and the man bandaging his arm stands for accident insurance.

VÖRÖSMARTY TÉR

This wide pedestrian space (*map p. 428, C3*) stands at the southern extremity of Lipótváros. It hosts a busy Christmas market in December and the Book Week in June but is known most of all for being home to the **Gerbeaud *pâtisserie***. Founded by Henrik Kugler on József nádor tér, it moved here in the 1880s. When Kugler retired his left his business to the Swiss-born Emile Gerbeaud, whom he had met in Paris. Gerbeaud introduced many new confections to Hungary. 'How I'd love to be rich,' muses Attila József in one of his most famous poems, 'Just for once to eat roast goose, to go around in fancy clothes and splurge five forints on a *kugler*.' Five forints was a lot of money in those days (c. 1916). A *kugler*, also known as a *mignon*, is a small cake covered in an icing of coloured sugar or melted chocolate, popularised by Henrik Kugler. You can get them in many Hungarian cake shops but alas, at the time of writing, not at Gerbeaud, which had moved into macaroons. Their signature delicacy is the *Gerbeaud szelet* (Gerbeau Slice), a layered rectangle of ground walnuts and apricot jam topped with chocolate.

THE GERBEAUD: PLACE OF CODED ASSIGNATIONS

An urban legend clings to the Gerbeaud *patisserie*. In the 19th century it was a fashionable resort, patronised by women of blue blood and their marriageable daughters, whom they hoped to thrust before the eye of eligible young men. In the 20th century, the predation is said to have been the other way round. Wealthy elderly ladies knew that if a young man audibly ordered a certain cake accompanied by a glass of soda water, then he was signalling his availability. Versions differ as to whether the code words were cake and soda or coffee with a certain number of sugar lumps, or whether it depended how you laid down your fork. There is even a school of thought that places the intrigue not in the Gerbeaud but in the Anna Café on Váci utca, on the other side of Vörösmarty tér. But still the basic idea remains: that there was a code and that the elderly ladies and their would-be escorts knew it. If any of this was ever true, it is now the stuff of the past. Like all such very famous places (the Sacher in Vienna, Florian in Venice), the Gerbeaud today is mainly popular with tourists and struggles to retain a local clientèle. Its high prices at any rate have banished the nymphomaniac dames and their gigolos (if they ever existed) to the further recesses of the city.

The Gerbeaud building is a Neoclassical structure by József Hild overlaid with an Art Nouveau carapace by Sándor Fellner (1912). Today the cake shop and café occupies the entire ground floor and the Michelin-starred Onyx restaurant is around the corner.

Vörösmarty tér takes its name from the poet Mihály Vörösmarty, whose statue (Ede Kallós and Ede Telcs, 1908) stands in the centre of the square. Vörösmarty's great poem, the *Szózat*, written in 1836 and set to music in 1843, is something of a second national anthem in Hungary, an appeal to undaunted patriotism. Beneath the Carrara marble **seated statue of Vörösmarty**, a limestone sculpture group shows people of all ages and stations singing the patriotic song. Its first line is carved beneath them: 'Be unyieldingly true to your country, O Magyar'. To protect the sculptures from frost, the monument is wrapped tightly in plastic in winter.

The buildings around the square have, over the years, been subject to fire and war and other torments, and today form a slightly heterogeneous ensemble. To the north, on the Dorottya utca and Vigadó utca corner, is the **former Futura building** (1938), with, over the entrance, Béla Ohmann's angel-borne coat of arms of the grain-trading company that first occupied it. On the east side, at no. 4, is the **Medimpex building**, formerly the town house of the textile magnate Leó Goldberger (*see p. 105*). The putti between the first-floor windows are all busily engaged in one or another stage of cloth-making. On the southeast corner is the **former Luxus department store** (1911), by Giergl and Korb, the architects of the Liszt Academy. It was designed as a mixed-purpose building, with retail space at street level and luxury apartments at the top. Opposite it, on a site once occupied by the German Theatre, is a modern version of a mixed retail and residential block, clad in glass panels (György Fazakas and Jean-Paul Viguier, 2007).

To the southwest, on the corner of Váci utca and Deák utca, is Ignác Alpár's monumental **former Pesti Hazai Első Takarékpénztár** (Savings Bank), Hungary's first national financial institution, founded in 1839. Alpár considered the building (1911–15) to be his masterpiece. At the time of writing, it was occupied by Budapest's Hard Rock Café. On the corner facing Váci utca and Türr István utca is a plaque commemorating the **Vác Gate**, the northern gate of medieval Pest, which stood here until 1789. Its site marks the boundary of Lipótváros and the Belváros, the inner city.

EATING AND DRINKING IN LIPÓTVÁROS

RESTAURANTS

fff **Borkonyha**. Michelin-starred restaurant that manages to retain a friendly, informal feel. Excellent food, lively atmosphere. Essential to book. Closed Sun. *Sas u. 3. T: +36 1 266 0835, borkonyha.hu. Map p. 428, C3.*

fff **Costes Downtown**. Michelin-starred restaurant, city centre offshoot of the original Costes in District IX. Essential to book. *Vigyázó Ferenc u. 5. T: +36 1 920 1015, costesdowntown.hu. Map p. 428, C2.*

fff **Onyx**. Michelin-starred restaurant, part of the Gerbeaud mini-empire. *Vörösmarty tér 7–8. T: +36 30 508 0622, onyxrestaurant.hu. Map p. 428, C3.*

fff **Baraka**. Gourmet French-Asian restaurant lovingly run by husband-and-wife team David and Leora Seboek. Some unusual and sometimes daring combinations. Dinner only. Closed Sun. *Dorrotya u.. T: +36 1 200 0817, barakarestaurant.hu. Map p. 428, C3.*

fff **Mák Bistro**. Talented young chef fronts a team serving experimental fine cuisine of a consistently excellent standard. Best to book. Closed Mon. *Vigyázó Ferenc u. 4. T: +36 30 723 9383, mak.hu. Map p. 428, C2.*

ff **Biarritz**. Restaurant of long standing, faintly French in atmosphere. Competent cuisine. Outdoor dining in fine weather. *Balassi Bálint u. 2. T: +36 1 311 413, biarritz.hu. Map p. 428, C1.*

ff **Café Kör**. Lively, popular bistro-style restaurant serving Hungarian cooking. The menu is written up on brown paper: as dishes sell out, they are crossed off. A sworn favourite with many. Closed Sun. *Sas u. 17. T: +36 1 311 0053, cafekor.net. Map p. 428, C2.*

*ff***Liberté**. Stylish-looking café-restaurant on the site of a historic coffee house. Breakfast, brunch, lunch and dinner (no dinner Sun). *Aulich u. 8. T: + 36 30 715 4635, libertebudapest. com. Map p. 428, C2.*

*ff***Elysée**. Popular café-bistro, a recreation of a well-known 1930s' coffee house, on Kossuth Lajos tér right in front of the Parliament. *Kossuth Lajos tér 13–15. T: +36 1 786 4306, elysee.hu. Map p. 428, C1.*

ff **Pomo d'Oro**. The 'Via Italia' comprises a popular *trattoria*, a delicatessen and a wine bar. Reliable Italian cuisine. *Arany János u. 9. T: +36 1 302 6473, pomodorobudapest.com. Map p. 428, C2.*

f–ff **Börze**. Bright, light café-restaurant in an attractive vaulted space on the corner of Szabadság tér, serving breakfasts, a weekday lunch menu and *à la carte* bistro meals and salads. *Nádor u. 23. T: +36 1 426 5460, borzeetterem.hu. Map p. 428, C2.*

f–ff **Kispiac**. Next to the Hold utca market. A tiny temple to meat. Good for a carnivorous lunch. Closes 10pm. *Hold u. 13. T: +36 1 269 4231. Map p. 428, C2.*

f–ff **Mazi**. Friendly Greek restaurant very close to Parliament. The name means 'together'. Mezes and moussaka. *Alkotmány u. 19. T: +36 70 203 4990. Map p. 428, C2.*

f–ff **Terv Presszó**. Deliberately retro, still with its old neon sign and serving Hungarian cuisine. *Nádor u. 19. T: +36 1 781 9625. Map p. 428, C2.*

CAFÉS, BARS AND SNACKS

DropShop on Balassi Bálint utca (*map p. 428, C1*) and **DiVino** on Szent István tér (*map p. 428, C2*) are both excellent places to taste wines by the glass. **Carpe Diem** at Zoltán u. 9 (*map p. 428, C2*) is also good.

For a quick lunch snack, there are stalls and eateries in the **Hold utca market** (*map p. 428, C2*). For coffee and cake, there is the famous **Gerbeaud** (*see p. 167*).

The **lobby bar in the Four Seasons** (*map p. 428, C2–C3*) is open until 12.30 at night, with a short selection of main courses. Very useful (and pleasant) for dinner after a concert.

District V: Belváros

The Belváros, literally Inner City, is the small area of central Pest that once stood within the embrace of the medieval city walls. The network of streets and buildings is more warren-like than the spaciously-planned Lipótváros further north. The principal sights are around the Károlyi-kert garden; Váci utca (the main street); and the lovely promenade along the Danube, at the end of which is the graceful Elisabeth Bridge and the Inner City Parish Church, with some interesting medieval and Renaissance works of art.

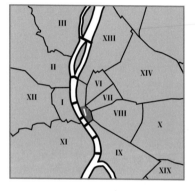

VÁCI UTCA

Váci utca (*map pp. 428–9, C3–D4*), a long, pedestrianised shopping street, runs in a more or less straight line through the entire length of the Belváros. It takes its name from the Vác Gate, the entrance in the city walls which stood at its northern end. Outside it ran the carriage road to the town of Vác on the Danube. The street has always been popular with tourists and in high season it can be very crowded. It has been many decades since any of the retail spaces were occupied by genuine shops. There is a handful of international brands, plenty of restaurants and cafés and a large number of souvenir outlets. At no. 7 is the **Anna Café**, which opened here as the Anna presszó in 1954 and was once popular with writers and actors (many of them hoping to be talent-spotted—though the original *presszó* had a reputation for broking other kinds of deal too; *see p. 167, Coded assignations*).

Architecturally, Váci utca preserves some interesting buildings. At no. 9 is **Philanthia**, a former florist (in business as such until very recently; at the time of writing it seemed to have become a year-round Christmas trinket shop), decorated in Art Nouveau style by Albert Kálmán Kőrössy in 1906. Next door at no. 11/a is Gyula Pártos and Ödön Lechner's **Thonet House** (1899), of cast iron and glazed ceramic, and next to that, at

INNER CITY PARISH CHURCH
Neoclassical funerary monument
by István Ferenczy.

KULTSÁR
ISTVÁNNAK
A'
NEMZETISÉGRE
BUZGÓ SERKENTŐNEK
KESERGŐ ÖZVEGYE

SZÜLETETT
MDCCLX
MEG HALT
MDCCCXXVIII

no. 11/b, a fine house by Sámuel Révész and József Kollár (1912). The exterior lamps are suspended from the mouths of bronze lions. On the **corner of Váci utca and Régi posta utca** (left) is another building by Kőrössy, in conjunction with Géza Kiss. At the very top, under the eaves on the corner elevation, you will see the date 1912–13 and a relief of the Hungarian Crown: the ancestor of the building on this site was the famous Magyar Korona coffee house. At **Régi posta u. 13**, sandwiched between older buildings, is a slim and elegant Modernist block by Lajos Kozma (1937) with a relief of a post coach (by Margit Kovács) over the door. Back on Váci utca, the elaborate **no. 15**, in a mélange of Art Nouveau, neo-Gothic and neo-Venetian styles (Lajos Hofhauser and Géza Majorossy, 1901), is also of interest. The ground-floor level is of carved oak.

ON & AROUND SZERVITA TÉR

Szervita tér (*map p. 428, C3*) is named after the Servite Order, whose church stands here. The **Church of St Anne** (Belvárosi Szent Anna templom; *open Mon–Sat 10–6.30, Sun 8.30–6.30; closes for around 30mins at lunch time*) was built between 1725 and 1732 (János György Paur and János Hölbling), after the Servite monks received permission to built a monastery and church here. The façade and bell-tower were altered in the 19th century. The interior preserves the opulent furnishings and overpowering atmosphere of the Austro-Hungarian ecclesiastical Baroque. The altarpiece shows the Virgin as a child with her parents, Joachim and St Anne. Of particular note are the gilded wooden carvings: the statues in the sanctuary of St Joseph, St John the Baptist and St Stephen of Hungary; and the pulpit with its carvings of the Evangelists. The church today is in the care of priests of Opus Dei. The Servite monastery was demolished under Communism (a hotel and apartments were under construction on the site at the time of writing).

The east side of the square (also a building site when this book went to press) was the site of the town house where Count László Teleki committed suicide in 1861 (*see p. 242*). Opposite, on the west side of the square, are four remarkable surviving buildings. At **no. 2** is a building (1908) clad in marble with metal studs imitating rivets in the Vienna style of Otto Wagner. The architects were the brothers Zsigmond and Dávid Jónás. Next to it, in marvellous contrast, is the **former Török Bank building** (Ármin Hegedűs and Henrik Böhm, 1906), with high windows culminating in an undulating roof pediment enclosing a tympanum filled with a Miksa Róth mosaic of the Virgin Mary, protectress of Hungary, surrounded by Hungarian heroes including Rákóczi, Széchenyi and Kossuth. At no. 5 is the **Rózsavölgyi building** (Béla Lajta, 1910–11), with stained-glass hoods above the doors and bronze plaques at pavement level embossed with folk motifs. It houses a pharmacy, the old-established Rózsavölgyi music shop (from which the building derives its name) and the Rózsavölgyi café and literary salon on the first floor. The corner building at no. 6, now a fashion store, is the **former Brammer draper's shop**. It was opened on this site in 1927 by Ödön Brammer, who became famous for his worsted fabrics. These became more sought-after than ever when Ödön Brammer's son Pál married the beauty queen Böske Simon, who was crowned Miss Europe in 1929. The Brammers were hit hard by anti-Jewish laws and by the Holocaust. Their business was nationalised under Communism, but a draper's known as Brammer continued to operate here until around the turn of the millennium, when the premises were given over to fashion retail. The shop still preserves is lovely bevelled glass windows, its mahogany wall panelling and walnut and cherry wood furnishings, including beautiful long cutting tables, all the work of the carpenter Bernát Fischer. If off-the-peg designer garments are not what you are after and you must have a yard of velvet, the Kis Brammer ('Little Brammer'), spiritual successor to the original draper's, at Bajcsy-Zsilinszky út 23 (*map p. 429, D2*), will be able to help you.

BÉLA LAJTA

Béla Leitersdorfer (he later changed his name to Lajta) was born into a Jewish family in Óbuda in 1873. He studied at the Technical University in Budapest and for a time worked in the office of the Historicist architect Alajos Hauszmann. After a lengthy study tour of Europe (Rome, Berlin and London), he returned to Budapest in 1899. His talents were wide-ranging; he experimented with all fields, painting, sculpture, interior design. However, it was as an architect that he would make his name, going on to become a pioneer of the modernist idiom. One of his most famous buildings, the Rózsavölgyi Building on Szervita tér in central Pest, with its architectonic horizontal distinction between retail, office and residential space, is considered a precursor of Modernism in Hungary. Although Lajta is often regarded as the father of Hungarian Modernism, the glazed pyrogranite decoration on the upper floors of this building and his copious use of folk motifs on many of his other works, betray his connections with Ödön Lechner (*see p. 318*). In his early period, in fact, Lajta was an explicit follower of Lechner. Indeed, the two worked together (the Schmidl mausoleum in the Kozma utca cemetery is one famous result of their collaboration; *see p. 281*). Although Lajta was later to deviate from Lechner's style, the fascination with folk motifs never left him and they can be seen crowding across many of his façades and other surfaces, worked out in various ways: rounded and sinuous at first (the former Jewish Institute for the Blind; *see p. 321*); hieratic and geometric latterly (Vas utca school; *see p. 239*). Lajta died young, in 1920. As well as his commercial and official buildings, he also left behind him a wealth of funerary architecture, much of it in the cemetery on Salgótarjáni utca. Many architects gained experience and inspiration in his office, among them Béla Löffler and Miklós Román, and also Lajos Kozma, who was to design his master's simple, classical grave monument in the Kozma utca cemetery.

VÁROSHÁZ UTCA

From the north side of the church on Szervita tér, you can look down the length of **Városház utca** (*map p. 429, D3*), past a portal with Atlas figures bearing a globe (local government offices) to a green building where the street bends (the Pest County Hall). Its Corinthian first-floor loggia is by Mátyás Zitterbarth Jr. Around the corner, wedged between two streets, Gerlóczy utca and Vitkovits Mihály utca, is the pleasant

DEÁK TÉR

Detail of the 'Flood Chalice' donated to the Lutheran church on the square by the Jewish community, who had found shelter there from the 1838 floodwaters.

Kammermayer Károly tér, named after (and with a statue of) the eponymous first mayor of the united city when Buda, Pest and Óbuda were administratively joined as a capital in 1873. The statue is a bronze copy of the aluminium original. The attractive Gerlóczy café and restaurant is justly popular. The Holló Műhely in **Vitkovits Mihály utca** sells painted folk woodwork and ceramics.

DEÁK TÉR

Deák tér (*map pp. 428–9, C3–D3*) is a busy traffic hub straddling districts V and VII. The Fifth District side of it, the west, is largely occupied by the so-called 'Insula Lutherana', an island of the Lutheran faith. A grey marble sculpture (Tamás Vigh, 2009) commemorates Gábor Sztehlo, a Lutheran minister who saved many Jews from the Arrow Cross (the Hungarian Nazis) and whose name is particularly associated with his work with orphans. Behind the sculpture rises the **Lutheran Church** (Evangélikus templom), built on the site of a former chapel which came into being soon after Joseph II's 1782 Edict of Tolerance granted freedom of worship to non-Catholics. The present church, consecrated in 1811, was designed by Mihály Pollack with later additions by József Hild. A plaque commemorates Lajos Kossuth, Hungary's most celebrated Lutheran, who baptised his two sons here. The church is usually only open for services or when concerts are held here.

Next door to the church, in the former Lutheran school house (where Sándor Petőfi studied for a year in 1833–4), is the **Lutheran Museum** (Evangélikus Múzeum; *open Tues–Sun 10–6, evangelikusmuzeum.hu*), with an interesting display on Lutheranism in Hungary (captions also in English, though difficult to read as they are printed in pale grey on transparent plastic). An exceptional item is the so-called Flood Chalice, a silver Communion cup of Viennese make, presented to the Lutheran church after the great flood of 1838, in gratitude from the Jewish community, to whom the church—which, being on higher ground, had remained dry—offered sanctuary. A beautifully executed relief on the bowl of the cup shows the church on Deák tér surrounded by floodwaters, with people on a raft making for its front steps.

Beyond the museum, on Sütő utca overlooking Szomory Dezső tér, is the **Lutheran High School**. Like many Lutheran schools in Hungary, its roster of past alumni—of whom several were Jewish—is impressive. Theodor Herzl, the founder of modern Zionism, was just one of many illustrious pupils to pass through these halls.

Underneath Deák tér, in the underpass, is the **Millennium Underground Museum** (*open Tues–Sun 10–5*), tracing the history of Budapest's first metro line (*see p. 193*).

ELISABETH BRIDGE & MÁRCIUS 15. TÉR

The graceful white **Elisabeth Bridge** (Erzsébet híd; *map p. 428, C4*) was designed by Pál Sávoly and opened in 1964. A plaque on the Pest side notes that it is Hungary's first ever cable-stayed bridge. Its predecessor on the same site was a chain bridge, opened in 1903 and named after Empress Elisabeth, wife of Franz Joseph and champion of the Hungarians (*see p. 16*), who had been murdered in Geneva five years previously. The bridge was blown up by the Germans in 1945, as they retreated from Pest to Buda. Of all the similarly destroyed Budapest bridges, Elisabeth Bridge was the only one not to be reconstructed according to its original design. Construction of both Elisabeth Bridges necessitated urban redevelopment on the Pest side. The Inner City Parish Church (*described below*) now stands uncomfortably hemmed in, with a car park occupying the area under the bridge flyover. Urban legend holds that the church was in fact moved further to the left to accommodate the bridge. This is not the case, although when Elisabeth Bridge was being planned, the church was deemed to be in the way and consultations were held with American engineers. There was even talk of demolishing it altogether.

MÁRCIUS 15. TÉR

This spacious square, which stretches on both sides of Elisabeth Bridge, was given its name (March 15th Square) in 1948, commemorating the centenary of the date in 1848 when the anti-Habsburg uprising began. Before that it was known as Eskü tér, after the coronation oath (*eskü*) taken here by Franz Joseph in 1867. After his coronation in the Matthias Church, the new king rode across the Chain Bridge to Pest. Here, on a specially constructed podium, he intoned the promise to uphold the laws, rights, freedoms and constitution of Hungary and her fellow nations. 'Long live the King!' was proclaimed three times, after which the procession returned to Széchenyi tér for the *kardvágás* (*see p. 161*).

The part of Március 15. tér on the lower (north) side of the bridge is particularly attractive, laid out as a public park. Facing the river is the **Piarist school**, recently restituted to the teaching order, with the Kiosk bar and restaurant occupying its ground floor. Just behind, on Piarista utca, is the **Százéves Étterem** ('Hundred-year-old Restaurant'), in a fine Baroque town house (András Mayerhoffer, 1755) with a portal borne by atlantes. Incised in the paving stones is an undulating line representing the Danube, with the Roman forts and camps which lined its course also marked. March 15th Square was the site of one such camp, **Contra Aquincum**, whose remains still lie under the square (seen through thick glass). The site was strategically important, and one of the main crossing points on the river. Roman Pannonia lay on one side, and on the other barbarian territory belonging to the Sarmatian Jazyges. The first Roman camp was built in the 2nd century AD. In the 3rd/4th century it was remodelled as part of Diocletian's programme of defence reinforcements along the empire's border (the Sarmatians had invaded Pannonia in 260). The name of the camp occurs both as Contra Aquincum (since it on the other side of the river from the Roman town of the same name) and Contra Teutanum on Tautantum, since it stands directly opposite Mons Teutani (Gellért Hill), chief cult centre of the Eravisci. On the grass close by stands István Tar's 1971 bronze fountain with figures symbolising the Roman-barbarian struggle.

THE INNER CITY PARISH CHURCH

Map p. 428, C3. Open 9–4.30, until 8pm on Sun. No visits during services. Fee. belvarosiplebania.hu.

The Inner City Parish Church (Belvárosi Nagyboldogasszony Főplébániatemplom), dedicated to the Assumption of the Virgin, is the finest and most interesting church in Pest. The first church on the site was built in the 12th century. For many years this was the only parish church in Pest. Part of the Roman fort of Contra Aquincum lies beneath it. It was rebuilt, to its current dimensions, in the 14th century. The Gothic remains seen today date from that time. During the early part of the Ottoman occupation it was used as a mosque. Later it was returned to the population as the only permitted place of Christian worship. After the reconquest in 1686, only the east end was in a usable state. In the early 18th century, following a fire, the church was rebuilt. The nave and

INNER CITY PARISH CHURCH
Renaissance tabernacle (early 16th century).

west end were completely remodelled, in the Baroque style, at this time. The church was again repaired following damage in the Second World War.

Exterior of the Inner City Parish Church

The current west façade is Baroque while the east end remains Gothic. The south and north sides present an amalgamation of the two styles. The **west door (1)** is surmounted by a statue group representing the Holy Trinity. On the south side, facing the car park, remains of the old Gothic **south doorway (2)** (blocked up) can be seen. The Gothic **north door (3)** still also partly survives (also blocked up). The small door in the bay next to it is the old **doorway to the crypt (4)**, fittingly surmounted by a skull and crossbones. At the east end is a **sculpture of St Florian (5)**, patron saint of fire fighters (Antal Hörger, c. 1723). It was erected here following the fire that destroyed much of the old church.

Interior of the Inner City Parish Church

The interior is spacious, with a barrel-vaulted nave and Gothic rib vaulting in the chancel. Numbering in the text below corresponds to the plan opposite.

(A) Renaissance tabernacle: The beautiful tabernacle in red marble within a grey limestone frame, with skilfully executed architectural perspective, dates from the 1500s. It is thought to be the work of an Italian master. Originally designed to hold Communion bread, it now contains a reliquary of St Elizabeth of Hungary (*see p. 223*; she was betrothed to Ludwig, Margrave of Thuringia, in this church in 1211). The inscription notes that the tabernacle was the gift of András Nagyrévi, parish priest from 1480–1506 and, since 1492, titular bishop of 'Thermopylae'. The semicircular tympanum shows the Risen Christ between angels.

(B) Baptistery: The font has an interesting cone-shaped lid surmounted by a bronze statue group by Béni Ferenczy (1955). On the west wall is a plaque commemorating Baron István Beniczky and his wife Valeria, who both died in the shipwreck of the *La Seyne*

between Java and Singapore in 1909. The couple were just coming to the end of an extended honeymoon and the young bride was expecting her first child. The *La Seyne* had collided with another vessel and sank in under five minutes, in shark-infested waters.

(C) Kray memorial: A black marble plaque adorned with a gilt lion couchant commemorates Baron Pál Kray (d. 1804), artillery general in the Austrian army, veteran of the Seven Years War, victor against the Turks in Transylvania and against Napoleon's army in Italy, where the French dubbed him '*Le terrible Kray*'. Later defeats on the Rhine led to his dismissal.

(D) Chancel: The **high altarpiece** is a folding polyptych by Pál Molnár-C. (1948). When open it shows the *Assumption of the Virgin* surrounded by scenes of the life of Christ. When closed (during Lent) it shows the *Crucifixion* surrounded by scenes of the *Way to*

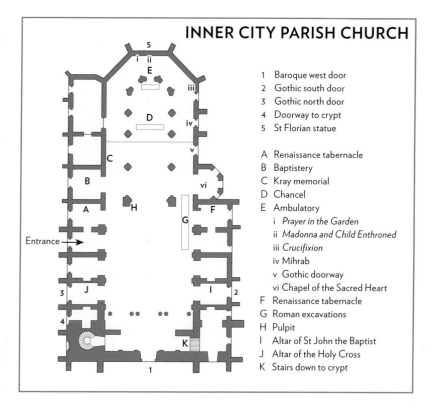

INNER CITY PARISH CHURCH

1 Baroque west door
2 Gothic south door
3 Gothic north door
4 Doorway to crypt
5 St Florian statue

A Renaissance tabernacle
B Baptistery
C Kray memorial
D Chancel
E Ambulatory
   i *Prayer in the Garden*
   ii *Madonna and Child Enthroned*
   iii *Crucifixion*
   iv Mihrab
   v Gothic doorway
   vi Chapel of the Sacred Heart
F Renaissance tabernacle
G Roman excavations
H Pulpit
I Altar of St John the Baptist
J Altar of the Holy Cross
K Stairs down to crypt

Calvary, Deposition and *Entombment.* The predella panels show the *Wedding at Cana* (left) and *Last Supper* (right). The gable has triangular images of saints: left to right, they are St Paul, St Margaret of Hungary, St Gellért, St Stephen of Hungary, St Ladislas, Prince Imre, St Elizabeth of Hungary, St John the Baptist. From the ceiling hangs a **Crucifix**, also by Molnár-C. (1949), showing Christ robed as High Priest. The large stone **altar** was installed to comply with the provisions of the Second Vatican Council's stipulations about priests facing their flock when serving Mass. It contains relics of St Gellért.

(E) Ambulatory: The outer wall is lined with Gothic recesses, some of which preserve remains of frescoes. There is a fragmentary 15th-century ***Prayer in the Garden* (i)** with the cloth of Veronica above and a trefoil aumbry. The old Lady Chapel has a beautiful 14th-century fresco of the ***Madonna and Child Enthroned* (ii)**, only brought to light in 2010. On the left inner side of the recess is the figure of a bishop. Beyond a 15th-century fragment of the ***Crucifixion* (iii)** is an Ottoman **mihrab (iv)** or prayer niche, indicating the direction of Mecca. A **Gothic doorway (v)** shows the entrance to the little rib-vaulted oratory above the **Chapel of the Sacred Heart (vi)**. The oratory is well seen from the centre of the nave crossing.

(F) Renaissance tabernacle: This lovely work forms a pair with the tabernacle opposite. It was donated by the city of Pest and is dated in the inscription: 1507. The same red marble and grey limestone are used and the same lovely architectural perspective device leads the eye towards the cupboard that once held the Host but which now has a reliquary of St Ladislas. The tympanum has a figure of Christ bound, flanked by Instruments of the Passion (lance and vinegar sponge), the Madonna and St John.

(G) Roman excavations: Beneath the floor, under perspex, can be seen traces of the Roman military fortress that once stood on this site.

(H) Pulpit: An interesting work, a fusion of Empire and neo-Gothic elements, designed by Pest's great Neoclassical architect János Hild. It was made in 1808–9 by the master carpenter Fülöp Ungradt.

(I) Altar of St John the Baptist: The carved and gilded altar surround contains a painting of the *Baptism of Christ*. In the gable is a carved scene of the *Assumption*. The altar was dedicated by the Guild of Fishermen (18th century). St Andrew, patron saint of fishermen, is represented in one of the supporting statues (left).

(J) Altar of the Holy Cross: The elaborate Baroque altar (1761) shows the Crucified Christ with, below him, Mary Magdalene kneeling on a blue globe, and the Madonna and St John the Evangelist. Opposite it, very difficult to see well because of the narrowness of the space, is a fine Neoclassical monument to István Kultsár, writer, publisher and theatre director, a great promoter of the Hungarian language. It is the work of István Ferenczy (1828).

(K) Stairs to the crypt: Excavations completed in 2014 have made accessible the crypt where, on the right-hand side, you can see remains of the Roman *castrum*. The crypt itself is first documented in 1699, when it was constructed by Jakab Proberger, master brewer of Pest, as his own burial place. The crypt was later extended, probably during work following the fire of 1723.

PETŐFI TÉR & THE DUNA CORSO

Petőfi tér (*map p. 428, C3*), which opens out onto the Danube promenade, is dominated by a **statue** of the heroic poet (Miklós Izsó, completed by Adolf Huszár, 1882), standing in a pose derived from the *acclamatio* of Classical statuary, where emperors are shown addressing their troops. In Petőfi's case it calls to mind the declaiming of his *National Song* (*Nemzeti dal*), which is said to have happened on 15th March 1848 on the steps of the National Museum. Though Petőfi did not in fact recite the poem on this occasion, it was printed in a shop nearby on 15th March, together with the people's 'Twelve Points' (*see p. 15*). The street which runs into Pest from Elisabeth Bridge, splitting Március 15. tér in two, is called Szabad sajtó út, 'Free Press Road', in memory of this. The Petőfi statue is the focus of patriotic gatherings of all kinds and its base is decorated with wreaths and flags on 15th March, one of Hungary's principal national holidays.

Behind the statue is a small **park** with more monuments, including a marble candle commemorating the 1932–3 famine in Ukraine and a brick lattice-work stele decorated with a cross erected to mark the 85th anniversary of the Armenian massacres by the Turks. Facing the square on the other side of the road is the **Hungarian Orthodox Cathedral**, dedicated to the Dormition of the Virgin (*open Wed 2–5, Fri 1–5, Sat 3–7, Sun 12–5, hungary.orthodoxia.org*). Building began after 1790 to designs by József Jung, though the façade with its two spires was added by Miklós Ybl in 1873 (one of the spires was destroyed in the Second World War). The iconostasis dates from 1797–1800 and the earliest icons are the work of an artist from Vienna, Anton Kuchelmeister.

SÁNDOR PETŐFI

Sándor Petőfi (1823–49) is Hungary's national poet, his verses learned by heart by generations of school children, his name the most popular on any city street atlas. He was the first poet in Hungary to use (in Wordsworth's phrase) 'the real language of men'. His verses stirred the nation's heart during the time of the Hungarian anti-Habsburg uprising. His *Nemzeti dal* (*National Song*) captured the mood of the times with its rousing call to throw off the chains of servitude:

> *Magyars arise, the homeland calls!*
> *The time is ripe, it's now or never!*
> *Shall we be free or forever in thrall?*
> *That is the question. Answer together:*
> *To the gods of the Magyars*
> *Our vow is sure,*
> *Our vow is sure that slaves we shall be*
> *No more!*

Petőfi took up arms in the ensuing War of Independence, in the service of General Bem (*see p. 75*). His poem *In Battle*, written in March 1849, describes his intoxication with the gun smoke and the stench of blood. 'One idea troubles me,' he had written in 1846, 'the thought of dying in a soft bed.' He need have had no worries on that score. He fell at the Battle of Segesvár (Sighișoara) on July 31st, and though his body was never found, it is assumed that he died on the field. A cult of the hero quickly grew up around him. When his widow, Júlia Szendrey, remarried just a year after his death, the poet János Arany wrote a stinging ballad entitled 'Soldier's Widow', in which the ghost of the dead hero appears at his successor's wedding banquet. 'Be happy,' it says, 'It's easy for those like you, who forget so soon.' The nation has never forgotten Petőfi, and visitors to Hungary cannot remain long unaware of him: his name and features occur so often on plaques, reliefs, street signs and commemorative sculpture of all kinds.

THE DANUBE CORSO

The upper Danube embankment, pedestrianised between Elisabeth Bridge and the Chain Bridge, takes the form of a promenade known as the Danube Corso (Dunakorzó; *map p. 428, C3*). It faces west, which makes it particularly popular on sunny days in early spring, when people sit on benches strung out along the route, enjoying the first warmth of the sun after the long Central European winter. The views of the bridges, the river, Gellért Hill and Castle Hill, are superb.

From Petőfi tér the promenade leads north past the **Marriott Hotel** (József Finta, 1969), which stands on the site of the Hungaria, a grand hotel destroyed during WWII. From the late 19th century, when the Danube embankment was built up, until the Second World War, the Corso was a favourite place of recreation. Fashionable hotels in the area included not just the Hungaria but the Carlton, the Bristol, the Europa and the Queen of England. It was a place to see and be seen and the hotels also harboured illustrious guests. Wagner stayed at the Hungaria in 1875, the year in which a joint concert of his and Liszt's works was given in the Pest Vigadó just a few steps further on. The great politician Ferenc Deák (*see p. 250*) used the Queen of England as his Pest residence and would receive guests there for political discussions and advisory meetings. Today the Corso is as popular as ever. It becomes more crowded and animated as it opens into **Vigadó tér**, a wide space always filled with visitors. In the centre is a paved garden surrounded by benches and clipped yews, with a fountain of two boys playing in the water (Károly Senyei, 1896) mounted on a base of pink Tardos marble. The fountain was once the centrepiece of a popular garden restaurant. Between the wars the Hangli Kiosk was a popular café here. In business until 1945, it is still alive in popular memory. Behind is the **Pest Vigadó**, a concert hall and exhibition space. The current building (Frigyes Feszl, 1859–65; rebuilt after damage in WWII; restored 2014) replaces an earlier concert hall that was destroyed during the War of Independence of 1848–9. Feszl's style aimed to create a Hungarian architectural vernacular, Romantic and Eclectic with hints of Orientalism.

Moored on the river at Vigadó tér is the ***Kossuth* paddle steamer**, partly a restaurant (the Vén Hajó) and partly a museum. Built in 1913 at the Ganz shipyard in Budapest and originally called the *Archduke Franz Ferdinand*, she was a market boat, bringing growers and vendors into town to sell their produce. The small museum (*free*), arranged on the bottom deck, has information about Danube shipping and you can also look down beneath the deck to see the *Kossuth*'s huge paddle wheel and pistons.

From Vigadó tér the Corso is lined with cafés, all with outdoor tables enjoying the splendid views of Buda. The Dunacorso café building escaped war damage and gives and idea of the aspect of the entire promenade before 1944–5. There are also several **statues** here. László Marton's popular bronze *Kiskirálylány* (*Little Princess*, 1990), modelled on his own daughter, sits on the railings. Pál Pátzay's standing female entitled *Danube Wind* (1937) is nearby, outside the Intercontinental Hotel (József Finta, 1981). A little further on is a genre statue of the artist Ignác Roskovics painting the Danube. Real paintings by Roskovics can be seen in St Stephen's Basilica and the church of St Ladislas in Kőbánya.

The Corso ends in **Eötvös tér**, with a statue (Adolf Huszár, 1879) of Baron József Eötvös, Minister for Education in the revolutionary government of 1848 and again under Andrássy in 1867. Although critical of Kossuth's politics of confrontation with Austria, Eötvös was at the same time radically democratic, strongly in favour of the emancipation of peasants. His Education Act established compulsory elementary schooling in 1868 and the previous year he had been instrumental in implementing the Jewish Emancipation Act. His radical Nationalities Bill of 1867, which would have given a degree of autonomy and language rights to Hungary's large number of non-Magyar citizens, was vehemently opposed and eventually watered down, a development which only stored up trouble for the future.

THE DANBUE IN BUDAPEST

The Danube river has, over the years, functioned as military frontier and transport route, pleasure ground for cruise ships and source of danger from floods. It has been—and still is—both obstacle and resource, opportunity and threat. In Roman times the river marked the *limes*, the border between civilisation and Barbaricum, and fortresses were strung out along it to defend the empire. Before the age of metalled roads and rail, the river was a key means of travel: this is how Gisela of Bavaria arrived, by boat from Regensburg, when she married King Stephen in the late 10th century. The year 1838 is engraved deep in Budapest's heart, for it was in March of this year, after the first thaw, that the river broke its banks, inundating both Buda and Pest and claiming many lives.

Historically the Danube was also an important source of food. Below Elisabeth Bridge, near the modern Irányi utca, was an open space called Hal tér ('Fish Square'), in the centre of which the Guild of Fishermen had erected a statue. In Buda above Margaret Bridge, a building facing the river on the corner of Harcsa utca ('Catfish Street') is decorated with a bronze fisherman pulling in a net. Further upstream around Árpád Bridge, the Vizafogó ('Sturgeon-catcher') district (*map p. 421, C4*) is named in memory of the fish from the Black Sea for whom this area was a spawning ground.

Today the river mainly presents a benign face (though sandbags were placed along the embankments when it threatened the city in June 2013). Cruise ships and pleasure boats dock at Vigadó tér and a public transport line of water buses also serves commuters.

BELVÁROS SOUTH OF ELISABETH BRIDGE

Szabad sajtó út (*map p. 428, C3*), a busy road that cuts the Belváros in two as it delivers traffic to and from Elisabeth Bridge, is lined with grand and imposing buildings that—perhaps because of the busy nature of the road—have been struggling for some years to find a role. Framing the view of the bridge are the twin **Klotild Palaces** (Korb and Giergl, 1899–1902), sometimes known as Klotild and Matild. On the ground floor of the palace on the south side was the famous Belvárosi Kávéház, which opened in 1901 and which, under Miklós Rónai, was the first establishment in the city to reopen for business after the Siege of Budapest in early 1945 (Miklós Rónai's son Egon Ronay made his name as a food critic in England). In its heyday the Belvárosi ranked with the great coffee houses of Budapest and was unique in not being home to any single clique (politicians from opposing factions could be spotted there). At the time of writing it was being renovated as a hotel by the Turkish Öyzer group and there were plans to reinstate the café. The northern Klotild Palace is now the Buddha Bar Hotel. Further north again stands the magnificent Moorish-Gothic **former Párizsi Udvar**, built for the Inner City Savings Bank in 1913 (Henrik Schmahl). This too is to reopen as yet another luxury hotel. Still further north, on the corner of Szép utca, a plaque commemorates the **site of the Landerer and Heckenast printing shop**, which on 15th March 1848 was stormed by patriotic rebels who used its press to print Sándor Petőfi's *National Song* and the people's 'Twelve Points', before converging on the National Museum (*see p. 15*).

ON AND AROUND FERENCIEK TERE

The rectangular Ferenciek tere (Square of the Franciscans; *map p. 429, D3*), free from traffic and with odd street lamps looking like blighted trees, opens off Szabad sajtó út.

The first **Franciscan church** on this site was founded by Béla IV in the 13th century. Under the Ottomans it became the Sinan Bey mosque. After the reconquest it returned to Christian worship, being formally restored to the Franciscans in 1690. The church and adjoining friary were entirely rebuilt in the Baroque style and consecrated in 1743. The Franciscans were banished again under Communism, returning in 1990. Above the entrance door is a relief of the Franciscan emblem of crossed stigmatised hands. On the exterior wall facing Kossuth Lajos utca is a bronze relief (Barnabás Holló, 1905) showing Miklós Wesselényi saving people from the flood of 1838. The high altar was donated in the 1740s by Antal Grassalkovich (*see p. 330*), in memory of his second wife. It is possible to visit the crypt (*open Mon–Sun 8–12*), where Count Lajos Batthyány was buried after his execution in 1849 (plaque). His body was exhumed in 1870 and ceremonially reinterred in Kerepesi Cemetery. Eyewitness accounts of the exhumation mention that, though the body was in an advanced state of decay, Batthyány's luxuriant beard was still fully recognisable.

Outside the church is the **Fountain of the Naiads** (1835; incorrectly labelled Fountain of the Nereids *in situ*). Ferenciek tere is also home to the stunningly decorated Kárpátia restaurant (*see p. 189*), some good cafés including the popular Ibolya presszó, and the **ELTE University Library** (Egyetemi Könyvtár) with its colourful dome, the best work of Antal Szkalnitzky (1876).

Cúria utca leads west into Veres Pálné utca, where at no. 4–6 an **Endre Ady museum** (*open Wed–Sun 10–5*) has been arranged in the apartment where the great poet (d. 1919) lived during the last two years of his life. Diagonally opposite, under a plane tree, is a seated **statue of Veres Pálné** (György Kiss, 1905). Mrs Pál Veres, née Hermin Beniczky, was a campaigner for women's education. In 1869, with the support of Ferenc Deák, she set up the first school that aimed to give girls an equivalent education to boys. She devised the curriculum herself.

THE SOUTHERN SECTION OF VÁCI UTCA

South of Elisabeth Bridge, Váci utca is quieter than in its northern part, although the closer you get to the Central Market Hall at the far south end, the more crowded it becomes. It is lined on both sides with some exceptionally fine buildings. At no. 38 on the left, near the top of this section, the **MKB bank building** was once the Royal Hungarian Officers' Club, hence the knights and halberdiers in the niches. The Femina hairdresser opposite preserves a sign from the great age of painted shop signage. Further along, on either side of the former Wüsztner Pension on the corner of Irányi utca, are two fine buildings. The one at **Irányi u. 15** was designed by Ödön Lechner (1910–11) and its exterior cladding is studded with mock rivets, Otto Wagner style. At Váci u. 42 is the Art Nouveau house (Jámbor and Bálint, 1908) commissioned by the doctor Sándor Korányi, decorated with green pyrogranite tiles with motifs of stylised foliage.

Diagonally opposite is the grey and white façade of the **Church of St Michael** (Szent Mihály-templom; *open 9–6*), with its conventual buildings attached. The church, which belonged to the Dominican Order, was founded at about the same time as that of the Franciscans, in the early 13th century. When Joseph II dissolved the mendicant orders in the 1780s, the church passed to a teaching order of nuns (in Hungarian the Angolkisasszonyok or 'English Maidens') founded in the 17th century by the Englishwoman Mary Ward. Today known as the Congregatio Jesu, the sisters still occupy part of the old friary next door. The present church was built in 1747–55, on the site of its predecessor which had not survived the Ottoman occupation. It was badly affected by the flood of 1838: the plaque at the head of the nave on the right shows the water level well above head height. The ceiling painting in the sanctuary shows St Michael triumphing over the Devil. On the (not very successful) *trompe l'oeil* balustrade stands a peacock, symbol of immortality. The altarpiece shows the Virgin offering the Rosary to St Dominic. The organ (1801, remade by Rieger in 1893) has a fine sound and the church is often used for concerts. The organ loft is borne by splendid demi-atlantes.

On two corners of Nyáry Pál utca stand fine Bauhaus buildings (**Váci u. 48 and 49**). At Nyáry Pál u. 4 a plaque commemorates Imre Kovács (*see p. 340*). Further up the street is red-brick building with what looks like a Doric temple on its roof. It is the **Apáczai Csere János School** (Kálmán Reichl, 1912–13). On the fourth corner of Nyáry Pál utca is a simple Neoclassical building by József Hild (1837). Next to it, the house at **Váci u. 52** (Nagy and Benedict, 1910; in a very poor state at the time of writing) preserves naive reliefs and mosaics of birds and pots of flowers. The fine entrance doors survive and there are stucco ribs in the hallway with a running design of long-beaked birds. The bird motif continues on the wrought-iron stair rail.

Further down Váci utca, at **no. 62–4**, is Imre Steindl's imposing New Town Hall (1870–5), built to replace Hild's old town hall, which stood near Elisabeth Bridge. It is slightly too large for the street and difficult to appreciate as a result.

From this point on, Váci utca becomes more crowded, especially in high season, with groups of visitors spilling off cruise ships and heading to and from the Central Market Hall (*see p. 264*). All the retail space is now given over to cafés, restaurants and souvenir shops.

UNIVERSITY CHURCH
Detail of the inner west doors showing a phoenix with grapes.

SZERB UTCA AND VERES PÁLNÉ UTCA

Szerb utca, which opens off Váci utca to the east (*map p. 429, D4*), is more peaceful. On the left, a gateway in the old wall, shaded by a maple tree, leads into the pretty cobbled courtyard of the **Serb Church of St George** (*open for services*). A church was founded here after the Great Serbian Migration of 1690 (*see p. 326*). The current building dates from 1733 and is by András Mayerhoffer. The tower is slightly later. On the street corner is a ceramic tabernacle of the titular saint slaying the dragon.

At **Veres Pálné u. 17** is the Nikola Tesla Serb-language High School (Sándor Fellner, 1907), with reliefs high up on the façade celebrating its founder, Sava Tekelija (Hungarianised as Tököly). On the opposite side at **no. 24**, the Pázmány University Theology Faculty occupies a house where Sándor Petőfi lived in 1844. **No. 9**, on the corner of Nyáry Pál utca, is an early work by Ödön Lechner (1874). The façade is enlivened by statues of the Magyar chieftains in niches. The corner oriel window is borne on a ram's head.

PAPNÖVELDE UTCA AND EGYETEM TÉR

Papnövelde utca (Seminary Street; *map p. 429, D4*) takes its name from the priests' training college at no. 7. On the corner of Cukor utca you can admire Reichl's Functionalist-Neoclassicist **Apáczai Csere János High School** from closer quarters.

Attached to the seminary is the **University Church** (Egyetemi Templom; *usually open during the day*), with a fine Baroque interior. Officially dedicated to the Nativity of the Virgin, it was built in 1725–71 by András Mayerhoffer. Hungary's revolutionary parliament held sessions here in 1849. The interior is rich with faux marble and *trompe l'oeil* wall painting, the latter the work of Johann Bergl. The church doors are particularly fine, richly carved (restored in 2017). Other fine woodwork includes the pews, still with their carved doors (those in the first three rows) and the stalls in the sanctuary. The carved and gilt pulpit is the work of Lipót Antal Conti. Under the pulpit is a plaque commemorating Bishop Ottokár Prohászka, who was taken ill while preaching here in 1927 and died the following day. Prohászka's strenuously-held views on the incompatibility between Christianity and Judaism have caused him to stand accused of stoking Hungarian anti-Semitism between the wars. The high altarpiece is an icon of the Black Madonna, beneath which is a sculpture group depicting the *Birth of the Virgin*, to which feast (8th Sept; Kisboldogasszony in Hungarian) the church is dedicated. Mary is depicted as a golden baby.

On the wide, spacious **Egyetem tér** (University Square), with a fountain and outdoor seating, stands the Law Faculty of ELTE University, with a WWI memorial on the part of the façade nearest the church.

THE KÁROLYI PALACE AND KÁROLYI-KERT

The handsome, Neoclassical Károlyi family palace now houses the **Petőfi Literary Museum** (PIM; *map p. 429, D3–D4; open Tues–Sun 10–6, pim.hu*), which hosts frequent exhibitions, book launches and literary festivals. A pleasant café and restaurant operates in the north wing, with seating outside in the courtyard. The building dates from 1832–40, built on an existing 18th-century core. On the Henszlmann Imre utca flank (south) is a **relief showing the arrest of Count Lajos Batthyány** (József Ispánki, 1941), which took place in this house on 8th January 1849. The female figure might be Batthyány's wife, Antónia Zichy, but may equally well (or is perhaps more likely to be) her sister, Karolina Zichy, who was married to György Károlyi (whose palace this was) but who was also Batthyány's lover. The two Zichy girls were intelligent, politically ardent, beautiful and popular. Sándor Petőfi wrote of them in shimmering terms, as 'two fairy flowers, pole stars of our benighted land'. (The Hungarian, *tündérvirág*, does literally mean 'fairy flower', but may also allude to the flowers of the epimedium family, also known as 'horny goatweed' for their aphrodisiac properties.)

On the opposite (north) flank of the building, facing Ferenczy István utca, is another relief, a **bust of Mihály Károlyi**, President of Hungary during the People's Republic of 1918–19 (*see p. 246*). It was set up here in 1963. The text (in lettering that is very difficult to read) says: 'This house was the birthplace, in 1875, of Mihály Károlyi, dedicated fighter for Hungarian independence and the liberation of the Magyar worker. President of the first Hungarian People's Republic. He presented this house, which the Counter Revolution had confiscated in 1920 and which liberated Hungary restored to him, to the workers of Hungary for use as a cultural centre.'

KÁROLYI PALACE
Relief showing the arrest of Count Lajos Batthyány.

THE KÁROLYI-KERT AND MAGYAR UTCA

Behind the Károlyi palace, its former garden is now a public park, the **Károlyi-kert** (*map p. 429, D3; open daily 8–sunset*). With flower beds, a playground, a fountain and the usual array of commemorative statuary, it is overlooked by attractive buildings. The one at Ferenczy István u. 20 was designed by Alfréd Hajós (*see p. 292*).

Magyar utca runs along the line of the old Pest city walls (*see p. 228*) and some of the houses have surviving sections in their inner courtyards and stairwells. At no. 26 the shopfront of the old Molnár and Moser pharmacy is preserved. No. 28 once housed the Lamacs inn, where Sándor Petőfi often dined and which became the haunt of Mihály Vörösmarty's National Circle (Nemzeti Kör), publisher of Petőfi's poems. Magyar utca was also known for its brothels. A notorious one was the Maison Frieda at no. 29. In 1906, members of the Eighty Club, a British liberal political group, paid a visit to Hungary and run up a substantial bill in Magyar utca, which they then refused to pay on the grounds that they were guests of the Hungarian government.

On Magyar utca in the other direction, at no. 8–10, is Miklós Ybl's **Unger-ház**, at the time of writing very shabby. An important example of Rundbogenstil and the first Pest house to have central heating, it was built in 1852 for Henrik Unger. The first Unger to settle here was Benedek, a blacksmith whose descendants became prosperous members of the Pest bourgeoisie, even aristocracy. They were connected to the architect Mihály Pollack and a great-granddaughter was wed to István Széchenyi's son Ödön. On the site of the old smithy, a later descendant built the Astoria Hotel. By this time the family had Hungarianised their name to Magyar, the name that the street now also bears.

EATING AND DRINKING IN THE BELVÁROS

RESTAURANTS

fff **Babel**. Fine dining restaurant where the cuisine in inspired by the chef's native Transylvania. Dinner only. Closed Mon. *Piarista köz 2. T: +36 70 600 0800, babel-budapest.hu. Map p. 428, C3.*

ff-fff **Kárpátia**. Magnificent old place, with opulent neo-Gothic design and wall painting, in business since 1877, offering traditional Hungarian cuisine ceremonially served under silver domes. It's grand without being slick and the experience comes complete with a gypsy band. *Ferenciek tere 7–8. T: +36 1 317 3596, karpatia.hu. Map p. 429, D3.*

f-fff **Centrál**. Successful recreation of a *belle époque* coffee house. You can come here for breakfast, lunch and tea, or sit for hours over a single coffee if you so desire. Poetry-writing is positively encouraged. Hungarian-international menu. Good cakes, good atmosphere. *Károlyi u. 9. T: +36 1 266 2110, centralkavehaz.hu. Map p. 429, D3.*

ff **Gerlóczy**. Justly popular café and brasserie offering breakfast, lunch and dinner. Choices range from simple quiche and salad to leg of lamb with all the trimmings. Good wine list, excellent atmosphere, superb location. *Gerlóczy u. 1. T: +36 1 501 4000, gerloczy.hu. Map p. 429, D3.*

ff **Károlyi**. Traditional Hungarian restaurant in the courtyard of the former Károlyi palace. Goulash soup, stuffed cabbage and *somlói galuska* can all be found here. Pleasant, peaceful outdoor dining in fine weather. *Károlyi Mihály u. 16. T: +36 1 328 0240, karolyietterem.hu. Map p. 429, D3.*

ff **Kiosk**. Shabby-chic restaurant and events space with a large outdoor terrace, in part of the old Piarist conventual complex near the Danube. The menu is modern Hungarian. Home-made cakes and ice cream. *Március 15. tér. T: +36 70 311 1969, kiosk-budapest.hu. Map p. 428, C3.*

CAFÉS, BARS AND WINE BARS

Csendes is a lively café-bar, restaurant and night spot, popular with students, on the site of the former Fiume literary coffee house. (closed Sun). Around the corner is the delightful **Csendes-társ** (open daily), a tiny wine bar with seating outside by the Károlyi Garden gates (*corner of Ferenczy István u. and Magyar u.; map p. 429, D3*). The **Astoria Hotel** has a spacious and pleasant café (excellent freshly-squeezed grapefruit juice) on the ground floor (*map p. 429, D3*).

The **Cultivini** wine bar (*Párisi u. 4; map p. 428, C3, closed Mon*) operates a tasting card system (you help yourself from special dispensing machines).

The **Három Holló** café (*Szabad sajtó út; map p. 428, C3*) aims to be a modern successor to the famous 'Three Ravens' on Andrássy út, the favourite haunt of the poet Endre Ady.

The espresso and brew bar **Madal** has one of its three branches on Ferenciek tere (*map p. 429, D3*). The long-established **Ibolya Presszó** café is next door.

District VI: Terézváros

The Sixth District, home to the magnificent Opera House on the grand Andrássy út avenue, began life in the late 18th century as a suburb of Pest. It was named Terézváros in 1777, after the empress Maria Theresa and her patron saint, Teresa of Avila (to whom the parish church was subsequently dedicated). Fresh impetus in the second half of the 19th century (when Andrássy út was laid out and the Opera House constructed) filled the upper reaches of the district with fine villas. The Liszt Music Academy, with its famous Art Nouveau interior, is also a major landmark.

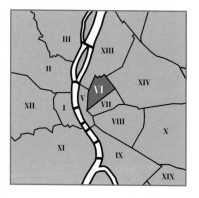

ANDRÁSSY ÚT

Andrássy út (*map p. 429, D2–F1*), the broad avenue that runs through central Pest from Erzsébet tér to Heroes' Square, was, in its heyday, the Champs Elysées of Budapest, grand, glamorous and graceful, a superb example of late 19th-century urban planning. According to the writer Gyula Krúdy, Andrássy út was to Budapest what the Danube is to Hungary: its oxygen-delivering artery. It runs in a straight line for some 3km, widening as it goes, with the houses that line it changing in character from contiguous urban mansions at the lower end to free-standing suburban villas at the top.

The idea to create a new street came from Gyula Andrássy, Hungary's first Prime Minister under the Dual Monarchy, aimed at relieving overcrowding on Király utca, which at the time was the main thoroughfare of populous Terézváros. Not without argument, Andrássy's plan was accepted and work began in 1872. A great many smaller, early 19th-century apartment houses were demolished to make way for the new avenue, and the vacant land was divided into building lots. Initially known as Sugár út (Radial Avenue), the street was named after Andrássy in 1885, by which year all the lots had been apportioned and the façades of the new buildings were standing. The official

NAGYMEZŐ UTCA
Trompe l'oeil painted backdrop in the old Manó Mai photography studio.

opening took place in May. After a lengthy lapse in the 20th century, when the avenue was successively Stalin Street, Hungarian Youth Street and People's Republic Street, it readopted the name Andrássy út in 1990. Metro line M1 (yellow), the *Földalatti*, runs under the street throughout its length (*see opposite*).

LOWER ANDRÁSSY ÚT

The lower section of Andrássy út is the commercial section. Here, on both sides, the street is lined by an unbroken row of handsome façades, with shops on the ground floors and residential apartments above. The families who built the houses would have retained the first floor for their own use, creating truly palatial apartments there. The flats on the other floors were let—but these were also extremely well appointed; the Andrássy út mansions were different entirely from the mansion blocks elsewhere in the city, where handsome exteriors often belied a reality of cramped tenements within.

Those who purchased the lots at the lower end of Andrássy út were not aristocrats (though many had been ennobled for their achievements); instead they were wealthy merchants, financiers and industrialists and they employed some of the finest architects, artists and craftsmen to create a street where every façade presents an elegant neo-Renaissance aspect and combines with those beside it to create a harmonious entity. Set into the pavement in front of the main entranceways, brass plaques give the date of construction and the name of the architect. Reading them reveals a roster of names from the 1870s and 1880s: Ybl, Quittner, Freund, Feszty, Czigler, Unger and Kallina. The list of their patrons, the families who commissioned these splendid residences, shows who was making money in Hungary at the time and in what sectors: no. 3: Saxlehner (mineral water); no. 7: Hochstein (banking); no. 8: Schossberger (tobacco and sugar); no. 10: Stern (distilling); no. 12: Krausz (milling and malting); no. 14: Kreische (salami); no. 21: Sváb (grain trading); no. 24: Lewy (leather); no. 27: Fischer and Sonnenberg (haulage); no. 28: Gschwindt (cognac and rum).

A few of the buildings keep their front doors open, and you can go in to see the old courtyards and stairwells. **No. 8**, the Schossberger mansion, has been renovated as a hotel. It still preserves its Károly Lotz frescoes in the entrance vault, but renovation has done away with many old features. It came too late to save the Miksa Róth stained-glass inner doors, which had long since, sadly, been smashed. The beautiful sculpted lampstand that once graced the stairwell has also disappeared. **No. 12**, the Krausz-palota, was built by Zsigmond Quittner for the industrialist Baron Lajos Krausz in 1884. The **Miniversum model railway** (featuring a number of Hungarian and Austrian landmarks in miniature; *miniversum.hu*) occupies part of the ground floor and the courtyard. **No. 16**, originally built for the banker Ede Loisch, was famous in the early 20th century as the home of the Wolfner and Singer booksellers. A plaque commemorates the painter István Farkas (born István Wolfner), who inherited the business after the death of his father. Farkas died in Auschwitz in 1944.

Beyond the Opera House (*described below*), the handsome palace at **no. 24** was once home to the Három Holló (Three Ravens) tavern, frequented by the poet Endre Ady. A plaque in the doorway commemorates this (Géza Csorba, 1937; restored 1960 with addition of Communist star; cleaned 2017). It shows a nude male on the deck of a ship and the words '*Röpülj hajóm*', taken from one of Ady's poems ('Fly, little boat; new horizons shimmer before you.'). **No. 26** (designed by Ármin Schubert, though the pavement plaque has question marks) was the home of a beautiful chemist's shop, founded by Sándor Török in 1878. Known as the Opera Pharmacy, it survived until 2008, when the Madison perfumery opened here instead. The chemist's furnishings and delicate curving staircase have been preserved. The Opera Pharmacy's first premises were on the other side of the street at **no. 29**, a pleasing building by Rezső Ray Sr with wrought-iron balconies bearing the letter S. It was built for the spice and fine foods merchant Ede Szenes (born Köhler, of which Szenes is a mirror translation), who sold his business to the patissier Emile Gerbeaud. Gerbeaud opened a café here which, in its heyday, became known as the **Művész** ('Artist', still its name today) and was popular with artists and writers. Today it is largely patronised by foreign visitors to the city. (Sándor Török, incidentally, was apprenticed to his father at the Holy Spirit Pharmacy on Király utca; its furnishings are now in the Semmelweis Medical Museum; *see p. 59*).

THE FÖLDALATTI

The Földalatti, literally 'Underground', designated as metro line 1 (yellow), was built in 1894–6, in time to transport people to the City Park for Hungary's Millennium festivities of 1896, celebrating a thousand years of Magyars in the Carpathian Basin. The first underground railway in continental Europe and the second in the world after London's Metropolitan Line (the third if you count Istanbul's Tünel funicular), it is a cut-and-cover construction only a few metres under ground, with no pedestrian underpasses between the lines: you have to know which side of the road you will be travelling on and use the entrance on that side; you can't cross the tracks below street level (the trains follow normal road rules; they drive on the right). The trains have always been powered by electricity. Franz Joseph ceremonially declared the Földalatti open on 3rd May 1896 and travelled on it himself a few days later. The stations, with their attractive brown-and-white Zsolnay tiles, were renovated in 1995. To learn more about the history of the line, visit the Földalatti Museum in the underpass at Deák tér (*map p. 429, D3; open Tues–Sun 10–5*).

THE OPERA HOUSE

Map p. 429, D2. Closed for renovation at the time of writing; performances are held at the Erkel Theatre (for programmes, see opera.hu). Tours of the building were still available while work is in progress (for details, see operavisit.hu).

The Hungarian State Opera (Magyar Állami Opera) occupies a magnificent neo-Renaissance building by Miklós Ybl, one of the most prolific and successful of Pest's 19th-century architects. A tavern of ill-repute is said to have stood here, blocking the way for the site's development, until Baron Frigyes Podmaniczky, who was in charge of public works, personally chased away the ruffians who haunted it. Construction began

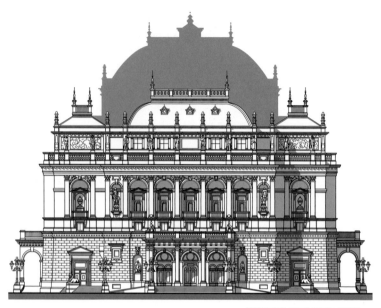

HUNGARIAN STATE OPERA HOUSE

in 1875. Progress was slow due to funding problems, but this had the advantage of allowing Budapest to learn from the disastrous fire at the Vienna Ringtheater in 1881, in which hundreds of people lost their lives. As a result, the Budapest Opera House was fitted with the very latest safety designs, involving all-metal, hydraulic stage machinery (the equipment lasted for almost 100 years). The Opera finally opened in September 1884, with a performance conducted by Ferenc Erkel, the institution's first musical director and composer of a number of operas with Hungarian national themes. Franz Liszt had been commissioned to write a work for the opening but because it included elements of the *Rákóczi March*, the 18th-century Hungarian rebel melody, it was not performed (his *Hungarian Rhapsody no. 15* is based on the theme). Seated statues of both composers now flank the entrance porch.

The Opera has had many distinguished directors, including Gustav Mahler and János Ferencsik. During the Siege of Budapest in 1944–5, thousands of people found refuge in the huge cellars. In the immediate post-war era the state granted the Opera large subsidies, both for prestige and to allow prices to be kept affordable for ordinary people. Prices are still low compared to London or La Scala, for example, but are not as cheap as they used to be.

The decoration of the Opera House

The exterior of the Opera House is decorated with statues of famous composers, Greek gods and demigods and four of the Muses: Erato (Mime), Terpsichore (Dance), Melpomene (Tragedy) and Thalia (Comedy). The painted interior, where the

OPERA HOUSE
Detail of the decoration in the vault of the *porte-cochère*.

iconographical references to Apollo and the Muses continue, is by Bertalan Székely, Mór Than and Károly Lotz, whose *Apotheosis of Music* fills the dome of the auditorium. Beneath it hangs a huge chandelier made in Mainz in 1884.

THE FORMER BALLET INSTITUTE AND ÚJSZÍNHÁZ

Opposite the Opera House is the **Drechsler-palota**, an early building by Ödön Lechner (1886, with Gyula Pártos), built for the Hungarian State Railways' pension fund. The ground floor tenant was the well-known Drechsler coffee house, hence the building's name. Lechner was fully aware of the risks of having won a commission in such a prominent spot and endeavoured to create a building that, while fine in its way, would not be seen as attempting to overshadow the Opera House. 'The lady-in-waiting may be more beautiful than the queen,' he is quoted as having remarked, 'but she must not upstage her'. It is debatable whether the lady-in-waiting did turn out to be lovelier. Early photographs of Lechner's building show a handsome pile with slender turrets, somewhat reminiscent of a French château. Clumsy restoration has spoiled the proportions. A ballet school moved into the building in the 1930s and after WWII it became home to the State Ballet Institute, which continued to occupy the premises until 2002. Since then there have been repeated attempts to turn it into a luxury hotel, but at the time of writing it was still empty.

Behind the Drechsler-palota, on Paulay Ede utca, is Béla Lajta's **Újszínház** (New Theatre, 1909), formerly the Parisiana night club. The building has been much altered over the course of its existence. Lajta's solemn grey marble façade, a sort of Art Deco incarnation of a rock-cut temple, is topped by a gilded attic storey with sculpted priestesses. It was restored to its original aspect in 1989. The auditorium retains the neo-Empire character given to it by László Vágó in the 1920s.

NAGYMEZŐ UTCA

Nagymező utca (*map p. 429, D2*) is known as the 'Broadway of Budapest' for its many theatres. On its northern section, the pavement is full of plaques bearing the footprints and shoe prints of famous Hungarian actors. The **Operetta Theatre** at no. 17 was built as the Somossy Orpheum by the Viennese firm of Fellner and Helmer in 1894. The Somossy seized the headlines in 1896 when, one hot August night, the young officer of hussars Marquess Artúr Csáky-Pallavicini blew his brains out for love of Ethel, a member of the Barrison Sisters burlesque troupe. Born in Denmark, the sisters emigrated to America and had come to Budapest to perform in the Millennium year of 1896. They were known for their tousled blonde curls, high-pitched voices and risqué lyrics ('Would you like to see my pussy?'). Five of the members were actual sisters. Ethel appears to have been English and to have been recruited by the girls to allow them to take occasional evenings off.

MAI MANÓ HÁZ
Nagymező u. 20. Open daily except holidays 11–7. Bookshop.
The Mai Manó House of Hungarian Photographers was built in 1894 for the *K. und K.* court photographer Manó Mai, who was particularly known for his portraits of children. The exterior of the building is lavishly decorated with Zsolnay pyrogranite. There is a pleasant café on the ground floor (the spaces on either side of the entrance were always conceived as commercial lets). Tiles in the hallway spell out the word 'Salve'. On the mezzanine floor, just beyond an iron gate with a stylised letter M, is the bookshop. More stairs lead up to the first floor, where the Mai family lived. The huge Venetian mirror in what is now the ticket office, the glass-panelled sliding door that divides the exhibition space, and the staircase with its wood and brass banister rail are all original. On what appears to be the top floor (the building in fact has eight storeys) is the photographer's studio, filled with natural light and preserving two painted backdrops (restored in 1998). From the window you have a good view of József Róna's sculpted female nudes on the façade.

In 1931 the house was purchased from Manó Mai's son by the composer Sándor Rozsnyai and his wife Mici. Under her stage name of Miss Arizona, Mrs Rozsnyai ran a famous nightclub here, enthusiastically described by Patrick Leigh Fermor in *Between the Woods and the Water* ('Did the floor of the Arizona really revolve? It certainly seemed to. Snowy steeds were careering round it at one moment, feathers tossing: someone said he had seen camels there, even elephants...'). The Rozsnyais were deported to concentration camps in 1944. The Hungarian Photography Foundation began the process of taking over the rents of the flats here in 1996. The House of Hungarian Photographers opened in 1999 and hosts excellent exhibitions.

THE CAPA CENTER

On the south side of Andrássy út, at no. 11 Nagymező utca, is the **Radnóti Theatre** with a statue of the poet outside it (Imre Varga, 2009). The striking Art Deco building at **no. 3** (Andor Vajda and Lajos Gyenes, 1912) once housed the newspaper offices of the *Neues Politisches Volksblatt*. The artist Sándor Bortnyik also had a studio here. Opposite, at no. 8, is the **Capa Center** (Capa Központ; *open daily 11–7, capacenter.hu*), occupying a huge, well-lit exhibition space built by the collector Lajos Ernst in 1912. The main doors are decorated with stylised tulips and stained-glass panels of flowers. The entrance is through the right-hand door, flanked by copies of the famous relief busts of Matthias Corvinus and his consort Beatrix of Aragon (*see pp. 43–4*). In the hallway are sober black and brown marble benches by Ödön Lechner and a bright, Fauvist stained-glass window designed by Rippl-Rónai fills the half-landing with dancing pools of coloured light. Many artists lived in the building, including Adolf Fényes. The Capa Center houses temporary exhibitions as well as a small, representative selection of the work of Hungarian-born war photographer Robert Capa, including famous images of the Spanish Civil War.

The central part of the building formerly housed the Tivoli Cinema, with an impressive Art Deco lobby. At the time of writing, plans for a **Capa Museum**—the world's first permanent exhibition dedicated to the photographer—had been announced.

TERÉZVÁROS PARISH CHURCH

Open Mon–Sat 7.30–12 & 3–7; Sun June–Aug 7.30–1 & 4.30–7.30, Sept–May 8.30–1 & 4.30–7.30.

The church, which takes the form of an aisleless basilica, was built in 1801–11 to designs by Fidél Kasselik on the site of a wooden chapel. The statue high up on the façade, representing Teresa of Avila to whom the church was dedicated in 1822, is by Lőrinc Dunaiszky. The interior layout is by Mihály Pollack (1824–31) and the steeple by Miklós Ybl (1871). The high altarpiece of the *Ecstasy of St Teresa* dates from the late 1820s.

ANDRÁSSY ÚT TO LISZT FERENC TÉR AND OKTOGON

On the site of the Terézváros Club, the tall building at Andrássy út 39, the **Párizsi Nagy Áruház**, was commissioned in 1909–11 by Samuel Goldberger as a department store on the Parisian model. It was Budapest's second such store; the first, also called the Párizsi and also owned by Goldberger, was on Rákóczi út but burned down in 1903. The Andrássy út store, with its late Art Nouveau lines, glass-fronted lifts and glassed-in courtyard, was a glamorous novelty in the Budapest of the time. The exterior façade is decorated with a frieze of wild animals, and male statues flank the large clock. One of the statues is heroically nude, clutching a caduceus and what looks like a money bag. The other, naked except for a workman's apron, holds symbols of the engineer and architect's trade. Both rather comically sport contemporary facial hair (curving moustaches and a trimmed beard). The ballroom of the old clubhouse, at the back of the building, exquisitely frescoed by Károly Lotz (*Apotheosis of Budapest*, 1885), has been preserved and until recently functioned as a café. At the time of writing the building was undergoing restoration. To the right of the main entrance, a lift in the lobby takes you up to the 360 rooftop bar, which offers good panoramic views of the city.

A short way further down Andrássy út, at no. 45, is the **Írók Boltja** (Writers' Bookshop), on the corner of Liszt Ferenc tér. One of the best bookshops in Budapest, it was the home of the famous Japán Kávéház, a literary coffee house frequented by many writers and artists, including Ödön Lechner and József Rippl-Rónai.

Liszt Ferenc tér (*map p. 429, D2*), lined with cafés and restaurants and with a tree-filled park in its centre, was one of the first parts of Budapest to develop as a centre for nightlife in the early 1990s. It is still lively today, but somewhat in decline. The statues in the centre are of the poets Endre Ady (Géza Csorba, 1960) and Attila József (Ferenc Gyurcsek, 2006), and of the composer Franz Liszt (László Marton, 1986), shown at an imaginary piano, hair flying wild. The square has been named after Liszt since 1907, when the Academy of Music opened at the far end.

THE LISZT ACADEMY

The Liszt Academy of Music (Zeneakadémia) is one of Budapest's finest concert halls and also its premier music teaching institute. Both Bartók and Kodály taught here. When the Academy was founded, in 1875, Franz Liszt was its first president (at that time the premises were further up Andrássy út; *see p. 200*). The current building, to designs by Flóris Korb and Kálmán Giergl, dates from 1904–7. Above the main entrance is a seated statue of Liszt (Alajos Stróbl) and on either side are high reliefs of putti demonstrating the development of music. The work of Ede Telcs, they seem to be inspired Luca della Robbia's cantoria in Florence.

Restored in 2013, the building has one of the most memorable Art Nouveau interiors in Budapest (*for tours, see zeneakademia.hu/guided-tours*). On the ground floor is Aladár Körösfői Kriesch's two-part fresco presenting an allegory of secular and sacred music. The first-floor mural, *The Fountain of Art*, is also by him (the bearded figure on the far right is Lajos Kossuth, half concealed since he was still *persona non grata*; he never made his peace with Franz Joseph. As you climb the stairs, note the beautiful deep blue eosin-glazed newel posts by the Zsolnay manufactory. These are said to symbolise water bubbles and in fact there is marine symbolism everywhere. The theme is the rising of the human spirit out of water to air and light, the realm of Apollo, as represented by the grand main auditorium, which rises through three storeys and where the cove of the ceiling is covered with gilded laurel leaves (the gilded mesh is in fact a gloriously disguised ventilation grille). In the centre, glass lozenges are inscribed 'Harmony', 'Beauty', 'Rhythm', 'Poetry', 'Melody', 'Imagination': abstract concepts of perfection. The gallery is a reinforced concrete structure by the acknowledged master of the medium Szilárd Zielinski (his first name, comfortingly, translates as 'sturdy').

OKTOGON AND THE NAGYKÖRÚT

The busy road junction known as **Oktogon** (*map p. 429, D2*) takes its name from the shape given to it by the chamfered ends of the buildings on each of its four corners.

LISZT ACADEMY
Musical putti by Ede Telcs.

Two of them once held famous coffee houses on their ground floors. Of these, one is now a bank and the other a Burger King. In 1936, following a promise by Mussolini to help Hungary regain territory lost after WWI, the Oktogon was renamed Mussolini Square. It became November 7th Square in 1950 (the date of the Russian Revolution). Its non-political, descriptive name was reinstated in 1990.

Oktogon marks the end of the lower section of Andrássy út, which is divided from the upper section by the **Nagykörút** or 'Grand Boulevard' (*see below*), Budapest's equivalent of the Vienna Ringstrasse (*körút* literally means 'ring road'). On the further side of the körút (look right as you face the Heroes' Square end of Andrássy út) is a building modelled on Florence's Palazzo Strozzi (**Teréz körút 13**). It was built by Alajos Hauszmann in 1884 for the Batthyány family.

THE NAGYKÖRÚT

The Nagykörút, laid out from 1872, takes the form of a single wide avenue curving through Pest in an arc between Petőfi Bridge at its south end and Margaret Bridge in the north. Its sections are named according to the parts of town that it passes through, which in turn are named after members of the Habsburg dynasty: Ferenc körút in Ferencváros (Ninth District); József körút in Józsefváros (Eighth District); Erzsébet körút in Erzsébetváros (Seventh District) and Teréz körút in Terézváros (Sixth District). In each district, the main parish church is dedicated to a saint who shares the same name: St Francis of Assisi, St Joseph, St Elizabeth of Hungary, St Teresa of Avila. The only part of the Nagykörút not to follow this pattern is Szent István körút in Lipótváros (Fifth District), which has been named after St Stephen (István) since 1937. The main church of Lipótváros is St Stephen's Basilica, though when that church was first planned, the intention had been to dedicate it to St Leopold (Lipót). Lipótváros' dual identity can be traced to this change of plan.

ANDRÁSSY ÚT FROM OKTOGON TO VÖRÖSMARTY UTCA

After Oktogon, Andrássy út gets wider. The houses here are still predominantly palatial apartment blocks, but many of them were also built to house civic, public and educational institutions. Make a detour to the left to see the **Rosenberg-ház** at Eötvös u. 29, a building by Béla Málnai (1911, recently restored), an interesting example of pre-Modernism.

Andrássy út 60, built by Adolf Feszty for the painter Izsák Perlmutter, is now the **House of Terror** museum (Terror Háza; *map p. 429, E2; open Tues–Sun 10–6, terrorhaza.hu*). Painted gunmetal grey, its roofline fringed with a huge overhang stencilled with the Communist star and the emblem of the Fascist Arrow Cross (the work of Attila F. Kovács), it is dedicated to the victims of totalitarian persecution. From 1937 the house was used as an Arrow Cross headquarters and subsequently as a prison and interrogation centre by the Communist State Security. Black and white photographs of those who suffered here are fixed to the rustication below the ground-floor windows. A plaque commemorates Cardinal Mindszenty (*see p. 151*), who was tortured in this building. Cells where many unfortunates were kept in solitary confinement have been recreated in the basement. György Pálóczi Horváth's *The Undefeated* contains an lengthy account of his experiences here and the cruel means by which his gaolers attempted to extort a 'confession' from him. Outside the building, planted in astroturf between the main body of Andrássy út and its side lane, is a **lump of the Berlin Wall**, donated to Hungary in 2010.

On the corner of Andrássy út (right) and Vörösmarty utca is the **old Liszt Academy**. It contains the Liszt Memorial Museum, a recreation of the apartment where the composer lived in 1881–6 (*open Mon–Fri 10–6, Sat 9–5, closed Sun and holidays, lisztmuseum.hu*). The building is still used for concerts and holds regular exhibitions.

A detour up Vörösmarty utca to the right (southeast) leads to **Hunyadi tér**, ringed with once-fine, now dilapidated buildings. One of these is Győző Czigler's Market Hall of 1897, one of a series of covered markets built at this time (*see p. 264*). The façade is adorned with masks of wild boar and oxen, all of them in a sorry state of decay. An outdoor produce market operates in the square outside (*Mon–Sat 7am–2pm*).

On Vörösmarty utca in the other direction, at no. 51, is the **Scottish Presbyterian church of St Columba**, founded by Church of Scotland missionaries in 1841. The missionaries were on their way to Palestine, but when one of their members fell from a camel they were forced to turn back. They came to Pest to evangelise the city's Jews, but on learning that Scottish engineers were at work on the new Chain Bridge, they found a securer role for themselves as chaplains to the workforce. The church continues to thrive (*for more details and service times, see scottishmission.org*).

VÖRÖSMARTY UTCA TO KODÁLY KÖRÖND

The proud but besmirched building at **Andrássy út 69** (Adolf Láng, 1877) was the former Kunsthalle or Műcsarnok, in use for art exhibitions until the new Műcsarnok was built on Heroes' Square. Today it forms part of the University of Fine Arts and a section of it is occupied by the **Puppet Theatre** (Bábszínház; *budapestbabszinhaz.hu*). You can go inside to admire the fine, columned entrance hall with its painted vaults and stained glass. The building next door is also part of the university and is in fact its original building (Alajos Rauscher, 1877). The façade is decorated with attractive sgraffito in tones of dark grey, red and gold, with medallions of artists by Bertalan Székely.

On the other side of Izabella utca, **Andrássy út 73–75** has a dramatic corner relief by János Zsákodi Csiszér commemorating railway workers who lost their lives in WWI. A companion relief on the Rózsa utca corner was put up in 1946 to mark the centenary of the first Hungarian railway line, from Pest to Vác. The vast edifice was built for the Hungarian railway company in 1876 (Gyula Rochlitz) and continued to be occupied by them until they sold it in 2009. At the time of writing it was still empty.

The end of the middle section of Andrássy út is signalled by the wide traffic junction known as **Kodály körönd** (Kodály Circus; *map p. 429, E1*). Originally known simply as 'The Circus', it was ignominiously named after Adolf Hitler in 1938. It became simply 'Körönd' again after the war, and adopted the name Kodály after its famous resident in 1971. Four magnificent palaces in eclectic architectural styles are placed around it. At the time of writing they were in varying states of repair. At the lower end on the right is a *palazzo* built as rental apartments for the Hungarian railway company (József Kauser, 1885). It was seriously damaged by fire and evacuated in 2014. Opposite, on the lower left side of the circus, is a slightly earlier palace (1881) also built for the railway company. The architect was Gusztav Petschacher, who designed many Andrássy út buildings, and it has sgraffito decoration on the façade by Bertalan Székely (similar to his work on the Fine Arts University). The magnificent wrought-iron gates and railings are by the workshop of Gyula Jungfer. At the upper end of the circus are Hübner Court (left) and Andrássy Court (right), both by Gyula Bukovics (1884–5). The latter contains the **Kodály Museum**, in the composer's former apartment (*open Wed–Fri by appointment at least two days in advance; T: +36 1 352 7106, kodalymuzeum@lisztakademia.hu*). The painter Jenő Barcsay also lived here. In front of each palace, on a patch of lawn, are statues of Hungarian heroes who distinguished themselves in the fight against the Ottomans: Miklós Zrínyi (József Róna, 1902), György Szondy, Bálint Balassi and Vak Bottyán (László Marton, Pál Pátzay and Gyula Kiss Kovács, 1958–9). The three later statues replaced two that were taken to Heroes' Square to substitute banished Habsburgs and one that was removed from public view altogether (Count János Pálffy, an army general who fought on the Habsburg side against the troops of Ferenc Rákóczi in the early 18th century).

KODÁLY KÖRÖND TO MUNKÁCSY MIHÁLY UTCA

Beyond Kodály körönd, Andrássy út becomes leafier, lined by maturer trees and with rows of detached villas with gardens at the front, often surrounded by fine iron railings. This was the aristocratic end of the street—the Pallavicini, Erdődy and Edelsheim Gyulai families all had property here. Many of the old villas are now occupied by embassies.

No. 98 on the left, with fine front doors, is the former Pallavicini palace (Gusztáv Petschacher, 1885). At the time of writing it was home to the MagNet Community Centre (specialising in self-awareness and spirituality), with the MagHáz restaurant and tea house attached.

Take a detour down **Bajza utca** to the left to see two impressive Art Nouveau houses, the **Léderer-ház** at no. 42 (Zoltán Bálint and Lajos Jámbor, 1902) and the **Baruch-ház** next to it, by the same architects (1899). The latter, rendered in pink, has door and window surrounds decorated with deeply moulded vines, artichokes and other fruits and trees. The overall effect is extremely rich, almost reminiscent of the Spanish plateresque style. Under the overhanging eaves of the Lederer house are mosaics designed by Károly Kernstok and executed by Miksa Róth showing huntsmen with leashed tigers, later encountering a group of naked maidens. The frieze culminates with a solitary moustachioed lute player. All extremely extraordinary.

Back on Andrássy út, at no. 112 on the corner of Munkácsy Mihály utca, is the **Kogart House**, hosting exhibitions from the collection (mainly modern and contemporary Hungarian art) of the businessman Gábor Kovács (*open Mon–Fri 10–5; kogart.hu*).

THE SCHIFFER VILLA

Map p. 429, E1. Munkácsy Mihály u. 19/b. Open Mon–Thur 8–4.30, Fri 8–2, Sat by appointment (T: +36 1 472 6342). Free.

Standing at some distance from the street, at the bottom of what would once have been its garden, is the Schiffer Villa, slightly ponderous and even seemingly uninteresting from the outside, but an extraordinary treasure trove within. Since the 1990s it has been the headquarters of the Hungarian Customs and Tax Authority and a museum on the subject is arranged on the first and second floors.

The house, in a late Secessionist style, was built in 1910–12 by József Vágó for the wealthy railway magnate and patron of the arts Miksa Schiffer, who lived here with his wife, Sarolta Grünwald, and four daughters. Vágó designed both the exterior (inspired by the Palais Stoclet in Brussels, by Josef Hoffmann) and the interior furnishings; the result is a *Gesamtkunstwerk* very much in the manner of the Wiener Werkstätte. The exterior has been considerably altered. An upper floor has been added, which destroys the proportions and makes it seem ungainly. The corner tower has also been re-modelled, but the cladding, in heavy composite ashlar, is the original.

Beautiful stained glass with a repeated pattern of swallows allows light to filter into the entrance lobby. From here, you go up steps into the main hall, the centrepiece of the villa. At the top of the steps is a statue of a seated male nude by Miklós Ligeti, part of the original furnishings. There was formerly a marble fountain in the centre of the floor (bronze statuettes belonging to it are now in the Hungarian National Gallery). To the right, between the doors (inlaid with beautiful wood and mother-of-pearl marquetry), is a Carrara marble *jardinière* borne on stout yellow columns and decorated with carved reliefs of male and female nudes. The walls are clad in deep green Zsolnay tiles picked out with red studs in imitation of rivets. A tall window completely fills the left wall, its stained-glass panels (reproductions) designed by Károly Kernstok and showing women and children in a pastoral, Elysian setting. Above the stairs is a painted tableau,

SCHIFFER VILLA
Detail of the stained-glass window by Károly Kernstok.

also by Kernstok, with a portrait of Schiffer (now very dark and difficult to see). Some of the door handles still bear the monogram 'SM', as does the window in the former study, where photos show the villa as it appeared in Schiffer's day. The large painting that hung here, *Summer* by Béla Iványi Grünwald, and another that hung in the main salon, a famous work by József Rippl-Rónai showing Mrs Schiffer and her daughters in the garden of their summer villa, are both now in the Hungarian National Gallery.

There is lovely stained glass in all the rooms on the main floor, much of it continuing the theme of bird life. The aim of the villa's entire design was to show how art can lift mankind heavenwards. The customs and excise and tax-collection exhibits (captions also in English) are interesting and include material on smuggling and its detection. One curiosity among the confiscated items is a bottle of an unidentified spirit in which floats a huge cobra with a scorpion in its mouth.

Wooden stairs lead up to a gallery overlooking the hall and the Kernstok window. The former bedrooms and sitting room open off it and there is an outdoor balcony with columns clad in bright green Zsolnay pyrogranite, in bold floral designs. Mrs Schiffer's bedroom has matching inlaid doors (and a particularly fine surviving door handle) and, above where her bed once stood, a copy of István Csók's *Spring*, which features girls in diaphanous pink gowns under a blossom-laden cherry tree. The original has survived and hangs in the National Gallery.

THE EPRESKERT AND SONNENBERG VILLA

Opposite the Schiffer Villa, on the corner of Kmety utca, is the **Epreskert** (Mulberry Garden; *map p. 429, E1*). This atmospheric place, shaded by trees and filled with collapsing sculptures and statues shedding limbs, is a vestige of the mulberry groves that once covered this part of town, planted by the municipality. In the late 19th century, artists began to set up studios here and the colony became famous. The garden, which is occasionally open to the public, is now owned by the Fine Arts University. Overlooking the garden at Munkácsy Mihály u. 23 (corner of Bajza utca) is the former **Sonnenberg Villa**, a fine example of Hungarian Art Nouveau, built as a family home for the wealthy merchant and haulage contractor Imre Sonnenberg (his offices were at the lower end of Andrássy út, at no. 27). Around the main doorway are Symbolist female sculptures by Géza Maróti. The villa itself is the work of Albert Kálmán Kőrössy (1904), who also designed the **Ferenc Kölcsey High School** a little further down the street at no. 26 and whose own villa lies not far away at Városligeti fasor 47 (*see p. 206*). The proportions of the Sonnenberg Villa were damaged when a third floor was added in the 1970s. In the 1930s one of the tenants in the building was the engineer István Egri, known for his central heating and plumbing systems: Alfréd Hajós (*see p. 292*) employed him to plumb his swimming pool complex on Margaret Island. In 1944 the Arrow Cross raided the Sonnenberg house and Egri's son was smuggled out of Budapest by his nanny, Mária Szabó. Bravely facing the opprobrium of appearing to be an unmarried mother, Mária took him to her home village in western Hungary, passing him off as her own child. She was declared a Righteous Gentile in 1995.

THE FERENC HOPP AND POSTAL MUSEUMS

On the other side of Andrássy út, at no. 103, is the **Ferenc Hopp Museum of Southeast Asian Art** (*map p. 429, E1; open Tues–Sun 10–6, last tickets at 5.15; hoppmuseum.hu*). Hopp, the manager of an ophthalmology company, was also a traveller and collector. He left his villa (built by Schubert and Hikisch in 1877) and his collection to the state with the aim that the ensemble should become a museum. It hosts excellent temporary exhibitions and there is a pleasant garden at the back. **Andrássy út 105**, with its wooden gable, is by the Swiss-born architect Rezső Ray Sr. At no. 111, on the further corner of Munkácsy Mihály utca, is the **Andrássy Hotel**, designed as a Jewish boys' home by Alfréd Hajós (*see p. 292*). A plaque on the Munkácsy Mihály utca façade commemorates Lajos Gidófalvy, who saved the inmates of the home from the Arrow Cross.

The Postal Workers' Cultural Centre at **Benczúr u. 27** occupies the former villa of Lajos Egyedi (originally Lajos Stern), heir to his father's distilling fortune. Lajos became known as a horse breeder but was unsuccessful in business and committed suicide in 1927. His brother Artúr came to a similar tragic end when he was strangled by his own son-in-law after failing to pay the young man's debts. The villa has a garden at the back where concerts are held (and beneath which, according to legend, lies buried one of the descendants of Kincsem the wonder mare; *see p. 316*). On the second floor is the **Postal Museum** (*map p. 429, F1; open Tues–Sun 10–6, postamuzeum.hu*), tracing the history of postal services, telegraphy, telephony and radio in Hungary. Exhibits include examples of 'American padlocks' used for securing mail bags, a PTT pneumatic tube system, still in working order, and a copy of the first Budapest telephone directory of 1882. Subscribers were mainly larger businesses. Almost alone among the smaller entrepreneurs is the architect Rezső Ray—but it is perhaps not surprising that he should have been an early adopter; after all, he designed the Telephone Exchange building on Baross utca (*see p. 241*). Also on display at the time of writing was an engine-assisted delivery tricycle of 1900, of the type devised by János Csonka (*see p. 123*). The vehicle belongs to the Transport Museum, which was waiting for a new home when this book went to press. When the new site is ready (*see p. 274*), the tricycle will be exhibited there.

At Benczúr u. 16 is the **Austrian Embassy**, the last Budapest residence of Raoul Wallenberg (at the time, the house belonged to László Olcsay; *see p. 317*). Wallenberg (*see p. 300*) left the building in January 1945 in the company of a Russian army major, never to be seen at liberty again.

MUNKÁCSY MIHÁLY UTCA TO HEROES' SQUARE

Back on Andrássy út, on the corner of Munkácsy Mihály utca, is a handsome pair of villas purchased in 1894 and 1919 respectively by the wealthy industrialist Manfréd Weiss, for himself and his daughter Margit (Daisy). **No. 114** (Vilmos Freund, 1877) has a front porch supported by caryatids. **No. 116** (Mór Kallina, 1877) was bought by Weiss in 1894. Weiss' son-in-law, Ferenc Chorin, was deported to Mauthausen after the German takeover of Hungary in 1944 but the family managed to negotiate their freedom in exchange for all their worldly wealth, which was appropriated by the Nazis. The Chorins escaped to Portugal and then to the US.

World War Two damage caused some of the villas along the upper stretch of Andrássy út to be demolished; in their place came new buildings reflecting an entirely modern aesthetic. At the far end of the street on the right, the building on the corner of Dózsa György út (*map p. 429, F1*) is the **Serbian Embassy**. Originally the Babocsay Villa, it was built by Aladár Árkay in 1906 in the Hungarian Secession style, with a corner dome, undulating gables and stucco floral fantasias. No two windows were alike. It was stripped down and squared off by Lajos Kozma in the 1920s. Between the 4th and 22nd November 1956, when it was the Yugoslav Embassy, Imre Nagy and his supporters took refuge here until they were arrested and taken to Romania (*see p. 91*). Opposite, on the other corner of Andrássy út, is the Albanian Embassy and next to it the Café Kara, where people come to smoke shishas and drink Turkish tea (the Turkish and North Cyprus embassies are nearby).

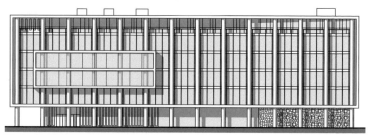

MÉMOSZ BUILDING, DÓZSA GYÖRGY ÚT FAÇADE

VÁROSLIGETI FASOR

This wide, tree-lined street (*map p. 429, E2–F1*), parallel to Andrássy út, divides Terézváros from Erzsébetváros, the Sixth District from the Seventh. In spirit, because of its graceful villas, its boulevard atmosphere and its cluster of embassies, Városligeti fasor belongs with Andrássy út.

The **Calvinist church** (Fasori Református templom) at no. 7 is the work of Aladár Árkay (1913). The huge portal is decorated with Zsolnay pyrogranite tiles with black, yellow and white motifs inspired by folk art. The interior has windows by Miksa Róth.

Just off the Fasor, at **Bajza u. 10**, is a house by József Fischer, built in 1936 for clients who had apparently wanted a castle (they got a Bauhaus villa instead).

On the corner of Bajza utca and Városligeti fasor are the **Lutheran church and High School** (Fasori Gimnázium). The first Lutheran school in Pest, on Deák tér, became too small to accommodate its growing number of pupils and plans were laid for a new centre in the outer reaches of Pest, where there was more room for expansion. The project was put out to tender and although the designs of Lajos Schodits were initially chosen, the commission eventually went to Samu Pecz. Both church and school were built in 1905, the church in Pecz's signature neo-Gothic style. The school, like its forerunner on Deák tér (*see p. 175*), has had a number of exceptional pupils pass through its doors. Among them are the mathematician John von Neumann, the poet György Faludy and Nobel prizewinners Eugene Wigner (atomic physics) and John Harsányi (game theory).

Opposite the church, the villa at **no. 20** was built in the 1890s for the wrought-iron master Gyula Jungfer (he made his own gates; note the intertwined initials). Another notable villa on Városligeti fasor is **no. 47**, an Art Nouveau masterpiece of 1899–1900, built by the architect Albert Kálmán Kőrössy as his own residence. The façade is rich in decoration: especially fine are the twin peacocks and the plaster relief in the gable, with allegorical figures of Painting, Sculpture and Architecture. The figure of Architecture is shown working on this very villa. Recently restored, the building is occupied by various offices and forms part of the curiously-named Resonator Park, a business complex which also includes the next-door house, the former studio and home of the photographer György Klösz, born in Darmstadt, who made his name in Hungary and is particularly known for his late 19th-century shots of Budapest streetscapes. The villa was built for Klösz in 1894–5 (Ármin Schubert and Lajos Hikisch). The third floor is an addition of the 1920s, also for the Klösz family.

Across the road is something of a very different kind: the **MÉMOSZ building** (Lajos Gádoros, Gábor Preisich et al, 1948–50), formerly the headquarters of the National Union of Building Workers. This superb example of modern architecture, its side elevation adorned with a frieze of happily toiling male and female workers (István Tar, 1949), was pronounced an execrable example of the decadent Western style in 1951.

NYUGATI STATION

The turreted building of Nyugati Railway Station (Nyugati pályaudvar; *map p. 429, D1*) stands at the top of Teréz körút. The first steam locomotives in Hungary began service in 1846, running between Budapest and Vác, a distance of 34km. In the decades that followed, Budapest grew hugely and the railway station, now surrounded by the swelling city, rapidly became too small. A tender for a new building was announced, won in 1870 by August de Serres and Gustave Eiffel. The new terminus was completed in 1877 (the framework bears plaques embossed with the Eiffel company name), constructed around the original pitched-roofed building, whose shape still determines the outline of the central steel and glass hangar (the glazier was probably Sigmund Roth, father of the stained-glass artist Miksa Róth). The name Nyugati ('Western') was adopted in 1891, not because of the region served by the trains, but from the name of the company that financed its construction (Magyar Nyugati Vasút). At the time of writing, Nyugati was run down and shabby (with plastic model crows in the ticket office, in an attempt to deter feral pigeons), but some fine and interesting features remain: note the once-grand entrance (beside Platform 10) to the former Royal Waiting Room, its doorway surmounted with the words *Viribus Unitis* ('With Forces United'), adopted by Franz Joseph as the motto of the Dual Monarchy.

Railway enthusiasts will also enjoy the Children's Railway (*see p. 132*) and the Railway History Park (Vasúttörténeti Park; *see p. 322*). The Hungarian railway company offers special charter journeys on old trains. For details, visit the MÁV Nosztalgia office here, beside Platform 10, or consult their website (*www.mavnosztalgia.hu*).

ON AND AROUND NYUGATI TÉR

Nyugati tér, the square on which the station stands, is bisected by a busy road and tramline, undercut by the metro and its underpasses, and traversed by a swooping overpass, built in 1980. In 2010 the 1000% group of artists (*www.thousandpercent. org*) decorated the pillars of the flyover with the words *Én, Te, Ő, Mi, Ti, Ők*, the personal pronouns in Hungarian. Opposite the station, on the site of the once-famous London Hotel, is the tinted glass Skála Metró shopping centre (György Kőváry, 1984), part of the portfolio of the Romanian-Hungarian businessman Sándor Demján, who also owns the huge WestEnd City Center shopping mall (József Finta, 1999), which stretches along Váci út behind the railway station.

The **Radisson Blu Béke Hotel** at Teréz körút 43 (corner of Szondi utca) was once the famous Britannia, with a glass-domed ballroom and Shakespeare-themed murals by Jenő Haranghy (1937). The dome partly survives, as do the paintings. Haranghy's wife served as the model for one of the figures in his *Merchant of Venice* scene.

A few blocks away at Izabella u. 94 (*map p. 429, D1*), is the **Lindenbaum House**, with an elaborate Art Nouveau façade by Frigyes Spiegel (1896–7), crowded with symbols of the elements Earth and Air. Earth is represented by the tree and the dogs. The golden woman striving to rise from Earth to Air is held back by Vanity (the peacock) and Temptation (the snake). Above her shines the Day (a golden sun) and Night draws a veil over a darkening sky, against which birds fly in formation. The next-door house would once have represented the companion elements of Water and Fire but its decorations, destroyed in WWII, have not been restored.

EATING AND DRINKING IN TERÉZVÁROS

RESTAURANTS

ff–fff **Krizia**. Italian restaurant run by Graziano, a chef from Bergamo, and serving delicious seasonal dishes. Weekday lunch menu. Truffles in season. Closed Sun. *Mozsár u. 41. T: +36 1 331 8711, ristorantekrizia.hu. Map p. 429, D2.*

ff **Két Szerecsen**. Popular, lively bistro serving snacks, tapas and an appetising selection of full meals. Good wine selection too. *Nagymező u. 14. T: +36 1 343 1984, ketszerecsen.hu. Map p. 429, D2.*

ff **Klassz**. Restaurant operated by the Bortársaság wine retailer, with a small wine store attached. Excellent location on Andrássy út. Excellent wine selection. Good food. *Andrássy út 41. T: +36 1 599 9490. Map p. 429, D2.*

ff **Café Bouchon**. Bistro-style restaurant offering traditional Hungarian cooking with international influences. Good wines. Closed Sun. *Zichy Jenő u. 33. T: +36 1 353 4094, cafebouchon.hu. Map p. 429, D2.*

Liszt Ferenc tér (*map p. 429, D2*) is lined on both sides with places to eat and drink. Many of them cater expressly to foreign visitors, but their kitchens stay open late, which is useful after an evening at the Music Academy.

CAFÉS AND BARS

For cocktails, go to **Boutiq'**, elegant and snug, a real classic cocktail bar (*Paulay Ede u. 5; closed Sun and Mon; cash only; map p. 429, D2*).

The **Mai Manó Café**, on the ground floor of the House of Hungarian Photographers (*Nagymező u. 20; map p. 429, D2*), has a pleasant café-bar.

The **360 Bar** is a panoramic roof terrace at the top of one of the finest buildings on Andrássy út, good for afternoon or evening drinks. They have special 'igloos' in winter. Open from 2pm. *Andrássy út 39 (take the lift to the top). T: +36 30 356 3047. Map p. 429, D2.*

NYUGATI STATION

District VII:
Erzsébetváros

Erzsébetváros, traditionally Pest's Jewish quarter, grew up in the 18th century as a suburb beyond the old city walls. Development was slow at first: in 1734, only eleven houses are recorded in an area that was still largely rural. This rapidly changed after the Edict of Tolerance (1782), when non-Catholics settled here and buildings went up along the main thoroughfares, Király utca and Dob utca. Erzsébetváros received its formal identity in 1882, when it was named after the Empress Elisabeth, wife of Franz Joseph. Its inner area is still traditionally the Jewish district and recently also became known as the Party District, for its many bars and eateries and its well-known ruin pubs (*see p. 354*). A number of blind fire walls have become vehicles for some interesting street art.

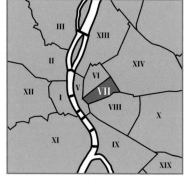

DEÁK TÉR & KIRÁLY UTCA

The busy Deák tér (*map pp. 428–9, C3–D3*), divides Erzsébetváros from the Belváros or inner city. On the Erzsébetváros side it is dominated by the huge, sherry-yellow former **Anker Insurance building** (you can still make out where the old lettering stood on the architrave), built in 1910 by Ignác Alpár. The writer Antal Szerb, author of *A Guide to Budapest for Martians* and *Journey by Moonlight* (one of the great Hungarian novels of the 20th century) was born in a house somewhere on this square in 1901, into an assimilated Jewish family. Szerb and his father converted to Roman Catholicism in 1907 and the young Antal received a Roman Catholic education. His godfather was the prominent (and later controversial; *see p. 187*) bishop Ottokár Prohászka. Despite this, as Fascism and Nazism intensified, Szerb was made to feel the effect of the anti-Jewish laws. His *History of Hungarian Literature* was banned and in 1944 he was sent

GREAT SYNAGOGUE
Detail of the Memorial Willow Tree. Each leaf is inscribed with the name of a Holocaust victim.

to a forced labour camp in west Hungary, where a few months later he was beaten to death by his warders. This is only one of many terrible Hungarian Holocaust stories. Erzsébetváros was the site of the Jewish Ghetto in the latter part of WWII.

THE JEWS OF PEST

Jewish history in the area occupied by today's Budapest goes back many centuries, as Roman-era tombstones decorated with menorahs show. In the Middle Ages, Jewish communities were variously tolerated, encouraged or expelled, depending on royal zeal or financial requirements. After the recapture of Buda from the Turks in 1686, however, the Christian victors adopted a restrictive policy and the Jewish communities dispersed. As the situation became more relaxed in the early 18th century, immigrant communities returned: major contributors to the early commercial character and success of Pest were the Jewish and Greek merchants. While the Greeks could live in the inner city (and many did, in the environs of Vörösmarty tér), the Jews settled in what is now Erzsébetváros.

Detail of the 4th-century tombstone of a Jewish family of Roman Pannonia, featuring two incised menorahs (in the National Museum).

When restrictions were lifted, after the Edict of Tolerance of 1782, the numbers of Jews in Pest swelled dramatically. Figures from the turn of the 19th century record some two hundred families; in two decades this number grew to well over a thousand. The great market they held on the site of present-day Deák tér caused the square to be known as the *Judenmarkt*. Formal emancipation of Jewish citizens came after the Compromise of 1867. Full recognition of the faith as a *religio recepta* (*see p. 370*) came in 1895.

While it has become customary to speak of Erzsébetváros as 'the Jewish district', the truth is that there were many areas of Pest that had sizeable Jewish populations; around Teleki tér in the Eighth District, for example, or in Újlipótváros in District XIII. A century ago, Jewish people represented almost a quarter of the population of Budapest and could be found at almost all levels of society and in most parts of the city. Many of them lived largely assimilated lives; some were from families that had converted to Christianity in order to prosper under Habsburg rule, but it is not uncommon to find families where some members converted and others did not. Unlike Jewish populations in other countries of Central Europe, the Jews of Hungary largely spoke Hungarian rather than Yiddish. They viewed themselves as Hungarians who professed the Jewish faith. In the decades between their emancipation and WWI, their contribution to the artistic, literary, commercial and scientific life of the nation was enormous.

After the First World War, Hungary went from being co-ruler of a vast empire to a severely truncated nation state. Tolerance of multi-ethnicity dwindled and Jews found themselves the targets of anti-Semitism. This became especially pronounced after the collapse of the Communist government of 1919. The concept of *fajvédés* (protection of racial purity) began to take root and a *numerus clausus* law limiting university entrance was introduced in 1920. More laws, restricting the number of Jews who could take up university places or work in certain professions or at certain levels in business, were passed in 1938–9. In the early 1940s, many Jews were dragooned into forced labour camps. On 19th March 1944, the Nazis took over Hungary. The deportations began and Jewish property was confiscated and looted. In November, the Jews of Budapest were confined within a ghetto, surrounded by a hastily erected wooden barricade. Conditions were freezing and insanitary and some ten thousand died. There are memorials to this wall in two places, at Király u. 15 and Dohány u. 32, and a mass grave in the courtyard of the Great Synagogue is now a Garden of Remembrance.

After WWII many of those who survived, mistrustful of Hungary, became Zionists and many emigrated. Today, Jewish life has returned to the city and the community is active and vocal.

KIRÁLY UTCA AND MADÁCH TÉR

Narrow, crowded, busy, grimy **Király utca** (*map p. 429, D3*) has been narrow, crowded, busy and grimy for most of its bustling history. It was its very narrowness that prompted the construction of Andrássy út, the great wide boulevard that pushes outwards to City Park, in order to relieve congestion on this thoroughfare that marks the northern border of Erzsébetváros.

On the corner of Király utca and Károly körút are the **Madách-házak**, two matching blocks borne on square columns and joined by a wide archway. Tall and imposing, of red brick with undressed window apertures, the only adornments are the wrought-iron balcony rails and the antefixes on the roofline. They are the work of Gyula Wälder, to an original design by Aladár Árkay. Seen from a distance—from Gellért Hill, for example—they appear enormous. Built in 1938, in a monumental style reminiscent of Mussolini-era Rome, they were intended as the gateway to a wide thoroughfare running parallel to Andrássy út and cutting right through the heart of the Jewish district, but WWII intervened and the project was never completed. The development tails off at the back of Madách tér, ending ingloriously in a modern office building. The unfinished complex stands on the site of the Orczy-ház, a teeming three-storey building filled with Jewish businesses, flats, shops, a prayer house and school. There were also warehouses here, coffee shops, cellaring facilities and lodgings for commercial travellers: in its heyday, the Orczy-ház must have had something of the atmosphere of a Levantine caravanserai.

Inside the courtyard of **Király u. 15** (go right through to the back) is a section of wall, in alternate courses of stone and brick, marking the boundary of the former Ghetto. A plaque in the form of a map shows its contours, bounded by Károly körút, Dohány utca, Kertész utca and Király utca. The building, now in a very dilapidated state, once housed the Blaue Katze burlesque theatre and nightclub, a source of many a salacious rumour concerning crowned heads and cocottes.

The Gothic-Romantic **Pekáry-ház** (Ferenc Brein, 1847–8) at no. 47 (corner of Csányi utca) was once the home of the writer Gyula Krúdy.

RUMBACH SEBESTYÉN UTCA

At Rumbach Sebestyén u. 11–13 is Otto Wagner's beautiful **Rumbach Street Synagogue** (*map p. 429, D3*), built in 1869–72 for a semi-conservative congregation (*see below*), in a Moorish style reminiscent of the Great Mosque at Córdoba. The façade has three narrow stilted arches between slender towers, with terracotta moulding and alternating bands of red brick and yellow plaster. It was badly damaged in WWII and was for long in a sadly ruinous state. It is now once again the property of the Budapest Jewish community and restoration was underway at the time of writing.

JEWISH DENOMINATIONS IN BUDAPEST

There are three synagogues in inner Erzsébetváros, arranged on the map in the form of a triangle. At the base are the Great Synagogue on Dohány utca and the Rumbach Street Synagogue just to the west of it. At the apex is the synagogue on Kazinczy utca. These three places of Jewish worship represent three denominations of Hungarian Jewry, which since the defeat of Nazism, and the fall of Communism with the return of freedom of worship, now once again play their part in the spiritual life of the city.

The Kazinczy utca synagogue is usually referred to as the Orthodox Synagogue. After the National Jewish Congress of 1868–9, a schism occurred which split Hungarian Jewry into two major sectarian groups known as Orthodox and Neologue. The conservative Orthodox were more numerous in the provinces than in Budapest. Their traditions come partly from the Ashkenazim and partly from the Hasidic world. The Neologue denomination, to which the Great Synagogue belongs, is a reformed form of Judaism which evolved to serve the needs of assimilated Budapest Jewry.

Some communities rejected the two-way split and adhered to the unified Jewish position, refusing to join either of the groups. In reference to the situation before the 1868 Congress, they took the name 'status quo ante'. The Rumbach Street Synagogue served this congregation. There are functioning status quo ante synagogues on Bethlen Gábor tér (*map p. 429, F2*) and at Hegedűs Gyula u. 3 (*map p. 428, C1*).

The Chabad Lubavitch movement, a branch of Hasidism with an active outreach programme, maintains a synagogue and yeshiva on Vasvári Pál utca (*map p. 429, D2*) and synagogues in Óbuda (*see p. 104*) and at Károly körút 20 (*map p. 439, D3*).

From the synagogue, continue up Rumbach Sebestyén utca, past a blind wall on the left with a mural of a Rubik Cube (the text claims that after one turn you only ever need 20 more to solve it), and look right to see, at **no. 6**, a façade studded with bright ceramic tiles with folk motifs. Built in 1913–15 by the Román brothers, it once housed the Budagant glove manufactory—but gone are the days when you looked through the street-facing windows to see ladies industriously stitching; today it is a hostel.

On the left-hand corner of Rumbach Sebestyén utca and Dob utca is a large, red-brick **former electricity substation** (1969), one of three in the city by Ernő Léstyán. The little square that opens out along its length is called **Carl Lutz Park**, in memory of the Swiss diplomat who saved many Jews during WWII. Memorials include a striking two-figure statue group (Tamás Szabó, 1991), showing the Angel of Mercy descending to rescue a bound captive, and a small rock carved with a sentence from Lutz's own diary: 'This having to make snap choices of who to save—it's insanity. Where is God?'

CARL LUTZ AND THE RIGHTEOUS GENTILES

Carl Lutz (1895–1975) was vice-consul at the Swiss Embassy in Budapest from 1942 until the end of WWII. Prior to that he had served in Jaffa, in what was then Palestine. When the Nazis began the transport of Budapest Jews to concentration camps, he set up over 70 safe houses in the city (one of them was the famous Glass House; *see p. 153*), where Jews could shelter under neutral Swiss diplomatic protection, and issued safe-conduct documents for Jews wishing to leave the country. He had secured permission to issue 8,000 of these but managed by various ruses to produce a good many more. In total he is credited with saving over 62,000 lives and is honoured as Righteous Among the Nations. His actions are said to have so infuriated the Germans that they contemplated having him killed. The stretch of Danube embankment above Margaret Bridge bears his name.

The decision to rename sections of the Danube embankment was taken in 2010. Other parts of it commemorate Raoul Wallenberg (*see p. 300*); Jane Haining (a Church of Scotland missionary who died in Auschwitz); Angelo Rotta (papal nuncio and leader of the Catholic resistance to the Nazis in Budapest; Gábor Sztehlo (Lutheran pastor who saved many Jews, particularly children); Friedrich Born (Swiss representative of the Red Cross in Budapest during WWII); József Antall Sr (lawyer and politician who saved the lives of many Polish Jews); Ángel Sanz Briz (Spanish diplomat who saved the lives of some 5,000); Bl. Sára Salkaházi (Catholic sister and saviour of many Jews, executed by the Arrow Cross) and Margit Slachta (the founder of the Sisters of Social Service, of which Salkaházi was a member. Slachta likewise saved many Jewish lives. She was also the first Hungarian woman MP, elected in 1920.).

THE GREAT SYNAGOGUE & JEWISH MUSEUM

Map p. 429, D3. Open 10–dusk daily except Sat; closes at 1.30pm on Fri. A single ticket gives entry to the Synagogue, Jewish Museum and Garden of Remembrance. In high season there can be lengthy queues at the ticket desks. You will be asked to pass through a security check before entering the precinct. Men will be given a paper kippah for entry to the synagogue. Guided tours begin inside the synagogue building; national flags show the location of tours in different languages. greatsynagogue.hu.

Rising magnificently on its corner site on Herzl Tivadar tér (named after the founder of modern Zionism, Theodor Herzl, who was born in a house on this site in 1860) is the Dohány Street Synagogue, also known as the Great Synagogue (Nagy Zsinagóga), the most famous Jewish place of worship in Budapest.

THE GREAT SYNAGOGUE

Built in 1854–9 by Ludwig Förster under the supervision of Ignác Wechselmann, this was the first purpose-built synagogue for the Jews of Pest. It is not only the largest synagogue in Europe but the second largest in the world (after Temple Emanu-El in New York). It is also one of the oldest monumental buildings in Pest, pre-dating the Academy of Sciences (1867), the Opera House (1884), the Parliament (1902) and St Stephen's Basilica (1906). The only building of a comparable size built before this synagogue and still standing is the National Museum (1847). Its dimensions and date say much about the confidence and sense of security of Budapest Jews in the second half of the 19th century.

Like Förster's earlier synagogue in Vienna, the style here is distinctly Moorish. Its entrance is a rounded archway beneath a huge rose window. On either side rise two octagonal towers topped with onion domes. The synagogue is home to a reformed or 'Neologue' congregation (*see p. 214*): an Orthodox synagogue would not have towers and in the interior there are other features which mark a departure from the strict tradition. The bimah, for example, a raised platform behind gilded railings, is placed at the east end, to which all eyes are drawn by its magnificence. In an Orthodox synagogue the bimah would normally be sited exactly in the centre. Here it is reminiscent of the sanctuary of a Christian church, perhaps a sign that the architects of Dohány Street Synagogue were gentiles. The magnificent Ark of the Torah, a temple in miniature crested with gilding, is by Frigyes Feszl. Behind and on either side rises the organ, another element not found in an Orthodox synagogue. The synagogue also has a choir, yet another departure from orthodoxy.

The decoration on the walls, ceiling and windows is brightly colourful and geometric, with eight-pointed stars a prominent motif. A double-tiered women's gallery is borne on slender columns.

THE JEWISH MUSEUM

The museum building (*entrance from inside the synagogue precinct with the same ticket*) dates from 1930 and stands on the site of the house where Theodor Herzl was born. Its collection is rich, formed of items either donated or salvaged from synagogues destroyed in the Holocaust. As a result, the provenance of some of the articles on display is unknown. There are prayer books, liturgical vestments, temple lamps, kiddush cups, seder plates and articles relating to Jewish high holidays and funeral rites. A row of stained-glass windows was donated by prominent members of the Budapest Jewish community. Among the donors' names is that of Leó Goldberger (*see p. 105*), on the window showing *Jacob's Dream*. The final wall on the first floor is a mizrah wall, facing east. Through a window to the left of it, as a plaque points out, you can see the site of the gate of the old ghetto, erected in the winter of 1944. Don't miss the tiny silver commemorative badge with a bust of Theodor Herzl, made in Israel in 1960, the centenary of his birth in a house on this site.

On the upper floor is an exhibition of precious objects, including a 'Congress Album' presented to József Eötvös in gratitude for his initiative in organising the Hungarian National Jewish Congress of 1868–9.

·BUDAY·GOLDBERGER·LEO· ÉS·NEJE·SZÜL. POPPER·IDA·

JEWISH MUSEUM
Stained-glass window of *Jacob's Dream*, donated by Leó Goldberger (1930s).

THE GARDEN OF REMEMBRANCE

In the harsh winter of 1944–5, when the Ghetto was set up here and Jews were confined within it, many died of hunger and cold and were buried in the Synagogue garden, which effectively is now a Holocaust mass grave. Simple **granite plaques** commemorate those whose lives were lost. Archive photographs on the columns of the covered walk show Herzl's house (on the site of the present museum) and the liberation of the Ghetto by Soviet troops in January 1945. Many of the dead were never identified.

At the end of the Garden is the **Heroes' Temple** (László Vágó and Ferenc Faragó, 1931), dedicated to those who lost their lives in WWI. Beyond it is a further garden and cobbled court with the **Memorial Willow Tree** (Imre Varga, 1990), its metal leaves inscribed with Holocaust victims' names. It is a gift of the Emanuel Foundation, set up by the actor Tony Curtis in memory of his father, Emanuel Schwartz, who was a Hungarian emigré to the US.

At the back of the courtyard is a plaque commemorating the dismantling of the ghetto walls by the 'liberating Soviet army'. This is a rare surviving example of such phraseology on a public monument: whatever else the Soviets may have brought to Hungary, it was certainly liberation and the chance of life for the city's Jewish population.

The large building on the far (east) side of the courtyard is the **Goldmark Hall**. Built in 1929, it is named after Károly Goldmark (1830–1915), a cantor's son who went on to become a composer of enormously popular operas. After 1938, when the anti-Jewish laws hindered Jews from appearing on stage, the Goldmark Hall was one of the few places open to them. Concerts are still held here. The building also houses the national rabbinical offices.

The exit turnstile takes you out into **Wesselényi utca** (note the symbols of the Tribes of Israel on the façade of Goldmark Hall; István Örkényi Strasser, 1931). From the street you can look back into the Garden of Remembrance. Against the railings are cut-out figures of prominent Hungarian Jews, including the journalist Joseph Pulitzer, doctor Frigyes Korányi, industrialist Manfréd Weiss, author Antal Szerb, pharmacist Gedeon Richter, poet Miklós Radnóti and architect Marcell Komor. The last four were victims of the Holocaust.

THE ASTORIA CORNER & DOHÁNY UTCA

On the **corner of Károly körút and Rákóczi út** (*map p. 429, D3*) are two remarkable buildings, similar yet different. The first is an apartment block built in 1939 as rental property for the Academy of Sciences. With its cylindrical tower, it was designed by Dezső Hültl. The Tisza shoe company has premises on the ground floor, selling sports and casual shoes designed and handmade in Hungary (*see p. 355*). Adjoining it is a slightly earlier apartment block, the **Georgia-ház** (Ede Novák and Béla Barát, 1935), with a tall clock tower. The **East-West Business Center** on the other side of the road, with a polygonal tower, was planned to harmonise with these buildings (note the gold 'Scythian' stag on its front-facing gable end). Built in 1989–91, it was the first such modern office block in post-Communist Budapest.

    Rákóczi út is busy and not particularly pleasant to walk along, but dip down it to see **no. 14**, an interesting late Art Nouveau/early Modernist building of 1912 by the Löffler brothers (who designed the Orthodox synagogue; *see p. 220*). On the roofline, looking fixedly down at the crowds below, are four extraordinary colossi by the sculptor Géza Maróti. Just beyond at **no. 18**, on the corner of Kazinczy utca, is the former Erzsébetváros Bank, a 1912 work by Béla Lajta.

    Behind Rákóczi út, at **Dohány u. 22** (*map p. 429, D3*), is the **former Árkád Bazár** toy emporium (László and József Vágó, 1908), its corner elevation an interesting mixture of angle and curve. The exterior cladding is fixed with rivets in the style of the Viennese architect Otto Wagner and the façade decorated with images of children and toys (girls with dolls and boys with rocking horses). Much of the tiling is now sadly lost. Diagonally opposite, at **no. 13** is the Magvető publishing company's café and bookshop, a modern incarnation of the literary coffee house. At **Síp u. 17** is the **Menorah House** (so-called for the designs on its balcony railings), built in 1908 by the Löffler brothers. The entrance door is particularly fine, with bird and Tree of Life motifs.

DOHÁNY UTCA
Detail of László and József Vágó's former toyshop façade (1908).

At **Dohány u. 32–34** is another **memorial of the Ghetto wall** (*for the one on Király utca, see p. 213*) Concrete panels with a map attached commemorate where the wall stood. Past a kosher mini-market, just beyond the corner of Nyár utca (*map p. 429, E3*), at **Dohány u. 44**, is the façade of the **former Hungária Fürdő baths** (Emil Ágoston, 1907–10). The main limestone relief of voluptuous nudes wallowing in water is the original (restored 2010), the others are reconstructions since the building had fallen into a bad state of decay. The Latin motto reads *Corpora sana dabunt balnea* ('Baths give clean bodies'). The baths closed in the 1920s and the building became a hotel, which is once again its function today. The adjoining building at **no. 46**, with the Mr XL outsize menswear shop, is by László Vágó (1929).

THE 'PARTY DISTRICT'

A large part of the Seventh District between Károly körút and the Nagykörút is familiarly known as the *Bulinegyed* or Party District. It is filled with cafés, bars and eateries of all kinds and it is here too that you will find many of Budapest's famous 'ruin pubs' (*see p. 354*). In high summer in some parts of the area, tourists far outnumber locals. Much of the district is still very dilapidated: local opinion is divided on the bars and clubs. When they first appeared, they were lively, fun and a uniquely Budapest phenomenon. With their popularity came crowds, noise and trash. There have been protests about street noise, drugs and obscene behaviour and many feel that the area has become impossible to live in. Others argue that the injection of life is necessary to a district where retail and commercial businesses were struggling and where many residential properties were in dangerously poor repair. Although a referendum in 2018 was inconclusive, discussions were still underway about the district's future when this book went to press, with hopes that a solution can be found that helps both the resident and the transient population. Amidst the roistering and the morning-after-the-night-before atmosphere, these streets preserve some interesting monuments.

DOB UTCA AND THE GOZSDU UDVAR

Dob utca (*map p. 429, D3*) runs through the heart of the Party District and is lined on both sides with restaurants and bars. A brave survival from simpler days is **Fröhlich**, a kosher pastry shop at no. 22. The long arcade known as the **Gozsdu udvar** opens at no. 16 and runs through to Király utca. Designed by Győző Czigler and built in 1901, with funds provided in the will of the wealthy Romanian lawyer Emanuel Gojdu (Gozsdu in Hungarian), it was partly a residential and partly a commercial development. Its courtyards and ground-floor spaces now make up a lively parade of shops, cafés, bars and restaurants. The tomb of Emanuel Gozsdu (1802–70) is in Kerepesi Cemetery.

KAZINCZY UTCA AND KLAUZÁL TER

Dob utca crosses Kazinczy utca about halfway along its length. This cobbled street is the heart of Orthodox Jewish Erzsébetváros. The Jewish character of the shops and businesses is not as pronounced as it once was but there is a kosher restaurant at no. 33, a kosher café and bakery at no. 28 (Tel Aviv Café), a ritual bath (mikveh) at no. 16, and it is not uncommon to see people adhering to Orthodox dress codes: the men in fedoras and married women wearing wigs. It was also on this street, at no. 55 in 1836, that József Schneider invented the Hungarian playing card design, with its characters from the story of William Tell. The rebel Tell, it is believed, was a coded expression of Hungary's own (at that time taboo) revolutionary impulses.

The **Orthodox Synagogue** (*map p. 429, D3; open daily except Sat; fee*) was built in 1911–13 to designs by the Löffler brothers. It has been lovingly restored following war damage and subsequent neglect. The interior is opulently decorated: the ceiling is a cerulean blue studded with stars; the beams holding up the women's gallery are painted with motifs of pitchers; the magnificent east wall is clad in coloured marbles with a motif of blessing hands. The niche of the Torah ark is flanked by green fluted columns. Everywhere in the synagogue the motif of the menorah is repeated, either sculpted, painted or in glass. It is often shown as five-branched—an inaccurate representation but one which cannot be attributed to the fact that the architects were gentiles: they were not. It is perhaps because no menorah can deign accurately to replicate the gold candlestick that was looted from the Second Temple by the Romans in AD 70. The bimah (decorated with delicate carved designs) is exactly in the centre of the interior space. Following Orthodox tradition too, weddings here are celebrated out of doors. There is a huppah, or wedding canopy, in the courtyard at the rear.

A little way beyond the synagogue, at no. 21, the **Electrotechnical Museum** (Elektrotechnikai Múzeum) occupies a former substation. The display is charmingly old-fashioned and partly interactive (*open Tues–Sun 10–5, until 6pm in summer; entrance on the right of the courtyard; ring the bell*). In the courtyard are a number of old neon signs, removed from shopfronts around the city.

KAZINCZY UTCA
Stylised menorah motif in the terrazzo floor of the Orthodox Synagogue vestibule.

Returning to Dob utca, turn right to reach Klauzál tér. On your way, you pass the back of the Orthodox Synagogue and the building of the **former Orthodox school**, also designed by the Löffler brothers (1912). A kosher butcher operates here.

Klauzál tér (*map p. 429, D3*), a large square with a playground in its centre, was at the heart of the Ghetto of 1944–5. Many of the dead were buried here; like the garden of the Great Synagogue (*see above*), it is another mass grave of the Holocaust. At the east side is a market hall (*open daily from 7am*), built in 1897 (restored 2015). It houses a supermarket and a mixture of permanent shops and itinerant stalls.

Further up Dob utca towards the Nagykörút, the corner building at Kertész u. 36 (*map p. 429, E2*) is home to the **Fészek Klub**. Built by Vilmos Freund in 1867 for the Pest Jewish Women's Association, it offered accommodation to orphaned girls as well as a soup kitchen. The club was founded here in 1901. Its name, literally 'Nest', is an acronym formed from the Hungarian words for painter, architect, sculptor, musician, singer and actor: an artists' club, in other words. Among its founders were the painters Gyula Benczúr, Adolf Fényes and József Rippl-Rónai, the sculptor Alajos Stróbl and the architect Ödön Lechner. Today the Fészek has lost a lot of its lustre. The inner courtyard restaurant, whose architecture is derived both from Brunelleschi's Florence and early Christian Rome, is now a Cuban-themed bar.

ERZSÉBETVÁROS BEYOND THE NAGYKÖRÚT

At the corner of the Nagykörút and Dohány utca is the famous **New York Coffee House** (*map p. 429, E3*), in a grandiose Eclectic pile built for the New York Life Insurance company in 1894. The architect was Alajos Hauszmann, with Flóris Korb and Kálmán Giergl. The lamps around the entrance are borne by bronze fauns. In its heyday the

DOB UTCA

Façade mosaic by Zsigmond Vajda and Miksa Róth, on the Dob utca Primary School, showing girl pupils singing, knitting and making a tapestry. The text being stitched is the first line from Vörösmarty's patriotic *Szózat*: 'Be unyieldingly true to your homeland, O Magyar.'

New York was the most celebrated of all Budapest's literary coffee houses (*see pp. 349–50*). In 2001 the building was bought by the Italian Boscolo hotels company. The interior décor, with magnificent solomonic columns, is partly intact but the New York now largely trades on its former fame and caters almost exclusively to tourists.

A POST OFFICE, A SCHOOL AND A THEATRE

On the corner of Dob utca and Hársfa utca (*map p. 429, E2*) is a fine **Post Office building** (Gyula Rimanóczy, 1939), its façade adorned with statues (Gábor Boda, 1940). The corner figure represents St Stephen. To the left facing Dob utca is an ancient Magyar messenger (with carrier pigeon). Facing Hársfa utca are allegories of Politics (represented as King Andrew II, who in 1222 promulgated the *Golden Bull*, a charter somewhat resembling the English *Magna Carta*); Art (modelled on Rimanóczy, the building's architect); the Army, Science, Technology and Agriculture. Inside is the **Stamp Museum** (Bélyegmúzeum; *Hársfa u. 47, open Tues–Sun 10–6, belyegmuzeum. hu*), which will be of interest not only to philatelists but also for the chance it gives to see more of the interior of this fine building. The walls are decorated with specially commissioned Zsolnay tiles, with a perforated design to make them look like stamps.

Further up Dob utca, at no. 85, is an **Art Nouveau primary school** building (Ármin Hegedűs, 1905–6) with colourful mosaic decoration of boys and girls at play (by Zsigmond Vajda and Miksa Róth). Beautifully restored, the scenes show boys learning geography, playing soldiers and catching butterflies while the girls, clad in spotless pinafores, sing and do needlework. In the centre, boys and girls together are enjoying a game of Squeak, Piggy, Squeak.

In the sharp angle where Izabella utca and Rejtő Jenő utca meet is the **Magyar Színház** theatre (*map p. 429, E2*). This was the Nemzeti (National) Theatre until the construction of the new National Theatre on the Danube (*see p. 269*). It is housed in a striking building of the mid-1960s, its façade decorated with a relief in Zsolnay pyrogranite. Inside is a mosaic mural of a Greek chorus by Jenő Barcsay.

RÓZSÁK TERE

Rózsák tere is dominated by the great neo-Gothic Church of St Elizabeth of Hungary (Árpád-házi Szent Erzsébet plébániatemplom; *map p. 429, F2*). Its twin bell-towers, fitted with clocks that never quite seem to tell the same time, rise high into the sky (76m). In front of the church, which is approached across a wide forecourt paved in yellow *keramit*, is a statue (József Damkó, 1931) of the titular saint with roses in the fold of her cloak, an allusion to the miracle associated with her (*see below*).

ST ELIZABETH OF HUNGARY

Elizabeth (1207–31) was the daughter of the Hungarian king Andrew II. At a young age she was married to Louis, Landgrave of Thuringia, who died of fever in Otranto, where he had been planning to take a boat to the Holy Land on Crusade. His death was a great blow to Elizabeth. She took a vow of celibacy and devoted herself to charitable works, founding a hospital at Marburg where she worked in person, ministering to the sick. The miracle of the roses is said to have taken place when she was observed taking food to the poor. Accused of hiding stolen treasure in her cloak, she was ordered to open it. On doing so, the bread rolls tumbled out in the form of red and white roses.

The first church was built in the 1880s, on the site of a poorhouse. Its congregation swiftly outgrew it and in 1895 Franz Joseph laid the foundation stone for its successor, which was completed in 1901 to the designs of Imre Steindl. It contains fine metalwork by Gyula Jungfer (the aluminium and bronze crown-shaped candelabrum over the crossing, as well as the elaborate font lid) and Miksa Róth, by whom there are six surviving stained-glass windows at the east end. These show saints important to the Hungarian Christian tradition: St Margaret (*see p. 293*), St John the Almoner (whose relics were presented to King Matthias by the Ottoman sultan), St Adalbert (10th-century Bohemian missionary to the Magyars), St Stephen (*see p. 156*), St John of Capestrano (*see p. 34*) and St Gertrude (mystic saint of Thuringia, where Elizabeth of Hungary lived after her marriage). All the other windows by Róth and his workshop were destroyed in WWII. The mayor's choir stalls, on the left of the chancel, are by Károly Lingel, a carpenter from Germany who set up a workshop in Budapest in the 1860s, moving to Rózsa utca, very close to this church, in 1872. The Lingel company suffered after nationalisation but was re-founded in 1997.

Close by, in a small park at the junction of Izabella utca and Alsó erdősor, is a bronze **sculpture of a Great Dane** with carefully cropped ears (Gyula Maugsch, 1937). It is a portrait of a dog named Dr Fool, who was the favourite pet of the lawyer and civil servant Károly Némethy.

MIKSA RÓTH MUSEUM

Map p. 429, F2. Nefelejcs u. 26. Open Tues–Sun 2–6, rothmuzeum.hu. Metro line M2 or M4 to Keleti pályaudvar, then take Exit C.

The museum occupies the building where the great glass artist Miksa Róth had his studio and manufactory, and where he and his family also lived. The entrance is through the courtyard (the manufactory occupied the building at the back). The ticket office is on the first floor, where the studio was (note the lovely mosaic fireplace). The family lived on the floor above, where three rooms are preserved as they were in Róth's day. All the furniture and ornaments are the originals.

MIKSA RÓTH

Miksa Róth was born in 1865, the son of Sigmund Roth, a Hungarian Jewish glazier and glass painter who died bankrupt in 1885, leaving a wife and seven children. Miksa and his younger brother Manó learned their trade at their father's side but it was Miksa who was to make his name from it, taking over the workshop in 1884. He was fortunate in his timing; the medievalist craze of the era had made stained glass fashionable and Róth spent some time studying the Gothic cathedrals of Europe. At the time there were a number of workshops in Hungary producing painted glass but it was the manufactory of Miksa Róth that became the most sought-after. Among the earliest Budapest public buildings which have windows by his hand are the Agricultural Museum (1896) and the Parliament (1890). In the 1890s, Róth introduced the opalised style of Louis Comfort Tiffany to Hungary. After winning silver at the Paris World's Fair in 1900, Róth's work became greatly in demand, not only for public commissions from both church and state but in private villas too. Many a stairway or winter garden was adorned with his lovely designs of flowers, birds and nymphs, either naturalistic or in a more geometricised, Jugendstil manner. The Gresham Palace and Liszt Academy both have glass by Róth (both 1907). Róth worked closely with a number of artists and architects: with Ödön Lechner in the former Postal Savings Bank; with Kernstok in the Schiffer Villa; with Rippl-Rónai in the Ernst Museum; and with the artists of the Gödöllő artists' colony.

In 1939, anti-Jewish laws forced Róth to close the workshop. The news of his nephew, Artúr Elek's suicide in April of 1944 seems to have precipitated a crisis and he simply lost the will to live. He died in June leaving no successor. His brother Manó is thought to have died in the Holocaust and his artistically-inclined grandson, treated as a class enemy by the Communists, emigrated to the US in 1956. His eldest daughter Amália continued to live in the house on Nefelejcs utca until her death in 1989.

The display includes a great many examples of glass in a variety of styles. There are portraits (including *Woman in a Purple Hat* and the splendid portrait of a bourgeois lady and her sons, both c. 1885), ecclesiastical glass, domestic glass (two panels of a dining room door showing fish and a boar's head being served), glass with geometric and floral designs, glass imitating painting (*Nocturnal Landscape with Lilies*, 1898) and glass mosaic (including the striking 1898 relief mosaic of a pomegranate tree, with ripe eosin-glazed pomegranates breaking open on the bough). The winning entries for the

1900 Paris World's Fair, *Pax* and *Sunrise*, are also on show. Pax's hair and helmet are of Tiffany-style opal glass.

EATING AND DRINKING IN ERZSÉBETVÁROS

There is no shortage of places to eat and drink in the Seventh District. It is home to hundreds of cafés, bars and restaurants. New places are opening all the time: some endure, a number do not. While Erzsébetváros remains the 'Party District', this is a trend that is likely to continue. The list below mainly features longer-established places.

RESTAURANTS

ff–fff **Fausto's**. Excellent Italian restaurant established here by Fausto Di Vora in the 1990s and still impeccable. Choose between the informal *osteria* or the more elegant *ristorante*, next to each other at the same address, opposite the Great Synagogue. Closed Sun. Ristorante also closed Sat lunchtime. *Dohány u. 3–5. T: +36 1 269 6806, fausto.hu. Map p. 429, D3.*

f–ff **Kőleves**. A kosher butcher operated at this address from 1914. It was never nationalised and closed down only recently. The Kőleves restaurant and beer garden doesn't serve pork and you will often find cholent (*sólet*, a Jewish bean stew) on the menu. This was one of the earliest places to open in the Party District and is still one of the best. *Kazinczy u. 41. T: +36 1 322 1011, kolevesvendeglo. hu. Map p. 429, D3.*

f–ff **M**. Small, simple, friendly place offering homely Central European cooking. Cash only. Closed Mon. *Kertész u. 48. metterem.hu. Map p. 429, E2.*

f–ff **Sáo**. Popular Vietnamese-Chinese food bar in the Gozsdu udvar. Friendly and lively. Excellent dumplings. Best to book. *Holló u. 10. T: +36 319 4099. Map p. 429, D3.*

f **Kádár Étkezde**. A beloved survival, a tiny, old-fashioned place serving cheap hot lunches. Traditional Magyar Jewish cooking. *Klauzál tér 9. T: +36 1 321 3622. Map p. 429, E3.*

CAFÉS, BARS AND WINE BARS

Doblo is a popular wine bar in an atmospheric brick-vaulted building in the heart of the Jewish district (*Dob u. 20, budapestwine.com; map p. 429, D3*). Another excellent wine bar is **Kadarka** at Király u. 42 (*kadarkabar. hu, map p. 429, D2*). **Pharma**, at Kazinczy u. 35 (*map p. 429, D3*), is a tiny cocktail bar designed to resemble a pharmacist's shop.

Fröhlich is a long-established kosher patisserie still in business at Dob u. 22 (*open 9–6, closes at 2pm on Fri, closed Sat; map p. 429, D3*).

Solinfo (a lamp shop with a café) serves coffee, cakes, breakfasts (eggs on toast) and light snack meals. It has a mixed clientèle: students, locals, tourists with suitcases in tow (*Wesselényi u. 6, entrance on Rumbach utca; map p. 429, D3*).

District VIII: Józsefváros

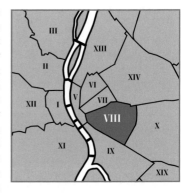

The Eighth District, Józsefváros, takes its name from Emperor Joseph II, the son and successor of Maria Theresa. It is one of the oldest districts of Pest and today one of the most ethnically diverse, with Roma and Chinese communities as well as small numbers of Africans and Arabs. The district's population has always been mixed: historically it was both an aristocratic area, filled with the town palaces of Hungary's noble families, and a manufacturing district, notorious for the damp squalor of its workers' housing. Cheap rents also made it popular with artists and writers. Sándor Petőfi lived here at various addresses; Attila József went to school here; Ferenc Molnár's much-loved novel *The Paul Street Boys* is set here. The bohemian flavour still lingers today, in the many bars, clubs and peculiar dens and hangouts. Though its association in the popular imagination with violence, prostitution and the underworld is hard to dislodge, Józsefváros is also a district of science and learning, home to a large number of hospitals and university campuses. It is here too that you will find the Hungarian National Museum.

ON & AROUND MÚZEUM KÖRÚT

The **Astoria Hotel** stands at a busy crossroads (*map p. 429, D3*), on the site of the Hatvan Gate in the Pest city walls. The hotel was purpose-built in 1914 (Rezső Hikisch and Emil Ágoston) on the site of the Unger family smithy (*see p. 188*) as well as of a coffee house and inn that was popular with politicians and writers, including Sándor Petőfi (*see p. 181*), who had lodgings next door. In its heyday the Astoria was one of the grandest and most exclusive hotels in the city. It was here that the Aster Revolution began in 1918, when from his room on the upper floor Count Mihály Károlyi (*see p. 246*) addressed a crowd in the street below. The hotel then became the headquarters of the National Council, which was replaced in 1919 by Béla Kún's Soviet-style Republic of Councils.

KEREPESI CEMETERY
Detail of the mausoleum of Lajos Kossuth.

Múzeum körút, the busy thoroughfare which leads from Astoria to the National Museum, describes an arc which traces the line of the medieval city walls. As you head south towards the museum, you pass Fekete Udvar at **no. 5**, a pleasant coffee bar (*see p. 259*). Next door at no. 7 is the dilapidated **Unger-ház**, in Rundbogenstil with box balconies borne by griffins and a decoration of eight-pointed stars. It is an early work (1852) by Miklós Ybl, built for the Unger family (*see p. 188*). Its inner courtyard, paved with wooden blocks, goes all the way through to Magyar utca. Inside the courtyard is the Könyvudvar bookshop, which makes the boast of being the cheapest in the city. The block of flats at no. 9 was a **Lottery House** (*see p. 267*). Just beyond it, look down Ferenczy István utca to see (on the right) a small section of the **medieval city wall** itself. Further on, past the **Központi Antikvárium** second-hand bookshop (still retaining its old owl shop sign), another vestige of the walls, a fine crenellated section, is preserved in the courtyard of no. 21.

On the other side of the main road is the **ELTE University Humanities faculty**, in yellow-and-red chequerwork brick, built in 1880–3 by Imre Steindl, better known as the architect of the Parliament building. Under its Tuscan Doric loggia, behind railings and encased within another set of protective bars, is a **pendulum clock** dating from 1912. At one time it had the reputation as the only reliably accurate timepiece in the city (it also has a dial showing the seconds) and passers-by would stop here to set their watches by it. Next door at **no. 10** were the headquarters of the Holy Cross Society (Szent Kereszt Egyesület), a Catholic organisation founded during WWII to offer legal and financial support to Jews. Its secretary, Gábor Ervin, was himself of Jewish descent (related to the poet Heine on his mother's side). To demonstrate solidarity, he attached the yellow star to his cassock. He was seized by the Arrow Cross in 1944 and shot into the Danube. The **Múzeum kávéház** at no. 12, in business since 1885, still offers traditional Hungarian cuisine.

THE HUNGARIAN NATIONAL MUSEUM

Map p. 429, D4. Múzeum körút 14–16. Open Tues–Sun 10–6. Photography allowed on purchase of a separate photo ticket. Café and shop. mnm.hu.

The Hungarian National Museum (Magyar Nemzeti Múzeum) occupies a stately and imposing building, Budapest's best example of Neoclassical architecture, artistically significant but also nationally iconic as the scene of a popular gathering on 15th March 1848, when the poet and freedom-fighter Sándor Petőfi addressed a massed crowd in the forecourt, a rally that marked the beginning of the anti-Habsburg revolution. The museum building's status as a symbol of national identity is strengthened by the fact that the country's 19th-century governing bodies used it as a place of congress: the Upper House of the National Assembly met here in 1848; the Lower House in the early 1860s; and after the establishment of the Dual Monarchy in 1867, the Upper House once again assembled here until the inauguration of the new Parliament

HUNGARIAN NATIONAL MUSEUM

building beside the Danube. The National Museum steps are still a focal point during Hungarian national celebrations.

HISTORY OF THE MUSEUM AND ITS BUILDING

The museum's beginnings date from 1802, when Count Ferenc Széchényi (father of the great István Széchenyi; *see p. 164*) donated his personal collection of prints, manuscripts, books, coins, medals, antiquities and paintings to the nation. Five years later, partly in line with a growing trend for public museums following models in Oxford, London, Paris and Rome, and partly born of an ever-more urgent sense of Hungarian nationhood, an institution was founded to embody the great idea and land was purchased on this site in 1813. The present building was completed in 1847, to designs by Mihály Pollack. Austerely graceful, it stands well placed on a curve in the street, a landmark from both sides of the road. Access is through two sets of gates placed left and right of centre, within an iron railing designed by Miklós Ybl.

A wide flight of steps leads up to an octastyle Corinthian portico. In the tympanum is an allegorical frieze showing Pannonia offering laurel crowns to Art and Science (right) and History and Reputation (left). It is the latter two with which the museum now largely deals, having evolved to become the leading institution devoted to Hungarian history (and, inevitably, politics). The collection is continuously augmented.

THE GARDEN

The museum is surrounded by a spacious garden, shaded by trees whose ancestors (the limes) were donated in the 1850s by Baron Simon Sinas, from his Gödöllő estate (*see p. 332*). A recent programme of re-landscaping and replanting has aimed to create a place of public recreation in the English park style. The garden is adorned with statuary and memorials, including a column from the Roman Forum donated by Italy in 1929, a copy of the *Apollo Belvedere*, a statue of the founder, Ferenc Széchényi, in the robes of the Order of the Golden Fleece (János Istók, 1902) and, in front at the very centre—making an unobstructed view of the main façade impossible—an outsize monument to the poet János Arany (Alajos Stróbl, 1893; restored 2018). On the left side of the steps, on the rear of the parapet, is a plaque erected in 1900 to Sándor Petőfi, who 'declaimed on this spot the first song of Hungarian freedom'. The song alluded to is his famous *Nemzeti dal* (*see p. 181*), which he did indeed compose in Pest in 1848 although it did not form part of his address to the crowd here on March 15th of that year. Copies of the poem had been run off the press hours before, together with the Twelve Points (*see p. 15*). Under the pattering rain of that historic March afternoon (surviving copies of the Twelve Points are visibly rain-spattered), the patriotic assembly coagulated into a revolutionary mob, streaming from here across the Danube to free Mihály Táncsics from his prison on Castle Hill (*see p. 30*). In his diary, István Széchenyi writes of 'the Furies which Batthyány and Kossuth have let loose...'

THE COLLECTIONS

As you walk into the museum, beneath the towering portico ceiling, spare a glance for the floor, which is paved with slabs of red Tardos marble, particularly rich in fossil life. The museum's collections are arranged on three floors, accessed from the central Doric-columned hall. The holdings are divided into four separate displays: the Roman (and medieval) lapidarium in the basement; the archaeological collection and the Coronation Mantle on the ground floor; and the first-floor display covering Hungary's history from the founding of the state to the fall of Communism.

THE ROMAN LAPIDARIUM

The basement displays a few fragments of **medieval stonework**, after which you pass through the small café and down another flight of stairs to the Lapidarium, a beautifully presented collection of **Roman sarcophagi, altars, tombstones and other stone fragments**, all excellently labelled. The huge room is well lit and very little visited; you might even find that you have the rich collection to yourself. In the centre of the floor is a mosaic pavement from the grand apsidal hall of a Roman villa at Baláca, near Veszprém. The entire picture space is filled with symmetrical geometric designs, with a figurative element right at the top: a bird pecking at berries on a branch. Outside the main room, a narrow chamber has sculptures and a relief from the Budaörs Mithraeum (*for the cult of Mithras, see p. 112*).

The star Roman exhibit is the extraordinary **Sevso Treasure**, which at the time of writing was destined shortly to go on display here. The Treasure comprises 14 pieces of 4th/5th-century Roman silver, found in a cache in the 1970s, packed into a copper cauldron. The silver, which has had a turbulent history, was acquired by the Hungarian government in two tranches in 2014 and 2017. The finest piece is the huge Hunting Plate, a salver with a central roundel showing figures dining under a canopy. The whole design is of silver-gilt with the details picked out in niello. Circling the roundel is the following inscription: H[A]EC SEVSO TIBI DVRENT PER SAECULA MVLTA POSTERIS VT PROSINT VASCVLA DIGNA TVIS ('May these vessels remain with you for centuries, Sevso, and serve your descendants worthily'). Sevso was probably a wealthy Romanised Celt who lived in one of the villas in the neighbourhood of Lake Balaton: the word 'PELSO', the Roman name for the lake, features on the plate, along with a tiny Chi Rho: Sevso must also have been a Christian.

THE AGE OF THE GREAT MIGRATIONS

Inconspicuously signed on the ground floor is the 'Archaeological Exhibition', which also goes under the title 'On the East-West Frontier'. Neither name adequately suggests the riches that are displayed here. The exhibition traces the history of settlement and waves of migration into and out of the territory of historic and present-day Hungary. It is superbly displayed, well captioned and should on no account be missed.

The arrangement is chronological, beginning with the Stone and Copper Ages. Alongside the usual tools, utensils and fertility idols made of clay, stone and bone are some lovely gold adornments. Tools, weapons and accoutrements from the Bronze Age are shown alongside more gold pieces of exquisite quality, including fine torcs and bracelets. With the Iron Age comes the culture of the nomadic **Scythians** of Eastern Europe and the Central Asian steppe (8th–5th centuries BC). Two *kurgan* (tumulus) cremation burials in east Hungary have yielded examples of the stylised animal art for which the Scythians are known: displayed back to back are two magnificent gold and electrum shield bosses in the form of stags, one seated, the other standing and pawing the ground. Both have splendid antlers.

The **Roman-era display** gives a vivid picture of the comfortable lives of the Romanised Celtic elite. Finds from two chariot burials are particularly impressive, as is the silver-gilt helmet studded with glass-paste cabochon gems, found in Március 15. tér (*map p. 428, C3*), site of the Roman fort of Contra Aquincum. Sarmatian objects, from the peoples across the Danube, are shown alongside the Roman finds.

The Romans' nemesis, the Huns, crossed the Volga c. 370 and by the early 5th century had established themselves in the Carpathian Basin. Other tribes were on the move at this time too: Suebi, Vandals, Goths, Heruls, Sarmatians and Gepids. The **Gepid royal treasure** from Transylvania (Szilágysomlyó/Șimleu Silvaniei), consisting of enamelled gold ornaments including a huge fibula set with onyx, is truly extraordinary. It is presumed to have been hidden for safety sometime in the late 5th century and was discovered in 1889.

In the mid-6th century the Gepids were displaced by the arrival of the **Avars**. Skilled horsemen from the plains of Eurasia, they introduced the iron stirrup to Europe (examples shown). They in turn were subsumed by the **Franks**, who conquered and Christianised them in the early 9th century. Also on the move at this time were the **Magyars**, who initially allied themselves with the Franks and conducted joint skirmishing expeditions throughout much of the 9th century. With the death of Arnulf, king of the eastern Franks, the Magyars seem to have seen their chance. They overran much of the Frankish territory between 895 and 902 and conducted raids deep into Europe before finally consolidating in the Carpathian Basin. Their weapons and metalwork look primitive in comparison with what has gone before; but they were also excellent horsemen—and horsewomen, as attested by the attractive iron and bronze bit for a lady's horse (restored), with stylised animal-head decoration.

THE CORONATION MANTLE

A dimly-lit, temperature-controlled room on the ground floor (*ask to be let in*) houses the precious Coronation Mantle (*Koronázási palást*), part of the regalia of the kings of

Hungary and dating from the reign of the very first king, St Stephen (r. 1000–38; *see p. 156*). The mantle, of richly embroidered silk and gold thread, is in fact an ecclesiastical cope, donated by King Stephen to the great basilica in Székesfehérvár, southwest of Budapest, which he caused to be built and which became the church where Hungarian kings were crowned and buried (it was destroyed by the Ottomans). At some point in the late 12th century the cope became the royal coronation mantle and Hungarian kings were crowned in it right up until the investiture of the last king, Charles IV, in 1916. The other pieces of the Hungarian coronation regalia, which include the famous Crown of St Stephen, are at present housed in the Parliament building (*see p. 141*).

The mantle has been much restored over the centuries, notably after 1853, when it was discovered in a wet and mouldering state in a rusty chest, where it and the rest of the coronation regalia had been buried after the failure of the 1848–9 War of Independence, to prevent them from falling into Habsburg hands.

The decorative scheme is in three bands, with a fourth part framed by a wide V at the top. Here, in the centre, within a mandorla, is *Christ Triumphant* (48), crushing beneath his feet two monsters representing Evil. At either side, within smaller mandorlas (partially obscured by the elaborate collar piece, attached later), are the *Virgin Orans* (in prayer) (46), with symbols of the Evangelists in roundels; and *Christ Blessing* (47), also with symbols of the Evangelists.

The uppermost horizontal band has a procession of full-length standing prophets (27–44). Below these are the twelve Apostles (14–26), shown seated between columns, with a central *Christ in Majesty* (20). The Latin text running along the narrow band between the prophets and Apostles gives the date, 1031, and records the cope's donation to the church of St Mary in Székesfehérvár ('Alba') by King Stephen and Queen Gisela.

Along the hem are half-figures of martyrs, in roundels separated by tendrils of foliage and pairs of birds. The two central roundels show **Queen Gisela (6)** and **King Stephen (8)**, the only known contemporary likeness of him (if true to life, he had large eyes, rather prominent ears, and wore a neatly trimmed beard). Between them on the vertical band is a much smaller roundel with a figure thought to represent **Prince Imre (7)**, the heir to the throne and Stephen and Gisela's only surviving son, who was to die in a hunting accident later in the same year that the cope was made (1031).

The silver chest displayed in this room, which contained Queen Zita's coronation gift of 50,000 gold crowns, was designed by Count Miklós Bánffy in 1916. King Charles IV's matching chest forms part of the display on the first floor.

THE HISTORY OF HUNGARY EXHIBIT

The main permanent exhibition, covering the history of Hungary from the foundation of the state in 1000 to the fall of Communism in 1989, is arranged in an enfilade of rooms on the upper floor. Before going in, take time to admire the grand columned staircase hall with its **fresco cycle** by Mór Than and Károly Lotz (1874–5). In the style of Raphael, it is filled with both allegorical figures and famous faces from Hungarian history. On the ceiling above the door through which you enter the exhibition space sits the Virgin crowned with a circlet of stars (identical in conception to the EU flag)

THE CORONATION MANTLE

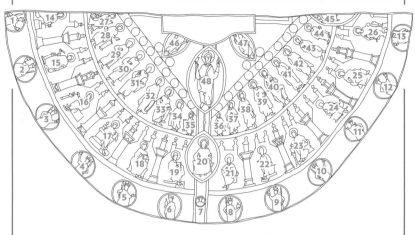

LOWER ROW: MARTYRS
1 Too worn to identify
2 St Cosmas
3 St Damian
4 St George
5 St Vincent
6 Queen Gisela
7 ?Prince Imre
8 King Stephen
9 St Stephen
10 St Clement (Pope Clement I)
11 St Sixtus (Pope Sixtus II)
12 St Cornelius (Pope Cornelius)
13 St Lawrence

MIDDLE ROW: APOSTLES
14 St Peter
15 St Paul
16 St John
17 St Thomas
18 St James
19 St Philip
20 *Christ in Majesty*
21 St Bartholomew
22 St Matthew
23 St Jude
24 St Simon
25 St Thaddeus (or Jude; he appears twice)

26 St Andrew

UPPER ROW: PROPHETS
27 ?Hosea (conjectural, not confirmed by scholars)
28 Nahum
29 ?Isaiah
30 Unnamed
31 'Principium et Finis' (Christ)
32 Daniel
33 Haggai
34 Zechariah
35 Malachi
36 Micah
37 Jonah
38 Obadiah
39 Jeremiah
40 Alpha and Omega (Christ)
41 Ezekiel
42 Too worn to identify
43 Joel
44 Amos
45 Lost mandorla of the ?*Annunciation*

TOP
46 *Virgin Orans*
47 *Christ Blessing*
48 *Christ Triumphant*

and flanked by female manifestations of Justice, Religion and the Arts and Sciences (signed by Lotz). Below that is a frieze by Than showing Art and Science flanked by István Széchenyi (right) and the Palatine Joseph (left). On either side of the door, against a brilliant gold ground, are two large female figures, one shown tending a flame and the other nurturing an oak tree. Beside the latter stands a fine large watering can.

Highlights of the collections

The display is chronological and mainly well-labelled. At the time of writing there were plans to refresh and reorganise it. A selection of highlights is given here.

From the days of the Árpád-dynasty kings (11th–13th centuries) come two exceptional crowns. The first, the so-called **Monomachos Crown**, was found by a farmer in present-day Slovakia in 1861. It takes the form of seven Byzantine cloisonné enamel plates, probably of the mid-11th century, showing the emperor Constantine IX Monomachos in the centre flanked by his wife, the empress Zoe (left), and her sister Theodora (right). On either side of the empresses are very unusual representations of female ribbon-dancers (a similar plaque in the V&A is held to be a forgery) and beyond these, smaller plaques with allegorical representations of Truth (ΑΛΙΘΗΑ) and Humility (ΤΑΠΙΝΟΩ). The second is the **Margaret Island Crown**, which was found in the ruins of the Dominican convent there. It is a circlet of linked silver-gilt plates studded with gemstones and decorated with *fleurs de lys*, six-petalled rosettes and beautifully executed trios of maple leaves in a style which is clearly French-inspired. It has been suggested that it came from the grave of Stephen V (d. 1272), the brother of St Margaret.

The **Jankovich Saddle** (c. 1408–25) of carved bone, which according to legend once belonged to Count Dracula, shows St George (in an enormous helmet) slaying the dragon along with courtly scenes. A second, similar saddle shows Phyllis riding Aristotle. The beautiful inlaid **choir stalls from Nyírbátor** in northeastern Hungary date from 1511, just before the Ottoman conquest. Fully Renaissance in spirit, they are the work of a Florentine master. Two of the panels show bookcases open to reveal volumes of poetry and philosophy, including one by Dante.

From the defeat at Mohács in 1526 and the subsequent period of **Ottoman occupation** come the spurs of the ill-fated King Louis II (*see p. 11*), a photograph of a mass grave at the Mohács battle site (one skeleton is memorably prostrate on its back, its arms thrown up above its head) and a portrait of Suleiman the Magnificent in the manner of the Titian portrait in the Kunsthistorisches Museum in Vienna.

The region (and later principality) of **Transylvania** remained independent of Ottoman rule and the museum displays some of the huge gold ducats that were minted by the princes as tribute money in order to secure this precarious autonomy. Also from Transylvania is the enormous tomb chest of Prince György Apafi (d. 1635) by the stone carver Elias Nicolai. Wall cases have examples of 17th-century goldsmith's work by the great Transylvanian master Sebastian Hann: particularly fine is the cup with Solomon and the Queen of Sheba. Another piece by Hann, a silver-gilt tankard, shows the Judgement of Solomon. There is also an elaborate, gem-studded brooch by him, the size of a large bread roll. Rather poignant is the painted wooden **chair**

carved by Ferenc Rákóczi during his exile in Turkey after the failure of his rebellion against Habsburg rule. For a man of action and ambition, life in the woodshed and the workshop must have been forlorn and dull.

The display moves from here through the enlightened despotism of Maria Theresa and her sons in the 18th century to the age of Széchenyi and Kossuth, and 1848 and its aftermath. **Mementoes of Széchenyi** include his English silver snuff box engraved (in Hungarian): 'Virtue Honour Homeland Health'. From 1848 comes the **printing press** belonging to the firm of Landerer and Heckenast which was used to print the nation's Twelve Points (*see p. 15*), summed up at the bottom of the list as the recipe for 'Equality, Freedom, Fraternity'—echoes of the French Revolution which can hardly have been expected to inspire conciliatory feelings in the Habsburg rulers, who had lost a prominent member of their family to the guillotine (Maria Theresa's daughter Marie-Antoinette).

Mór Than's portrait of Mihály Pollack shows the architect with his designs for the National Museum building. This ushers in a display on the development of **civic society** in Hungary: the age of Hungarian language reform, of vernacular theatre and literature, of applied arts, domestic manufacture, and advances in industry and science. All this culminates at the turn of the 19th century in a cacophony of political voices, both radical and reactionary, hectoring the public from posters (many of them masterpieces of design). The First World War and the Communist government of Béla Kun are followed by the deliberate wholesomeness of the Horthy years. Propaganda is everywhere, running like an oil slick throughout the **20th century**. Meanwhile, in the countryside, the gendarmes on patrol and the peasantry impoverished (as evidenced by some superb photographs from a suppressed exhibition of 1932).

The blandishments of the Second Vienna Award (*see p. 18*), the disaster of the Second World War, the Holocaust and the ensuing Stalin and Rákosi years are well covered. On display is the door of Imre Nagy's prison cell and the hand and ear of the hated statue of Stalin that was pulled down in 1956 (*for more on the statue, see p. 317; for Imre Nagy, see p. 91*). The display ends with the 'Goulash Communism' of János Kádár and the opening of the Austrian border in 1989.

THE PALACE DISTRICT

The area immediately behind the National Museum is known as the Palace District (*Palotanegyed*) from the many former aristocratic town houses that it contains. The fortunes of this area, originally marsh and grazing land, changed forever after the great 1838 flood. Fields and farms were swept away and the developers, buoyed by increasing economic prosperity, moved in. The architect Miklós Ybl gained many of the building commissions and the character of the district has largely been shaped by his aesthetic and that of his associates. The palaces of wealthy patrician families stood shoulder to should here: at one time the Batthyány, Esterházy, Festetics, Almássy, Pálffy, Degenfeld, Wenckheim, Károlyi, Odescalchi, Zichy and Bánffy families all had town residences here, to say nothing of the bankers and other plutocrats who followed in their wake, causing the area also to be dubbed the 'magnates' quarter'.

BRÓDY SÁNDOR UTCA AND POLLACK MIHÁLY TÉR

Bródy Sándor utca (*map p. 429, D3*) runs past the north edge of the National Museum garden. At no. 4, next to the pleasant Caffè Torino, is the **Ádám-ház**, built in 1875 by Antal Weber. At the time, Weber was newly returned from a study tour of Italy and Italian influence is clear to see in this building. The frescoes in the loggia are by Károly Lotz. Opposite no. 6, fixed to the railings of the National Museum garden, is a plaque showing the level of the Danube waters during the 1838 flood. At no. 8 is the neo-Renaissance **Italian Cultural Institute**. The roofline is adorned by a sculpted Crown of St Stephen because the building was originally made for the Chamber of Deputies, the lower of the two houses of the Hungarian parliament. The building was designed by Miklós Ybl and construction began in 1865. Some 800 people worked on it and despite a strike for higher pay by Hungarian carpenters (which led to the importing of Austrian furniture), the building was complete by the following spring. MPs met here (the Upper House met in the National Museum opposite) until the new Parliament building beside the Danube opened in 1902.

The building at **Bródy Sándor u. 5–7**, formerly home to Magyar Rádió's public broadcast studios, bears a plaque commemorating 1956. It was here that the first shots were fired, on October 23rd, after protesters mobbed the building, calling for the withdrawal of Soviet troops and unbiased radio broadcasting.

Opening off Bródy Sándor utca is **Pollack Mihály tér**, named after the architect of the National Museum. Miklós Ybl's name is writ large here: the fine corner building, the former Festetics Palace, is his (1862), now home to the Andrássy University, a private, German-language institution founded in 2001. The wrought-iron railings of the palace's former garden survive, with a 1980s' glass building behind them (scheduled for demolition). The palace on the corner at the other end, formerly belonging to the Károlyi family, is also by Ybl (1863–5), built in the style of a French château with a grand *porte-cochère*. It was gutted by fire in 1945 but at the time of writing was due to be restored. Between the two is the former Esterházy Palace (Sándor Baumgarten, 1865). In 1946–8 it served as the residence of the President of the Republic.

Around the corner at Múzeum u. 3 (with a California Coffee outlet on the ground floor) is a mansion built for Jenő Freystädtler Pasha after 1896. The title pasha was awarded him for his part in constructing the Turkish railways. Freystädtler was notoriously extravagant: the lavish palace here had its own private fencing court and gossip abounded about the statues of his lovers in gold, silver and bronze.

AROUND MIKSZÁTH KÁLMÁN TÉR

Ötpacsirta utca leads out of Múzeum utca past the former Almássy Palace on the left, now home to the Hungarian Architects' Association (with a café and restaurant). The orange building next to it, the former Pálffy Palace, now houses part of the **Ervin Szabó Library**. The main library building (*open Mon–Sat*) is straight ahead on Reviczky utca, in the former Wenckheim Palace (Artúr Meinig, 1887–91), a largely neo-Baroque

SZABÓ ERVIN TÉR
István Szentgyörgyi's 'Fountain of Justice' (1928).

edifice occupying a corner site. When the library is open you can go inside to admire the glassed-in courtyard, where there is a self-service café (*closed weekends*). You can sit here with a coffee and look up at three floors of Rococo mansion rising above you. The main door (through which you came) is surmounted by a carved helmet decorated with laurel branches and four horse heads.

The original main entrance of the Wenckheim mansion (with elaborate wrought-iron gates by Gyula Jungfer) is on the corner elevation overlooking an isosceles triangle of pristinely-kept lawn in whose centre rises the **Fountain of Justice**, erected in 1928, according to the inscription by 'grateful Hungarians to Viscount Rothermere, worthy son of Great Britain'. Rothermere, a pioneer of tabloid journalism, co-founder of the *Daily Mail* and *Daily Mirror* newspapers, was vocal in his opposition to the provisions of Trianon (*see p. 17*) and championed a movement to revise the treaty under the slogan 'Justice for Hungary'.

Reviczky utca, a pleasant cobbled street lined with handsome houses, leads into **Mikszáth Kálmán tér**, an attractive square full of places to sit out in summer, always lively thanks to the cluster of universities nearby. It boasts a statue of the portly novelist who lived on the square and who gives it its current name. The building at no. 1 has a plaque commemorating the chemist János Irinyi, inventor of the noiseless, non-explosive match, which he patented in 1836. He founded a match factory on this site in 1839. The plaque, by János Horvay, has a high relief of a studious nude (strategically draped) grinding substances in a mortar—no doubt phosphorous and lead oxide to make the famous match heads.

From Mikszáth tér it is a very short walk up Krúdy utca to **Lőrinc Pap tér** (*map p. 429, E4*). On one side is the former Zichy Palace, now a hotel. Opposite it is the Jesuit Church of the Heart of Jesus (**Jézus Szíve templom**; *open early mornings until 9am, and afternoons at varying times, see jezusszive.jezsuita.hu*). Built in 1880–90 by József Kauser, it was funded by public subscription, the money collected largely thanks to the zeal of Count Nándor Zichy, whose statue looms large in the small square outside. The church is mainly neo-Romanesque, although the high altar, with its lifesize statue of Christ, is neo-Gothic. The inscription around the top of the triumphal arch reads: 'Learn of me for I am meek and lowly in heart' (*Matthew 11:29*). A plaque at the end of the north aisle commemorates two Jesuit priests taken from here to internment camps by the Communists in 1949–50. Both died in captivity.

On the corner of Krúdy utca and the Nagykörút is György Kiss's small genre sculpture known as the '***Little Rascal***' (*Kiscsibész*, 1885, erected in 1927). It shows a young street urchin caught by a guard dog in the act of stealing a cockerel.

SZENTKIRÁLYI UTCA AND UPPER BRÓDY SÁNDOR UTCA

Szentkirályi utca (*map p. 429, E4–E3*) leads north out of Mikszáth Kálmán tér past one of the campuses of the Péter Pázmány Catholic University. Just beyond the junction with Bródy Sándor utca, at no. 18 on the right, a simple Classicist town house has been given a five-storey extension by the architect Imre Makovecz, an exponent of Organic Architecture whose work, at its best, takes elements of Ödön Lechner, Károlyi Kós and Antoni Gaudí and turns them into something that could almost have sprung from nature. This piece of eclectic Post-Modernism (the Parthenon meets Hansel and Gretel) is probably not his finest.

Further up Bródy Sándor utca, at no. 15, is the **'Chimney Sweep House'**, built in 1855 by Károly Hild (brother of the famous Neoclassical architect József Hild) for a wealthy burgher who had no qualms about making a public display of the source of his fortune (the statue of a chimney sweep, at the time of writing in sore need of restoration). Opposite, at **no. 30/b**, the young János Kádár lived as a sub-tenant of a certain Ottó Róna and his wife Mária in 1944. Mária Róna became Mrs Kádár in 1949. She worked at the Post Office for the State Security authority, steaming open people's letters. At **no. 36** (opposite the junction with Horánszky utca) is the house where the great novelist Mór Jókai lived for two years and where his first wife, the tragedienne Róza Laborfalvi, died in 1886. The little **Budapest Cukrászda** (est. 1957) offers cakes and biscuits at no. 23.

VAS UTCA
Detail of the exterior decoration on Béla Lajta's
School of Trade building (1912).

On the opposite side, at **no. 46**, is a house built by Jenő Freystädtler (*see 236*) for his actress mistress. When she had exhausted his fortune, she left him (but kept the house) and accommodated her former lover's fallen sister Flóra in one of its flats. Flóra shared her brother's libidinous reputation but her career could only last as long as her youth and beauty. She ended her days abandoned and in penury.

Bródy Sándor utca ends in **Gutenberg tér**, with a little central garden. At the far end is the 'Gutenberg Otthon', apartments built for the Union of Printers in 1906. It is a work of the Vágó brothers.

VAS UTCA AND THE ST ROCH HOSPITAL

At Vas u. 9 stands the **István Széchenyi School of Trade** (Béla Lajta, 1912), built of brick with stone adornments, a great mass of soaring verticality, with owls (sculpted by Ödön Moiret) decorating the pilasters between the two entrance bays. Above the door is inscribed the Latin motto: 'We learn for life, not for school'. The carvings are inspired by Hungarian folk art: flowers and other decorative elements mingle with symbols of commerce, travel and trade: birds in flight, a steam train, ships in full sail and a zeppelin. The right-hand entrance bay was in very poor repair at the time of writing.

Vas utca leads into the busy Rákóczi út. Turn left to see the neo-Moorish **Uránia Cinema** at no. 21, built by Henrik Schmahl in the 1890s as a night club and vaudeville theatre. If you turn right you come to the **St Roch Hospital** (Szent Rókus Kórház), where Ignác Semmelweis (*see p. 60*) once worked. His Carrara marble statue (Alajos Stróbl, 1906) stands opposite the main entrance: a grateful mother and her bevy of but-for-him-motherless babes cluster around his feet. The sculptor used his own wife as a model for the mother. The chapel attached to the hospital (*open Mon–Fri 7–12*), dedicated to St Roch, patron saint of plague sufferers, was built in 1711 after pestilence had swept the city. The building was modified and its tower added later in the 18th century. Above the side door is a carving with the Latin motto *Pestarum calamitosorum domicilium*: 'refuge for the destitute of Pest'. The entire chapel was rebuilt after it was destroyed by bombs in WWII. The destruction revealed the foundations of a medieval three-lobed structure, which are now preserved in the crypt. A fruit and vegetable market operates in the square on Saturday mornings.

As you admire the little chapel, you might find yourself regaled with recorded music from the Hangszer Pláza (Instrument Plaza) across the road. This is appropriate enough, since the nearby traffic junction, **Blaha Lujza tér**, is named after the actress and singer Lujza Blaha (1850–1926), 'the nation's nightingale', who was a member of the company of the People's Theatre (Népszínház), which stood here. The building was demolished in the 1960s during construction of the metro.

JÓZSEFVÁROS BEYOND THE NAGYKÖRÚT

Harminckettesek tere (also written '32-esek tere'; *map p. 429, E4*), a bulge in Baross utca east of the Nagykörút, is named after Maria Theresa's 32nd infantry regiment, founded in 1741. A large monument to their war dead of 1914–18 (István Szentgyörgyi, 1933) takes the form of a bronze infantryman hurling a grenade. On the plinth is a relief of the famous scene from the 1741 Diet of Pressburg, when Maria Theresa appealed to her Magyar subjects for aid in her struggle against Prussia (*see p. 13*).

Baross utca leads to **Horváth Mihály tér**, where the road forks. In the interstice is the church of St Joseph (Józsefvárosi plébániatemplom), with a statue of the saint holding the Christ Child in his arms at the top of the façade between the twin towers, which end in octagonal bell-cotes. The statue is dated 1820, though construction of the church began in the 1790s and alterations continued to be made over the following century. At the time of writing it was much in need of restoration. In the little garden in front is a statue (Béla Radnai, c. 1914) of Péter Pázmány (1570–1637), Archbishop of Esztergom and a leading figure of the Hungarian Counter-Reformation, after whom Budapest's Catholic University is named. On the right as you look back down Baross utca is the **former Józsefváros Telephone Exchange**, a fine late Art Nouveau building (Rezső Ray Jr, 1910–12) clad in red brick (the structure is of reinforced concrete) with stone dressings, statues and reliefs by József Damkó. The reliefs, appropriately, take communication as their theme, with the Chain Bridge, a man yodelling, two telegraph poles and a child holding a receiver to his ear.

Further north along József körút is **Rákóczi tér** (*map p. 429, E3*), once notorious for its prostitutes but now remodelled and greatly smartened up, with a station of metro line M4 (green). At the back is a covered market (*open daily except Sun, closes 1pm on Sat*), one of a series of similar halls that were built in Pest in 1896 (*see p. 264*). Rákóczi

BAROSS UTCA
Detail of the reliefs by
József Damkó on Rezső Ray's
former Telephone Exchange
building (1910–12).

tér today spreads a thin veneer of gentrification over an area of Józsefváros that is still poor and deprived. The prostitutes have not gone away; they have beaten a retreat to more distant streets.

NÉPSZÍNHÁZ UTCA

The long, straight **Népszínház utca** (*map p. 429, E3–F3*), with a tramline running up its centre, leads out of Blaha Lujza tér through a poor and in some parts derelict part of town, past a string of once-fine, now dilapidated buildings. The chamfered building at **no. 22**, on the corner of Kiss József utca, was built by József Vágó as rental apartments for the Polgári Brewery in 1906. At the very top is a huge mosaic featuring dray horses and scenes of brewing and beer drinking. Opposite (**no. 25**), on the corner of Fecske utca, is another house by Vágó, together with his brother László, decorated with incised courtly scenes.

Népszínház utca leads to two inner city parks. The first, **II. János Pál Pápa tér** (Pope John Paul II Square) is home to the **Erkel Theatre**, an important venue for opera and ballet (*opera.hu*). It opened in 1911 as the Népopera (People's Opera) but the building has since been altered out of all recognition from the original. In 1912 the Ballets Russes gave their first performance in Hungary here. At that time the square was named after the politician Kálmán Tisza. In 1946 it was renamed Köztársaság tér (Republic Square). In 2011 it took the name of the Polish pope. On the south side of the square, linked together by a parade of low shops, are three Modernist housing blocks by József Fischer, Bertalan Árkay, Farkas Molnár and others (1934).

At the end of Népszínház utca (past **nos. 35 and 37**, dilapidated but interesting buildings by Béla Málnai and the Löffler brothers, respectively 1912 and 1911) is the triangular **Teleki tér** with its covered market (opened in 2013, replacing earlier ramshackle stalls and booths). A pleasant public park opened here in 2014. The paved area outside its main entrance is populated with genre statues, including one of a lamplighter and his dog. There has always been a market here. In the late 18th century, when the Pest city walls were demolished and the city began to expand into the countryside beyond, this area was left free and used as a cattle fair. In the 19th and early 20th centuries the vicinity was full of pedlars and rag-and-bone men, many of them Jewish: between the end of the 19th century and the 1940s, Józsefváros had the highest concentration of Jewish residents in the city. As a result, it was here, immediately after the Nazi takeover in March 1944, that the first pogrom was carried out and the deportations began. A plaque opposite the side flank of the market hall commemorates this. Of the numerous prayer houses that existed around the square, many of them simple rooms in apartment blocks, there is a lone survivor, at no. 22. Teleki tér is also known for its Roma population, many of whom traditionally worked as musicians in the inns and bars that surrounded the market. The well-known Szakcsi Lakatos family of jazz musicians have roots on Teleki tér. For much of the 20th century the square was known for its fleamarket, the ancestor of today's Ecseri piac (*see p. 356*). Teleki tér takes its name from Count László Teleki (1811–61), who served in 1848 as Hungary's ambassador to France. After years of exile, he committed suicide in his Pest town house, unable to bear the prospect of constitutional bargaining with Austria and Franz Joseph.

TELEKI TÉR
Attila Mészáros' *Lamplighter* (2014), with the market hall in the background.

KEREPESI CEMETERY

Map p. 427, C4. Open daily 10–5. Entrance on Fiumei út. Metro line M2 (red) or M4 (green) to Keleti pályaudvar, from where it is a short walk down Festetics György utca and Fiumei út. nori.gov.hu/nemzeti-sirkert.

Kerepesi Cemetery, officially Fiumei úti Temető (Fiume Road Cemetery), is not only Hungary's national pantheon, home to the last resting places of its most celebrated sons (and a few famous daughters); it is also one of the loveliest burial grounds in Europe, its walks shaded by noble trees, its glorious dead resting under monuments of sculpture that act as a lexicon of some of the finest names associated with that art in Hungary. Many of the sculptors and architects who designed the funerary monuments are themselves buried here under monuments designed and sculpted by other famous artists. The cemetery opened in the mid-19th century and is still in use today. Much of it is very well kept and the graves are easy to find. Other parts, particularly the outer northeast corner and the far south, are in a sad tangle. The descriptions below (A–H) are of the major mausolea and burial plots. There is also a selected listing (*see the plan on p. 248*) of graves of those who feature prominently in this guide.

(A) Árkádsor: This dumbbell-shaped double arcade of mausolea and crypts has a high platform at each end, surmounted by a dome. In the dome above the grave of the 1848–9 general Artúr Görgei (8; *see opposite*) is a **mosaic of the *Resurrection*** by Aladár Körösfői-Kriesch. Humbled figures labelled *Erőszak* ('Force') lay down their spears and crouch beneath the Risen Christ. On either side three male figures and three female raise their arms in acclamation. A turreted city awaits, a Magyar Jerusalem inspired by the architecture of Transylvania (where the artist often travelled for inspiration). The plaster model for this composition is in the Town Museum in Gödöllő (*see p. 334*).

Opposite the *Resurrection* dome is the **dome of the *Entombment***. As you walk along the row of arcades, note the Kilián and Eisele family tombs, inspired by Canova, showing figures at the door of a sepulchral chamber, the work of Miklós Ligeti. **Ignác Alpár's tomb** (9) is embellished with reliefs of his major buildings: the Hungarian National Bank, Stock Exchange and Vajdahunyad Castle. The far right-hand cupola shows the *Last Judgement* (by János Stein, a pupil of Károly Lotz).

(B) Mausoleum of Lajos Batthyány: When Count Lajos Batthyány (1807–49), first Prime Minister in Hungary's independent government of 1848, was executed for high treason in the barracks on what is now Szabadság tér, there was no question of giving him a hero's funeral. His body was quietly buried in the crypt of Pest's Franciscan church. Three years after the Compromise, in 1870, it was reinterred here with full pomp, in an enormous mausoleum planned by Albert Schickedanz (and never fully completed). Tomb robbers in 1987 made off with Batthyány's ceremonial sword and other valuables.

GÖRGEI, MALIGNED HERO

Artúr Görgei (1818–1916), at once the hero and the villain of the Hungarian War of Independence against the Habsburgs, began life as the third son of an impoverished nobleman from Upper Hungary (now Slovakia). Following his father's wishes he studied at a military academy, though as a young man his real loves were mathematics and chemistry, at which he excelled. Fate had nevertheless not planned a laboratory career for him. Enflamed by patriotism, he enlisted in the Hungarian revolutionary army in 1848 and changed the spelling of his name from Görgey to Görgei (a less aristocratic form). Lajos Kossuth noticed the young soldier's talent and promoted him to the rank of general. He went on to win a string of battles (including the recapture of Buda, by siege, in May 1849). Already in April, alarmed by the Hungarian victories, Franz Joseph had appealed to Russia for aid. By August 1849, after a disastrous defeat at Temesvár (now Timişoara, Romania), it became clear that Hungary could not prevail against Austria and Russia combined. Kossuth resigned as head of the government and fled Hungary, placing Görgei in full political and military command, in the hope that he would be able to make a bargain with the Russians. Görgei appealed to them but their position had already been decided: they would only accept an unconditional surrender. Hungary laid down arms on 13th August. Thanks to Russian intercession, the Austrians spared Görgei's life, but all of his commanding officers were executed (the 'Arad Martyrs') and Görgei was sent into exile in Klagenfurt. Later, in a vindictive letter written from his own exile, Kossuth accused Görgei of treachery. The accusation found support: Mihály Vörösmarty wrote a poem calling Görgei a base wretch who had betrayed his country and calling down God's eternal wrath upon his soul. It was only in the 1880s that Görgei's rehabilitation began. Despite it, however, he has never gained the honour in Hungary that he probably deserves.

(C) Pantheon of the Workers' Movement: This solemn and magnificent example of propaganda architecture is approached by a path between flanking low tombs, giving the ensemble the air of a Socialist Realist Temple of Karnak. Today it is almost Ozymandian in its desolation. Famous sons of Hungary deemed too precious to be forever tarnished by a Stalinist or proletarian reputation (László Rajk and Attila József) have been disinterred and reburied elsewhere. Empty concavities in the grass reveal where they once lay.

The Pantheon, designed by József Körner (1958–9), is formed of a series of stone screens, like theatre wings, adorned with low reliefs by Zoltán Olcsai-Kiss of heroic workers standing up to the forces of their bourgeois-capitalist-imperialist enemies. At the back is a statue group (also by Olcsai-Kiss) showing three young worker martyrs. The wording above them reads: 'They lived for Communism and the people'. Metal doors enclose chambers where the ashes of working-class heroes and the Party faithful now rest in peace. Some of them still have streets or public places named after them (Leó Frankel, the Workers' Movement activist, and Ervin Szabó, the social scientist, librarian and translator of Marx and Engels into Hungarian). Here too is Gyula Derkovits, painter and graphic artist and Communist Party member.

The red granite **grave of János Kádár** (1912–89) (77) is slightly subsiding on one side thanks to a scandal in 2007 when grave robbers broke it open and removed some of the remains, including his skull. 'Hallowed ground is no place for murderers and traitors' was scrawled on the wall of the adjacent Pantheon. The culprits were never found (nor the skull recovered). Nevertheless, the grave still receives copious floral tributes.

(D) Graves from 1956: There are two plots. Graves of those who fought on the Soviet side, no longer conspicuously fêted, are buried in a circular sunken garden (Dii), today largely untended. Those who stood up against the regime are buried in a flowery field festooned with tributes (Di).

(E) Mausoleum of Mihály Károlyi: Count Mihály Károlyi, President of Hungary in 1919 (*see below*) lies buried in one of the cemetery's most striking tombs: a stone altar protected by a dome-shaped, open-sided metal canopy (Lajos Skoda, 1962–3).

MIHÁLY KÁROLYI, THE 'RED COUNT'

Count Mihály Károlyi (1875–1955) was born into one of Hungary's wealthiest landowning families. Fond of gambling and fast cars as a young man, he was also an avid reader, soon captivated by Marx. He developed into a pacifist, an opponent of Hungary's close ties with Germany, a champion of universal suffrage and of the breaking up of the vast aristocratic estates. He married the dashingly left-wing Katinka Andrássy, granddaughter of the great Gyula Andrássy, and formed his own radical political party. In 1918 Austria-Hungary lost the First World War. Károlyi and his National Council were swept to power by the Aster Revolution that erupted from the upheavals of military defeat, imperial collapse and disastrous harvests causing acute shortages of food. King Charles IV stepped down and Hungary proclaimed itself a republic with Károlyi initially as Prime Minister and later, in January 1919, as the country's first president. Suffrage by secret ballot was extended and freedom of the Press and freedom of assembly were granted. In March 1919, Károlyi made his grand gesture, voluntarily dividing up his own estates.

The Károlyi administration faced many problems. He believed that he could defuse the ethnic tensions between Hungary and her subject Romanians, Serbs, Czechs and Slovaks but they were making their own arrangements, hungry for independence. Meanwhile, hunger and shortages were rife and the victorious powers, deep in peace talks in Paris, were intent on dismembering Hungary, partly in line with secret treaties and promises made while the war was still raging. Béla Kun had also returned from the Soviet Union, with an arsenal of new ideas to try out on the nation. Under pressure, Károlyi resigned and the Communist Republic of Councils was formed, in March 1919.

During the Horthy years Károlyi, widely regarded as a naive ideologue whose political weakness had allowed both the dismemberment of Greater Hungary and the Communist takeover, was forced into exile. He returned home after WWII and in 1947–9 served as Hungarian ambassador in Paris. Disaffection with the hardline Soviet regime led to a second exile. He died in France. Originally buried on the Isle of Wight, his remains were reinterred here in 1962.

KEREPESI CEMETERY
Pantheon of the Workers' Movement.

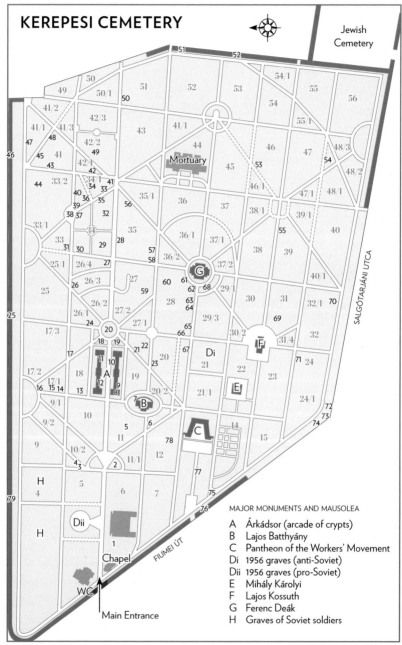

KEREPESI CEMETERY

Jewish Cemetery

MAJOR MONUMENTS AND MAUSOLEA

A   Árkádsor (arcade of crypts)
B   Lajos Batthyány
C   Pantheon of the Workers' Movement
Di   1956 graves (anti-Soviet)
Dii   1956 graves (pro-Soviet)
E   Mihály Károlyi
F   Lajos Kossuth
G   Ferenc Deák
H   Graves of Soviet soldiers

LIST OF NOTABLE BURIALS

Black numbers on the plan show the graves listed below. Numbers in blue are plot numbers.

1 Apponyi hearse
2 Martinovics and the 'Hungarian Jacobins'
3 György Ráth (by Géza Maróti)
4 Szilárd Zielinski (sarcophagus by Gyula Wälder, with a relief of the Margaret Island water tower by Jenő Bory); Alajos Hauszmann (design by Dezső Hültl, with a relief of the royal palace); Sándor Wekerle
5 László Rajk (by Imre Varga; reburial)
6 István Bethlen (cenotaph)
7 Dezső Hültl
8 Artúr Görgei
9 Emil Unger, Unger family
10 Ignác Alpár
11 Gyula Jungfer
12 Gundel family
13 Vilmos Zsigmondy
14 Gábor Döbrentei
15 Antal Szkalnitzky
16 The brother, parents, wife and son of Sándor Petőfi (by Jenő Bory)
17 Miklós Ligeti (by Jenő Bory)
18 Lujza Blaha
19 Endre Ady (by Géza Csorba)
20 Mór Jókai (by Richárd Füredi and Jenő Lechner)
21 Gyula Gömbös
22 Gyula Pártos
23 Albert Schickedanz (by Ödön Moiret)
24 Alajos Stróbl (own design)
25 Imre Steindl
26 János Horvay (own design)
27 Gerbeaud family (by János Horvay)
28 Gyula Wälder
29 Mór Kallina (by Aladár Árkay)
30 Zsigmond Jónás
31 János Pásztor (own design)
32 István Réti (by Béni Ferenczy)
33 Miklós Ybl (by Alajos Stróbl); Frigyes Feszl; Tivadar Puskás
34 Miklós Izsó; Adolf Huszár
35 Zsigmond Móricz (by Ferenc Medgyessy); Mihály Babits (by Béni Ferenczy)
36 Ignác Semmelweis (cenotaph, by Albert Schickedanz); Ferenc Medgyessy (own design); Jenő Barcsay; Lajos Kozma; Noémi Ferenczy (by Márta Lesenyei); Benedek Virág

37 György Zala
38 Mihály Munkácsy (by Ede Telcs)
39 Tivadar Csontváry (by Jenő Kerényi)
40 Károly Ferenczy (by Béni Ferenczy); Béni Ferenczy; Gyula Krúdy (by Miklós Borsos); János Kmetty, Béla Uitz; Zsigmond Kisfaludi Strobl (own design); Sándor Bortnyik
41 Mihály Táncsics
42 István Olcsai-Kiss (own design)
43 Frigyes Karinthy (by Miklós Borsos)
44 Ede Kallós
45 Zoltán Bálint
46 Henrik Kugler
47 Béla Iványi Grünwald
48 Miklós Radnóti (cenotaph)
49 Dezső Kosztolányi
50 Flóris Korb (by Kisfaludi Strobl)
51 Samu Pecz
52 András Mechwart (by Ede Telcs)
53 Gusztáv Petschacher
54 Artúr Meinig
55 Kálmán Reichl
56 Attila József (reburial)
57 István Csók (by István Szentgyörgyi)
58 Adam Clark
59 György Hevesy
60 József Antall
61 Károly Lotz (by János Pásztor)
62 Károly Kammermayer
63 János Fadrusz (own design)
64 Ödön Lechner
65 Győző Czigler
66 Miklós Barabás (by Ede Telcs)
67 Rezső Hikisch
68 Ferenc Erkel (by Ede Kallós)
69 Heroes of 1848–9
70 Géza Maróti (own design)
71 Antal Szerb (reburial)
72 János Balassa (by József Engel)
73 Abraham Ganz (by Miklós Ybl)
74 Lőrinc Dunaiszky
75 János Arany (by Alajos Stróbl, Kálmán Gerster and Mór Kallina)
76 Mihály Vörösmarty
77 György Lukács; Mrs Béla Kun (Irén Gál)
78 János Kádár
79 Emanuel Gozsdu

(F) Mausoleum of Lajos Kossuth:
Lajos Kossuth, Hungary's greatest
revolutionary hero (*see p. 144*), died
in Turin in 1894 at the age of 91. His
body was brought back to Budapest and
buried here. Franz Joseph, who after
the Compromise agreement of 1867
had given amnesty to so many of his
enemies, would not permit any public
mourning for Kossuth from members of
the armed forces or government bodies.
To the end of his life, Kossuth had
refused to acknowledge Franz Joseph
as his sovereign or himself as Austro-
Hungarian. Plans for a grand and fitting
mausoleum were nevertheless put in
hand and (despite squabbling among
the jury) the commission was given
to Kálmán Gerster and Alajos Stróbl.
The monument, guarded by snarling
lionesses, features a bronze figure of
Genius taming a lion and a mourning
allegory of Hungaria. The coffin under
the baldachin is empty: Kossuth's
remains are in the richly-decorated
interior (*no admission*).

Behind the mausoleum are the graves
of Honvéd heroes, members of the
National Guard who fought for Hungary
in 1848–9. Most of the graves were
transferred here from Buda, when the
cemeteries there were closed and the
land developed.

(G) Mausoleum of Ferenc Deák: The
'Nation's Sage', Deák (1803–76) lies in
a beautiful neo-Renaissance *tempietto*
erected in 1887 to designs by Gerster
and Stróbl, who later continued their
collaboration on the mausoleum of
Kossuth (*see above*).

Ferenc Deák, lawyer, liberal
politician and Minister of Justice in the
independent government of 1848, was a
voice of restraint amid the nationalistic
intransigence and hot-headed bluster
of the mid-19th century. His weapon
was passive resistance but he was also
a believer in the value of constitutional
monarchy, seeing union under the
Austrian crown as Hungary's best
means of survival and stability given
the aspirations of the other nations
within the portion of the empire under
Hungarian dominion. It was Deák who
successfully steered Hungary through
the negotiations of 1867, leading to the
Compromise agreement with Austria,
despite the famous 'Cassandra letter'
which Kossuth wrote from exile,
accusing him of taking Hungary down
a path that would lead to the 'death
of the nation', preventing her from
being mistress of her own destiny. The
Dual Monarchy that Deák ushered in
ultimately led to the great decades of
Hungarian prosperity between 1867
and WWI. But he also understood the
Hungarian spirit. 'A nation so prone to
revolt,' he mused, 'will it ever be able
truly to value peace and the blessings it
brings?'

(H) Graves of Soviet soldiers: The
large plot containing the graves of
Russian soldiers who fell during the
battle for Budapest in WWII is pristinely
maintained. Against the perimeter wall
are the graves of members of other
Orthodox churches. Emanuel Gozsdu
(Romanian Orthodox; d. 1870), who
built the Gozsdu udvar in District VII
(*see p. 220*) lies under a fine canopied
mausoleum (79). A short way beyond
is another, similar monument, in very
poor condition, rusting and collapsing,
the mausoleum of the Greek-Hungarian
leather magnate Anasztáz Lyka (d. 1871).

FIUMEI ÚT

One of the reliefs showing the perils of the workplace on the
former Social Insurance building (János Zsákodi Csiszér, 1930).

FIUMEI ÚT

Opposite the main entrance to Kerepesi Cemetery, at **Fiumei út 19**, is a building
housing state pension insurance offices (*map p. 429, F3*). Formerly the Social
Insurance building (Marcell Komor et al, 1930–1, restored), it is covered with reliefs
by Béla Markup, Gyula Maugsch and János Zsákodi Csiszér depicting work and its
potential dangers, thus demonstrating the advisability of taking out insurance.

On the corner of Salgótarjáni utca is the **ex-Józsefváros railway station** (disused).
At the time of writing there were plans to open a museum here, the Sorsok Háza
(House of Destinies), commemorating the deportation of the Jews, partly reusing
the old station buildings and partly in a new complex designed by Attila F. Kovács,
incorporating old railway track and wagons. Two towers are linked by a bridge shaped
like an elongated Star of David. Beneath it, a 'Space Light' is positioned to illuminate
the night sky (when in operation, air traffic control will need to be alerted). Lack of
consensus among government ministers and failure to reach an agreement with the
Jewish community had stalled the project at the time of writing.

THE JEWISH CEMETERY ON SALGÓTARJÁNI UTCA

*Map p. 427, D4. Tram 37 or 37A from Blaha Lujza tér/Népszínház utca to Salgótarjáni
utca, temető (four stops). Open daily except Sat April–Oct 8–4, Nov–March 8–3. Maps
of the cemetery, and kippahs for men, are available in the entrance courtyard.*

The Jewish section of Kerepesi Cemetery, divided from the gentiles' graveyard by
a wall, dates from 1874. By the early decades of the 20th century, space was already
scarce and most Jewish burials took place at Kozma utca (*see p. 281*). Badly neglected
since WWII, the cemetery is now beginning to revive and restoration is underway.

The tram stops right outside the **gatehouse**, which is fashioned like that of a moated
castle, complete with mock portcullis. It is the work of Béla Lajta (1908). You go
through this and cross an inner courtyard to enter the cemetery precinct. Most of the
graves take the form of simple headstones or granite obelisks, but there are also some
fine mausolea. The oldest grave markers are in Hebrew only; a few are in German.

Some areas of the cemetery are completely overgrown, the smaller graves lost under a thick tangle of undergrowth while grander tombs have collapsed into amorphous heaps of masonry fragments.

An enfilade of fine crypts backs onto the west (left-hand) wall, behind which can be seen the tops of the Christian memorials of Kerepesi. Here you will find the splendid black granite **mausoleum of the Sváb family,** by Béla Lajta (1909), guarded by twin swans with their heads bowed. Further up, on the other side of the path, is the **Guttmann tomb,** also by Lajta (1908), guarded by a pair of lions. Still further up, on the left, is the Neoclassical tomb of the great industrialist **Manfréd Weiss** (d. 1922)and his wife Alice Wahl. The inscription proudly commemorates 'the noblest of men, Baron Manfréd Weiss of Csepel, member of the Upper House, founder of the Csepel Steelworks.'

Memorials against the north boundary wall include the obelisk of the textile manufacturer **Gerson Spitzer** (d. 1868; *see p. 104*) and, at the far end, the grand **mausoleum of the Hatvany-Deutsch dynasty** (*see below*), in the form of a Doric temple on a tall podium.

Before you leave, seek out the simple grave of the great painter **Adolf Fényes** (d. 1945): a limestone slab with no headstone and the briefest of inscriptions. It is in the first plot to the right as you enter the cemetery, behind the large Mauthner tomb.

THE HATVANY-DEUTSCH DYNASTY

The Deutsch family had a long lineage in Hungary, even tracing their ancestry back to the days of Matthias Corvinus, when they are said to have been financiers to the royal court. The founder of the family's modern fortunes was Ignác Deutsch (1803–73), a patriotic Hungarian Jew, veteran of the 1848–9 war, who built steam-powered mills and bought land around the town of Hatvan in east Hungary, where he planted sugar beet. After the beet fields came sugar refineries, which made Ignác's grandson Sándor (1852–1913) one of the wealthiest of Hungary's late 19th-century magnates. He went on to co-found the National Association of Industrialists (GYOSZ). Ennobled in 1908, he took the title Baron Deutsch of Hatvan. One of his sons, Lajos Hatvany (1880–1961), was an expert on the poetry of Sándor Petőfi and one of the founders of the influential literary periodical *Nyugat.* Lajos' brother, the painter Ferenc Hatvany (1881–1958), formed a huge and valuable collection of artworks by Hungarian, Italian, French and Spanish masters (including Impressionist masterpieces and some famous El Grecos). This was dispersed in 1944–5. Many works are missing; claims respecting others are still unsettled. Some made their way to the Budapest Museum of Fine Arts. In the 1920s Ferenc Hatvany had bought the Lónyay palace on Castle Hill, overlooking Pest (a grand work of the 1870s by Ybl, it was destroyed in WWII and a project to rebuild it began in 2000). Both brothers left Hungary: Lajos fled first to Vienna in 1919 (he had been a member of the National Council after the Aster Revolution in 1918). Accused of publishing national slurs in the Horthy years, he was pardoned but fled the country again, to Paris and then England, in 1938 (he returned to Budapest in 1947); Ferenc died in Lausanne. Another member of the family (also with a splendid art collection, of porcelain, looted by the Soviets) was Baron Joseph Hatvany-Deutsch, who bought the former Erdődy palace, also on Castle Hill (*see pp. 31–2*), in 1912.

JEWISH CEMETERY
Detail of the Guttmann tomb (1908).

KELETI STATION AND BAROSS TÉR

Keleti pályaudvar, the Eastern Railway Station (*map p. 429, F2–F3*), stands on Baross tér, a spacious plaza named after Gábor Baross (1848–92), Minister for Transport and Trade, who developed Hungary's transport networks, railways and postal service during the time of the Dual Monarchy. He is commemorated by a magnificent **statue** (Antal Szécsi, 1898), isolated on its own island in front of the railway station, flanked by allegorical figures of Agriculture and Industry, its plinth adorned with reliefs of railways and shipping. The station itself presents a bold façade, emblazoned with the date of its completion, 1884, and boasting statues of two British pioneers of the railway industry, James Watt (inventor of the steam engine) and George Stephenson (builder of the first railway, the Stockton–Darlington line, in 1825). The four smaller statues represent Industry, Domestic Manufacture, Agriculture and Commerce. The curving steel framework of the main station concourse has a span of 44m. Inside, immediately on the left, is the Baross Terem restaurant. The offering is very basic but the setting gives a sense of how grand the station once was.

At Baross tér 20, on the corner of Rottenbiller utca, is a block of flats built in 1960 as a **Lottery House** (*see p. 267*), one of several across the city.

THE CORVIN DISTRICT & LUDOVICEUM

The Corvin District (Corvin negyed) takes its name from the **Corvin Cinema** (Corvin Mozi; *map p. 429, E4*), a handsome, yellow-and-white odeon-shaped building which has been in operation since 1922. Miklós Horthy was present at its inauguration, for which Dezső Kosztolányi composed a poem. The building is by Emil Bauer, who also designed the tiered fountain to the left of the steps, inspired by the papyrus capitals of ancient Egyptian temple architecture.

The exterior is decorated with stone ravens with rings in their beaks, the emblem of Matthias Corvinus, Hungary's great Renaissance king, from whom the cinema takes its name and who is celebrated in two bas-reliefs by József Róna on either side of the main entrance steps. They are designed to show the two sides of Matthias' character: warrior and man of culture. On the left, he is depicted surrounded by savants and on the right, the elders of Vienna submit to his rule, offering him the keys of the city (the majesty of the king is somewhat compromised by the fact that the frame into which the relief is inserted now cuts off the top of his head).

The cinema's exterior walls are festooned with plaques commemorating the events of 1956, when the cinema precinct—chosen because it was difficult to enter and easy to defend—was one of the focal points of resistance against the Soviet tanks. To the right of the entrance steps is a bronze statue of a boy with a rifle (Lajos Győrfi, 1996), commemorating the *Pesti srácok* or 'Pest lads', the teenage boys who joined the anti-Soviet resistance. The Corvin today (as well as being a successful multiplex) is a popular rendezvous spot: people often choose the steps as a place to meet. Around

KELETI STATION
Detail of the main frontage, with the statue of 'Agriculture'.

the curved sides are shops and cheap cafés, and there are more of the same in **Corvin sétány**, the broad plaza beyond the long, covered Corvin Plaza shopping mall.

Corvin sétány was pushing ever outwards at the time of writing, part of a long-planned scheme to redevelop what for decades was a very run-down part of the city. Many of the flats in the old apartment buildings had only communal toilets and were drastically in need of refurbishment. The decision to tear them down and replace them with modern blocks has been controversial, not least since it has entailed re-housing most of the old inhabitants elsewhere. The people moving into the new flats are not long-time Józsefváros residents and the area is rapidly taking on a new flavour. A few old houses still survive, like stump teeth in a jaw filled with implants, and there have been valiant attempts at creating community gardens in the remaining vacant lots.

THE BOTANICAL GARDEN
At the perimeter of the district is the 'Fűvészkert', the ELTE University Botanical Garden (*map p. 429, F4; open April–Oct daily 9–5, Nov–March 9–4; fuveszkert. org*), increasingly overlooked by new apartment blocks but nonetheless a lovely and tranquil island of calm in this strange Bermuda Triangle of a district. Here you will find a herb garden, a rock garden, a rose garden, a Southeast Asian garden, fruit trees, a lily pond, a palm house and greenhouses with ferns, orchids, tropical and sub-tropical plants including various insectivorous species. Information in the garden is in Hungarian only, but experts will be happy to see the botanical names in Latin. Here too is the house from which Endre Bajcsy-Zsilinszky was deported for the second time by the Nazis, in November 1944.

ENDRE BAJCSY-ZSILINSZKY
Endre Bajcsy-Zsilinszky was born in 1886 into a family of lawyers and teachers. He followed the family footsteps and studied law, but his early interest in politics and social issues meant that as well as setting up in practice, he also became involved in local government. In the chaotic aftermath of WWI he was one of the founders of the Hungarian National Defence League, an anti-Communist body that also aimed to prevent Hungary from being stripped of territory. During the government of Béla Kun, he went into hiding and after Kun's fall became the editor of a national socialist newspaper, explicitly Christian and in favour of ethnic homogeneity. Together with Gyula Gömbös, he founded the Hungarian National Independence Party. Increasingly, however, his views began to diverge from those of the extreme right and by the early 1930s he was editing *Szabadság* (*Freedom*), an anti-national socialist weekly. From this he went on to join the Independent Smallholders' Party, concerned with land reform, and was elected to Parliament on this ticket. During WWII he remained a vocal opponent of Nazism. After the German takeover of Hungary in 1944, he was arrested, attempted to resist and was wounded in the scuffle (the coin that saved him from the bullet is preserved in the National Museum). Released a few months later, he actively worked to organise the defence of Budapest in alliance with the Soviets. He was arrested by the Arrow Cross in this villa, where he and his wife had taken refuge. He was summarily tried and hanged on Christmas Eve, 1944.

THE LUDOVICEUM

The busy Nagyvárad tér traffic junction (*map p. 427, C5*), with its university buildings and hospitals, is dominated by the 89m high **Semmelweis University Theory Block** (Semmelweis Egyetem Elméleti Tömb), Hungary's first skyscraper (László Wagner, 1963–76) and still one of its tallest buildings. Opposite are a hall of residence and teaching block of the **Public Service University**.

Facing the green triangle of Ludovika tér is a handsome Neoclassical building with two sentry boxes flanking its front entrance: the former Ludovika Military Academy or **Ludoviceum**. In 1808 Hungary began to undertake the training of its own army officers and this building, by Mihály Pollack (1830–6), was the home of the Officer Training Corps until 1872. Variously repurposed since, it is now the National Public Service University (Nemzeti Közszolgálati Egyetem). Behind it stretches the **Orczy-kert** (Orczy Garden), laid out in the late 18th century in the manner of an English park by the Orczy barons (ancestors of the Baroness Orczy, author of the *Scarlet Pimpernel*, published in 1905). At the time of writing it was being replanted and was to be partly used by the university and partly open to the public. Its amenities include a boating lake, a children's playground and a horse riding track.

THE NATURAL HISTORY MUSEUM

Map p. 427, C5. Metro line M3 (blue) to Klinikák or Nagyvárad tér. Open daily except Tues 10–6. Last tickets 30mins before closing. Photography permitted on purchase of a photo ticket. Café and shop. nhmus.hu.

Occupying a building on the site of the Ludoviceum stables is the Natural History Museum. A line of huge mineralogical samples marks the entrance.

The history of the institution goes back to the founding of the National Museum by Count Ferenc Széchényi (*see p. 229*), whose wife's collection of Hungarian minerals formed part of his donation to the nation. A few years later this was joined by a zoological collection. In 1818 the Palatine Joseph purchased the botanical collection of Pál Kitaibel. These holdings were augmented throughout the 19th century by donations and acquisitions of items assembled during that great age of human inquiry. The various departments continued to operate under the aegis of the National Museum until 1949, when an independent National History Museum was set up. Much of the material continued to be exhibited in the National Museum building and valuable holdings (including the entire Africa exhibit) were lost in the 1956 Uprising, when the building became caught in the crossfire. The great hunter and writer Zsigmond Széchenyi at once set about gathering replacement artefacts: his valuable library of hunting literature is now also held by the museum.

Since its inception the museum has struggled to find a permanent home and it still operates at a variety of locations. Its exhibition space has been at the Ludoviceum since 1996. The collections are well displayed despite the somewhat cramped conditions. As with Natural History museums throughout the world, you can expect to share your visit with large numbers of children.

NATURAL HISTORY MUSEUM
Miocene-epoch limestone with fossil scallop shells, from the Tétény plateau.

The displays

Above the ticket hall hangs the **skeleton of a fin whale** (*Balneoptera physalis*). The permanent exhibition consists of a model of a coral reef and, on the upper floors, three displays devoted to rocks and minerals, fossils and biodiversity.

The **rocks, minerals and gemstones** collection includes pieces of meteorite, a case of beautiful luminous minerals and well-displayed and labelled examples of the many types of rock that are to be found in the earth's crust, including bright lemon yellow Sicilian sulphur, various corundums (from which rubies and sapphires are made) and delicate wavelite, which forms crystals like little parasols. A wall caption notes that there are more colours to be found in the mineral world than in the light spectrum.

Lost Worlds exhibits **fossil remains** of shells, ferns, trees (including cycads), belemnites, crinoids and other prehistoric creatures. Part of the display is devoted to Hungarian dinosaur remains, from isolated species such as the huge *Magyarosaurus dacus* (in appearance similar to an apatosaurus) and the armoured *Hungarosaurus tormai*. The **biodiversity display** attempts to cover the vast array of life forms on earth, from mosses and molluscs to mammals, with particular focus on the Carpathian Basin.

EATING AND DRINKING IN JÓZSEFVÁROS

RESTAURANTS

f–fff **Oinos**. Bar and bistro occupying a wing of the Rákóczi tér market hall, on the corner of Déri Miksa utca. Despite the Greek name, it is an Italian restaurant, offering a wide range from pizza and pasta to *filetto di manzo*. Good wines. *Rákóczi tér 7. T: 06 70 770 9803, oinos.hu. Map p. 429, E3.*

ff **Rosenstein**. Popular family restaurant close to Keleti Station.

Traditional Hungarian and Jewish cooking leavened with a little Mediterranean influence. The meat is sourced from their own farm. *Káposztás cvekedli*, a pasta and cabbage dish, features on the dessert menu, in true old-fashioned Hungarian style. Closed Sun. *Mosonyi u. 3. T: +36 1 333 3492, rosenstein.hu. Map p. 429, F3.*

f–ff **Építész Pince**. Seating in a cosy vaulted cellar in winter and in the courtyard of the old Almássy town house in summer. Weekday lunch menu. Good-value Hungarian cooking with a faint international flavour. The building is also home to the Hungarian Architects' Association, hence the restaurant's name ('Architects' Cellar'). Closed Sun. *Ötpacsirta u. 2. T: +36 1 266 4799, epiteszpince.hu. Map p. 429, D4.*

f **Csiga**. Facing Rákóczi tér, a relaxed, very low-key place offering coffee, drinks, simple full meals and a weekday lunch menu. *Vásár u. 2. T: 06 30 613 2046. Map p. 429, E3.*

CAFÉS AND BARS

Fekete Udvar, at Múzeum körút 5 (*map p. 429, D3*), is a nice place to take a break at one of the little tables clustered around the marble well head. As you sip your coffee, spare a thought for the toiling housemaids who would once have filled their heavy pails here. Above you rise two storeys of flats joined by an interior suspended walkway with pretty wrought-iron railings.

Lumen, a café at Mikszáth Kálmán tér 2–3 (*map p. 429, E4*) is open daily for coffee, drinks and sandwiches. They also hold photography exhibitions.

At Bródy Sándor u. 2, close to the National Museum (*map p. 429, D3–E3*), is **Caffè Torino** (seating outside in warm weather), which serves coffee, cakes, sandwiches and simple pasta. It's good for a mid-morning drink or a light lunch. Further up at no. 9 is the **Tasting Table**, where you can buy and taste wine, accompanied by selections of Hungarian cheese and charcuterie. For tastings, booking is advised (see the website for details; open daily noon–8pm; *T: +36 30 720 8197, tastehungary.com*). At Bródy Sándor u. 23 is the **Budapest Cukrászda**. It has no seating but is a good place to buy a sweet snack to eat as you go. They bake excellent biscuits (the lavender ones are particularly good). With **Coffee Stand Gutenberg** (Békési utca; *map p. 429, E3*), coffee-to-go (in disposable cups) has arrived in Budapest. It opened in 2018.

Further out, beyond the Nagykörút, is **Cintányéros**, a small, atmospheric place for drinks and light snacks (a contemporary take on the traditional *borozó*, where wine was served loose, measured out by the ladle) in a 19th-century block that still bravely survives amid the bulldozers of the Corvin district. Coffee, wine, spritzers, *pálinka* or fruit cordial accompanied by grilled *debreceni* sausage, cold meats, cheese or sandwiches. Cash only. Opens at 5pm. *Bókay János u. 52 (corner of Tömő utca). T: +36 1 797 7396. Map p. 427, C5.*

BAKÁTS TÉR
Head of St Francis by Alajos Stróbl (1927).

District IX: Ferencváros

T he Ninth District, Ferencváros or Francis Town, is one of the more sparsely populated of Pest's districts. Formerly industrial in character, it is home to the Central Market Hall, the National Theatre and Müpa concert hall, as well as Ödön Lechner's great Museum of Applied Arts. The Ferencváros football team, popularly known as Fradi, was founded here in 1899. Buses also leave from here for the well-known Ecseri flea market (*see p. 356*).

HISTORY OF FERENCVÁROS

The first settlement in the area now occupied by Ferencváros was Szentfalva, a village beside the Danube close to where the Central Market Hall now stands. Early records date from the days of the Árpád kings but it is thought that the area was first occupied long before. Deserted after the Ottoman occupation, it only began to be resettled after the Habsburg reconquest of 1686. The site of today's Kálvin tér, where the city gate stood, became a market place and many inns sprang up to accommodate the drovers and herders who brought their livestock up from the Great Plain. The district became increasingly built up and in 1792 acquired the name Ferencváros, Francis Town, after Franz I, who had come to the throne in the same year. After the 1838 flood, which swept away 80 percent of Ferencváros's buildings, reconstruction began, following a strict urban plan. From the mid-19th century the character of Ferencváros became increasingly industrial, with the setting up of factories, foundries and leather and carpentry workshops. In the outer district, beyond Boráros tér, there were steam-powered mills and a large slaughter house. The main customs house was established here on the Danube bank and a transport network by rail and water ensured the supply of goods and raw materials. By the end of the century many thousands of families had moved to the area in search of work, greatly swelling the population. Overcrowding in hastily-built, insalubrious tenements became endemic and the district was predominantly a poor, working-class one. Poverty was exacerbated by the disaster of

WWI. The industrial character of the area made it the target of aerial raids in WWII. Today many of the old industrial lots have been cleared, making way for modern residential development and even for gated communities (with names like Allure Residence), which have become popular in recent years.

ON & AROUND KÁLVIN TÉR

The gateway to the Ninth District is Kálvin tér (*map p. 429, D4*). On its west side, just under the arch that links the two halves of the Korona Hotel, a red marble relief of a knight in armour marks the site of the **Kecskemét Gate**, beyond which the open highway led east to the towns of the Great Plain.

The open space immediately outside the gate, once a burial ground, then a haymarket, is named for its **Calvinist church**, still the focal point of the square (although the space has been badly remodelled since WWII). Though there has been a Calvinist community in Pest since the 16th century, it was only able to exist formally and with its own church premises after Joseph II's Edict of Tolerance in 1782. The church here (*only open for services*) was built in 1816–30 to designs by József Hofrichter, with a later entrance porch by József Hild. It was paid for largely thanks to the efforts of Hermina of Anhalt, second wife of the Palatine Joseph, who was present when the foundation stone was laid. She died the next year, aged 19, of puerperal fever following the birth of twins. Initially buried here, her coffin was removed to the Palatine Crypt (*see p. 49*) after the great flood of 1838.

Many of the paving stones around the entrance to the metro here are inscribed with quotations from Protestant theologians, chiefly Calvin, Luther and Zwingli. A relic of the days of the old market place is the building at no. 9, the **former Two Lions inn** (the lions are still there above the doorway), now the Café Intenzo. In the pleasant inner courtyard is a female statue representing the Sava river, belonging to the Danube Fountain designed for the centre of Kálvin tér by Miklós Ybl. The rest of the fountain was destroyed in WWII but a reworking of it now stands in Erzsébet tér (*see p. 166*).

In the **Kálvin tér underpass** is a sculpture of a cleft rock (Gyula Illés, 1983) evoking the dismantled Kecskemét Gate which stood on this site. On the right is a carving of a small cat. People stroke its tail for luck.

RÁDAY UTCA

Ráday utca (*map p. 429, D4*), semi-pedestrianised for much of its length, leads south out of Kálvin tér. Small neighbourhood shops have almost all disappeared and the street presents an unbroken string of cafés, bars and restaurants, including the Michelin-starred Costes at no. 4 (*see p. 271*). Two long-established bars, Paris, Texas and Pink Cadillac at **no. 22 and no. 26**, are in interesting Art Nouveau buildings of 1910. A plaque notes that the sculptor János Istók once lived at no. 22, which was designed by Rezső Waczula. No. 26 has a good stained-glass panel above the entrance to its inner courtyard.

RÁDAY UTCA
Figurine of Isis nursing Horus (2nd/3rd century) in the Bible Museum.

At no. 28, on the corner of Köztelek utca, is the **Bible Museum** (Biblia Múzeum; *open Mon–Fri 10–6, Sat 10–5; bibliamuzeum.com*), occupying the basement of a Christian bookshop. The small display (handbills available) traces the loci of the Bible (Egypt, Babylon, the Holy Land and Rome) with information boards and numerous artefacts, most of them replicas but also including some pieces from the collection of the Museum of Fine Arts. The small 2nd/3rd-century statuette of *Isis lactans*, showing Isis breastfeeding the infant Horus, is a particularly interesting illustration of the conflation of iconographies that existed among the mystery religions of late antiquity. There is also a replica of a Roman soldier's helmet found at Alsóhetény (southwest Hungary), with the Chi-Rho christogram on the nose guard. On the ground floor is the Ráday Collection of early printed books and Bibles.

A little further up the street, the building at no. 32 stands on the site of Hungary's first ever champagne factory, which was opened by Ignác Prückler in 1834.

Back in the other direction, on the corner of Erkel utca, at Ráday u. 18 (entrance from Erkel utca), is the **Ferencváros Local History Museum** (Ferencvárosi Helytörténeti Gyűjtemény; *open Tues–Fri 12–6, Sat 10–2*), which holds regular exhibitions. Its building is a block of former rental apartments built by Miklós Ybl for Count György Károlyi in 1875–6. In the other direction, Erkel utca leads down to the Central Market Hall past the Barokk Antikvitás cellar shop at no. 8, an Aladdin's Cave of bric à brac.

ON & AROUND FŐVÁM TÉR

Fővám tér (Customs Square; *map p. 429, D4*), formerly Só tér (Salt Square), with Közraktár utca (Central Warehouse Street) and Só utca (Salt Street) hard by, are all names that allude to the commerce that went on here: goods were brought in by river and rail, duties were paid and storage and onward shipping was arranged. The square is dominated by the old **Chief Customs House** (Fővámház), the stone for whose construction came here by boat. Now it is one of the buildings of the Corvinus University Economics Faculty (commonly known as Közgáz). Built in 1870–4 by Ybl, in a Historicist, neo-Renaissance style, its façades are adorned with allegorical statues. Those overlooking the Danube are Titans and Olympians representing Law and Order (Themis, with Fasces); Power (Hercules); Science (Minerva, with a sword); Fortuna (representing railways); Neptune (shipping, with a wheel); Vulcan (heavy industry, with a hammer); ?Rhea (with a cogwheel); Ceres (textiles); Hermes (trade) and ?Pomona (prosperity, with fruits). The building behind is the old salt warehouse and administrative offices (1890). Access was by rail at embankment level and by boat from the river directly to the basement.

Behind the Customs House, on **Csarnok tér**, obscured behind a concrete hotel in a curious sub-Gaudíesque style, stands Léstyán Ernő's 1960s' red-brick former electricity substation. Both are on a site where finds were discovered in 2016 showing that occupation of this area, which later became the medieval village of Szentfalva, may go as far back as the Bronze Age.

CENTRAL MARKET HALL
Map p. 429, D4. Open Mon 6–5, Tues–Fri 6–6, Sat 6–3.
This magnificent red-and-yellow brick structure, known in Hungarian as the Nagycsarnok ('Great Hall'), is the largest covered market hall in Budapest, with neo-Gothic details on the façade and a roof clad in colourful Zsolnay tiles. It was built to designs by Samu Pecz in 1897.

> ### BUDAPEST'S COVERED MARKET HALLS
> In 1896, a series of architecturally similar market halls was built to give a permanent home to traders who until then had sold their wares from outdoor stalls. The Great Market Hall, on Fővám tér in District IX, was market hall no. 1 (recorded in Roman numerals on the façade). The others, all in Pest, were at Rákóczi tér (District VIII, no. II; *map p. 429, E3*), Klauzál tér (District VII, no. III; *map p. 429, E2*), Hunyadi tér (District VI, no. IV; *map p. 429, E2*) and Hold utca (District V, no. V; *map p. 428, C2*). All still survive. The last market hall, no. VI, on Batthyány tér in Buda (*map p. 428, B2*), was built in 1902. It is now a supermarket.

The Central Market Hall today is one of Budapest's most popular tourist attractions, on the itinerary of every coach tour and cruise ship group, not to mention the independent tourists, who also come here in great numbers. In the basement (where the stalls were formerly supplied directly by river boats) are a number of fishmongers. Meat and fresh produce are on the ground floor. As you come in through the main doors, the row on the far right used to be known as the *gazdagsor* ('Rich Row') because it sold more exotic produce as well as fruit and vegetables out of season, for higher prices. Recently more of the stalls here have been given over to souvenir articles, though costermongers are still plentiful elsewhere in the market.

On the upper level, under the splendid steel roof structure, are stalls selling souvenirs; in high season it can be crowded and hot.

SZABADSÁG BRIDGE

Szabadság híd, or Liberty Bridge (*map pp. 428–9, C4–D4*), the third permanent bridge across the Danube after the Chain Bridge and Margaret Bridge, was built in 1896, the year of the 'Magyar Millennium' (*see p. 368*). It originally bore the name Franz Joseph Bridge, after the reigning monarch. Franz Joseph was present at the opening ceremony—indeed, he had personally banged into place the final rivet (a special silver one). Like all the bridges at the time, a toll was charged for its use (two toll booths survive, on either side of the bridge on Fővám tér). Like all the bridges too, it was blown up in 1945 by the retreating Nazis. Whereas its companion bridge, Erzsébet híd, was rebuilt to a completely new design, Szabadság híd was faithfully reconstructed, partly with pieces dredged from the river and reconstituted. It opened in 1946 as Liberty Bridge, a name it has since retained. On top of its tall finials perch Turul birds (*see p. 372*), wings outstretched. In recent years it has become customary to close the bridge to traffic on some summer weekends, when it is given over to pedestrians and picnickers (with the proviso that no one is to climb up to the Turuls).

THE BÁLNA TERRACES

The shopping and leisure centre known as the **Bálna** ('Whale'; *map p. 429, D4*) is an interesting example of fusion architecture. A pair of 19th-century brick customs warehouses have been given a billowing glass extension by the Dutch architect Kas Oosterhuis (2013). The terrace cafés put out chairs and tables on warm days.

Közraktár utca has a number of buildings reflecting the work and productivity ethic of Ferencváros. At no. 22, on the corner of Zsil utca, there is a relief of iron workers by Ö. Fülöp Beck. The building at no. 30, part of the RiverPark office complex, is the former headquarters of the Hangya Production, Sales and Consumers' Co-operative, built c. 1920 to earlier plans by Dénes Györgyi (construction was delayed by WWI).

ÜLLŐI ÚT & BAKÁTS TÉR

Leading southeast out of Kálvin tér, Üllői út (*map p. 429, D4–E4*) may be shabby but its buildings have housed some famous names: Raoul Wallenberg had offices at no. 2–4 (destroyed in WWII); Mihály Tancsics (*see p. 30*) lived at no. 23 in 1880–1; Dezső Kosztolányi wrote his poem *Üllői úti fák* (*Üllői út Trees*) at no. 21 (plaque); Miklós Ybl lived here in 1851–71, when he was at work developing the area, in an apartment block built for Count György Károlyi by Mihály Pollack a decade or so previously; and the poet Arany János lived on the corner of Üllői út and Erkel utca (Erkel u. 20) in 1860–4.

THE MUSEUM OF APPLIED ARTS

Map p. 429, E4. Closed for restoration at the time of writing. imm.hu.

The well-known landmark building housing the Museum of Applied Arts (Iparművészeti Múzeum), with its eye-catching yellow and green tiled roof, was designed by Ödön Lechner in conjunction with Gyula Pártos and was opened by Franz Joseph in 1896 as part of the grand finale of the Hungarian Millennium celebrations. It is an important example of Hungarian Secessionist architecture and one of the finest illustrations of Lechner's aim to create a uniquely Hungarian building idiom. It also marks a departure from the traditional choice of a Historicist style—Neoclassical, neo-Gothic, neo-Renaissance or neo-Baroque—for prominent public buildings: the plans submitted to tender bore the title 'Hungarians look East'. The design uses of traditional folk motifs and the interior has a distinctly Mughal feel. Some early commentators did not like the building; today it is recognised as one of the major architectural sights of Budapest.

The museum collection was founded in 1872, making it the third of its kind in the world (after the V&A in London and the MAK in Vienna). The aim, in line with the Arts and Crafts movement in Britain, was to promote the development of Hungarian applied arts and artisanal manufacture and to educate public taste. It coincided with the contemporary craze for World's Fairs, from where many of the early acquisitions came. The very first pieces of the collection were acquired when the director of the National Museum donated non-Hungarian antiquities. Archduke Joseph Karl then gave pieces of the 18th-century porcelain collection of his father, the Palatine Joseph's first wife, Alexandra Pavlovna. The second director of the museum, György Ráth, was also a collector. During his tenure (1881–96) many fine items of furniture as well as sculpture and *objets d'art* came to the museum. Ráth's own villa, just off Andrássy út, was also something of a show-home, with furniture by Albert Schickedanz. On Ráth's death in 1905, his wife presented the villa and its contents to the state.

The museum closed in late 2017 for a lengthy process of renovation and restoration (it is hoped that it will reopen in 2021), which will include replacing the lantern on top of the dome, restoring and cleaning the pyrogranite decorations, completing the quadrangle with the addition of a new wing joining Hőgyes utca, and creating a roof terrace (in accordance with the original designs). While work is in progress, the museum plans to open an exhibition in the György Ráth villa (Városligeti fasor 12; *map p. 429, E2*), focusing on the museum's Art Nouveau holdings and featuring pieces from Ráth's collection. For details and updates, see the museum website (*given above*), which also has an excellent online database of Ráth's collection. Ráth is buried in a fine Secessionist-Symbolist tomb in Kerepesi Cemetery (*see p. 249*). Standing at a fork in the pathways between the graves, it features a tripartite sculpture of the goddess Hecate, traditionally a guardian of thresholds and crossroads.

Close to the Applied Arts Museum, at Hőgyes Endre u. 3, is a small **Unitarian chapel**, consecrated in 1929. In the wake of the dismemberment of Hungary after WWI, many Unitarians came to Budapest from Transylvania. In 2001 the chapel adopted the name of the most internationally famous Hungarian Unitarian, Béla Bartók, as part of its official title.

At the junction of Üllői út with the Nagykörút are two modern buildings diagonally opposite each other, both of them built as **'Lottery Houses'** (*see below*).

LOTTERY HOUSES

From the late 1950s, as part of the reconstruction programme to replace buildings lost to war damage or to the crossfire of 1956, a number of so-called *Lottóházak* or Lottery Houses were built: residential blocks whose flats were awarded as prizes in the national lottery. The buildings were typically hasty constructions, going up in the space of a single year—but certainly worth the price of a single lottery ticket to a poorly-paid worker, many of whom  won the chance to move from the countryside to Budapest. Over 20 Lottery Houses were built across the country between 1959 and 1973, as well as hundreds of holiday flats in locations such as Lake Balaton. The Lottery House on the corner of Ferenc körút is one of the earliest (Miklós Csics, 1959). The first lucky winners received the keys to their apartments here in 1961 at a televised event. The lottery block diagonally opposite went up in 1962. Both houses stand on the site of heavy fighting during the 1956 revolution. Other Lottery Houses in Budapest are at Múzeum körút 9 (*map p. 429, D3*), Baross tér 20 (*map p. 429, F3*), Frankel Leó út 76 (*map p. 424, D2*) and Margit körút 27 (*map p. 428, B1*). Look for the identifying circular metal plaques on the façades, bearing the words 'Lottó Ház'.

BAKÁTS TÉR

Tucked away behind the Nagykörút, between the river and the wide swing of Petőfi Bridge, Bakáts tér (*map p. 427, B5*) is a pleasant enclave, one of the few 'squares' in Budapest that really is a square, rather than a traffic junction or transport hub. It is surrounded on all sides by interesting façades: note the curious green turret on no. 3 (corner of Ráday utca) and the Art Nouveau **former Schöpf-Merei Hospital** at no. 10 (Emil Tőry, 1906). The square takes its name from Tamás Bakócz, Archbishop of Esztergom, whose funerary chapel (in Esztergom) is one of the few surviving Renaissance monuments in Hungary. In the centre of Bakáts tér stands the neo-Romanesque **church of St Francis of Assisi** (Bakáts téri templom), by Miklós Ybl (1879), built to replace an earlier church destroyed in the great Danube flood of 1838. On the exterior north wall, in a niche decorated with low reliefs of birds, is a bust of St Francis by Alajos Stróbl (1927). A plaque on the east end commemorates victims of the 1956 revolution. In the interior, the crossing and sanctuary have frescoes by Mór Than and Károly Lotz and at the head of the south aisle is a statue of St Anthony of Padua by Béni Ferenczy (1950).

FERENCVÁROS BEYOND THE NAGYKÖRÚT

DANDÁR UTCA

At Dandár u. 1, on the corner of Soroksári út, is the **Zwack distillery and museum** (*map p. 427, B6*). The family firm, now in its sixth generation, dates the production of its famous herb liqueur, Unicum, to the reign of Joseph II, who was prescribed it by his court physician, Dr Zwack, as a remedy for indigestion. Upon taking a sip of it, the monarch is said to have exclaimed, 'Doktor Zwack, das ist ein Unikum!'. The epithet stuck. The first Unicum distillery was in central Pest; it moved to this Ferencváros site in 1892. The company is still in family hands, largely thanks to the late Peter Zwack, who escaped Budapest in 1948 and returned in 1988. Peter's son Sándor took over in 2008. It is possible to take tours of the Zwack distillery and there is also a museum and shop (*for details, see zwackunicum.hu*). The recipe for Unicum, which is still sold in the traditional globular bottles, is a closely-guarded secret.

At no. 5 are the **Dandár Baths** (Dandár Gyógyfürdő), a small spa complex in a building of 1929–30 by Gyula Rimanóczy, with an Art Deco street façade in dark brick and Bauhaus-inspired lines at the back facing the garden, where there are two thermal pools and the statutory female nude (shown towelling her hair). The indoor pools occupy a high-ceilinged semicircular hall. The Dandár opened in 1930 as a public bath house (where working-class families would go to wash). It became a spa (for health and leisure rather than simple hygiene) in 1978, though the complex still preserves a very local character: many of the customers are elderly people with doctors' notes. There are very few tourists. (*For practical details and opening times, see p. 357.*)

THE ATTILA JÓZSEF MEMORIAL SPACE

This little **literary museum** (*Gát u. 3; open Tues–Fri 10–6, Sat–Sun 10–5; ring the bell; map p. 427, B6–B5*) is arranged in a room in the house where the poet Attila József was born in 1905. This is not the exact flat (it is uncertain which one that was). Mementoes include manuscript poems and letters and a few personal items (his propelling pencil). Captions are all in Hungarian. Born to a Greek Catholic father and a Calvinist mother, Attila was baptised into his father's faith in the church on Kálvin tér is this district. The father later abandoned his family. The flat where Attila and his sisters grew up would have been very simple, consisting of a single room with a kitchen. The building was recently renovated and the exhibition reorganised in 2015. Before renovation, the house was apparently 'full of rats, much more like it would have been in Attila József's day'. Photographs of the poet's mother, Borbála, from a village on the Great Plain, show her to have been beautiful. After her husband left her, she found work as a washerwoman and char lady. She died in 1919. One of the best known of all Hungarian poets, loved by the Communists for being a son of the working class, still admired today for the beautiful, hard-edged simplicity of his style, Attila József never knew material fortune during his short life. He died under the wheels of a train—probably suicide—in 1937.

Diagonally opposite the museum is a **neo-Romanesque church** (Antal Hofhauser, 1903), a Lazarite foundation dedicated to the Dutch Jesuit saint Peter Canisius.

THE LUDWIG MUSEUM, MÜPA AND NATIONAL THEATRE

The **Ludwig Museum** (*map p. 427, B6; open Tues–Sun 10–8, ludwigmuseum.hu*) is one of a number of art galleries around the world that bear the Ludwig name: the Budapest museum was founded in 1996 to house artworks donated in 1989 by the art collectors Peter and Irene Ludwig (the couple's money came from chocolate manufacturing). The Ludwig Museum has become Hungary's national collection of contemporary art, housing works from the 1960s to the present day. The focus is on young Hungarian artists though the collection, which is continually being augmented with new acquisitions, also includes works by a great many international names. In addition to the permanent holdings, the Ludwig also hosts frequent temporary shows. It occupies the riverside wing of the **Müpa** concert hall and performance space, which offers a wide-ranging programme that includes classical music, opera, jazz, world music, theatre and dance (*for programmes, box office opening hours and ticket information, see mupa.hu*). The building (Zoboki, Demeter and Partners, 2005) is known for its fine acoustics and is an important example of contemporary architecture in the city.

North of the Müpa is the **National Theatre** (Nemzeti Színház; Mária Siklós, 2002). For many years, ever since their building on Blaha Lujza tér was demolished after WWII, the National Theatre company had no satisfactory home, nor could a site be agreed on. The present building was completed in just 15 months. It was much criticised at first but people seem to have got used to it. Outside it on the ground is a symbolic representation of the demolition of the old theatre building. The small Ziggurat Gallery holds temporary exhibitions.

GULAG MEMORIAL

In front of the Ferencváros railway station, on the corner of Fék utca and Remíz utca (*map p. 427, C6*), is the Gulag Memorial (Málenkij robot-emlékhely; *tram 51 from Mester utca/Ferenc körút, map p. 427, B5*), commemorating Hungarians who were deported to Soviet labour camps at the end of WWII. The atmospheric exhibition, with photographs and other memorabilia, occupies a concrete bunker (*open by appointment; malenkij@mnm.hu*), originally an air raid shelter for the directors of the Hungarian railway company. A railway wagon with sculpted figures of deportees now adorns its exterior.

THE HOLOCAUST MEMORIAL CENTER

Map p. 427, B5. Holokauszt Emlékközpont. Open Tues–Sun 10–6, last tickets 1hr before closing. hdke.hu.

Designed in 2004 by István Mányi and his studio, the Memorial Center occupies a secluded courtyard backed by the main façade of a former synagogue (seen at the end of the tour). To the right is the Wall of Remembrance, eight metres high and bearing over 170,000 victims' names. The total number of Hungarian victims is over half a million; research is ongoing to complete the database. The entrance to the exhibition is on the

HOLOCAUST MEMORIAL CENTER
The synagogue.

left of the courtyard, under the leaning 'Tower of Lost Communities' which bears the names of the 1,441 Hungarian towns and villages which because of the Holocaust no longer have a Jewish community.

One Holocaust victim in ten and one Auschwitz victim in three was Hungarian. The centre is dedicated to their memory. The express aim is not only to remember Jews, but all the victims, including anti-Nazi objectors of other faiths. Space is given throughout the display to the persecution and killing of Roma. The story told here is nevertheless essentially a Jewish one: never before in the history of mankind had the leaders of a state made it their policy to exterminate every member of a people.

The story is told through photographs, wall texts, contemporary newssheets and family histories on audio loops which the visitor can follow all the way to the end. Exhibits include crude anti-Jewish propaganda from the Hungarian national front, photographs of the Budapest Ghetto and a room devoted to Auschwitz, the camp to which most of the Hungarian victims were taken. The final room offers horrifying and moving video footage of the liberation of the camps and a section on reprisals and calling to account (there is a photograph of Ferenc Szálasi, the Hungarian Nazi leader, on the scaffold). The tour ends in the synagogue. Over the triumphal arch is inscribed, with horrible irony, 'Love thy neighbour as thyself', in Hungarian and Hebrew. Built by Lipót Baumhorn in 1924, this was the second largest synagogue in Budapest. During the war it served as an internment centre. It was restored as part of the Memorial Center in 2004.

Close to the Holocaust Center, at **Berzenczey u. 11** (*map p. 427, B5*), is the house that Ödön Lechner built as his own residence, in 1895.

EATING AND DRINKING IN FERENCVÁROS

RESTAURANTS

fff **Costes**. Michelin-starred restaurant, the first in Hungary to receive the accolade. Soberly smart, with a dress code. Dinner only. Closed Mon and Tues. *Ráday u. 4. T: +36 1 219 0696, costes.hu. Map p. 429, D4.*

ff-fff **Petrus**. Michelin Bib Gourmand restaurant: gourmet food for reasonable prices. The décor is a bit gimmicky and the service erratic but the food is good French bistro fare (snails, *boeuf bourgignon, confit de canard*). Closed Sun and Mon. *Ferenc tér 2-3. T: + 36 1 951 2597, petrusrestaurant.hu. Map p. 427, B5.*

ff **Borbíróság**. Informal, popular restaurant serving Hungarian cuisine with international influences. Changing weekly specials, excellent wine list. Right behind the Central Market. *Csarnok tér 5. T: +36 1 219 0902, borbirosag.com. Map p. 429, D4.*

ff **Café Intenzo**. Relaxed café-restaurant. Hungarian and international dishes. Weekday lunch menu. In fine weather the seating spills into the interior garden (with a statue from the old Danube Fountain; *see p. 262*) and onto the street outside.

Kálvin tér 9. T: +36 1 219 5243, cafeintenzo.hu. Map p. 429, D4.

CAFÉS AND BARS

The **Monyó** pub serves good craft beers by the Monyó brewery, still operating in the Kőbánya district, Budapest's historic brewing heartland (*Kálvin tér 7; map p. 429, D4; closed Sun*). The **Rombusz-kert** beer garden, on an empty plot at Ráday u. 10 (*map p. 429, D4*), is informal and fun in summer (it retreats inside a plastic marquee in winter).

You can get drinks and simple meals in the cafés in the **Bálna building** (*map p. 429, D4*). On the riverward side is the Esetleg Bistro (seating and deckchairs overlooking the Danube in fine weather). On the other side is BeoPlay, which serves good coffee (in the Bang & Olufsen shop—perhaps a curious combination, but the background music is relayed through top-quality speakers).

The **Malom Bistro**, in the courtyard of the old Hungária flour mill, is open at lunchtime for snacks and sandwiches (*Soroksári út 48; map p. 427, B6*).

Districts X & XIX: Kőbánya & Kispest

K őbánya and Kispest are separate districts but linked in the public mind because they give their name to the southern terminus of the M3 (blue) metro line, Kőbánya-Kispest, familiarly abbreviated to Köki. Kőbánya is historically famous for its breweries; Kispest is perhaps best known for its football team. Both are outlying areas, scarcely visited by tourists. For the curious traveller, there is plenty to see. Both districts are interesting architecturally: here you will find a magnificent church by Ödön Lechner, beautiful mausolea in the

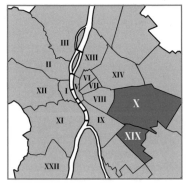

Kozma utca Jewish cemetery, and a housing estate built on the English Garden City model.

KŐBÁNYA

Kőbánya means 'quarry', and the first fortunes of the area derived from its rich seams of limestone. Almost all the major buildings of Budapest—the Chain Bridge, Opera House, Academy of Sciences, St Stephen's Basilica, Parliament—have Kőbánya limestone either deep at the heart of their structure or decorating their exteriors, or both. Ox carts laden with stones would lumber into town, scattering fine dust as they went and leaving a white film upon the road surfaces. Fehér út (White Road; *map p. 419, B1*) takes its name from this phenomenon. Along with the quarries, the area became known for its pigs and its fattening farms. Vines were also cultivated. In the 1830s, a lawyer, agriculturalist and viticulturalist by the name of József Havas bought a number of vineyards and set up Hungary's first brandy distillery here. Brandy, limestone and pigs gave way to beer in the later 19th century (*for the story of the breweries, see p. 280*).

KŐBÁNYA
The Lutheran church of 1931, with
post-war housing forming a backdrop.

Kőbánya today is a mix of historic buildings, derelict industrial plots and post-war housing estates. Vestiges of past brewing wealth can still be seen and felt, although today this is a poor part of town. The area to the west, around Százados út and Hős utca (*map p. 427, D4*), has a reputation for drug crime (Katalin Karády, singer and star of the Hungarian silver screen, was born here in 1910, the daughter of a shoemaker from the Százados út slum). Further east the district opens out. The roads are not busy and there are plenty of pleasant, breezy parks. Though it does not feel high up or appear to be on any kind of slope, Óhegy ('Old Hill') is in fact at nearly the same elevation as Buda Castle and at one time was covered in vines. The area might feel like a suburb but—as Kőbánya patriots are proud to point out—it lies almost at the geographical centre of greater metropolitan Budapest.

Getting to Kőbánya

The most direct route is by bus no. 9 from Nyugati station, Deák tér, Astoria or Kálvin tér to Szent László tér (map p. 419, A1), its penultimate stop. Alternatively, take metro line M2 (red) to Puskás Ferenc Stadion and then bus 95 or 195 to Kápolna utca (map p. 419, A2). NB: When you get out of the metro, the bus stop you need is on the corner of Kerepesi út and Hungária körút. Make sure you are heading away from the distant hills and the Arena Hotel.

Bus no. 9 runs along Kőbányai út (*map p. 427, C5–D5*), the entire length of which is taken up with a sprawling **Asian emporium** of booths and stalls, many of them run by Budapest Chinese, occupying an old industrial site. Electronic goods, clothes, food and more are available at cheap prices. Further on is the **Északi Járműjavító**, a former railway repair yard with a large central hangar designed by the Eiffel company. The complex was being refurbished at the time of writing to house workshop space and rehearsal rooms for the Opera House and Erkel Theatre, and the relocation of the **Transport Museum** (*currently closed*) to this site had been announced.

THE CHURCH OF ST LADISLAS

Map p. 419, A1. Open Mon–Sat 9–12 & 2.30–7, Sun 8–6.45.

The Church of St Ladislas (Szent László plébániatemplom) is the most important monument in Kőbánya and one of the finest churches in Budapest, the work of the great architect of the Hungarian Secession Ödön Lechner, himself the grandson of a Kőbánya brick manufacturer: as a boy he spent many summer holidays modelling the local clay. The church was built in 1892–1906, naturally enough of Kőbánya limestone, and combines all the characteristic elements of Lechner's style: copious decoration using Hungarian folk motifs and elements derived from Oriental art, and liberal use of glazed ceramics from the Zsolnay manufactory. Though the architecture is in part inspired by European Romanesque and Gothic traditions, its amalgamation of these with Persian, Indian and traditional Hungarian elements make it a work of architecture *sui generis*, impossible to classify.

KŐBÁNYA
The Church of St Ladislas.

Outside the church, in a little planted area beside Kőrösi Csoma Sándor út, is a **statue of Lechner** (Ildikó Zsemlye, 2014) with a model of the church beside him. In the garden directly in front of the church's main entrance is a colossal, stern-faced statue of the titular saint, **Ladislas I** (r. 1077–95), the great warrior king, consolidator of Hungary's power and strengthener of her borders, who instigated the canonisation of King Stephen and Prince Imre and who was himself canonised in 1192.

Exterior of the church

The church's slender **spire** (83m) makes it the third tallest church in Hungary and is a landmark for miles around. The domes and roof are clad in coloured tiles by the Zsolnay manufactory. The dome ribs and gables are richly crocketed and the gables have angel finials and central reliefs of the Eye of God. In the lunette above the main door is a **mosaic by Miksa Róth** showing Christ between the Virgin and St Ladislas with the legend: *Porta patet vitae; Christus via vera: venite* (The gate of life lies open; Christ is the true way: Enter). The **doors** themselves, both the main pair and those on either side, are decorated with delicate metal overlay that almost looks like something from a Hindu temple. The north door has a mosaic of the *Madonna and Child*; the south door a mosaic of Melchizedek holding bread and wine.

Interior of the church

The interior is spacious, a light and airy nave with two aisles and a clerestory, the walls, columns and vaults, with their moulded decorations, painted white on white. This colour scheme dates from post-war restoration and is not original. Lechner's church would have been coloured in warm tints of ochre. Every element—lamps, holy water stoups, wall sconces, the gates around the entrance vestibule—has been designed for this space. In the first north chapel, the Zsolnay ceramic **font** glitters like a giant reliquary casket. The pulpit and all the side altars are likewise clad in Zsolnay majolica and pyrogranite, to designs by Ottó Tandor. The colour scheme is very delicate: pale apricot, cream, light blue and gold—in some ways evocative of a luxury ladies' powder room. The **pulpit** is adorned with angels and Apostles and above it hangs an enormous sounding board like a towering papal tiara. At the head of the north aisle is the **St Anthony Chapel** with a mosaic altarpiece of the titular saint. At the head of the south aisle is the **St Margaret Chapel** with lovely ceramic angels adorning the altar and a painted altarpiece by Ignác Roskovics. Roskovics also painted the **high altarpiece** of St Ladislas. At the bottom of the south aisle is the **Easter Sepulchre**, with an altar above it surmounted by turreted ceramic tabernacles. The **stained-glass windows** are mostly reproductions of the Miksa Róth originals that were destroyed in WWII. Many are dated and include the names of the donors. At the head of the north aisle is a window with a reproduction in glass of Gyula Benczúr's *Baptism of Vajk*, a famous painting in the Hungarian National Gallery (*see p. 45*).

St Ladislas enjoys an active musical life and concerts are often held here. The **organ**, by the firm of Otto Rieger, is the original of 1899, a remarkable survival. The concert organist Xavér Varnus, who was born in Kőbánya, sometimes plays here.

ON AND AROUND SZENT LÁSZLÓ TÉR

Szent László tér (*map p. 419, A1–A2*), the square on which the church stands, is bisected by the busy Kőrösi Csoma Sándor út. The square once hosted the Hungarian-Soviet Friendship Monument, which was daubed with 'Russkies go home!' and toppled in 1956. It is now in the Memento statue park (*see p. 125*) and instead the square features the monumental **Hungarian Altar** (Tibor Szervátiusz, 1996), put up to commemorate Hungary's 'millecentenary'. It consists of three limestone monoliths with naïve reliefs of Árpád (with the Turul bird behind him), the Virgin and St László. Stones carved with outlines of Scythian stags (*see p. 231*) bear the dates 896 (the Magyars' occupation of the Carpathian Basin) and 1996. Also on the square, on the corner of Halom utca, is a modern building housing the **Kőbánya Cultural Centre** (Kőbányai Kulturális Központ). There are WCs, a very simple buffet selling drinks and snacks and, around the top of the walls in the foyer, interesting copies of advertising posters from the various Kőbánya breweries as well as old photos of the district, including one showing the Csősztorony (*see p. 279*) in the midst of vineyards.

Further along Kőrösi Csoma Sándor út, at no. 28–34 on the corner of Ónodi utca (*map p. 419, A1*), is another, later building by Ödön Lechner (probably in conjunction with József Vágó), the **Szent László High School**, which opened in 1915. It has a fine corner entranceway with a giant order of fluted columns, and on the side flanks, relief medallions of children.

MARTINOVICS TÉR

On Káplona utca, where it meets Martinovics tér (*map p. 419, A2*), stands the brown-brick **Lutheran Church**, a striking round building (János Frecska, 1931) with a tall, slim bell-tower thrusting into the sky like one of Kőbánya's factory chimneys. Martinovics tér is noisy at noon, when the bells from this church and those from the **Calvinist church** in nearby Ihász utca (a fine building of 1897–1900 by Lajos Schodits) ring out together. The house at **Martinovics tér 4** was built by the architect Richárd Schöntheil as his own home in 1911. Schöntheil's best-known work is just a few paces away, on the corner of Cserkész utca and Román utca: the **Mindenki temploma** (Church for All), which was built in 1909–11 as Kőbánya's synagogue. It has stout cyclopean walls and domed turrets, and wrought-iron gates now adorned with the word 'Sion'. Following years of abandon and decay, it was taken over by a congregation of Pentecostal Christians in 1991. A charming local story explains the church's unusual name: some time before the Second World War, an elderly Christian widow was found praying here. Upon being questioned by the rabbi, she replied that she was too frail to walk far and that this was the closest house of prayer to her home. The rabbi responded that she was free to come whenever she pleased, 'for truly this is a temple for all'.

Also on Martinovics tér, in a modern building marked 'Tűzoltó Múzeum', is the **Firefighting Museum** (*open Mon–Thur 7.30–4, Fri 7.30–2, Sat 8.30–4; closed Sun; entrance on Káplona utca; the building is a working fire station; ask to see the museum, which is on the first floor; free*). The captions are all in Hungarian but the exhibits and photographs largely speak for themselves. The display begins with firefighting in Roman days (with a reproduction of the water organ found in the firemen's barracks at Aquincum; *see p. 109*). Mechanisation began with the invention of the fire hose in Holland in 1672. Nineteenth-century memorabilia includes a photograph of István Széchenyi's son Ödön as commander-in-chief of the Ottoman fire brigade. Árpád Feszty's tragic genre painting *Kárvallottak* (*The Bereft*, 1866) shows a family standing disconsolately amid the still-smoking ruins of their house. Everything has been consumed in the blaze except for a painted wooden trunk, on which the grandfather morosely sits. Particularly good is the collection of early gas masks, including the 1844 prototype invented by the Hungarian military engineer Károly Kőszeghi-Mártony. Photographs of conflagrations line the stairway and on the ground floor is a collection of old fire engines.

At the top of Kápolna utca stands the eponymous *kápolna* (chapel). The tiny little building with its onion-domed bell-tower stands on a natural rocky outcrop now planted with aloes and lavender. It was built in 1739–40 by a stonemason of Italian descent, Lipót Antal Conti. By the late 19th century, the population of Kőbánya had outgrown the **Conti Chapel** (*map p. 419, A2*) and moved to Ödön Lechner's new church of St Ladislas. The chapel today serves a Uniate congregation.

AROUND CSAJKOVSZKIJ PARK

Csajkovszkij Park (Tchaikovsky Park; *map p. 419, A2*) was once the garden and grounds of the **Havas Villa**, an attractive (but at the time of writing derelict) Neoclassical building built in 1856, probably by Károly Hild, for the lawyer-turned-brandy-distiller József Havas. Havas later sold his estate to Jakab Perlmutter (ancestor of the painter Izsák Perlmutter), who set up Kőbánya's second brewery here. That brewery was bought by Antal Dreher in 1862 and the Havas Villa, extended by Frigyes Feszl in the 1870s, was used as the house of the owner/manager until the breweries were nationalised after WWII. The **old brewery premises** (also very run-down at the time of writing) can be seen from Halom utca. The wing that faces the street (designed by Frigyes Feszl) was the old stable block. The top floor, where there is no glass in the apertures, was the hayloft. Opposite, at Halom u. 37/b, is the **Kőbánya Local History Museum** (Helytörténeti Gyüjtemény; *open Wed and Fri 10–2, Thur 2–6. NB: At the time of writing the museum was planning to move to a new location at Fűzér u. 32; map p. 419, A2*). The collection is formed entirely of donations and includes relics of Kőbánya's past as a centre of the brewing, brick-making (there is a brick stamped with Frigyes Feszl's 'FF' monogram), porcelain manufacturing (look for the 'Drasche' mark) and pharmaceuticals industries, as well as items from the old Kőbánya lamp factory and examples of hewn Kőbánya limestone. An interesting piece is the commemorative cup from a dinner of the local '48 Club. Until the Compromise of 1867, the 1848 War of Independence could not be openly celebrated and Hungarian patriots would meet in private assemblies. This silver cup has a lid topped with a head of Kossuth.

To see more of the old brewery, walk up Ászok utca (*ászok* is a lager beer, fermented slowly and at very cool temperatures as opposed to the higher temperatures required

KŐBÁNYA
The district in its industrial heyday, with the spire of St Ladislas vying with
the smokestacks of the Dreher brewery.

for an ale; the process was commercialised in Hungary by the Dreher family), which turns into steps and a rough path which takes you right round the old factory precinct. At the beginning of the path there is a fine view to the left of the spire of St Ladislas. From Előd köz (*map p. 419, B2*) you have a good view of the **old malt house** with its serried chimneys, still with their crown-shaped cowls in a double layer, one to draw off steam, the other smoke. The patch of rough ground here is punctured by ventilation shafts for the **system of tunnels** beneath. Kőbánya is undermined by over 30km of tunnels. On certain days they are open to the public and it is also possible to see them on guided tours (in Hungarian). Scuba diving to the areas of tunnel now submerged is also a possibility (*see titanbuvar.hu;* images on the website show old pieces of brewery equipment preserved under crystal clear water). During the Second World War, a section of the tunnel labyrinth was used as a secret aeroplane factory.

At Ihász u. 39 is the **Kőbánya Reservoir** (Kőbánya Víztározó; *map p. 419, B2*), surrounded by a small arboretum. Its beautiful brick-vaulted cistern was built in 1868 and supplied water to the main pump house on today's Kossuth Lajos tér in central Pest. Open days are sometimes held here.

At the junction of Harmat, Kőér and Gitár streets, overlooking Óhegy Park, is a white building with a spiral stair leading to the top of a tower on its roof. This is the **Csősztorony**, built by Ferenc Brein and Lőrinc Zofahl in 1844 as a watchtower from which the vineyards (in what is now the park) could be surveyed. Today it has a pleasant café and beer garden behind it.

JÁSZBERÉNYI ÚT AND THE DREHER BREWERY

The pronounced bend in the road where Kőrösi Csoma Sándor út becomes Jászberényi út is known as the **Éles sarok** (Acute Angle; *map p. 419, B1*). A 1956 memorial commemorates the gallant resistance that was put up here against the invading Soviets. On top of the fence behind the bus stop is a Socialist Realist sculpture group of female grape harvesters (László Garami, 1954). At the time of writing the kneeling woman had been robbed of her bunch of grapes and pruning knife.

The flight path to and from Budapest airport comes past here and planes fly quite low overhead. A short way further along Jászberényi út is the **Dreher Brewery** (*map p. 419, B1*), the sole survivor of the many breweries that once populated Kőbánya. Today it is owned by the Japanese Asahi firm. Tours of the brewery can be organised and there is also a small **beer museum** (*Jászberényi út 7–11; open Mon–Fri 9–4; for updates and details of brewery tours, see dreherzrt.hu*).

HISTORY OF THE KŐBÁNYA BREWERIES

Brewing in Kőbánya dates back to the 1850s. When quarrymen working the limestone hit springs of pure water, it was discovered that this, coupled with the underground tunnels opened up by the workmen, offered an ideal environment for cellaring and for sprouting barley (malting). In 1854 two partners, Ágost Barber and his brother-in-law Károly Klusemann, set up a brewery on Jászberényi út (the site now occupied by the Asahi-Dreher concern). It was a move which proved successful and which inspired others to follow. Antal Dreher, the 'King of Beer', soon set up a brewing business here, on the now-derelict Halom utca site. In the 1890s, accidents in the quarries caused their closure. Meanwhile, the railway had come to Kőbánya and land formerly given over to vines became too valuable to be used for agriculture. Though phylloxera is often blamed for the demise of the Kőbánya vineyards, it is likely that economics and commercial opportunity were the true cause. Vines may well have continued to thrive in the soil here, which is sandy and thus inimical to the phylloxera louse. An outbreak of swine fever, plus a burgeoning human population which could not live side by side with a hundred thousand hogs, led to the closure of the piggeries. Kőbánya became a brewers' monopoly. Six breweries were in operation by the early 20th century: Dreher, the Első Magyar Részvény (formerly Barber and Klusemann), Polgári, Király, Haggenmacher and Fővárosi.

The Dreher family, originally from Bavaria, moved their brewing operations first to Austria and then, in 1862, to Kőbánya, where they found fame and fortune under the younger Antal (Anton) Dreher, grandson of the founder. In the 1920s, Antal's son Jenő (Eugen) merged the brewery with the former Barber-Klusemann (Első Magyar Részvény) and Haggenmacher operations and became a huge conglomerate, producing 75 percent of Hungary's beer. After the First World War, times were much harder. The Treaty of Trianon deprived Hungary of two thirds of her territory and with it went an important beer-drinking market. The Dreher brewery was inventive, introducing new products to make use of their yeast and malt: brandy, liqueurs, chocolate (turning the drayhorse stables into cowsheds) and a meat substitute called

Sertamin, a yeast extract developed in tandem with Gedeon Richter, who had set up Hungary's first pharmaceutical factory on Cserkész utca in 1907. Not all the breweries survived the lean years. Those that did were nationalised under Communism and became a single state entity. The brewery on Jászberényi út readopted the Dreher name in 1997. Owned first by the SABMiller group, it was bought by Asahi in 2016. Their brands include Dreher, Kőbányai, Arany Ászok and Pilsner Urquell.

At no. 47 Maglódi út is the once-fine former Fővárosi Serfőzde, built in 1912. The finials on its gateposts are shaped like barrels. Subsequently used by the Globus canning factory, it is now the **M47 Enterprise Park**, rather a grand name for such a shabby enclave. At the time of writing the buildings badly needed attention. Note the fine medallions of King Matthias Corvinus, the company trademark. The mosaic likenesses of the king are thought to be by the Anglo-Venetian firm of Salviati, Jesurum & Co. The eosin-glazed wreaths that enclose the mosaics are by Zsolnay. Micro-breweries were in operation here at the time of writing (*see Monyó, p. 271*).

KOZMA UTCA JEWISH CEMETERY

Beyond map p. 419, B1. Marked on map p. 431, E3. Tram 28 from Blaha Lujza tér to Izraelita temető, the last stop (journey time 40mins). If you are coming from Kőbánya, take the same tram from Szent László tér (journey time 20mins). Open April–Oct daily except Sat 8–4, Nov–March closes 1hr earlier. Posted on the inner gate is a map of the cemetery showing the numbered sectors. You can also ask for a printed copy in the office inside the mortuary building.

This scarcely-visited, marvellously atmospheric, secret garden of a place is the largest, most populous Jewish cemetery in Hungary, with thousands of graves. Although many of the tombs are neglected and many areas are completely overgrown, it is still in use, and the various sectors are filled with graves old and new, in a wide variety of styles, some of them artistic and architectural masterpieces. Many illustrious men and women are buried here. The cemetery was opened in the early 1890s.

EXPLORING THE CEMETERY
In front of you as you enter is the bright white, Moorish-style **mortuary**, designed by Vilmos Freund in 1891. It is decorated with sculpture by Alajos Stróbl, who also provided the lions that guard the **Brüll mausoleum**, which stands against the perimeter wall to the right. Some of the mausolea here are exceptionally fine and are the chief glories of the cemetery. Sadly many of them are desperately in need of refurbishment and there are fears that the decorative elements—Zsolnay tiles and glass and mosaics by Miksa Róth—will be lost or fall prey to thieves.

Close to the Brüll mausoleum is the famous **Schmidl mausoleum** (1903), by Ödön Lechner and Béla Lajta, covered entirely in blue pyrogranite and blue glazed brick, with moulded reliefs of urns from which sprout luxuriant plants with mosaic flowers and nodding poppy heads. The gates are fashioned to look like the boughs of a willow

KOZMA UTCA JEWISH CEMETERY
Detail of the Griesz mausoleum
mosaics by Béla Lajta (1906–8).

tree. A beautiful flowering tree against a gold mosaic ground adorns the interior. Schmidl was a wealthy dealer in exotic imported goods. Further on, around the corner, is the **Adler-Wellisch mausoleum**, also decorated with mosaics, and beyond that the fine **Griesz mausoleum**, another work by Béla Lajta (1906–8), the interior magnificently adorned with mosaic lions, date palms and stained-glass panels of birds. In its opulence it is reminiscent of the Room of King Roger in Palermo. Next to it is the **tomb of Béla Bedő** (d. 1916), who commissioned the famous Art Nouveau Bedő-ház in central Pest (*see p. 148*).

In the line of mausolea that leads in the other direction from the mortuary is a **tomb of the Goldberger family** (with a plaque commemorating Leó Goldberger, who died in Mauthausen; *see p. 105*); the **Grósz mausoleum**, with motifs of grapes and wheat and beautiful ceramic willow trees (Jámbor Lajos and Zoltán Bálint, 1905); and the lovely **mausoleum of the Konrád Polnay family**, by Gyula Fodor.

Other burials here include the photographer Manó Mai (sector 10 row 4), the architect Lajos Jámbor (sector 7 row 3), Olympic swimmer and architect Alfréd Hajós, the painter Izsák Perlmutter and Béla Lajta himself. The great architect lies in sector 3J (beside the path where sector 3J meets sectors 7 and 8), under a plain classical stele topped by an urn. It was designed by his pupil, Lajos Kozma. On the opposite side of the path is the tomb of Lajta's parents, Dávid and Teréz Leitersdorfer. It has a curious shape, almost like a bread oven, and is decorated with incised hearts and the words, 'Here lies benevolence and love.' Next to it is the tomb of Lajta's older brother Henrik.

ÚJ KÖZTEMETŐ

Map p. 431, E3. Tram 28 from Blaha Lujza tér to Új Köztemető (journey time c. 40mins). If you are coming from Kőbánya, take the same tram from Szent László tér (journey time 20mins). Open daily from 7 or 7.30am until dusk.

The Új Köztemető, or New Public Cemetery, is one of the largest burial grounds in Budapest. It opened in 1886 and was laid out to designs by Győző Czigler. Plot 301, in the far northeast corner, is where Imre Nagy and others executed after 1956 were buried ignominiously as traitors to their Party (*see p. 91*). The plot was transformed into an honoured and hallowed patch of ground after Nagy's reburial in 1989.

KISPEST

Kispest, the city's 19th district, only became part of the capital with the formation of Budapest's greater metropolitan area in 1950. It is a largely residential area, characterised by leafy streets of simple, low-rise housing. Its main attraction for the visitor is the workers' housing estate known as the Wekerletelep—although football fans will know that the great Hungarian striker Ferenc Puskás was born here in 1927. Puskás went on to become an Olympic gold medallist, captain of the 'Mighty Magyars' or 'Golden Team' in the 1950s. After he defected from Hungary, he played for Real Madrid; but his home team was Kispest-Honvéd and when he died, in 2006, he was given a state funeral in St Stephen's Basilica.

WEKERLETELEP

The Wekerletelep (Wekerle Estate; *map p, 431, D3*) was begun in 1908 in response to a growth in the demand for housing in the rapidly growing city. Many people came up from the countryside in search of work (the architect Dezső Zrumeczky's father was one such case) and this estate, the only one of its kind in Budapest, conceived on the English Garden City model, was aimed at making the transition from country to town not too stark for the new arrivals. The housing stock is of two main types: single-storey semi-detached or terraced cottages for two to four families or two- or three-floor houses with flats for six to twelve families. The flats in each case are of varying sizes. Over a thousand houses were built here, between 1908 and 1925 (progress was interrupted by WWI). The estate is named after Sándor Wekerle, who was prime minister at the time and who brought the project to fruition.

The idea for a Garden City type of development, as opposed to rows of tenement blocks, had been proposed to the government by the architect Róbert Fleischl, who subsequently designed a number of houses in the estate (those known as the F-type). The layout and planning of the main square was supervised by Károly Kós until 1913. The Wekerle Estate consists of streets arranged geometrically around this square (now called Kós Károly tér), originally a low hillock. The entire area was planted with fruit trees, currant bushes and flowers, and each house has its own plot. Four main streets radiate out from the sides of the square: Pannónia út to the sections north and south, and Hungária út running east and west. Architects besides Kós involved in designing the houses include Dezső Zrumeczky, Róbert Fleischl, Lajos Schodits and Béla Eberling (who worked together), Gyula Wälder, Dénes Györgyi and Aladár Árkay.

Today the estate is a flourishing community where people like to live. It has kindergartens, schools, a cultural centre, two churches and a market (*daily except Sun from early morning until early afternoon, on Gutenberg körút*). The houses are all very characterful, and though some are shabby, the public spaces are excellently kept. It is common to see gardeners and groundsmen at work here.

Getting to the Wekerletelep
Metro line M3 (blue) to Határ út, from where it is a brisk 10min walk up Pannónia út. To avoid the walk, take bus 99, 194 or 199 from directly outside the metro station to Kós Károly tér. Bus 99 will also take you directly back to town, to Blaha Lujza tér.

If you choose to walk from the metro station, pause to look at the semi-detached cottages at **Pannónia út 1**, with their small front gardens and catenary arcades. They are by the partnership of Schodits and Eberling. On the other side of the road are two examples of houses by Fleischl, **nos. 4 and 6**.

KISPEST
Doorway in the Wekerle Estate.

KÓS KÁROLY TÉR

One of the stepping stones commemorating the achievements of the polymath
Károly Kós: in this case, publishing. *A Ház* was an architectural periodical.

KÓS KÁROLY TÉR

This spacious square lies at the heart of the Wekerletelep. The garden in the centre, behind railings, is planted with flower beds and shady trees. It is a pleasant place to sit, with a bandstand, a fountain and a children's playground. The square is overlooked by some of the most monumental buildings of the estate. Those on the east side, **nos. 2 and 3**, were designed by Károly Kós himself. With characteristic parabolic arches, steeply pitched roofs and a turret like a Transylvanian fortified church, they are linked by the wide arch of the **Kós kapu** (Kós Gate). No. 3 houses a pleasant cake shop and café, occupying a former butcher's. The corner building, **no. 4**, is by Schodits and Eberling. It became famous in Hungary when it was used in a popular TV soap opera. **No. 5** is by Dénes Györgyi and **no. 6** by Gyula Wälder.

At the west side of the square is the great, weather-boarded **Zrumeczky Gate** (restored 2008), by Dezső Zrumeczky, who had moved to Kispest as a child. His father set up in business as a haulier.

In the garden is a **statue of Kós** (László Péterfy), dating from 1987, the year when the square was named after its architect. The engraved paving stones leading to the statue act as commemorative plaques for Kós's achievements in the fields of architecture, graphic art and literature. Behind the central fountain is a bust of Sándor Wekerle, erected in 2008, the estate's centenary year.

On the northeast corner of Pannónia út (Kós Károly tér 16) is the **Munkás Szent József templom**, the church of St Joseph the Worker. Built in 1930, it is slightly later than the other buildings in the estate. Its interior walls are covered with frescoes from the 1940s and '50s.

EATING AND DRINKING IN KŐBÁNYA AND KISPEST

KŐBÁNYA

The *f* **Torockó Vendéglő** at Martinovics tér 2 (*torockovendeglo. hu; map p. 419, A2*) has been family-run for over 30 years (and in business for a lot longer, since 1906; it proudly markets itself as Kőbánya's oldest hostelry). The food is traditional Hungarian (sometimes they have rooster testicle stew on the menu). The interior décor is basic but the cooking is good (and in fine weather you can sit in the pleasant garden at the back). The beers, as might be expected, are all from the Dreher brewery. In fact, most of the bars and restaurants in this part of town have a Dreher sign outside them.

Behind the Csősztorony is the *f* **Csősztorony Bisztró** (*Harmat u. 31; map p. 419, B2*), where you can enjoy a coffee, a beer or a simple meal (grilled meat, fried fish, salad). Open spring–autumn in fine weather.

For craft beers by **Monyó**, made in the old brewery on Maglódi út, you need to go to Kálvin tér (*see p. 271*).

KISPEST

In the Wekerletelep, for a very local, extremely simple, time-stood-still sort of experience, there is the *f* **Wekerle Étterem** at Pannónia út 15. The *cukrászda* (café and cake shop) at **Kós Károly tér 3** serves coffee and cake. In the Zrumeczky building at no. 11 Kós Károly tér is the *f* **Éléskamra** health food restaurant, with a health food shop next door.

At the other end of the estate, at Andy Endre út 37 (walk to the east end of Hungária út and turn right) is the *f-ff* **Nótafa Vendéglő**, which has been in business since the 1900s and still offers traditional, no frills Hungarian cooking (*notafavendeglo. hu*).

Margaret Island

Margaret Island, 2.5km long, divides the Danube into two channels between Margaret and Árpád bridges. 'Margaret Island is Budapest's cameo,' wrote the 19th-century novelist Mór Jókai, 'a gem made more precious by cutting.' He was right. In its pristine state of silty mudflat and willow thicket, the island may possibly have had attractions, but in its man-made incarnation of public park, with noble trees grouped around closely-mown lawns, shady walks and sunny cafés, flower beds and fountains, it is many times more appealing. In summer the river embankments fill with sunbathers, sprawled on the stones like seals. There are bikes for rent, swimming pools, tennis courts and a popular running track. There is also a mini zoo, a spa hotel, an open-air theatre and the ruins of the Dominican convent where St Margaret, a princess of the House of Árpád, lived out her brief but exemplary life.

MARGARET BRIDGE

The exceptionally wide Margaret Bridge (Margit híd; *map p. 428, B1–C1*), accommodating cars, trams, pedestrians and cyclists, was the second permanent bridge to be built across the Danube. The original bridge was completed in 1876, three years after the union of Buda, Óbuda and Pest. Its designer was the French engineer Ernest Gouin. In the first year of the bridge's life, the poet János Arany wrote his ballad '*Híd-avatás*' ('Inauguration of the Bridge'). There is no poet-laureate-style bombast and it does not celebrate a great feat of engineering. Instead it is a doleful catalogue of suicide: the bridge rapidly became a last resort for those wishing to end their lives.

The bridge is angled in the centre and connected to Margaret Island by a linking arm, which was built in 1900. Until then, access to the island was by boat. The bridge was widened in the 1930s, blown up during WWII, reconstructed much more soberly in 1947, then given a lengthy makeover in 2009–11, in a bid to restore some of the lost splendour. The lamp-stands with their winged dragons date from the renovation, as do the yellow-painted iron railings and the sculpted St Stephen's Crowns. The crosses on top of the crowns present an irresistible temptation to vandals: they are perpetually being knocked off and then patiently replaced.

MARGARET ISLAND
The Palatinus Baths.

HISTORY OF MARGARET ISLAND

In the early Middle Ages the island (which in fact was several smaller islands, separated by channels) was known as *Insula Leporum*, Hare Island, and was used as a royal hunting reserve by the Árpád kings. In the 12th and 13th centuries, grants of land were made to the Premonstratensians and Franciscans, both of whom had religious houses here. At the north end was a castle belonging to the Archbishop of Esztergom, all trace of which has disappeared. In 1241–2, the Mongols ravaged Hungary and King Béla IV is said to have vowed that if he was victorious over them, he would dedicate his daughter Margaret to God. At the age of three she was given into the care of Dominican nuns, later entering the convent that her father built here. It enjoyed great prestige under his patronage and came to eclipse the two other religious establishments. By the end of the century the entire island belonged to the nuns. Margaret remained in the convent until her death in 1270. The island was named after her in the 19th century.

During the period of Ottoman rule, the island became depopulated and its buildings were destroyed. After the recapture of Buda in 1686, it passed to the Franciscan order of the Poor Clares. They erected a small chapel here, dedicated to Margaret, but their convent was on Castle Hill and the island was little used except as a place of pilgrimage to the chapel. Following the suppression of the religious orders by Joseph II, Margaret Island passed into the hands of the Habsburg Archduke Alexander, son of Leopold II and Palatine of Hungary. Following his death (aged only 22) after an accident at a fireworks display, his brother, the Palatine Joseph, took over the island in 1795 and had vines and rare trees planted, laying out a great part of it in the English manner. Wine harvest festivals were held here in the first half of the 19th century. After the failure of the 1848–9 Hungarian rebellion, József Szekrényessy, a wealthy lawyer and supporter of Széchenyi, rented the island for national celebrations, in an effort to sustain and stimulate Hungarian culture and artistic and intellectual life.

After the Compromise of 1867, the island became a popular watering place, open to the public upon payment of an entry fee, and poets and writers came to enjoy the tranquillity. In 1908 the island was made over to the state, as a public park in perpetuity. Entry fees were abolished after WWI. It has been open and free to all ever since.

EXPLORING MARGARET ISLAND

Map p. 424, D1–D2. Detailed map on p. 420. The island is accessed from its two ends: from Margaret Bridge at the south end (closest public transport Tram 4/6 to Margit híd Margitsziget) and from Árpád Bridge at the north. Bus 26 runs the length of the island; its termini are Árpád híd and Nyugati Station. The description below begins at the island's southern tip.

Centenary Monument: The bronze **Centenary Monument** (*Centenáriumi emlékmű*; István Kiss, 1972) commemorates the hundredth anniversary of Budapest, the capital city that was formed in 1873 from the union of Pest, Buda and Óbuda. The monument is shaped like a tulip bud, open at the side. Flanking the opening, forming a sort of entranceway, are two bronze tree stumps studded with nails, such as were created by travelling apprentices (*see p. 67*). The sculptor's signature appears on the left-hand stump. Inside, the monument appears like a collage of *objets trouvés*, except that everything is fashioned from the same bronze. Medals, coins, daggers, tokens for crossing the Danube bridges, helmets, mortar shells, cogwheels and a battered teddy bear all trace the history of Budapest from the days of the medieval guilds through the age of steam and iron to the wars and revolutions—and ultimate peace—of the 20th century.

Behind the monument is a large circular **fountain**, very popular on hot days, when people sit around the rim catching the water droplets blown on the breeze and watching while its automated jets perform hourly aquabatic stunts accompanied by music from the loudspeakers positioned around the perimeter. The fountain is drained in winter.

Hajós Alfréd Swimming Pool: The entrance to the swimming complex is through a well-proportioned red-brick building designed by Alfréd Hajós in 1930. More than just an architect, Hajós (1878–1955) was also an Olympic swimming champion. At the age of 18 he won gold in the 100m and the 1200m events at the first modern Olympic Games, in Athens in 1896. At the 1924 Paris Olympics (during the days when arts competitions also formed part of the Games), he won silver for a stadium design. Hajós continued with his architectural career and went on to design a number of Bauhaus-influenced buildings in Budapest. Opposite the entrance to the pool complex is a bronze statue (Gyula Palotai, 1955) of a female swimmer tucking her hair into her cap.

Franciscan Friary ruins: The friary was founded here in the 13th century. With the advent of the powerful Dominican sisters, the Franciscans' influence began to wane and their holdings of land became much smaller. Nevertheless, they remained here until their church and friary were destroyed by the Ottomans. In the late 18th century, Archduke Joseph, Palatine of Hungary, built himself a summer villa over what remained. The villa was later turned into a hotel and boarding house, and some of Budapest's greatest writers (including Gyula Krúdy) took rooms here. The building was damaged beyond repair in the Second World War and demolished in 1949.

Palatinus Baths: The Palatinus Baths (*Palatinus strandfürdő*) is the earliest outdoor bathing complex in Budapest, in operation since 1919. The baths immediately proved popular and were extended in 1937 by István Janáky. The geometric, columned exterior front dates from this time, as does the wave pool (though its mosaics are from the 1960s). The female statue outside the main entrance (*Woman Sunbathing*) is a 1967 recarving of an original by Géza Csorba, destroyed in WWII. The large mural, a 2017 repainting of a 1937 original by István Pekáry (faintly in the style of a Mughal miniature), shows men on a boar hunt on the left and ladies bathing on the right, attended by their waiting women. Peasants are at work in the background and a great many deer, duck, egrets and other creatures also inhabit the scene. It is an illustration of Endre Ady's poem 'The Wedding of King Dal's Daughters', which is set beside the Sea of Azov. The baths offer a variety of pools, open all year (*see palatinusstrand.hu*).

Rose Garden: Tucked into the bushes at the south end of this regularly planted space is a seated statue of the writer Imre Madách (Tibor Vilt, 1973). Madách is best known for his play *Az ember tragédiája* (*The Tragedy of Man*, 1861), which in 15 scenes follows Adam, the archetypal man, from his creation through the various ages of human history and achievement, into space and the future. Adam's errors (caused largely by his covetousness and pride) and his disillusion (caused largely by humanity's fallen state) are always underpinned by a tenacious, unbreakable seam of hope—and by Eve, who keeps reappearing in various guises to spur him ever onward. Metal thieves (to whom Margaret Island is particularly vulnerable) have twice removed Madách's arms, but lizard-like he continues to grow new ones.

Zoo: A small enclosure close to the rose garden (the cries of peacocks might alert you to its existence) gives sanctuary to numerous birds and small mammals, mainly native Hungarian species. The zoo's rescue centre specialises in the rehabilitation of birds and animals injured in the wild. A particularly delightful sight in spring are the nesting storks. The zoo is very popular with small children. When it is open (*April–Oct; free*) you can go inside. Otherwise the animals and birds can be seen through the railings.

Dominican Convent ruins: It was here that Margaret, a royal princess of the House of Árpád, daughter of Béla IV and the island's namesake, spent most of her short life. In what was once the nave of the convent church, a red marble slab under a maple tree marks the spot where her tomb once lay (it and her remains were smuggled to Bratislava after the Ottoman invasion). Nearby a little brick-built shrine, filled with votive offerings, testifies to her enduring popularity.

ST MARGARET OF HUNGARY

St Margaret (Szent Margit), a royal princess of the House of Árpád, was born in 1242 in a castle on the Adriatic coast, in present-day Croatia. Her mother was Maria Laskarina, daughter of the Byzantine emperor Theodore Laskaris, and her father Béla IV, King of Hungary. At the time of Margaret's birth, the Mongols had completely overrun King Béla's realm and he vowed that if by some miracle the hordes could be defeated, he would dedicate his newborn child to God. The miracle duly occurred: the Mongols retreated. At the age of three, Princess Margaret was entrusted to the care of Dominican nuns. When she was twelve she moved to the Dominican convent which her father had built for her on Hare Island and it is here that she took her vows of perpetual claustration. It appears that she entered into her sequestered life with dutiful enthusiasm. She refused the hands of two royal suitors. Records paint her as a fierce ascetic, deliberately depriving herself of food and sleep, choosing the most nauseating menial tasks and enthusiastically mortifying her flesh (a cilice associated with her is preserved in the Semmelweis Medical Museum; *see p. 60*). Broken in health and physically exhausted, she died in 1270 at the age of just 28. A magnificent tomb was made the following year. It immediately became a pilgrimage site and miracles were reported. The process of beatification was begun in 1276 by the Dominican pope Innocent V. She was finally canonised by Pius XII in 1943.

MARGARET ISLAND
Tympanum sculpture of the Chapel of St Michael, sole survivor of the
plethora of religious houses that once dotted the island.

Muvészsétány: The 'Artists Promenade' was planned in 1963. Busts of writers, painters and sculptors line all the walks in this part of the island. The sculptures repeatedly fall prey to thieves and have to be replaced. New busts are constantly added to the pantheon, sometimes used as vehicles for political statements. The bust of the controversial novelist Albert Wass, for example, has a map of the 'Greater Hungary' (Hungary's pre-Trianon outline) on its plinth.

Water Tower (*Víztorony*): This graceful former water tower, 57m high, was built in 1911 by the architect Rezső Ray Jr and the engineer Szilárd Zielinski. It is one of Hungary's earliest reinforced concrete structures. An open-air theatre functions at its base, offering a range of programmes during the Summer Festival. The tower itself has a look-out gallery offering superb panoramic views of surrounding Pest and Buda (*usually open May–Sept*). The tower has become the symbol of the Budapest Waterworks.

Chapel of St Michael (*Szent Mihály kápolna*): This small neo-Romanesque church (Kálmán Lux, 1930–1) stands on the foundations of a 12th-century chapel which was incorporated into a later (13th century) monastery of Premonstratensian (Augustinian) canons. With the arrival of the Dominican nuns a couple of decades later, strife broke out between the two religious houses concerning land rights. The chapel was completely destroyed during the Ottoman invasion, though its 15th-century bell was found nearby when the tree under which it had been hidden came down in a storm in 1914. It was rehung when the chapel was rebuilt. The relief over the main entrance shows St Michael Archangel weighing souls. The legend reads *Ignosce Domine*: 'Lord forgive me'.

The hotels: The Grand Hotel and Thermal Hotel are sister establishments under the same management, linked to each other by an underground corridor. In the early 20th century, the Budapest city council bought Margaret Island from the Habsburgs and turned it into a public park. It rapidly became a fashionable resort, known for its polo ground, restaurants and sports facilities, as well as for its hot springs. In its heyday the **spa**, housed in a building by Miklós Ybl, was one of the most beautiful in the city. It was badly damaged in the Second World War and again by flooding in the 1950s and was replaced by the current modern construction (Gyula Kéry, 1979). In its courtyard stands a bronze statue group entitled *Lovers* (József Ilosfai, 1980). The **Grand Hotel** was also designed by Ybl, with additions made in 1926 by Gyula Wälder. Renovations in the 1980s and subsequently have removed much of its original character. Both hotels have outdoor cafés and bar terraces. A curiosity of Margaret Island is that the Danube water around its shores never freezes at the level of the Thermal Hotel, because of the warm springs that bubble up here.

Japanese Garden (*Japánkert*): This is a pleasant spot, a collection of small rockeries with a string of artesian-fed thermal pools, home to terrapins and goldfish. Two bronze statues stand in the pools: *Seated Girl* (Imre Csikász, 1911, copy) and *Boy Crayfisher* (Miklós Ligeti, ?1890s).

Musical Fountain (*Zenélő kút*): This ornamental bandstand and drinking fountain is a replica of a public fountain of 1820–2 that once stood in Marosvásárhely (now Târgu Mureş, in Transylvania). The original, which played music by water power, was destroyed in a snowstorm in 1836. A century later this replica was erected here, powered by electricity. Its dome is crowned by a bronze statue of Neptune, which revolves through 360° in 24hrs. There are marble basins and water spouts on three sides. Recorded music issues from the roof at 15-minute intervals.

EATING AND DRINKING ON MARGARET ISLAND

Margaret Island lacks a good restaurant. The so-called Casino, originally a restaurant built by Ybl, was reconstructed (of concrete and to a simplified design) in 2017 but at the time of writing it was available for hire and no longer offered refreshment. There are stalls at various points all over the island (at all times of year, though far fewer in winter) selling drinks and snacks. The two hotels also have cafés and restaurants. Margaret Island is also a lovely place to take a picnic.

District XIII: Újlipótváros

The Thirteenth District, of which Újlipótváros is a part, stretches north along the Danube from the Pest side of Margaret Bridge. Lively and local, it is probably the nearest Budapest comes to having a New York-style neighborhood or Spanish *barrio*. It is not strictly a tourist area—there are no major sights here—but it is visited instead for its interesting architecture, for its historical associations (*see below*) and for its atmosphere.

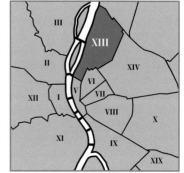

HISTORY OF ÚJLIPÓTVÁROS

In its name—New Leopold Town—Újlipótváros defines itself as being distinct from its near neighbour and near namesake on the other side of the Nagykörút. While old Leopold Town (Lipótváros, the Fifth District) is filled with wide stately streets lined with wide stately buildings, new Lipótváros presents a regular chequerboard of streets where the eye is led to the vanishing point past streamlined Bauhaus geometry articulated here and there with Art Deco ornament. Only laid out from the late 19th century, this was an avant garde district between the wars, with a sizeable Jewish population. In late 1944, the so-called International Ghetto was set up here, in the area around Szent István Park. Safe houses belonging to neutral Sweden and Switzerland, and claiming diplomatic immunity, offered sanctuary to many. The district also had a large number of the so-called '*Csillagos*' houses, where Jews forced to wear the yellow star were compelled to live before they were transferred to the Ghetto around Klauzál tér (*for more on this, see p. 299*).

Újlipótváros today has a relaxed and friendly charm. Still full of small, owner-managed shops and businesses, it is a place where local families choose to live (though prices have risen in recent years), a place where there is a strong community feeling. People often bump into people they know, greet each other in the streets and stop to chat. Sometimes familiarly known as 'Lipócia' (which sounds like the name of a separate country) because of its self-contained atmosphere, the district is host to the ever-more-popular Pozsonyi Piknik street festival in late summer.

XIII., VISEGRÁDI U.
53

VISEGRÁDI UTCA
Relief of a lamp-bearer.

ON & AROUND JÁSZAI MARI TÉR

Jászai Mari tér (*map p. 428, C1*) lies right beside Margaret Bridge. Facing the Danube is a tall development with corner domes, the **Palatinus Houses** (Emil Vidor, 1911), built for the Palatinus construction company, which built many of Hungary's railways. The apartments were originally very luxurious, with a central vacuum cleaning system and—so it is said—hot water pumped directly from the thermal source on Margaret Island. The company offices were at Jászai Mari tér 6 (later a Swiss safe house). Vilmos Grünwald, founder of Palatinus, later hired the railway engineer Miksa Schiffer, his brother-in-law, whose beautiful villa still partly survives (*see p. 202*).

Just off the square, between the Danube embankment access road and the road that runs under Margaret Bridge, set into the pavement, is a **mosaic by Anna Stein** (1990), the 'Sin Crying out for Vengeance'. The reference is to the Holocaust and to the four types of sin mentioned in the Bible as being outrages so grave that when the victims cry to the Lord, the Lord is sure to hear them. Murder is the first of these: 'And the Lord said unto Cain, what hast thou done? The voice of thy brother's blood crieth unto me from the ground' (*Genesis 4:10*). The Danube bank here is one of the places from which Jews and anti-Nazis were shot into the river in 1944. A story attaches to the Swiss vice-consul Carl Lutz (*see p. 215*), who is said to have leaped into the water to save a woman who was wounded but not killed. The embankment here is now named after him.

POZSONYI ÚT & SZENT ISTVÁN PARK

Pozsonyi út (*map p. 428, C1*), the heart of Újlipótváros, is lined with cafés, restaurants and independent, owner-managed shops. There are also plenty of fine and interesting buildings.

At **no. 1** (corner of Budai Nagy Antal utca), a plaque commemorates the ceramicist Margit Kovács and the poet Miklós Radnóti, both of whom lived here. Radnóti moved here on the day of his wedding in 1935, to a small flat on the second floor of what was then a new apartment block, built in the previous year. He died in 1944, shot during a forced march back to Hungary from a Serbian copper mine. His widow survived the war and lived here until her death in 2014. She was 101. Not far away, in a wall niche on the corner of Hollán Ernő utca and Katona József utca, is a **sculpture of St Florian**, an example of Margit Kovács's work.

Újlipótváros is an area of Budapest where you will see a clean sweep of Modernist architecture, expressing an aesthetic that is very different from the nostalgia of the 'Third Baroque' (*see p. 24*). At **no. 23** is a fine Modernist building (István Hámor, 1937) with balconies occupying a wide projecting bay, three to a floor, shielded by wood-framed glass panels, all with a square central roof light. **No. 41** (corner of Herzen utca; *map p. 426, A2*) is by Hugó Gregersen with sculpture by Alice Lux (1937). There are friezes by Lux over both entrances and elegant balcony rails on the upper floors.

At the **junction of Pozsonyi út with Victor Hugo utca and Wahrmann Mór köz** are two interesting corner buildings of the 1940s. Both have characteristic rounded window mouldings; one of them (Gyula Jakobik, 1940) has balconies fitted across a receding-angled front. The corner building at **Pozsonyi út 53–55** (with the Sarki Fűszeres café and delicatessen on the ground floor) is known as the **Vasaló-ház** ('Flatiron Building', inspired by the famous New York tower). It has a relief over the door and a beautiful entrance hall: look through the glass to admire the curve of the stair, the radiator surround and bell console. It is another work by István Hámor (1942).

On the opposite side of Pozsonyi út is the **Dunapark House (nos. 38–42)** by Domány and Hofstätter (1937). The same architects also designed the Weiss Manfréd apartment building in Buda (*see p. 76*) and the projects are similar in some details. Built as apartments for the Alföld Sugar Factory, the Dunapark development was both modern and luxurious, with a communal roof garden. The lobbies are clad in delicate pink marble with chrome steel fixtures. No. 42 has a special storeroom marked '*Gyermekkocsik*', for perambulators, and a marble ramp for buggies and wheelchairs. The politician Anna Kéthly, Social Democrat MP (first elected in 1922) and later a victim of hardline Communist persecution, lived here. No. 40 also has a fine entranceway and twin exterior lamps on either side of the door. Both these sections of the building were Swedish protected houses in late 1944. Renovations in the 1970s removed many of the original features. The Dunapark café and restaurant occupies the ground floor of no. 38. It reopened here in 2007, as far as possible to the original streamlined design.

SAFE HOUSES AND '*CSILLAGOS*' HOUSES

In June 1944 a ruling was passed compelling the Jews of Budapest to move to the so-called *Csillagos-házak* ('Yellow Star Houses'), which were scattered all across the city. The conditions of life in such a house are described by the writer and politician Miksa Fenyő in his diary entry for 25th June 1944: 'Jews can only leave the Yellow Star Houses between 2 and 5 o'clock, and even then only to go to the doctor, to wash or go shopping. They are crammed into the flats four or five to a room, with one kitchen and WC between 15 or 20 people. Reduced to a state of complete torpor, they suffer horribly from the heat, unable even to leave their rooms to go for a walk (they are not allowed in parks and public spaces). They are not permitted to receive visitors, on trams they have to use the wagons and they may not set foot inside Christian homes.'

In November 1944, the Ghetto was set up in the Seventh District (*see p. 213*) and all Jews were ordered to move there. Some managed to find places in the Safe Houses (*Védett házak*) set up under Swiss or Swedish diplomatic protection. Most of these were in the Thirteenth District around Pozsonyi út, the so-called International Ghetto. Today they are marked with curved kite-shaped plaques. The building at Pozsonyi út 15–17 (corner of Raoul Wallenberg utca), with a fine symmetrical façade by Imre Szőke (1936)—and today a good café—was one such. Although the neutral countries who set up the safe houses did their best to protect those who took refuge within them, the status of these buildings was always precarious and no Jew was ever completely safe from raids organised by the Arrow Cross death squads.

SZENT ISTVÁN PARK

The apartments in the handsome buildings of Szent István Park, surrounding a leafy playground (*map p. 426, A2*), are some of the most desirable in this district, especially those with Danube views. At **no. 16** a plaque commemorates the architect József Fischer and his wife Eszter Pécsi. Fischer is mentioned as instrumental in the rebuilding of the bomb-damaged city after 1945. Pécsi was the first woman in Hungary to qualify as an engineer. The house at **no. 25** has a plaque to Tom Lantos (1928–2008), the only Holocaust survivor to become a member of the US Congress. Fronting the Danube is a public park with a large sculpture of the ***Snake Slayer***, a naked man in combat with a serpent, a copy of a monument to Raoul Wallenberg by Pál Pátzay (1949).

RAOUL WALLENBERG AND HIS MEMORIALS

Raoul Wallenberg (1912–?), scion of the Swedish industrial and banking family, was accredited to the Swedish Legation in Budapest from July 1944, his operations financed by Roosevelt's War Refugee Board. He boldly and heroically saved thousands of Jews from the German Nazis and Hungarian Arrow Cross, not only issuing them with Swedish documents but also at times intervening personally. Wallenberg disappeared in January 1945 during the Siege of Budapest. He was arrested by the Red Army, accused of being a spy, and taken to the Soviet Union. Ironically, it was Wallenberg himself who had naively sought contact with the Soviets; he appears to have willingly left his apartment near City Park with Major Demchenko, after which his movements are unclear. In 1957, the USSR announced that Wallenberg had died in Lubyanka prison ten years previously. Many continued to cling to the hope that he could still be alive (in fact various sightings were reported). In 2000, Moscow announced that Wallenberg had been executed. Because of the Soviet involvement in the case, the Wallenberg story was never properly investigated in Communist Hungary. The statue of the *Snake Slayer* in Szent István Park, an allegory of Man combating Evil, was taken down on the eve of its unveiling and set up instead outside the Biogal pharmaceutical factory in Debrecen, east Hungary, where its symbolism was interpreted as Man combating Disease. For years the only memorial to Wallenberg in Budapest was the street in District XIII that bears his name. Then in 1987, Imre Varga's statue went up on Szilágyi Erzsébet fasor (*see p. 85*). The fact that its location is far from the former Ghetto and from the centre of Wallenberg's Pest operations indicates the sensitivity that still persisted. It was not until 1999 that this replica of the original *Snake Slayer* was erected in its first-designated site, Szent István Park. It was paid for with contributions from Biogal, which had been bought by an Israeli firm who wanted to keep the original monument in front of the Debrecen factory premises.

SZENT ISTVÁN KÖRÚT & PANNÓNIA UTCA

Szent István körút (*map p. 428, C1*) is lined on either side with tall, late 19th-century buildings. On the corner of Pannónia utca is the **Vígszínház theatre**, a reconstruction of the 1896 eclectic neo-Baroque original by Fellner and Helmer, which suffered a direct hit in WWII. Its ticket office and props store are on Pannónia utca (you sometimes see people wheeling racks of costumes or carting stage sets to and fro). Beyond it, at **Szent István körút 16**, is a handsome apartment house by Alfréd Wellisch, with a fine wrought-iron entrance gate and hallway lamp, and frescoes by Károly Lotz in the shallow vault above. The entranceway preserves its pretty floor tiles and there are putti over the lateral doors marked '*Lift*' and '*Főlépcső*' (main stairway). Wrought-iron corner balconies rise through four storeys in the inner courtyard, which preserves a central fountain. There are shops in the courtyard so it is accessible during business hours.

Round the corner, at **Visegrádi u. 3**, is a synagogue. Nothing on the exterior of the building gives this away, but the Pesti Súl has operated here, in a former private apartment, since 1948. It serves a modern Orthodox community.

At **Katona József u. 21** is a plaque commemorating Gedeon Richter, founder of the pharmaceutical company that bears his name. A pioneer pharmacist, he patented a number of successful drugs but despite this was stripped of his director's post and forbidden access to his own factory following the introduction of stringent anti-Jewish legislation in 1942. For a time he was hidden by Raoul Wallenberg. In December 1944 he was taken from this house by the Arrow Cross and shot into the Danube. He was 72 years old. At Katona József u. 2 is a monumental red-brick **electricity substation**, one of three built by Ernő Léstyán in the 1960s.

PANNÓNIA UTCA

Walking northwards up Pannónia utca (*map p. 428, C1*), you will notice that in the space of the very first block, the 19th century ends and the 20th century begins. There are some exceptional early 20th-century façades here, in a rich combination and juxtaposition of styles: Bauhaus or Art Deco or something more eclectic.

At **no. 6** (Dávid and Zsigmond Jónás, c. 1909), look up to see pairs of lovely wrought-iron peacocks. **No. 12** (Béla Barát and Ede Novák, 1928) is a restrained building in dark red brick with brown stone dressings. Shallow angled balconies are supported each by a single central console. At **no. 9**, built by the Löffler brothers for the printer Ödön Lőbl in 1915, the style is 'stripped Venetian' with a three-light corner window on the top floor. Above the main entrance is a terracotta-coloured screen, reminiscent of a columbarium.

The elaborate main entrance bay of **no. 18, the Phőnix House** (also by the Jónás brothers, 1929), gives onto a wide central garden overlooked by myriad flats. The garden stretches all the way through to Tátra utca, the parallel street (where the bird named above the entrance is not 'Phőnix' but 'Turul'). At **no. 20**, the Phőnix Patika pharmacy preserves its original neo-Neoclassical furnishings, also of 1929.

STOLPERSTEINE

There are examples of *Stolpersteine* all over Budapest, but nowhere more densely than in the Thirteenth District. These 'Stumbling Blocks', conceived and executed by the German artist Gunter Demnig, take the form of small brass plaques commemorating victims of Nazi persecution, set into the pavement in front of the houses where they lived or worked. To paraphrase Rabbi Johanan and the Jerusalem Talmud: if a person's name is incised on an object, that person will never be forgotten. Demnig laid his first *Stolperstein* in Cologne in 1995. The first Budapest example was laid in 2007. The number of such plaques so far laid, and the diffuse nature of the project (there are *Stolpersteine* in more than 20 countries), make this the largest commemorative monument in the world (*for more on the phenomenon, see www.stolpersteine.eu*).

Pannónia u. 19 (Frigyes Spiegel and Endre Kovács, 1929) is built of brick with protruding central bays and four decorative balls on the roofline. **No. 24** opposite, with its alternating balconies and elegant balcony rails, is by Hofstätter. **No. 23**, on the corner of Radnóti utca (Béla Jánszky and Tibor Szivessy, 1927), was built for the transport agent Ignác Heisler. Note the ship and locomotive in roundels and the terracotta statues of *Fortune* and *Hermes* beside the main doorway. The owner's initials (HI) and the date (1927) are worked into the ironwork of the front doors.

At **Radnóti Miklós u. 19/b** is a house by Szivessy's pupil Artúr Wigdorovits (1927). The influence of the master is clear in the use of moulded decoration. Opposite is a pair of widely contrasting buildings: one top-heavy with articulation, the other characterised by horizontal and vertical lines (the only oblique element is the front door handle).

And for something completely different, walk on one block to Radnóti Miklós u. 18, where you will find the **Pinball Museum**, an entire basement filled with games machines (*open Wed–Fri 4–midnight, Sat 2–midnight, Sun 10–10, flippermuzeum.hu*). Many of the machines are from the 1980s and '90s. The oldest are the table football and table ice hockey sets. There is also an original 'Humpty Dumpty' pinball machine of 1947. Made by the Chicago-based firm of Gottlieb, it was the first to introduce the system of button-operated 'flippers' at the bottom of the playfield.

The late Art Nouveau building at **Pannónia u. 30** (Miklós Román and István Jelinek, 1914) is decorated with putti riding bears and dogs. The pink building next to it (**Radnóti Miklós u. 25**) is by Miklós Román and his brother Ernő, dating from a year earlier. Both brothers were in the circle of Béla Lajta.

LEHEL TÉR

The neo-Romanesque **Church of St Margaret** on Lehel tér (*map p. 426, B2*), by István Möller (1931–3), is modelled on the ruins of the medieval abbey church at Zsámbék (*see p. 338*), which Möller also restored. Some of the funds for its construction were donated by Lord Rothermere, the British newspaper magnate and vocal supporter of the revision of the Treaty of Trianon. Unless there is a service in progress, you can only get into the vestibule, from where you can peer at the interior through the glass of the main doors. The beautiful stained-glass windows are by the workshop of Miksa Róth.

The Lehel Csarnok **market hall**, at Váci út 9, is a bulky, kitsch building by László Rajk (2002), painted in bright primary colours and for some reason evoking a ship. Prices here are very reasonable; this market is a long way from the tourist trail. The café next to the Lotto shop on the first floor serves good coffee.

EATING AND DRINKING IN ÚJLIPÓTVÁROS

RESTAURANTS

ff **Khan**. Asian (Vietnamese, Chinese, Thai) restaurant, sister establishment to Sáo in the Gozsdu udvar. Very popular. Best to book. Kitchen closes at 10pm. *Ipoly u. 3. T: +36 20 451 1737. Map p. 426, A1–A2.*

ff **Kiskakukk**. Traditional Hungarian restaurant: goulash soup, veal in paprika sauce, strudel. A place to come for a leisurely meal. *Pozsonyi út 12. T: +36 1 786 3439, kiskakukk.hu. Map p. 428, C1.*

f **Bécsiszelet Kisvendéglő**. Traditional and very simple lunch place on the district's liveliest street. The name means Wiener Schnitzel but the offering is wider than that. Weekday lunch menu. Very small interior space, seating outside in fine weather. *Pozsonyi út 14. T: +36 20 823 0920. Map p. 428, C1.*

f **Firkász**. The name ('Scribbler') is a slang word for journalist and the walls of this place are plastered with old news cuttings. Popular at lunchtime when they do a good-value buffet. Popular with locals. *Tátra u. 18. T: +36 1 789 4661, firkasz.hu. Map p. 428, C1.*

f **Norbi Étkezde**. A traditional *étkezde*, a tiny place serving hearty Hungarian lunches, also available to take away. Queues can form on the days when they do beef chasseur (*vadas marha*). *Tátra u. 5. Map p. 428, C1.*

CAFÉS AND BARS

Sarki Fűszeres. The 'Corner Grocery' is a delicatessen and café occupying the ground floor of Budapest's 'Flatiron Building'. Breakfasts, lunchtime sandwiches, after-work drinks. Outdoor seating in fine weather. *Pozsonyi út 53–55. T: +36 1 787 7868. Map p. 426, A2.*

Dunapark. Café (and restaurant) on the ground floor one of Pozsonyi út's most elegant apartment blocks of the 1930s (*see p. 299*), with outdoor seating overlooking Szent István Park. *Pozsonyi út 38. T: +36 1 786 1009, dunaparkkavehaz.com. Map p. 426, A2.*

My Green Cup. Excellent coffee (sister café of My Little Melbourne on Madách tér), croissants, sandwiches. A good place to take a break. *Pozsonyi út 15. Map p. 428, C1.*

Madal. Espresso and brew bar (one of three in Budapest). Makes good coffee and good cheesecake. *Hollán Ernő u. 3. Map p. 428, C1.*

District XIV: Zugló

Heroes' Square is the Hungarian Pantheon, a monumental public space adorned with statues of the nation's most fêted heroes and animated at all times of year by groups of tourists. The grandiose Museum of Fine Arts building lies to one side. Behind it lies City Park, the green lung of Pest, home to the famous Széchenyi Baths and the architectural pastiche known as the Vajdahunyad Castle. The streets nearby preserve some fine examples of early 20th-century architecture.

HEROES' SQUARE

The huge open space known as Heroes' Square (Hősök tere; *map p. 429, F1*), attractively paved with a grey and white geometric pattern, was laid out in 1896 by the architect Albert Schickedanz as a parade ground for the celebrations to mark Hungary's Millennium, the year when the country celebrated a thousand years since Árpád and the Magyar tribes had first occupied the Carpathian Basin. In the centre of the square is a tall Corinthian column surmounted by a statue of the Archangel Gabriel (by György Zala) holding aloft St Stephen's Crown and the Apostolic Cross. Gabriel is said to have appeared to Pope Sylvester II in a dream, telling him to send a crown to the king of Hungary, to legitimise his position as one of the defenders of Christendom. Today that crown is displayed in the Hungarian Parliament (*see p. 141*). Grouped around the column, in mounted file, are the seven Magyar chieftains. At the front rides Árpád (György Zala, 1912), then moving clockwise they are Kond, Ond, Tétény (also known as Töhötöm), Tas, Huba and Előd (all by Zala, 1928). A frieze of oak leaves runs below them. The ensemble was restored in 1996 for the 'millecentenary', 1,100 years since the Magyars arrived in their new homeland. Behind the column is a two-part hemicycle adorned with statues, as follows:

HEROES' SQUARE
The statues between the columns
are Charles I and Louis the Great.
Above is the Chariot of War.

Left-hand section: On the attic level are allegorical figures (György Zala, 1906) representing Work (with a scythe) and Abundance (sowing seed and holding a basket of fruit) and helmeted War in his biga (two-horse chariot). Below, between the columns, are statues of seven Hungarian kings with accompanying reliefs of famous events in their reigns:

1: **St Stephen** (Károly Senyei, 1911), receiving his crown from Pope Sylvester II (György Zala, 1912);

2: **St Ladislas** (Ede Telcs, 1911), defeating the Cuman (Zala, 1909);

3: **King Kálmán** (Richárd Füredi, 1906), banning the burning of witches (1955);

4: **Andrew II** (Senyei, 1912), leading a Crusade to the Holy Land (Zala, 1912);

5: **Béla IV** (Miklós Köllő, 1905), vowing to rebuild the nation after the Mongol raids (Zala, 1912);

6: **Charles I** (György Kiss, 1905), defeating Ottokar on the Marchfeld (Zala, 1912);

7: **Louis the Great** (Zala, 1927), entering Naples in 1348 (Zala, 1913).

Right-hand section: At the top another, more sedate biga is occupied by a female figure bearing a palm frond, an allegory of Concord (Zala, 1908). The statues at the other end represent Knowledge (with a laurel branch) and Glory (the nude male holding a gilded Nike, surely inspired by Canova's statue of Napoleon with the same attributes, now in London). Beneath are seven more statues. Originally all of monarchs, the five last (statues of Habsburgs) were substituted with Hungarian heroes during the Republic of Councils (after WWI). Reinstated under the regentship of Miklós Horthy, they were once again removed after WWII. This explains the later dates of some works:

1: **János Hunyadi** (Ede Margó, 1906), defeating the Turks at Belgrade (Zala, 1912);

2: **Matthias Corvinus** (Zala, 1905), surrounded by savants (Zala, 1909);

3: **István Bocskai** (Barnabás Holló, 1903), fighting imperial mercenaries (László Marton, 1955);

4: **Gábor Bethlen** (György Vastagh, 1902), making a pact with the Czechs

(István Szabó, 1955);

5: **Imre Thököly** (Jenő Grantner, 1954), defeating Habsburg-allied troops (Grantner, 1946);

6: **Ferenc Rákóczi**, being welcomed home by a peasant army (both by Zsigmond Kisfaludi Strobl, 1955);

7: **Lajos Kossuth**, calling the people of the Great Plain to arms (both by Kisfaludi Strobl, 1955).

In front of the Árpád statue, behind low railings, is a **cenotaph** commemorating all Hungarian heroes who have laid down their lives. Tourists take turns to photograph themselves posing on it. Behind it (between it and the Árpád), a metal plaque on the ground marks the spot where in 1878 the mining engineer Vilmos Zsigmondy dug a 971m borehole, piercing a spring of thermal water (74°C) and thus paving the way for the creation of the Széchenyi Baths.

Heroes' Square is flanked by Neoclassical buildings: the Museum of Fine Arts (*see below*) and the **Műcsarnok** (Palace of Art; *open Tues–Sun 10–6*), a Neoclassical exhibition hall designed by Albert Schickedanz and Fülöp Herzog in 1896 as part of the new layout of Heroes' Square for the Hungarian Millennium. The tympanum is filled with a mosaic commissioned in 1938 from Jenő Haranghy to celebrate another millennium, that of the death of St Stephen, founder of the Hungarian state.

THE MUSEUM OF FINE ARTS

Map p. 429, F1. The museum was closed for major renovation work at the time of writing. For updates, see szepmuveszeti.hu.

The Museum of Fine Arts (Szépművészeti Múzeum) is one of the leading galleries of European art in the world, home to an astonishingly rich collection of painting, sculpture and antiquities. The building was designed by Albert Schickedanz and Fülöp Herzog and completed in 1906. Its style is an eclectic compendium of Revivalist architecture, with elements of neo-Romanesque, Neoclassical, neo-Renaissance and neo-Baroque. The collection comprises antiquities from ancient Egypt, Greece and Rome; paintings from the 13th–20th centuries; and prints and drawings.

EGYPTIAN COLLECTION

This interesting and representative collection was formed partly through Hungarian archaeological expeditions to Egypt and partly from acquisitions and donations. It opened at the Museum of Fine Arts in 1939, with the transfer of the National Museum's holdings of Egyptian antiquities. Highlights include a relief fragment from the tomb of the priest Haunefer (3rd millennium BC); the serene limestone head of a man with a tightly curled wig very painstakingly worked (13th century BC); and a statuette of Imhotep, decorated with gold, electrum and silver overlay (7th/6th century BC), which once belonged to the collector and museum director György Ráth (*see p. 266*). There is also the painted mummy case of a priestess of Amun (c. 1000 BC) and a 3rd-century BC Ptolemaic gold necklace tightly strung with gold plaques of the hippopotamus-headed goddess Taweret, protectress of women in childbirth.

CLASSICAL ANTIQUITIES (GREEK, CYPRIOT, ETRUSCAN, ROMAN AND COPTIC)

There are many treasures among the holdings here. Those that particularly stand out are the Grimani Jug, a 5th-century BC Corinthian bronze oinochoë with a marvellous Silenus figure occupying half the spout; a 4th-century BC red-figure vase decorated with Dionysiac scenes by the Brooklyn-Budapest painter, who was at work in Lucania in Magna Graecia (southern Italy); the 3rd-century BC *Budapest Dancer*, a graceful Hellenistic statue of a girl with superbly rendered drapery (the head is a reintegration); a large Cycladic idol of the Spedos type, dating from the 3rd millennium BC; and a small terracotta model of an intimate embrace between a couple lying on a bed, beneath a striped blanket (Mycenaean, 14th–13th centuries BC).

OLD MASTERS COLLECTION

The Old Masters section is particularly rich, formed around the core collection of Count Miklós Esterházy (1765–1833), which was acquired by the nation in 1871. It ranges over most of Europe but is particularly well-endowed with works of the Italian school.

Italian School highlights

The great diversity of the collection makes choosing highlights difficult. Some paintings not to miss include an exquisite panel by Sassetta, from the dismembered Arte della Lana altarpiece made for the Sienese guild of wool merchants in 1423. Showing St Thomas Aquinas at prayer, it is one of seven predella panels now dispersed around the world (two are in Siena, one in the Vatican and one in Melbourne). The lovely *St Stephen* by Ghirlandaio was once part of a polyptych (1494). There are three beautiful Madonnas: by Giovanni Antonio Boltraffio (a member of Leonardo's studio in Milan); Correggio (1534), where the breastfeeding Christ is shown interrupted by a cherub offering fruit; and Raphael (the famous, unfinished *Esterházy Madonna* of 1508). Lorenzo Lotto's *Sleeping Apollo and the Muses* (1545–50) is a delightful painting showing the god fast asleep in a woodland grove. The Muses, taking full advantage of the situation, have cast all seriousness aside—along with their clothing, which lies strewn at Apollo's feet—and are cavorting merrily in a nearby stream. Bronzino's *Venus, Cupid and Jealousy* (c. 1545) is a variant of the similar allegorical work in the National Gallery, London. The *Portrait of a Man* by Sebastiano del Piombo (c. 1512–14) is only partly successful (there is something wrong with the sitter's neck), though the background is particularly fine. However, it is famous for the tragic consequences of its arrival in Hungary. It was bought in 1895 by Károly Pulszky, curator of the Esterházy collection, but a scandal broke out when it was alleged to be a forged Raphael. Pulszky never recovered from the damage done to his reputation. He emigrated to Australia, where he committed suicide in 1899. There are paintings of the Bolognese school (Annibale Carracci) and Venetian works by Veronese, Tintoretto, Titian (portrait of Doge Marcantonio Trevisan, 1553–4), Sebastiano Ricci and Tiepolo (his large-scale *St James the Greater*, 1750, shown mounted on a quite extraordinary horse: white with a luxuriant black curling mane and My-Little-Pony eyes).

Netherlandish, Flemish and Dutch Schools highlights

There is a lovely *Nativity* by Gerard David (c. 1485) and a triptych of the *Way to Calvary, Crucifixion and Resurrection* by Hans Memling and his workshop (c. 1480–5), which has a charming grisaille *Angel Gabriel* and *Virgin Annunciate* on the reverse of the side panels: when closed they form an Annunciation scene. Joos van Cleve's *Madonna and Child* (1515–20) shows Christ symbolically drinking red wine. The splendid *Sermon of John the Baptist* by Peter Brueghel the Elder (1566) is placed in a contemporary setting. People are perching in trees to hear the oration and figures in the crowd below include a turbanned Muslim, two friars and a gypsy palm-reader. Later works include some fine still lifes and symbolic genre scenes (*In the Barber's Shop* by Teniers the Younger, 1636) and a number of works by Van Dyck, including an excellent portrait of an elderly married couple (c. 1620), dressed in black with splendid white ruffs. There is a typical skating scene by Hendrik Avercamp (early 17th century), landscapes by Jacob van Ruisdael, the tranquil *Cattle in a River* by Cuyp (c. 1650) and still lifes with the stock symbolism of transience and corruptibility.

Spanish School highlights
The collection is known first and foremost for its exceptional number of works by **El Greco** (*Penitent Magdalene, Agony in the Garden, Annunciation*). There are also representative works by Velázquez, Jusepe de Ribera, Francisco de Zurbarán (a tender *Holy Family* of 1659), Murillo and Goya.

SCULPTURE COLLECTION

The collection illustrates the development of European sculpture from the Middle Ages to the 19th century. Perhaps the most famous item is the **small bronze of a horse and rider** attributed to **Leonardo da Vinci**, which was acquired in Rome by the Neoclassical sculptor István Ferenczy, when he went there to study under Thorvaldsen. There is also a *Man of Sorrows* by **Verrocchio** (c. 1470) and a lovely terracotta group of *Christ and St Thomas* by **Luca della Robbia** (1463–5), showing Thomas touching the wound in the Risen Christ's side. Traces of the original paint remain. The head of St Thomas is particularly beautiful (the head of Christ is unfortunately missing). There are some fine examples of Austrian Baroque-era sculpture by Georg Raphael Donner and Franz Xaver Messerschmidt.

ART AFTER 1800

The Museum has three landscapes by Monet, a portrait by Renoir, and two Gauguins. One of them is a lovely early work, *Snowy Garden* (1879), full of silence and serenity and very unlike the more famous Tahitian scenes, represented here by *Black Pigs* (1891). By the Viennese artist Hans Makart is *Nessus Abducting Deianeira* (1873–4), which makes copious use of the blue tints of which the artist was so proud. By the Munich Secessionist artist Franz von Stuck is the highly representative *Kiss of the Sphinx* (1895). There are works by Cézanne, Chagall, Kokoschka, Maurice Denis (founder of the Nabis) and many others. Sculpture includes Anthony Caro's *Catalan Song* (1987–8) and Rodin's magnificent *Eternal Spring* (1901), designed for his Gates of Hell but not used in the final composition. It shows Paola and Francesca in a swooning embrace.

PRINTS AND DRAWINGS

The wide-ranging collection of prints and drawings encompasses European graphic art from its early beginnings to the present. Many well-known names are represented, including Albrecht Dürer, Leonardo da Vinci, Raphael, Rembrandt, Van Gogh and Cézanne. Items from the collection are usually displayed on a rotating basis or as part of temporary exhibitions.

VÁROSLIGET: CITY PARK

Behind Heroes' Square a road bridge leads over the boating lake (an ice rink in winter) to the Városliget or City Park (*map p. 429, F1*). Formerly an area of boggy marsh, it enters the records in 1241, when the Mongol leader Batu Khan staged a false retreat, luring the Hungarian troops here, only to surround them and shoot them down. In the later Middle Ages it was part of the Rákos Field, where the Hungarian Diet met. The land was given to the city of Pest by Leopold I in the 17th century, at which time the marshes and grazing lands gave way to plantations of mulberry trees. The area was landscaped in the late 18th century and its bogs were turned into lakes. Pest citizens took refuge here from the great flood of 1838 and again from fighting during 1849. For most of the 19th century the Liget was famed as a pleasure garden. It hosted the National Exhibition of 1885 and the Millennium Exhibition of 1896, for which many of the grand buildings that still stand today were built.

Plans were afoot at the time of writing to turn the Liget into a Museum Quarter, involving the construction of at least three new exhibition spaces and the realignment of many of the current roads and paths. A group calling themselves the 'Liget Defenders' had set up camp in the park, protesting at the felling of trees. The description below was of the status quo at the time of going to press (*for updates, see ligetbudapest.hu*).

In summer the Liget can be very busy with tourists around focal points such as the Vajdahunyad Castle and Széchenyi Baths, but it is peaceful in certain pockets and elderly men still find it congenial around the fringes to meet up and play cards.

THE BOATING LAKE AND ICE RINK

The **ice rink** opens in late November and stays open throughout the winter. During the rest of the year it is a **boating lake**, with a variety of small craft for hire (*for details, see mujegpalya.hu*). The attractive **club house** is by Imre Francsek Sr (1894).

The lake also has an ornamental section with a fountain, overlooked by a café and restaurant with tables on the water. Here and elsewhere in the park you will come upon playfully painted benches, a voluntary initiative of 2013. Just outside the restaurant (Robinson), close to Állatkerti körút, is a small, seemingly pointless, **concrete bridge**. The underground railway (Földalatti; *see p. 193*) built to bring visitors to the Millennium exhibition here in 1896 rose above ground at this point, and a station for the Budapest Zoo stood here. The bridge allowed passengers to cross the tracks.

THE BUDAPEST ZOO

Map p. 426, B2–C2. Állatkerti körút 6–12. Open daily 9–dusk. zoobudapest.com.
The Budapest Zoo (Állatkert) is open all year round and extremely popular with families and young children. Many of the animals hibernate, but there is plenty to see at all seasons. The enclosures are as animal-friendly as the condition of captivity can allow and animals do breed here (an elephant calf was born in 2017). The predecessor of the Zoo, the Municipal Zoological and Botanical Gardens, opened in 1866 on the initiative of the Academy of Sciences and in particular of János Xantus (1825–94), a

BUDAPEST ZOO
Elephant and mahout by Gyula Maugsch (1912).

natural scientist who spent much of his life in the United States. The species living here today represent a great part of the spectrum of life on Earth, from mammals to scyphozoa (jellyfish). The architecture of the Zoo is also of some importance. As you queue for your ticket, notice the mandrils on the columns by the ticket booths. The main entrance (Kornél Neuschloss, 1912) has a dome surrounded by polar bears and an archway adorned with alternating owl and wolf heads and a mosaic of cacti, orange trees, palms and an egret. Flanking it are twin pairs of stone elephants with mahouts between them, sculpted by Gyula Maugsch. The street railings also have repeated stylised wrought-iron outlines of stags, a bear and cubs and etched birds (many of them faded from repeated over-painting). The famous Elephant House, with its Zsolnay pyrogranite decoration, is also the work of Neuschloss. Károly Kós and Dezső Zrumeczky designed the Australia House (formerly the Bird House), the Madagascar House (formerly the Monkey House) and the India House (formerly the Tiger House). The Pannon Park biodome was under construction at the time of going to press.

THE CAROUSEL

Near the back of the Széchenyi Baths (*see below*) are three Moorish kiosks selling coffee, ice cream and souvenirs. Beyond, on the opposite side of the road, is the delightful **Carousel** (Körhinta; *open April–Sept 10–6*), built in 1906, a survivor of the funfair that operated here in various guises from the early 19th century until 2013. Carved and painted wooden horses and chariots with bugle-blowing, torch-bearing outriders, whirl round and around to the music of Vienna waltzes under a ceiling painted with scenes of summertime trysts under Chinese lanterns and wisteria blooms.

East of the Carousel, at the edge of Hungária körút, is a magnificent wooden **rollercoaster** (Hullámvasút), built in 1922.

THE SZÉCHENYI BATHS

Map p. 426, C2. Metro line M1 (yellow) to Széchenyi fürdő. The description below deals with the history of the building, its architecture and decoration. For opening times and practical details, see p. 358.

The vast and beautiful Széchenyi Baths are one of the Liget's most famous and popular attractions. Ten years after plans to create a bathing establishment in Pest were formally agreed in 1868, the engineer Vilmos Zsigmondy dug a borehole which struck an artesian well of thermal water. Building began in 1909, posthumously to the plans of Győző Czigler (he had died in 1905). The resulting grand and eclectic building, the largest bathing complex in Europe, opened in 1913. Its waters are reputed to be good for spinal complaints. The baths were extended in 1927 by Imre Francsek Jr, with the addition of the swimming pool.

In front of the main façade, to the right as you face it, is the **Szent István ívókút** (pump room), housed in a glass pavilion (*open daily except Sun*), where you can drink the curative water. Overlooking it on the other side of the road is Antal Szécsi's 1895 **bust of Vilmos Zsigmondy**, the engineer who drilled the borehole.

SZÉCHENYI BATHS
Centaur capturing a triton. Detail of the fountain by József Róna.

THE BUILDING

Czigler's main entrance, facing the park, takes you into the **Dome Hall**, with leather upholstered benches, metalwork by Gyula Jungfer, a mosaic ceiling by Miksa Róth and Zsigmond Vajda showing Helios driving the chariot of the Sun, putti by Géza Maróti, and József Róna's Centaur Fountain, behind which is a Tree of Life mosaic of acanthus fronds recalling that in the Lateran Baptistery in Rome. The entire **Czigler wing** and its thermal pools are decorated with Zsolnay ceramic tiles with a variety of marine themes.

The rear wing of the building, facing the zoo, is part of Imre Francsek's 1927 extension, housing the **outdoor bathing facility**. It is in one of the hot pools here that clusters of elderly men famously like to play chess in the water. A statue group of *Leda and the Swan* (Dezső Lányi, 1916) stands over this pool, with water gushing from beneath it in twin jets. The entire complex is covered with statuary by various artists, including Géza Maróti, Ede Telcs, János Pásztor and Ferenc Sidló.

VAJDAHUNYAD CASTLE

The so-called Vajdahunyad Castle (Vajdahunyad vár; *map p. 426, C2*) was built to the designs of Ignác Alpár as a temporary structure for the 1896 Hungarian Millennium Exhibition. The idea was to present in one single building the variety of architectural styles to be found in Hungary and her Crown Lands. The building proved so popular that Alpár was commissioned to reconstruct it in permanent form. It was completed in 1907. The area on which it stands is surrounded by water, giving the impression of a moat. The right-hand section is based on the 15th-century Vajdahunyad Castle in Transylvania (today Hunedoara, Romania), from which the whole complex takes its name. Beside the road that leads to the castle from Kós Károly sétány is a statue of Alpár in the guise of a medieval master builder (Ede Telcs, 1931).

The **left-hand gate tower** pays tribute to the architecture of Upper Hungary (present-day Slovakia). Through the gate, on the left of the courtyard, is the Romanesque wing, with the **Ják Chapel**, a smaller, squatter version of a 13th-century Benedictine abbey church (still standing) in western Hungary. The doorway has elaborate zigzag moulding and statues of Christ and the Apostles in niches above it.

Opposite is the Gothic wing, with the **Vajdahunyad section** (Alpár is commemorated with a medallion on the part that now houses the souvenir shop), augmented by a copy of the famous **clock tower of Segesvár** (Sighișoara, Romania). Between the Romanesque and Vajdahunyad wings, on a stone bench, is a **statue of Ignác Darányi**, a former Minister of Agriculture who was instrumental in re-building Hungary's wine industry after the phylloxera outbreak in the 1870s. The Latin inscription reads: *Si monumentum quaeris, circumspice* ('If you require a monument, look around you')— and indeed, the Agricultural Museum is close by. The work is signed 'Kisfaludi Strobl', but it is in fact a modern re-casting of the original, which was melted down for its metal when the giant statue of Stalin (*see p. 317*) was made.

The Agricultural Museum occupies the **Baroque wing** of the castle complex. Opposite the entrance is a statue (Miklós Ligeti, 1903, on a base by Zoltán Bálint and Lajos Jámbor) of the cowled **Anonymus**, author of the 13th-century *Gesta Hungarorum*, chronicler of 'the most glorious King Béla'. The pen he holds in his right hand is polished to a gleam: people rub it for luck and to cure writer's block. On the back of the statue, at the time of writing, a member of the Anonymous activist group had printed in neat white letters: 'We are Anon, we are legion, we do not forgive, we do not forget'. A homeless person's blanket was folded away on a shelf inside the plinth.

THE AGRICULTURAL MUSEUM

The Agricultural Museum (Mezőgazdasági Múzeum; *map p. 426, C2; open summer Tues–Fri 10–5, Sat–Sun 10–6, one hour shorter in winter; mezogazdasagimuzeum.hu*) has a permanent collection arranged on three floors. The main display on the ground floor traces the **development of Hungarian agriculture** from prehistoric times to the early 20th-century land reforms. Exhibits include a reconstructed yurt, the first steam threshing machine to be used in Hungary (built in Lincoln, England, in 1852), a stuffed *mangalica* pig (*for more on the famous breed, see p. 348*) and a small

VAJDAHUNYAD CASTLE
Ignác Alpár's reproduction of the Romanesque church of Ják.

but interesting display on wheat breeding (as a result of improvements to the native, weak-stemmed stock, Hungarian wheat was voted best in the world at the 1933 World Wheat Exhibition in Canada).

Other exhibitions on the ground floor cover **plants**, **forestry** and the **domestication of animals** and, in the basement, **viticulture and wine-making**. On the upper floor are displays on **fishing and hunting** (enormous numbers of antlers)

Also on the upper floor, accessed up the grand main stairway, is the **National Horse Exhibition**, which explores man's long relationship with the animal that, from its domestication sometime in the 7th–5th millennium BC until well into the last century, was indispensable for agriculture, warfare, transport, leisure and sport. A special display looks at racehorses, notably Kincsem, the miracle chestnut mare (1874–87) who won all 54 of the 54 races she ran (England's Goodwood Cup was one of them). Budapest's Kincsem Park racecourse is named after her. Her skeleton is preserved entire in a glass case: on her lower left hind leg you can see the bony growths which forced her to retire from racing. The 2017 film *Kincsem* is based on the story of the wonder mare and her owner, the stud farmer Ernő Blaskovich.

OLOF PALME SÉTÁNY AND DÓZSA GYÖRGY ÚT

Olof Palme sétány, named after the Swedish Prime Minister assassinated in 1986, leads past the neo-Renaissance **Olof Palme Ház**, formerly a Műcsarnok (Palace of Art) built by Ferenc Pfaff for the National Exhibition of 1885. The fine building, of brick with colourful pyrogranite decoration, rapidly became too small and was superseded by the new Műcsarnok on Heroes' Square. Among the decorative elements are busts of Titian and Raphael. At the time of writing there were plans to restore it.

West of the Olof Palme Ház, in the angle formed by the junction of Olof Palme sétány with Zichy Mihály út, is a statue (Miklós Ligeti, 1908) of a huntsman with a pair of field glasses, dressed in a Norfolk jacket: the ill-fated Crown Prince Rudolf, only son of Franz Joseph, who shot himself in a suicide pact with his mistress in 1889. Opposite, on the other side of Olof Palme sétány, is a smooth lump of granite commemorating another assassinated Swedish politician, the Foreign Minister Anna Lindh, who was stabbed to death by an attacker in 2003.

A short way to the northeast of the Olof Palme Ház, surrounded by an iron railing, is the **Fuit stone**. It is the grave of a man who requested in his will that no name, date or detail of any kind should appear on his headstone, only the Latin word *Fuit*: 'He was'. The ruse has ensured that his identity has been fully researched and preserved for posterity. The anonymous man is Jakab Horváth, a lawyer who undertook the defence of the Hungarian Jacobins (*see p. 56*). He died in 1809.

DÓZSA GYÖRGY ÚT

This wide avenue, which today is named after the peasant rebel leader György Dózsa (*see p. 59*), forms the western border of the Liget. It has a number of memorials along its length. A mound topped with a painted Crucifix, opposite the Damjanich utca junction, marks the site of the Regnum Marianum church, hit by a bomb in 1944 and demolished in 1951 when Felvonulási tér, a wide space for Stalinist public parades, was laid out. A short way further north, opposite the Városligeti fasor junction, is the **1956 monument** (an ensemble of rusty palings), on a site once occupied by the statue of Stalin that was famously torn down in 1956.

THE TOPPLING OF THE STALIN STATUE

A colossal statue of Stalin, 25m high and standing on a huge ceremonial tribune, was erected on this spot in 1951. The bronze from which it was made was obtained by melting down earlier monuments commemorating men who had come to be considered unsuitable role models or class enemies (the former Prime Minister Count Gyula Andrássy, for example). On the evening of 23rd October 1956, the first day of the Hungarian Uprising, massed crowds set about the  task of pulling the Stalin statue down. This was the most symbolic event of the entire revolution—doubly so as the statue refused to disappear completely. Despite the use of multiple tools and some heavy machinery, the crowds only managed to topple the top three-quarters, leaving Stalin's massive pair of boots in place (now replicated in the Memento Park; *see p. 125*). The rest of the statue was hacked into small pieces. Two of them, a hand and an ear (*illustrated*), are now preserved in the National Museum. Other parts were re-melted down to form part of the re-cast monument to Andrássy that once again stands outside the Parliament building.

The third memorial, opposite the MÉMOSZ building (*see p. 206*) and standing on the site of Pál Pátzay's statue of Lenin (*see p. 126*), is the **Time Wheel** (Időkerék), the world's largest hourglass, erected to mark Hungary's entry into the EU in 2004. Sadly, time has got the better of it: when this book went to press it was no longer working and one of its panes of glass was cracked. There were plans to erect a large new building here to house the **Museum of Ethnography**, displaced from Kossuth Lajos tér in 2017. It was projected to open in 2020.

REMARKABLE BUILDINGS NEAR THE VÁROSLIGET

The street at the far south edge of the Liget, running into Dózsa György út, is Ocskay László út. His name is linked to the **ELTE Radnóti Miklós Gyakorlóiskola**, a school just a few steps away on Cházár András utca (no. 10, on the corner of Abonyi utca; *map p. 426, C3*). The school originally belonged to Pest's Jewish community, with a synagogue attached. During the war it was occupied by a detachment of Jewish forced labourers, employed in making clothes for the German army. Attached to the exterior wall are two plaques commemorating the bravery of László Ocskay, the captain who was placed in charge of the camp and who managed to prevent the thousands of Jewish workers from being murdered. The building itself (1923–31; badly in need of restoration) is a fine Art Deco work designed by Béla Lajta, though it was completed after his death by Ármin Hegedűs. It reuses elements seen in Lajta's Vas utca school building (*see p. 239*). The doorcases of the three tall, narrow-arched entranceways are decorated with carvings of owls, trains, motor cars, zeppelins, sailing ships, windmills and factory buildings, arranged in a different order each time so that each element is at eye level at least once. At the summit is the Star of David. The red-brick, vertically soaring façade has a pattern of two menorahs picked out in protruding bricks between the narrow arches. The ironwork of the doors themselves is fashioned to depict the symbols of the Twelve Tribes of Israel. Surviving stained-glass windows from the building are now preserved in the Jewish Museum next to the Great Synagogue.

The Dominican church of **Our Lady of the Rosary** (on the corner of Cházár András utca and Thököly út (Antal Hofhauser, 1915; *only open for services*), has fine stained glass by the workshop of Miksa Róth and frescoes by Béla Kontuly in the transepts.

THE SIPEKI BALÁS VILLA

At the east end of the Városliget, you might see a greater than usual number of people walking with the aid of white sticks: there is a sensory garden for the blind here (Vakok kertje), surrounded by a circular railing. Close by, the former Sipeki Balás Villa, a highly original building of 1905–7 by Ödön Lechner, is now occupied by the Hungarian Federation for the Blind and Partially Sighted (*Hermina út 47; map p. 426, C2; open weekdays 8–6, other times by appointment; international@mvgyosz.hu*). Béla Sipeki Balás was a legal adviser at the Ministry of Justice and secretary of the Association for the Blind. He left the house to the association in his will and it has been used by them ever since. This is a rare chance to examine a Lechner building at close quarters.

LECHNER AND HIS BUILDINGS

Ödön Lechner (1845–1914), often called the Gaudí of Budapest, was a patriotic genius who set out to devise a uniquely Hungarian architectural style. He believed that the origins of Hungarian culture were in the East, not the West, and that Hungarian models of beauty were informed by the Orient. Though his work is often bracketed with Art Nouveau, and though he loved colour, texture and exuberant ornament, his aesthetic has little in common with the world of whiplash fronds of foliage and lissom female forms. Lechner was a true original. His surfaces are often articulated in what he called the 'Persian carpet style', with exposed brickwork or applied ceramic elements used to create symmetrical stylised patterns. He makes copious use of folk motifs—hearts, pomegranates and tulips—all from somewhere deep in Hungary's lost Oriental subconscious. His work met with a mixed reception from contemporaries. Enthusiastically received by certain sections of the public, it was reviled by traditionalists. His best-known buildings in Budapest are the former Post Office Savings Bank (now the State Treasury; *see p. 152*), the Museum of Applied Arts (*see p. 266*) and the church of St Ladislas in Kőbánya (*see p. 275*).

The villa's asymmetrical exterior is rendered in pink and cream, resembling a delectable strawberry blancmange. Though somewhat shabby at the time of writing

SIPEKI BALÁS VILLA
Detail of the wall fountain in the conservatory.

(the dove that surmounts the roof turret had only a single wing), many details survive, such as the wrought-iron holders for planters and window boxes and the moulded concrete bench in shades of pink and grey. Even the guttering is specially fashioned: moulded concrete with drainage spouts at ground-floor level and lead adorned with tulips and roses above. The hood over the front door is reminiscent of the Paris Metro stations of Hector Guimard. The front door handle is original.

On the ground floor you can visit the front hall, lit by tall wide windows and with a marble fireplace adorned with deep blue Zsolnay tiles. Off it opens the conservatory, which still preserves its double iron-framed window and lead wall fountain (somewhat crumpled but mainly still intact). The other ground-floor room is a long salon divisible by sliding doors (still with the original handles).

A wide flight of marble stairs leads up to a columned gallery, its balustrade supported by stout colonnettes with a beautiful streaked blue, pink and violet eosin glaze and with neo-Romanesque capitals, again the work of Zsolnay. The walls are covered to dado level with moulded plaster painted in mossy green and gold to imitate eosin-glazed ceramic. There are niches for statues. The ceilings and door- and window-surrounds are articulated with characteristic Lechner stucco details. On the stair wall, opposite the little minstrels' gallery, is a stucco frame enclosing a painting of a May Day scene. Sipeki Balás and his wife threw their house open for the season every year on the 1st of May, hosting frequent musical events.

The **Roheim Villa** next door (no. 45) is where the former Prime Minister István Tisza was murdered during the Aster Revolution of 1918.

AJTOSI DÜRER SOR
The Festival of Venus on Olympus (detail), designed by
György Zala for his own villa (1899).

AJTOSI DÜRER SOR, STEFÁNIA ÚT AND HERMINA ÚT

On the corner of Ajtosi Dürer sor and Stefánia út (**Ajtosi Dürer sor 25**) is the villa built for the sculptor György Zala (1901, Lajos Jámbor, Zoltán Bálint and Ödön Lechner), with a crowd of moulded figures by Zala above the main first-floor window. On the corner of Zichy Géza utca and Abonyi utca (**Zichy Géza u. 10**) is a twin-turreted fairytale palace of a villa (1899) built by the great portrait painter Philip de László, on the basis of sketches that he had produced (so it is said) to impress the parents of his intended bride, Lucy Guinness. Diagonally opposite it is the back carriage entrance to the **Stefánia Palota** (Meinig Artúr, 1895), which has its main façade at Stefánia út 34–36. It is now the Hungarian Army Cultural Centre (the Regiment Restaurant occupies part of the modern wing). The old palace building was originally the Park Club, a favourite resort of the blue-blooded and the well-to-do until the end of the Second World War. Around the corner at **Izsó u. 5** is Béla Lajta's Malonyay Villa (1906; now the Romanian Cultural Institute), in which he breaks away from Lechnerism and turns instead to the English Arts and Crafts movement for inspiration.

Stefánia út crosses the busy Thököly út, where at **no. 61**, standing in a balcony at the side (hidden by trees in summer) is a mysterious sculpture of a woman by Miklós Ligeti (1903). Beyond Thököly út, at Stefánia út 14, is Ödön Lechner's **Geological Institute** (Földtani Intézet, 1899; *map p. 426, D3*). Mighty Atlas figures, moustachioed and with the braided hair of ancestral Magyars, hold aloft a globe on its roof. Opposite it, at **no. 65/c** (*access down a tarmac path*), is an early work by Lajos Kozma: dark puce with cream-coloured moulded peacocks.

On the corner of Ajtosi Dürer sor and Hermina út (*map p. 426, C2*) are two buildings inspired by Lechner's Persian carpet style. The first (no. 37) is the **Blanka Teleki High School** (1901–2). Adjoining it is the **Institute for the Blind** (Vakok Intézete; 1904). Ceramic fronds of Hungarian folk-inspired flowers and foliage adorn the façade. Both are the work of the same architects, Sándor Baumgarten and Zsigmond Herczegh.

At Hermina út 23 is the **Hermina Chapel**, built in honour of the Palatine Joseph's daughter Hermina, a nun, who died at the age of 24 (*see pp. 49–50*). Begun 1842, it was completed in 1856. At the inaugural ceremony, Liszt led the choir in his *Esztergom Mass*.

TWO BUILDINGS BY BÉLA LAJTA

Beyond the railway line, on the corner of Korong utca, is the marvellous **former Jewish Institute for the Blind** (*map p. 426, D2*; now a physiotherapy school for the disabled), built in 1908 with funds provided by the wealthy but childless Ignác Wechselmann, who stipulated that the blind and partially-sighted children cared for by his new institute should be Jews and Christians in equal proportion. Lajta's building is a fusion of Art Nouveau and Art Deco, adorned with the folk motifs that are so common in his work and which were inspired by his research trips to Transylvania. The street railings (at the time of writing sadly corroded) are thronged with stylised birds of many kinds and have inset panels of text in Braille, including the first lines of Vörösmarty's *Szózat* (*see p. 168*) and of Psalm 1. The lampstands on either side of the main steps are profusely decorated; the one on the right, with stylised stags' heads, bears the words: 'May God give sight to the eyes'. The entrance doors, with very

FORMER JEWISH INSTITUTE FOR THE BLIND
Detail of the doorway, designed by Béla Lajta (1908).'Thou shalt not put
a stumbling block before the blind, but shalt fear thy God' (Leviticus 19).

shallow carvings of birds and flowers, have glass panes decorated with menorahs. Here too there is text, from the books of Isaiah, Leviticus and Exodus. On the far right of the door frame are the words: 'The Lord gives sight to the blind'.

Two blocks further on, at Amerikai út 57, is another Béla Lajta building, the **Institute of Neurosurgery**, formerly the Hevra Kadisha Hospice (1911).

THE RAILWAY MUSEUM & AEROPARK

Housed in an old railway depot, the **Railway History Park** (*beyond map p. 426, C1; Vasúttörténeti Park; Tatai u. 95; open April–Oct; vasuttortenetipark.hu*) boasts over a hundred old locomotives, wagons and carriages, as well as a working turntable. The museum's proudest possession is the teak dining car of 1912 that was once attached to the Orient Express. The oldest working steam locomotive dates from 1870. The chrome steel and powder blue 'Silver Arrow' was built in 1968 as the private train of Party Secretary János Kádár, who famously hated flying. It is said that Kádár dismissed plans to import a Mercedes engine for the train, insisting that it be built exclusively of Hungarian-made parts. The air-conditioning system, however, did come from beyond the Iron Curtain. Kádár's sleeping compartment, with its own shower, was no. 8. The museum is extremely popular with children and offers a range of interactive programmes, carriage rides, etc. Some of the carriages can be rented for private parties, organised by MÁV Nosztalgia (*mavnosztalgia.hu*).

The **Aeropark** is a small outdoor museum of old aeroplanes on the approach road to the airport (*open April–May, Sept–Oct daily 9–6, June–Aug Mon–Thur 9–6, Fri–Sun 9–8, Nov–March Sat–Sun 10–4; aeropark.hu; bus 200E from Kőbánya-Kispest on metro line 2. Stay on the bus until it begins its return journey from the airport and get off at the first stop, Repülőmúzeum*). Aircraft on show include old Soviet Ilyushins and Tupolevs.

EATING AND DRINKING IN ZUGLÓ

fff **Gundel**. Famous, historic restaurant in a fine building created for the 1896 Hungarian Millennium celebrations. Károly Gundel took over the business in 1910. Under him it became a household name and many of the dishes he invented have passed into the Hungarian canon: Gundel pancake (*Gundel palacsinta*, stuffed with rum and walnuts and drizzled with chocolate sauce) is a famous example. Today you pay a lot to eat *à la carte* in Gundel, but they offer more moderately priced tasting menus and Sunday brunches. *Gundel Károly út 4. T: +36 1 889 8111, gundel.hu. Map p. 426, B2.*

ff **Bagolyvár**. Family restaurant set up in 1913 to cater to visitors to the Zoo. Today it is still doing just that. Eat inside under the lofty wooden rafters or outside overlooking the Zoo. Classic Hungarian cooking. *Gundel Károly út 4. T: +36 1 889 8127, bagolyvar.com. Map p. 426, B2.*

ff **Robinson**. Restaurant, café and steak house (char-grilled Tuscan beef), on an island terrace in the City Park lake. Hungarian-Mediterranean fusion cuisine. Very pleasant out on the water in warm weather. *City Park Lake. T: +36 1 422 0222, robinsonrestaurant.hu. Map p. 426, C2.*

f **Kertem**. Popular summer beer garden and grill, with live music and a fun atmosphere. The plans to develop City Park have forced it to be itinerant in recent years. At the time of writing it was outside the Olof Palme-ház (but may have to move again). For updates, check the Kertem Facebook page. Open April–Sept.

f **Nyereg**. Kiosk-like place offering drinks and a simple snack menu, overlooking the City Park lake. *Városliget körút 2. T: +36 1 351 5217, nyeregitato.hu. Map p. 426, C2.*

f **Pántlika**. Retro canteen evoking the spirit of the Communist era. Order at the bar; you will be called when it is ready. The menu features *bableves* (bean soup) and *rántott sajt* (fried breaded cheese) and other Hungarian fast food, plus pulled pork sandwiches, burgers and tortillas. It began life as an information booth and is the only surviving pavilion from the Budapest Trade Fair, which used to take place in Városliget until it outgrew the space and moved further out of town. The roof is shaped like a Soviet red star (apparently the Hungarian astronaut Bertalan Farkas has verified this from space). The ceramic-chip floor is typical of the period. Among the furnishings is a standard lamp that once belonged to János Kádár. Checked oil cloths, slatted chairs, paper lanterns overhead in summer. Opens at midday. *Edge of City Park (opposite the Sipeki Balás Villa, Hermina út 47). T: +36 70 376 9910, pantlika.hu. Map p. 426, C2.*

Day Trips from Budapest

This chapter describes three excursions: to the riverside town of Szentendre (north of Budapest); to the small town of Gödöllő, east of the city; and to Zsámbék, with its famous Romanesque priory ruins in the hills to the west. All are served by public transport, either train or bus—and, in the case of Szentendre, by river boat up the Danube.

SZENTENDRE

The picturesque little town of Szentendre, situated beside the Danube c. 20km north of Budapest, is a popular destination for day trips. It can be accessed by suburban railway (HÉV) or by boat. It is particularly pleasant on sunny days in autumn, when the woods behind the town and on the island opposite it are turning to auburn and gold, and you can sit beside the river on the wide *Duna korzó*, the Danube promenade. Szentendre was formerly home to a large Serbian Orthodox population and a number of fine churches survive. The cobbled streets are home to numerous galleries and museums.

Getting to Szentendre

By HÉV: *Trains (line 5) leave from Batthyány tér and Margit Híd (map p. 428, B2 and B1). Journey time approx. 40mins. You will need a standard transport ticket, valid until the Békásmegyer stop (the Budapest city boundary), and a suburban railway extension ticket from Békásmegyer to Szentendre, available from machines at the stations or on the train.*

By boat: *Boats leave from the Batthyány tér landing stage (map p. 428, B2). Journey time to Szentendre is 2hrs and back again is 1hr. You can combine the two transport methods: travel up by train and return by boat (for timetables, see mahartpassnave.hu).*

HISTORY OF SZENTENDRE

There has been occupation on the site of Szentendre since prehistoric times, as attested by finds from the Bronze Age and Iron Age. In the 1st century AD the Romans built

SZENTENDRE
Icon of St John the Baptist (18th century)
in the Belgrade Church museum

SZENTENDRE

a riverside fort here, defending their border, and the settlement was known first as Ulcisia and then, from the 4th century, as Castra Constantia. Unlike Aquincum (*see pp. 97 and 108*), it never grew into an established town, though the hills were dotted with veterans' villas and in fact the largest villa complex so far found in the former province of Pannonia was here. After the Romans, the site seems to have been occupied by the Lombards and in the 9th century the Magyars used the remains of the Roman fort. Today's town grew up around a monastery, established in the early 13th century and dedicated to St Andrew (patron saint of fishermen and also the name of the monarch at the time, Andrew I). The town's name, Szent (St) Endre (Andrew), derives from this.

Migrations of Serbs began in the late 14th century, as they fled west from the advancing Ottomans, and other Balkan migrants followed them. The town became depopulated following the Ottoman invasion of Hungary and it was only after the reconquest that the Serbs returned, in the Great Migration of 1690, settling here in large numbers under their patriarch, Arsenije III, who was invited here by Leopold I, when he granted the Serbs religious freedom. They immediately set about building churches for their several communities, at first of wood and later, from the 18th century, of stone, in the Baroque style with elaborate Rococo interiors. Most of these have now been adapted for use by Catholic or Protestant congregations but the Serbian Orthodox cathedral, or 'Belgrade Church', survives.

In the 19th century the Serb population was joined by Germans, Slovaks and Hungarians. The surrounding hillsides were planted with vines and, until the phylloxera outbreak of the 1870s, winemaking was a mainstay of the economy. In the early 20th century Szentendre gained fame as an artists' colony. You will see plaques on houses all over town commemorating the artists who lived and worked here. One of the great names of the Nagybánya school (*see p. 369*), Károly Ferenczy, also lived in Szentendre. His son Béni (sculptor) and daughter Noémi (tapestry designer) were born here.

EXPLORING SZENTENDRE

THE ROMAN LAPIDARY GARDEN

The lapidary garden (Római kőtár; *open weekdays 9–4*) is a short walk from the HÉV train station, along the busy main road (the 11). Behind a chicken-wire fence is a small collection of tombstones, sarcophagi and sarcophagus fragments, relics of the Roman fortress of Ulcisia. One particularly fine fragment shows a guardian of the Underworld leaning on what looks like a hockey stick, in fact a representation of an inverted torch, symbolising the flame of life extinguished.

A stepped path beside the Római kőtár bus stop leads behind the lapidary garden and into town (turn right at the T-junction keeping the two church towers on either side of you). Paprikabíró utca soon becomes cobbled and leads down to the main Kossuth Lajos utca and the canalised Bükkös stream. To your left is the main square (*described below*). To the right, at Kossuth Lajos u. 5, is the Ferenczy Museum.

SZENTENDRE'S ART MUSEUMS

The Szentendre school of painting, which aimed to continue the traditions of the Nagybánya artists' colony, came into being in the 1920s, when Nagybánya (in Transylvania) was severed from Hungary and awarded to Romania by the Treaty of Trianon. The Szentendre artists included Imre Ámos, Jenő Barcsay, János Kmetty and Béla Czóbel, all of whom have museums named after them in Szentendre today. They are run as a single institution by the Ferenczy Múzeumi Centrum (*muzeumicentrum. hu*). Not all were open at the time of writing and not all of them had permanent collections on view. For up-to-date information and opening times, consult the website. At the time of writing the museums that could be visited were as follows:

Ferenczy Museum (*Kossuth Lajos u. 5*): In the courtyard is a copy of Béni Ferenczy's tombstone of Egon Schiele. The museum hosts temporary shows and a permanent collection of material related to the Ferenczy family.

Szentendrei Képtár (Szentendre Gallery; *Fő tér 2–5*): Housed in the Merchants' House on the town's main square. It hosts temporary shows.

Czóbel Museum (*Templom tér 1*): Housed in the former boys' school on the hill above the main square. It has a permanent collection of works by the artist Béla Czóbel.

Vajda Museum (*Hunyadi u. 1*): The artist Lajos Vajda lived in Szentendre and the museum that bears his name hosts temporary exhibitions.

Margit Kovács Museum (*Vastagh György u. 1*): Home to a permanent collection of works by the ceramicist Margit Kovács.

Művészet Malom (*Bogdányi u. 32*): The 'Art Mill', housed in a former sawmill, is a gallery of contemporary art.

MANK Gallery (*Bogdányi u. 51*): The Magyar Alkotóművészeti Közhasznú company, abbreviated (somewhat unfortunately in English) to MANK, is an artists' co-operative with studios and a temporary exhibition space on the site of a former TB sanatorium, where the Szentendre artists' colony set up studios in 1929.

LOCAL HISTORY MUSEUM

Housed in a cellar diagonally opposite the Margit Kovács Museum is the Helytörténeti Gyűjtemény or Local History Museum (*NB: Often kept locked; ask at the Kovács Museum or in the Képtár on the main square if they can open it for you.*) The display is excellent, covering Szentendre's history from prehistoric times to the 20th century. Highlights are a Roman gold *solidus* with the head of Valentinian II; a fragment of wall-painting from the large 3rd–4th-century *villa rustica* on the site of the Skanzen open-air museum; and a chest thought to have belonged to Mátyás 'Rab' Ráby. The 'Prisoner' Ráby gives his name to a restaurant and a town square in Szentendre. A former Habsburg imperial informant-turned-Magyar sympathiser, he was arrested here in 1784, then released five years later thanks to the clemency of Joseph II. When Joseph died the following year, Ráby found himself forced to flee. He settled in Strasbourg.

DUMTSA JENŐ UTCA AND FŐ TÉR

The main street of Szentendre is the pedestrianised Dumtsa Jenő utca, named after the town's first mayor. It is lined with boutiques and bars and at no. 14 is the **Szamos Cukrászda** (patissier), famous for its marzipan figurines. There is a small museum attached.

THE SZAMOS STORY

Cafés and cake shops bearing the Szamos name are frequently to be found in Budapest. There is one on Kossuth Lajos tér, right in the centre of the city opposite Parliament. Szamos is famous across Hungary for its colourful marzipan figurines, as well as for its chocolates and other sweet pastries. The story began in Szentendre, with a young pastrycook's apprentice by the name of Mladen Savić (b. 1918), who went to learn his trade under József Auguszt in Krisztinaváros (*see p. 93*). It was here that he mastered the art of making figures (mainly roses) out of marzipan. As a master pâtissier he worked for Gerbeaud (*see p. 167*) and, after nationalisation, for state confectioners. He quickly became famous for his marzipan confections. In the 1970s he set up a small factory in Pilisvörösvár, in the hills not far from Szentendre, and in 1987 opened the first Szamos shop (Mladen Savić had by this time Hungarianised his name to Mátyás Szamos). Szamos is now an international business, with a website where you can buy the sweetmeats online. Mátyás Szamos died in 2002 and is buried in Szentendre, in the Serbian Orthodox cemetery.

Dumtsa Jenő utca leads into Fő tér, the main square of town, with the old Serbian **Merchants' Cross** in the centre and the Merchants' House (now the Szentendre Gallery) occupying most of one side. Here too is the famous **Blagoveshtenska Church** (Church of the Annunciation), founded by Greek merchants. The current Baroque building, which replaces a wooden predecessor, was consecrated in 1754

SZENTENDRE LOCAL HISTORY MUSEUM
Fragment of Roman wall-painting from a 3rd–4th-century *villa rustica*.

and it has been suggested that the architect was András Mayerhoffer, who designed the Serb church in Pest. No longer used for worship, it can be visited and is known for its elaborate Rococo iconostasis. The building next door to it is the former Serbian Orthodox school.

From Fő tér, narrow stepped streets lead up to Templom tér, the **citadel**, site of the Roman fort and medieval monastery, now occupied by the Roman Catholic church of St John the Baptist. This is the oldest church in Szentendre (*not open except for services*).

THE SERBIAN ORTHODOX CHURCH AND THE SZÁNTÓ HOUSE

On Alkotmány utca is the crimson-and-cream Serbian Orthodox Church, known as the Belgrade Church, with attached museum (*open Tues–Sun 10–4*). The **museum collection**, on two floors, includes ecclesiastical vestments and church furnishings and plate (including two fine wedding crowns) from Szentendre and other Serb centres in Hungary. There is a display of the reconstructed iconostasis from the destroyed Serb church in Buda and a collection of 18th-century icons, including a winged *St John the Baptist* from Esztergom. The **Belgrade Church** has fine carved exterior doors and Tardos marble memorial tablets featuring a skull and crossbones below a shallow shrine niche. The Rococo iconostasis has the *Annunciation* on the central doors into the sanctuary and a representation of the Trinity above them.

An unnamed street leading north from Alkotmány utca has a plaque on the corner commemorating the painter Károly Ferenczy, who lived here. The house was the birthplace of the twins Noémi (tapestry designer) and Béni Ferenczy (sculptor). A little further up the street, on the left, is the **Szántó Jewish Memorial House** (*open April-Oct Tues–Sun 11–5*), a tiny museum and synagogue in the courtyard of the former house of the Szántó family, created by György Szántó in memory of his parents, who perished in the Holocaust, and completed by György's son in 1998. It was the first new synagogue to be consecrated in Hungary after WWII. It contains a small collection of secular and religious objects, including photographs of the vanished Jewish community of Szentendre and a particularly pretty 19th-century silver etrog holder.

THE OPEN-AIR MUSEUM (SKANZEN)

Open April–early Nov Tues–Sun 9–5. skanzen.hu. Local buses connect the HÉV station to the Skanzen stop. Bus times are given on the Skanzen website; it is worth checking them and aiming for a specific bus because services can be intermittent.

Occupying the site of a 3rd–4th-century Roman *villa rustica*, the open-air ethnographic museum, known as the Skanzen after the museum's Swedish prototype, which opened in Stockholm in 1891, is a collection of village houses and other examples of Hungarian vernacular architecture collected from around the country. It is a popular tourist attraction and hosts many folklore/fakelore shows and other rustic events. The museum is well kept and very enjoyable to visit with children.

GÖDÖLLŐ

The small town of Gödöllő (pop. 32,000), some 30km east of Budapest, is chiefly visited for its 18th-century château, a former palace of the Habsburgs and a favourite resort of the Empress Elisabeth. The town was known for its early 20th-century artists' colony and is also home to the Szent István Agricultural University. The important pilgrimage church of Máriabesnyő is close by.

Getting to Gödöllő

Gödöllő can be reached by the HÉV suburban train H8, which leaves every 15–30mins from Örs Vezér tere, the eastern terminus of metro line M2 (red). A single ticket will take you to the Budapest city limit at Ilonatelep. From there you need a suburban railway extension ticket to Gödöllő, available in advance from machines at the station or from the guard on the train. The best stop for the royal palace is Gödöllő, Szabadság tér. Journey time c. 45mins. The S80 mainline rail service to Hatvan, from Budapest's Keleti Station (map p. 429, F2–F3), also stops at Gödöllő (journey time 30–45mins).

HISTORY OF GÖDÖLLŐ

Gödöllő was anciently settled and Roman remains have been found here. However, it only rose to prominence in the early 18th century with Antal Grassalkovich, a lawyer and financial administrator at the court of Maria Theresa, tasked with organising the reallocation of property after the ousting of the Ottomans. He purchased the Gödöllő estate in the 1730s and set about building a residence for himself. He was created Baron, then Count, and Gödöllő was raised to the status of market town. Grassalkovich died in

GÖDÖLLŐ
Detail of the statue of Antal Grassalkovich
holding the architectural design for his manor house.

1771. Neither his son nor grandson, both also Antal, paid much attention to Gödöllő and its fortunes ebbed once again. During the anti-Habsburg War of Independence of 1848–9, after the Hungarian victory at nearby Isaszeg, Lajos Kossuth held meetings in the château to discuss the future course of the conflict and the deposing of the Habsburgs. In the mid-18th century the estate was briefly in the possession of the banker Georgios Sinas (whose son Simon donated lime trees from Gödöllő to the new National Museum garden in Budapest) but it was only in 1867 that the town became truly prosperous once again, after the château was presented to Franz Joseph and Elisabeth as a coronation gift. The royal couple—especially Elisabeth—spent much time here. A new railway line running northwards from Budapest was directed through Gödöllő for their convenience and a gasworks was set up here to provide lighting for the railway and the palace. Suddenly Gödöllő became not only economically successful but also fashionable. The aura of royalty made it a popular resort, with a club house, a bathing lido, hotels and restaurants. Gödöllő declined again after WWI, though it flourished during the Horthy years, when the Regent used the palace as a residence and, in 1933, organised the Boy Scouts' international jamboree here. Under Communism, Gödöllő was industrialised, with a factory making electricity meters, and the Agricultural University was also set up here. Since those days Gödöllő has suffered from rather unimaginative modern development and it lacks a truly attractive old centre. Nevertheless, it is well worth a visit for its historical and artistic associations.

EXPLORING GÖDÖLLŐ

THE ROYAL PALACE

Open March–Oct Mon–Wed 9–5, Thur 10–8, Fri–Sun 10–6; Nov and Dec Mon–Thur 10–4, Fri–Sun 10–5. Tickets 1hr before closing. In Jan and Feb the palace has more restricted opening; see website for details (kiralyikastely.hu). The Baroque theatre, stables and reconstructed Horthy bunker can only be seen on guided tours.

The pink, grey and cream Palace of Gödöllő stands beside the main road, surrounded by trees. Begun by Count Antal Grassalkovich in the 1730s and extended and partially remodelled by his successors, it is a neo-Baroque château of considerable charm. The central block, by András Mayerhoffer, has two long wings extending on either side at the rear, in a manner that has come to be known as the Gödöllő style: instead of having a grand *cour d'honneur* at the front, the wings enclose a paved courtyard at the back, more intimate and secluded and suited to family life. It was renovated and fitted out for Franz Joseph and Elisabeth under the direction of Miklós Ybl. Elisabeth was particularly fond of Gödöllő, a place which she found much more congenial than Vienna. She enjoyed hunting and country sports here, and spent much of her time with her horses in the palace stables. After her murder, the palace was little used by the Habsburg family, though Franz Joseph and his successor Charles IV came here occasionally. It was used as an army hospital both at the time of the Republic of Councils in 1919 and during the Romanian occupation. Under Miklós Horthy it was once again used as an official residence; the Regent enjoyed riding and hunting in the neighbouring woods and entertained important guests here, including Ribbentrop,

King Vittorio Emanuele III and Edward, Prince of Wales. During WWII it was occupied first by Nazi and then by Soviet troops. The Soviets continued to occupy parts of the building until 1991. The main wing became an old people's home in 1958. As may be imagined, the events of the 20th century took a vast toll on the palace. None of its furnishings or flooring and almost none of the interior fittings were left intact. Restoration, the first phase of which was completed in 1996, has taken the form of complete reconstruction, based on surviving fragments and on photographs and other documents. The result is surprisingly successful, with fine ceramic stoves, Rococo panelling painted white and picked out in gold, and furnishings and paintings carefully chosen to evoke the life and times of the Grassalkovich and Habsburg families.

Interior of the palace

The Small **Dining Room** has a table laid with a Herend dinner service in the design of broad orange bands known as the Gödöllő pattern. The grandest room is the **Salle d'Honneur**, designed c. 1758 by Maria Theresa's court architect Nicolò Pacassi. Five huge windows with pier glasses between them overlook the gardens. The room is often used for concerts and events. On one side of it is **Franz Joseph's study** and on the other **Elisabeth's small salon**, with two fine paintings from the Hungarian National Gallery: *Elisabeth Repairing St Stephen's Mantle* and *Elisabeth and Archduchess Gisela at Gerbeaud*. **Elisabeth's study** is hung with silk in her favourite shade of violet. Her **bedroom**, with just one window and a deep alcove for the bed, was originally built for the visit to Gödöllő of Maria Theresa in 1751.

The rooms in the opposite wing are taken up with **Habsburg family portraits** (*Franz Joseph* by Gyula Benczúr and *Elisabeth beside the Bier of Deák* by Mihály Zichy); an **Empress Elisabeth memorial exhibition**, with photographs, personal effects and a commemorative plaque by Ö. Fülöp Beck; and a display on the **history of the palace** after Elisabeth's death. There is a portrait of Horthy by Philip de László (1927).

The route to the exit takes you past the shop, WC and café.

The park

Originally a formal garden in the French style, the park was landscaped in the English manner by the wife of Antal Grassalkovich III in 1817. Today it is a very pleasant place to stroll, much enjoyed by local families, and there are plenty of benches. It contains some fine trees (including a giant Redwood behind the small octagonal pavilion on its hillock), a small palm house and garden shop, and György Zala's 1907 **statue of Maria Theresa** that originally stood in Heroes' Square in Budapest (*see p. 306*). It was brought here in 2011. As you look back at the palace, the wing on the left was the former coach house. The stables were on the right.

The lower park

At the edge of the lower park, across the road from the palace, is a **statue of Grassalkovich** (2013) spreading open a roll of architect's plans. The park is crossed by the **Rákos-patak stream**, which runs from here to Budapest, where it empties into the Danube. The trees include a row of ancient limes. Behind the Grassalkovich statue,

GÖDÖLLŐ TOWN MUSEUM

Plaster model by Aladár Körösfői Kriesch for his *Resurrection* mosaic in Kerepesi Cemetery.

the attractive building with a green lattice-work porch and veranda formerly housed guard rooms and administrative offices for the palace and estate. It is now home to the **Karácsonyház**, a Christmas market (open from the beginning of November).

THE TOWN MUSEUM AND ARTISTS' COLONY

On the opposite side of the main road from the modern House of Arts concert hall and exhibition space is a large yellow building, formerly the manor house (before Grassalkovich built his château) and after that a hotel, home to the town's main social club with a ballroom on the first floor. It now houses the **Town Museum** (*Városi Múzeum; open Wed–Sun 10–4; godolloimuzeum.hu*), with a local history display, an exhibition on the Boy Scouts jamboree, votive icons and statuettes from Máriabesnyő (*see below*), material on trades and crafts in the town and a very interesting section on the Gödöllő artists' colony, which includes drawings, paintings, stained glass, tapestries, sculpture and furniture by many of its members, including its founder, Aladár Körösfői Kriesch. His plaster model for the mosaic dome over the tomb of Artúr Görgei in Kerepesi Cemetery (*see p. 244*) is preserved here. Görgei led the Hungarian troops to victory at the Battle of Isaszeg, just outside Gödöllő, in April 1849.

THE GÖDÖLLŐ ARTISTS' COLONY

The colony of artists associated with Gödöllő was founded by Aladár Körösfői Kriesch in 1901. Among their number were the graphic artist Laura Kriesch (Aladár's sister), the sculptors Ferenc Sidló and Ödön Moiret, painters Jenő Remsey and Sándor Nagy (husband of Laura Kriesch), designer Ede Torockai Wigand, architect István Medgyaszay and the sisters Mariska and Carla Undi. The colony was greatly influenced by the English Pre-Raphaelites; in fact a book on Ruskin and the Pre-Raphaelites, written by Aladár Körösfői Kriesch and dedicated by him to a member of his circle, Róza Frey (sister of Remsey's wife Vilma), is part of the museum display.

The creative ethos of the colony was akin to that of both the Arts and Crafts movement in Britain and the German Nazarene painters, as well as other artists' colonies of the period such as the one at Worpswede in northwest Germany. The drawings and paintings produced in Gödöllő, often with a medieval theme or subject matter from the realm of myth and fairytale, have echoes of Aubrey Beardsley, Kate Greenaway and Arthur Rackham.

The colony was occupied with the entire spectrum of artistic production: painting, drawing, architecture, sculpture, literature and furniture design, with a particular emphasis on textiles. Many of the male members married women from the weaving workshop, set up by Körösfői Kriesch in 1904.

On the street where many of the artists lived, now Körösfői Kriesch Aladár utca, you can see the old weaving school at no. 47, with Körösfői Kriesch's former home opposite it at no. 28. A little further up at no. 36 is a large yellow-brick house with huge studio windows, designed for Sándor Nagy by István Medgyaszay. Today it is occupied by offices and has been greatly altered. Sándor Nagy and Laura Kriesch bravely tried to keep the weaving school going after WWI but the colony lost its impetus and could not survive the death of its charismatic founder in 1920. The Gödöllő Applied Arts Workshop (GIM; *gimhaz.hu*) now continues the tradition, holding regular exhibitions of work by its artists in their house and garden at Körösfői Kriesch Aladár utca 15–17.

THE ROYAL WAITING ROOM AND AGRICULTURAL UNIVERSITY

A waymarked path leads through the lower park, across the Rákos-patak stream. The waymarks on the trees have the red-and-white stripe of the main trail that crosses Pest County and the crossed M of the Marian Way, indicating that you are on a pilgrimage route (the basilica of Máriabesnyő is on the outskirts of town; *see below*). At the end of the park, you come out at the terminus of the HÉV, at Gödöllő's railway station. The current building is modern, of red brick. Standing incongruously beside it is the much larger Royal Waiting Room (*open daily 10–6*), a neo-Renaissance structure built in 1882. The building has three rooms: a central one with archive photographs; Franz Joseph's waiting room to the right, containing photographs of royal and imperial trains and a model of a locomotive; and Elisabeth's waiting room to the left, papered in yellow and containing busts of the royal couple. There is a café (*closed in winter*).

A footbridge leads over the railway line to the grounds of the **Szent István Agricultural University**. Its main building is a neo-Baroque former college of Premonstratensian canons, built in the 1920s. In front of it is an equestrian statue of Prince Kálmán (József Róna, 1931), son of Andrew II and benefactor of the Premonstatensians. He died of wounds sustained in battle against the Mongols in 1241.

Keeping the building to your left and the modern Premontrei Auditórium to your right, take the path signposted 'Botanikus kert', which leads up through scruffy woodland to another tarmac road, across which is the entrance to the university's **Botanical Garden** (*open Mon–Thur 8–4, Fri 8–2, closed weekends and school holidays*). Also on the university campus, in Block B (just beyond the modern Mechanical Engineering Faculty, which is fronted by a giant copper ear of wheat; István Kiss, 1977), is the **Museum of Agricultural Machinery** (*open Mon–Fri 9–4, Sat 9–2*).

OTHER SIGHTS OF GÖDÖLLŐ

Apart from his château, Antal Grassalkovich adorned his fiefdom with a number of **statues** in the Counter-Reformation spirit. A statue of St John of Nepomuk (*see p. 69*) stands outside the eastern boundary wall of the palace. On the other side of the main road and railway line, in Szabadság tér, is a statue of the Assumption. Further north is the **Erzsébet Park**, a public park named after Empress Elisabeth, with a memorial statue by József Róna (1901) at the end of an avenue of lime trees. Near the entrance to the park is a painted Calvary (János Mayerhoffer, 1771), with statues of the Crucified Christ and the two thieves placed on top of a stepped gloriette standing in for the hill of Golgotha. The park is particularly proud of its periwinkles.

Grassalkovich is buried in the lower church of the **pilgrimage basilica of Máriabesnyő** (*bus 469 or 474 from the main bus station, on the main road beyond the House of Arts, to Máriabesnyő, templom*). The yellow-and-white Baroque church, standing in a grove of trees beside the main road, was built (by János Mayerhoffer) on the spot where an ivory *Madonna and Child*, presumably a survival from the abandoned medieval church on the site, was found in 1759. The statue is now housed within the main altarpiece of the upper church (*both churches open during the day, but no access beyond the vestibules*). The church is a focus of large pilgrimages on 15th August (Feast of the Assumption) and 8th September (Nativity of the Virgin). A footpath behind the church leads round to the **cemetery**, where Count Pál Teleki is buried (plot 12; beside the main path that leads up to the cemetery chapel). Teleki, who organised the Gödöllő scouting jamboree in 1933, was Hungary's Prime Minister from 1939 to 1941. He committed suicide following the Hungarian invasion of Serbia (*see p. 18*).

Gödöllő also has a large **arboretum**, on the Isaszeg road (*open daily April–Oct 8–6, Nov–March 8–4*).

ZSÁMBÉK

Situated some 30km west of Budapest, in a wine-growing area at the foot of Nyakas-hegy hill, the small town of Zsámbék is visited chiefly for the atmospheric ruins of its Romanesque priory, which stand high above the main streets and are a landmark for many miles.

ZSÁMBÉK
Relief commemorating the expulsion of the Swabians in 1946.

Getting to Zsámbék

Zsámbék is served by a large number of regional buses run by Volánbusz (volanbusz. hu). Nos 783, 784, 785, 786, 787 and 795 leave from Széna tér (map p. 428, A1); nos 777 and 799 leave from Kelenföld railway station (map p. 430, B3). Services are regular throughout the day. Journey time is between 35mins to 1hr depending on time of day and traffic conditions. Tickets from the driver. The most convenient stop is Zsámbék, Szent István tér.

HISTORY OF ZSÁMBÉK

Zsámbék has been inhabited since Palaeolithic times. Blessed with an abundance of water, it was a place of relative importance after the foundation of the Hungarian kingdom in 1000, since it lay on a route between the temporal and spiritual capitals of Székesfehérvár and Esztergom. Its real flowering began in the 11th century, when Béla III presented the village and its land to a certain Aynard, a Norman knight in the retinue of his second wife, Margaret. It was Aynard who built the church and priory (*see below*). After the Mongol raids, a castle was built. Zsámbék was taken by the Ottomans in 1541, the year they captured Buda. In 1689, three years after the Habsburg reconquest, Zsámbék was purchased by the Zichy family, who built their château on the site of the medieval castle. To restore the population, which had fled or died out under the Ottoman occupation, Swabian settlers arrived, bringing with them the skills of wine-making and forestry. In the reprisals that followed WWII, many were expelled from Hungary and

ZSÁMBÉK
Ruins of the Romanesque priory church.

their place in Zsámbék was taken by Hungarians from the Great Plain. Zsámbék today has schools and some industry (Wavin, making plastic piping). Though officially a town since 2009, it still has the air of a large village. The cobbled and stepped streets leading up Nyakas Hill to the priory ruins are particularly pretty in spring and summer. The roadside wells preserved in some of the streets attest to the number of natural springs.

EXPLORING ZSÁMBÉK

THE PRIORY CHURCH

Open Tues–Sun March–late Oct 10–6; otherwise 10–5. Closed Mon. Fee.

The stepped Erzsébet lépcső, flanked by Stations of the Cross, is one of the approaches to the magnificent ruins of the Romanesque priory church, which stand high above the town on the lower slopes of Nyakas Hill, a landmark for many miles.

King Béla III gave Zsámbék to the French knight Aynard, who had come to Hungary in the train of Béla's second wife, Margaret, daughter of Louis VII of France and widow of Henry of England (eldest son of Henry II and Eleanor of Aquitaine). It was Aynard who built the church and priory, c. 1220, placing it in the charge of Premonstratensian canons. It was transferred to the Paulines in 1475 during the reign of Matthias Corvinus, following a fire. The buildings survived the Ottoman occupation but were badly damaged by earthquake in 1763, after which the site was pillaged for building stone. The remnants became one of the romantic sights of Hungary until István Möller set about restoring and reconstructing parts of them in 1889. Kálmán Lux continued the work in the 1930s. Today the priory is a gaunt and evocative ruin, its surviving bell-tower a pigeon roost. Traces of carving survive at the spring of the vaults. A cellar museum within the grounds has photographs and lapidary fragments.

THE CONVENT GARDEN AND TURKISH WELL

From the scruffy square where the buses terminate, a paved marketplace opens out, backed by the old **Zichy Palace** (being restored at the time of writing), on the site of the medieval castle. On the right is a low **relief commemorating the expulsion of the Swabians** in 1946 (*see overleaf*). From the back of the market square (turn right), there is access to the **Convent Garden** (Zárdakert), created by the nuns who occupied the Zichy Palace in the early 20th century. It is now a small public park with ponds and trees, including plane, ash and willow. The ponds are fed by the so-called **Turkish Well** (*Török kút*), a large public fountain popularly credited to the Ottomans (though it might in fact be later). It supplied the village drinking water until the 1960s.

THE LAMP MUSEUM AND SWABIAN PEASANT HOUSE

The main street of Zsámbék is Magyar utca, a wide thoroughfare bisected by a stream and with the typical arrangement of houses on either side, built end-on to the road with a yard and outhouses in front. As you walk down it, look back for fine views of the priory ruins and the spire of the parish church. At no. 18, in a traditional village house with a veranda and porch running down the side (note the stucco roses on the porch columns), is the **Lamp Museum** (Lámpamúzeum; *open Tues–Sun from 10, T: 06 20 502*

6682, *mizsambekunk.hu*), with over a thousand types of lamp, organised by type. There are candlesticks (including two menorahs), nightlights, bicycle lights, train lights, lanterns, a 1950 Hungarian prototype camping gas stove with built-in illumination, chandeliers and gasoliers and many types of oil lamp, some with attractive porcelain bases (including a Meissen and a Zsolnay example, both of c. 1870). The lighting of the display cabinets and the rooms themselves is provided by neon tube and LED strip (though these are not captioned). The museum is proud of its 1995 entry in the Guinness Book of Records. A curiosity (not a lamp) is the 500-year-old whetstone for sharpening swords, from the Zichy Palace.

In the south of town, at Bicskei u. 12, is an old **Swabian peasant house** with a polychrome relief of St Vendel, patron saint of shepherds, on the street-facing elevation. It is open two weekends a month.

THE HUNGARIAN SWABIANS

The Swabians (*Svábok*) were ethnic Germans (mainly from Baden-Württemberg and Bavaria) who were invited to Hungary in the 18th century to colonise depopulated areas of the Danube basin. With them they brought skills such as metalworking and viticulture. After WWII they were accused of collective crimes against the nation. Imre Kovács, leader of the Peasants' Party, said in a speech in April 1945: 'The Swabians came with a bundle on their backs; let them go the same way. By their every action they have demonstrated their solidarity with Hitler's Germany.' A few months later, it was announced that all those who in the latest census had identified as German, claimed German as their mother tongue, or who had reverted from a Hungarianised surname to a German one were to be deported. The deportations, ratified by Imre Nagy (*see p. 91*), who wanted to redistribute Swabian farms as part of his land reforms, began in 1946. About a quarter of a million were deported. Those who were able to claim Communist allegiance were reprieved. Their culture and language survived in some parts of the country, where in living memory it was not uncommon to hear elderly people speaking German. Today, many of the streets of Zsámbék have the Swabian name posted up alongside the Hungarian.

The **Ground-Based Air Defence Branch Museum**, in an old missile base, is on the outskirts of town (*best reached with your own transport*). It exhibits military vehicles, tanks and missile launchers. (*Open April–mid Oct Tues–Sun 10–6. For details, see zsambekinfo.hu.*)

EATING AND DRINKING IN SZENTENDRE, GÖDÖLLŐ AND ZSÁMBÉK

SZENTENDRE

There are dozens of places to eat and drink in Szentendre, both in the higher town and right on the Danube bank.

Adria Café. Serves Greek and Balkan food. Garden open in fine weather.

Kossuth Lajos u. 4. T: 06 20 448 8993, adriacafe.hu.

Szamos. Café and confectioner selling the famous marzipan (*see p. 328*). *Dumtsa Jenő u. 12–14. szamos.hu.*

GÖDÖLLŐ

f **Novo Café**. In the House of Arts. In fine weather, its terrace is a pleasant place to sit with a drink, overlooking the lower park. *Szabadság út 6. muza. hu.*

f **Palazzo Pizzeria**. Simple place in the railway station building at the Szabadság tér HÉV stop. *Szabadság tér 2. T: +36 28 420 688, pizzapalazzo.hu.*

f–ff **Erzsébet Szálloda**. Art Nouveau building on the corner of the main square and Dózsa György utca. Has a café and restaurant. *Dózsa György út 2. T: +36 28 816 819, erzsebetkiralyneetterem.hu.*

f–ff **Smarni**. Hungarian fusion cooking in an attractive old building between the House of Arts and the Karácsonyház. For dessert, try the eponymous *smarni* (*Kaiserschmarren* or *császármorzsa*) waffle-style chopped pancake topped with jam. It was a favourite of Franz Joseph. *Szabadság út 4. T: +36 20 270 1239, smarnietterem.hu.*

ZSÁMBÉK

f **Dióhej**. Delightful café and bistro, with a cellar for use in winter, as well as a cosy bar area. Their caramel cappuccino is welcome in winter. In summer you can sit outside with a cool drink. Simple snack meals also available. *Corvin János u. 5. T: 06 70 362 5136.*

f **Mátyás Terasz**. In an old wine cellar, with a panoramic outdoor terrace enjoying fine views of the church ruins. Serves drinks and full meals. In winter only open at weekends and Wed–Fri evenings. *Corvin János u. 20. T: 06 30 964 3088.*

f–ff **Ez meg Az Bisztró**. On the main street very close to the Lamp Museum, the 'This and That Bistro' serves salads, pasta and Hungarian favourites such as *borjúpaprikás* (veal in paprika sauce). *Magyar u. 19. T: 06 70 362 5136.*

LOCAL SPECIALITIES

Zsámbék is known for its crispy **wafers** (*ostya*), made by the firm of Ziegler. They have a shop on the village outskirts, at the end of Magyar utca (opposite the supermarket). The wafers come in a variety of flavours: cheese, caraway, chili and more. The shop also sells a variety of other delicacies and has a café.

Zsámbék was also known for its **wine**: the old Swabian cellar row, in Józsefváros utca (just east of the main Petőfi Sándor utca) has been looked after by a local association since 2005 (interesting as a monument; no wine is to be had, sadly). For thriving local producers, visit the nearby village of Tök (just before Zsámbék if you approach on bus 795), where you will find a small enclave of cellars and the Nyakas winery (*for details, see nyakas. hu*). Tök also gives its name to the dish known as *töki pompos*, an Alsace-style *tarte flambée* topped with onions and sour cream.

For **Szentendre marzipan**, see p. 328.

Practical Information

PLANNING YOUR TRIP

CLIMATE AND WHEN TO GO

The Budapest climate is characterised by hot summers, very short springs, long lingering autumns and cold winters. Not every year brings much snow but temperatures will regularly register minus figures. During the coldest months, public statuary is wrapped in protective layers and fountains are drained and switched off. Spring arrives in April and temperatures quickly become warmer. May and June are lovely months. July is very hot but a delightful time to be in the city, since life spills out of doors and bars and cafés set up tables on the Danube bank and in squares and parks all over town. August is the main holiday month and many locals will be away. Late September and October often bring a warm Indian summer (*vénasszonyok nyara*; old ladies' summer), perhaps the best weather of all for sightseeing.

DISABLED TRAVELLERS

Budapest has made great efforts in recent years to make more places accessible to those with restricted mobility. There are lifts to Castle Hill, for example, and many more ramps and wheelchair-friendly doors than there used to be. Disabled-friendly WCs are available in the larger museums and thermal baths. The transport company, BKK, has introduced a fleet of low-floor buses. For details, see their website (*bkk.hu*).

TOURIST OFFICES AND VISITOR INFORMATION

The two main city-centre tourist offices, run by Tourinform, are on Sütő utca (near Deák tér in Pest; *map p. 428, C3; open daily 8–8*) and on Castle Hill (*Tárnok u. 15; map p. 428, B2; open daily 9–6*). There are also information desks at the airport. For more details, see *tourinform.hu* and *budapestinfo.hu*. A good general website with information for the visitor, including historical background as well as practical tips, is maintained by We Love Budapest (*welovebudapest.com*).

THE BUDAPEST CARD

The Budapest Card, valid in several permutations (24h, 48h, 72h etc.), gives free use of all public transport within the city limits, free entry to a number of museums and other discounts. It can be bought online or over the counter, from Tourist Information offices and other outlets. For details, see *budapest-card.com*.

GETTING AROUND

TO AND FROM THE AIRPORT

Budapest's Liszt Ferenc Airport is just over 15km outside town to the southeast. There are two terminals, 2A and 2B, but both occupy different ends of the same building, so it is easy to walk from one to the other.

Access by taxi: Outside the Arrivals hall is the official taxi booth, with cars run by Fő Taxi. This is a reliable service. You should ignore any touts who approach you with offers of taxi rides, even (or perhaps especially) if they brandish badges saying 'Official Taxi': they are not. At the taxi booth, tell the cashier where you want to go. He/she will give you the number of your cab, which will arrive within a few minutes, and a receipt, which you should give to the driver. The journey is metered and charged accordingly. Expect to pay 8–10,000 Ft to the centre, depending on destination and traffic.

Access by public transport: Bus no. 200E runs from 4am to 11pm to and from the Kőbánya-Kispest metro terminal (metro line M2, blue). There is also a direct bus, no. 100E, which runs to and from Deák tér/Károly körút (*map p. 429, D3*). Normal transport tickets are valid for the 200E (available from the airport post office). For the 100E you need to purchase a special ticket. For details, see the airport website (*bud.hu*) and the public transport website (*bkk.hu;* click on *repülőtéri busz*).

Access by shuttle bus: For details of the 'miniBUD' shuttle bus service, see the airport website (*bud.hu*) or the shuttle's own site (*minibud.hu*).

TRANSPORT IN BUDAPEST

Public transport, by a mixture of bus, tram, trolley bus, metro, suburban train and river boat, is efficient and excellent. There is a website (*bkk.hu*) and an app, BKK Futár, which if you have roaming is worth downloading. Most services run from early in the morning until about 10.30 or 11pm (the metro runs slightly longer), after which a network of night buses takes over.

TRANSPORT TICKETS

If you are in Budapest for a couple of days and intend to use public transport frequently, it might make sense to purchase a Budapest Card (*see above*). The public transport company, BKK, also offers day passes and 72h passes. There is a weekly pass too, to purchase which you must provide ID. You can also buy single tickets per journey, or ten tickets *en bloc* (which confers a discount). The same types of ticket are valid for buses, trolley buses, trams, the metro and HÉV suburban trains. They are available from all metro stations and major transport stops, usually from automated machines. Some newspaper kiosks and newsagents also sell tickets. Tickets are not normally available from the drivers of vehicles, except on bus services which have front-door boarding only. If you do buy from the driver, you will pay a slightly higher price.

   If you are travelling with a ticket rather than a pass or the Budapest Card, you need to validate it when you begin your journey. Machines for doing this are at the top of the escalators in the metro or on board the vehicle in the case of trams, buses and suburban trains. On the older buses and trams, the machines are not automatic: slot your ticket into the black funnel at the top and pull it manually towards you. It will punch the ticket. Inspectors sometimes board vehicles to check tickets and you will be fined if you cannot show one. On front-door boarding buses you must punch your ticket in front of the driver or show him your pass. There is no system of turnstiles.

Tickets are valid for a single journey on one line, regardless of the number of stops. If you change line, you need to validate a new ticket (unless you have purchased a transfer ticket, which is very slightly cheaper, but a fiddly system unless you know exactly what journeys you are going to be making).

THE METRO

There are four underground lines. The M1 (yellow), known as the Földalatti, runs the length of Andrássy út (*see p. 193*). M2 (red) and M4 (green) serve stations in both Buda and Pest. M3 (blue) was being renovated at the time of writing and at certain times was operating a limited service, supplemented by buses. There is a map of the metro lines on p. 432.

SUBURBAN TRAINS

The HÉV, or suburban railway, is mainly useful for visiting outlying areas of the city or places beyond the metropolitan border. Outside the city limits, a supplementary ticket is needed, available from machines at the stations or sometimes from the guard on the train. Within the city borders, normal transport tickets are valid. A map of the HÉV network is given on p. 432.

DANUBE BOATS

The public transport company, BKK, runs **river boats** (lines D11, D12 and D14) on the Danube. A separate kind of ticket is needed for these. Services are not very frequent and are useful mainly for commuters.

The Hungarian shipping company Mahart offers **pleasure cruises** to the Danube Bend, Visegrád and Esztergom and also runs boats to and from Szentendre. For details, see the website (*mahartpassnave.hu*).

The **River Ride amphibious bus** wallows its way up and down the Danube three or four times a day (tours last approx. 90mins). The pick-up point is on Széchenyi tér (*map p. 428, C2*). For details, see the website (*riverride.com*).

TAXIS

Budapest used to have an enviably excellent taxi system. Taxis are still good value but now, at peak times, they can be difficult to find and waiting times have increased. Attempts to regulate the market have made taxis pricier and scarcer but have unfortunately not managed to reduce the number of crooks (the so-called 'hyena taxis') who unscrupulously rob foreigners. All officially licensed taxis charge according to the meter and there is a fixed tariff per kilometre. You can pick taxis up at taxi tanks or order a cab by phone (the latter option gives a surer likelihood of an honest fare).

Reliable taxi companies include City Taxi (*T: +36 1 211 1111*), Fő Taxi (*T: +36 1 222 2222*) and 6x6 (*T: +36 1 666 6666*). Taxi companies are distinguished mainly by the different design of their roof lights. Hailing cruising cabs in the street is possible but you need to be sure who you are flagging down.

Uber was not legal in Hungary at the time of writing but the Estonian company Taxify (*taxify.eu*) is present in Budapest.

BY BICYCLE AND ELECTRIC CAR

The public bike-sharing system known as Bubi, sponsored by MOL, the Hungarian oil company, has docking stations throughout the city. For details of how to use them and a map of the docking stations, see *molbubi.bkk.hu*. Electric (and petrol) cars can be rented through MOL Limo (*mollimo.hu*). You need to register, with images of your driving licence, 24hrs before you want to use a car.

There are also companies that rent scooters, segways, Renault Twizys and other e-cars. Cycle rickshaws are for hire on Margaret Island.

ACCOMMODATION

Accommodation is plentiful in Budapest and as demand has risen in recent years, so has supply grown to meet it—and indeed continues to do so, with new hotel developments being approved all the time. The offering covers the full scale, from five-star luxury to the most basic hostel; nevertheless, Budapest is still short on hotels of genuine charm, distinction and individuality. The listing below is restricted to just twelve choices across all categories, with priority given to convenience and location. Prices are per double room per night in high season.

ffff   100,000 Ft and above
fff   50–100,000 Ft
ff   30–50,000 Ft
f   around or under 30,000 Ft

ffff **Four Seasons**. Luxury hotel in the Art Nouveau Gresham Palace (*see p. 161*), located directly opposite the Chain Bridge. The building has fine original ironwork and stained glass in the stairways. Immaculate service. Pool and wellness centre. *Széchenyi István tér 5–6. T: + 36 1 268 6000, fourseasons.com. Map p. 428, C2–C3.*

fff **Callas House**. The spacious rooms (25 in all) occupy the upper floors of a 19th-century mansion by Vilmos Freund, next to the Opera House on Andrássy út. The décor is sober and sedate, in keeping with the building. The Art Deco Callas restaurant is on the ground floor. *Andrássy út 20. T: + 36 1 354 0794, callashouse.com. Map p. 429, D2.*

fff **Corinthia**. Luxury hotel in an elegant building on the Nagykörút with comfortable rooms, a grand main stairway and a fabulous spa and swimming pool. Décor is stylish without being shrill. *Erzsébet körút 43–49. T: + 36 1 479 4000, corinthia.com. Map p. 429, E2.*

***ff–fff* St George Residence**. A variety of suites of different sizes are on offer in this 18th-century former inn, built on medieval foundations on one of the prettiest streets of Castle Hill. The décor is classic—cherry wood, drapes and mirrors—in keeping with the age of the building. *Fortuna u. 4. T: +36 1 393 5700, stgeorgehotel.hu. Map p. 428, A2.*

***ff* Astoria**. Historic hotel, the oldest purpose-built hotel in the city, opened in 1914. The first general manager had worked for the Waldorf Astoria in New York, hence the hotel's name. Clean but unexciting rooms. Handsome café. Part of the Danubius group. *Kossuth Lajos u. 19–21. T: +36 1 889 6000, danubiushotels. com. Map p. 429, D3.*

***ff* Brody House**. Acclaimed shabby-chic guest house beside the National Museum. Welcoming, attentive staff. Cool design. *Bródy Sándor u. 10. T: + 36 1 266 1211, brody.land. Map p. 429, D3.*

***ff* Lánchíd 19**. Superb position on the Danube bank in Buda, close to the Chain Bridge. A member of the Design Hotels group, recently renovated, with self-consciously modern interiors. *Lánchíd u. 19. T: + 36 1 457 1200, lanchid19hotel. com. Map p. 428, B3.*

***ff* Moments**. Occupying a 19th-century Andrássy út mansion, built by Adolf Feszty for the Schossberger family of tobacco and sugar magnates. Completely modernised but—despite the daft name—still a historic location. *Andrássy út 8. T: + 36 1 611 7000, hotelmomentsbudapest.hu. Map p. 429, D2.*

***ff* Palazzo Zichy**. Former patrician palace on a tiny square in a lively part of the Eighth District. The exterior has been preserved; the interior is almost entirely modern. *Lőrinc Pap tér 2. T: +36 1 235 4000, hotel-palazzo-zichy.hu. Map p. 429, E4.*

***f–ff* Gerlóczy Rooms deLux**. Budapest needs more places like this. Light and airy, tastefully designed rooms above a popular café/brasserie on a small, inner city square, perfectly positioned for sightseeing. *Gerlóczy u. 1. T: +36 1 501 4000, gerloczy.hu. Map p. 429, D3.*

***f* ROOMbach**. Well-run 3-star accommodation in a modern block in the old Jewish quarter. *Rumbach Sebestyén u. 14. T: +36 1 413 0253, accenthotels.com. Map p. 429, D3.*

***f* Victoria**. Slim modern building on the Danube bank in Buda. The great draw are the rooms on the front, which have stunning river views. Clean and well located. *Bem rakpart 11. T: + 36 1 457 8080, victoria.hu. Map p. 428, B2.*

FOOD & DRINK

There are hundreds of restaurants in Budapest. Most of those in the centre of town serve a generic kind of modern European cooking, a fusion of local and Mediterranean influences, with fewer carbohydrates and more fresh vegetables than the traditional Budapest bill of fare would have offered. Classic Hungarian food includes plenty of meat (particularly pork, goose, chicken and game), lots of curd cheese and sour cream, and plenty of paprika spice. It is still possible to find purist Magyar places to eat—and in fact they are becoming ever more precious because of their increasing rarity. Hungarians generally like to eat a hot meal at lunchtime, with a simple cold supper in the evening. There is no tradition of a long lunch break to accommodate this; instead many restaurants offer quick, cheap, two-course lunch menus. There is also the *étkezde*, literally 'eatery', a small place with traditional one-pot meals. Many now also offer takeaway.

A short, selective listing of places to eat is attached to each chapter in this guide. The aim has been to choose authentic places where Hungarians go. Where possible, websites have been included but many of the smaller establishments have a Facebook page in place of a website. Price categories are as follows:

fff   Main courses over 6,000Ft
ff   Main courses generally between 3,000 and 6,000Ft
f   Main courses generally under 3,000 Ft

Starters

A Hungarian meal typically begins with soup. In summer this might be a cold fruit soup, usually made from sour cherries (*meggy*). In winter, there is the hearty *gulyásleves* (goulash soup), a rich mix of meat, vegetables and paprika, traditionally cooked in a cauldron over an open fire. It takes its name from the cattle-herders (*gulyás*) of the Great Plain, who lived and ate out of doors, and is now registered as a 'Hungarikum' (*see p. 355*). The *Jókai bableves* is another filling soup, made with beans, vegetables and pork knuckle, often served with a swirl of sour cream (*tejföl*). *Halászlé* is the Hungarian answer to *bouillabaisse*: a rich fish soup made from a mixture of carp, catfish and other freshwater species, often served in a mini-cauldron and deep red in colour from the copious use of ground paprika.

Other traditional starters are the *vegyes tál* or *vegyes ízelítő* (mixed appetiser), a plate of sliced tomato, cucumber, red onion, sweet paprika and different types of ham (*sonka*), sausage (*kolbász*) and salami. The *téliszalámi* (lit. 'winter salami') made by the firm of Pick is another Hungarikum, although salami-making was in fact introduced to Hungary by the Italians in the mid-19th century. In Kőbánya (District X), around the bus station on Állomás utca, is a building with a corner tower, one of a number in the area. It is said that buildings like this were once smokeries for salami, made here by Ármin Herz, who had learned the recipe during his time as a sailor. Sliced goose liver (*libamáj*), served in its own dripping with raw onion, is another traditional dish.

Main courses

On a traditional menu these will be divided into *frissensültek* (cooked to order) and *készételek* (ready meals). The *frissensültek* will be different cuts of meat, fried, roasted or grilled, sometimes breaded. Look out for dishes made from *mangalica* (pron. 'mongalitsa') pork. The mangalica is a Hungarian breed of woolly pig (a domestic and wild cross breed) that yields a highly marbled meat particularly suited for pork steaks. The *szürkemarha* grey cattle, whose beef is highly prized, are another Hungarian breed. Most places now also offer a few vegetarian choices.

Készételek might include stuffed cabbage (*töltött káposzta*), savoy cabbage leaves stuffed with minced pork and served in a rich paprika sauce; and various types of *pörkölt*, stews made from pork (*sertés*), beef (*marha*), lamb (*bárány*), wild boar (*vaddisznó*) or tripe (*pacal*). They are traditionally eaten with *galuska* or *nokedli*, flour-and-water gnocchi. *Lecsó* is a sort of Hungarian ratatouille, made of onions and paprika.

Hungarian fish dishes are made from freshwater varieties. *Harcsa* (catfish) is stewed with paprika. The finest of the lake fish is the *fogas* (pike perch).

Vegetables

Hungarian main courses are traditionally accompanied by simple salads of tomato, cabbage, cucumber or lettuce, and often with pickled vegetables (*savanyúság*), depending on the season. May is asparagus month and many restaurants offer special asparagus menus, using both the white and the green varieties. The Hungarian vegetable *par excellence*, however, is paprika.

PAPRIKA

Hungary's most famous cooking ingredient was brought to the country by the Ottomans. To begin with it was known as 'Turkish pepper' and even believed to be poisonous. Instead it was grown as an ornamental plant. In the 18th century, when trade embargoes during the Napoleonic Wars made pepper unavailable, paprika, cultivated in the sunny climate of Szeged, in south Hungary, began to be used as a seasoning. Today, ground paprika powder from Szeged is designated a 'Hungarikum' (*see p. 355*). It can either be hot (*erős, csípős*) or mild (*édes*). Raw paprika, sliced crossways or lengthways, is a popular accompaniment to plates of cold meat. The long, thin green and red ones are hot. The cone-shaped yellow ones (called *TV paprika*, standing for *töltenivaló*, 'good for stuffing') and long, broad red ones (*kápia paprika*) are mild and crunchy. In summer you will find the deep red *pritamin*, rounded in shape and sweet to taste. The small round *alma paprika* ('apple paprika'), is often pickled. All year round you will find bell peppers: known as *kaliforniai paprika*, they are not native. Paprika is a rich source of Vitamin C, and in fact it was while eating a piece of raw paprika that Hungarian Nobel Prize-winning chemist Albert Szent-Györgyi first discovered and isolated the vitamin.

Desserts

Pancakes (*palacsinta*) are popular desserts, served filled with curd cheese (*túró*), apricot jam, ground walnuts (*dió*) or chocolate sauce. Strudel (*rétes*), with a variety of fillings, is also commonly offered. *Somlói galuska* is a dessert of pieces of sponge soaked in brandy and served with raisins, whipped cream and chocolate sauce.

Hungarian street food

Hungary had a street food culture long before wagons serving pulled pork and soup-in-a-bun became commonplace in cities further west. Look out for stands offering *lángos*, a deep-fried disc of batter the size of a small pizza, topped with sour cream, garlic or grated cheese.

Kürtőskalács is a sweet snack, a twined tall cylinder of sugared dough coated with a cinnamon-, coconut-, walnut- or other-flavoured sugar glaze. They are cooked over coals on a special spit and originally were a treat reserved for weddings and other feast days, particularly in Transylvania. Today they have become a standard feature of the city's street food scene and an English name has even been invented for them: 'chimney cake'. There are stands selling them in many markets and they always make an appearance during street festivals. In fact, both *lángos* and *kürtőskalács* are beginning to have dedicated shops devoted to the single article.

Along the Danube on **Római part** (*see p. 114*) you will find stalls selling fried and grilled sausages and fish, served with bread and mustard and side orders of pickled cabbage, paprika, beetroot or gherkins.

COFFEE HOUSES, CAFÉS AND PÂTISSERIES

'The Hungarian cannot do without the coffee house,' says Joseph Kahn in his *Illustrated Guide to Budapest* (1891). 'On Sunday afternoons the space in the fashionable coffee houses seems too limited for the accommodation of the crowds which besiege them'. Budapest is famous for its coffee house culture (at the turn of the 20th century there were some 500 such establishments in the city).

COFFEE AND THE COFFEE HOUSE

Coffee was introduced to Hungary by the Ottomans and the first coffee houses were in Buda. Hungarians developed a taste for the bitter brew in the 18th century, after the reconquest, but the heyday of the coffee house was in the late 19th century. It is difficult to overestimate the role they played at this time. The poet, novelist and journalist Dezső Kosztolányi wrote verses apostrophising the New York Coffee House, evoking a world of strong black coffee, tobocco smoke and late nights. The late 19th-century coffee house had a reputation as a male preserve, somewhere to go to get fed, and then to drink, smoke, talk, write and play billiards. Artists and writers had regular tables reserved for them; politicians would sit deliberating amidst the cigar smoke; each coffee house had its regulars and its clique. Women were not debarred; nor were children. But to preserve their hair and their clothing from the penetrating smell of smoke, ladies often chose to patronise the pâtisserie (*cukrászda; see below*) instead.

Many coffee houses were humble places but a good few of them were architecturally outstanding. The famous New York Coffee House (*map p. 429, E3*), built in 1884 at the corner of Erzsébet körút and Dohány utca as an investment by the New York

Insurance Company, was the grandest of all, adorned with marble, metalwork, glass and gilding. The regulars had tables in the gallery overlooking the 'deep end', the lower floor where the billiard tables were (and later, after 1920, a restaurant). According to legend, to ensure that the New York would never shut, the novelist and playwright Ferenc Molnár threw its keys into the Danube. The coffee houses became famous as a hotline for news, gossip and the dissemination of ideas. Already in 1848 they had played a role in fomenting revolutionary zeal: taverns such as the Pilvax, in central Pest (*Petőfi Sándor u. 7*), had been used as meeting places by Sándor Petőfi and his circle. The writer Frigyes Karinthy once measured how quickly it would take a joke to travel across the river by telling it in a coffee house in Buda, and an hour or so later strolling into a coffee house in Pest, where the same joke was relayed to him. According to Ferenc Molnár, it was this capacity for underground communication that made the coffee houses so unpopular with the Communists: when they came to power in 1948, they had those that had not been destroyed in the fighting closed down.

Times change but never entirely. In the heyday of the New York, regulars were provided with pens and paper and were allowed to sit for hours on end over just a single coffee. Journalists would use the coffee house as their editorial office. Today, a plethora of hipster cafés has sprung up across town where co-workers and creatives sit over their laptops, updating their Instagram feeds on the free wifi and scarcely spending a forint.

Types of coffee

Traditionally, coffee is served either as a single shot (*presszó káve*), a double shot (*dupla presszó*), or American style, with more water (*hosszú kávé*). It can be taken with or without milk (*tej*), but if you want fresh milk, and you want it warm, you need to ask for it. Otherwise your espresso may arrive with a plastic pot of creamer and a twist of sugar. Cappuccino is also available everywhere, though it is not always expertly made and sometimes is indistinguishable from a *café au lait* (*tejes kávé*). In the newer places, the flat white and (less frequently) the *cortado* have been introduced.

Traditional coffee houses: None survive in a wholly traditional form. Locals no longer use the coffee house in the way they used to and all of the survivors have found their way onto major tourist itineraries, a circumstance which has inevitably ossified them in one sense and internationalised them in another. The **New York** (*map p. 429, E3*), attached to the Boscolo Hotel, has been re-designed and now operates more as a restaurant and must-see sight than as a true coffee house. Certainly no starving writer could afford to spend all day here (though he or she might find quite a lot of material for poetry, fiction or travelogue). The interior is still spectacular. The **Centrál** (*Károlyi Mihály u. 9; map p. 429, D3; centralkavehaz.hu*) was re-founded in 1999 and is the closest modern approximation to a traditional coffee house. The **Művész** (*Andrássy út 29; map p. 429, D2; muveszkavehaz.hu*) has a venerable history and protected interior furnishings but is more of a pâtisserie than a coffee house.

Modern espresso and brew bars: The 'brew bar' or 'brew lab' concept has found receptive ground in Budapest: the coffee is made by hand, without an espresso machine (by the AeroPress, Chemex, V60 or other methods). It means a longer wait, but the results are worth it. A selection of brew bars (they also offer espresso) includes **Madal** (*madalcafe.hu*), at various locations: on Ferenciek tere near Elizabeth Bridge (*map p. 429, D3*), on Hollán Ernő utca in District XIII (*map p. 428, C1*) and on Alkotmány utca near Parliament (*map p. 428, C2*). **Espresso Embassy** (*Arany János u. 15; map p. 428, C2*) is similar.

Fekete Udvar near the National Museum (*Múzeum körút 5; map p. 429, D3; feketekv.hu*) serves artisanal coffee and sandwiches in an atmospheric courtyard. **Kontakt Coffee**, in another central Pest courtyard (*Károly körút 22; map p. 429, D3; kontaktcoffee.com*), has a Florentine Marzocco coffee machine. All of the last three are in District V. **My Little Melbourne** (*District VII, Madách Imre út 3; map p. 429, D3*) is another good place. It has a sister establishment, **My Green Cup** (*District XIII, Pozsonyi út 15; map p. 428, C1*).

PÂTISSERIES AND BAKERIES

Bakers historically were divided into three types: those who baked bread; those who also made white rolls and brioche; and those who made fancy pastries stuffed with ground walnuts, dried and candied fruit and poppy seed. With the advent of refrigeration came cakes and gâteaux filled with cream. The pâtisserie (*cukrászda*) was originally a place where you bought items to take away (as Daubner and the Budapest Cukrászda still are). Gradually, some of them evolved into grand and genteel establishments, of which **Gerbeaud** on Vörösmarty tér was the most celebrated (*see p. 167*). Other fine cukrászdas in Budapest, all in Buda, include the **Ruszwurm** on Castle Hill (*see p. 53*), **Auguszt** near Széll Kálmán tér (*see p. 93*) and **Daubner** (*see p. 93*). The offering in a *cukrászda* covers the whole spectrum of the pastrychef's art: creamy gâteaux, fruit jellies, delicate sponges and dainty biscuits. *Esterházy torta* (made with ground walnuts) and *krémes* (millefeuille and vanilla custard) are popular.

A *cukrászda* is different from a *pékség* (bakery), which sells not only bread but different types of *pogácsa* (savoury scones), *túrós táska* (a choux pastry case filled with sweet curd cheese and raisins) and *kakaós csiga* (a snail-shaped pastry coil layered with chocolate). In recent years French-style croissants and *viennoiseries* have proliferated, but traditional Hungarian baked goods are still widely available.

HUNGARIAN WINE

Hungary is the 17th largest wine producer in the world and viticulture has a long history here. The Romans certainly made wine and the colonising Magyars probably had knowledge of it too. They brought with them their own indigenous word for it: *bor*. Following depopulation during the Ottoman period, Hungary was resettled in the 1700s by the so-called Swabians, immigrants from Germany who brought wine-making skills with them. Their partial expulsion after WWII had an impact on local wine production, as did the disastrous collectivisation of the Communist years. Today Hungarian wine has found a new lease of life and enjoys enormous local popularity.

Production volumes are relatively small (and most of the consumption is domestic) and many of the native grape varieties are little known outside Central Europe. This makes these wines all the more fun to explore and get to know.

HUNGARIAN WINE REGIONS

There are seven wider wine regions, each with a community of mainly small winemakers vinifying both noble, Old World grapes and a broad palette of indigenous varieties. The Great Plain region supplies mainly mass-market, supermarket wines. The other six regions are as follows:

North Transdanubia: The rolling hills west of Budapest produce fresh, aromatic whites and light, fruity reds, including some excellent Pinot Noir. Producers to look out for include Etyeki Kúria (good Sauvignon Blanc and Pinot Noir), Szentesi (a champion of indigenous varieties), Törley (a well-known producer of sparkling wine), Pannonhalma (wines from Hungary's oldest Benedictine abbey).

Sopron: In Hungary's far west, this region specialises in the Kékfrankos grape (light reds) and has also been a pioneer of organic winemaking. Weninger is a reliable producer.

The Pannon Region: This large region encompasses a number of important sub-regions producing some of Hungary's finest reds. The vineyards are centred on the towns of Szekszárd and Villány, and though production is highly vintage-specific, in good years the wines can be remarkable. From Szekszárd, look out for wines by Heimann, Márkvárt and Takler, as well as rosés by Dúzsi. In Villány, key producers are Gere, Gábor Kiss, Sauska and Vylyan.

Eger: The northern town of Eger is the home of Bull's Blood, which at its best is a light, spicy blend always with a predominance of the Kékfrankos grape. The white blend known as Egri Csillag is made largely of indigenous varieties. The Szent Andrea winery makes wines of great interest and elegance.

Balaton: The shores of Hungary's great lake, where the water reflects the sun onto the volcanic vineyard slopes, is home to some very attractive wines, both white and red. From the village of Csopak come some of the finest whites made from the Olaszrizling variety (Jásdi is a good producer of these). Konyári and Ikon on the south shore turn out some good reds. The volcanic Badacsony sub-region produces lean, high-acid whites as well as some beautiful luscious Rieslings (from Villa Sandahl). Other producers to try include Gilvesy, Gella Villa, Figula and Villa Tolnay. Kreinbacher, in the sub-region of Somló, makes some of Hungary's best sparkling wine.

Tokaj: Tokaj, in Hungary's far northeast, is historically renowned for its dessert wines, given depth and intensity by the 'noble rot' or botrytis that, when conditions are right, affects the grapes, allowing for the production of Aszú, the famous sweet wine. Falling global demand for sweet wines, however, together with unreliable botrytisation, have meant that Tokaj is now reinventing itself as a producer of dry whites and even sparkling wines alongside its fine sweet Aszús. The two grapes that form the basis of all Tokaj wine are Furmint and Hárslevelű. The sweet wines are categorised as Late Harvest, Szamorodni (wines where *aszú* and non-*aszú* berries are vinified together unselected, as they come off the vine) and Aszú (sweet wine containing a certain proportion of berries infected by noble rot). Aszú is further categorised by *puttony* number, traditionally the number of hods of *aszú* berries that went into the vat. The sweetest, 6-puttonyos wines can have as much as 180g/l of residual sugar. At the time of writing, some of the finest Tokajs, both sweet and dry, were being made by Balassa, Bardon, Disznókő, Gizella, Kaláka, Oremus, Royal Tokaji, István Szepsy (the most famous and admired of all the winemakers) and Tállya.

WHERE TO TASTE WINE

Hungarian wine is tasted by the decilitre (just as meat is purchased by the dekagram). *Fehér* is white, *vörös* is red, *rozé* is rosé. Wines can be *száraz* (dry), *félszáraz* or *féledés* (off-dry or semi-sweet) and *édes* (sweet).

Wine bars with a good atmosphere and a wide offering include: **DropShop** (*District V, Balassi Bálint u. 27; map p. 428, C1; dropshop.hu*); **DiVino** (*District V, Szent István tér 3; map p. 428, C2; divinoborbar.hu*); **Kadarka** (*District VI, Király u. 42; map p. 429, D2; kadarkabar.hu*); **Cultivini** (*District V, Párizsi u. 4; map p. 428, C3; cultivini.com*); **Doblo** (*District VII, Dob u. 20; map p. 429, D3; budapestwine.com*) and **Palack** (*District XI, Szent Gellért tér 3; map p. 428, C4; palackborbar.hu*).

Wines by the glass and flights of wine are available at Carolyn and Gábor Bánfalvi's **Tasting Table** (*District VIII, Bródy Sándor u. 9; map p. 429, D3; tastehungary.com*). **Klassz** (*District VI, Andrássy út 41; map p. 429, D2*) is a restaurant run by the wine retailer **Bortársaság** (*bortarsasag.hu*), attached to one of their shops. Bortársaság has several other retail outlets in the city. Another good wine store is **Radovin** (*District XIII, Pannónia u. 17/b: map p. 428, C1; radovin.hu*). If you are travelling with hand-luggage only but want to take some wine home, there is a reasonable selection at Budapest airport.

In summer, Hungarians like to drink refreshing white or rosé wine spritzers (*fröccs*). The proportions are: *Nagyfröccs* (2dl wine + 1dl soda); *Kisfröccs* (1dl wine + 1dl soda) and *Hosszúlépés* (1dl wine + 2dl soda).

PÁLINKA

Pálinka, the Hungarian equivalent of schnaps, is a double-distilled spirit made from orchard fruit, typically plum (*szilva*), pear (*körte*), apricot (*barack*), sour cherry (*meggy*) and quince (*birsalma*). It is drunk as an aperitif or digestif, in small thimblefuls, often downed in one go. It should not be served chilled, as this obscures the fragrance and taste. A good *pálinka*, after the initial alcohol burn, should leave behind a lingering scent and memory of high summer. Traditionally, *pálinka* is a rural drink—perfect for aiding the digestion of village cuisine—but some of the speciality *pálinkas* made today retail for prices that only prosperous urban pockets can afford.

NON-ALCOHOLIC DRINKS

Hungarians are very fond of fresh lemonade (*limónádé*) and cordials (*szörp*) made of mint, elderflower, lavender etc., which are delicious and widely available.

THE RUIN PUB PHENOMENON

The first of the now-famous 'ruin pubs' (*romkocsma*) appeared in the early 2000s, in derelict, often condemned 19th-century buildings in the Seventh District. When a building was demolished or revamped, the ruin pub moved on, to squat on a different site. The first ruin pubs were extremely simple beer garden-type places, occupying the inner courtyards of the old apartment buildings, with a makeshift bar and a jumble of old, beaten-up chairs and tables, gravel strewn on the floor and fairy lights strung overhead. Because they were out of doors, they were a summer phenomenon, relaxed and cheap and extremely informal, springing up *ad lib*. The ruin pub since those days has become one of the reasons visitors come to Budapest, and as a result many of them have become permanent, year-round fixtures, their existence now guaranteeing the survival of the once-to-be-demolished buildings. The ruinousness is artfully contrived and many have expanded to include dance floors, hostel accommodation, indoor bars, performance stages and restaurants. On Akácfa utca (*map p. 429, D2*), the once-low key Fogas Ház has, since its recent merger with Instant, become an enormous, labyrinthine complex with a Berlin-style techno nightclub called Lärm ('Din'—a name that is self-descriptive). The ruin pubs are a Budapest phenomenon and should be experienced. Be prepared for crowds (rowdy stag parties if you are unlucky) and for many of the guests to be non-Hungarian. **Szimpla Kert** (*District VII, Kazinczy u. 14; map p. 429, D3*) is the original ruin pub (though not in its original location), the place which spawned the entire concept and a host of imitators. It is still probably the best. **Kőleves** (*District VII, Kazinczy u. 37–39; map p. 429, D3*) is not strictly a ruin pub, being more of a restaurant with ruin pub-style garden, but it has a good atmosphere and good food. **Anker't** (*District VI, Paulay Ede u. 33; map p. 429, D2*) is another good choice, cavernous and throbbing but less chaotic. (*For a full listing, in English, see ruinpubs.com.*) Seasonal, **pop-up outdoor bars** are a summer phenomenon. There is one at the foot of Gellért Hill (*see romkert.eu*).

SHOPPING & MARKETS

Antiques: Falk Miksa utca, just off Kossuth Lajos tér (*District V, map p. 428, C1*) is the best place to go. The whole street is an almost unbroken parade of antique shops and auction houses. Many of them have smartened up in recent years but one or two still retain an old treasure-trove feel and bargains can still sometimes be found.

Books: For an excellent selection of books and magazines in English, go to **Bestsellers** (*District V, Október 6. u. 11; map p. 428, C2; bestsellers.hu*). The best general bookstore is **Libri** (*libri.hu*), with many branches across town that have an English-language section. **Írók Boltja** is a fine literary and academic bookshop (with an English-language section) at Andrássy út 45 (*District VI, map p. 429, D2*). **Antiquarian books** and prints are available from shops on Múzeum körút (*District V, map p. 429, D3*).

Chocolate: Artisanal chocolates made by the Bonbon Manufaktúra in east Hungary are sold at **Cadeau** (*District V, Veres Pálné u. 8; map p. 429, D3*). **Rózsavölgyi** is also excellent (*District V, Királyi Pál u. 6; map p. 429, D4*), as is **Stühmer** (*District XIII, Pozsonyi út 9, map p. 428, C1; District XI, Bartók Béla út 18, map p. 425, D6 and District VI, Teréz körút 36, map p. 429, D2*), which aims to revive the tradition of Friedrich Stühmer, a Hamburg chocolatier who set up a factory in Budapest in 1868.

Clothing: Sports and casual shoes are handmade by **Tisza**, established in the town of Martfű, on the Tisza river in south Hungary, in 1942 (*tiszacipo.com*). The shoes (and now also bags and a line of clothing) all bear the trademark logo of a capital T. There is an outlet at the Astoria crossroads (*Károly körút 1; map p. 429, D3*). Opposite, the **Bognár glove store** sells gloves handmade in Pécs, also in south Hungary (*Károly körút 4; map p. 429, D3*).

Folk art: Potters, weavers and other craftsmen set up stalls at street fairs throughout the year. At the National Dance House Convention (*Táncháztalálkozó*), held annually in spring, there is always a good variety of stands. The **Holló Műhely** (*Vitkovics*

Mihály u. 12; map p. 429, D3) sells hand-painted furniture, mirrors, jewellery boxes and other smaller items.

'Hungarikum' souvenirs: For a truly Magyar memento, look out for products marked with the 'Hungarikum' logo. This accolade is awarded to products that somehow also encapsulate an essential Hungarianness. Many of them are to be found in the field of gastronomy: **Tokaj wine**, **Szamos marzipan** (*see p. 328*), certain types of **salami**, acacia blossom **honey**, ground **paprika** from Szeged, **mangalica** pork products, **goulash soup** and **Túró Rúdi**, a delectable stick of curd cheese enveloped in chocolate. It can be found in all supermarkets: choose from the traditional Pöttyös brand (with a red-and-white spotted wrapper) or its recent rival made by Cserpes, a successful artisanal dairy.

The bottled wine spritzer **Vasuta fröccs** (white or rosé) is another Hungarikum, the brainchild of former engineer György Vasuta.

Hungarica that are non-gastronomy-related include **Ilcsi cosmetics** made from natural herbal extracts, available from their District II store at Bem József u. 7 (*map p. 428, B1*), **Herend porcelain** (several shops in Budapest, *herend.com*) and **Zsolnay ceramics** (they also have a number of shops around town, *zsolnay.hu*). Antique Zsolnay and Herend pieces are also available from many of the shops on Falk Miksa utca (*map p. 428, C1*).

Jewellery: For distinctive silverware, particularly rings and chunky pendants, go to Wladis, the retail outlet of metalworker and designer Vladimir Péter (*Falk Miksa u. 13; map p. 428, C1*).

MARKETS

There are many **produce markets** in Budapest, some of them in handsome late 19th-century covered market halls (*see p. 264*). The **Ecseri fleamarket** (*Nagykőrösi út 156; open Mon–Fri 8–3, Sat 5–3, Sun 8–1; map p. 431, D4*), where vendors in both fixed and temporary stalls offer furniture, paintings, sculpture, carpets, lamps, clocks and watches and bric à brac galore still offers a few genuine bargains.

In recent years Budapest's **Advent and Christmas markets** have become a destination in their own right, as they have long been in Vienna. This means that they can get very crowded at weekends, as groups come specifically to visit them, but on weekdays they are quieter and atmospheric, with stalls selling crafts, jewellery, pottery, textiles and Christmas decorations. There is always plenty of food on offer: fried sausages and roast vegetables, strudel, mulled wine. The biggest markets are in District V, on Vörösmarty tér (*map p. 428, C3*) and Szent István tér (*map p. 428, C2*; with a spectacular hourly light show against the façade of St Stephen's Basilica). Smaller, less touristy markets are held in the outer districts, such as Óbuda (Fő tér; *map p. 421, B3*).

THERMAL BATHS

Budapest is famed for its spas, and rightly so. In the thermal baths that line the Danube—the Gellért, Rudas, Király, Lukács and Veli Bej—you swim in water that 8–10,000 years ago fell as rain and entered the karstic system of limestone caverns in the Buda Hills (*for more on this fascinating world, a visit to the caves is recommended; see p. 84*). There are two main sources of thermal water under the city: the springs at the foot of Gellért Hill (*map p. 425, D5*) and those opposite the Lukács Baths (*map p. 424, D2*).

VISITING THE BATHS: GENERAL

All of the baths work on similar lines. In most cases, there is a flat fee for entrance. Some baths charge more at weekends, or less for afternoon visits, or allow you to buy a ticket for an entire day or just a couple of hours. In many cases you will be given the choice between a cabin or a locker. If total privacy while changing is important to you, ask for a cabin (you will have to pay a bit more). With your ticket you will be given a plastic 'proxy watch' which lets you through the turnstile and opens and locks your cabin or locker. In some cases you will be told the number of your cabin, in others you choose your own from among the free, empty ones, and in still others you hold your proxy watch to the electronic allocator unit on the wall of the changing room and the number of the cabin allotted to you will be displayed (your watch will only work with that cabin). In each bath house, there are attendants on hand to help you. All information about opening times, prices and special treatments can be found on the baths' websites. All the baths have buffets, of varying quality.

NB: Children under 14 are not allowed into the thermal water.

What to take

Bring a towel, flip-flops, soap and shampoo, a comb, a small bag to carry money to spend in the buffet, a swimming costume and swimming cap (obligatory for the cold-water swimming pools). If you have long hair, you will be asked either to tie it up or to wear a cap (in the thermal pools too). Hairdryers are usually provided.

PRACTICALITIES, BATH BY BATH

The entries below give details of the facilities offered by each bath, including websites to check access and opening times. For information on the history and architecture of each establishment, see the entries in the relevant chapters of this guide.

Dandár: Supplied originally with water brought across the river in casks from the Gellért, but now from its own purpose-drilled borehole. This is a very local bath house, frequented by a mainly elderly clientèle, often with doctors' notes. There are hot pools of 36°C and 38°C, both outside and inside, as well as a cold plunge pool inside. The buffet is in the basement. No swimming pool. *District IX. Dandár u. 5. Map p. 427, B6. en.dandarfurdo.hu.*

Gellért: The entrance to the spa is on the right-hand side of the Gellért Hotel building, round the corner. The facilities comprise an indoor pool in a beautiful columned hall with a glass roof that can be opened in summer. At one end is a hot pool and at the other, on either side, are the entrances to the thermal and steam baths. These used to be segregated, men on the right and women on the left, but are now unisex. Both have two large thermal pools (temperatures between 35° and 40°C), a cold plunge pool and steam room. Though both are lavishly decorated, the former men's baths are much finer, with mosaic inlay and coloured glazed ceramic details by the Zsolnay manufactory. Above the indoor pool is the buffet, with a wide terrace giving onto the outdoor swimming pool, which has a wave machine. There is ample space for sunbathing and on an upper level is a hot tub and sauna. *District XI. Kelenhegyi út 4. Map p. 427, A5. gellertfurdo.hu.*

Király: Unisex Ottoman-era baths between Margaret Bridge and Batthyány tér. From the ticket office you are directed upstairs to the changing lockers, and then back down again to the bathing pools. The central domed hall is very fine, with a warm water-pool in the centre and a hot pool at the side. At the back is the steam room, with a cold plunge pool just outside it. This is the one bath that, at the time of writing, had not been renovated and, in the Turkish thermal section at least, there is a real sense of the ages. This atmosphere is less appropriate in the massage and treatments sections: the facilities look outdated and cheerless. In the garden courtyard there is a small hot tub and loungers where you can relax with a drink from the buffet. It is scruffy but pleasant. *District II. Fő u. 84. Map p. 424, D3. kiralyfurdo.hu.*

Lukács: The Lukács is the bath house that most has the air of a medical facility (and it is popularly used as such: you will see plenty of people doing underwater gym classes). Though neither as opulent as the Széchenyi nor as ancient as the Király (though it does preserve the remains of an Ottoman powder mill), its water is regarded as the most efficacious (it is important not to stay in it too long).

Entrance to the ticket office is either from the Danube side, or from Frankel Leó út past the columned pump room (where you can get mugs of the water to drink). Beyond it you pass through a cobbled courtyard shaded by plane trees. Against a wall is a statue of St Luke on a solomonic column and on the walls themselves, numerous plaques placed in thanks for cures received.

The interior is labyrinthine. There is an outdoor thermal bubble bath and whirlpool; an indoor thermal section with pools ranging from 24°C to 40°C; saunas; areas for massage and mud treatments; and two outdoor swimming pools (cap obligatory), adorned with the statutory female nude (kneeling at the brim to fill a water jar). Behind her is a plaque listing the famous people who have enjoyed the waters here, among them Zoltán Kodály. A tall outdoor stairway leads up to the fitness terrace and sun terrace, a pleasant place to occupy a lounger, either in the sunshine or under the plane-tree shade, overlooking the rooftops. *District II. Frankel Leó út 25–29. Map p. 424, D2. lukacsfurdo.hu.*

Széchenyi: Know before you go if you want a locker or a cabin. The side entrance leads to lockers only. For cabins, enter by the main door. The locker option means that you change in a wooden cabin, then move your things to a locker which you secure with your proxy watch.

The indoor baths offer a succession of different bathing halls. A beautiful columned steam room, with a central large pool, is followed by a succession of plunge pools and saunas, all variously decorated. The clientèle is a mix of locals and tourists (in high summer it is almost all tourists, except in the early morning). The Széchenyi also specialises in 'sparties', thermal carousing sessions.

The stuccoed buffet has a small and quite pricey offering. There are other refreshment stalls around the outdoor pools, which comprise a swimming pool (cap required) and two warm-water pools (one of them with a whirlpool). It is by one of these that men famously congregate to play chess. *District XIV. Állatkerti körút 9–11. Map p. 426, C2. szechenyifurdo.hu.*

Rudas: Decide which sections you want to visit: you can get a ticket to the entire complex (thermal section, swimming pool and wellness centre), or just to part of it. The thermal baths consist of a lovely Ottoman domed pool with triangular corner pools around it (*NB: This has separate men's and women's days: men on Mon and Wed–Fri, women on Tues, mixed on Sat–Sun*). You will be given a sheet and a modesty cloth; you do not need your own towel. (Nor do you need a swimsuit on segregated men's or women's days, but some bathers wear them.)

The swimming pool is in a large, light hall surrounded by double arcades. The wellness centre includes a sun terrace and hot tub on the roof overlooking the Danube. There is a buffet selling basic snacks. *District I. Döbrentei tér 9, just at the Buda end of Elizabeth Bridge. Map p. 425, D5. rudasfurdo.hu.*

Veli Bej: The Veli Bej baths are attached to a hospital run by the Brothers Hospitallers but the bathing complex is open to the public on a separate basis (*open mornings and afternoons, closed in the middle of the day; consult the website for up-to-date opening hours*). It is popular with a younger age group than the other Turkish baths. When you buy your ticket you will also be given a locker number. There are cabins to change in; the locker is for safe storage of your belongings (a similar arrangement to the Széchenyi; *see above*). Your ticket allows you to stay in the baths for 3hrs.

The baths are arranged in a square, with the domed Ottoman bath house in the centre. On either side are: to the left, the saunas and rainforest shower; to the right, the jacuzzi and heated swimming pool. The café is outside the bathing area, in the entrance hall. *District II. Árpád fejedelem u. 7. Entrance is from the Danube side, through the café. Map p. 424, D2. www.irgalmasrend.hu/site/velibej/home.*

SWIMMING POOLS

Budapest has a number of swimming pools. The two loveliest are the **Palatinus** on Margaret Island (*map p. 424, D1; palatinusstrand.hu*), with outdoor swimming pools, adventure pools and a wellness centre; and **Csillaghegy**, fed by a natural spring, in a very pleasant garden and known since Roman times (*District III. Pusztakúti út 2–6; accessible by HÉV suburban train line H5. Beyond map p. 430, C1. csillaghegyistrand.hu*).

ENTERTAINMENT, FESTIVALS & EVENTS

English-language listings of concerts can be found on the Koncert Kalendárium website (*muzsikalendarium.hu*). For listings in all categories, see *est.hu*. The Opera House was closed for renovation when this book went to press and performances were taking place at the Erkel Theatre (*see opera.hu*). For the Liszt Academy concert programme, see *zeneakademia.hu* and for the Müpa events space, see *mupa.hu*. Hungary has many fine orchestras and vocal ensembles. Look out in particular for concerts by the Budapest Festival Orchestra. Works by the two great Hungarian classical masters, Bartók and Kodály, invariably form part of any musical programme.

Plays and films in English are often screened at the Uránia Film Theatre (*see urania-nf.hu for details*). Tickets for all events can be bought at the venues' box offices but generally online as well. The 'Ticket Master' website (*jegymester.hu*) can be very useful.

HUNGARIAN FOLK MUSIC

Hungary has an important and distinctive folk tradition, kept alive by a large number of bands and dance ensembles. Stars such as the singer Márta Sebestyén, the Muzsikás ensemble and jazz-folk saxophonist Mihály Dresch still perform live and are also now handing on the baton to a host of talented newcomers. You can try your hand at folk dancing at one of the Táncház (Dance House) teaching sessions, or simply turn up to listen to a concert. **Fonó** is a well-known venue (*District XI, between Etele út and Andor utca; map p. 430, B3; see fono.hu for precise directions and programmes*). Traditional instruments include the *cimbalom* (dulcimer), *tilinkó* (a wooden pipe), violin, viola and *gardon* (a sort of cello that is hit with a stick). For information on concerts, Dance House sessions and events, see the Dance House Guild website (*tanchaz.hu*).

GYPSY MUSIC AND ROMA MUSIC

The music played by gypsy ensembles, a traditional accoutrement of many restaurants and taverns (now much rarer in Budapest than formerly), is known as *cigányzene* (lit. 'gypsy music') and takes the form of short pseudo-folk songs, *nóták*, similar in theme and cadence to the real thing, either merry or doleful and many of them well-known repertoire staples. A party of diners enjoying the music will often request a favourite *nóta* and join in with the singing, sometimes raucously if they are well enough watered. If you request a tune (the ensembles have a wide repertoire which includes all the international evergreens), it is customary to show your appreciation with a small tip.

Roma music, played by bands or soloists of Hungary's Roma minority, can also be enjoyed in Budapest. Well-known names from recent decades include Kalyi Jag, Mitsoura, Kálmán Balogh (and his cimbalom band) and Romano Drom, who use traditional instruments like the milk churn and spoons. Félix Lajkó plays music of many genres, including Roma and Balkan. The 100 Tagú Cigányzenekar (lit. the 'Hundred-member Gypsy Orchestra), known in English as the Budapest Gypsy Symphony Orchestra, gives regular concerts of classical music (particularly Brahms and Strauss). They have received the 'Hungarikum' accolade (*see p. 355*).

FESTIVALS AND EVENTS

Budapest is a lively city and there are events going on throughout the year, both across the capital and locally, for example in the 'Piknik' street festivals, held for example on Bródy Sándor utca in May or on Pozsonyi út in late summer. We Love Budapest (*welovebudapest.com*) maintains a complete listing, with dates and links. A few highlights are given below, ordered as far as possible by season (though of course dates and venues are subject to annual change).

Spring: The **Spring Festival** in March–April offers music, theatre and dance at venues across town (*btf.hu*). Musicians and dance troupes from all over the Carpathian Basin converge on Budapest for the **Dance House Festival** (*tanchaztalalkozo.hu*). Millenáris Park hosts the **International Book Festival**. The **Margo Festival of Literature** (*margofeszt.hu*) is held in spring and autumn.

Summer: Brain Bar Budapest, in early June, sees innovators and mould-breakers from across the world converge on the city for a series of lectures and debates (*brainbar.com*). **Múzeumok Éjszakája**, the 'Night of Museums' (*muzej.hu*), has been held every midsummer since 2003. Museums keep their doors open long into the night and there is also the opportunity to visit some places not normally open to the public.

A single wristband gains you entry to all the participating institutions. Summer is also the season of the **Hungarian Grand Prix** and the enormously popular **Sziget music festival**, always with star headliners, on the 'Island of Freedom', Óbudai-sziget (*szigetfestival.com*). There is also an open-air **festival on Margaret Island** and crowds line the Danube to watch the **Red Bull Air Race**. August 20th is **St Stephen's Day**, when the saint's Holy Right Hand (*see p. 159*) is solemnly paraded around town. The celebrations culminate in a spectacular fireworks display on the Danube.

Autumn: The **Budapest Wine Festival** is held in the precincts of the royal palace on Castle Hill in early September. Stalls from leading Hungarian wineries offer tastings of their range (*aborfesztival.hu*). The **Jewish Cultural Festival**, centred around the Great Synagogue, is a week-long celebrations of Jewish music, dance, art and literature, with performers from Hungary and beyond. September also sees Heroes' Square turned into a race track, with grandstands in front of the two museums, for Hungary's answer to the Siena Palio: the **National Gallop** (Nemzeti Vágta; *en.vagta.hu*), with horse racing and jumping as well as Hungarian stunt riding and carriage contents. If you miss it and feel like a day out at the races, Budapest's racing track is at Kincsem

Park (*map p. 431, D2; kincsempark.hu*).

In October **CAFe Budapest** (*cafebudapestfest.hu*) is a two-week contemporary arts festival. The annual **Art Market Budapest** in Millenáris Park brings Hungarian and international contemporary artists and photographers together in a four-day fair (*artmarketbudapest.hu*).

Autumn draws to a close with **St Martin's Day** (Szent Márton napja), November 11th, customarily the day when the first wines of the year's vintage are released. It is also traditional to eat goose. Restaurants across town offer St Martin's Day menus of goose broth, goose liver and confit of goose leg served with red cabbage.

Winter: Advent and Christmas markets are a big part of the Budapest winter season (*see p. 356*). A **Chinese New Year concert** (Nagy Kínai Újév) is held in February at the Müpa concert hall and the **Mangalica Festival** (*mangalicafesztival.hu*) in Szabadság tér celebrates the native breed of woolly pig (*see p. 348*), from nose to tail. This is also the time of the **Carnival Gala season** at the Opera House and Erkel Theatre. Speeches, military processions and tricolour cockades honour **Hungary's National Day** on 15th March, the anniversary of the beginning of the 1848–9 anti-Habsburg Revolution.

LANGUAGE

Hungarian has certain affinities with Turkish and Finnish but ultimately is a language in a category of its own, with no close relatives. The Hungarians inhabit a lonely linguistic island surrounded by a sea of Slav, Germanic and Romance tongues.

Hungarian names are given surname first (Kovács Emma). In this guide, they are given in the more customary European style of given name followed by surname, unless the name is used as the name of a street or square, in which case it is written Hungarian-style. The suffix -*né* means 'Mrs'. Kovács Pálné = Mrs Paul Kovács (the usage is becoming less popular among younger women, who tend to keep their own names).

The stress in Hungarian always falls on the first syllable of a word and pronunciation is phonetic, according to the following rules:

Vowels

a   similar to the *o* in 'hot'
á   like the *a* in 'arm'
e   as in 'ten'
é   like the *a* in 'say'
i   as in 'sit'
í   like the *ee* in 'seek'
o   like the *o* in 'old'
ó   longer than the above, similar to the *oo* in 'door'
ö   a short schwa, like the *a* in 'pizza'
ő   longer than the above, similar to the *u* in 'fur'
u   like the *u* in 'put'
ú   like the *u* in 'rule'
ü   like the *u* in the French '*tu*'
ű   like the above but longer

Consonants

Pronounced as in English with the following exceptions:

c   *ts*
cs   *ch*
g   always hard, as in 'grass'
gy   like the soft *du* of 'during'
j   like the *y* in 'yellow'
ly   like the *y* in 'yellow'
ny   like the *gn* in 'cognac'
s   like the *sh* in 'sheep'
sz   like the *s* in 'sleep'
ty   like the soft *t* in 'tune'
zs   like the *g* in 'beige'

SOME USEFUL WORDS

nyitva	open	nagy	large
zárva	closed	kis, kicsi	small
Vigyázz!	Caution!	hosszú	long
tolni	push	rövid	short
húzni	pull	jó	good, OK
mosdó	WC	rossz	out of order, wrong
Hölgyek/Nők	Ladies		
Férfiak	Gents	Köszönöm!	Thank you
szabad	free, allowed	Jó reggelt!	Good morning
foglalt	engaged, occupied	Jó napot!	Good day
gyerek	child	Jó estét!	Good evening
felnőtt	adult	Jó éjszakát!	Good night
jobbra	right	Elnézést!	Sorry
balra	left	Viszontlátásra!	Goodbye
igen	yes	Szia!	Hi / 'Bye
nem	no		
tilos	forbidden	cukrászda	cake shop, pâtisserie

Hungarian	English	Hungarian	English
étterem	restaurant	hétfő	Monday
kávéház	coffee house	kedd	Tuesday
kávézó, presszó	café	szerda	Wednesday
vendéglő	simple restaurant	csütörtök	Thursday
söröző	beer bar	péntek	Friday
patika	pharmacy	szombat	Saturday
piac	market	vasárnap	Sunday

Hungarian	English	Hungarian	Number
fasor	avenue	egy	1
ház	house	kettő	2
hegy	hill	három	3
híd	bridge	négy	4
kert	garden	öt	5
körút	ring road or boulevard	hat	6
korzó	corso, esplanade	hét	7
köz	alley	nyolc	8
lépcső	steps	kilenc	9
palota	palace	tíz	10
pályaudvar	railway station	húsz	20
	(abbreviated to pu.	harminc	30
	on maps and signs)	negyven	40
rakpart	quay, embankment	ötven	50
sétány	promenade	hatvan	60
templom	church	hetven	70
tér	square	nyolcvan	80
tó	lake, pond	kilencven	90
udvar	court, courtyard	száz	100
út	road	ezer	1000
utca	street		

ADDITIONAL INFORMATION

BUDAPEST WITH CHILDREN

Budapest is a child-friendly city and Hungarians are welcoming to children. There are plenty of things to keep them occupied: cycle rickshaws and the Palatinus swimming pool on Margaret Island; the zoo and carousel in City Park; the Budapest Eye ferris wheel; the Miniversum model railway on Andrássy út; a boat trip on the Danube. There are public playgrounds all over the city: one of the nicest is on Szabadság tér. Adults can admire the architecture while the children play in the sandpit or in the nearby interactive fountain. Note that the thermal baths are not open to children under 14.

CRIME AND PERSONAL SECURITY

The Tourist Office operates a 24-hour hotline where English is spoken (*T: +36 1 438*

8080). The main office in central Pest, at Sütő u. 2 (near Deák tér; *map p. 428, C3*), is open daily 8–8 and can organise help if you need it.

As in cities all over the world, pick-pocketing can be a problem. Don't carry valuables in handbags and take care on public transport, in crowded markets and around the main railway stations. Hungarian law requires everyone to carry some form of photo ID: it is best to keep your passport with you at all times.

The European emergency telephone number is 112.

MONEY AND ATMs

The Hungarian unit of currency is the forint. Note that there are no 1- or 2-forint coins in circulation. Sums are simply rounded up or rounded down. If you buy something costing 998 Ft, you will be charged 1000; alternatively, if your bill comes to 1,002 Ft you will only be asked for 1000.

ATMs are widely distributed across the city. It is better to use the ones attached to banks than the stand-alone cashpoints, which charge a higher commission. Credit and debit cards are generally accepted in Budapest and for smaller payments the contactless system is widespread.

OPENING HOURS

Museums and monuments: Hours of admission are given with individual entries in the text, but opening times often change, so always check before you visit. Almost all museums have websites. Ticket offices usually close 30–60mins before closing time. Museums are typically closed on Mondays (though not if it is a public holiday)

Shops and businesses: Most shops are open daily from 10am to 6pm. Smaller or more traditional establishments close for a couple of hours at lunchtime and are closed from 1 or 2pm on Sat and all day Sun. Larger shops and shopping centres are open on Sundays. Food shops often keep longer hours.

Places of worship: Churches and synagogues which are also tourist attractions have official opening times, given with individual entries in the text. An entrance fee is payable. The Matthias Church, Inner City Parish Church, Great Synagogue and Orthodox Synagogue are in this category. A couple of other churches are also kept open during the day: the University Church, the church on Szervita tér and St Ladislas in Kőbánya. Other churches and synagogues are open for services only, although in the case of many of the churches, you can go into the entrance vestibule and look through the main glass doors into the nave.

Church orientation: In church descriptions in this guide, the terms 'north' and 'south' refer to liturgical north (the left-hand side) and south (right-hand side), taking the high altar as being at the east end.

PHARMACIES

Some medicines that are widely available over the counter in other countries can only be bought on prescription in Hungary. It is advisable to bring any necessary supplies with you when you travel. At the time of writing there were two central pharmacies open round the clock. In Pest there is the Teréz Patika in District VI (*Teréz körút 41, T: + 36 1 311 4439; map p. 429, D2*) and in Buda the Széna Tér Patika (*Széna tér 1, T: + 36 1 225 7830; map p. 428, A1*).

PUBLIC HOLIDAYS

The main holidays in Hungary, when offices and schools are closed, are as follows:

1 January	New Year's Day
15 March	Start of the 1848 War of Independence
Good Friday	Easter long weekend
Easter Monday	Easter long weekend
1 May	Labour Day
Whit Monday	
20 August	Feast of St Stephen (Szent István)
23 October	Start of the 1956 Uprising
1 November	All Saints' Day
25 December	Christmas Day
26 December	Boxing Day

If the public holiday falls on a Tuesday or Thursday, the Monday before or the Friday following will also be taken as days off. A Saturday at some other time of year will be converted into a working day to make up for this. If the public holiday falls on a weekend, no compensatory day off is given.

Public transport operates to a Sunday schedule on public holidays. Buses and trams often sport little national flags.

PUBLIC TOILETS

Public toilets are not easy to find in Budapest and are not always in pristine condition when you do (though the newer ones are excellent). All museums have WCs. Otherwise you will need to visit a café or a hotel.

TELEPHONES AND THE INTERNET

Free wifi is widely available in hotels, restaurants and cafés. The country dialling code for Hungary is + 36. The city code for Budapest is 1. When making calls internally in Hungary, preface the number with 06 instead of 36 (though +36 will always work from a mobile).

TIPPING

Bills in restaurants sometimes include a service charge and sometimes not; it is always worth checking before you pay. If no service charge is included, it is customary to add 10–15 percent, not by leaving change on the table but by telling the person you are paying how much change you wish to receive or how much extra you are giving them. The same applies to taxi drivers.

Glossary of Terms

Ambulatory, section of a church curving around and behind the high altar

Annunciation, the delivering of the news to the Virgin that she is to bear the Son of God

Antefix, architectural ornament, usually of terracotta, traditionally placed at the roofline of Etruscan or Roman temples to hide the ends of the roof tiles

Apostles, those who spread the Christian word following the death of Christ, initially twelve in number (the disciples excluding Judas but with his replacement Matthias) and later including St Paul and his followers

Apse, wall recess, usually semicircular and vaulted, often at the end of an aisle or sanctuary at the liturgical east end of a church

Architrave, the horizontal beam placed above supporting columns, the lowest part of an entablature (*qv*); the horizontal lintel above a door or window

Arrow Cross, the Hungarian Nazi party (Nyilaskeresztes Párt in Hungarian), whose emblem was a Greek cross with arrow tips at the end of the arms. Under Ferenc Szálasi, they were in power from October 1944 until the end of WWII

Art Deco Stylised, often geometric art and architecture of the 1920s and '30s

Art Nouveau design style originating in the late 19th century, curving and feminine, asymmetrical, making use of floral motifs, leaves and vine tendrils

Assumption, the ascension of the Virgin to Heaven

Aster Revolution, revolution of October 1918 following the disintegration of the Austro-Hungarian empire into national blocs. The revolution brought Mihály Károlyi (*see p. 246*) to power in a republican Hungary after the resignation of the Prime Minister Sándor Wekerle and the stepping down of King Charles IV. The uprising took its name from the aster flowers (Michaelmas daisies) which the revolutionaries wore as their emblem

Atlas (pl. atlantes), sculpted figure or figures of the god Atlas, used as supporting columns

Attic, in architecture, the topmost storey, or the vertical wall above the top cornice used as a support for decoration and/or inscriptions

Aumbry, cupboard or recess in a church wall for storing ritual vessels

Baldachin, canopy supported by columns or other uprights

Basilica, originally a Roman building used for public administration; in Christian architecture, an aisled church with a clerestory (*qv*) and apse (*qv*)

Bas-relief, sculpture in low relief

Bauhaus, design school founded by Walter Gropius in Weimar, Germany, in 1919 and which came to be associated with clear, clean, Functionalism, the aim being to link art with industry, mass-produced affordability with aesthetics

Biedermeier, a term that refers to the period between 1815 (Congress of Vienna) and 1848 (outbreak of revolution), an era in Central Europe that was characterised by political stability and a growing middle class. The stability was ensured by a system of rigid central control and press censorship, and the spheres of painting, applied arts, literature and music, took mainly safe domestic, historical or natural history subjects as their themes

Biga, in Classicist sculpture, a two-horse chariot

Bimah, in a synagogue, the raised platform from which the Torah is read

Boss, on a shield, a convex attachment, usually of metal, placed in the centre to protect the wearer's hand

Cabochon, of a gemstone, smoothed and polished but not cut into facets

Caduceus, the rod of Mercury, the messenger god, a short staff around which twine two serpents

Caldarium (pl. caldaria), the hot room in an ancient Roman bath house

Capital, the top or head of a column

Caryatid, supporting column in the form of a sculpted female figure

Castrum, an ancient Roman military camp

Cenotaph, literally 'empty tomb', a monument to someone whose body is lost or buried elsewhere

Chancel, part of a church to the liturgical east of the crossing (*qv*), including the sanctuary, where the clergy officiate, and the choir

Chi-Rho, Christian symbol formed by the superimposition of the first two letters of Christ's name in Greek, X and P

Cilice, an instrument worn to mortify the flesh, typically taking the form of a tight metal band, spiked belt, garter or hair shirt, worn under ordinary clothing

Clerestory, uppermost part of the nave wall of a church, above the side aisles, pierced by windows

Cloisonné, type of enamel decoration, where areas of colour are partitioned by narrow strips of metal

Coffer, in a wooden or masonry ceiling, a recessed section or sunken panel

Columbarium, in an early cemetery, a walled area with niches for urns containing the ashes of the dead

Constructivism, art movement that originated in Communist Russia, a branch of Geometrical Abstraction and much used for social and propaganda purposes. It was supported by Trotsky, after whose fall it began to lose ground, eventually being supplanted by Socialist Realism

Contrapposto, a pose in which the body is twisted so that hips and shoulders balance each other, first used in Classical statuary

Corbel, projecting block, usually of stone, to support an arch or beam

Corinthian, ancient Greek and Roman order of architecture, a characteristic of which is the column capital decorated with sculpted acanthus leaves

Couchant, in heraldry, describes a recumbent posture

Cour d'Honneur, a monumental forecourt, often flanked by symmetrical side wings

Crenellated, of a wall or parapet, with alternate indented and elevated sections forming a battlement

Crocketed, of a spire, decorated along the ribs with curved elements of moulded foliage

Crossing, the part of a church where the nave (central aisle) and transepts (side arms) meet

Cyclopean, of a wall, made of large, rough-hewn blocks arranged as they fit, in uneven courses

Damascened, of metalwork, denoting an object typically of iron or steel inlaid with a pattern in other metals such as gold and silver

Diocletian window, large window in the shape of a demi-lune. It takes its name from apertures of the same shape in the Baths of Diocletian in Rome

Dionysiac, pertaining to Dionysus or Bacchus, the ancient Greek and Roman god of wine and revelry

Doric, ancient Greek order of architecture characterised by fluted columns with no base, and a plain capital

Dormition, the death of the Virgin, represented in art as a 'falling-asleep'

Easter Sepulchre, side chapel or arched recess in a church that is decorated at Easter time to evoke the tomb of Christ

Eclectic, type of architecture that evolved in the later 19th century, borrowing elements from more than one Historicist (*qv*) style, for example mixing neo-Baroque with neo-Renaissance forms

Electrum, a naturally-occurring gold and silver alloy

Emblema (pl. emblemata), central panel of a mosaic or ancient wall painting, often showing a well-known scene from mythology

Entablature, the continuous horizontal element (consisting of architrave, frieze and cornice) above the column capitals of a Classical or Neoclassical building

Eosin, in chemistry, a red fluorescent compound. Eosin ceramic glazes were pioneered in Hungary by the Zsolnay (*qv*) manufactory. At first, they were red or pink but later new colours were introduced: blue, purple and green

Eravisci, the Eraviscans, a Celtic people of ancient Transdanubia who had an important settlement on Gellért Hill. They were absorbed and assimilated by the Romans in the 1st century BC

Etrog, the citron, one of the ritual elements of the Jewish feast of Sukkot

Evangelists, the writers of the gospels, Matthew, Mark, Luke and John, often represented in art by their symbols: a man (or angel), a lion, a bull and an eagle

Fibula, a pin used to fasten clothing. It was an important element of the dress of the pre-Roman Celtic peoples. The finest examples are intricately fashioned and set with precious stones

Frigidarium (pl. frigidaria), the cold room in an ancient Roman bath house

Giant Order, order of architecture where the columns or pilasters have a vertical span of two or more storeys

Gothic, medieval architectural style that flourished in Europe from the 12th–16th centuries, characterised by pointed arches, vaulted interiors and traceried (*qv*) windows

Greek cross, a cross with vertical and transverse arms of equal length

Grisaille, painting in tones of grey

Hellenistic, ancient Greek culture of the period between the death of Alexander the Great (323 BC) to the victory of Rome over Antony and Cleopatra (30 BC)

Hemicycle, a semicircular structure or space

Historicist, architecture that reuses a style from the past: neo-Romanesque, neo-Gothic, Neoclassical, neo-Baroque or neo-Renaissance. It was particularly popular in the 19th century

Hungarian Millennium, the celebrations held in the year 1896 to commemorate a thousand years since the Magyars first occupied the Carpathian Basin. The main venue of the celebrations was City Park. Heroes' Square was laid out for the occasion and the first underground railway was built along Andrássy út to convey visitors to the park. In 1996, a 'millecentenary' was held

Hypocaust, ancient Roman heating system in which hot air was made to circulate under the floor and sometimes between double walls

Iconostasis, screen in a Byzantine church holding icons and also serving to separate the sanctuary from the nave and thus the clergy from the laity

Ionic, an order of Classical architecture identified by its capitals decorated with volutes (scrolls)

Keramit, durable, frost-resistant clay-based material, of a characteristic yellow ochre colour, that was widely used to pave road surfaces and line pavements

Kiddush, in Hebrew, 'sanctification', a blessing recited to mark Jewish holy days, after which wine may be drunk from a special goblet

Kippah, a skullcap

K. und K., abbreviation for *kaiserlich und königlich*, 'imperial and royal', a designation used during the period of the Dual Monarchy of Austria-Hungary

Lady Chapel, in a church, a chapel dedicated to the Virgin

Latin cross, cross where the vertical arm is longer than the transverse arm

Lunette, semicircular space in a vault or ceiling, often decorated with a painting or relief

Mandorla, tapered, almond-shaped aura around a holy figure (usually Christ or the Virgin)

Mascaron, decorative element in the form of a carved head or face

Menorah, in Jewish iconography, the seven-branched candelabrum

Mihrab, niche in the wall of a mosque indicating the direction of Mecca

Mikveh, Jewish ritual bath house or bathing pool

Millennium (*see Hungarian Millennium*)

Mithraic, pertaining to the cult of Mithras (*see p. 112*)

Monolith, monolithic, in sculpture or architecture, made from a single block of stone

Nagybánya, a town in Transylvania (now Baia Mare, Romania) which gave its name to the artists' colony founded there in 1896 by the painters Simon Hollósy, Károly Ferenczy and others. Its original focus was on naturalistic, *plein-air* painting. Other founder-members were Béla Iványi Grünwald, István Réti and István Thorma. Hollósy left the colony in 1902, after which its leading figure became Ferenczy. After the Treaty of Trianon in 1920, when Transylvania was given to Romania, many Hungarian artists left the colony. István Thorma was one who remained, opening it to art students from Bucharest

Necropolis, a cemetery, from the Greek meaning 'city of the dead'

Niello, a black substance composed of silver and lead inlaid into stone to make an incised design stand out

Nike, winged female figure representing Victory (*Nike* in Greek)

Numerus clausus, literally 'closed number', in a Budapest context referring specifically to the law of 1920 restricting university entrance along ethnic lines, a measure which particularly penalised Hungarian Jews

Oculus, round window or other aperture

Octastyle, of a Classical portico, having eight columns

Oinochoë, an ancient Greek type of pitcher for serving wine

Oppidum (pl. oppida), a fortified settlement, particularly of the ancient Celtic peoples

Opus quadratum, masonry of large

rectangular blocks laid without mortar

Organic architecture, building style of the 20th century, associated in Hungary with Imre Makovecz. Its forms imitate the shapes of nature and borrow from folk iconography and it aims to integrate built forms with the landscape around them

Palaeochristian, early Christian, dating from the first centuries after the faith took root

Panel apartments, blocks of flats made of prefabricated concrete panels, typically around 8–10 storeys high and grouped together in large housing estates, which began to appear in Budapest from the mid-1960s

Parabolic, of an arch, inverted U-shaped, broader at the base and tapering towards the top

Pauline, pertaining to a monastic order of Hungarian foundation (the only one), founded by the Blessed Eusebius in 1250 and named after Paul the Hermit, a 4th-century anchorite in the Egyptian desert

Pediment, gable above the portico of a Classical building; also above a door or window, either triangular in form or curved (segmental)

Pendentive, concave spandrel (*qv*) beneath the four 'corners' of a dome

Pier, a square or compound pillar used as a support in architecture

Pilaster, shallow pier or rectangular column projecting slightly from the wall

Polyptych, painting or tablet in more than three sections

Porte-cochère, canopied entranceway that allows a conveyance to drive up to a doorway and discharge its passengers under cover from the elements

Predella, narrow panel, usually divided into sections, each decorated with a separate scene, attached to the bottom of an altarpiece

Putto (pl. putti), sculpted or painted figure, usually nude, of a chubby male child, without wings

Pyrogranite, architectural faïence for exterior decorative use developed by the Zsolnay manufactory (*qv*). Fired at very high temperatures, the resulting glazed ceramic is resistant to heat and frost

Red-figure ware, Greek pottery style of the 6th–4th centuries BC where the figures appear in red against a black ground

Religio recepta, lit. 'received religion', a term used in the Habsburg lands to denote a faith that was recognised by public law and whose adherents enjoyed full freedom of conscience. Lutheranism and Calvinism were permitted after the Edict of Tolerance in 1782 and received full *religio recepta* status in 1791, together with Greek Catholicism. Unitarianism became a *religio recepta* 1848 and Judaism in 1895

Reliquary, casket, monstrance or other container for preserving and displaying the relics of a saint

Revivalist, in architecture, a reworking of a style from the past

Rococo, frothy, highly ornamented design style of the 18th-century

Roman School, group of artists who received scholarships to the Hungarian Academy in Rome from the late 1920s. Most were influenced by Classical and Renaissance models as well as by the anti-avant garde ethos of the Italian Novecento, and many brought an interesting fusion of styles to ecclesiastical commissions: altarpieces for the Jazz Age. Artists of the Roman School include Pál Molnár-C., Béla Kontuly, Vilmos Aba-Novák and Tibor Vilt

Romanesque, European architectural style

of the 7th–12th centuries, preceding the Gothic and typified by sturdy columns supporting round arches

Rovásírás, the runic script of the ancient Magyars, read from right to left

Rundbogenstil, literally 'round arch style', a type of Historicist architecture, neo-Romanesque in character, that was popular in Central Europe in the mid–late 19th century

Rustication, the robust effect given when grooves or channels are cut at the joints between slabs of masonry (ashlar) cladding

Sanctuary, in a church, the area at the liturgical east end, traditionally used by the clerics and the choir, while the congregations sits in the nave and aisles

Scythian, pertaining to the Scythians, ancient Eurasian nomadic peoples who flourished between the 9th and 1st centuries BC and who are known for their animal art featuring stylised beasts

Secession, art and architecture movement that began in response to the Vienna Secession of 1897, when a group led by Gustav Klimt officially left the Association of Artists. The Secession style in Hungary is broadly an equivalent of Art Nouveau, though as well as departing from Historicist, academic models it also sought to develop a distinctively Hungarian idiom. The name most readily associated with the movement is Ödön Lechner

Seder, Jewish feast, held on the first night of Passover, at which symbolic foods are traditionally eaten, served on a special Seder plate

Sedilia, in Gothic architecture, a stone bench or bank of seating divided into individual recesses, set into a wall

Serlian, describes a style of tripartite aperture with a taller central round-arched section flanked by two lower lateral sections with trabeated (square) tops. It was much used by the architect Palladio

Sgraffito, decorative technique whereby a surface is coated in two layers of contrasting colours and a design is scratched into the surface, revealing the colour of the layer underneath

Silenus, in Classical mythology, a drunken satyr, companion and mentor to Dionysus

Socialist Realist, style of figurative art that was predominant during the 1950s, the era of Soviet-style Communism. Its typical themes are happy family life, motherhood and toiling workers, both industrial and agricultural, portraying scenes of productivity and peaceful co-existence

Soffit, the underside of an arch

Solidus, late Roman gold coin. Its name is the origin of the French *sou*

Solomonic column, a twisted, 'barley sugar' column

Spandrel, surface between two arches in an arcade or the triangular space on either side of an arch

Spolia, ancient stones or other architectural elements that have been reused as construction material in more recent buildings

Stele (pl. stelae), upright stone slab with a commemorative function

Stigmatised, in Christian iconography, meaning bearing the stigmata, the marks of the wounds of Christ

Stilted arch, a rounded arch that rises vertically a short way, as if on stilts, before it begins to curve

Stoup, vessel for Holy Water, usually placed near the entrance of a church

String course, horizontal band of masonry, either plain or moulded, stretching across an elevation of a building

Stripped Classicism, also known as Grecian Moderne, a 20th-century architectural style which uses the forms of Greek Classical architecture without the attendant ornament

Swabians, German settlers (in Hungarian *Svábok*) who were invited to Hungary in the 18th century to recolonise parts of the country that had become depopulated under the Ottomans

Székely Gate, traditional wooden entrance gate from the Székely lands in east Transylvania, often elaborately carved and comprising a wide carriage entrance and smaller lateral opening for pedestrians

Tardos marble, reddish-pink metamorphosed limestone from quarries around the town of Tardos, northwest of Budapest. Popularly used in architecture, for floors, steps and wall revetment, it is characterised by the inclusion of numerous fossils

Tepidarium, the warm room in an ancient Roman bath house

Tondo, a circular painting or sculpture

Torc, chunky, rigid metal neck ring of the type worn by Celts, Gauls and other 'barbarians' at the time of Roman imperial expansion

Tracery, system of carved and moulded ribs within a window aperture dividing it into patterned sections

Transept, the side arm of a church projecting to the right (liturgical south) or left (liturgical north) of the nave

Trefoil, decorated or moulded with three leaf or lobe shapes

Triptych, painting or tablet in three sections, often hinged together

Triton, a sea god

Trompe l'oeil, literally, a deception of the eye: illusionist decoration, painted architectural perspectives, etc.

Türbe, an Ottoman mausoleum, consisting of a single domed room, typically octagonal, containing a cenotaph of the deceased. The actual burial is in the ground beneath

Turul, in Magyar mythology, a large, eagle-like bird that appeared in a dream to Emese, prophesying that rivers of water would flow from her womb. The dream was interpreted to mean that Emese's descendants would conquer many lands, including those once ruled over by Attila the Hun. Emese's son, Álmos, became leader of the seven Magyar tribes. Under Álmos' son Attila, the tribes entered the Carpathian Basin

Terrazzo, style of flooring made of stone or glass chips bound with a cement-like material, arranged in patterns and polished to a smooth finish

Tuscan Doric, a simplified variant of the Doric order (*qv*) that was popular in Renaissance and Neoclassical architecture. The columns are unfluted and stand on a base

Tympanum, the space formed between lintel and arch above a doorway; or the triangular space enclosed by a pediment (*qv*)

Villa rustica, ancient Roman farmstead; a villa with agricultural land attached; the centre of an agricultural estate

Yeshiva, a Jewish school for studies of the Talmud, Torah and other sacred texts

Zopf, style of late Baroque exterior decoration that takes its name from the defining feature of looped stucco swags resembling braids (*Zopf* in German, *copf* in Hungarian)

Zsolnay, ceramic ware, both decorative and architectural, made by the company of the same name in Pécs, south Hungary (*see p. 395*)

Glossary of Artists

The list below is not exhaustive but contains notes on many of the painters, sculptors, architects and other artists whose work is encountered in this book.

Aba-Novák, Vilmos (1894–1941). Painter, subject to a wide range of early influences. He trained under Adolf Fényes, spent time in the Nagybánya artists' colony and in 1928 won a scholarship to Rome. His ecclesiastical works are a testimony to this. His favourite themes later became urban and rural crowds—circus troupes, musicians, artisans' shops, busy markets—painted in bold shades of navy blue, yellow and scarlet with large shafts of black.

Ágoston, Emil (1878–1921). Architect, born Emil Adler. He studied at the Technical University, then in Italy and afterwards spent time in Paris and Berlin. In Budapest he is known for his blocks of rental apartments as well as the Astoria Hotel (probably his most famous work). Buried in the Kozma utca cemetery.

Almási Balogh, Loránd (1869–1945). Architect. After graduating from the Technical University, he worked under Ignác Alpár and Ödön Lechner. He later taught at the School of Applied Arts, a post he was forced to relinquish during the Republic of Councils in 1919. He built country houses for the aristocracy and well-planned workers' housing in Budapest.

Alpár, Ignác (1855–1928). Architect, born Ignác Schöckl, the son of a Styrian carpenter. After studying under Alajos Hauszmann, he went on to become one of the architects who did most to transform the face of Budapest in the late 19th century and first decade of the 20th, teaming up with well-known sculptors to produce buildings in a broadly Eclectic style. Vajdahunyad Castle, the National Bank and former Stock Exchange were all built to his designs. Buried in Kerepesi Cemetery.

Árkay, Aladár (1868–1932). Architect in the Secessionist and early Modern tradition. A graduate of the Budapest Technical University, he first worked for Fellner and Helmer (Operetta Theatre) and later assisted Alajos Hauszmann on the royal palace in Buda. He teamed up with his father-in-law, Mór Kallina: the Buda Vigadó is one of the results of their partnership. Surviving works by him include the Serbian Embassy at the end of Andrássy út (much altered), the Calvinist church on Városligeti fasor, and his own villa in Buda. His son, Bertalan Árkay (1901–71), completed his greatest work, the Városmajor Church.

Bálint, Zoltán (1871–1939). Architect, born Zoltán Bleyer. After completing his studies, he entered the studio of Korb and Giergl and then, in 1897, went into partnership with Lajos Jámbor. A number of surviving works attest to the success of their collaboration, among them the house near City Park built for the sculptor György Zala to designs by Lechner. Buried in Kerepesi Cemetery.

Barabás, Miklós (1810–98). Painter and printmaker, one of the greatest names of the Biedermeier age in Hungary, especially known for his portraits (he was highly sought-after), though he also produced charming genre scenes and landscapes. Buried in Kerepesi Cemetery.

Barát, Béla (1888–1945). Architect, known especially for the buildings he produced in partnership with Ede Novák, notably the Georgia-ház at the Astoria crossroads.

Barcsay, Jenő (1900–88). Painter and mosaicist, working in both figurative and abstract styles, in a distinctive modern idiom. He was a member of the Szentendre School. His funeral was the first one Kerepesi Cemetery, since Communism began relaxing its strictures, to have an overtly religious content.

Bauer, Emil (1883–1956). Architect. His Corvin Cinema is an interesting combination of the 'Third Baroque' and Modernism. Bauer left Hungary and settled in Australia. He died in Sydney.

Bebo, Károly (d. 1779). Sculptor and stucco moulder known for the work he carried out in Buda, in the Austrian Baroque style, when in the employ of the Zichy family.

Beck, Ö. Fülöp (1873–1945). Beck studied metalworking at the College of Applied Arts, a pupil of Albert Schickedanz. He won a scholarship to Paris and began his career as a medallist, though he is also known for his small sculptures and reliefs. His first initial, Ö, was added by himself and stands for *ötvös*, 'metalworker' in Hungarian. He produced designs for a set of coins to be used under the Republic of

Councils and after its fall was debarred from teaching in state institutions. Though he had converted to Christianity in 1917, he was interned by the Nazis in 1944, escaped and took refuge in the cellar of a friend's house, from which he disappeared without trace in 1945.

Benczúr, Gyula (1844–1920) Painter. He studied first in Munich, then in Italy and France and is one of the finest exponents of the Hungarian academic tradition of history painting; the National Gallery has a number of important works by his hand. He also excelled at portraiture, producing likenesses of many illustrious sitters, including Count Gyula Andrássy and Empress Elisabeth.

Benedict, Gyula (*see Nagy, Izsó*)

Berény, Róbert (1887–1953). Painter, born Róbert Backofen. He is one of the 'Hungarian Fauves', his style influenced by Matisse while a student in Paris. He was a member of the avant garde group known as the Eight. His first wife found a job as secretary to Béla Kun and in 1919 Berény designed his famous '*To Arms!*' poster. After the fall of the Republic of Councils he fled to Vienna, then Berlin, where he briefly courted the young Marlene Dietrich before meeting and marrying his second wife, a cellist. *Woman Playing the Cello* (1928) in the Hungarian National Gallery, perhaps his most famous painting, is a portrait of her.

Bernáth, Aurél (1895–1982). Painter. Over the course of a long career he experimented with a number of styles, both figurative and abstract, but the movement with which he is perhaps most closely associated is the Nagybánya artists' colony, where he studied before WWI. In the '20s he lived in Vienna and Berlin and came under the sway of German Expressionism. On his return to Hungary he went back to his roots, becoming a leading member of the post-Nagybánya Gresham Circle. He also worked at the Szolnok artists' colony.

Bierbauer, Virgil (1893–1956). Architect and architectural historian. He designed a number of buildings in partnership with Kálmán Reichl.

Böhm, Henrik (1867–1936). Architect. In 1896 he opened a joint practice with Ármin Hegedűs (the former Török Bank building is their most famous co-production).

Borsos, Miklós (1906–90). Born in Transylvania, the son of a watchmaker. His family fled to west Hungary during WWI. Originally he planned to be a painter but turned to sculpture after a trip to Florence. For many years he taught at the College of Applied Arts but lost his job on ideological grounds. He produced busts and portrait sculpture but much of his best work is abstract or symbolic.

Bortnyik, Sándor (1893–1976). Painter and graphic artist in the Constructivist circle of Lajos Kassák. He spent three years in Weimar in the 1920s, where the Bauhaus was to have a profound influence on him. In Budapest he set up an art school known simply as The Workshop (Műhely). His Communist beliefs never deserted him; between 1949 and 1956 he was director of the School of Fine Art. Buried in Kerepesi Cemetery (appropriately under a Constructivist headstone).

Bory, Jenő (1879–1959). Architect, sculptor and teacher, a pupil of Alajos Stróbl. He pursued a course of study abroad, learning to carve marble in Carrara. His most famous buildings are in his native city of Székesfehérvár but there are a number of sculptural works by his hand in Budapest, notably some fine tombs in Kerepesi Cemetery.

Brein, Ferenc (1817–79) Architect, born in Pest. He began work as apprentice to his father and soon won independent commissions. His style is generally Romantic though somewhat eccentric. In Budapest he is remembered for the Csősztorony in Kőbánya and the Pekáry House on Király utca.

Bukovics, Gyula (1841–1914). Architect and engineer, director of Miklós Ybl's planning office. Throughout his own architectural career he clung to his master's neo-Renaissance style. He designed a number of the palaces along Andrássy út as well as the Agricultural Ministry building on Kossuth Lajos tér.

Conti, Lipót Antal (1708–73). Stonemason and sculptor of Italian descent. He came to Pest in the 1730s and worked on a number of buildings in the developing city.

Csíkszentmihályi, Róbert (b. 1940). Sculptor and medallist, a pupil of Pál Pátzay and Iván Szabó, known for his commemorative public works as well as sculpture for churches.

Csók, István (1865–1961). Painter, a pupil of Bertalan Székely and Károly Lotz. He later studied in Paris, where the art of the Impressionists had a great influence on him, and before WWI spent a number of summers in Nagybánya. It was nonetheless not the landscapes of Transylvania that were to be his true inspiration but those of Lake Balaton. His works are known for their bold and unabashed use of colour. Buried in Kerepesi Cemetery.

Csontváry Kosztka, Tivadar (1853–1919). Painter, a pupil of Simon Hollósy, though his works bear no resemblance to his master's, nor to any other member of the Nagybánya school or indeed to the work of any artist. Naïve and brightly coloured, Csontváry's eccentric painting is in a category of its own. He set out to paint what he termed the 'Path of the Sun', experimenting with rendering many different types of light: sunlight, firelight, moonlight, electric light, the eruptions of Etna. He was unappreciated in his lifetime. It was only after 1930 that his art came to be studied and admired. There is a representative selection of his paintings in the Hungarian National Gallery. Buried in Kerepesi Cemetery.

Csorba, Géza (1892–1974). Sculptor, known for his simplified, direct style. He specialised in portraits of artists and writers, particularly of the poet Endre Ady: many likenesses can be seen across town, including the funerary monument in Kerepesi Cemetery, for which the sculptor received great acclaim.

Czigány, Dezső (1883–1937). Painter, born Dezső Wimmer. He studied in Nagybánya under Simon Hollósy and then in Paris, where he was influenced by Cézanne, among others. He was a member of the Eight and is known particularly for his self-portraits and still lifes. The Hungarian National Gallery has a good selection of his works. His personal life is complicated and dark. His first wife died in suspicious circumstances. His own life ended in suicide after he had first shot his second wife, his daughter and grandchild.

Czigler, Győző (1850–1905). Architect, born into a long line of architects of Swiss extraction. His first teacher was his father; later he pursued his studies in Vienna under Theophil Hansen and on study tour in Italy. In Budapest he produced Historicist works, notably the Saxlehner palace on Andrássy út. The Gozsdu udvar is also his design, as are the Széchenyi Baths. Buried in Kerepesi Cemetery.

Czóbel, Béla (1883–1976). Painter, a founding member of the Eight. He studied first in Nagybánya under Béla Iványi Grünwald and then in Munich and Paris. For a time he lived and worked in Szentendre (where there is a museum dedicated to him). Later he moved to a studio in the Műteremház on Gellért Hill.

Damkó, József (1872–1955). Sculptor. Studied first under Alajos Stróbl, then in Paris and Italy. In Budapest he produced architectural sculpture for Alajos Hauszmann and Rezső Ray Jr (former Józsefváros Telephone Exchange). He also received ecclesiastical commissions. His St John Capestrano (Castle Hill) and St Elizabeth of Hungary (Rózsák tere) capture zeal and modest piety respectively, in bronze and stone.

Domány, Ferenc (1899–1939). Architect, a pupil of Dezső Hültl. After working in Berlin he went into partnership with Béla Hofstätter in Budapest, then moved to London, where a promising career was brought to an end by his death from an overdose of sleeping pills.

Dunaiszky, Lőrinc (1784–1833). Trained in Vienna, he came to Budapest in the first years of the 19th century and worked as a jobbing sculptor in the burgeoning city. Two statues of titular saints for Pest district parish churches are by his hand, in Terézváros and Józsefváros. He also worked in Buda (Krisztinaváros). His style is a homely version of Neoclassicism. Buried in Kerepesi Cemetery.

Engel, József (1815–1901). Sculptor. His studies took him to Vienna, Munich, Paris and then London, where his *Amazons and the Argonaut*, commissioned by Prince Albert, was exhibited at the Great Exhibition of 1851. From London he went to Rome, where his classical style made him popular among Grand Tourists. In Budapest he is known for his monument to Széchenyi on Széchenyi tér. He also made portrait busts for the National Museum.

Fadrusz, János (1858–1903). Sculptor, originally trained as a locksmith. At the beginning of his career he worked as a woodcarver. He subsequently studied in Vienna and then worked in his native city of Pressburg (Bratislava). He moved to Budapest towards the end of his life, spending most of his time on an equestrian monument to Matthias Corvinus (in Cluj, Romania). The lions guarding the Lion Courtyard of Buda's royal palace are his.

Fellner and Helmer. Architectural studio founded in 1873 by two Viennese architects, Ferdinand Fellner and Hermann Helmer. They are known chiefly for their Historicist theatre buildings (almost 50 of them, in a number of countries). Their architectural practice broke up after WWI.

Fellner, Sándor (1857–1944). Architect. After studying in Budapest, Vienna and Paris, he returned to Hungary where his designs included public and private buildings, hotels, synagogues and funerary monuments. He died in the Budapest Ghetto in the winter of 1944.

Fényes, Adolf (1867–1945). Painter, born Adolf Fischmann, the son of a rabbi. He abandoned studying law to become an artist and was apprenticed to Bertalan Székely. After further studies in Paris he returned to Hungary and was one of the founders of the artists' colony in Szolnok on the Great Plain. His lovely, brightly-coloured, poignant works are well represented in the Hungarian National Gallery. During WWII he was one of the artists protected by Horthy, but after the Nazi takeover he was interned in the Budapest ghetto. He died just two days after its liberation. Buried in the Salgótarjáni utca cemetery.

Fenyves, István (*see Fried, Miksa*)

Ferenczy, István (1792–1856). Hungary's greatest Neoclassical sculptor, the son of a locksmith. He began making medals while working in Vienna. He journeyed on foot to Rome, where he stayed six years, studying under Bertel Thorvaldsen. It was in Rome that he acquired the famous small bronze horse and rider attributed to Leonardo and now in the Museum of Fine Arts. Examples of his work can be seen in the National Gallery and Inner City Parish Church. He died in poverty.

Ferenczy, Károly (1862–1917). Painter. Studied in Munich and then Paris, after which he settled in the town of Szentendre beside the Danube. He was a founder of the artists' colony in Nagybánya, Transylvania, in 1896, and was one of its most prominent members, known for his *plein-air* paintings suffused with sunlight and colour. His son **Béni Ferenczy** (1890–1967) was a sculptor; Béni's twin sister **Noémi Ferenczy** (1890–1957) was a tapestry designer. A superb double portrait of the twins, by their father (Béni in a truly hideous sweater), hangs in the National Gallery. Both twins absorbed the bohemian ideals of their artistic upbringing and both were politically active in the Workers' Movement. Noémi was appointed head of the Gödöllő weaving school (*see p. 335*) in 1919, during the Soviet-style Republic of Councils. Later she was imprisoned for Communist activity. Both she and Béni spent some years in exile during the 1920s and '30s. It was while he was in Vienna that Béni produced his funerary monument for Egon Schiele. All three artists are buried in Kerepesi Cemetery.

Ferretti, Bernardo (17C). Sculptor and stone carver from the Lake Como area of northern Italy who settled in Buda and was active there from around 1688.

Feszl, Frigyes (1821–84) Architect, a pupil of József Hild. His style is usually described as Romantic. His best-known work is the Pest Vigadó. He also worked for the Dreher family of brewers in Kőbánya.

Feszty, Árpád (1856–1914) Painter, born Árpád Rehrenbeck. As a young man he worked as a travelling actor, embarking thereafter on a wandering career in Munich, Paris, Venice, Vienna and finally Florence. Chiefly known for his genre scenes, he produced an acclaimed work for the Hungarian Millennium celebrations of 1896. The stage always makes itself felt in his oeuvre: there is something of a film set nature to many of his works. He married the foster daughter of the novelist Mór Jókai. Their daughter was the painter Masha Feszty (1895–1979). His older brother was the architect **Adolf Feszty** (1846–1900), known for his Pest town houses in the Historicist style, particularly on Andrássy út.

Finta, József (b. 1935). Architect, born in Transylvania. He came to Budapest during WWII. As a student his talents were soon recognised and he obtained a position with LAKÓTERV, the Communist state office in charge of designing residential buildings. He made his name as a designer of hotels with his monumental Duna Intercontinental on the Danube (now the Marriott) in 1969. During the '80s and '90s he built many office blocks, commercial buildings and more hotels, including the Forum (now the Intercontinental), the Kempinski on Erzsébet tér, the Bank Center on Szabadság tér and the WestEnd shopping mall behind Nyugati Station. The face of Budapest has been partly shaped by his aesthetic taste.

Fischer, József (*see p. 89*).

Francsek, Imre (1864–1920). Architect and planner, responsible for the layout of parts of Gellért Hill and City Park (the skating rink ticket hall). His son, **Imre Francsek Jr** (1891–1952/3), designed the outdoor extension to the Széchenyi Baths, after which he was appointed architect to the Shah of Iran. The last ten years of his life were spent in a Soviet labour camp. The exact date and location of his death are unknown.

Frecska, János (20C). Building engineer. Little is known of him but he has left a superb monument to himself in the form of the Lutheran church in Kőbánya.

Freund, Vilmos (1846–1922). Architect, the son of a prosperous grain trader, a prominent member of Pest's Jewish community. Among Freund's works are the mortuary in the Kozma utca cemetery and the Duna Palota, former Lipótváros clubhouse. He also built some of the mansions on Andrássy út. Buried in the Salgótarjáni utca cemetery (gravestone designed by Emil Vidor).

Fried, Miksa (1895–?). Architect who often worked in tandem with István Fenyves (1897–1957). Their joint projects from the 1930s are in a restrained Art Deco style. Their partnership did not survive WWII. Fried left the country around 1948. Fenyves went on to work for IPARTERV, the state-controlled planning office for industrial buildings.

Füredi, Richárd (1873–1947). Sculptor, a pupil of Alajos Stróbl, whom he assisted on a number of important building projects.

Gádoros, Lajos (1910–91). Architect and furniture designer, born Lajos Gonda, the son of a carpenter. He studied in Budapest (under Károly Weichinger) and in Germany, then worked in the studio of Lajos Kozma. His brand of clean-lined

Functionalism was particularly suited to public buildings. He also assisted Pál Sávoly on the construction of the new Elisabeth Bridge.

Giergl, Kálmán (1863–1954). Architect, member of a family of architects, painters and metalsmiths who settled in Hungary from the Tyrol in the mid-19th century. He met his future partner Flóris Korb in the studio of Alajos Hauszmann. Their Eclectic architecture can be seen in many places in Pest: Liszt Academy, former Luxus department store on Vörösmarty tér, Klotild palaces, New York coffee house building.

Gregersen, Hugó (1889–1975). Architect, son of the Norwegian-born engineer Gudbrand Gregersen. He designed plain, geometric buildings, often decorated with sculptures and reliefs by his wife, Alice Lux.

Györgyi, Dénes (1886–1961). Architect, a descendant of the Giergl family of architect and artisans. Before WWI he was a member of the Folk Revival group of architects led by Károly Kós. Between the wars, he moved to a distinctly Art Deco style, teaming up with sculptors such as Béla Ohmann to provide the decorative elements. Some of his designs are preserved in the Kiscell Museum.

Hajós, Alfréd (1878–1955). Architect, Olympic swimmer and footballer, born Arnold Guttmann. He was apprenticed to Ignác Alpár and Ödön Lechner. (*See p. 292.*) Buried in Kozma utca cemetery.

Hamon, Kristóf (1693–1748). Stonemason and master builder from Buda, father-in-law and predecessor of Máté Nepauer. His best-known work is the church on Batthyány tér.

Hámor, István (1895–1970). Architect, born István Hamburger. His works from the 1930s are in a modern, geometric

style, sometimes angular, sometimes streamlined, often with fine ironwork. After WWII he worked for LAKÓTERV, the state-controlled office that designed domestic buildings.

Haranghy, Jenő (1894–1951). Painter and graphic artist known for his designs for murals, posters and mosaics as well as for book illustration. He spent time with the artists' school in Nagybánya.

Hauszmann, Alajos (1847–1926). Architect, a contemporary of Ödön Lechner and Gyula Pártos. Unlike them, he remained true to the Historicist idiom. He joined the Technical University as assistant teacher under Antal Szkalnitzky, becoming a full teacher in 1872, after a sojourn in Italy where he studied Renaissance buildings. After the death of Miklós Ybl, he was appointed to complete the restoration and extension of the royal palace on Castle Hill, his most famous work (and featured in relief on his tombstone in Kerepesi Cemetery).

Hegedűs, Ármin (1869–1945). Architect, born Ármin Geiger. Together with Henrik Böhm he designed a number of buildings in Budapest around the turn of the 20th century (the former Török Bank building on Szervita tér is a famous example). Hegedűs was also one of the architects involved in the design of the Gellért Hotel and Baths. Buried in the Kozma utca cemetery.

Herzog, Fülöp (1860–1925). Architect. Studied in Vienna, then came to Budapest, where he went into partnership with Albert Schickedanz. He is known for his work on the design and layout of Heroes' Square.

Hikisch, Kristóf (1756–1809). Stone mason and master builder, active in Buda, where the house he built for himself survives on Batthyány tér.

Hikisch, Lajos (*see Schubert*).

Hikisch, Rezső (1876–1934). Architect, worked in the studio of Rezső Ray Sr. His best-known work in Budapest is the Astoria Hotel.

Hild, József (1789–1867). Architect. Born in Pest, the son of **János Hild** (c. 1766–1811), who drew up the urban plan for what is now the Lipótváros district of central Pest. József Hild studied chiefly under his father and also in Vienna, after which he went to Eisenstadt as assistant to the Esterházy family's court architect. Following the death of his father he undertook an extensive study tour in Italy. The hallmark of his work is a restrained and elegant Neoclassicism; he is one of Hungary's best exponents of the style. He played a great part in the rebuilding of Pest after the disastrous Danube flood of 1838, and though many of his buildings sadly do not survive, those that do give a sense of the grace and proportion that must have characterised the newly-rebuilt city. His younger brother **Károly Hild** was also an architect.

Hofhauser, Antal (1859–1923). Architect, an admirer of the buildings of the Middle Ages and pupil of Friedrich Schmidt, architect of the Vienna Rathaus. In his native Hungary, Hofhauser designed a number of neo-Gothic churches.

Hofstätter, Béla (1891–1944). Architect. He studied at the Technical University before opening his own studio and going into partnership with Ferenc Domány. Together the two architects designed some of Pest's most luxurious apartment blocks of the 1930s. It appears that while living in one of them, Hofstätter fell victim to an Arrow Cross death squad.

Holló, Barnabás (1865–1917). Sculptor, a pupil of Alajos Stróbl. He made his name with his reliefs of the *Founding of the Academy of Sciences* and *Great Flood of 1838*. After that he produced sculptures for the Parliament and monuments for public squares. He had a studio in the Várkert Bazár.

Hollósy, Simon (1810–79). Painter, one of the most influential and formative figures of Hungarian 19th-century art. He studied first in Munich, where he gathered like-minded young artists around him and founded an independent school, flying in the face of traditional academic painting. Later he went on to found the Nagybánya artists' colony with Károly Ferenczy and others, although he himself left the colony in 1902, setting up on his own in the sub-Carpathian region of present-day Ukraine. The eccentric painter Tivadar Csontváry was one of his pupils. His works can be seen in the Hungarian National Gallery.

Horvay, János (1874–1944). Sculptor, born János Hoppl. Studied in Vienna, then worked as assistant to József Róna. He went on to specialise in likenesses of Lajos Kossuth: best known is the monument outside Parliament. In a very different vein—though also profoundly melancholy—is his small group of a shepherd piping to his flock in Erzsébet tér. Buried in Kerepesi Cemetery, under a monument of his own design.

Hültl, Dezső (1870–1946). Architect and teacher, exponent of the retrospective, conservative style that was popular in the cowed and defeated Hungary of the 1920s. His later works, though modern in form, never completely depart from historical models. Buried in Kerepesi Cemetery.

Huszár, Adolf (1843–85). Sculptor. His are the statue of József Eötvös at one end of the Danube Corso and the statue of Petőfi at the other, which he completed after his master Miklós Izsó's death. His own early death meant that his statue of Deák on

Széchenyi tér was in turn completed by his pupils.

Istók, János (1872–1972). Sculptor, a pupil of Alajos Stróbl. His lifesize bronze statue of Count Ferenc Széchényi in the garden of the National Museum (1902) won him acclaim and an award. The heroic Bem statue on Bem tér is also his.

Iványi Grünwald, Béla (1867–1940). Painter, born Béla Grünwald. He studied first in Budapest under Bertalan Székely and Károly Lotz (which he did not enjoy) and then in Munich (which he did). Together with István Csók he left Munich for Paris, where he met Károly Ferenczy. The next years were productive, spent partly in Paris and partly in Hungary, where he worked side by side with another friend, the sculptor Ede Kallós. In 1896, Grünwald and Ferenczy, with Simon Hollósy, founded the Nagybánya school. Grünwald converted to Christianity and married the daughter of a Uniate priest. He is known for his naturalistic and *plein-air* painting as well as for stylised, Secessionist landscapes and still lifes. His death was caused by a heart attack, on hearing that Nagybánya had been restored to Hungary under the terms of the Second Vienna Award (*see p. 18*). Buried in Kerepesi Cemetery.

Izsó, Miklós (1831–75). Sculptor. After a rackety early life spent fighting in the 1848–9 War of Independence and then going into hiding, he learned stone-carving as assistant to István Ferenczy, subsequently pursuing his studies in Vienna and Munich. His greatest monument in Budapest is the statue of Petőfi on Petőfi tér. Left unfinished at his death, it was completed by his pupil Adolf Huszár. Buried in Kerepesi Cemetery.

Jámbor, Lajos (1869–1955). Architect, born Lajos Frommer. He worked first in the studio of Alajos Hauszmann and then under Ödön Lechner. He worked together with Zoltán Bálint, producing houses and villas in the Hungarian Secessionist style. Buried in the Kozma utca cemetery.

Janáky, István (1901–66). Architect, known for his work on Margaret Island (Palatinus Baths) and on Castle Hill (reconstruction of the royal palace). His son, **István Janáky Jr** (1938–2012), designed the *Time Wheel* at the edge of City Park.

Jankovits, Gyula (1864–1932). Sculptor. Studied in Munich and Vienna. He is best known for the monument to St Gellért on Gellért Hill and for the two busts—often passed by but little looked-at—outside the Academy of Sciences. Portrait sculpture was one of his specialities.

Jánszky, Béla (1884–1945). Architect. He studied at the Technical University under Frigyes Schulek, then began his career in the studio of József Fischer. The combination of Romantic and Modernist precepts is interesting—and well seen in the designs he carried out in partnership with Tibor Szivessy.

Jónás, Dávid (1871–1951). Architect who worked together with is brother **Zsigmond Jónás** (1879–1936). Their work fuses modern trends with elements of Neoclassicism and the French Empire and *retour d'Egypte* styles.

Jungfer, Gyula (1841–1908). Ironworker, descended from a family of immigrant German smiths. His workshop was famous and sought-after during the boom years of the Dual Monarchy. Wrought-iron gates by him, as well as iron and bronze screens, candelabra, door handles and other elements, adorn the Széchenyi Baths, Szabó Ervin Library, Parliament and many other buildings. Buried in Kerepesi Cemetery.

Kallina, Mór (1844–1913). Architect. Born in the present-day Czech Republic, he worked in Vienna under Otto Wagner, with whom he came to Budapest when Wagner was commissioned to design the Rumbach Synagogue. At the time (1870) there was plenty of work in Buda and Pest and the young architect soon had his hands full. In partnership with his son-in-law Aladár Árkay, he built the Buda Vigadó. His Historicist designs enjoyed an enthusiastic reception from aristocratic and ecclesiastical patrons. Buried in Kerepesi Cemetery.

Kallós, Ede (1866–1950). Sculptor. Studied in Budapest and Paris. He is known for his commemorative sculpture, much of which, being in Hungary's former Crown Lands, was destroyed after 1920 (his statue of Kölcsey on Batthyány tér is a 1938 recasting of a lost work from Transylvania, for example). The monumental statue group on Vörösmarty tér is also his (with Ede Telcs), as is the gravestone (with bronze relief of woman and weeping willow) of the national composer Ferenc Erkel in Kerepesi Cemetery, where Kallós himself also now lies.

Kassák, Lajos (1887–1967). Constructivist artist, poet and political activist. After dropping out of school, Kassák worked as a locksmith's assistant, taking a variety of factory jobs after that. As a member of the Workers' Movement, he organised strikes and demonstrations, for which he was blacklisted. He embarked on a self-tailored Grand Tour of Europe on foot, visiting museums and galleries by day and sleeping in doss-houses by night. On his return to Hungary he began to publish poems and short stories in literary journals. He took a strongly anti-war stance during the build-up to WWI. When the war ended, he joined the Communist Party and became editor of the radical arts periodical *Ma* ('Today'). After the fall of the Republic of Councils 1919, he fled to Austria, continuing to edit *Ma* from Vienna and publishing works by avant-garde artists and writers such as Cocteau, Schwitters and Le Corbusier. He also began to experiment with graphic art himself, designing many of the magazine's covers. Kassák returned to Hungary in 1926 and despite clashes with the authorities (he was charged with inciting public unrest and taken into custody more than once) he continued to publish novels and stories addressing social problems such as unemployment and the plight of the rural peasantry. He also married his partner of 20 years, the actress and reciter of Dadaist poetry Jolán Simon. The marriage was not a success and Simon took her own life in 1938. After WWII, Kassák held a number of exhibitions and his poetry was intoned at Party rallies. But his independent cast of mind meant that he was always destined to fall foul of authority. He had more sympathy with the Social Democrats than the Communists and when Hungary became a one-party state, he was evicted from the Communist Party. In 1956, he came out on the side of the revolutionaries, after which his movements were closely monitored. Though permitted to exhibit privately, he was not allowed to mount public shows. It was not until 1967, the year of his 80th birthday, that he was finally rehabilitated and given the official state recognition he had always known he deserved. He died soon afterwards.

Kasselik, Fidél (1770–1830). Architect and master builder. Born in Austria, he became a Pest citizen in 1795. He designed many buildings in the Neoclassical style for the newly developing city. His son **Ferenc Kasselik** (1795–1884) was also an architect, apprenticed to his father.

Kauser, József (1848–1919). Architect. He was first apprenticed to his father before pursuing his studies abroad. Working in a Historicist style, he carried out a number of public commissions in Budapest.

Kerényi, Jenő (1908–75). Sculptor, a pupil of Jenő Bory, alongside whom he subsequently taught. His works are expressive and stylised (though he was also capable of Realism, as shown in his 1951 *Ostapenko*, now in the Memento Park) and he was especially known for his ability to suggest dynamic movement.

Kernstok, Károly (1873–1940). Painter. He studied in Munich under Simon Hollósy and later in Paris. Influenced by Fauvist art, particularly Matisse and Cézanne, he was one of the founders of the Eight. Before WWI he worked with a number of architects, including József Vágó (Schiffer Villa). Because of his political affiliation with the Soviet-style Republic of Councils, he lived in exile in Berlin between 1919 and 1926. On his return he was active in the artists' group known as KUT (New Association of Artists).

Kisfaludi Strobl, Zsigmond (1884–1975). Tenacious and flexible sculptor who pursued a successful career spanning many changes of regime, gathering international recognition along the way. His works include female nudes, portraits, funerary monuments and commemorative public works. Some have been destroyed or removed. One that has stood the test of time is the Liberation Monument on Gellért Hill, a 20th-century take on the Classical Victory figure.

Kiss, Géza (1878–1944). Architect, known mostly for his collaboration with Albert Kálmán Kőrössy.

Kiss, György (1852–1919). Shepherd lad-turned-sculptor, known for his genre pieces and portraits. The seated marble statue of Veres Pálné in Central Pest is his, as is the *'Little Rascal'* sculpture of the chicken thief on József körút. György Zala invited him to contribute to the Heroes' Square sculptures. *King Charles I* (Károly Róbert; *illustrated on p. 305*) was the result.

Kiss, István (1927–97). One of the favoured sculptors of the Communist era, the son of a rural blacksmith. He studied at the School of Fine Art under Zsigmond Kisfaludi Strobl and Pál Pátzay. His breakthrough came while still a student, when he won a competition to design a monument to the peasant hero György Dózsa (it stands at the western foot of Castle Hill). His most iconic work is his monument made to celebrate the 50th anniversary of the Republic of Councils. It, like many of his sculptures, is now in the Memento Park.

Kmetty, János (1889–1975). Painter. Studied in Budapest under Károly Ferenczy, then went on study tour to Paris, where the art of Cézanne and the Cubist works of Picasso and Braque made a great impression on him. He was a member of the circle that formed around Lajos Kassák and was a member of the KUT (New Association of Artists) as well as of the Szentendre artists' colony. Buried in Kerepesi Cemetery.

Komor, Marcell (1868–1944). Architect, born Marcell Kohn, the son of a rabbi. After graduating from the Technical University, he worked under Czigler, Hauszmann and Ödön Lechner, whom he assisted on the Museum of Applied Arts and Geological Institute projects. The years between the Hungarian Millennium (1896) and WWI were a fruitful period, when he gained a number of commissions in partnership with Dezső Jakab. He shared Lechner's belief in the need for Hungarian architecture to find its own indigenous style. Seized by the Arrow Cross, he was marched to the Austrian border and murdered there in 1944.

Kontuly, Béla (1904–83). Painter, a pupil of István Réti. Together with his wife, Hajnalka Fuchs (a designer of stained-glass windows), he received a scholarship to the Hungarian Academy in Rome. He went on to produce many notable paintings and frescoes for churches in Hungary.

Körner, József (1907–71). Architect, known as an exponent of Socialist Realism. He studied at the Technical University and was a founder-member of the Hungarian branch of CIAM. His international socialist style was not greatly in favour before WWII, though he did build private houses and retail spaces. After the Communists came to power, he received commissions for a number of public buildings in Budapest, including the Pantheon of the Workers' Movement in Kerepesi Cemetery.

Korb, Flóris (1860–1930). Architect, long-time assistant to Alajos Hauszmann. He is best known as the partner of Kálmán Giergl, with whom he designed the Liszt Academy and other buildings. Buried in Kerepesi Cemetery.

Körösfői-Kriesch, Aladár (*see p. 335*).

Kőrössy, Albert Kálmán (1869–1955). Architect, chiefly known for his works in the French and Belgian Art Nouveau style (Philanthia flower shop, Sonnenberg Villa, Walkó-ház), though also influenced by Ödön Lechner. Born into a wealthy Jewish family, he studied first in Budapest and then at the Ecole des Beaux Arts in Paris. In the early 20th century he worked in

partnership with Géza Kiss. After WWI he gave up architecture and worked as a civil servant for the Budapest municipality.

Kós, Károly (1883–1977). Architect, the leading light of a group of young students known as the Fiatalok (Dezső Zrumeczky and Györgyi Dénes, with whom Kós worked in Budapest, were also members). He was inspired by the Arts and Crafts movement and the work of Charles Rennie Mackintosh and Frank Lloyd Wright. His Folk Revival style, which borrows from the architecture of Transylvania, has some affinities with the National Romantic architecture of Scandinavia. He was also a writer, author of *Az Országépítő* (*The Nation Builder*), a novel about King (and Saint) Stephen.

Kovács, Margit (1902–77). Ceramicist, known for her small-scale, naïve and doll-like polychrome figures. There is a museum devoted to her work in Szentendre.

Kozma, Lajos (1884–1948). Architect and interior designer, born Lajos Fuchs (*see p. 89*). Buried in Kerepesi Cemetery.

Lajta, Béla (1873–1920). Architect, born Béla Leitersdorfer (*see p. 173*). Buried in the Kozma utca cemetery.

László, Philip de (1869–1937). Painter. Born Fülöp Laub, the son of a Jewish tailor. In later life he converted first to Catholicism and then, on his marriage to Lucy Guinness, to Protestantism. He studied in Hungary under Károly Lotz and Bertalan Székely and then in Munich and Paris. A British subject from 1914, he became one of the foremost portrait painters of his age. His sitters included monarchs (Franz Joseph, Kaiser Wilhelm II, Alfonso XIII of Spain, Sawai Singh, Maharajah of Jaipur), prelates (Pope Leo XIII; in the Hungarian National Gallery), heads of state (Roosevelt, Coolidge,

Miklós Horthy; in Gödöllő) and many others. His work was completely out of favour under Communism; today in Hungary he is still relatively little known.

Lechner, Ödön (*see p. 318*). Buried in Kerepesi Cemetery.

Lesenyei, Márta (b. 1930). Sculptor, a pupil of Pál Pátzay and Zsigmond Kisfaludi Strobl. In the 1950s she produced sculptures of women and children, a theme then much in favour with the Communist art commissars. She has produced a large body of works with Christian themes as well as war memorials and funerary monuments.

Ligeti, Miklós (1871–1944). Sculptor, a pupil and then assistant of Alajos Stróbl. He studied in Vienna and Paris, where he met and was influenced by Rodin. His works include genre pieces, architectural sculpture (royal palace), some fine Canova-esque funerary monuments (Kerepesi), portrait sculpture (Harry Hill Bandholtz in Szabadság tér) and the famous *Anonymus* in City Park (winner of a competition, though it completely split the jury). His own funerary monument is one of the most original in Kerepesi Cemetery, the work of Jenő Bory.

Löffler, Sándor (1877–1962) and **Löffler Béla** (1880–late 1930s). Architects, brothers. They opened an office in 1906. Plans known by them include domestic, industrial, commercial and religious buildings, many with rich decoration in a geometricised, late Art Nouveau style, though also demonstrating the influence of Béla Lajta in the use of stylised folk motifs. Their most famous work is probably the Orthodox synagogue on Kazinczy utca. After WWII Sándor settled in Australia. Béla's last years are uncertain: he is known to have gone to Paris and afterwards possibly to Jerusalem.

Lotz, Károly (1833–1904). One of the great History painters of the mid–late 19th century, known for his canvases as well as frescoes of historical and allegorical subjects, to be seen in many of Budapest's most important buildings. Much of his decorative work takes inspiration from the so-called 'grotesques' of Nero's Domus Aurea in Rome, schemes of wall painting that include patterns of flowers, sphinxes, birds, human figures etc., against a light ground. He was also a fine portraitist.

Lux, Alice (1906–88). Sculptor, best known for figurative works made to decorate buildings. She worked in partnership with her husband, the architect Hugó Gregersen.

Lux, Kálmán (1880–1961). Architect and conservator. Studied at the Technical University, then worked under István Möller. He worked on the Rock Chapel inside Gellért Hill and on excavations and restoration of the monastic and church buildings on Margaret Island.

Makovecz, Imre (1935–2011). Architect, profoundly influenced by the Folk Revival style of Károly Kós and himself an exponent of Organic Architecture, aiming to make the built environment conform to the patterns and shapes of nature. His designs for a church in Krisztinaváros (not built) have echoes of Gaudí's Sagrada Família. MAKONA, the studio which he co-founded in 1983, was the first Western-style architects' practice in Communist Hungary. A house in the Buda Hills, which Makovecz had intended to use as his own home, can be visited (*Városkúti út 2; map p. 422, C3; see makovecz.hu for details*).

Málnai, Béla (1878–1941). Architect. Studied at the Technical University, then worked under Ödön Lechner and Béla Lajta. He is an important exponent of Hungarian pre-Modernism. The

Rosenfeld building on Eötvös utca combines Art Deco lines with archaising Classical forms (a temple portico and Diocletian window).

Markup, Béla (1873–1945). Sculptor, a pupil of Alajos Stróbl. His first notable success was the pair of lions flanking the main Parliament steps. He also produced busts and portrait sculpture.

Maróti, Géza (1875–1941). Sculptor, born Géza Rintel. Many buildings are decorated with works by Maróti (Liszt Academy, Gresham Palace, Széchenyi Baths). He collaborated with Secessionist and early Modern architects at the turn of the 20th century, including Béla Lajta (Újszínház), Albert Kőrössy (Sonnenberg Villa, Walkóház) and the Löffler brothers (Rákóczi út 11). In the late '20s he worked in the USA. A later journey to the Holy Land resulted in ambitious plans for a rebuilding of Solomon's Temple. He also produced a design for a reconstructed lost city of Atlantis. He is buried in Kerepesi, under a monument of his own design.

Marschalkó, János (1818–77). Sculptor, born in what is now Slovakia. He studied in Vienna and undertook an extensive European study tour before settling in Budapest. He produced some of the statuary for the Széchenyi Baths and completed some works that had been left unfinished by István Ferenczy. He is best known for the lions on the Chain Bridge. His wife belonged to the Giergl dynasty of architects and artisans (Kálmán Giergl was her nephew).

Marton, László (1925–2008). Sculptor, a pupil of Béni Ferenczy and Pál Pátzay. Many examples of his work can be seen in parks, squares and prominent public places across the city. His most popular works are probably the *Little Princess* beside the no. 2 tramline in central Pest

and the statue of Attila József, also on the Danube bank, below Parliament.

Maugsch, Gyula (1882–1946). Sculptor and medallist, known for the elephant sculptures at the entrance to the Zoo in City Park. He also produced some of the reliefs on the former Social Insurance building on Fiumei út.

Mayerhoffer, András (1690–1771). Master builder, born in Salzburg. He became a Pest citizen in 1724 and is known for his Baroque churches and Baroque/ Rococo country palaces. His son, **János Mayerhoffer** (1721–80) pursued the same career.

Medgyaszay, István (1877–1959). Architect, born István Benkó. He studied under Imre Francsek Sr and at the Technical University and was an enthusiastic convert to reinforced concrete. His work is a fusion of many influences, including Hungarian folk styles, Oriental and Egyptian forms. He designed studio villas for members of the Gödöllő artists' colony. Under Communism he was branded an architect of the Horthy era and his reputation suffered.

Medgyessy, Ferenc (1881–1958). Sculptor. Born in east Hungary, he undertook study tours to Paris and Florence before settling in Budapest. His work shows affinities with that of Aristide Maillol, with thickset female nudes a favourite theme. He produced public sculpture, reliefs and small statuettes (the *Fat Thinker* and *Woman Scrubbing*). Much of his work shows an archaising tendency and an interest in ancient sculptural forms.

Meinig, Artúr (1853–1904). Architect, born in Germany. After studying in Dresden, he worked for the Fellner and Helmer firm of theatre architects in Vienna. He came to Budapest in 1883 and made a career for himself building town houses and country châteaux for the nobility, typically in the neo-Baroque style. Buried in Kerepesi Cemetery.

Moiret, Ödön (1883–1966). Sculptor and medallist, a member of the Gödöllő artists' colony. His works are characterised by a mystic blend of influences from mythology and Christianity. After WWII he lived in Vienna.

Möller, István (1860–1934). Architect and teacher, a specialist in the Middle Ages and known particularly for his work in the field of conservation.

Molnár-C., Pál (1894–1981). Painter, born Pál Molnár. He added the final C to his surname in honour of his mother, Jeanne Contat, a Swiss governess in the service of a well-to-do-Hungarian family. He studied in Budapest, then in Switzerland and Paris and was a member of the KUT (New Association of Artists). In 1928 he won a scholarship to the Hungarian Academy in Rome. He was a prolific artist and his oeuvre is very varied, ranging from pen-and-ink cartoons to large murals of religious subjects. He also experimented with Metaphysical art in the manner of De Chirico and painted some interesting landscapes, sometimes serene, sometimes sinister. His Novecento-inspired ecclesiastical works are particularly characteristic (Inner City Parish Church). His former home and studio can be visited (*see p. 124*). Molnár-C. is first and foremost a happy artist. On the experience of getting up to begin a new day's painting, he wrote, 'I wake up every morning as excited as a bridegroom who is about to rejoin his bride.'

Molnár, Farkas (*see p. 89*).

Munkácsy, Mihály (1844–1900). Painter, born Mihály Lieb in Munkács (Mukachevo, modern Ukraine). He grew up in straitened circumstances and was apprenticed to a carpenter. In 1866 he won a scholarship to Paris, which marked a turning point in his fortunes. In France he made influential friends, found artistic inspiration, and won an important gold medal at the Paris Salon. He married the widow of a French baron and in 1881 painted his *Christ before Pilate*, which was shown in Europe and the US. It and his later *Golgotha* were purchased by John Wanamaker in 1887, for over $100,000 each. Munkácsy was the first Hungarian artist to make an international name for himself. Both paintings, together with a third work, an *Ecce Homo*, are now in the Déri Museum in Debrecen, east Hungary. Buried in Kerepesi Cemetery.

Nagy, Izsó (1848–1926). Architect who worked in partnership with Gyula Benedict (1876–1934), working in the Secessionist style. Both are buried in the Kozma utca cemetery.

Németh, Pál (1913–59). Architect, a graduate of the Technical University. Active during the decade following WWII and known for his clean-lined, faintly Bauhaus-inspired buildings, in the 1950s adhering to Socialist Realist principles.

Nepauer, Máté (1719–92). Austrian-born master builder who was active in Buda, where he died. He married the widow of Kristóf Hamon and took over the latter's unfinished projects. His name is associated with a number of Baroque churches.

Neuschloss, Kornél (1864–1935). Architect. As a young man, he worked in France, taking part in the restoration of châteaux. After serving in WWI, he taught at the Ludoviceum (Military Academy). His designs include public and domestic buildings but his best known (and best loved) works are the Elephant House and main entrance of the Budapest Zoo.

Novák, Ede (1888–1951). Architect, a graduate of the Technical University. He worked in partnership with Béla Barát and the pair made their name with the Georgia-ház at the Astoria crossroads in 1935. Novák also worked with István Hámor. A number of Budapest apartment blocks of the 1920s and '30s were designed on his drawing board. Novák survived WWII thanks to Swiss and Swedish protection.

Nyíri, István (1902–55). Architect. He spent his formative years in the studio of Gyula Wälder before opening his own practice. He became known for his modern designs and was awarded the Ybl Prize in 1953. Nyíri was also a farmer. After nationalisation his land became the Gödöllő Agricultural University's model farm.

Ohmann, Béla (1890–1968). Sculptor, ceramicist and teacher. He worked with the architect Dénes Györgyi, producing architectural sculptures, made stylised sculpture for churches (Városmajor, Pasaréti tér) and other public sculpture with a Christian theme. After WWII he fell from favour.

Olcsai-Kiss, Zoltán (1895–1981). Sculptor. He served time as a prisoner in Siberia, then joined the Hungarian Red Army. With the fall of the Republic of Councils, he fled into exile, returning to Hungary only at the end of WWII. He received teaching posts and numerous commissions, becoming a favoured artist of the regime. The Pantheon of the Workers' Movement in Kerepesi Cemetery is his. His own grave is also in Kerepesi, in the sculptors' and artists' plot.

Pártos, Gyula (1845–1916). Architect, born Gyula Puntzmann, a contemporary of Ödön Lechner, alongside whom he studied in Berlin and with whom he afterwards worked in partnership. Many notable works were produced by their joint office, among them the Museum of Applied Arts building. Buried in Kerepesi Cemetery.

Pásztor, János (1881–1945). Sculptor. Studied in Budapest and Paris and went on study tour to Italy. The influence of Rodin and of the Classical world is equally felt in his oeuvre. His post-WWI work is of a different type, excellently illustrated by the equestrian monument to Rákóczi outside Parliament, self-consciously heroic, the sculptural equivalent of the 'Third Baroque' architectural movement (*see p. 24*). Pásztor died in the Siege of Budapest. His funerary monument in Kerepesi Cemetery, a nude female stargazer (his own work), was formerly in the garden of the Budapest observatory.

Pátzay, Pál (1896–1979). Sculptor, winner of many awards, including two Kossuth Prizes. As a young man he spent time in Nagybánya with the Ferenczy family (the sculptor Béni Ferenczy was a near contemporary). In Budapest he was a member of the circle that formed around Lajos Kassák (*see p. 382*). He served a term in prison for his involvement with the Republic of Councils. During WWII he gave shelter to Jews, earning for himself the title of Righteous Gentile. He taught at the School of Fine Art for the rest of his career. To accompany the statue of Stalin at the edge of City Park he made a sculpture of Lenin, erected in 1965, which gained him his second Kossuth Prize. It is now in the Memento Park.

Paur, János György (1692–1752). Master builder, born in Bavaria. He became a Pest citizen in 1721 and was a member of the city stonemasons' guild. He is known for his Baroque churches (and is buried in the crypt of one of them, the church of St Anne on Szervita tér).

Pecz, Samu (1854–1922). Architect. Pecz received a Lutheran education in Pest at the school on Deák tér. He later studied in Vienna under Theophil Hansen and on his return to Hungary, worked under Frigyes Schulek on the restoration of the Matthias Church. The neo-Gothic aesthetic was to remain close to his heart, as can ben seen in his churches, market halls and the National Archives building. He also designed the a new, larger premises for the Lutheran school on Városligeti fasor, together with its church. He worked on the buildings of the Technical University, where he was a teacher. Buried in Kerepesi Cemetery.

Petschacher, Gusztáv (1844–90). Architect. Born in Vienna, he came to Budapest to assist with the development of Andrássy út, going on to produce some of its finest Historicist, neo-Renaissance buildings, notably on Kodály körönd. Buried in Kerepesi Cemetery.

Pfaff, Ferenc (1851–1913). Architect. Studied at the Technical University under Imre Steindl. He spent most of his career as architect for the Ministry of Transport, building railway stations all over Hungary and the Crown Lands. In Budapest he is known for the former Palace of Art, now Olof Palme Ház in City Park and, also in the City Park, for the former Transport Museum building (which at the time of writing there were plans to reconstruct).

Pollack, Mihály (1773–1855). Architect, born in Vienna, the son of a master builder. After working alongside his cousin Leopold Pollack in Milan, he came to Pest in 1798. In 1808 he was appointed to the Beautification Committee (*see p. 23*). He is one of the great Neoclassical architects of early 19th-century Hungary, his most famous work the Hungarian National Museum.

Preisich, Gábor (1909–98). Architect, a graduate of the Technical University. He worked for a time under Emil Bauer and was in the circle of the CIAM and Bauhaus architects. He is known for his clean, Modernist style. He collaborated on a number of projects with Lajos Gádoros.

Quittner, Zsigmond (1859–1918). Architect who worked in a broadly Historicist and afterwards Secessionist style, designing some of the mansions on Andrássy út and also, with the Vágó brothers, the Gresham Palace (Four Seasons Hotel). Buried in the Salgótarjáni utca cemetery. His son **Ervin Quittner** (1895–1945), also an architect, designed buildings in the Bauhaus style. Deported after the Nazi takeover, he died in Dachau.

Rajk, László (b. 1949). Architect, son of the Communist leader László Rajk who was executed after a show trial in 1949. Rajk Jr studied at the Technical University and after that in Canada, France and New York. His style is highly original and individual. He has also worked in set design (including for the Oscar-winning *Son of Saul*) and as a politician and political activist.

Ray, Rezső (1876–1938). Architect. After studying in Lausanne and Munich, he returned to Budapest to take over the studio of his father, **Rezső Ray Sr** (1845–99), who had moved to Hungary from Switzerland in 1868. The elder Ray built villas and apartment blocks as well as some public buildings (Lukács Baths). Rezső Ray Jr worked in a number of styles—Historicist, Art Nouveau and early Modernist—always apparently interested in exploring new avenues and technologies.

Reichl, Kálmán (1879–1926). Painter and architect. He studied painting in Nagybánya under Simon Hollósy and architecture at the Technical University. He later became a teacher. His work makes use of Classical forms in a modern idiom. Buried in Kerepesi Cemetery.

Réti, István (1872–1945). Painter, born in Nagybánya, where the famous artists' colony was later set up. He studied in Munich under Simon Hollósy and then in Paris. On Kossuth's death he travelled to Turin and made a famous drawing of the great hero (*see p. 144*) on his bier. After the colony was established in his native Nagybánya in 1896, he was an important member of the group. Buried in Kerepesi Cemetery.

Rieger. Organmakers, founded by Franz Rieger in 1884 in what is now the Czech Republic. Rieger's sons Otto and Gustav opened a sister manufactory in Budapest in 1894. It continued in operation until it was nationalised under Communism. After re-privatisation, it became the Aquincum Organ Factory.

Rippl-Rónai, József (1861–1927). Painter and designer, studied in Munich and then Paris. His Paris years were formative and productive. He was one of the Nabis (works by him are held in the Musée d'Orsay). He worked in a variety of styles, Post-Impressionist and Art Nouveau among them, and developed his own version of pointillism, using bold colours and very large dots. The National Gallery has a good collection of his paintings and drawings.

Rimanóczy, Gyula (1903–58). Architect, a pupil of Gyula Wälder. Before 1930 his works were faintly orientalising, notable for their sculptural brickwork. In the '30s he worked in a Bauhaus-inspired style. The church and bus station on Pasaréti tér are his masterpieces.

Román, Miklós (1879–1945). Architect, born Miklós Rennberger. Together with his brother, **Ernő Román** (1883–1959), he designed numerous apartment buildings, articulated with folk motifs and other stylised figurative and geometric designs.

Róna, József (1861–1939). Sculptor. Trained initially as a carpenter, then studied in Vienna. He is known for his biblical and mythological themes and for the erotic charge of many of his works. He produced architectural sculpture and reliefs, statues and fountains, as well as large-scale commemorative works (*Eugene of Savoy* on Castle Hill; *Empress Elisabeth* in Gödöllő).

Roskovics, Ignác (1854–1915). Painter. He studied in Budapest and Munich and shortly after opening his own studio, in 1882, exhibited a *Descent of the Holy Spirit* which gained him great acclaim. He went on to be much sought-after as a painter of religious works. He also produced genre scenes and illustrations for books.

Róth, Miksa (*see p. 224*).

Schickedanz, Albert (1846–1915). Architect. He worked under Antal Szkalnitzky and Miklós Ybl in the 1860s and at the end of the decade won the commission to design the mausoleum of Lajos Batthyány (*see p. 244*). His second great commission, in conjunction with Fülöp Herczog, was the laying out and design of Heroes' Square in 1896. Buried in Kerepesi Cemetery.

Schmahl, Henrik (1846–1912). Architect, born in Hamburg. He worked in Budapest alongside Miklós Ybl, producing Historicist buildings (Andrássy út) but is more particularly known for his neo-Venetian Gothic designs (Uránia Film Theatre).

Schodits, Lajos (1872–1941). Architect, teacher and writer. He collaborated on a number of projects with Béla Eberling.

Schöntheil, Richárd (b. 1874). Architect whose Art Nouveau works can be seen in Kőbánya. Chief of these is the former synagogue and the house he built as his own residence. There are several other small villas in the neighbouring streets, many of them signed and dated. The date of Schöntheil's death is unknown, though he is recorded as a director of the Therápia Steam Bathing Company, at Hölgy u. 12 (also in Kőbánya), in 1913 and at an address in Buda in 1943.

Schubert, Ármin. Architect and builder who worked in partnership with Lajos Hikisch in the latter part of the 19th century. They seem to have had their own design studio although they also executed designs by other architects.

Schulek, Frigyes (1841–1919). Architect and teacher at the Technical University. He studied in Vienna under the neo-Gothic specialist Friedrich Schmidt. His own Historicist style embraced both the neo-Gothic and neo-Renaissance. His most famous works are on Castle Hill, where he restored and reintegrated the Matthias Church and designed the Fishermen's Bastion.

Senyei, Károly (1854–1919). Sculptor. Studied in Munich and on his return to Hungary worked with György Zala: two of the sculptures in Heroes' Square are his (*St Stephen* and *Andrew II*). He also made numerous allegorical and symbolic statue groups. Alongside his monumental works, he is known for genre sculpture, notably for fountains, and often featuring figures of children.

Sidló, Ferenc (1882–1954). Sculptor. Studied under Alajos Stróbl, then in Vienna and Munich. After a spell in Rome, he settled in Gödöllő as a member of the artists' colony there (*see p. 335*). Until the end of his life he taught at the School of Fine Art. He is known for his Symbolist works.

Somogyi, József (1916–93). Sculptor, a pupil of Zsigmond Kisfaludi Strobl (among others) and for many years rector of the School of Fine Art. He produced a number of figurative public bronzes of human and animal subjects, many with a characteristic rough-hewn surface.

Spiegel, Frigyes (1866–1933). Architect. He began his career in the studio of Vilmos Freund. He is known for his works in the Art Nouveau style.

Steindl, Imre (1839–1902). Architect, best known for the Parliament building on the Danube bank. Other works by him include the church on Rózsák tere and the ELTE University building on Múzeum körút. The frost-resistant 'pyrogranite' ceramic made by the Zsolnay factory and much used for exterior decoration on buildings of the period was developed by Zsolnay in tandem with Steindl. Its original name was 'Steindl-clay'. Buried in Kerepesi Cemetery.

Stróbl, Alajos (1856–1926). Sculptor. Trained in Vienna, then found work in Budapest during its boom years, at first making decorative sculpture to adorn buildings. The statues of Liszt and Erkel and the two sphinxes outside the Opera House are examples of his early works. He soon became sought-after and received numerous commissions. Today his works can be seen all over town. They include the equestrian statue of St Stephen and the Matthias Fountain on Castle Hill; the colossal *János Arany* in front of the National Museum; and the statue of the titular saint in the sanctuary of St Stephen's Basilica. Ennobled in 1913, he is buried in Kerepesi Cemetery.

Szabó, Iván (1913–98). Sculptor. Studied at the School of Fine Art under Jenő Bory and then worked in Ferenc Medgyessy's studio. He identified himself as a Socialist sculptor from the 1930s and was also an enthusiastic folk dancer.

Szécsi, Antal (1856–1904). Sculptor in the academic style, best known for his statue of Gábor Baross outside Keleti Station. The figures on the pediments of the Saxlehner mansion (Andrássy út 3) are derived from Michelangelo's Medici tombs in Florence.

Székely, Bertalan (1835–1910). Painter in the academic tradition. He studied in Vienna, Dresden and Munich and produced numerous canvases and murals dealing with themes from Hungarian history.

Szentgyörgyi, István (1881–1938). Sculptor, metalworker and teacher at the School of Fine Art. He studied in Zurich and Brussels. His works are often very direct, devoid of allegory. He is known for fountains, military memorials and other public sculpture. His *István Nagyatádi Szabó* on Kossuth Lajos tér is interesting: stiff and frozen in expression, like an Archaic kouros with clothes on.

Szervátiusz, Tibor (b. 1930). Sculptor, born in Cluj, Transylvania, but resident in Hungary since the 1970s. His works, both small- and large-scale are often in a naïve, folk-inspired style.

Szinyei Merse, Pál (1845–1920). Painter. He studied in Munich and produced some well-known Romantic *plein-air* scenes (*Skylark, Picnic in May*). Family difficulties (the death of three children from diphtheria, divorce) induced him to give up painting for a long spell, until one of his works was purchased by Franz Joseph. From then on he was sought-after and successful. He is credited with introducing Impressionism to Hungary.

Szivessy, Tibor (1884–1963). Architect. His eclectic style mixes elements of the Secession, Art Deco, Modernism and the early Renaissance. He is particularly known for the works carried out in partnership with Béla Jánszky.

Szkalnitzky, Antal (1836–78). Architect. After studying in Berlin and Munich he was active in the rapidly developing Pest of the post-Compromise era. He oversaw the construction of the Academy of Sciences building. Buried in Kerepesi Cemetery.

Sztehlo, Lili (1897–1959). Painter, best known for her painted glass windows, especially for churches. She was one of the scholarship artists at the Hungarian Academy in Rome, together with her husband, the architect Aladár Árkay, with whom she collaborated. Her style, like many of the Roman School artists, blends elements of the Italian Novecento with more avant garde styles.

Tándor, Ottó (1852–1913). A pupil of Imre Steindl and later head of his architects' office. He worked on the Parliament and, with Ödön Lechner, the church of St Ladislas in Kőbánya.

Tar, István (1910–71). Sculptor, a pupil of Jenő Bory. He was active both as a sculptor and teacher and in organising and running artists' societies and associations. A number of his public works, both Realist and Expressionist, can be seen in Budapest. He died in a car crash.

Telcs, Ede (1872–1948). Sculptor. The son of a provincial shoemaker, Telcs studied in Budapest and Vienna before joining the studio of György Zala. He is known particularly for his human figures. Works by his hand adorn the Liszt Academy, Ritz-Carlton Hotel (re-made) and Széchenyi Baths, and examples of his funerary sculpture can be seen in Kerepesi Cemetery. The *St Ladislas* on Heroes' Square is his, as is the statue of Ignác Alpár in City Park. He collaborated with Ede

Kallós on the Vörösmarty monument in Vörösmarty tér. He managed to survive the Holocaust, partly in a Swedish safe house in Pest.

Than, Mór (1828–99). Painter, a pupil of Miklós Barabás. During the 1848–9 War of Independence against the Habsburgs he worked as a war artist. Afterwards he undertook a lengthy study tour in Europe, following which he returned to Hungary and began work with Károly Lotz, producing decorations and fresco cycles for numerous buildings in the capital.

Uitz, Béla (1887–1972). Painter and graphic artist, a pupil of Károly Ferenczy. Afterwards he joined the circle of Lajos Kassák. Forced to emigrate after the fall of the Republic of Councils, he went to the Soviet Union where he was greatly influenced by Russian Constructivism, the style that was to shape his own. He remained true to his Communist principles throughout his life. Buried in Kerepesi Cemetery (with a Communist star on this gravestone).

Unger, Emil (1839–73). Architect, grandson of Mihály Pollack and a descendant of the Unger family of blacksmiths (*see p. 188*). After completing his studies in Pest and Berlin, he trained under Miklós Ybl and Antal Szkalnitzky. The patronage of Ybl (who built the Unger-ház for his uncle) helped him greatly and he became one of the leading architects in the project to develop Andrássy út. He died tragically young. Buried in Kerepesi Cemetery.

Vágó, László (1875–1933). Architect. Worked in Ignác Alpár's studio before starting his own joint practice with his brother, **József Vágó** (1877–1947). Their designs span the Art Nouveau and Art Deco periods and are rich in decorative detail. József Vágó designed the Szent László High School in Kőbánya together with Ödön Lechner. His Schiffer Villa is an example of a *Gesamtkunstwerk* in the Viennese manner. László Vágó co-designed the Heroes' Temple in the Great Synagogue precinct.

Vajda, Zsigmond (1860–1931). Painter, a pupil of Károly Lotz and Bertalan Székely, whose style he followed closely. He worked on frescoes in the Parliament and produced designs executed by Miksa Róth for the Széchenyi Baths and Dob utca school.

Varga, Imre (*see p. 107*). His son **Tamás Varga** (b. 1953) is also a sculptor.

Vasarely, Victor (*see pp. 105–6*)

Vastagh György (1868–1946). Sculptor, a pupil of György Zala. He produced portrait sculpture and animal sculptures as well as a number of large-scale equestrian monuments on Castle Hill, including the Hadik statue. His Görgei monument was damaged in WWII and melted down (now remade by László Marton). The *Horse-breaker*, usually outside the royal palace, was being restored at the time of writing. Another colossal equestrian statue, used as the funeral monument of Gyula Gömbös in Kerepesi Cemetery, was smashed in 1946.

Vaszary, János (1867–1939). Painter. Studied in Munich and then Paris, which was to have a profound influence on him. His early works are in a Symbolist, Art Nouveau style. After WWI he was a founder-member of KUT (New Association of Artists). Later he moved in a more Post-Impressionist and Fauvist direction, in some of his works showing an affinity with Raoul Dufy. He also produced pastels and watercolours, inspired by Parisian society and the *demi-monde*, as well as the seaside resorts of the Mediterranean. He produced religious works too, in Expressionist slashes of colour.

Vidor, Emil (1867–1952). Architect, one of the most important figures of the late Secession and transition to Art Deco and streamlined Modernism. The Bedő-ház is one of his best-known works.

Vilt, Tibor (1905–83). Sculptor, a pupil of Kisfaludi Strobl. He won a two-year scholarship to Rome and his early works can be grouped with the Hungarian Roman School. There are stylised reliefs by his hand in Buda (Pasaréti tér church, Lövőház utca). Later he experimented with abstract sculpture. He took part in the 1956 Uprising and was only rehabilitated in the 1960s, after which the state rewarded him with support and numerous commissions.

Waczula, Rezső (d. 1923). Architect and engineer who designed a number of late Art Nouveau buildings in Pest in the years before WWI. After serving in the war (he reached the rank of lieutenant), it appears that he gave up architecture: in the defeated and truncated Hungary of the time, commissions were hard to come by. Instead he made a career for himself in the police force and seems to have set up a training scheme for police dogs.

Wälder, Gyula (1884–1944). Architect. István Nyíri and Gyula Rimanóczy trained in his studio. A study tour of Italy left him with a love of the Baroque and the Classical world; his 'Third Baroque' school building on Villányi út is an example of the retrospective style of the immediate post-WWI era. He later turned his hand to more monumental projects, taking over the Madách complex after the death of Aladár Árkay (and introducing Baroque and Neoclassical elements into the design). Buried in Kerepesi Cemetery.

Wagner, László (1911–87) The first Hungarian architect to use the curtain wall and also the architect of the first Hungarian skyscraper (the Semmelweis University tower at Nagyvárad tér, begun in 1963).

Wagner, Nándor (1922–97). Sculptor, known for his work in cast stainless steel. He lived in Sweden after WWII, returning there after 1956. In the 1970s, he moved to Japan, remaining there for the rest of his life.

Wechselmann, Ignác (1828–1903). Prussian-born architect who supervised the construction of many of Budapest's important buildings of the time, including the Great Synagogue on Dohány utca under Ludwig Förster, whose assistant he had been in Vienna. He was one of the first Jews to practise the profession in Budapest, even before their formal emancipation in 1867. In later life his eyesight failed him and he donated a large sum of money to an institute for the blind (*see p. 321*). Buried in the Salgótarjáni utca cemetery.

Weichinger, Károly (1893–1982). Architect and designer, a faculty director at the Technical University (during his tenure a number of successful architects graduated from the school, including József Finta). His architectural works include public, domestic and ecclesiastical buildings. One of the houses in the Napraforgó estate is his, as are the conventual buildings built for the Paulines on Gellért Hill.

Wellisch, Alfréd (1854–1941). Architect. After studying in Vienna and Paris, he made a lucrative career for himself in Budapest, winning both public, commercial and private commissions. His son **Andor Wellisch** (1887–1956) was also an architect. He changed his surname after the war to Vécsey.

Ybl, Miklós (1814–91). The most successful and representative architect of Budapest's golden era of expansion and development as co-capital of the Dual Monarchy. Pupil of Mihály Pollack. Beginning with many commissions for the Károlyi family, he rose to become the most popular architect in Pest for members of the aristocracy wishing to build town houses. He also received commissions for important public buildings, notably the Opera House and Basilica of St Stephen. Buried in Kerepesi Cemetery.

Zala, György (1858–1937). Sculptor. A scholarship took him to Vienna to study, from where he went on to Munich. His early works are portraits. His career break came when he was appointed to make the sculptures for the new Heroes' Square millennial monument, from 1896. After that he became the sort of sculptor laureate of Budapest's golden age. By his hand are the statue of Empress Elisabeth at the Buda end of Elisabeth Bridge and the monuments to Andrássy and Tisza outside Parliament (both re-made).

Zichy, Mihály (1827–1906). Painter and graphic artist, known for his portraits, Romantic canvases, literary illustrations and erotica. He spent much of his life in Paris and served as court painter to Tsars Alexander II and Alexander III. His duties to the latter prevented him from contributing artworks to the Hungarian Millennium celebrations of 1896. He died in St Petersburg.

Zielinski, Szilárd (1860–1924). Architectural engineer known for his pioneering use of reinforced concrete. He studied in Germany, Great Britain and France, where he worked for the Eiffel company. He taught at the Technical University, and built bridges and water towers (notably that on Margaret Island). Buried in Kerepesi Cemetery.

Zofahl, Lőrinc (c. 1791–1863). Architect and builder of tenement blocks in the rapidly-expanding Pest of his day.

Zrumeczky, Dezső (1883–1917). Architect in the Folk Revival style, a talented partner of Károly Kós. He moved to Kispest as a child, after his father fell on hard times and came to the capital to look for work. He died young, of pleurisy.

Zsákodi Csiszér, János (1883–1953). Sculptor. Studied in Paris under Rodin and in Budapest under György Zala. He is known for his commemorative statues, war memorials and reliefs.

Zsolnay, Vilmos (1828–1900). Potter and ceramicist from Pécs in south Hungary whose manufactory became one of the most famous in the country. It shot to prominence in the late 19th century with designs not only for portable *objets d'art* but also for its ceramic tiles and architectural faïence. The material used for the exterior elements is known as pyrogranite: 'pyro' because it is fired at very high temperatures; and 'granite' because of its resulting durability, resistant to frost, damp and also acid pollution. Zsolnay also invented the eosin glaze, which he developed in tandem with the chemist Vince Wartha. It gives the effect of an iridescent, metallic sheen and comes in a variety of colours, the most popular of which (certainly for smaller household ornaments) are the deep scarlet and the blue-green. The Zsolnay firm is still in operation, known for its ornamental ceramics and teaware.

Rulers of Hungary

KINGDOM OF HUNGARY

House of Árpád

St Stephen I (István)	1000–38
Peter	1038–41
Aba Sámuel	1041–4
Peter (second reign)	1044–6
Andrew I (András)	1046–60
Béla I	1060–3
Salamon	1063–74
Géza I	1074–7
St Ladislas I (László)	1077–95
Coloman (Könyves Kálmán)	1095–1116
Stephen II	1116–31
Béla II	1131–41
Géza II	1141–62
Stephen III	1162–72
Ladislas II (anti-king)	1162–3
Stephen IV (anti-king)	1163–5
Béla III	1172–96
Imre	1196–1204
Ladislas III	1204–5
Andrew II	1205–35
Béla IV	1235–70
Ladislas IV	1272–1301
Andrew III	1290–1301

Various dynasties

Wenceslas (of Bohemia)	1301–5
Otto (of Bavaria)	1305–7
Charles I (Károly Róbert) (of Anjou)	
	1308–42
Louis I, the Great (Lajos)	1342–82
Maria	1382–85

Charles II	1385–6
Maria (ruled jointly with Sigismund)	
	1386–95
Sigismund of Luxembourg	1387–1437
Albert (of Habsburg)	1438–39
Vladislas Jagiello	1440–4
Ladislas V (of Habsburg)	1444–57
János Hunyadi (not crowned)	1446–53
Matthias Corvinus	1458–90
Vladislas II Jagiello	1490–1516
Louis II	1516–26
John Zapolya	1526–40

TRIPARTITE HUNGARY

Royal Hungary (House of Habsburg)

Ferdinand I	1526–64
Maximilian I	1564–76
Rudolf II	1576–1608
Matthias II	1608–19
Ferdinand II	1619–37
Ferdinand III	1637–57
Ferdinand IV (jointly)	1647–54
Leopold I	1657–86

Vilayet of Buda (Ottoman Empire)

Pashas of Buda	1541–1686

Transylvania

Princes of Transylvania	1570–1690
Ferenc Rákóczi	1704–11

AUSTRIAN EMPIRE

House of Habsburg

Leopold I	1686–1705
Joseph I	1705–11
Charles III	1711–40
Maria Theresa	1740–80

House of Habsburg-Lorraine

Joseph II	1780–90
Leopold II	1790–92
Franz I	1792–1835
Ferdinand V	1835–48
Franz Joseph	1848–1916

REPUBLIC OF HUNGARY

Lajos Kossuth	May–August 1849

DUAL MONARCHY OF AUSTRIA-HUNGARY

Franz Joseph	1867–1916
Charles IV	1916–18

HUNGARIAN DEMOCRATIC REPUBLIC

Mihály Károlyi	Jan–March 1919

REPUBLIC OF COUNCILS (HUNGARIAN SOVIET REPUBLIC)

Béla Kun	March–August 1919

REGENCY

Miklós Horthy	1920–44

NAZI OCCUPATION

Ferenc Szálasi	1944–5

HUNGARIAN REPUBLIC AND PEOPLE'S REPUBLIC

Zoltán Tildy	1946–8
Árpád Szakasits	1948–9
Mátyás Rákosi	1949–1956
Ernő Gerő	1956
János Kádár	1956–88
Károly Grósz	1988–9

REPUBLIC OF HUNGARY   1989–

Since 1989 Hungary has been a democratic republic, its government headed by a Prime Minister and with a President as its head of state. The word 'Republic' was dropped from the official name in 2011. Pre-2011 Hungarian coins, for example, say '*Magyar Köztársaság*' (Hungarian Republic). Post-2011 coins say '*Magyarország*' (Hungary).

Index

Explanatory or more detailed references are given in bold. Numbers in italics are picture references. For more detailed entries on artists, architects and sculptors, refer to the Glossary of Artists on p. 373

SELECT BIBLIOGRAPHY

Andrássy, Dorottya. *Az Országház építéstörténete*. Budapest, 2016

Baji, Etelka, Csorba, László. *Kastélyok és mágnások*. Budapest, 1994

Bardoly, István, ed. *The Coronation Mantle of the Hungarian Kings*. Budapest, 2005

Bartos, Erika. *Budapest titkai*. Budapest, 2016

Berza, László, ed. *Budapest Lexicon*. Akadémiai Kiadó, 1993

Bolla, Zoltán. *A magyar art deco építészet* (2 vols). Budapest, 2016, 2017

Buzinczky, Géza, ed. *Élet az óvóhelyen: vári ostromnaplók*. Budapest 2003

Carlberg, Ingrid. *Raoul Wallenberg*. London, 2016

Cartledge, Bryan. *Mihály Károlyi and István Bethlen*. Haus, 2009

Dent, Bob. *Budapest 1956: Locations of Drama*. Europa, 2006

Erdődy, Gábor. *Magyar szabadelvűek: Batthyány Lajos*. Új mandátum, 1998

Faludi, Ildikó. *Guide to Gödöllő*. Gödöllő, 1995

Fényi, Tibor. *Róth Miksa üvegfestményei*. Budapest, 2005

Fenyő, Miksa. *Az elsodort ország*. Park Kiadó, 2014

Frojimovics, Komoróczy, Pusztai, Strbik, eds. *Jewish Budapest*. CEU Press, 1999

Gábor, Eszter. *Andrássy út*. Budapest, 2002

Gellér, Katalin. *The Art Colony of Gödöllő*. Gödöllő, 2001

Gerenday, Ágnes. *Árpád-házi Szent Erzsébet plébániatemplom*. Budapest, 1993

Gerle, János, Ferkai, András, Vargha, Mihály, Lőrinczi, Zsusza. *Építészeti kalauz*. 6BT, 1997

Guba, Ildikó. *'A halál nem program': Buday-Goldberger Leó élete*. Óbudai Múzeum, 2014

Hámori, László. *Károlyi Mihály, a földosztó*. Népszava Könyvkiadó, 1946

Heathcote, Edwin. *Budapest: A Guide to 20th-century Architecture*. Ellipsis, 1997

Hegedűs, András, *Az idők tanúja: a pesti Nagyboldogasszony-templom története*, Budapest 2016

Kahn, Joseph. *An Illustrated Guide of Budapest*. Légrády, 1891

Kapronczay, Károly. *Semmelweis*. Budapest, 2003

Ludmann, Mihály. *A Magyar szobrászat mesterei*. L'Harmattan/Kossuth Klub, 2015

Mátéffy, Balázs. *A Szent Korona*. Budapest, 2003

Nagy, Mihály. *Lapidarium. Guide to the Archaeological Exhibitions in the Hungarian National Museum*. Budapest 2012

Pálóczi Horváth, George. *The Undefeated*. Eland, 1993

Ráday, Mihály, ed. *Budapesti utcanevek*. Corvina, 2013

Saly, Noémi, ed. *A régi pesti városfal mentén*. Fekete Sas, 2015

Stevens, Mary Elizabeth. *Letters from Hungary* (ed. Katharine Armstrong). DRP, 1999

Széchenyi, István. *Napló* (ed. Gyula Viszota). Gondolat, 1978

Széll Kálmánné Vörösmarty, Ilona. *Emlékeim*. Budapest, 2017

Vágó, Ádám. *A Kárpát-medence ősi kincsei*. Hungarian National Museum, 2015

Verrasztó, Gábor. *Budai históriák*. Napkút 2010–16

Zombory-Moldován, Béla. *The Burning of the World*. New York Review of Books, 2014

Köztérkép public artworks database: *kozterkep.hu*; Óvás!: *lathatatlan.ovas.hu*; Fortepan photo archive: *fortepan.hu*; Rubicon history journal: *rubicon.hu*; Hungarian Electronic Library: *mek.oszk.hu*; Hungarian Catholic Lexicon: *lexikon.katolikus.hu*

KEY TO MAP SYMBOLS

Ⓓ Commuter boat service

✡ Synagogue

☦ Orthodox church

Ⓜ Metro

♟ Catholic church

♝ Uniate church

Ⓗ Suburban train (HÉV)

♁ Lutheran church

♠ Presbyterian church

⌂ Statue or monument

✹ Calvinist church

∩ Cave

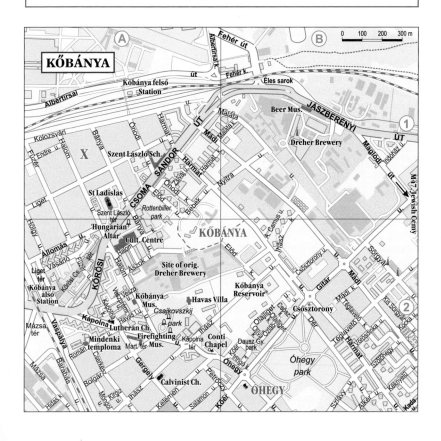

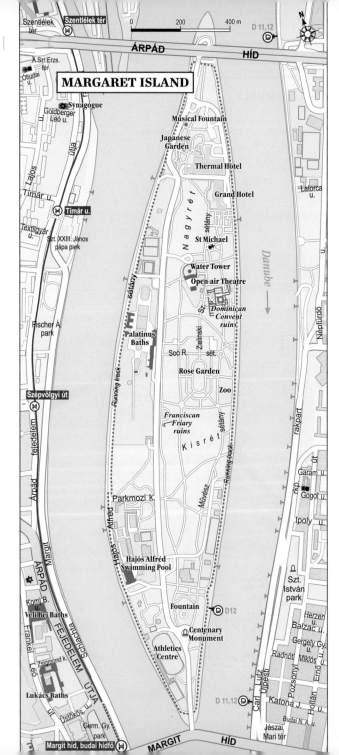

MARGARET ISLAND

Szentlélek tér
Szentlélek tér

Á.Szt.Erzs. tér
Óbudai u.

Synagogue
Goldberger Leó u.

Lajos utja

Musical Fountain

Japanese Garden

Thermal Hotel

Grand Hotel

Latorca u.

Tímár u.
Tímár u.

Textilgyár u.
Szt. XXIII. János pápa park

N a g y r é t

sétány

St Michael

Water Tower

Open-air Theatre

Sz.

Dominican Convent ruins

Danube →

Zielinski

Fischer Á. park

Palatinus Baths

Soó R.   sét.

Running track

Rose Garden

Zoo

Szépvölgyi út

Franciscan Friary ruins

K i s r é t

sétány

Running track

Garam u.

Gogol u.

Ipoly u.

Parkmozi K.

Művész

rakpart

Hajós

Alfréd

Árpád fejedelem

Hajós Alfréd Swimming Pool

Szt. István park

Herzen u.

Balzac u.

Gergely Gy. u.

Radnóti Miklós u.

Pozsonyi út

Ernő

Fountain   D12

Komj. B. u.
Veli Bej Baths

Centenary Monument

Athletics Centre

Carl Lutz

Újpesti

Katona J.

Budai N. A. u.

Jászai Mari tér

Frankel Leó út
Zsigmond k.

ÁRPÁD
Margit híd
FEJEDELEM
UTJA

Lukács Baths

Üstökös u.

Germ. Gy. park

Margit híd, budai hídfő

MARGIT   HÍD

0   200   400 m

ÁRPÁD   HÍD

D 11,12

Népfürdő

D 11,12

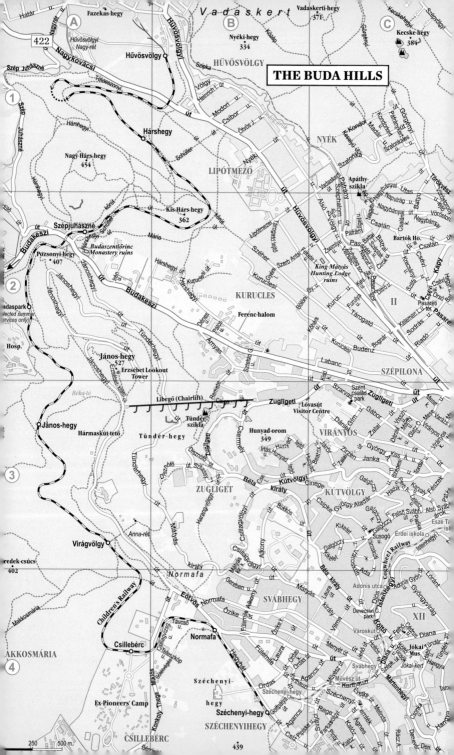

CASTLE HILL & DISTRICT I

0   100   200   300 m

CENTRAL BUDAPEST

BUDAPEST OVERVIEW

Sikátorpuszta

HUNGARORING

431

Csömör

KISTARCSA

RÁKOS-PALOTA

ÚJPALOTA

XV

XIV

ZUGLÓ

Bosnyák tér

RÁKOS-SZENTMIHÁLY

XVI

CINKOTA

SZABADFÖLD

NAGYTARCSAI ÚT

Naplás

Újszász

MÁTYÁSFÖLD

RÁKOSLIGET

KEREPESI

Kincsem Park

p.419

Rákos-p.

KŐBÁNYAI

KÖRÖSI CSOMA S.

X

KŐBÁNYA

Harmat

JÁSZBERÉNYI

PESTI

Kozma

Jewish Cemetery

Helikopter

RÁKOS-KERESZTÚR

XVII

CSABAI ÚT

PESTI

pliget

Gyömrői

Új köztemető

FERIHEGYI

REPÜLŐTÉRRE

Gyömrői

Csévéző

VEZETŐ

Baross

FERENC-VÁROS

Wekerle-telep

Hungária

NAGYKŐRÖSI

XIX

KISPEST

ÜLLŐI

PEST-ERZSÉBET

XX

Ecseri Market

PESTSZENT-LŐRINC

Liszt Ferenc Airport

XVIII

Béke tér

PESTSZENTIMRE

VECSÉS

SOROKSÁR

M5

XXIII

Vecsés

út

0   1   2   3   4   5 km

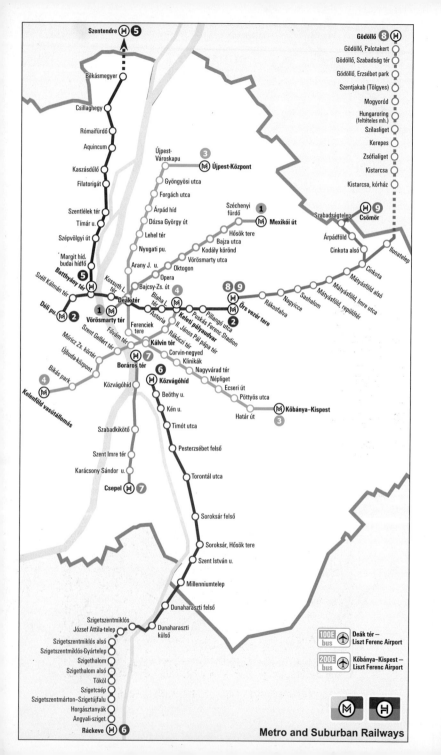

Metro and Suburban Railways